HANDBOOK ON DIGITAL CORPORATE COMMUNICATION

Handbook on Digital Corporate Communication

Edited by

Vilma Luoma-aho

Professor of Corporate Communication, Jyväskylä University School of Business and Economics (JSBE), Finland

Mark Badham

Senior Lecturer, Leeds Business School, Leeds Beckett University, UK

EE Edward **Elgar**
PUBLISHING

Cheltenham, UK • Northampton, MA, USA

© Vilma Luoma-aho and Mark Badham 2023

All rights reserved. No part of this publication may be reproduced, stored in a retrieval system or transmitted in any form or by any means, electronic, mechanical or photocopying, recording, or otherwise without the prior permission of the publisher.

Published by
Edward Elgar Publishing Limited
The Lypiatts
15 Lansdown Road
Cheltenham
Glos GL50 2JA
UK

Edward Elgar Publishing, Inc.
William Pratt House
9 Dewey Court
Northampton
Massachusetts 01060
USA

A catalogue record for this book
is available from the British Library

Library of Congress Control Number: 2023934063

This book is available electronically in the **Elgar**online
Business subject collection
http://dx.doi.org/10.4337/9781802201963

Printed on elemental chlorine free (ECF)
recycled paper containing 30% Post-Consumer Waste

ISBN 978 1 80220 195 6 (cased)
ISBN 978 1 80220 196 3 (eBook)

Printed and bound in the USA

Contents

List of figures		viii
List of tables		ix
List of contributors		x
Foreword by Joep Cornelissen		xiii
List of cases and/or illustrative examples		xv

1   Introduction to the *Handbook on Digital Corporate Communication*   1
Mark Badham and Vilma Luoma-aho

PART I   DIGITALLY-INFLUENCED CHANGES TO LEGACY FUNCTIONS

2   Digital corporate communication and internal communication   18
Rickard Andersson, Mats Heide and Charlotte Simonsson

3   Digital corporate communication and brand communication   34
John M. T. Balmer

4   Digital corporate communication and media relations   51
Daniel Vogler and Mark Badham

5   Digital corporate communication and corporate reputation   64
Elanor Colleoni, Stefania Romenti and Grazia Murtarelli

6   Digital corporate communication and CSR communication   78
Lina Gomez-Vasquez

7   Digital corporate communication and financial communication and
investor relations   91
Alexander V. Laskin and Christian P. Hoffmann

8   Digital corporate communication and stakeholder relationship management   103
Linjuan Rita Men, Marc Vielledent, Cen April Yue and Alvin Zhou

9   Digital corporate communication and measurement and evaluation   118
Sophia C. Volk and Alexander Buhmann

PART II   DIGITALLY-INFLUENCED ISSUES AFFECTING ORGANIZATIONS

10   Digital corporate communication and issues management   135
Laura Illia and Elanor Colleoni

11   Digital corporate communication and activism   152
Maureen Taylor

v

vi *Handbook on digital corporate communication*

12   Digital corporate communication and paracrises and AI   165
       Timothy Coombs and Sherry Holladay

13   Digital corporate communication and crisis life cycles   179
       Augustine Pang and Jerena C. K. Ng

14   Digital corporate communication and complaint management   193
       Sabine Einwiller and Wolfgang Weitzl

15   Digital corporate communication and hostile hijacking of organizational crises   208
       Sofia Johansson, Howard Nothhaft and Alicia Fjällhed

16   Digital corporate communication and brandjacking and character assassination   222
       Sergei A. Samoilenko and Quentin Langley

PART III   CORPORATE COMMUNICATION'S ADOPTION OF
             DIGITAL TECHNOLOGIES

17   Digital corporate communication and digital transformation of
       communication functions and organizations   238
       Ansgar Zerfass and Jana Brockhaus

18   Digital corporate communication and social media influencers   253
       Nils S. Borchers

19   Digital corporate communication and gamification   266
       Jens Seiffert-Brockmann and Ariadne Neureiter

20   Digital corporate communication and artificial intelligence and future roles   281
       Alexander Buhmann and Anne Gregory

21   Digital corporate communication and extended intelligence   297
       Chris Galloway and Lukasz Swiatek

22   Digital corporate communication and algorithmic leadership and management   311
       Polina Feshchenko, Niilo Noponen, Vilma Luoma-aho and Tommi Auvinen

23   Digital corporate communication and visual communication   326
       Chiara Valentini and Grazia Murtarelli

24   Digital corporate communication and voice communication   343
       Alex Mari, Andreina Mandelli and René Algesheimer

PART IV   CORPORATE COMMUNICATION'S RESPONSE TO
            DIGITALLY-INFLUENCED EFFECTS IN SOCIETY

25   Digital corporate communication and organizational listening   357
       Jim Macnamara

26   Digital corporate communication and the market for big data   371
       Gregor Halff and Anne Gregory

27	Digital corporate communication and public diplomacy *Jérôme Chariatte and Diana Ingenhoff*	384
28	Digital corporate communication and public sector organizations *Hanna Reinikainen and Chiara Valentini*	400
29	Digital corporate communication and co-productive citizen engagement *Louis Pierre Philippe Homont, María-José Canel and Vilma Luoma-aho*	413
30	Digital corporate communication and disinformation *Mirko Olivieri, Rosa-Maria Mäkelä, Stefania Romenti and Vilma Luoma-aho*	426

PART V   FUTURE DIRECTIONS

31	Conclusion: future roles of digital corporate communication *Vilma Luoma-aho, Mark Badham and Alina Arti*	440

Index   449

Figures

1.1	The four parts of the *Handbook*	9
3.1	Total corporate brand communication mix	42
9.1	The basic management cycle and types of evaluation	120
9.2	A framework of M&E in digital corporate communication	123
10.1	Issues lifecycle	142
10.2	Monitor broadness of issues vs convergence of issues	144
10.3	Digital collectives during the #deleteuber boycott	147
11.1	The grid of network building strategies and tactics	156
13.1	Crisis life cycle phases	181
13.2	Digital crisis life cycle framework	185
13.3	Trajectory in dialogic communication	187
14.1	Process model of complaining behaviour	197
17.1	Dimensions of the digital transformation of communication functions and departments	243
17.2	Action fields for corporate communication supporting organizational change	245
20.1	Predicted level of AI penetration into the profession by 2023: mapping the 50 skills identified in Global Alliance's Global Body of Knowledge (GBOK) with AI	285
22.1	Sociotechnical dynamics in algorithmically mediated organizational context	315
23.1	The four realms of digital visual experience	334
24.1	Digital voice communication (DVC) framework	345
26.1	A taxonomy of responses to big data's externalities	378
27.1	Listening and evaluation compass	390
30.1	Share of online fake news related to Covid-19 in the period January–May 2020	432

viii

Tables

5.1	Chronological sequence of the events regarding users' backlash against D&G in 2018	72
8.1	Relationship maintenance strategies, indicators, types, and outcomes	106
8.2	Access, voice, and engagement before and after digital technologies	109
9.1	Digital KPIs for M&E in digital corporate communication	125
10.1	Disciplines studying issues management	137
10.2	Changes in stakeholders' segmentation in the digital communication era	138
10.3	Changes in issues prioritization	140
17.1	Drivers for the organization-wide digital transformation	248
17.2	Potential agenda for research on the digital transformation of corporate communication	249
18.1	Advantages of and challenges in strategic influencer communication as described by corporate communicators	259
23.1	Visual social semiotics functions of images, key features and implications for communication managers	331
25.1	Elements of an 'architecture of listening' in an organization	362
25.2	Methods for digital organizational listening	362
29.1	Madrid City Council's and citizens' new possibilities to engage in co-production via the Madrid Móvil app	419
29.2	Notices received and solved (Madrid Móvil versus non-Madrid Móvil)	420
29.3	Notices received and solved (traditional channels versus digital channels)	421
30.1	Definitions from academic studies about disinformation	428
30.2	Different types of fake news (Tandoc et al., 2018)	429
30.3	The EU's policy framework and instruments for tackling disinformation	433

ix

Contributors

René Algesheimer is in the Department of Business Administration at the University of Zurich (Switzerland).

Rickard Andersson is in the Department of Strategic Communication at Lund University (Sweden).

Alina Arti is in the Jyväskylä University School of Business & Economics at the University of Jyväskylä (Finland).

Tommi Auvinen is in the Jyväskylä University School of Business & Economics at the University of Jyväskylä (Finland).

Mark Badham is in the Leeds Business School at the Leeds Beckett University (UK).

John M. T. Balmer is in the Brunel Business School at Brunel University London (UK).

Nils S. Borchers is in the Institute of Media Studies at the University of Tübingen (Germany).

Jana Brockhaus is in the Institute of Communication and Media Studies at Leipzig University (Germany).

Alexander Buhmann is in the Department of Communication and Culture at BI Norwegian Business School (Norway).

María-José Canel is in the University Complutense of Madrid (Spain).

Jérôme Chariatte is in the Department of Communication and Media Research at University of Fribourg (Switzerland).

Elanor Colleoni is in the Department of Business, Law, Economics and Consumption at IULM University (Italy).

Timothy Coombs is with the Centre for Crisis and Risk Communications (USA).

Joep Cornelissen is in the Department of Business-Society Management, Rotterdam School of Management, at Erasmus University (The Netherlands).

Sabine Einwiller is in the Department of Communication, Faculty of Social Sciences, at the University of Vienna (Austria).

Polina Feshchenko is in the Jyväskylä University School of Business & Economics at the University of Jyväskylä (Finland).

Alicia Fjällhed is in the Department of Strategic Communication at Lund University (Sweden).

Chris Galloway is in the School of Communication, Journalism and Marketing at Massey University (New Zealand).

Contributors xi

Lina Gomez-Vasquez is in the Department of Communication at the University of Tampa (USA).

Anne Gregory is in the Huddersfield Business School at the University of Huddersfield (UK).

Gregor Halff is in the Faculty of Social Sciences at Vrije Universiteit Amsterdam (The Netherlands).

Mats Heide is in the Department of Strategic Communication at Lund University (Sweden).

Christian P. Hoffmann is in the Institute of Communication and Media Studies at Leipzig University (Germany).

Sherry Holladay is an independent researcher.

Louis Pierre Philippe Homont is in the University Complutense of Madrid (Spain).

Laura Illia is in the Department of Communication and Media Research, Faculty of Economics and Social Science, at the University of Fribourg (Switzerland).

Diana Ingenhoff is in the Department of Communication and Media Research at University of Fribourg (Switzerland).

Sofia Johansson is in the Department of Journalism, Media and Communication at Gothenburg University (Sweden).

Quentin Langley is in the Gabelli School of Business at Fordham University (USA).

Alexander V. Laskin is in the Public Relations program at Quinnipiac University (USA).

Vilma Luoma-aho is in the Jyväskylä University School of Business & Economics at the University of Jyväskylä (Finland).

Jim Macnamara is in the School of Communication at the University of Technology Sydney (Australia).

Rosa-Maria Mäkelä is in the Jyväskylä University School of Business & Economics at the University of Jyväskylä (Finland).

Andreina Mandelli is in the SDA Bocconi School of Management (Italy).

Alex Mari is in the Department of Business Administration at the University of Zurich (Switzerland).

Linjuan Rita Men is in the College of Journalism and Communications at the University of Florida (USA).

Grazia Murtarelli is in the Department of Business, Law, Economics and Consumption at IULM University (Italy).

Ariadne Neureiter is in the Department of Communication at the University of Vienna (Austria).

Jerena C. K. Ng is in the Lee Kong Chian School of Business at Singapore Management University (Singapore).

xii *Handbook on digital corporate communication*

Niilo Noponen is in the Jyväskylä University School of Business & Economics at the University of Jyväskylä (Finland).

Howard Nothhaft is in the Department of Strategic Communication at Lund University (Sweden).

Mirko Olivieri is in the Center of Marketing Researches, Università Cattolica del Sacro Cuore (Italy).

Augustine Pang is in the Lee Kong Chian School of Business at Singapore Management University (Singapore).

Hanna Reinikainen is in the Centre for Consumer Society Research at the University of Helsinki (Finland).

Stefania Romenti is in the Department of Business, Law, Economics and Consumption at IULM University (Italy).

Sergei A. Samoilenko is in the Department of Communication at George Mason University (USA).

Jens Seiffert-Brockmann is in the Department of Business Communication at the Vienna University of Economics and Business (Austria).

Charlotte Simonsson is in the Department of Strategic Communication, Lund University (Sweden).

Lukasz Swiatek is in the School of the Arts and Media, Faculty of Arts, Design and Architecture, at the University of New South Wales (Australia).

Maureen Taylor is in the School of Communication at the University of Technology Sydney (Australia)

Chiara Valentini is in the Jyväskylä University School of Business & Economics at the University of Jyväskylä (Finland).

Marc Vielledent is Strategy Branch Chief, United States Special Operations Command (USA).

Daniel Vogler is in the Research Center for the Public Sphere and Society at the University of Zurich (Switzerland).

Sophia C. Volk is in the Department of Communication and Media Research at the University of Zurich (Switzerland).

Wolfgang Weitzl is in the Digital Business Institute, Faculty of Business and Management, at the University of Applied Sciences Upper Austria (Austria).

Cen April Yue is in the Department of Communication at the University of Connecticut (USA).

Ansgar Zerfass is in the Institute of Communication and Media Studies at Leipzig University (Germany) and in the Department of Communication and Culture at BI Norwegian Business School (Norway).

Alvin Zhou is in the Hubbard School of Journalism and Mass Communication at the University of Minnesota (USA).

Foreword by Joep Cornelissen

The explosion of digitally mediated forms of communication, such as social media, digital communication platforms and online collaborative tools, is a game-changer for corporate communication. As a function that became established in many organizations in the 1980s and 1990s, corporate communication used to follow a command-and-control model with messages being issued from the top of the organization, and with the task of communication professionals being to ensure that this happens in a seamless and coordinated manner. If executed to perfection, organizations would in turn be able to create strong reputations, trust and goodwill with the very stakeholders upon whom its livelihood depends.

This model, whilst still alluring perhaps, is no longer workable. In fact, organizations who continue to use it as an overarching logic very much risk alienating themselves from their stakeholders, who do not want to be talked to in that way, and who in any case may use digital sources of information other than those messages coming from the organization itself to form an image or reputation of the organization. Digitalization has fundamentally altered the dynamics of corporate communication. As this *Handbook* comprehensively shows, this change is profound and existential, going to the heart of what corporate communication is, or rather is quickly turning into. Digitalization has changed its basic functions such as branding, internal communications, crisis communication and media relations, as well as all the operational processes within it. Managing crises online, for instance, is drastically different from the traditional model of trying to manage an unfolding crisis and its aftermath via legacy media and following the rhythms of the traditional news cycle.

However, prior to this *Handbook*, there was no single resource that covered this fundamental change in a comprehensive and detailed manner. This volume therefore plugs an important gap; it brings together academic and practitioner experts on digital corporate communication from around the world, covering all the different functions, practice areas and digitalization-related developments in an in-depth manner. It is a stellar achievement that two of the field's thought leaders, Vilma Luoma-aho and Mark Badham, have managed to bring together in a single volume all the research-based evidence and insights from practice on this important topic. Academic readers will find the broad overview and research-based insights that they seek and those who are more geared towards practice will get the practical advice and guidance that they are looking for.

A particularly compelling aspect of the *Handbook* is that it puts the digitalization trend in perspective in the context of society. With algorithms and machine learning at the centre of the business models of many organizations as part of a digital form of capitalism that is fast becoming mainstream, digitalization has far-reaching consequences for stakeholders and citizens in society. Those consequences are perhaps most patently observable in the surveillance and data harvesting tactics of the big tech corporations such as Alphabet (which owns Google) and Meta (which owns Facebook), although the trend itself is omnipresent in smaller and bigger companies, and in the private and public sectors of society alike. As this *Handbook* astutely shows, corporate communication professionals are not innocent bystanders, but are very much implicated in this trend, requiring of them that they combine proficiency in the use of digital tools with constant ethical vigilance in ensuring that the use of these tools is on

xiii

xiv *Handbook on digital corporate communication*

every occasion not harmful to individual users and do not produce negative consequences for society. The lessons provided in the fourth section of this *Handbook* go a long way towards helping professionals think through this ethical dimension to digital corporate communication.

Professor Dr Joep Cornelissen
Editor-in-Chief, Organization Theory
Academic Director, Executive Master in Corporate Communication
Department of Business-Society Management
Rotterdam School of Management, Erasmus University
The Netherlands

List of cases and/or illustrative examples

Chapter 2	Swedish Transport Administration
Chapter 3	British Monarchy
Chapter 4	Global Strategic Communications Council (GSCC)
Chapter 5	Dolce & Gabbana
Chapter 6	Nutresa
Chapter 7	SAP SE
Chapter 8	Mondelez
Chapter 9	UNICEF
Chapter 10	#deleteuber
Chapter 11	Asia Pulp and Paper (APP) company
Chapter 12	VW
Chapter 13	NETS (Singaporean electronic payment service provider) and Havas Worldwide Singapore (advertising agency)
Chapter 14	Gucci
Chapter 15	SAS (Scandinavian airline)
Chapter 16	McDonald's and Boeing
Chapter 17	Siemens Healthineers (global medical technology company)
Chapter 18	Unilever
Chapter 19	Nissan, Google and Deloitte
Chapter 20	Vodafone
Chapter 21	City of Sydney (local government authority)
Chapter 22	Deliveroo France
Chapter 23	Heineken
Chapter 24	Burger King, Nike, Alibaba and McDonald's
Chapter 25	Achmea (multinational insurance and financial services company)
Chapter 26	The EU's General Data Protection Regulation (GDPR), the California Consumer Privacy Act, the 'Honest Ads Act', and the Open Algorithms (OPAL) project
Chapter 27	Presence Switzerland (public diplomacy unit at the Swiss Federal Department of Foreign Affairs)
Chapter 28	Finnish Tax Administration
Chapter 29	Madrid City Council
Chapter 30	European Union

1. Introduction to the *Handbook on Digital Corporate Communication*
Mark Badham and Vilma Luoma-aho

WHY THIS BOOK?

The future of corporate communication is unreservedly digital. Indeed, due to digital technology's incremental yet ubiquitous influence on this field over the years, digital corporate communication (DCC) is already here, and it has been nudging the profession and its professionals towards changes in attitudes, skills, strategies and priorities. Some changes have been seismic, such as the way social media networks and digital platforms have democratized corporate communication, empowering digitally savvy stakeholders and disempowering organizations, often challenging old fashioned attitudes to stakeholder relationships and communication. Now, all kinds of stakeholders, from investor activists to past employees, can and do take over organizations' communication reins, steering organizational communication in new and uncharted directions, shifting organizational roles from gatekeeping (Shoemaker, 1991) to gatewatching (Bruns, 2005, 2011). For example, collectives of organizational hateholders (Luoma-aho, 2015) frequently are hijacking communication campaigns by taking over corporate hashtags in social media and retargeting them against corporations. A corporate crisis forming among posts in one Facebook account can spread fast and furiously across online social networks, damaging a corporation's reputation within hours.

These are both exhilarating and challenging times for practitioners and scholars within the profession. As masses of individual consumers and stakeholders master emerging means of 24/7 communication enabled by technology, so must the professionals of communication. New services, devices, apps and software are emerging onto the market to help organizations solve existing and future communication challenges. Many organizations are responding proactively to the opportunities these present. Increasingly, customers are interacting with chatbots on corporate websites, enabling organizations to be continuously 'open for business' 24/7, as illustrated in this *Handbook*'s cover image. In 2023, TikTok influencers are creatively collaborating with organizations who share their values and passions. Google Assistant is telling coffee lovers where their branded coffee was grown and roasted. Employees are proactively advocating for their employers' social causes in their personal social media posts. At the same time, the ease of clicktivism and the superficial world of social media and data privacy concerns is contributing to masses of passive and disengaged stakeholders who fail to see the value added by technology.

This volume is titled *Digital Corporate Communication* in recognition of these omnipresent, significant and fast-changing influences, both positive and negative, of digital technologies on the communication profession and on the external economic, cultural and societal forces shaping it. Despite this, academic studies to date have not been well integrated into a coherent research perspective. This *Handbook* argues that current theorizing on digitalization in the corporate communication literature has not yet adequately defined *digital corporate*

1

communication (DCC) or addressed the wide spectrum of digitalization's effects on and role in corporate communication (for a recent exception, see Brockhaus et al., 2022). Accordingly, there is an evident need for a thoughtful collection of current DCC research that extends and refines our understanding of how digital technologies, devices and platforms (e.g., beyond the dominant focus on social media) are reshaping corporate communication with various stakeholders. This *Handbook* meets that need by illuminating established and emerging theories, concepts, processes and practices related to DCC in terms of their fit to meet future challenges.

This volume builds a foundation for this emerging research by drawing on contributions from scholars across the globe who are carving out niche scholarly expertise in specialist areas of corporate communication influenced by digital technologies. Their research sheds light on how the discipline can best respond to the digital-driven opportunities and challenges facing it as a research community, a profession, and as individual and collective members of wider society. Accordingly, this *Handbook* provides an extensive overview of current knowledge of corporate communication from a digital point of view. It brings concepts and theories to life via case examples located in each chapter, which serve to illustrate theorizing in different cultural, socio-political and organizational contexts.

WHAT IS CORPORATE COMMUNICATION?

Insight into DCC first requires a clear understanding of corporate communication. The term *corporate communication* began in the scientific discourse in the 1970s, emerging from the older discipline and practice of public relations. At the time, corporate communication was sometimes understood as 'corporate public relations' (Lerbinger, 2019), beginning as public relations practised by industry and commerce (Kitchen, 1997) when the role of business began to rise in society and in higher education institutions (e.g., when business schools began to flourish). Accordingly, because of their unique needs and challenges, business organizations and business schools demanded new approaches to public relations and thus different communication-related tools and activities.

Corporate communication today is linked not only with the discipline of public relations, but also with strategic communication, communication management, organizational communication and marketing communications (e.g., van Riel, 1995; van Riel and Fombrun, 2007). The names of these disciplines are often used loosely and interchangeably in practice and research (Christensen and Cornelissen, 2011; Cornelissen, 2017; Gregory and Fawkes, 2019; Hallahan et al., 2007; Heath and Gregory, 2015), which suggests they have the same meanings. However, from a scholarly perspective, each discipline has its own loosely connected body of research and thus scholarly community that has developed over time and from which nuanced differences between them have both emerged and merged.

This chapter explains and defines corporate communication through six distinguishing attributes: (1) the communicating entity, (2) the purposive nature of communication, (3) the management of communication, (4) the object of communication, (5) the overall emphasis on communication, and (6) the goal of communication. Although these key attributes are interlinked and thus interdependent, they are separated here as distinct building blocks from which a coherent definition may emerge.

1. **Communicating entity**: Corporate communication has long since shed its business-only focus. For almost two decades now, corporate communication has been linked to all communications not only in large multinational corporations, but also in small-to-medium enterprises (SMEs) and public sector and not-for-profit organizations (Oliver, 2004). Accordingly, although corporate communication retains strong links to commerce, it also embraces other types of organizations, such as governments, public sector agencies, NGOs, trade associations and social movements. For this reason, the word *organization* as the communicating entity is a key component in forming a definition of corporate communication.

2. **Purposive nature of communication**: The question of the purposive nature of communication points to the wider ontological theorization of communication agency. Corporate communication is linked to the idea that communication professionals working for or on behalf of organizations may actively intervene in organizational communication processes and thus communicate on purpose for strategic reasons. According to Christensen and Cornelissen (2011, p. 384), "corporate communication research is mostly focused on the controlled handling and organization of communication". For this reason, the word *strategic* is an important component in shaping a corporate communication definition.

3. **Management of communication**: The word 'corporate' in the term *corporate communication* emphasizes that any type of organizational entity ideally should present a unified, coherent organizational or 'corporate' message by coordinating all forms of its communication to provide a consistent organizational image to all its stakeholders (van Riel, 1995). Corporate communication is identified as a core management function responsible for coordinating all communications (Christensen and Cornelissen, 2011, p. 386) under one banner, department or discipline to both external and internal stakeholders. Thus, corporate communication has been seen as having the ability to 'orchestrate' the varying messages and communication activities emanating from within the organization (van Riel, 1997).

    Corporate communication scholarship also acknowledges that an organization may speak with many different voices simultaneously to build and maintain legitimacy in a complex world. In other words, organizations may differentiate their messages to adapt to different audiences (Hill and Winski, 1987; Onkvisit and Shaw, 1987), strategically communicate in ambiguous ways (Eisenberg, 1984) to accommodate multiple conflicting interpretations and expectations of diverse stakeholders and manage multiple identities (Cheney, 1991).

    A corporate communication perspective also understands that organizational messages often do not emanate from organizations themselves; increasingly, stakeholders initiate messages affecting organizations (e.g., when they complain about an organization or its products and activities) as well as join other stakeholders' conversations in which organizational messages are discussed and debated. This describes collective stakeholder-to-stakeholder communication in which organizational intangible assets such as reputation and legitimacy are discursively inflated, debated and deflated. For this reason, corporate communication, and strategic communication scholars more recently, have begun to question how much agency communication professionals have over communication in this context. Emerging participatory-type communication and stakeholder-centric communication approaches suggest that organizations should value stakeholders' offline

4   *Handbook on digital corporate communication*

and online conversations about organizational matters, even from hateholders (Luoma-aho, 2015), and for this reason should seek to participate in them to listen to (Macnamara, 2017), learn from (Macnamara, 2017), and even love (Badham, 2020) them. Nevertheless, emerging from corporate communication theory is the perspective that at least some level of management of communication is imperative, which is why the word *management* is a key component in an emerging definition of corporate communication.

4. **Object of communication**: One of the distinctions between public relations and corporate communication is centred around the object of communication: publics, audiences, stakeholders and society. Distinctions between these terms are important. Predominantly, public relations scholars consider publics to be "groups of individuals who face a similar problem, recognize it, and organize themselves to address it, regardless of whether they have a direct interest in any organization involved with the issue" (Valentini, 2021, p. 9). Thus, publics often may be considered to be temporary and somewhat separate from organizational interests and ties, particularly when compared to stakeholders.

    Although both corporate communication and public relations disciplines may be separated by their unique approach to the object of organizational communication, the concept of audiences suggests that they are spectators in organization-managed, one-directional communication processes and recipients of organizational messages and thus they have limited agency in these processes. While public relations traditionally refers to 'target audiences', which suggests they are viewed as assets to be used for organizational purposes, corporate communication tends to refer to 'stakeholders' who are dependent on and affect and are affected by organizations and their activities and communication either directly or through intermediaries (Freeman, 1984; Luoma-aho and Paloviita, 2010). This approach to stakeholders indicates corporate communication's interest in treating them as more equal partners in the business of the organization and conducting communication with them in interactive, participatory ways. Thus, corporate communication aims to simultaneously engage with stakeholders while being mindful of prioritizing the organization's overall strategy.

    Increasingly, organizations are stepping forward as socio-political actors in society, entering public debates as advocates for and opponents against causes and issues. In this way their public statements reflecting their point of view are designed to contribute to public opinion in society. Thus, society has become one of the objects of communication for corporate communication professionals. Accordingly, the words *stakeholder* and *society* are important components contributing to an emerging corporate communication definition.

5. **Overall emphasis on communication**: As indicated in its name, the discipline of corporate communication focuses predominantly on communication. While public relations is focused predominantly on an organization's management of its relationships with various publics (organization–public relationship research dominates public relations scholarship), corporate communication tends to emphasize at its core the management of an organization's communication with its stakeholders. In other words, while public relations emphasizes an organization's management of relationships with key publics, corporate communication's emphasis is on managing communication for relationships with key stakeholders. Thus, corporate communication is seen as a management function within an organization that seeks to oversee and coordinate communication between and with

stakeholders. Thus, the word *communication* is important in the definition of corporate communication.

6. **Goal of communication**: While the word 'relations' in the term public relations indicates this discipline's strong focus on an organization's relational 'ties' with target audiences (Beger, 2018), corporate communication theory does not tend to accentuate organization–stakeholder relations (for *OSR theory*, see Badham, 2020) as a goal of communication. There are exceptions, of course (e.g., van Riel, 1995, p. 26). Favourable relations with stakeholders and the general public in society are considered an important intangible asset of organizations (Canel et al., 2020; Zerfass and Viertmann, 2017) that corporate communication professionals should seek to nurture and acquire. Other organizational intangible assets that corporate communication actions contribute to include organizational legitimacy (Suchman, 1995), identity (van Riel and Balmer, 1997) and reputation (Barnett et al., 2006). The importance of these different tangible and intangible assets will vary by sector, organization type, as well as the society surrounding the organization. Interestingly, in the digital realm the value of intangible assets appears to be gaining in importance, as digital platforms make reputation and social capital more visible for stakeholders. Although tangible communication outputs such as press releases, tweets and website content are important, these are simply ways to achieve intangible assets, which are considered more important to organizational management. Accordingly, *the maintenance of organizational intangible assets*, as an end goal of communication, is a key term in the formation of a corporate communication definition.

For the purposes of clarity, and taking the above definitions, conceptual ideas, key attributes and key terms (italicized below) into account, corporate communication can thus be defined analytically and in encompassing terms as:

> An *organization's strategic management* of *communication* with internal and external *stakeholders* and more broadly within *society* for the *maintenance of organizational tangible and intangible assets*.

The next section examines how the digital world is shaping corporate communication, which suggests that a new, refined definition is required to contribute to a holistic understanding of the discipline.

WHAT IS DIGITAL CORPORATE COMMUNICATION (DCC)?

Digital Corporate Communication Practices

Although 87 per cent of executives surveyed by Gartner in 2018 agree that 'digital' is an important priority for business, communication leaders struggle to understand the meaning of 'digitalization' and the role they should play as businesses seek to prioritize digitalization (Bryan, 2018). However, the emerging communications field known as CommTech (Communication Technology) is very much focused on addressing the challenge of how digital technologies can modify communication processes along the whole stakeholder journey with the organization (e.g., Arthur W. Page Society, 2021; Brockhaus et al., 2022; Weiner, 2021). CommTech's specific focus is on using digital tools, techniques and data to enable organizations to personalize

6 Handbook on digital corporate communication

closer engagement with stakeholders, such as by creating and delivering content and managing and analysing feedback.

The Arthur W. Page Society for Global Communication Executives (a leading professional association for senior public relations and corporate communication executives and educators) lists communication technology as one of the most urgent development areas for global brands and organizations in the 2020s. The Society's CommTech guide (Arthur W. Page Society, 2021) states that a CommTech system is built on three elements: the technologies available to us, the skills needed to make use of these technologies, and the methods to enculturate the use of these technologies.

The 2021 European Communication Monitor (Zerfass et al., 2021) reports that a vast majority of communication practitioners across Europe emphasize the importance of digitalizing stakeholder communication processes (87.7 per cent) and building a digital infrastructure to support internal workflows (83.9 per cent). Three out of four communication departments and agencies acknowledge they are relatively experienced in using external digital platforms for stakeholder communication and in providing collaboration platforms for their team members. However, only 60 per cent of communication departments and agencies in Europe have well-developed approaches for digitalizing their communication processes. Of concern is that about 40 per cent of practitioners across Europe believe their department or agency is not adequately digitalizing stakeholder communication processes and building digital infrastructure such as supporting internal workflows within a communication department or agency. To address this digital communication immaturity, Brockhaus et al. (2022) developed a framework to help practitioners to uncover and evaluate the level of digital maturity of communication departments and agencies.

Digital Corporate Communication Research

The increasingly widespread use and abuse of digital technologies for communication purposes by organizations, their stakeholders and wider society has led to a plethora of academic communication studies examining the nexus between digital technologies and communication approaches, processes and practices. As society and the organizations within them gradually come to terms with the ubiquitous nature of digital technology in our everyday lives, the rate at which we are studying and thus trying to make sense of the impact of digital technologies on communication within and by organizations is rapidly expanding. Recent examples of such studies include Brockhaus et al. (2022), Etter et al. (2019, 2021), Ewing et al. (2019), Freberg (2020), Lutrell et al. (2021), Wilson et al. (2020), and Wright and Hinson (2017).

Academic research in corporate communication has so far focused predominantly on new media and channels enabled by digital technology, such as social media, internet and websites (Duhé, 2017). Studies examining how organizations and stakeholders use social media as a communication tool have become one of the more dominant research areas in corporate communication. Other focal points of research include how digital technologies are shaping ways in which organizations and stakeholders communicate (for *digital dialogic principles and communication* see Capriotti et al., 2021 and Zhou and Xu, 2021; for *digital channels* see Oltarzhevskyi, 2019), interact (for *digital activism* see Ciszek, 2016; for *digital social advocacy* see Chalmers and Shotton, 2016), and relate (for *digital communicative organization–stakeholder relationships* see Lock, 2019). Scholars have recently begun to examine how big data and digital technology (e.g., AI and automation) are reshaping practices in corporate

Introduction 7

communication from the perspective of practitioners (e.g., Bajalia, 2020; Cacciatore et al., 2017; Wiencierz and Röttger, 2019; Wiesenberg et al., 2017; Zerfass et al., 2020).

However, despite this growing body of research, only a few corporate communication studies (with a heavy focus on the digital effects shaping corporate communication) explicitly refer to *digital corporate communication* (see e.g., Etter et al., 2019) or *online corporate communication* (García García et al., 2017; Oksiutycz and Kunene, 2017). In comparison, public relations studies refer to *digital public relations* (Huang et al., 2017; Kim et al., 2010; Sommerfeldt et al., 2012; Yaxley, 2012; Zhou and Xu, 2021), *online public relations* (Kitchen and Panopoulos, 2010; Ye and Ki, 2012), and *internet-related public relations* (Khang et al., 2012; Ye and Ki, 2012) when examining new media, social media, websites and the Internet. This *Handbook* addresses the need for a single body of published knowledge under the nomenclature of *digital corporate communication* to contribute to the widening knowledge gap in this increasingly important research and practice topic.

Another challenge is that a search through corporate communication studies back to 2010 reveals that a definition of digital corporate communication has not yet emerged. Marketing scholarship has defined digital marketing and legitimized it as a field of research (see Kannan and Li, 2017), yet corporate communication has not defined digital corporate communication despite the breadth of research in this area. Accordingly, in order to present a unified and coherent meaning of DCC to various internal stakeholders (e.g., corporate communication scholars and practitioners), external stakeholders (e.g., colleagues in other disciplines and practices), and wider society, a definition of DCC is needed and provided here.

But first, definitions of *digital*, *digitalization* and *digital transformation* also are needed. Unfortunately, like other professions and fields of study, corporate communication practitioners and scholars tend to rather loosely refer to these terms. Indeed, *digitization* and *digitalization* are sometimes used synonymously despite having different meanings. For this reason, interpretations and definitions of these concepts are offered below from both academic and professional practice points of view to try to shed light on a DCC point of view and to formulate a DCC definition.

Digital Technologies, Digital Infrastructures and Digitalization Processes

Definitions of *digital* in *The Oxford English Dictionary* (2022b) relate to numerical digits and their use in representing data in computing and electronics as well as to "signals, information and data represented by a series of discrete values (commonly the numbers 0 and 1), typically for electronic storage or processing". A synthesis of the definition of *digital*, in its adjective form, from both *The Oxford English Dictionary* (2022b) and *The Merriam-Webster Dictionary* (2022a) describes a type of device, image or period of time or space characterized by its electronically-enabled function, formation, storage, iniquitousness and empowerment; and, as a noun, the term refers to a medium in a digital format or a mechanism or device characterized or operated by digital technology. Typically, *digital* is contrasted with analogue.

The terms *digital platform* and *digital infrastructure* often are used synonymously. A digital platform is a corporate-owned digital media infrastructure (software-based or hardware-based) intended for users to share and co-create content for social purposes (e.g., YouTube, Facebook, Twitter) (Schwarz, 2017). As utilities that generate new societal functions and business opportunities, they also "facilitate complex multisided market exchanges (between media consumers, license holders, content creators, telecoms operators, investors) by way of digital

8 *Handbook on digital corporate communication*

automation" (Schwarz, 2017, p. 377). The dual nature of these infrastructures both empowers and constrains user interaction and expression (Eriksson et al., 2017).

Although there are many slightly differing definitions of *digitalization*, they predominantly refer to a social or socio-technical process. Communication scholars Brennan and Kreiss (2016), two of only a few communication scholars to offer a definition of digitalization, refer to it as "the way in which many domains of social life are restructured around digital communication and media infrastructures" (2016, p. 556). In information systems literature, one of the first scholars to offer clarity of digitalization, David Tilson, defined it as a socio-technical process in which digital technologies, which are integrated into or consist of software, platforms, information systems and devices, are integrated into processes, structures, capabilities and products. In this process, digital technologies become embedded into an overall digital infrastructure (Tilson et al., 2010). More recently, Legner et al. (2017) defined digitalization in the information systems context as "the manifold socio-technical phenomena and processes of adopting and using these technologies in broader individual, organizational, and societal contexts" (2017, p. 301). Within a more social context, when "interactions move away from analogue technologies (snail mail, telephone calls) to digital ones (email, chat, social media), both work and leisure domains become digitalized" (Bloomberg, 2018, p. 3).

Although *digitization* and *digitalization* are both processes, they are quite different in meaning. Frenzel et al. (2021) found a tendency in information systems research to define digitization as a technical process of data conversion, generation, storage, or processing. Information systems scholars Legner et al. (2017) define digitization as "the technical process of converting analogue signals into a digital form, and ultimately into binary digits" (2017, p. 301). In contrast, digitalization has mainly been referred to in the literature as "a socio-technical phenomenon, the use of digital technologies, and their influence on societies, businesses, and personal lives" (Frenzel et al., 2021, p. 7). This *Handbook* prefers the concept of digitalization, as it more aptly applies to the process in which digital technologies transform both corporate and corporate communication practices with the aim of improving communication with organizational stakeholders and in society more generally.

From an organizational point of view, digitalization is designed to transform organizational life. Indeed, digital transformation is one of the most important challenges for organizations of all types and sizes in the coming decades (Hess et al., 2016; Nadkarni and Prügl, 2021). Digital transformation is understood as "the intercept of the adoption of disruptive digital technologies on the one side and actor-guided organizational transformation of capabilities, structures, processes and business model components on the other side" (Nadkarni and Prügl, 2021, p. 236). In their McKinsey report, Bughin et al. (2019) define digital transformation as "an effort to enable existing business models by integrating advanced technologies" (2019, p. 1). In sum, according to Bloomberg (2018), "we digitize information, we digitalize processes and roles that make up the operations of a business, and we digitally transform the business and its strategy" (2018, p. 5).

Definition of Digital Corporate Communication (DCC)

This *Handbook* presents the argument that although *digital technologies* are a key contributing factor shaping significant changes in corporate communication processes and practices, these technologies also contribute to *digital infrastructures* and overall *digitalization processes* which in turn also influence corporate communication processes and practices. Accordingly,

Introduction 9

the following attribute is integrated into the earlier framework of six features forming a definition of corporate communication:

7. **Digital effects shaping communication**: The intersection of digital technologies, digital infrastructures and digitalization processes is identified as the main three-fold factor forming and shaping digital corporate communication in significant ways.

As such, taking these seven attributes of corporate communication and their related key terms into account, the following definition of DCC is offered:

> An organization's strategic management of digital technologies, digital infrastructures and digitalization processes to improve communication with internal and external stakeholders and more broadly within society for the maintenance of organizational tangible and intangible assets.

HOW IS THIS *HANDBOOK* STRUCTURED?

This *Handbook* is divided into four over-arching sections covering (1) digitally-influenced changes to legacy corporate communication functions, (2) digitally-influenced issues that corporate communication must address, (3) corporate communication's adoption of digital technologies, and (4) corporate communication's role in managing digitalization's effects in society. As shown in Figure 1.1, this *Handbook* follows the four spheres of digital development in corporate communication.

Figure 1.1   *The four parts of the Handbook*

10 *Handbook on digital corporate communication*

Part I: Digitally-Influenced Changes to Legacy Functions

Overall, the chapters in this first section deal with how digital technologies, digital infrastructures and digitalization processes are influencing long-standing, traditional core functions and strategic activities of corporate communication within different types and sizes of organizations. In short, the chapters in this section address the question: *How are digital technologies changing older practices within corporate communication?*

With an illustrative example of the Swedish Transport Administration, the chapter on internal communication investigates how digital communication tools and platforms offer organizations new possibilities for communication between organizational members through the reciprocal influence these tools/platforms and humans exert on each other. With a look at the British Monarchy as an illustrative example, the chapter on branding presents the Total Corporate Brand Communication model, which illuminates how digitally-influenced stakeholder communication can be accommodated into digital brand communication. Referring to the Global Strategic Communications Council (GSCC) as an illustrative example, the chapter on media relations examines how, despite the digital transformation of both journalism and media relations practices, news media outlets remain an important intermediary through which organizations can reach stakeholders with carefully crafted messages. Through the illustrative example of the Italian fashion house Dolce and Gabbana, the chapter on corporate reputation explores how emotionally-charged positive, negative and neutral social evaluations of organizations expressed in social media constantly shape organizations' reputations over time in these digital arenas; it also examines the role of fake news and AI applications in reputation formation. The chapter on investor relations and financial communication looks at the multinational enterprise software company SAP SE and examines how the effects of digital technologies on corporate relationship management with sophisticated and financially powerful stakeholders are shaping new roles for investor relations officers as data scientists and expert listeners. While social media has allowed organizations to create interactive and personalized experiences about diverse corporate social responsibility (CSR) topics and activities with different stakeholders, the popularization of social media also has enabled stakeholders to discover new and powerful ways to force organizations to be more accountable and report their commitments to environmental and socially responsible efforts; the chapter about CSR communication illustrates all this with the example of Nutresa, the leading processed food company in Colombia. Through the illustrative example of the multinational confectionary company Mondelez, the chapter on stakeholder relationship management explores how the evolution of digital communication technologies contributes to a stakeholder-centric approach to cultivating enhanced, meaningful relationships with stakeholders while also opening organizations up to direct critique from hateholders. Finally, through the UNICEF measurement framework case study, the chapter on measurement and evaluation examines how digital technologies offer advantages for measuring corporate communication (e.g., real-time automated data collection and analysis) as well as challenges (e.g., with data-based profiling).

Part II: Digitally-Influenced Issues Affecting Organizations

The chapters in this second section examine how corporate communication is responding to and dealing with digitally-shaped societal issues and stakeholder challenges impacting organizations. Organizational crises can emerge when stakeholders such as activists hijack

Introduction 11

organizational messages and when stakeholders' complaints about products and services are not managed well. Thus, organizations addressing rising issues that can affect their intangible assets require a deep understanding of how to take advantage of digital technology to manage diverse stakeholder relationships and respond to complaints. In short, chapters in this section address the question: *How is corporate communication dealing with digitally-influenced issues and challenges affecting organizations?*

The chapter on issues management, illustrated through the case example of the #deleteuber boycott, explores how organizations use digital technology to strategically monitor, analyse and respond to emerging socio-political issues important to stakeholders. The chapter on activism explores how activists make use of digital tools to target organizations across supply chains to achieve their socio-political aims; it examines this phenomenon through the illustrative example of the Asia Pulp and Paper (APP) company. Through the VW Golf case study, the chapter on the rise of paracrises and AI examines how to integrate digital channels into crisis and paracrisis communication and how AI offers the potential to identify crisis risks as well as actual crises. Using the illustrative example of the Singaporean electronic payment service provider NETS, along with its advertising agency Havas Worldwide Singapore, the chapter on crisis communication and crisis life cycles shows how digitally-driven communication tactics can be adopted at each stage of a crisis life cycle to help corporate communication professionals manage crisis communication more effectively. Referring to the case example of the Italian fashion house Gucci, the chapter on complaint management examines how the corporate communication function can mitigate consumer criticism or complaints about organizations and their products or services before they collectively escalate into socially-mediated crises in digital arenas. Referring to the Scandinavian airline SAS case, the chapter on hostile hijacking of organizational crises examines how organizations can prepare for and respond to hostile hijacking of organizational crises in digital arenas from ideologically motivated disinformation operators by looking out for four tell-tale signs. The related chapter on brandjacking and character assassinations examines how dissatisfied activists weaponize social media affordances to disrupt organizations' narration through character assassination of organizational leaders and hijacking organizations' communication campaigns; it illustrates this through the two illustrative examples of McDonald's and Boeing.

Part III: Corporate Communication's Adoption of Digital Technologies

In the third section, scholars explore how corporate communication practitioners are making use of (and should make more use of) digital infrastructures, digitalization processes and digital technologies, such as artificial intelligence, gamification, voice assistants and image-based apps, as well as manage algorithm-enhanced leadership and social media influencers. In short, these chapters address the question: *How is corporate communication embracing and adopting digital technologies and the influential actors mastering them?*

Drawing on the illustrative example of the global medical technology company Siemens Healthineers, the chapter covering digital transformation of the corporate communication function examines how the function of corporate communication is building digital infrastructures for communication management purposes and thus digitally transforming itself in the process. The chapter on social media influencers examines how an influencer relations approach and corporate influencer programmes helps corporate communicators harness the disruptive power of influencers, empowered through online social networks, to their advan-

12   *Handbook on digital corporate communication*

tage; it draws on the illustrative example of a Unilever influencer campaign in Germany. Using case examples such as Nissan, Google and Deloitte, the chapter on gamification explores how corporate communication can apply the application of game elements in non-game contexts to offer stakeholders a new kind of participatory storytelling experience that may deepen organization–stakeholder relationships. Presenting a Vodafone case study, the chapter on AI and its implications for corporate communication roles and responsibilities examines how corporate communication roles will be reshaped as many of the operational tasks are automated and infused with AI, how roles can become more strategic, and proposes an ethical guardian role within organizations. Referring to the local government authority for Sydney (Australia) as a case study, the chapter on extended intelligence (EI) explores how EI (the idea that AI can extend human intelligence), which includes machine learning, chatbots, augmented reality and virtual reality, are disrupting corporate communication while also offering more interactive and immersive organization–stakeholder communication experiences. Through the illustrative example of Deliveroo France, the chapter about algorithmic leadership explores how, through AI and automated technologies, algorithms that increasingly perform many management and leadership functions previously executed by humans require corporate communication professionals to integrate interactive communication and emotional engagement in unique, complex social communication processes. The chapter discussing visual communication examines how corporate communication is creating a visual content architecture to more effectively serve organizations' visual communication with stakeholders, and illustrates this through the case of the Dutch brewing company Heineken. The chapter covering voice communication investigates how voice platforms such as Amazon Alexa (and Alexa for Business) offer novel communication and relational opportunities within, between and beyond organizations; examples such as McDonald's 'I'm Lovin' it' audio signature are offered for illustrative purposes.

Part IV: Corporate Communication's Response to Digitally-Influenced Effects in Society

In the fourth section, chapters examine corporate communication's response to technology's critical effects in society, such as the ubiquity of big data and resulting disinformation, polarization and hegemony, as well as the complementary effects in society, such as corporations' improvement of their home country's images across global audiences as well as public sector organizations' use of digital technology to co-produce public services with their citizens. Thus, organizations are looking to better understand how to listen to stakeholder concerns in society so they can better manage stakeholder relations and respond to both negative and positive effects in society, such as through diplomacy, citizen engagement and public sector communication. In short, chapters address the question: *How is corporate communication dealing with the effects of digital technologies in society?*

Through the illustrative case of the multinational insurance and financial services company Achmea, the chapter on organizational listening examines principles and approaches for effective listening in and by organizations, digital technologies that facilitate organizational listening methods, and the resulting benefits these afford organizations and their stakeholders. Drawing on multiple examples such as Facebook allegedly skirting the European Union's GDPR laws, the chapter on the market for big data presents the perspective that, as a producer and beneficiary of the big data market, corporate communication contributes to corporate organizations' hegemony over stakeholders. The chapter on digital public diplomacy of

Introduction 13

nation-states and connected voices explores how digitalization is enabling corporations to interact with global stakeholders who evaluate them based on the image of their country of origin, and how this process enables these corporations to shape the international diplomatic discourse; an illustrative case study of Presence Switzerland, the specialized public diplomacy unit at the Swiss Federal Department of Foreign Affairs, is presented. Using the Finnish Tax Administration as an illustrative example, the chapter covering public sector organization (PSO) communication examines how the traditional text-based, one-directional informational communication approach of many PSOs is being challenged by citizens' expectations of real-time dialogue with them, albeit often spiced with emotion-infused digital memes, and how a more contemporary online, interactive, visual and intimate approach may be more suited to citizens' expectations. The chapter covering co-productive citizen engagement, through a case study of the Madrid City Council's smartphone app, examines how digital technology improves the way PSOs can listen to, communicate with, and engage in real time information exchange with citizens to enhance joint efforts for the co-production of public services. Finally, referring to the case of the European Union's response to a Covid-19 vaccine disinformation campaign, the chapter on disinformation explores how exponential growth in social media as a source of information has enabled the spread of disinformation and yet also how these same digital channels can be used by organizations to address concerns of stakeholders and strengthen relationships of trust.

The final chapter, in Part V, concludes with recommendations for future research directions.

REFERENCES

Arthur W. Page Society (2021). *CommTech Guide*. https://commtechguide.page.org/getting-started-in -commtech-from-professional-to-pathfinder/a-new-profession-emerges/.

Badham, M. (2020). Love wins: A love lens approach to cultivation of organization–stakeholder relationships. In R. Tench, A. T. Vercic, and S. Einwiller (eds.), *Joy: Using strategic communication to improve well-being and organizational success*, Advances in Public Relations and Communication Management Vol. 5 (pp. 3–20). Bingley: Emerald Publishing.

Bajalia, A. (2020). Where are we now? Public relations professionals discuss measurement and evaluation. *Public Relations Journal*, *13*(2).

Barnett, M., Jermier, J., and Lafferty, B. (2006). Corporate reputation: The definitional landscape. *Corporate Reputation Review*, *9*, 26–38.

Beger, R. (2018). *Present-day corporate communication: A practice-oriented, state-of-the-art guide*. Singapore: Springer Nature.

Bloomberg, J. (2018). Digitization, digitalization, and digital transformation: Confuse them at your peril. *Forbes Magazine*, 29 April. https://www.forbes.com/sites/jasonbloomberg/2018/04/29/digitization -digitalization-and-digital-transformation-confuse-them-at-your-peril/?sh=189c02682f2c.

Brennan, J. S. and Kreiss, D. (2016). Digitalization. In K. B. Jensen and R. Craig (eds.), *The international encyclopedia of communication theory and philosophy* (pp. 1–11). Wiley Online Library.

Brockhaus, J., Buhmann, A., and Zerfass, A. (2022). Digitalization in corporate communications: Understanding the emergence and consequences of CommTech and digital infrastructure. *Corporate Communications: An International Journal*, volume ahead-of-print. DOI:10.1108/CCIJ-03-2022-0035.

Bruns, A. (2005). *Gatewatching: Collaborative online news production*. New York: Peter Lang.

Bruns, A. (2011). Gatekeeping, gatewatching, real-time feedback: New challenges for journalism. *Brazilian Journalism Research Journal*, *7*(2), 117–136.

Bryan, J. (2018). *What digitalization means for corporate communications*. Gartner, 17 September. https://www.gartner.com/smarterwithgartner/digitalization-means-corporate-communications/.

Bughin, J., Deakin, J., and O'Beirne, B. (2019). Digital transformation: Improving the odds of success. *McKinsey Quarterly* (October).

14 *Handbook on digital corporate communication*

Cacciatore, M. A., Meng, J., and Berger, B. K. (2017). Information flow and communication practice challenges: A global study on effective responsive strategies. *Corporate Communications: An International Journal, 22*(3), 292–307.

Canel, M. J., Luoma-aho, V., and Barandiarán, X. (2020). Public sector communication and public-valued intangible assets. In V. Luoma-aho and M. J. Canel (eds.), *Handbook of public sector communication* (pp. 101–114). Malden, MA: Wiley-Blackwell.

Capriotti, P., Zeler, I., and Camilleri, M. A. (2021). Corporate communication through social networks: The identification of key dimensions for dialogic communication. In M. A. Camilleri (ed.), *Strategic corporate communication in the digital age* (pp. 33–51). Bingley: Emerald Publishing.

Chalmers, A. W. and Shotton, P. A. (2016). Changing the face of advocacy? Explaining interest organizations' use of social media strategies. *Political Communication, 33*(3), 374–391.

Cheney, G. (1991). *Rhetoric in an organizational society: Managing multiple identities*. Columbia: University of South Carolina Press.

Christensen, L. T. and Cornelissen, J. (2011). Bridging corporate and organizational communication: Review, development and a look to the future. *Management Communication Quarterly, 25*(3), 383–414.

Ciszek, E. L. (2016). Digital activism: How social media and dissensus inform theory and practice. *Public Relations Review, 42*, 314–321.

Cornelissen, J. (2017). *Corporate communication: A guide to theory and practice* (5th ed.). London: Sage Publications.

Digital (2022a). *Merriam-Webster online dictionary*. https://www.merriam-webster.com/dictionary/digital.

Digital (2022b). *Oxford English online dictionary*. https://www-oed-com.ezproxy.jyu.fi/view/Entry/52611?redirectedFrom=digital#eid.

Duhé, S. C. (ed.) (2017). *New media and public relations* (3rd ed.). New York: Peter Lang.

Eisenberg, E. (1984). Ambiguity as strategy in organizational communication. *Communication Monographs, 51*, 227–242.

Eriksson, M., Fleischer, R., Johansson, A., Snickars, P., and Vonderau, P. (2017). *Spotify teardown: Inside the black box of streaming music*. Cambridge, MA: MIT Press.

Etter, M., Winkler, P., and Glozer, S. (2019). New responsibilities for digital corporate communication. In M. Morsing, U. Golob, and K. Podnar (eds.), *CSR Communication Conference 2019: Conference Proceedings*. Izdajatelj: Faculty of Social Sciences, University of Ljubljana.

Etter, M., Winkler, P., and Pleil, T. (2021). Public relations and social media. In C. Valentini (ed.), *Public relations*, Handbook of Communication Science Vol. 27 (pp. 159–174). Berlin: De Gruyter.

Ewing, M., Men, L. R., and O'Neil, J. (2019). Using social media to engage employees: Insights from internal communication managers. *International Journal of Strategic Communication, 13*(2), 110–132.

Freberg, K. (2020). Social media for strategic communication: Creative strategies and research-based applications. *Journal of Public Relations Education, 6*(2), 200–204.

Freeman, M. E. (1984). *Strategic management: A stakeholder approach*. Cambridge: Cambridge University Press.

Frenzel, A., Muench, J. C., Bruckner, M. T., and Veit, D. (2021). *Digitization or digitalization? Toward an understanding of definitions, use and application in IS research*. AMCIS 2021 Proceedings.

García García, M., Carrillo-Durán, M. V., and Tato Jimenez, J. L. (2017). Online corporate communications: Website usability and content. *Journal of Communication Management, 21*(2), 140–154.

Gregory, A. and Fawkes, J. (2019). A global capability framework: Reframing public relations for a changing world. *Public Relations Review, 45*(3), 1–13.

Hallahan, K., Holzhausen, D., Van Ruler, B., Verčič, D., and Sriramesh, K. (2007). Defining strategic communication. *International Journal of Strategic Communication, 1*(1), 3–35.

Heath, R. E. and Gregory, A. (2015). Introduction: Defining strategic communication – groundings, forewarnings, and calls to action. In R. E. Heath and A. Gregory (eds.), *Strategic communication* (pp. xxxi–xxxvi). London: Sage Publications.

Hess, T., Matt, C., Benlian, A., and Wiesboeck, F. (2016). Options for formulating a digital transformation strategy. *MIS Quarterly Executive, 15*(2), 123–139.

Hill, J. S. and Winski, J. M. (1987). Goodbye global ads: Global village is fantasyland for big marketers. *Advertising Age*, 16 November, 22–36.

Huang, Y.-H. C., Wu, F., and Huang, Q. (2017). Does research on digital public relations indicate a paradigm shift? An analysis and critique of recent trends. *Telematics and Informatics*, *37*, 1364–1376.

Kannan, P. K. and Li, H. (2017). Digital marketing: A framework, review and research agenda. *International Journal of Research in Marketing*, *34*(1), 22–45.

Khang, H., Ki, E. J., and Ye, L. (2012). Social media research in advertising, communication, marketing, and public relations, 1997–2010. *Journalism & Mass Communication Quarterly*, *89*, 279–298.

Kim, S., Park, J. H., and Wertz, E. K. (2010). Expectation gaps between stakeholders and web-based corporate public relations efforts: Focusing on Fortune 500 corporate websites. *Public Relations Review*, *36*(3), 215–221.

Kitchen, P. J. (1997). Was public relations a prelude to corporate communications? *Corporate Communications: An International Journal*, *2*(1), 22–30.

Kitchen, P. J. and Panopoulos, A. (2010). Online public relations: The adoption process and innovation challenge, a Greek example. *Public Relations Review*, *36*(3), 222–229.

Legner, C., Eymann, T., Hess, T., Matt, C., Böhmann, T., Drews, P., Mädche, A., Urbach, N., and Ahlemann, F. (2017). Digitalization: Opportunity and challenge for the business and information systems engineering community. *Business & Information Systems Engineering*, *59*(4), 301–308.

Lerbinger, O. (2019). *Corporate communication: An international and management perspective*. Hoboken, NJ: John Wiley & Sons.

Lock, I. (2019). Explicating communicative organization-stakeholder relationships in the digital age: A systematic review and research agenda. *Public Relations Review*, *45*(4), 1–13.

Luoma-aho, V. (2015). Understanding stakeholder engagement: Faith-holders, hateholders and fakeholders. *Research Journal of the Institute for Public Relations*, *2*(1). https://instituteforpr.org/understanding-stakeholder-engagement-faith-holders-hateholders-fakeholders/.

Luoma-aho, V. and Paloviita, A. (2010). Actor-networking stakeholder theory for corporate communications. *Corporate Communications: An International Journal*, *15*(1), 47–69.

Lutrell, R., Emerick, S., and Wallace, A. (2021). *Digital strategies: Data-driven public relations, marketing, and advertising*. Oxford: Oxford University Press.

Macnamara, J. (2017). Creating a 'democracy for everyone': Strategies for increasing listening and engagement by government. The London School of Economics and Political Science. https://www.lse.ac.uk/media-and-communications/assets/documents/research/2017/MacnamaraReport2017.pdf.

Nadkarni, S. and Prügl, R. (2021). Digital transformation: A review, synthesis and opportunities for future research. *Management Review Quarterly*, *71*(2), 233–341.

Oksiutycz, A. and Kunene, S. J. (2017). Contribution of online corporate communication to brand reputation among millennials in the Vaal region. *Communicatio*, *43*(3–4), 74–94.

Oliver, S. M. (ed.) (2004). *Handbook of corporate communication and public relations: Pure and applied*. London: Routledge.

Oltarzhevskyi, D. O. (2019). Typology of contemporary corporate communication channels. *Corporate Communications: An International Journal*, *24*(4), 608–622.

Onkvisit, S. and Shaw, J. J. (1987). Standardized international advertising: A review and critical evaluation of the theoretical and empirical evidence. *Columbia Journal of World Business*, *22*, 43–55.

Schwarz, J. A. (2017). Platform logic: An interdisciplinary approach to the platform-based economy. *Policy & Internet*, *9*(4), 374–394.

Shoemaker, P. J. (1991). *Gatekeeping*. London: Sage Publications.

Sommerfeldt, E. J., Kent, M. L., and Taylor, M. (2012). Activist practitioner perspectives of website public relations: Why aren't activist websites fulfilling the dialogic promise? *Public Relations Review*, *38*(2), 303–312.

Suchman, M. C. (1995). Managing legitimacy: Strategic and institutional approaches. *Academy of Management Review*, *20*(3), 571–610.

Tilson, D., Lyytinen, K., and Sørensen, C. (2010). Research commentary—digital infrastructures: The missing IS research agenda. *Information Systems Research*, *21*(4), 748–759.

Valentini, C. (ed.) (2021). *Public relations*, Handbook of Communication Science Vol. 27. Berlin: De Gruyter.

16 *Handbook on digital corporate communication*

van Riel, C. B. M. (1995). *Principles of corporate communication.* Upper Saddle River, NJ: Prentice Hall.

van Riel, C. B. M. (1997). Research in corporate communication: An overview of an emerging field. *Management Communication Quarterly, 11*, 288–309.

van Riel, C. B. M. and Balmer, J. M. T. (1997). Corporate identity: The concept, its measurement, and management. *European Journal of Marketing, 31*, 341–355.

van Riel, C. B. M. and Fombrun, C. (2007). *Essentials of corporate communication: Implementing practices for effective reputation management.* London: Routledge.

Weiner, M. (2021). *PR technology, data and insights: Igniting a positive return on your communications investment.* London: Kogan Page.

Wiencierz, C. and Röttger, U. (2017). The use of big data in corporate communication. *Corporate Communications: An International Journal, 22*(3), 258–272.

Wiesenberg, M., Zerfass, A., and Moreno, A. (2017). Big data and automation in strategic communication. *International Journal of Strategic Communication, 11*(2), 95–114.

Wilson, C., Brubaker, P., and Smith, B. (2020). Cracking the snapcode: Understanding the organizational and technological influences of strategic social media adoption. *International Journal of Strategic Communication, 14*(1), 41–59.

Wright, D. K. and Hinson, M. D. (2017). Tracking how social and other digital media are being used in public relations practice: A twelve-year study. *Public Relations Journal, 11*(1), 1–30.

Yaxley, H. (2012). Digital public relations: Revolution or evolution? In A. Theaker (ed.), *Public relations handbook* (4th ed., pp. 411–422). Abingdon: Routledge.

Ye, L. and Ki, E. (2012). The status of online public relations research: An analysis of published articles in 1992–2009. *Journal of Public Relations Research, 24*(5), 409–434.

Zerfass, A., Buhmann, A., Tench, R., Verčič, D., and Moreno, A. (2021). *European Communication Monitor 2021. CommTech and digital infrastructure, video-conferencing, and future roles for communication professionals. Results of a survey in 46 countries.* Brussels: EUPRERA/EACD.

Zerfass, A., Verhoeven, P., Moreno, A., Tench, R., and Verčič, D. (2020). *European Communication Monitor 2020. Ethical challenges, gender issues, cyber security, and competence gaps in strategic communication. Results of a survey in 44 countries.* Brussels: EUPRERA/EACD.

Zerfass, A. and Viertmann, C. (2017). Creating business value through corporate communication: A theory-based framework and its practical application. *Journal of Communication Management, 21*(1), 86–91.

Zhou, A. and Xu, S. (2021). Digital public relations through the lens of affordances: A conceptual expansion of the dialogic principles. *Journal of Public Relations Research,* 33(6), 445–463.

PART I

DIGITALLY-INFLUENCED CHANGES TO LEGACY FUNCTIONS

2. Digital corporate communication and internal communication

Rickard Andersson, Mats Heide and Charlotte Simonsson

INTRODUCTION

Digital internal communication is not a new phenomenon – it has existed as a practice in organizations since the early 1970s and the use of digital technology in our daily work life has been growing gradually since then. However, the Covid-19 pandemic with its initial outbreak in early 2020 caused a sudden and disruptive change in the sense that it brought about an exponential increase in the use of digital communication tools and platforms in corporations across the globe. As regional and national lockdowns forced large numbers of staff members to work from home, managers and coworkers rapidly had to acquaint themselves with digital communication and develop new practices for cooperation, work and communication (Ruck and Men, 2021). Consequently, while internal communication gradually has become digitalized since the dawn of the information age in the 1970s, there is no doubt that the Covid-19 pandemic accelerated this change. And while electronic or digital communication tools and platforms are nothing new, the pace of innovation and constantly improved quality of digital platforms and tools ensure that they will continue to become an indispensable part of internal communication to ensure successful coordination and organizing.

The ongoing digitalization is still haunted by unrealistic assumptions of what technology per se can do to increase the efficiency of work processes and communication with stakeholders. For example, internal social media may be rich with potentials such as collective learning, relationship building, dialogue and participatory communication, but several scholars argue that in most cases these potentials have not been reached yet (Heide, 2015; Madsen, 2017, 2018). What is important to consider is that communication technology and digital communication tools and platforms offer several new *affordances* (Gibson, 1979; Hutchby, 2001) (i.e., possibilities for action) to organizational members, but that it is the reciprocal influence that communication technology and humans have on each other that constitutes novel forms of internal communication.

This chapter gives an overview of earlier research on digital internal communication. It also discusses what is changing in organizations as an effect of digital internal communication and what will remain the same. Further, it problematizes and discusses the possible negative implications of an increasing use of digital tools before concluding with some suggestions for future research.

DEFINITIONS OF THE TOPIC AND PREVIOUS STUDIES

The importance of internal communication for organizations has been emphasized by researchers for several decades (e.g., Clampitt and Downs, 1993). Despite this, Verčič et al.

(2012) concluded in 2012 that internal communication is in its infancy both as a practice and academic topic. However, the body of research on the topic is steadily expanding, and research on internal communication has increased exponentially since 2011 (Lee and Yue, 2020). As a result of this expansion, a growing number of definitions have been proposed. For example, Welch and Jackson (2007, p. 193) proposed a definition of internal communication as:

> the strategic management of interactions and relationships between stakeholders within organisations across a number of interrelated dimensions including, internal line manager communication, internal team peer communication, internal project peer communication and internal corporate communication.

Kalla (2005) defines integrated internal communication as "all formal and informal communication taking place internally at all levels of an organisation" (p. 304), intended to cover all communication processes within the organization. As is evident, the two definitions approach and conceptualize internal communication somewhat differently. Welch and Jackson (2007) emphasize the strategic management of internal communication (see also Men and Bowen, 2017), distancing themselves from perspectives focusing on organizational communication processes as such. It is also important to notice that Welch and Jackson (2007) use the term 'stakeholders' within the organization. From a philosophical standpoint, one may wonder what constitutes the organization if coworkers are perceived as 'stakeholders'. This understanding of organization originates from a functionalist perspective, where the organization is understood as an objective entity that exists independent of employees (Burrell and Morgan, 1979) (i.e., managers and coworkers). In a functionalist view of organization, communication is reduced to a tool for transmitting information from senders to receivers (Putnam, 1983; Putnam and Boys, 2006). What is also characteristic of functionalist research on organizations is a focus on solving practical problems and taking a managerial perspective (i.e., helping managers to increase efficiency). Kalla (2005) instead contributes to a processual understanding of internal communication, thereby offering a complementing understanding. However, Kalla still views communication as something going on 'inside' an already existing organization. While different, these three definitions have in common that they treat organizations as objects or reified identities where messages are transmitted between internal senders and receivers.

However, already towards the end of the 1960s, the American organizational psychologist Karl E. Weick (1969) maintained that organizations come into existence and are reproduced by communication processes. Later, the interpretive turn in organizational communication initiated a process view of communication and challenged the dominating view of organizations as social facts that exist 'out there'. Hence, according to a social constructionist perspective, communication is not only a variable or transmission of communication. Putnam (1983) states that communication creates and recreates social structures that constitute an organization. This concise review of two different definitions of internal communication highlights that both management-centred and process-centred perspectives on internal communication exist. The two definitions reviewed capture essential elements of internal communication.

However, this chapter proposes a two-fold definition of internal communication as: (1) the formal and informal communication between organizational members (managers and coworkers) taking place through various communication modes (digital media such as email, intranet and video meetings, but also various face-to-face meetings and print media; and (2) the strategic management and administration of internal communication. This definition thereby combines a process-centred and management-centred understanding of internal communication in

20 *Handbook on digital corporate communication*

a single definition. Additionally, by not referring to communication as taking place 'inside' an already given organization, the definition emphasizes that organizations, rather than being pre-given entities, are continuously constituted, negotiated and contested in and through communication. Furthermore, this definition of internal communication considers not only formal communication, but also what Barnard (1938/1968) defines as the informal organization; that is, the interaction between organizational members taking place outside the formal communication structures such as staff meetings and line management communication. It should also be noted that leadership communication (i.e., communicative interaction between managers and coworkers) is regarded as a vital part of digital internal communication. Thus, rather than drawing a distinction between internal communication and leadership communication, the latter is here considered as a vital, if not the most important, part of internal communication. In a similar vein, Men (2014a, 2014b) has called for a stronger focus on the role of leadership in internal communication systems. However, this does not mean that communication professionals do not have a vital role in internal communication. On the contrary, they have several important roles – as communication coaches to leaders and coworkers, as producers of formal communication mediated via internal channels and platforms, and as strategic managers and developers of internal communication processes (Heide and Simonsson, 2014; Zerfass and Franke, 2013). The second part of the definition (i.e., "the strategic management and administration of internal communication") intends to capture this vital work. However, given that managers and coworkers nowadays are expected to take greater responsibility for communication, it is not explicitly stated in the definition that the strategic management and administration of internal communication is a concern for communication professionals only.

It is important to address that while this chapter discusses internal communication, assuming a clear boundary between an organization's internal communication and the external communication is problematic given that these are closely intertwined communication processes (Cheney and Christensen, 2001), influencing each other to the extent that it would be counter-productive to treat them as totally distinct processes. This blurring is further enhanced through digital media as it has made it easier for coworkers to make their voice heard through social media (e.g., Ravazzani and Mazzei, 2018). However, while it is relevant to problematize the distinction between external and internal communication, there are many communication events and media (e.g., workplace meetings, newsletters, intranets and internal social media) that are intended for organizational members (managers and coworkers) only. And while the communication taking place in and on these channels and platforms can (and often does) extend beyond the network of organizational members, narrowing the scope of the chapter to the communication processes involving organizational members, and the strategic management and administration of those processes, is necessary to maintain clarity.

Defining Digital Internal Communication

Before proposing a definition of *digital internal communication*, it is important to clarify the distinction between *digitization* and *digitalization* to provide a more nuanced understanding of digital internal communication. The chapter follows Brennen and Kreiss' (2016) definition of digitization as "the material process of converting analogue streams of information into digital bits" (p. 1), and digitalization as "the way many domains of social life are restructured around digital communication and media infrastructures" (p. 1). Thus, in short, the term digitization refers to the process of converting analogue information into digital bits, while the term digitalization refers to the various implications of digital media and digital technologies for society, organizations and the social world in general. In an organizational context, digitization changes organizational processes, such as the dissemination of information, through reducing limitations of time, space, location, or resources (Leonardi and Treem, 2020). In contrast, Leonardi and Treem suggest that digitalization takes place when organizations take advantage of the digitization of organizational processes to develop new forms of organizing, such as remote work arrangements, or virtual team collaboration enabled through, for example, communication platforms and internal social media (ISM). Thus, while digitization can refer to the process of turning the analogue office noticeboard into a digital noticeboard available on the intranet, digitalization necessitates more profound changes in organizing.

Following the two-fold definition of internal communication and the clarification of the impact of digitization and digitalization on organizing, digital internal communication is in this chapter defined as: *the formal and informal communication between organizational members taking place through various digital communication modes, and the strategic management and administration of digital internal communication.* 'Organizational members' here refers to managers and coworkers, and examples of digital communication modes are email, intranet and video meetings. Similar to the definition of internal communication, by not referring to communication as taking place 'inside' the organization, this definition stresses that organizations are continuously constituted, negotiated and contested in and through communication rather than pre-existing independently of communication.

Previous Studies on Digital Internal Communication

When it comes to previous studies on digital internal communication, it becomes clear that various forms of computer-mediated communication (CMC), such as email, electronic billboards and group decision support systems, have been used in organizations since the 1970s and, since then, CMC also has been studied as a phenomenon (Hiltz and Turoff, 1978). CMC can be defined as "human communication between two or more individuals through the use of central computers that store and process message content and are connected to users in a communication network" (Rogers and Allbritton, 1997, p. 249). The early research on CMC in organizations emphasized positive effects, such as independence of time and space in work (Rogers, 1988) and more efficient cooperation (Orlikowski et al., 1999). However, researchers claimed early on that there is little evidence of changed organizational structure and increased productivity by the use of CMC. One explanation for the exaggerated expectations is unrealistic or even erroneous assumptions about human behaviour in organizational environments (Contractor and Eisenberg, 1990). Technology is viewed as an independent variable per se that can cause social and cultural changes – a reasoning described as technical determinism (Hirschheim and Klein, 1989) or as a technological imperative (Bloomfield et al., 1997). As noted above, this strong belief in the causal effects of technology per se still exists. Related to this is the still dominating transmission view of communication, which focuses on efficient transportation of information via a medium from a sender to receivers and that information per se is valuable; the more information, the better (Falkheimer and Heide, 2022).

In more contemporary studies on digital internal communication, one growing body of research concerns how digital communication tools such as internal social media, collaboration tools and strategy development tools influence aspects such as listening, coworker voice and strategizing (Gode, 2019; Madsen and Johansen, 2019; van Zoonen and Sivunen,

22 *Handbook on digital corporate communication*

2020). Other researchers have investigated how internal social media influences employee engagement (e.g., Ewing et al., 2019; Men et al., 2020). Another body of research in which the digitalization of internal communication is explored is workplace communication (Mikkola and Valo, 2019). Here, studies suggest that digital workplace communication platforms can provide new possibilities for communication and contribute to enhanced knowledge sharing and organizational learning, but that these platforms simultaneously risk reducing coworkers' willingness to share information and communicate on these platforms due to the increased visibility of communication that these platforms provide (Sivunen and Laitinen, 2019). Another study indicates that coworkers' job performance increases when they make use of both online and offline communication tools to interact with their workplace network to acquire relevant resources to carry out their tasks (Zhang and Viswanath, 2013). However, in their study of how the social bot Slackbot was used in virtual team interaction on the communication platform Slack, Laitinen et al. (2021) found that the bot, instead of contributing to process-optimization and more efficient task accomplishment, contributed to shift focus from the team tasks towards relational communication. Their study thereby highlights that the use of social bots in internal communication can facilitate and support socialization as well as social and relational needs. Yet another research area focuses on leaders' use of digital media, but much of this concerns social media and crisis management (Grafström and Lid-Falkman, 2017) rather than leaders' internal communication with coworkers. However, there are some recent studies that focus on leaders' communication on internal digital platforms (covering aspects such as frequency, clarity, listening, etc.) and how it is related to aspects such as performance, culture and trust (Cardon et al., 2019; Newman et al., 2020). Interestingly enough, Cardon et al. (2019) found that leaders in organizations with strong culture and high performance were active on internal digital platforms. Another study investigated how managers' computer-mediated communication can facilitate communication and connection among coworkers and contribute to a healthy workplace environment (Kelly et al., 2022).

WHAT IS CHANGING?

The most fundamental changes to internal communication processes brought about by digitalization are the gradual dissolving of time and space constraints (see Gulbrandsen and Just, 2020). This follows wider societal trends brought about by the information technological revolution beginning in the 1970s, and which, for example, sociologist Castells (2010) argues necessitates a reconceptualization of space and time. The understanding of space in the information age needs to be reconceptualized from the traditional understanding of it as the 'space of places' (that is, traditional physical places such as a city in which people live and interact with other people in the same place), to a 'space of flows' (that is, a new form of space located in communication flows that enables people to communicate in real-time across physical distances). The understanding of time, Castells suggests, must also be reconceptualized from the notion of time as an essential ordering device in society, as has been the case in pre-industrial and industrial societies, to an age in which the importance of time as an ordering device is made redundant given the immediacy, fragmentation, and dissolving of time due to the emergence of the 'space of flows'.

This gradual dissolving of space and time due to information technology has several implications for internal communication processes. For example, while traditional collaboration and communication between organizational members were highly dependent upon members sharing the same geographical location at the same point in time, communication platforms such as video meeting technologies and digital collaboration platforms enable individual organizational members to communicate online in a way that removes the time and space constraints. The dissolving of space and time limitations thus has several implications for internal communication. Below, these implications are discussed from both the perspective of managers and of coworkers.

Digitalization changes leadership both in terms of its role and how it is practised. Terms such as e-leadership (Avolio and Kahai, 2003; Braun et al., 2019; Liu et al., 2018) and digital leadership (Franco, 2020) have been used to capture this new kind of leadership. Digital leadership is frequently described as part of the fourth industrial revolution – a new technological epoch where big data, artificial intelligence, internet of things, automation etc. will radically bring new business models (Della Corte et al., 2020). The term digital leadership sometimes refers to leadership roles being responsible for the digital transformation, requiring capabilities such as entrepreneurship, innovation spirit, courage and open communication (Abbu et al., 2020; Della Corte et al., 2020). Other researchers put less emphasis on strong leaders and argue instead for a more relation-oriented leadership. Malakyan (2020), for example, claims that traditional, hierarchical leadership models are not relevant in the digital age. Increasing complexity calls for a shift from 'great man' theories and other leader-centred perspectives, to a stronger focus on leadership as a relational process and follower-oriented approaches to leadership (Jackson and Parry, 2011; Malakyan, 2020).

The term e-leadership seems not to focus so much on the link between digitalization and new business models, but rather on leaders' use of advanced information technology and how leadership and the organization of work is mediated by information technology (see e.g., Avolio and Kahai, 2003; Braun et al., 2019; Liu et al., 2018). Avolio and Kahai (2003) point out that e-leadership not only means that leader–follower communication takes place via advanced information technology, but also that information technology is used to collect, store and distribute information needed to support work and decisions. Doing leadership in an increasingly digitalized context has been part of many leaders' daily work for several years, but as mentioned above, there is still not much empirical research on leaders' actual communication practices mediated via new technology (Liu et al., 2018). Avolio et al. (2014) argue that "what we know about the interaction between AIT (Advanced Information Technology) and leadership still remains at the very nascent stages of development" (p. 105). Braun et al. (2019) conclude that much of the existing research on leaders' use of digital channels is focused on effective transmission of information and they are calling for a stronger focus on how coworkers perceive the changes towards more digitalized communication with their managers. In a recent study, Braun et al. (2019) found that coworkers still prefer face-to-face communication over email and telephone communication with their manager. There are also studies that focus on how coworkers perceive leaders' communication in digital media and its impact on aspects such as performance (Cardon et al., 2019; Newman et al., 2020). More studies from a coworker perspective are certainly needed, but also research on the interaction and the relational process between managers and coworkers in digital media.

Increased use of digital internal media means that coworkers have access to more or less the same information as managers, and the old saying of "information is power" is no longer valid (Avolio and Kahai, 2003). This, in combination with a stronger emphasis on self-leadership (Harari et al., 2021) and independent team work raises the question of the implications of these changes for the role of leadership. Braun et al. (2019) claim that leadership in virtual teams may be even more important than in physical settings to alleviate some of the detrimental processes that are enhanced in virtual and hybrid settings. Such settings may, for example, entail the loss of a bigger picture, or the loss of a sense of being part of an organizational context that goes beyond one's specific role or team of nearest colleagues. Work in silos has for a long time been a problem, but it may become an even bigger problem when organizational members do not share a common workplace on a daily basis. Although it has always been important, it may be even more crucial that leaders bring in the organizational perspective and facilitate collective sensemaking around issues such as the organization's vision and goals. Thus, leaders' role as information providers will further decrease, while their role as initiators and facilitators of sensemaking concerning bigger, collective matters will increase (Ruben and Gigliotti, 2016; Weick, 1995).

Given that a relation-oriented approach to leadership is becoming increasingly important, leaders' listening on internal digital platforms needs more attention. Scholars within the field of strategic communication and related fields have, in recent years, increasingly emphasized the importance of organizational listening (Macnamara, 2016, 2019). The Covid-19 pandemic and the subsequent increase of remote work has further highlighted the need to better understand how to listen remotely and how to use digital tools for this purpose. Interestingly enough, Cardon et al. (2019) found that listening was the communication behaviour of leaders that had the highest impact on the development of a positive culture (measured as high emotional capital) and strong organizational performance. Neill and Bowen (2021) demonstrated that there are many challenges to organizational listening, not least to close the feedback loop by communicating to coworkers how their ideas and concerns have been addressed. Personal relationships and initial trust are important for coworkers' willingness to share their concerns, but if the feedback loop is not closed there is a clear risk of creating a negative impact on trust and commitment.

Digital internal communication does not only have an impact on leadership and leaders' communication, but it may also change the communication roles and practices of coworkers. Most organizations seem to have been keener on applying social media in their communication with external stakeholders than internally, but more and more organizations use social media in their internal communication (Leonardi et al., 2013; Sievert and Scholz, 2017). Leonardi et al. (2013) underline that there are at least two aspects that make internal social media different from other communication forms and channels: "They provide people visibility into the communicative actions of others and the visible traces of those communicative actions persist over time" (p. 3). Social media platforms also enable multivocal communication, where voices act and communicate to, with, against, past and about each other (Frandsen and Johansen, 2017). Internal social media expand the range of people and texts that coworkers can learn from, but also give them a possibility to share their own viewpoints and knowledge across hierarchical levels, departments and geographical distances (Madsen, 2016, 2018). Internal social media can thus be used to build new or deepen already existing relationships (Sievert and Scholz, 2017) and may therefore work as a social lubricant (Leonardi et al., 2013). Madsen (2018) has argued that internal social media also may contribute to democratize organizations and flatten hierarchies. Democratic or participatory communication is often closely linked to dialogue, which is not primarily a matter of transporting information between senders and receivers but rather of transforming information and collective sensemaking processes (Deetz, 1995). The introduction of digital internal media means that a larger number of organizational members

Digital corporate communication and internal communication   25

have the opportunity to be involved in the sensemaking process, and the term 'multilogue' is sometimes used to highlight that it is a dialogue between many-to-many (Murphy, 2021; Rosén, 2021).

Other scholars have claimed that social platforms may have an impact on coworker engagement (Sievert and Scholtz, 2017) and also that the tools for social networking may increase workplace productivity (Bennett et al., 2010). However, introducing internal social media does certainly come with a lot of tensions and challenges. The above-mentioned aspects of visibility and persistence mean that coworkers are turned into reflective and sometimes strategic communicators on internal social media. Madsen (2018) argues that perceived safety and efficacy influence coworkers' willingness to share their ideas and experiences. If coworkers do not feel it is safe to voice their critique or if managers do not respond, they will not be active on internal social media (Madsen, 2018). However, if coworkers perceive they have a licence to critique, they may speak up and gain support from others, which may turn into a spiral of voice. Such a spiral can attract management attention and hence also influence strategic decisions (Madsen and Johansen, 2019).

Lastly, the accelerating digitalization has implications for formal and informal communication networks. That formal communication networks, such as formal work teams assigned a specific task, form an integral part of internal communication goes without saying. However, already in the 1970s, Allen's (1977) pioneering study of communication flows in science and engineering organizations highlighted the importance of informal communication networks. While formal communication networks are essential for reducing intra-organizational coordination requirements (Sosa et al., 2015), it is often difficult to foresee the formal communication requirements, especially for organizations that innovate or deal with very complex tasks. This is where informal communication networks play an essential role. Informal communication networks complement the formal communication networks and enable formal teams to coordinate with other teams in ways that enable task accomplishment. While communication technology has played an essential role in inter-organizational team coordination for several decades, and nowadays is very common (Gilson et al., 2015) the implications of the accelerating digitalization of internal communication open up several possibilities for improved communication and coordination between formal and informal communication networks. For example, online collaborative software such as Slack facilitate collaboration and open up new technological possibilities, such as the use of chatbots, in team communication (Laitinen et al., 2021).

WHAT REMAINS THE SAME?

Even if the fast digitalization of organizations has substantially changed and challenged many communication practices in organizations, some patterns and practices remain the same. First of all, the basic needs of humans will remain the same irrespective of whether communication is conducted with digital media or not. In other words, all humans have a profound need to be seen, heard and confirmed by others. The philosopher of dialogue Martin Buber (1923/1994) argued that humans exist in relationship to other humans, and gradually form and change their identity in interactions and dialogue with others. Hence, the human existence is truly based in dialogue (Asakavičiūtė and Valatka, 2020). Humans need others and various forms of relationships to exist and fulfil their basic human needs. In sum, humans' basic needs of communication remain the same, which implies that those needs also must be put in the limelight in the management of digital internal communication.

Second, it is important to challenge the assumption that everything in society and organizations changes rapidly. It is true that various forms of technology have developed in an accelerated pace during the history of mankind, but that does not automatically imply changed human practices or that technology is used as intended (cf. Zuboff, 1988). According to Donald Schön (1973), there is a force of dynamic conservatism in all organizations, i.e., "a tendency to fight to remain the same" (p. 30). Thus, human aspects in organizations such as communication, culture, leadership and coworkership change slowly, or maybe not at all (Madsen, 2021). For example, while internal social media offers new possibilities for dialogue in organizations, there are still only a few examples of when this has been successful. One reason for this is the intrinsic conflict between management's desire to be in control of internal communication and management's perception of social media as open and uncontrollable (Macnamara and Zerfass, 2012). Hence, if fundamental aspects of organizing, such as culture, communication climate, structure and leadership, are not changed or adapted to the new possibilities that digital tools and platforms entail, digital internal communication will not become characterized by free and open dialogue between organizational members (cf. Pekkala, 2020).

Third, the 'function' of communication remains the same in organizations whether it is online or offline. Ever since Barnard's seminal work *The functions of the executive* (1938/1968), communication has been considered a necessary element for successful organizing. While the gradual digitalization of internal communication processes has entailed fundamental changes to organizing processes, for example, the slowly dissolving space and time constraints, the fundamental functions of internal communication highlighted in our two-fold definition – (1) the very cooperation and coordination/organizing itself, and (2) the management intended to facilitate cooperation and coordination/organizing – remain the same no matter if communication is digital or analogue. Thus, while the digitalization of internal communication entails several new possibilities/affordances, challenges and risks, its fundamental role remains the same.

CRITICAL EXAMINATION

This section focuses on the following aspects of digital internal communication from a critical perspective: pseudo involvement, communication visibility/surveillance and availability.

By introducing new interactive channels, digital collaboration tools and communication platforms, and thereby enabling coworkers to make their voice heard, many managers take for granted that coworkers automatically will experience that they are participating in, for example, decision-making and strategy development. However, introducing digital tools that open up coworker participation is rarely enough. Instead, coworkers might experience such introductions and idealistic communication about their potential as merely another form of *symbolic* participation (Lewis, 2019). In other words, it becomes an illusion of participation, in which coworkers are provided an opportunity to contribute to the ritual of symbolic participation without any possibility to make a real impact on decision-making and the strategic direction of the organization. Such an approach can also be called window-dressing (i.e., a pseudo action) – it looks good that all coworkers are invited, but there is seldom any substantial change (Alvesson, 2013). Thus, managers must avoid falling into the trap of introducing digital platforms without making the effort to integrate them into decision-making processes and making sure to provide meaningful feedback to coworkers. Otherwise, coworkers will refrain from making their voice heard. Such pseudo action could also further cement the perception of a culture of silence in the organization (Parcham and Ghasemizad, 2017; Perlow and Williams, 2003). One important explanation of pseudo involvement is the phenomenon *immunity to change*. Kegan and Lahey (2009) claim that individual fears among managers and dynamic conservatism (see above) produce a powerful immunity to change. Many managers are afraid of losing power and control if they involve coworkers in decision-making. This implies that they do not dare to listen to coworkers or include them in decision-making since that may threaten their understanding of power.

As stated previously in the chapter, digital communication platforms and other interactive online channels contribute to increase the visibility of communication (Leonardi, 2014) and behaviour (Leonardi and Treem, 2020) since what is said and done online becomes visible for third parties. As suggested, this visibility has the potential to improve organizational metaknowledge (Leonardi, 2014), knowledge sharing and organizational learning (Sivunen and Laitinen, 2019). However, as pointed out by Sivunen and Laitinen, it also raises questions about surveillance and accountability as the visibility of communication for third parties such as managers makes it possible to monitor coworkers with or without their awareness. The possibility to identify trends on an aggregated level by utilizing data generated through coworkers' online communication and behaviour in corporate communication management decision-making to increase efficiency will contribute to the development of more sophisticated techniques for collecting, analysing and utilizing large quantities of data about coworkers' communication and behaviour. Thus, the possibility for managers to monitor coworkers' online communication and behaviour is important to study from more critical perspectives as well.

Another consequence of the digitalization of workplaces is increased availability. On the one hand, the use of advanced information technology makes it possible for both managers and coworkers in many organizations to choose where and when to work. On the other hand, this new flexibility also comes with an expectation to be available any time to fulfil the idea of the ideal worker (Thomason and Franczak, 2022). Reinke and Gerlach (2022) have studied availability expectations of both coworkers and nonwork contacts and how these predict employees' management of work and nonwork boundaries, as well as how these boundary management behaviours relate to well-being. To avoid the development of an 'always on' culture, it is important to discuss perceived and actual availability expectations within the work team and also make it explicit that team members are allowed to manage the boundaries between work and nonwork in different ways. Rather than forcing everyone into the same boundary management model it is better to give room for different employee preferences. Reinke and Gerlach (2022) also conclude that organizations could allow nonwork contacts and matters being taken care of while working. However, employees should openly discuss availability expectations with their nonwork contacts and find ways to bring those in line with their work responsibilities.

CASE STUDY: THE SWEDISH TRANSPORT ADMINISTRATION

An organization that has challenged traditional communication patterns and routines when it comes to management communication, an integral part of the internal communication, is the Swedish Transport Administration. This Swedish Government agency is responsible for the long-term planning of the transport system, and consists of 9,000 coworkers with regional offices in seven cities. The Swedish Transport Administration is led by a general director (GD) that is acknowledged for her genuine interest in communication. As a new GD, she toured the different sites with the goal of building relations, listening to and talking with the organizational members. After the tour, she implemented a new routine of a yearly gathering at the sites where coworkers were able, during a day, to meet and discuss issues and various strategic concerns with the GD and a couple of members of the board of directors. This meeting was named The Meeting Point, and most coworkers appreciated the opportunity to meet the directors and to discuss with other colleagues at different units. During the Covid-19 pandemic, the communication department, which is responsible for this meeting, had to consider and rethink how to implement The Meeting Point when most coworkers worked from home. They landed on the idea to implement a digital event named The Digital Meeting Point.

This meeting was held at several times, and started with a studio broadcasting with the GD, two representatives of the board and a host. The first meeting focused on the topic of the 'new normal' with a digital working environment. It is worth noting that the agenda was not related to the actual work tasks or strategies that are a common subject for similar large meetings. Rather, the agenda was focused on the experience and feelings of coworkers. The managers in the studio introduced their understanding of the past situation and described how they had perceived it, and this part of the programme ended with a film. Coworkers from different departments and regions had been divided into groups of five to six persons, and they met in a digital room to discuss some questions that were given by the organizer. The groups also had possibilities to send questions to the GD and the board members in the studio. Finally, the meeting ended with a shorter discussion in the studio where the managers replied to questions that were sent from the groups. This is a good example of how management communication can be conducted digitally and where the managers strive to establish an open communication climate by listening to coworkers in the organization. The senior management has also an important role model function for remaining managers in the organization. If senior management tries to listen more, both digitally and physically, and value and reward listening, there are greater possibilities to develop an open communication climate.

Furthermore, The Digital Meeting Point illustrates some of the possibilities that the dissolving of time and space constraints has for the internal communication. Following the novel use of a videoconferencing platform, the management group of the Swedish Transport Administration was able to communicate to all managers and coworkers simultaneously, regardless of their geographic location. The digital meeting format thus enabled the top management to be more visible in the organization even though the approximately 9,000 coworkers of the Swedish Transport Administration were distributed across the entire country. Given that the digital meeting format also enabled individual members of the top management group to enter the digital rooms and listen and participate in the discussions together with coworkers, the format thus also enabled the top management to interact with and listen to a larger number of coworkers than was possible before the introduction of the communication technology used for the event. However, it is important to stress that the communication technology used merely opens up possibilities. Without a communication department coming up with and initiating the idea of The Digital Meeting Point, a management group open to this kind of digital event, as well as middle managers, supervisors and coworkers willing to participate, the *affordances* (Gibson, 1979; Hutchby, 2001) (i.e., possibilities for action) provided by the communication technology would not turn these potentialities into actualities. Thus, as stated earlier in the chapter, the success of the digitalization of internal communication depends on so much more than just the digital tools and platforms per se, such as the organizational culture, internal trust, leadership/coworkership, and communication climate.

CONCLUSION AND FUTURE DIRECTIONS

Current research has only begun paying attention to the digitalization of internal communication and its implications for organizing. There are several issues in need of further exploration, and this concluding section therefore suggests three directions for future research.

One interesting direction is to examine the implications of digitalization for aspects such as organizational identification, organizational culture and intra-organizational trust. On the one hand, some studies indicate that certain features of digitalization, such as the utilization of social bots in internal communication, can have positive implications for relationship building (e.g., Laitinen et al., 2021). On the other hand, the gradual dissolving of time and space restrictions driven by digitalization and the possibility to work, and thus organize, from a distance potentially will have implications for aspects such as coworker identification, organizational culture and the possibility to build trust-based relations between organizational members.

Another interesting direction for future research is to further explore how the digitalization of internal communication facilitates aspects such as upward communication and listening. Will digital communication tools and platforms enable increased coworker participation in strategizing and decision-making, or will they merely be used for creating the illusion of participation? Digital communication tools and platforms certainly open up the possibility for more frequent interaction between management and coworkers. However, research indicates that new communication technology tends to be used as a medium for broadcasting and not as a way of building relationships or facilitating collective sensemaking (e.g., Cardon et al., 2019; Heide and Simonsson, 2021). Therefore, more research is needed on how these new technologies are being utilized to facilitate organizational listening, open strategizing, and coworker participation in decision-making.

The ongoing digitalization of internal communication highlights the reciprocal influence human action and technology have on each other. Therefore, researchers interested in digital internal communication would have much to gain from embracing theoretical perspectives that advocate ways of thinking about sociality and materiality as constitutive of *entanglements*, *assemblages*, or essential features of everything possible to identify and experience (Barad, 2003; Cooren, 2018; Orlikowski, 2007). Such theoretical perspectives that challenge the social-material dualism, such as socio-material perspectives or Cooren's (2018) *relational ontology*, offer promising theoretical lenses for researchers exploring digital internal communication.

REFERENCES

Abbu, H., Mugge, P., Gudergan, G., and Kwiatkowski, A. (2020). Digital leadership: Character and competency differentiates digitally mature organizations. *IEEE International Conference on Engineering, Technology and Innovation* (ICE/ITMC) (pp. 1–9).

Allen, T. J. (1977). *Managing the flow of technology*. Cambridge, MA: MIT Press.

Alvesson, M. (2013). *The triumph of emptiness: Consumption, higher education, and work organization*. Oxford: Oxford University Press.

Asakavičiūtė, V. and Valatka, V. (2020). Martin Buber's dialogical communication: Life as an existential dialogue. *Filosofija Sociologija*, *31*(1), 51–60.

Avolio, B. J. and Kahai, S. S. (2003). Adding the "e" to e-leadership: How it may impact your leadership. *Organizational Dynamics*, *31*(4), 325–338.

Avolio, B. J., Sosik, J. J., Kahai, S. S., and Baker, B. (2014). E-leadership: Re-examining transformations in leadership source and transmission. *The Leadership Quarterly*, *25*(1), 105–131.

Barad, K. (2003). Posthumanist performativity: Toward an understanding of how matter comes to matter. *Signs*, *28*(3), 801–831.

Barnard, C. I. (1938/1968). *The functions of the executive*. Cambridge, MA: Harvard University Press.

Bennett, J., Owers, M., Pitt, M., and Tucker, M. (2010). Workplace impact of social networking. *Property Management*, *28*(3), 138–148.

Bloomfield, B. P., Coombs, R., Knights, D., and Littler, D. (eds.) (1997). *Information technology and organizations: Strategies, networks, and integration*. Oxford: Oxford University Press.

Braun, S., Hernandez Bark, A., Kirchner, A., Stegmann, S., and van Dick, R. (2019). Emails from the boss—curse or blessing? Relations between communication channels, leader evaluation, and employees' attitudes. *International Journal of Business Communication*, *56*(1), 50–81.

Brennen, J. S. and Kreiss, D. (2016). Digitalization. In K. B. Jensen and R. T. Craig (eds.), *The international encyclopedia of communication theory and philosophy*. Chichester: John Wiley & Sons.

Buber, M. (1923/1994). *I and thou* (2nd ed.). Edinburgh: T&T Clark.

Burrell, G. and Morgan, G. (1979). *Sociological paradigms and organizational analysis*. London: Heinemann.

Cardon, P. W., Huang, Y., and Power, G. (2019). Leadership communication on internal digital platforms, emotional capital, and corporate performance: The case for leader-centric listening. *International Journal of Business Communication*. https://doi.org/10.1177/2329488419828808.

Castells, M. (2010). *The rise of the network society* (2nd ed.). Malden, MA: Blackwell.

Cheney, G. and Christensen, L. T. (2001). Organizational identity: Linkages between internal and external communication. In F. M. Jablin and L. L. Putnam (eds.), *Organizational communication: Advances in theory, research, and methods* (pp. 231–269). London: Sage Publications.

Clampitt, P. G. and Downs, C. W. (1993). Employee perceptions of the relationship between communication and productivity: A field study. *Journal of Business Communication*, *30*(1), 5–28.

Contractor, N. S. and Eisenberg, E. M. (1990). Communication networks and new media in organizations. In J. Fulk and C. W. Steinfield (eds.), *Organizations and communication technology* (pp. 143–172). London: Sage Publications.

Cooren, F. (2018). Materializing communication: Making the case for a relational ontology. *Journal of Communication*, *68*, 278–288.

Deetz, S. A. (1995). *Transforming communication, transforming business: Building responsive and responsible workplaces*. Cresskill, NJ: Hampton Press.

Della Corte, V., Del Gaudio, G., and Sepe, F. (2020). Leadership in the digital realm: What are the main challenges? In M. Franco (ed.), *Digital leadership: A new leadership style for the 21st century* (pp. 3–18). London: IntechOpen.

Ewing, M., Men, L. R., and O'Neil, J. (2019). Using social media to engage employees: Insights from internal communication managers. *International Journal of Strategic Communication*, *13*(2), 110–132.

Falkheimer, J. and Heide, M. (2022). *Strategic communication: An introduction to theory and global practice*. Abingdon: Routledge.

Franco, M. (ed.) (2020). *Digital leadership: A new leadership style for the 21st century*. London: IntechOpen.

Frandsen, F. and Johansen, W. (2017). *Organizational crisis communication*. London: Sage Publications.

Gibson, J. J. (1979). *The ecological approach to visual perception*. Boston: Houghton Mifflin.

Gilson, L. L., Maynard, M. T., Young, N. C., Vartiainen, M., and Hakonen, M. (2015). Virtual teams research: 10 years, 10 themes and 10 opportunities. *Journal of Management Studies*, *41*, 1313–1337.

Gode, H. E. (2019). Dynamics of employee ideation on internal social media from a communication perspective. Dissertation, Aarhus University, Aarhus.

Grafström, M. and Lid-Falkman, L. (2017). Everyday narratives: CEO rhetoric on Twitter. *Journal of Organizational Change Management*, *30*(3), 312–322.

Gulbrandsen, I. T. and Just, S. N. (2020). *Strategizing communication: Theory and practice*. Frederiksberg: Samfundslitteratur.

Harari, M. B., Williams, E. A., Castro, S. L., and Brant, K. K. (2021). Self-leadership: A meta-analysis of over two decades of research. *Journal of Occupational & Organizational Psychology*, *94*(4), 890–923.

Heide, M. (2015). Social media and internal communication: On wishful thinking of democracy in organizations. In W. T. Coombs, J. Falkheimer, M. Heide, and P. Young (eds.), *Strategic communication, social media and democracy: The challenge of the digital naturals* (pp. 45–53). Abingdon: Routledge.

Heide, M. and Simonsson, C. (2014). Developing internal crisis communication: New roles and practices of communication professionals. *Corporate Communications: An International Journal*, *19*(2), 128–146.

Heide, M. and Simonsson, C. (2021). What was that all about? On internal crisis communication and communicative coworkership during a pandemic. *Journal of Communication Management*, *25*(3), 256–275.

Hiltz, S. R. and Turoff, M. (1978). *The network nation*. Reading, MA: Addison-Wesley.

Hirschheim, R. and Klein, H. K. (1989). Four paradigms of information systems development. *Communications of the ACM*, *32*(10), 1199–1216.

Hutchby, I. (2001). Technologies, texts and affordances. *Sociology*, *35*, 441–456.

Jackson, B. and Parry, K. W. (2011). *A very short fairly interesting and reasonably cheap book about studying leadership*. London: Sage Publications.

Kalla, H. K. (2005). Integrated internal communications: A multidisciplinary perspective. *Corporate Communications: An International Journal*, *10*(4), 302–314.

Kegan, R. and Lahey, L. L. (2009). *Immunity to change: How to overcome it and unlock the potential in yourself and your organization*. Boston: Harvard Business Review Press.

Kelly, S., Dawkins, A., Rocker, K. T., Someshwar, S., and Penny, T. (2022). Supervisor computer-mediated immediate behaviors: Fostering subordinate communication. *International Journal of Business Communication*. https://doi.org/10.1177/23294884221085724.

Laitinen, K., Laaksonen, S.-M., and Koivula, M. (2021). Slacking with the bot: Programmable social bot in virtual team interaction. *Journal of Computer-Mediated Communication*, *26*(6), 343–361.

Lee, Y. and Yue, C. A. (2020). Status of internal communication research in public relations: An analysis of published articles in nine scholarly journals from 1970 to 2019. *Public Relations Review*, *46*(3).

Leonardi, P. M. (2014). Social media, knowledge sharing, and innovation: Toward a theory of communication visibility. *Information Systems Research*, *25*(4), 796–816.

Leonardi, P. M., Huysman, M., and Steinfield, C. (2013). Enterprise social media: Definition, history, and prospects for the study of social technologies in organizations. *Journal of Computer-Mediated Communication*, *19*(1), 1–19.

Leonardi, P. M. and Treem, J. W. (2020). Behavioral visibility: A new paradigm for organization studies in the age of digitization, digitalization, and datafication. *Organization Studies*, *41*(12), 1601–1625.

Lewis, L. (2019). *The power of strategic listening*. Lanham, MD: Rowman & Littlefield.

Liu, C., Ready, D., Roman, A., Wart, M. V., Wang, X., McCarthy, A., and Kim, S. (2018). E-leadership: An empirical study of organizational leaders' virtual communication adoption. *Leadership & Organization Development Journal*, *39*(7), 826–843.

Macnamara, J. (2016). Organizational listening: Addressing a major gap in public relations theory and practice. *Journal of Public Relations Research*, *28*(3–4), 146–169.

Macnamara, J. (2019). Explicating listening in organization–public communication: Theory, practices, technologies. *International Journal of Communication*, *13*, 5183–5204.

Macnamara, J. and Zerfass, A. (2012). Social media communication in organizations: The challenges of balancing openness, strategy, and management. *International Journal of Strategic Communication*, *6*(4), 287–308.

Madsen, V. T. (2016). *Internal social media: A new kind of participatory organizational communication? Two explorative studies of coworkers as communicators on internal social media.* Department of Business Communication, Aarhus BSS, Aarhus University.

Madsen, V. T. (2017). The challenges of introducing internal social media – the coordinators' roles and perceptions. *Journal of Communication Management*, *21*(1), 2–16.

Madsen, V. T. (2018). Participatory communication on internal social media – a dream or reality? *Corporate Communications: An International Journal*, *23*(4), 614–628.

Madsen, V. T. (2021). Internal social media and internal communication. In L. R. Men and A. T. Verčič (eds.), *Current trends and issues in internal communication* (pp. 57–74). Cham: Springer.

Madsen, V. T. and Johansen, W. (2019). A spiral of voice? When employees speak up on internal social media. *Journal of Communication Management*, *23*(4), 331–347.

Malakyan, P. G. (2020). Digital leader-followership for the digital age: A North American perspective. In M. Franco (ed.), *Digital leadership: A new leadership style for the 21st century* (pp. 59–82). London: IntechOpen.

Men, L. R. (2014a). Strategic internal communication: Transformational leadership, communication channels, and employee satisfaction. *Management Communication Quarterly*, *28*(2), 264–284.

Men, L. R. (2014b). Why leadership matters to internal communication: Linking transformational leadership, symmetrical communication, and employee outcomes. *Journal of Public Relations Research*, *26*(3), 256–279.

Men, L. R. and Bowen, S. A. (2017). *Excellence in internal communication management.* New York: Business Expert Press.

Men, L. R., O'Neil, J., and Ewing, M. (2020). Examining the effects of internal social media usage on employee engagement. *Public Relations Review*, *46*(2), 101880.

Mikkola, L. and Valo, M. (eds.) (2019). *Workplace communication.* Abingdon: Routledge.

Murphy, E. (2021). Investigating the multiple worlds of teaching through multiloguing. *Educational Technology and Society*, *4*(3), 153–159.

Neill, M. S. and Bowen, S. A. (2021). Ethical listening to employees during a pandemic: New approaches, barriers and lessons. *Journal of Communication Management*, *25*(3), 276–297.

Newman, S. A., Ford, R. C., and Marshall, G. W. (2020). Virtual team leader communication: Employee perception and organizational reality. *International Journal of Business Communication*, *57*(4), 452–473.

Orlikowski, W. J. (2007). Sociomaterial practices: Exploring technology at work. *Organization Studies*, *28*(9), 1435–1448.

Orlikowski, W. J., Yates, J., Okamura, K., and Fujimoto, M. (1999). Shaping electronic communication: The metastructuring of technology in the context of use. In G. DeSanctis and J. Fulk (eds.), *Shaping organization form: Communication, connection, and community* (pp. 133–171). London: Sage Publications.

Parcham, E. and Ghasemizad, A. (2017). The impact of organizational culture on employees' organizational silence in Shiraz University of Medical Sciences. *Journal of Health Management & Informatics*, *4*(1), 25–30.

Pekkala, K. (2020). Managing the communicative organization: A qualitative analysis of knowledge-intensive companies. *Corporate Communications: An International Journal*, *25*(3), 551–571.

Perlow, L. and Williams, S. (2003). Is silence killing your company? *Harvard Business Review*, *81*(5), 52–58.

Putnam, L. L. (1983). The interpretive perspective: An alternative to functionalism. In L. L. Putnam and M. E. Pacanowsky (eds.), *Communication and organization: An interpretive approach* (pp. 31–54). London: Sage Publications.

Putnam, L. L. and Boys, S. (2006). Revisiting metaphors of organizational communication. In S. R. Clegg, C. Hardy, T. B. Lawrence, and W. R. Nord (eds.), *The SAGE handbook of organization studies* (pp. 541–576). London: Sage Publications.

Ravazzani, S. and Mazzei, A. (2018). Employee anonymous online dissent: Dynamics and ethical challenges for employees, targeted organisations, online outlets, and audiences. *Business Ethics Quarterly, 28*(2), 175–201.

Reinke, K. and Gerlach, G. I. (2022). Linking availability expectations, bidirectional boundary management behavior and preferences, and employee well-being: An integrative study approach. *Journal of Business and Psychology, 37*, 695–715.

Rogers, E. M. (1988). Information technologies: How organizations are changing. In G. M. Goldhaber and G. A. Barnett (eds.), *Handbook of organizational communication* (pp. 437–452). Norwood , NJ: Ablex.

Rogers, E. M. and Allbritton, M. M. (1997). The public electronic network: Interactive communication and interpersonal distance. In B. D. Sypher (ed.), *Case studies in organizational communication 2* (pp. 249–261). New York: Guilford Press.

Rosén, M. (2021). *Social mättnad, relationell hunger: Strategis̜k kommunikation i förändring när matindustrin utmanas av folklig misstro*. Department of Strategic Communication, Lund University.

Ruben, B. D. and Gigliotti, R. A. (2016). Leadership as social influence: An expanded view of leadership communication theory and practice. *Journal of Leadership and Organizational Studies, 23*(4), 467–479.

Ruck, K. and Men, L. R. (2021). Guest editorial: Internal communication during the COVID-19 pandemic. *Journal of Communication Management, 25*(3), 185–195.

Schön, D. (1973). *Beyond the stable state: Public and private learning in a changing society*. New York: W. W. Norton.

Sievert, H. and Scholz, C. (2017). Engaging employees in (at least partly) disengaged companies. Results of an interview survey within about 500 German corporations on the growing importance of digital engagement via internal social media. *Public Relations Review, 43*(5), 894–903.

Sivunen, A. and Laitinen, K. (2019). Digital communication environments in the workplace. In L. Mikkola and M. Valo (eds.), *Workplace communication* (pp. 41–53). New York: Routledge.

Sosa, M. E., Gargiulo, M., and Rowles, C. (2015). Can informal communication networks disrupt coordination in new product development projects? *Organization Science, 26*(4), 1059–1078.

Thomason, B. and Franczak, J. (2022). 3 tensions leaders need to manage in the hybrid workplace. *Harvard Business Review Digital Articles*, 1–6. https://hbr.org/2022/02/3-tensions-leaders-need-to-manage-in-the-hybrid-workplace.

van Zoonen, W. and Sivunen, A. (2020). Knowledge brokering in an era of communication visibility. *International Journal of Business Communication, 60*(1). https://doi.org/10.1177/2329488420937348.

Verčič, A. T., Verčič, D., and Sriramesh, K. (2012). Internal communication: Definition, parameters, and the future. *Public Relations Review, 38*(2), 223–230.

Weick, K. E. (1969). *The social psychology of organizing*. Reading, MA: Addison-Wesley.

Weick, K. E. (1995). *Sensemaking in organizations*. London: Sage Publications.

Welch, M. and Jackson, P. R. (2007). Rethinking internal communication: A stakeholder approach. *Corporate Communications: An International Journal, 12*(2), 177–198.

Zerfass, A. and Franke, N. (2013). Enabling, advising, supporting, executing: A theoretical framework for internal communication consulting within organizations. *International Journal of Strategic Communication, 7*, 118–135.

Zhang, X. and Viswanath, V. (2013). Explaining employee job performance: The role of online and offline workplace communication networks. *MIS Quarterly, 37*(3), 695–722.

Zuboff, S. (1988). *In the age of the smart machine: The future of work and power*. New York: Basic Books.

3. Digital corporate communication and brand communication
John M. T. Balmer

INTRODUCTION

Whilst it is unquestionably a fact that the corporate brand and corporate communication fields are important, it is also indisputably the case that scholars and managers do not always fully realize the significance of these areas. Moreover, both fields, all too often, are narrowly conceived because of a tunnel vision approach. This chapter seeks to address this tunnel vision by illuminating the nature and importance of Total Corporate Brand Communication (TCBC). Arguably, this may have hindered an appreciation of the full strategic importance of the territory. Furthermore, for scholars of both corporate communication and corporate brand management some critically important perspectives have been overlooked. One of these perspectives is the TCBC domain: a perspective which accommodates, and melds, the increasingly important digital corporate communication, and corporate branding spheres. Digital corporate brand communication represents a new, and highly significant, vector by which we can more fully discern the critically important corporate communication territory.

However, a commonly held myopia in relation to TCBC has hindered the full power, and significance, of the corporate brand communication territory to be wholly realized. Consequently, this chapter, which has TCBC as its focus – and which accords importance to digital corporate brand communication – provides an antidote to this short-sightedness. It is an approach which builds on the extant panoptic Total Corporate Communication perspectives and accommodates new technological/digital viewpoints as well as the crucially significant corporate brand dimension. It is an approach which highlights, and illuminates, the strategic importance of the broad territory.

The reasons for a TCBC myopia are complex and varied. They include a failure to appreciate the breadth and depth of the territory; a failure to appreciate the communication impacts of an organization's corporate identity; a failure to appreciate the importance of organizational-focused word-of-mouth communication; a failure to appreciate the significance of customer and stakeholder feedback; a failure to appreciate digital, technological, and artificial intelligence perspectives; and, moreover, a failure to accord sufficient significance to an organization's corporate brand.

DEFINITIONS OF CORE CONCEPTS

Corporate Brands

The corporate brand concept dates back to, and was formally introduced in, the mid-1990s (Balmer, 1995). From its inception, some scholars have argued that corporate brands represent the most significant form of branding: a branding mode which is of considerable strategic importance (Balmer, 2001b, 2010; Balmer and Gray, 2003). From the 1990s onwards, a distinct literature on the territory slowly materialized (Balmer, 1995, 2001a, 2001b; Hatch and Schultz, 2001), and it became apparent that an organization's corporate brand represented a distinct, novel, and important platform on which an organization, and its customers/stakeholders, could have mutually durable and profitable exchanges and interactions (Balmer, 2012).

At its essence, a corporate brand can be viewed as an informal contract (sometimes termed a covenant) which affords bilateral links and relationships between an organization and its customers and stakeholders (Balmer, 2001a; Balmer and Greyser, 2003). Corporate brands are distinct from product brands because they are multidisciplinary in scope; have a stakeholder focus; and are underpinned by a corporate marketing perspective (Balmer, 1995, 2012).

Significantly, corporate brands have corporate identities as their foundations. A corporate brand develops out of an organization's corporate identity (an organization's distinguishing traits) and accommodates the perception of a corporate identity. Even when a clear corporate brand promise/covenant is established, a corporate identity is critical. This is because an entity's corporate identity actualizes, or makes real, the corporate brand promise/covenant (Balmer, 2012).

A strong corporate brand is meaningful since it serves as a powerful cornerstone for organizations (Balmer, 2001a). As such, a strong corporate brand both distinguishes and differentiates one organization from another. Thus, a corporate brand can be highly significant in terms of an organization's corporate navigation, positioning, and communication (Balmer and Gray, 2003). It also can be invaluable for customers and other stakeholders in distinguishing, and differentiating, one corporate brand from another. Corporate brands are valuable for corporations and stakeholders alike.

For corporations, a strong and consequential corporate brand can enhance the financial worth and value of an organization and, for instance, can burnish shareholder value. A strong corporate brand can be a flexible and powerful asset which can be borrowed (through franchising), as well as bought, or sold (Balmer, 2005).

Given the above, it is no surprise that a good deal of attention is afforded to corporate brands by scholars and managers alike. And this is for good reason; corporate brands often have considerable financial worth. For many organizations, their corporate brand is their primary corporate resource – a resource that is often prized by customers, employees, shareholders, and other stakeholders.

Total Corporate Communication

Total corporate brand communication melds together, as well as advances, the territories relating to total corporate communication and corporate brand management. It is an approach that is mindful of the digital corporate communication dimension as well. Consequently, this section provides a brief overview of the foundational total corporate communication field and discusses recent developments apropos the total corporate communication which accommodates the critically important digital corporate communication perspective.

Total Corporate Communication (TCC) came to the fore in the 1990s (cf. Balmer, 1995; Balmer and Gray, 1999). Underpinned by an unequivocal stakeholder orientation, TCC is cognizant that: (a) corporate communication is complex and multidimensional; and (b) is

36   *Handbook on digital corporate communication*

informed by the view that everything an organization says, makes or does (including third party commentary and narratives relating to an organization), has a corporate communication effect (Balmer, 1995, p. 35).

Thus, the total corporate communication approaches are differentiated from traditional one-way communication models which emphasize controlled communication. Moreover, TCC represents a nexus linking a company's corporate identity (a firm's distinguishing and defining traits) and stakeholder/customer images and reputations (Gray and Balmer, 1998). Images and reputations are important since they provide the foundations of stakeholders' identifications and behaviours which can meaningfully support the company's mission and purpose as evinced in its corporate identity (Balmer, 2008).

Originally, TCC had an overt corporate identity focus. Corporate identity as used here refers to an organization's distinctive and defining characteristics. (Importantly, corporate identity should *not* be equated with the visual representation of an organization which, more properly, should be termed 'corporate visual identification'.) Consequently, the TCC notion, to emphasize an earlier point, was underpinned by the perspective that "Everything an organisation does will in some way communicate the organisation's identity" (Balmer, 1995, p. 35).

The original TCC perspective was tripartite in character (Balmer and Gray, 1999). It comprised primary corporate communication (*emanating from the organization's corporate identity*), secondary corporate communication (*emanating from the organization's controlled corporate communication*) and tertiary corporate communication (*emanating from word-of-mouth stakeholder communication*).

These can be explained more fully as follows:

1. Primary Corporate Communication ('Corporate Identity Based Transmission Communication'). This encompasses the total corporate communication effects of an organization's corporate identity. This includes an organization's purposes, activities and behaviours, product and service quality, management style, employee behaviour, etc.
2. Secondary Corporate Communication ('Controlled Communication Based Transmission'). This encompasses the total corporate communication effects of an organization's controlled corporate communication (corporate advertising, corporate design, corporate public relations, public affairs, etc.
3. Tertiary Corporate Communication ('Word-of-Mouth Based Transmission'). This encompasses the total corporate communication effects of third party/uncontrolled communication, including narratives and dialogues, emanating from stakeholders, the media, competitors, and others.

Digital Corporate Brand Communication

Mindful of the definition of digital corporate communication as espoused in this *Handbook* (p. 9), the following delineation of digital corporate brand communication can be enumerated:

> Digital corporate brand communication denotes the strategic management of digital technologies in embodying and conveying an organization's corporate brand promise/covenant to customers and other stakeholders, whilst also providing accessible digital conduits for feedback from customers and other stakeholder groups.

WHAT IS CHANGING?

Developments in Total Corporate Communication: Accommodating Technological and Digital Perspectives

Developments in digital and artificial intelligence technologies are important dimensions of the new world of corporate communication. Their growth and importance have been inexorable and their use, increasingly, is ubiquitous. Digital technologies represent a new dynamic apropos company–customer/stakeholder interfaces. As such, they have transformed corporate marketing and societal interactions. This is especially the case amongst the post-2000 generations. Unquestionably, the new digital technologies represent new, and significant, corporate communication resources. Additionally, they represent an information resource as evidenced by the increasing utilization of cloud space which enables the collection and analysis of big data – data which is exchanged amongst organizations, networks, people, and governments on a regular basis. Big data represents a gold mine of customer insights which allows for more finely honed products and services. Moreover, it provides managers with descriptive, predictive, and prescriptive analytics (Chaturvedi and Verma, 2022). Whilst there can be positive outcomes relating to the above there can also be negative – and even dark – consequences as well.

Developments in the digital and artificial intelligence realms are meaningfully affecting, and shaping, company–customer/stakeholder relationships. As a result, they are moulding and influencing the ways in which individuals – and society at large – live, work, and interact. The new digital environment is important since it provides novel ways in which organizations can reach, inform, and engage with customers in the offering and selling of products and services (Juran et al., 2021). Digital technologies can also be efficacious in adding value to and strengthening brands (Chaffey and Smith, 2017). Moreover, they offer the potential for corporate brands and their customers to co-create the corporate brand promise more effectively (cf. Lahtinen and Närvänen, 2020; Ramaswamy and Gouillart, 2010). Co-creation activities can lead to the development of 3D printing, the creation of a non-fungible token (NFT), and even the development of a metaverse.

Unquestionably, the corporate marketing and corporate communication worlds are witnessing a digital and technology tumult (Balmer and Yen, 2017). In this new world, customers are becoming 'digital savvy' and the digital sphere represents "the biggest growth opportunity for companies" (Chuturvedi and Verma, 2022, p. 35). As such, the digital transformation is qualitatively different from earlier upheavals. The label 'the Fourth Industrial Revolution' has been applied to these developments (Schwab, 2015). The Fourth Industrial Revolution differs from earlier upheavals in several significant respects. Whereas the first industrial revolution began with the rise of mechanical manufacture in the eighteenth century, the second industrial revolution of the nineteenth century was triggered by the advent of mass production, the access to electricity, and the division of labour, and the third industrial revolution of the late twentieth century was triggered by automated production, electronics, and information technology (Schwab, 2015), the Fourth Industrial Revolution, which characterizes the early twenty-first century and which is grounded in digital technology and artificial intelligence, is ground-breaking in terms of its analytical and problem-solving qualities which are of a scale, speed, scope, and sophistication that has not, to date, been experienced (Balmer and Yen, 2017).

38 *Handbook on digital corporate communication*

Thus, the Fourth Industrial Revolution is in marked contrast to earlier revolutions which were transformative in terms of how products/services were created, supplied, and consumed. Consequently, this digital/AI revolution is transforming organizational life, consumer expectations and, of course, the domains of corporate communication, corporate marketing, and corporate branding. The Fourth Industrial Revolution holds the prospect of transforming the connectivity of billions of people via mobile and other devices: devices which have access to extraordinary processing capabilities (Schwab, 2015).

Just as Schwab (2015) identified four industrial revolutions, similar revolutionary developments have characterized marketing (Balmer and Greyser, 2006; Balmer and Yen, 2017). Balmer and Greyser (2006) noted how the First Marketing Revolution was underpinned by beneficial company–customer exchange relationships based on products/product brands; the Second Marketing Revolution was based on advantageous company–customer exchange relationships based on services/services brands; and the Third Marketing Revolution was grounded on mutually beneficial company–stakeholder exchange relationships based on corporate identities/corporate brands.

However, Balmer and Yen (2017) noted how the Fourth Marketing Revolution is mutually founded on beneficial company–stakeholder/stakeholder networks and exchange relationships based on digital technology. Exemplarily, over recent decades, the world has witnessed the ascendancy of the digital sphere. For example, the internet has emerged as an increasingly indispensable information gathering and marketing resource. Significantly, it is also a social resource. With the advent of digital corporate communication, there is the potential for organizations to marshal fine-tuned, and bespoke, corporate communication. The British Broadcasting Corporation's (BBC) news application, for instance, takes account of an individual's past selection of news stories, and general browsing behaviour, to provide a bespoke news service tailored to an individual's interests and tastes. However, whilst corporate communication messages are still very much within the purview of organizations, customers and other stakeholders can exert some control over which digital corporate communication they receive – for instance, by removing an app or by managing how it is used.

Conspicuously, the field of digital corporate communication not only increases the power of organizations and, to some degree, enhances the power of individuals (who can remove or restrict a digital application), it also can enhance the power of intermediaries such as providers of digital platforms. Moreover, digital corporate communication can be part of a company's service offering. For example, companies can send digital-based reminders and prompts to customers in both consumer and industrial markets. What's more, access to, and the quality of, digital applications ('apps'), smart meters, and the like, can be an important and sometimes critical part of a corporate or product brand offering. For example, consumers use smart meters to check and display energy consumption, comparable usage, and details of real-time costs. Digital corporate communication has also given rise to so called 'conversational agents'. Conversational agents represent a new mode of corporate communication between corporate brands and consumers. As such, corporate brands employ a digital voice to interact with customers. Sometimes also known as 'conversational commerce', a digital assistant often is the point of contact when an individual is engaged in buying activities (Chuturvedi and Verma, 2022).

Of course, some organizations have become 'fully digitalized' in terms of their corporate brand offering. News gathering and reporting organizations are cases in point. For example, the prominent 'newspaper' *The Independent* is totally digital, whilst the BBC, CNN, *Financial Times*, *Wall Street Journal*, and *Die Welt* have significant digital arms.

However, there are some downsides to digital corporate brand communication. For instance, an organization's corporate brand data, along with those of their customers, can be 'hacked' with data being harvested or even manipulated. Such activities also cause considerable distress to individuals (Elhai et al., 2017). Digital corporate brand content can be subject to 'digital hijacking' which can result in a warped corporate brand image being communicated. For example, activist groups have been known to be engaged in 'trolling' online discussions. Additionally, such groups have created fake profiles enabling them to hijack social media accounts. They have even been able to manipulate digital voting systems (Rone, 2022). Given the above, the same potentially could take place in relation to the digital corporate brand communication space. Furthermore, manipulated media, so-called 'deepfakes', allow individuals and groups to utilize media technology to change what an individual says on video. The consequence is that what is being said can be perceived to be authentic.

'Deepfakes' can be highly persuasive and powerful. To date, 'deepfakes' have already influenced political outcomes in certain countries (Pesetski, 2020). Thus, there is the potential for prominent figures, media influencers, and celebrity corporate brand endorsers to have their video material tweaked to say erroneous or disparaging things about a particular corporate brand.

Whilst noting the above problems which require constant vigilance on the part of organizations, given the inexorable use of digital technologies it is imperative for the corporate communication discipline to take account of, as well as accommodate, digital features. Alas, digital technologies have not always been afforded sufficient prominence and significance within the corporate communication territory.

Thus, the original tripartite TCC approach, detailed earlier, was amplified to a quadripartite perspective to accommodate technological advances as manifest apropos the internet of things (cf. Balmer and Yen, 2017). Logically, quaternary communication can be broadened to accommodate a broader technological palette which includes digital corporate communication. It can be seen to embrace analogous areas such as artificial intelligence. Thus, in addition to corporate identity based (primary), controlled communication (secondary), and tertiary communication, an additional communication vector – Quaternary ('Digital Based') Corporate Communication – was added (Balmer and Yen, 2017).

Quaternary ('Digital Based') Corporate Communication

Quaternary Communication is based on digital/new technology/artificial intelligence dimensions. It is broad in scope. Whilst it can be considered as a corporate communication vector (as with primary/'corporate identity based', secondary/'controlled', and tertiary/'word-of-mouth' corporate communication), arguably it is more akin to a galaxy of digital corporate communication. This is because corporate digital communication has wide boundaries and can be compared to a network spanning multifarious internet platforms, machines, cloud spaces, technologies, as well as peoples and organizations. Moreover, digital corporate communication serves as an information resource which assists in planning, learning, and the analysis of big data. In addition, particularly in relation to AI, it is imbued with automation, personalization, and predicting qualities (Kumar et al., 2019). It is a conduit by which there can be bilateral information exchange between organizations and customers/stakeholders. Furthermore, it

40 *Handbook on digital corporate communication*

can accommodate multilateral information exchange between customers and stakeholders. However, quaternary communication, whilst increasing the knowledge and power of organizations, is not absolute. This is because increasingly individuals can exercise control over data usage and, moreover, third party entities such as internet platform providers can be significant players apropos quaternary communication. Increasingly, internet suppliers sit at the intersection of corporate and customer/stakeholder communication. Also significant are the activities of bloggers and social influencers (Casais and Gomes, 2022). It is unquestionably a fact that consumer bloggers are valuable agents of influence marketing (Halvorsen, 2019). This, perhaps, explains why CEOs sometimes write blogs (Hanson, 2006) and why some organizations employ journalists to do the same (Hoffjan and Haidukiewicz, 2020).

However, in accommodating change, the corporate communication field not only needs to recognize the growing importance of digital corporate communication, but is also required to take account of the increased significance of the organization as a corporate brand. As such, there is a need to revisit and refigure the extant total corporate communication mix.

WHAT REMAINS THE SAME?

In one sense, the territory of digital corporate brand communication is characterized by continuity as well as change. As just mentioned, the corporate communication field needs not only to acknowledge the growing importance of digital corporate communication, but must also take account of the increased significance of the organization as a corporate brand.

Thus, certain verities endure, namely the importance of corporate communication, the significance of digital technologies, and the centrality of corporate brands to a good deal of organizational life. Given that TCBC regards an organization's corporate brand as providing a pivot on which an organization's corporate communications are centred, at this juncture it is worth recalling a few core corporate brand principles.

The first of these is that corporate brands are characterized by two forms of corporate brand ownership: *emotional ownership* and *legal ownership*. Both are important and both are prerequisites for strong corporate brands. Yet both are not always appreciated.

Emotional ownership is vested in customers and stakeholders who not only associate with but also define themselves in relation to a corporate brand. Consequently, they are predisposed to have an emotional sense of ownership with a corporate brand. The real power of corporate brands come from their emotional ownership by customers/stakeholders.

Legal ownership of a corporate brand is held by an organization. As such, an entity (or sometimes multiple entities) will have legal rights over a corporate brand name. Legal ownership necessarily entails a sense of responsibility on the part of managers who must demonstrate ongoing stewardship of the corporate brand (Balmer, 2010, 2012). Significantly, the CEO is, de facto, an organization's corporate brand manager (Balmer, 1995). Thus, managers need to give ongoing attention to the corporate brand to ensure it remains relevant, and attractive, for customers/stakeholders whilst ensuring it is valuable and profitable for an organization.

A second precept of corporate brands is the *importance of employees*. Thus, organizational members are critical in delivering the corporate brand promise (Balmer, 1995, 2001a). Consequently, everyone in an organization needs to have a sense of responsibility in delivering the corporate brand (Balmer, 2001a, 2012), and the entire organization needs to have a corporate brand-focused culture and to be corporate brand-orientated (Balmer, 2013).

Digital corporate communication and brand communication   41

For many stakeholders, a strong corporate brand provides a foundation on which a social identity can be shaped; a self-definitional meaning can be established; and where, in part, a stakeholder's identity can be moulded. For example, organizational members can have a profound sense of identification with a corporate brand (Balmer, 2013; Balmer and Podnar, 2021). For customers and other shareholders, corporate brands can be invested with emotional and promissory value, as encapsulated in the corporate brand promise/covenant.

The third, and final, corporate brand imperative is *the vital role of senior management and the CEO*. Given the central and strategic importance of corporate brands, corporate brand management is a senior management and, moreover, a CEO concern (Balmer, 1995). In addition, it needs to be a senior management responsibility given that corporate brand management is a complicated task. As such, managers must ensure they coordinate the organization's many activities and disciplines that are aligned with the corporate brand, as demonstrated in the ACID Test of corporate brand management (Balmer, 2012). Thus, a corporate brand orientation requires senior managers to see the corporate brand as a significant strategic resource and capability (Balmer, 2022). Moreover, they need to view corporate brand management as a strategic management imperative (Balmer, 2012).

Total Corporate Brand Communication Mix

Given the growing importance of corporate brands, and the desirability for organizations to be orientated around their corporate brands, account needs to be accorded to corporate brand communication apropos total corporate communication. Moreover, for corporate brand orientated entities, corporate brand communication can be a key corporate communication dimension. Given that a corporate brand, at its simplest and at its most fundamental, is a promise (or what is sometimes called a covenant) corporate brand focused communication can, usefully, be labelled Promissory ('Corporate Brand Based') Corporate Communication. Consequently, promissory corporate communication needs to encapsulate, and exemplify, the corporate brand promise/covenant. Where an organization has a corporate brand orientated corporate communication, the corporate brand promise/covenant, de facto, underpins all corporate communication endeavours. Thus, corporate brand based communication represents a common starting point and indeed, template, for an organization's corporate communication endeavours. Where two or more organizations share a corporate brand (cf. Balmer, 2012) there should be calibration apropos corporate brand communication.

Thus, just as Corporate Digital Communication (Quaternary Communication) has been accommodated within the total corporate communication mix, so should Corporate Brand Communication (Promissory Communication) where an entity has an explicit corporate brand orientation.

There is another significant corporate communication dimension which needs to be accommodated in the corporate brand communication mix: 'Feedback Based Communication'. This is a corporate communication dimension which accommodates communication feedback from customers and other stakeholders. Feedback has long been recognized as an important facet of communications. Such feedback is of value to organizations in appraising their overall corporate communication endeavours and in comprehending the perceptions held of the corporate brand. Thus, it can be invaluable in adjusting or refiguring those aspects of an organization's corporate brand communication which it can control as well as understanding, and accommodating, the effects of other corporate brand communication vectors. The 'feedback based' dimension of corporate brand communication may also be assigned the label *responsory corporate communication*. The origins of the word *responsory* are to be found in the Latin word *responsorium*, which means 'to answer'.

Figure 3.1 shows the total corporate brand communication mix which encompasses both corporate brand based ('promissory') corporate communication and feedback based ('responsory') corporate communication.

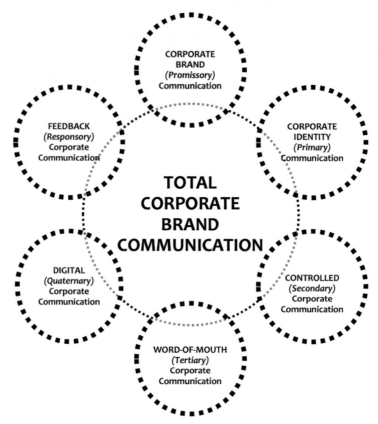

Figure 3.1   Total corporate brand communication mix

CRITICAL EXAMINATION

Undoubtably, digital corporate brand communication constitutes an important and meaningful advance in the realm of digital corporate communication. Digital corporate brand communication also allows for the communication and delivery of a corporate brand promise to be more finely honed and executed by organizations to better serve customers and other stakeholders. Unquestionably, it opens up both bilateral and multilateral corporate brand information exchange between organizations and stakeholders as well as between stakeholders and others. This can be empowering.

However, there are some downsides to this territory, and these represent the dark sides of digital corporate brand communication. For instance, digital corporate brand communication has empowered third party organizations who, progressively, have become integral to digital corporate brand communication. Digital platforms such as Google, YouTube, and Facebook are cases in point. More worryingly, the digital field has attracted the attention of authoritarian governments who have banned, or restricted, digital corporate brand communication. Certain governments have employed firewalls to 'regulate' digital communication, for instance (Burgers and Robinson, 2016). Notably, too, social media can be the cause of corporate brand crises and can materially impact on reputation (Etter et al., 2019). All the above has resulted in a loss of control on the part of organizations. The same can be true for individuals. As such, individuals can feel there has been a loss of control. They may also reason that opaqueness, rather than transparency, inhabits areas of the digital sphere where corners are dark and, sometimes, invisible.

Moreover, some corporate brands do not always demonstrate acceptable levels of digital corporate responsibility. Some company-based digital information systems have been shown to be untrustworthy. Consider ByteDance, which owns the app TikTok, who sold children's digital data and monetarized this data (Shephardson and Wang, 2021). Also consider Meta, which owns Facebook, who was accused of contravening privacy laws after sharing the information of 533 million users online (Meta's Facebook agrees to settle data privacy lawsuit, 2022). More seriously, the British Post Office, which knew that its Fujitsu Horizon computer system was faulty, used the faulty information from the system to accuse several hundred Post Office employees of false accounting, fraud, and theft. This resulted in the managers of Post Office branches being wrongly charged, and even imprisoned. Many suffered financial ruin and severe ill health (Peachey, 2022).

One unintended consequence of the rise of digital corporate brand communication is digital poverty and/or disenfranchisement. At one level this can be manifest in small organizations which do not have the wherewithal to fully embrace digital corporate brand communication. It can be a particular problem in business-to-business (B2B) organizations (Setkute and Dibb, 2022). Whilst many of those born after 1980 are likely to be conversant with the digital sphere, many older adults will be less adept. Moreover, many of those of retirement age will not be sufficiently au courant with digital mediums and technology and this can make them digitally disenfranchised. This has attracted little attention to date but warrants particular investigation (Nunan and Di Domenico, 2019). A similar picture is likely to characterize younger adults who are less educated and/or are socially disadvantaged. Similarly, large parts of the developing world will be the same. Therefore, for many organizations the socially responsible thing to do is not to be fully digitalized. Thus, digital corporate brand communication managers need to be sensitive to the above. As such, non-digital corporate brand communication can still be important as well as necessary for the reasons just delineated.

CASE STUDY: THE BRITISH MONARCHY AND TOTAL CORPORATE BRAND COMMUNICATION

The British Monarchy is one of the most famous, and enduring, corporate brands. British monarchs have a global presence and profile. Whilst attention is often focused on the person of the monarch or on the Royal Family, it is sometimes forgotten that the British Monarchy

44   *Handbook on digital corporate communication*

is an institution. Significantly, it is also a corporate brand. Indeed, the British Monarchy is colloquially referred to as 'the firm' by members of the Royal Family. As with many corporate heritage brands, it is a family business as well.

The British Monarchy is exceptional in that, as a corporate brand, it has entered the subconsciousness of thousands of people both in the UK and overseas over many years. Such is the importance and symbolic meaning of the monarchy to British life that many in Great Britain dreamt about meeting, or having tea with the Queen (the author is no exception in this regard).

Why can the British Monarchy be deemed to be exceptional in the global context? In part, this is because it is a corporate heritage brand whose roots go back to the ninth century. Furthermore, it is the most familiar and celebrated of all monarchical brands. Consequently, it is accorded a great deal of attention by the world's media. It is the last of the great 'imperial' monarchies and is surrounded by a good deal of pomp and ceremony. As such, British monarchs are the only European monarchs who still wear a crown.

Additionally, the monarchy's high international profile is because until the mid-twentieth century somewhere between a quarter and a third of the world's population were subjects of the British monarch. Today many of these historical links endure. By tradition, the British monarch is titular head of the 'British' Commonwealth which comprises 56 independent nations. For the main, these are countries which were once under British rule. Today, the Commonwealth comprises around a third of all mankind (Cannon and Griffiths, 1998, p. 632). Notably, one in three of the world's adults aged between 15 and 29 lives in a Commonwealth country (The Commonwealth, 2022). Of course, there is often considerable interest in the loves, romances, weddings, births, deaths, royal visits, and royal haute couture of 'The Royals'. Equally, the blunders, imperfections, shortcomings, rumours, and scandals, whether real or perceived, also garner considerable public and media interest. Notably, the monthly magazine *Majesty Magazine* takes an in-depth look at the British Monarchy.

The insatiable interest in the British Monarchy as a corporate brand is evidenced in various TV series and films. Some focus on the reign of Queen Elizabeth II and include the popular Netflix mega series *The Crown* along with the films *The Queen* and *A Royal Night Out*. Also of note is the highly irreverent and satirical Channel 4 fictional sitcom series on the Royal Family entitled *The Windsors*. Many other films concentrate on earlier monarchs including King George VI (*The King's Speech*); Queen Victoria (*Mrs Brown, Victoria and Abdul*, and *The Young Victoria*); King George III (*The Madness of King George*), and the eighteenth-century monarch Queen Mary (*The Favourite*). TikTok has a plethora of short videos on the monarchy (as does The Royal Family YouTube channel and the Royal Fashion YouTube channel).

Since time immemorial, with the exception of a fleeting period in the seventeenth century when England was, de facto, a republic, monarchs have reigned over the British people. However, with the passage of time, monarchy in Great Britain has undergone several transformations, from being a *theocratic*, then an *autocratic*, and then a *constitutional* monarchy (Balmer, 2009). Whereas, in the past, the monarchy had political power, today its power is primarily symbolic rather than political. However, the strength and significance of the British Monarchy's symbolic power should not be discounted. Symbolic power is a potent power.

The British monarch is unusual in that in addition to his or her role as British Head of State, he or she also wears the crown of other countries including Canada, Australia, and New Zealand. Therefore, the recently deceased British monarch, HM Queen Elizabeth II, was Queen of Australia, Queen of Canada, Queen of New Zealand, etc. Thus, the British monarch wears many crowns rolled into one. Interestingly, Queen Elizabeth, in her various realms, was Queen of around 100,000,000 people (Bogdanor, 1995).

Today, the British Monarchy has become the prototypical model of constitutional monarchy in which the monarch 'reigns but does not rule'. This monarchical form has been emulated by similar constitutional monarchies in Belgium, Denmark, Japan, Malaysia, Norway, the Netherlands, Spain, and Sweden, amongst others.

As a constitutional monarch, the British monarch has three principal functions. Consequently, the monarch is required to be dutiful, devoted, and dedicated (Balmer, 2009). *Dutiful* is the requirement for the monarch to honour the tenets of a constitutional monarch as head of state of a parliamentary democracy where the monarch must be seen to reign but not to rule. *Devoted* requires the monarch to be in the service of the peoples of the realm; and to celebrate their achievements; to empathize with them in times of adversity; and to highlight the plight of the ill, dispossessed, vulnerable, and/or forgotten. The *dedicated* monarchical trait requires a monarch to maintain the dignity, symbolism, and traditions of the institution.

Clearly, digital corporate communication is of crucial importance to the British Monarchy. Mindful of the total corporate brand communication mix outlined in this chapter, it is possible to illustrate how the mix pertains to the British Monarchy as follows.

Corporate Brand Based (Promissory) Corporate Communication of the British Monarchy

A cornerstone of the institution's corporate communication is focused on the associations linked to the British Monarchy as a corporate brand. For the author, this is encapsulated in the institution communicating the key tenets of the monarchy's corporate brand promise in terms of the monarch being *dutiful* to the constitution, *devoted* to the peoples of Great Britain, and *dedicated* to upholding the dignity of the monarchy. These three precepts can be viewed as representing the cornerstone of the British Monarchy as a corporate brand. Ideally, the monarchy's corporate brand based communication should serve as the cornerstone, or as what is sometimes called 'common starting points', for the institution's corporate communication endeavours.

Corporate Identity Based (Primary) Corporate Communication of the British Monarchy

This encapsulates the corporate communication effects of the British Monarchy's activities and behaviours in constitutional, social, and societal terms. Corporate identity signifies an organization's defining and distinguishing traits. Thus, what the British Monarchy does, and how it does it, represents a powerful form of corporate communication in its own terms. Whilst the person of the monarch is the main vehicle and focus of the above – with the late Queen following the dictum, 'to be seen is to be believed' – it can encompass those who serve as the monarch's representatives and may, for instance, include members of the Royal Family. It should be remembered that "Everything an organisation does, will in some way communicate the organisation's identity" (Balmer, 1995, p. 35).

46 *Handbook on digital corporate communication*

Controlled Based (Secondary) Corporate Communication of the British Monarchy

This comprises the controlled corporate communication of the British Monarchy which will be grounded in various corporate communication conduits under the direct control of the institution. Of course, this communication vector should also be mindful of corporate brand based communication and its emphasis on being dutiful, devoted, and dedicated. Furthermore, controlled based corporate communication entails a concern for the institution's varied constituencies. As such, there will be targeted corporate communication activities aimed at these groups. Given the unique modus operandi of the monarchy in addition to the more usual controlled communication vectors, importance is accorded to the monarch's visits, receptions, messages of support, occasional broadcasts (such as the monarch's Christmas Message), news stories and press releases, and other activities which would be comparable to corporate public relations. The rituals and ceremonies of the monarchy are also part of the institution's corporate communication. The above being noted, paid-for advertising is uncommon.

Word-of-Mouth Based (Tertiary) Corporate Communication of the British Monarchy

The monarchy does not control every aspect of its corporate communication. As such, tertiary communication takes account of communication about the institution from third parties. The most important of these will be the public, but will also encompass commentary from the media, politicians, and other key figures. Although the institution cannot control these narratives and dialogues, it must, all the same, be cognizant of them and take account of them. Word-of-mouth based corporate communication can have a discernible 'corporate communication effect'.

Digital (Quaternary) Based Corporate Communication of the British Monarchy

Quaternary corporate communication means the British Monarchy needs to take account of new forms of communication as evinced in digital based communication and encompasses innovative technology along with artificial intelligence. It is broad in scope and has wide boundaries. It can also be used as an information resource which assists in planning, learning, and the analysis of big data. Amongst the corporate communication team within the British Monarchy is a head of digital engagement who has responsibility for the British monarchy's website along with the institution's social media channels. The monarchy's YouTube 'Royal Channel' was started in October 2007; its first tweet dates back to April 2009; and shared photographs on Flickr commenced in April 2010. The British Monarchy's Twitter account, named @RoyalFamily, has about 4.8 million followers (as at 2022). The current head of digital communication understands the importance of digital corporate communication for the monarchy and believes it has promoted the Crown as a corporate brand as "a modern, forward-thinking organisation" (http://www.com.uk/meet-our-people-emma). However, the worldwide high profile and high public interest in the monarchy's digital sphere has its challenges:

> One of the great, but also at times nerve-wracking things about working in communications for the Royal Family, is that the reaction to our work is always high-profile: announcements make front page news, and Facebook posts reach tens of millions of followers. (http://www.com.uk/meet-our-people-emma)

As one blogger on the British Monarchy has presciently observed:

> The Monarchy wants to be where the people are, and the people – you and me – love it … The role of the British Monarchy today: not so much pomp and circumstance but socialization. Who doesn't want to socialize on the internet with Queens, Princes, and Duchesses? Granted they may not be tweeting or Facebooking individually, but I'll wager a bet they are very aware of what is written on their behalf and what people are writing in response. (ariherzog.com/blog)

During the coronavirus pandemic in the years following 2019, the monarchy was heavily reliant on digital corporate communication owing to the need to maintain social distancing. As such, virtually all the monarch's activities and communication went digital.

Feedback (Responsory) Based Corporate Communication of the British Monarchy

Direct communication from individuals and groups to the British Monarchy represents an important dimension of the British Monarchy's corporate communication. It can come in a variety of digital forms, such as social media and email, and by traditional forms such as postal correspondence. Feedback can also be solicited by the Crown from the public in terms of opinion surveys and be instigated by the monarch's personal representatives through Great Britain (e.g., the lord-lieutenants who can filter feedback to the institution).

CONCLUSION AND FUTURE DIRECTIONS

This chapter has explained the nature and significance of TCBC and outlined a sextuple framework. Broad in scope, the TCBC perspective accommodates several corporate communication perspectives which are not always accorded importance, such as digital corporate communication and corporate brand communication. Both are important and both need to be taken account of. Importantly, a growing number of organizations are according increased importance to their corporate brands and to their corporate brand promise. This is not only because corporate brands can be of significant strategic value for organizations, but also because corporate brands can be highly attractive to customers and other stakeholders. In terms of digital corporate communication, whilst it has increased the breadth and power of the corporate communication field for organizations, it has also greatly empowered stakeholders. Thus, it can be seen, in part, to have 'democratized' corporate communication – however, only in part. This is partially because digital corporate communication has increased the influence of 'third party' organizations and these organizations can also be seen to be part of the corporate communication process in a way that was not previously the case. What is apparent is that the corporate brand and digital spheres require a radical rethinking of corporate communication and its management.

Looking ahead, the digital world is pregnant with possibilities. One facet of this is the use of AI to augment the real world via extended reality (Chuturvedi and Verma, 2022). *Extended Reality* (ER) encompasses a variety of forms including augmented reality, virtual reality, and mixed reality.

Thus, focusing on the British Monarchy, *Augmented Reality* (AR) will enhance a person's experience of the institution. Consequently, digital corporate communicators can employ the services of designers and others to amplify a person's interaction with the institution through

48   *Handbook on digital corporate communication*

visuals, sound, and graphics. In the future, a person attending the changing of the guard at Buckingham Palace would be able to overlay their encounter with this ritual through digital means via the utilization of enhanced sensory effects. These enhanced digital sensory effects might include the smell of leather saddles and the scent of horses.

Virtual Reality (VR) allows for the monarch's digital corporate communication team to permit an individual to experience the monarchy from anywhere in the world. As such, through VR, it will be possible for an individual to have a virtual presence at real time events and ceremonies where the monarch is present. This might include 'witnessing' the more mundane, but important, visits by the monarch to hospitals, hospices, charities, and schools. It could include 'selected eavesdropping' on meetings between the monarch and the British prime minister and overseas ambassadors and high commissioners. It most certainly would include 'experiencing' the great royal occasions such as coronations, the State Opening of Parliament, the Trooping the Colour, and so on.

Finally, through *Mixed Reality* (MR) the monarch's digital corporate communication experts can allow individuals to suffuse their real-world experience with a virtual world experience. Thus, a person standing outside Buckingham Palace might be granted digital access to enter the palace gates and, eventually, find themselves wearing formal evening attire and seated opposite a princess at a state banquet for the president of Finland or the emperor of Japan. One problem of Extended Reality is that the real thing might seem lacklustre in comparison. However, for those with disabilities or sensory impairments, ER might prove to be a boon.

In bringing this chapter to a close, it is evident that the corporate communication landscape has increasingly morphed not only into a digital landscape but also a corporate brand landscape. Thus, there is a need to take account of both the corporate brand and digital realms and for them to be integrated. This chapter has shed light on the importance of these dimensions. Given the inexorable rise of digital technologies and the relentless recognition of the importance of corporate brands, the new domain of digital corporate brand communication will increase in importance. Today, we have reached a 'tipping point' where digital channels of corporate brand communication will grow in importance whilst some traditional corporate communication components will wane. As such, although this chapter has highlighted the nature and significance of digital corporate brand communication, this overview should be seen as not so much the end but, rather, as the end of the beginning.

REFERENCES

Balmer, J. M. T. (1995). Corporate branding and connoisseurship. *Journal of General Management*, *21*(1), 24–46.

Balmer, J. M. T. (2001a). The three virtues and seven deadly sins of corporate brand management. *Journal of General Management*, *27*(1), 1–17.

Balmer, J. M. T. (2001b). Corporate identity, corporate branding and corporate marketing: Seeing through the fog. *European Journal of Marketing*, *5*(3–4), 248–291.

Balmer, J. M. T. (2005). Corporate brand cultures and communities. In J. E. Schroeder and M. Salzer Morling (eds.), *Brand culture* (pp. 34–49). London: Routledge.

Balmer, J. M. T. (2008). Identity based views of the corporation: Insights from corporate identity, organisational identity, social identity, visual identity, corporate brand identity and corporate image. *European Journal of Marketing*, *42*(9–10), 879–906.

Balmer, J. M. T. (2009). Scrutinising the British Monarchy: The corporate brand that was shaken, stirred and survived. *Management Decision*, *47*(4), 639–675.

Digital corporate communication and brand communication   49

Balmer, J. M. T. (2010). Explicating corporate brands and their management: Reflections and directions from 1995 to the present. *Journal of Brand Management, 18*(3), 180–196.

Balmer, J. M. T. (2012). Corporate brand management imperatives: Custodianship, credibility, and calibration. *California Management Review, 54*(3), 6–33.

Balmer, J. M. T. (2013). Corporate brand orientation: What is it? What of it? *Journal of Brand Management, 20*(9), 723–741.

Balmer, J. M. T. (2022). Managerial corporate brand orientation: Explication, significance, and antecedents. *Journal of Brand Management, 29*(1), 1–12.

Balmer, J. M. T. and Gray, E. R. (1999). Corporate identity and corporate communications: Creating competitive advantage. *Corporate Communication: An International Journal, 4*(4), 171–176.

Balmer, J. M. T. and Gray, E. R. (2003). Corporate brands: What are they? What of them? *European Journal of Marketing, 37*(7–8), 972–997.

Balmer, J. M. T. and Greyser, S. A. (2003). *Revealing the corporation: Perspectives on identity, image, reputation, corporate branding and corporate-level marketing.* London: Routledge.

Balmer, J. M. T. and Greyser, S. A. (2006). Corporate marketing integrating corporate identity, corporate branding, corporate communications, corporate image and corporate reputation. *European Journal of Marketing, 40*(7–8), 730–741.

Balmer, J. M. T. and Podnar, K. (2021). Corporate brand orientation: Identity, internal images, and corporate identification matters, Journal of Business Research, *134*, 729–737.

Balmer, J. M. T. and Yen, D. A. (2017). The internet of total corporate communications, quaternary corporate communications and the corporate marketing internet revolution. *Journal of Marketing Management, 33*(1–2), 131–144.

Bogdanor, V. (1995). *The monarchy and the constitution.* Oxford: Oxford University Press.

Burgers, T. and Robinson, D. R. S. (2016). Networked authoritarianism is on the rise. *Security and Peace, 34*(4), 248–252.

Cannon, J. and Griffiths, R. A. (1998). *The Oxford illustrated history of the British Monarchy.* Oxford: Oxford University Press.

Casais, B. and Gomes, L. R. (2022). Fashion bloggers' discourse on brands under corporate crisis: A netnographic research in Portugal. *Journal of Fashion Marketing and Management, 26*(3), 420–435.

Chaffey, D. and Smith, P. R. (2017). *Digital marketing excellence: Planning and optimising your online marketing* (5th ed.). London: Routledge.

Chaturvedi, R. and Verma, S. (2022). Artificial intelligence-driven customer experience: Overcoming the challenges. *California Management Review.* https://cmr.berkeley.edu/2022/03/artificial-intelligence -driven-customer-experience-overcoming-the-challenges/.

Elhai, J. D., Levine, J. C., and Hall, B. J. (2017). Anxiety about electronic data hacking: Predictors and relations with digital privacy protection behavior. *Internet Research, 27*(3), 631–649.

Etter, M., Ravasi, D., and Colleoni, E. (2019). Social media and the formation of organizational reputation. *Academy of Management Review, 44*(1), 28–52.

Gray, E. R. and Balmer, J. M. T. (1998). Managing corporate image and corporate reputation. *Long Range Planning, 31*(5), 695–702.

Halvorsen, K. (2019). A retrospective commentary: How fashion blogs function as a marketing tool to influence consumer behavior – evidence from Norway. *Journal of Global Fashion Marketing, 10*(4), 398–403.

Hanson, K. (2006). Should the boss be blogging? *Strategic Communication Management, 10*(29), 6–7.

Hatch, M. J. and Schultz, M. (2001). Are the strategic stars aligned for your corporate brand? *Harvard Business Review, 79*(2), 129–134.

Hoffjan, O. and Haidukiewicz, O. (2020). Good journalist, bad blogger? A study on the labeling of paid content in blogs and journalism. *Communications, 45*(3), 350–362.

Juran, K., Seungmook, K., and Ki Hoon, L. (2021). Evolution of digital marketing communication: Bibliometric analysis and network visualization from key articles. *Journal of Business Research, 130*, 552–563.

Kumar, V., Rajan, B., Venkatesan, R., and Lecinski, J. (2019). Understanding the role of artificial intelligences in personalized engagement marketing. *California Management Review, 61*(4), 135–155.

Lahtinen, S. and Närvänen, E. (2020). Co-creating sustainable corporate brands: A consumer framing approach. *Corporate Communications: An International Journal, 25*(3), 447–461.

Meta's Facebook agrees to settle data privacy lawsuit (2022). *Reuters*, 27 August. https://www.reuters.com/legal/metas-facebook-agrees-settle-data-privacy-lawsuit-2022-08-26/.

Nunan, D. and Di Domenico, M. (2019). Older consumers, digital marketing, and public policy: A review and research agenda. *Journal of Public Policy & Marketing*, *38*(4), 469–483.

Peachey, K. (2022). Post Office scandal: What the Horizon saga is all about. *BBC News*, 22 March. https://www.bbc.com/news/business-56718036.

Pesetski, A. (2020). Deepfakes: A new content category for a digital age. *The William and Mary Bill of Rights Journal*, *29*(2), 503–514.

Ramaswamy, V. and Gouillart, F. (2010). *The power of co-creation*. New York: Free Press.

Rone, J. (2022). Fake profiles, trolls, and digital paranoia: Digital media practices in breaking the indignados movement. *Social Movement Studies*, *21*(1–2), 25–41.

Schwab, K. (2015). The Fourth Industrial Revolution: What it means and how to respond. *Foreign Affairs*, 12 December.

Setkute, J. and Dibb, S. (2022). "Old boys' club": Barriers to digital marketing in small B2B firms. *Industrial Marketing Management*, *102*, 266–79.

Shephardson, D. and Wang, W. (2021). ByteDance agrees to $92 million privacy settlement with U.S. TikTok users. Reuters, 25 February. https://www.reuters.com/article/us-bytedance-tiktok-lawsuit-idUSKBN2AP2O5.

The Commonwealth (2022). *Facts*. https://thecommonwealth.org/about/facts.

4. Digital corporate communication and media relations

Daniel Vogler and Mark Badham

INTRODUCTION

As an institution, the news media are one of the most dominant forces in Western democratic societies and have a powerful influence over the public formation of opinions about organizations (Carroll and McCombs, 2003; Deephouse and Heugens, 2009; Meijer and Kleinnijenhuis, 2006; Vogler and Eisenegger, 2020). Much research has focused on understanding the effects of media coverage on issues (e.g., issues management and corporate social responsibility (CSR) communication), crises (e.g., crisis communication), organizational reputation (e.g., corporate reputation management), an organization's finances (e.g., investor relations and financial communication), and relationships with stakeholders (e.g., stakeholder relationship management), including politicians and public servants (e.g., public affairs and public diplomacy). Research demonstrating mainstream news media's substantial effects on mass audiences has led to journalists being one of the primary target stakeholder groups of corporate communication (Grunig, 1990). Therefore, the news media have traditionally been a central focus of corporate communication practitioners and scholars and *media relations* was established as a specialized function within the broader corporate communication domain.

Digital technology has changed the function of media relations in significant ways. According to Chadwick (2017, p. 24) today's media environment is "far more diverse, fragmented, and polycentric, and new practices have evolved out of the rise of digital communication". The massive changes in the media environment and the rise of new means of digital communication have affected organization's media relations practices. In hybrid media environments 'new' media relations practices emerge from digital communication and merge with 'old' or legacy practices. For instance, press releases (also known as news releases or media releases) are now hosted on corporate websites (Pettigrew and Reber, 2010) and press conferences are streamed live on platforms such as YouTube and embedded in corporate social media accounts, which often makes them accessible not only to journalists but also to the wider public. Further, all these activities can be monitored and analysed with digital tools almost in real time and on a global scale in online corporate newsrooms (Atabek and Alikilic, 2020) and social media newsrooms (Zerfass and Schramm, 2014).

The process of digitalization is also fundamentally changing journalism, which in turn shapes media relations practices. News organizations are facing declining revenues from subscriptions and advertising, which has led to the diagnosis of a general crisis of the news business in many Western countries (Picard, 2014). As a consequence, journalists have had to cope with fewer resources and depend more on news content supplied by third-party sources such as corporations, which implies corporations' stronger influence over news content through the media relations function (Vogler and Schäfer, 2020).

52   *Handbook on digital corporate communication*

Legacy news media are confronted with declining audiences for their printed newspapers and linear broadcasting formats. Still, newspapers and television news programmes remain important information channels for some audiences (Reuters Institute for the Study of Journalism, 2021). Podcasts, for instance, have emerged as new forms to provide audio news to audiences (Nee and Santana, 2022). Furthermore, regularly updated news published 24/7 on websites and social media enable news media outlets to reach new, more diverse and larger audiences on a global scale and in real time (Rauchfleisch et al., 2020). Media relations practitioners have had to adapt to these digitally transformed practices, which have become increasingly hybrid through the integration of both traditional and new media (Bajkiewicz et al., 2011). At the same time, media relations, through its symbiotic relationship with the news business (Lee et al., 2018), continues to address the informational needs of offline audiences through legacy media.

DEFINITIONS OF THE TOPIC AND PREVIOUS STUDIES

As a corporate function, media relations involves the management of relations between an organization and the news media (Raupp, 2013). Media relations is an integral part of corporate communication (Argenti, 2006). Indeed, it is one of corporate communication's oldest functions. The news media have been viewed as an independent yet accessible channel through which organizations can disseminate corporate messages to mass audiences in a relatively efficient and cost-effective way (Grunig, 1990). Thus, communication professionals working for organizations have sought to specialize in building relationships with journalists for the purpose of influencing their news reports with corporate messages. This has led to the function of media relations being institutionalized in organizations' communication efforts (for an overview of media relations' influence on journalism, see Jackson and Moloney, 2015; Macnamara, 2014; Schönhagen and Meißner, 2016; Zoch and Molleda, 2014).

Within the field of corporate communication and its sibling discipline public relations, media relations scholars and practitioners have sought to understand journalists' news values (Boukes et al., 2022; Shoemaker and Reese, 2014), media logics (Esser, 2013), news routines (Shoemaker and Reese, 2014), journalistic ideals (Shoemaker and Reese, 2014), hierarchy of influences (Shoemaker and Reese, 2014), and news production processes for the purpose of further understanding how organizations may influence news coverage about them. In his journalist-centric media relations model, Pang (2010) posits internal and external influences on news media professionals. The internal influences include the individual journalist's working routines and mindset as well as the newsroom (or organizational) routines. The external influences consist of extra-media forces, for instance, legal constraints and media ideology (i.e., the larger ideological framework journalists work in).

Journalists' work essentially involves gathering news from credible sources and subsequently editing, producing and publishing/broadcasting it through their own channels. Media relations practitioners attempt to understand journalists and journalism so that they may be more effective in building relationships with media workers for the purpose of influencing their perspective of the organization and thus bend their gatekeeping authority (Lewin, 1943) to reflect the organization in a more favourable light in their news coverage. In doing so, these practitioners attempt to persuade journalists and media outlets that their organizations are a reliable, credible and authoritative source of valued news that they can draw on.

Because journalists rely on external sources for a regular and reliable supply of news content, media relations practitioners try to persuade journalists to treat them as a credible media source. Having then gained media standing (Gamson, 2004), organizations' distribution of information subsidies (Cook, 1998), such as press releases, fact sheets and backgrounders, to journalists becomes more effective. Multiple actors (e.g., corporations, politicians, activists and trade unions) typically compete to gain a voice in media reports relating to a topic or issue of importance to them. When considering the limitations of time, space and format in news production practices (Berger, 2001; Curtin, 1999), gaining media attention can be a very competitive process. Nevertheless, over time skilled media relations professionals can be relatively successful at gaining a voice in media coverage. Studies show that up to 75 per cent of the content of media reports, particularly business or financial news, is sourced from or significantly influenced by media relations professionals (Macnamara, 2014).

Despite their competing interests, media relations practitioners and journalists have a "symbiotic" relationship (Bentele and Nothhaft, 2008, p. 35; Currah, 2009, p. 66); one party supplies news content to the other and both parties benefit from this exchange. However, a key challenge in this exchange relationship is that, traditionally, journalists strongly defend their independence from external influences (Gans, 1979; Shoemaker and Reese, 2014). For this reason, scholars have also referred to the "love–hate" relationship between the two parties (Harcup, 2009, p. 72).

One way to respond to this tension is to understand journalists and media organizations as conduits, actors and arenas. First, as conduits (for a conduit or channel perspective, see Badham, 2019; McQuail, 2000; Wright, 1986), they can be useful in transmitting corporate messages in relatively unfiltered ways. A conduit perspective views media as 'earned' media (Badham et al., 2022b; Stephen and Galak, 2012). Accordingly, organizations have to earn favourable publicity via the news media; they strive to negotiate not only *how much* of the core corporate message can be embedded in news reports, but also *when* this message gets disseminated to news audiences.

However, media organizations and journalists may sometimes be viewed as actors or agents (Badham, 2019; McQuail, 2000; Page, 1996), shaping or framing news reports (de Vreese, 2005) in relatively active ways based on variables such as ideology and newsroom culture (Shoemaker and Reese, 2014). An actor perspective of media organizations and journalists views them as entities or agents independent of outside influence while selecting and editing news content.

A third approach views news media as a public arena (see Frandsen and Johansen, 2010, 2018; Luoma-aho and Vos, 2010), or facilitator of a plurality of news voices (Badham, 2019), in which organizations and audiences participate in discussion, dissemination, and even creation of news. Traditionally, organizations could submit letters to newspaper editors (known as 'letters to the editor') as largely unedited texts published alongside other audience-submitted texts, sometimes with contrary views. The participatory nature of social media and online discussion forums hosted on news sites enables spaces in which organizations and stakeholders can contribute to the formation of what is considered news (Badham et al., 2022b; Badham and Mykkänen, 2022). Thus, organizations are given opportunities to influence news discussions in these digital arenas.

The function of media relations is sometimes reduced to technical aspects like writing press releases, responding to informational requests by journalists and providing the news media with favourable information about the organization. However, media relations also includes

54 *Handbook on digital corporate communication*

tactical and strategic approaches (Pang, 2010) that seek to manage socio-political issues being discussed in society, mitigate the effects of corporate crises (Raupp, 2013), and contribute to longer-term intangible assets such as corporate reputation. Indeed, a media relations strategy must consider both proactive and reactive stances. On the one hand, organizations need a media relations function that can proactively build and execute media strategies linked to corporate strategies. On the other hand, an agile media relations strategy is needed to respond to journalists reacting to customer complaints and developing corporate crises.

A strategic approach also can play an important role in agenda-building (Weaver and Elliott, 1985) – the process that influences the formation of the salience of organizations, topics and issues on the news agenda (Berkowitz, 1992; Ragas et al., 2011) and which subsequently merges into the agenda-setting process (Kroon and van der Meer, 2020; McCombs and Shaw, 1972). The aim of the media relations function is to influence not only the media salience or presence of the organization in media reports, but also the tone of news about the organization. By selecting and framing topics in a certain manner, which some have described as 'spin' (e.g., Davies, 2009), media relations practitioners can influence the agenda of the news (Zoch and Molleda, 2006) and consequently also the agenda of the public (i.e., the media's agenda-setting role).

WHAT IS DIGITALIZATION CHANGING IN MEDIA RELATIONS?

Even though digitalization has significantly changed the media environment, legacy media continue to remain relevant. In hybrid media environments (Chadwick, 2017) new digital means of communication coexist alongside 'older' media but also interact with them. This is also true for media relations. New practices have emerged but have also merged with existing practices, while many practices remain rooted in traditional media relations. Journalists continue to demand press releases as the means through which organizations supply them with news content. However, the dissemination of press releases has changed. Instead of solely sending them to journalists via email (or by traditional mail before the Internet), press releases are hosted on organizations' websites, often in online newsrooms, making them permanently available and traceable, for instance, through search engines (Jung Moon and Hyun, 2014; Waters et al., 2010). Although press conferences are still staged in offline spaces and primarily aimed at journalists, today they are often streamed in real time, for instance, via YouTube or social networks, thus enabling them to reach larger audiences within and beyond news media (Jacobs, 2011). Increasingly, they are held online only, making them more accessible and affordable for journalists to attend.

Digitalization has also changed the interaction between media relations practitioners and journalists, again leading to hybrid forms of interaction. Communication through email has become the norm and is slowly replacing on-site face-to-face interaction or phone calls, even though both traditional practices remain important (Waters et al., 2010). Social media complements the toolbox of media relations; increasingly, media relations specialists also are using social media (e.g., Twitter and WhatsApp), such as through Twitter's direct messaging feature, to reach journalists with organizational content (Mashiah, 2021; Young, 2021). Media relation practitioners also engage in so-called media catching (Waters et al., 2010), which is changing the traditional process of pitching stories to news media. Instead of contacting lots of journalists "in hopes of gaining media placements, thousands of practitioners are being contacted at one time by journalists and others seeking specific material for stories, blog postings, and Web sites with upcoming deadlines" (Waters et al., 2010, p. 243).

Transformation of corporate communication in general and media relations specifically is taking place against this backdrop of an ongoing crisis of journalism (Picard, 2014). Even though news is still a sought-after commodity and the demand for reliable information is high in modern societies, most traditional media companies in Western countries face financial challenges. Consumers' willingness to pay for online news remains low in most countries (Reuters Institute for the Study of Journalism, 2021). At the same time, advertising revenues of most legacy media outlets in Western European countries are declining and the digital advertising market is dominated by large technology companies rather than news organizations (Lobigs, 2018). As a result, most players in the news industry are struggling to find a business model that will allow them to operate in today's digitally-enhanced world.

With the emergence of digital intermediaries (i.e., technology platforms such as Apple, Google and Facebook), the news media have on the one hand lost much of their primary gatekeeping power (Wallace, 2018) and have increasing difficulties in reaching certain audiences, for instance, young people who prefer to consume news in non-traditional ways. On the other hand, social media and search engines have boosted the way news is distributed to and accessed by larger audiences on an international scale (Rauchfleisch et al., 2020). Societal developments like citizen journalism (Allan and Thorsen, 2009) and crowdsourcing of news (Van Der Haak et al., 2012) have led to new feedback loops between news media and their audience (Kus et al., 2017). This process is accompanied by changing perceptions of journalists and journalism in the eyes of the public and certain stakeholder groups which is observable, for instance, in declining trust (Kalogeropoulos et al., 2015, 2019).

For a long time, the news media were the only viable avenue for organizations to reach a wide audience. However, digitalization introduced new mass and targeted communication channels (e.g., corporate media) that organizations have made use of (Etter et al., 2019), enabling them to address their stakeholders in more direct ways (Hutchins and Tindall, 2016). Nevertheless, more and more organizations have adopted technology to invest in their own (quasi-)journalistic products to reach their news media stakeholders (Pettigrew and Reber, 2010). Media relations activities are increasingly bundled and executed in social media and online corporate newsrooms – sections of organizational websites where press releases, fact sheets, photos, videos and other multimedia content are published for journalists' access (Zerfass and Schramm, 2014). The term *newsroom* implies that corporations no longer perceive themselves as mere providers of information exclusively for news media, but rather act as journalists themselves (Moss, 2021; Sherwood et al., 2017). For example, the emerging view is that an organization's stakeholders can easily access news about the organization on these online newsrooms. These newsrooms, combined with digital news dissemination and monitoring software platforms such as Mynewsdesk providing AI-based scanning of news stories, extensive journalist databases and SEO, enable media relations practitioners to easily monitor and measure outputs such as publicity and social media 'hits' almost in real time and on a global level.

Furthermore, digitalization has spawned a long tail (Anderson, 2006) of diverse news outlets catering to a wide range of niche audiences each with their own unique informational needs. Entrepreneurial journalists and editors have created digital native news media businesses (Salaverría, 2020) that are cost-efficient to launch and maintain, although their financial viability has been challenged in recent times. Media relations specialists are able to tailor and

56 *Handbook on digital corporate communication*

target corporate messages to quite diverse audiences via these digital-only news outlets. With this development, hybrid forms of media between the diverse poles of earned media and paid media (Badham et al., 2022b) have emerged. These forms of organization-sponsored content include advertorials (advertisements blended into editorial material), native advertising (advertiser-sponsored content designed to look similar to unpaid editorial content), and brand journalism (corporations producing journalistic content on their own sites).

Another change caused by digitalization of communication is that news media increasingly discover stories about organizations via social media. Social media empowers anyone anywhere to quickly report a problem caused by and/or affecting an organization simply by capturing an incident on a smartphone and posting the video or audio file as evidence of the problem via their personal social media accounts. From one such post, crises can emerge and spread through social media. Journalists are increasingly discovering these social media crisis incidents, investigating their nature, and producing their own versions of these crises in their news reports, thus further spreading the impact of these crises to new and wider audiences. In their study of crisis arena crossovers, Badham at al. (2022a) propose the Crisis Arena Crossover (CAC) framework as an analytical tool with which media relations and crisis communication professionals can gain foresight and strategic understanding of this phenomenon to help them deal with digital-led organizational crises.

WHAT REMAINS THE SAME?

In the digital age, personal relationships through direct one-on-one communication still matter in the media relations process. Media relations is a profession based on both personal and organizational influence. As such, not much has changed in the way individual media relations specialists build trusting professional relations with journalists through private meetings, phone calls and emails. These relationships set up a strong foundation for effective long-term influence in the agenda-building process.

In hybrid media systems new and old media coexist alongside each other. This is also true for the audience. The media diets of contemporary audiences are composed of a combination of digital and offline legacy media. Even though digital news consumption has become the norm, many people still receive information about the world through traditional channels, like newspapers and television (Reuters Institute for the Study of Journalism, 2021). So despite the increased importance of social media in society, journalism remains an integral producer and multiplier of information from and about corporations (Vogler and Eisenegger, 2020). Thus, the news media are still a viable channel for corporate messages, meaning that media relations is still a viable function today.

Because the news media still are capable of reaching large audiences, organizations continue their media relations efforts to convey their messages via news reports. Although organizations are able to reach stakeholders through social media and corporate publications and thus bypass journalistic gatekeepers, audiences generally value the editorial intervention and counter-balance of professional third-party intermediaries such as the news media. Thus, information about organizations and public issues in news reports are seen as credible (Nikolaeva and Bicho, 2011). Accordingly, because of journalism's long-standing claim of professional independence and objectivity, journalistic media are still viewed as legitimate actors in mass communication processes (Deephouse, 1996) and thus are critical actors in the formation of corporate reputations (Carroll and McCombs, 2003; Vogler and Eisenegger, 2020). For this reason, political and corporate leaders continue to hold press conferences and view relationships with journalists as important.

CRITICAL EXAMINATION

In recent years, corporate communication departments have been growing in staff numbers as the number of journalists has decreased. Journalists have been facing other challenges, such as limitations in the resources at their disposal. It is no wonder then that the corporate communication profession is full of ex-journalists whose insider knowledge gives them an advantageous influence in the agenda-building process. This has led scholars to diagnose a growing asymmetrical influence of organizations' media relations function on journalism (Jackson and Moloney, 2016; Vogler and Schäfer, 2020). The relative power dynamic between media relations and journalism, thus, has shifted towards media relations. But this is only one side of the coin; serious disadvantages for both corporate communication and the wider society evolve from journalism's weaker power in this dynamic (Meissner and Vogler, 2022). Media relations practitioners are frustrated by "the resulting dearth of institutional knowledge, influx of young, inexperienced reporters, and shallow stories" (Bajkiewicz et al., 2011, p. 329). Furthermore, journalism's limited gatekeeping capacity to influence what gets disseminated as news is enabling corporations with greater media relations resources (e.g., skills, budgets and network-spanning) to win public debates played out in news coverage (Jung Moon and Hyun, 2014). Also, specifically trained business journalists, who are equipped to deal with and understand increasingly complex financial and economic processes, are increasingly rare in editorial departments (Kalogeropoulos et al., 2015). Consequently, journalists are turning to outside sources, such as media relations departments within organizations, to help them make sense of corporations' business affairs.

Gaining audience attention is important for news outlets, who seek to attract a wider audience for their news by increasing traffic to their online news sites through social media (Badham and Mykkänen, 2022). Social media platforms like Facebook enable news outlets to use tactics such as "engineering headlines to include emotional directives for readers (to click or like and share) and creating digestible and relatable content that could be easily shared among users" (Caplan and boyd, 2018, p. 5). Such developments lead to declining news quality and indirectly result in increased reputational risks for corporations engaging with the media.

News published by media outlets on digital platforms leaves an interlinked and lasting data trail. The advantage for the media relations function is that this digital trail enables organizations to easily monitor news coverage about them and issues important to them, which is helpful to gauge public opinion and understand issues important to stakeholders. The disadvantage, however, is that corporate scandals published online can remain accessible to public view (almost) forever.

58 *Handbook on digital corporate communication*

CASE STUDY: A SECRETIVE MEDIA RELATIONS FUNCTION SHAPING THE CLIMATE DEBATE

In the lead-up to the COP26 climate talks in Glasgow in November 2021, a secretive network of media relations specialists worked behind the scenes to shape news coverage emerging from the event. For over ten years, the Global Strategic Communications Council (GSCC), a network of approximately 100 media relations professionals in more than 20 countries, had been promoting a climate change agenda in opposition to the climate agenda of fossil fuel companies. A news article published by *Politico* on 9 November 2021 exposed the GSCC, the media relations professionals working for it and the organizations sponsoring this network, its tactics and overall strategy. The article revealed that GSCC had been established to "push a unified message from a diverse group of sources" (Wheaton, 2021).

GSCC tactics included setting up press conferences for activists like Greta Thunberg, providing media training to activist groups, collecting science-based facts for selective distribution to journalists and crowdsourcing a database of climate-friendly journalists across the globe. GSCC members also helped journalists gain access to news content not normally accessible to them by delivering direct quotes from policy decision-makers in closed-door meetings at COP26. The fluid way in which these media relations professionals disseminated their climate change messages through news outlets shows how the media can be viewed as a *conduit* in organization–audience communication processes. These tactics not only involved the collection and distribution of raw information that serves as building blocks for news articles, they also included framing news stories with a strong bias towards the climate change agenda. In other words, their media relations actions were "whispering into journalists' ears about climate science – spoon-feeding them facts, figures, spin and quotes" (Wheaton, 2021).

This case illustrates how these media relations specialists became involved in the agenda-building process, discursively building and promoting the foundations of a climate change agenda for news outlets one tactic at a time. It also shows both the technical (e.g., collecting and distributing statements) and the strategic aspects of media relations (e.g., shaping news coverage of climate change over time through the presentation of a unified message from a diverse group of sources).

This case offers insight into the ways that digitalization of communication influences the media relations function. First, GSCC members prepared and disseminated a daily newsletter via email to "exhausted reporters in Glasgow trying to understand the confusing COP26 deliberations" (Wheaton, 2021). Emails aid in providing fast-breaking news to journalists who have daily and even hourly news production deadlines. Second, GSCC members were involved in "summarizing multiple negotiations tracks through a confidential online document shared with reporters"; online document-sharing platforms like GoogleDocs enable sanctioned individuals to collaborate in writing confidential texts and then provide private access to others. Third, GSCC maintained a skeletal website to offer some legitimacy for its existence, identity and purpose. Content on the website was deliberately scarce to maintain a level of anonymity. Finally, GSCC was able to use emails, text messaging software and video conferencing software such as Zoom to collaborate with multiple stakeholders across the globe and to mobilize and synchronize action.

This case also triggers ethical questions with implications for the trustworthiness of the media relations profession. For example, how transparent should organizations be about themselves and their media relations efforts, not only to journalists but also to the wider public? In this case, GSCC kept its purpose, people and sponsoring organizations – even to some extent its existence – hidden from journalists and the public. This was a secretive intermediary organization acting on behalf of multiple corporations and public sector entities who also remained anonymous, raising questions about the ethics involved in hiding the forces of powerful societal influence. Although corporate communication typically is a behind-the-scenes function within organizations – for instance, ghost-writing corporate messages on behalf of public figures such as CEOs – the media relations function typically is not hidden to journalists; press releases and other media relations tools are publicly available on organizational websites and contain the names and contact details of media relations practitioners and their employing organizations. However, in this case many journalists were not aware of the actors behind the messages that GSCC was feeding them. One potential resulting downside of this secrecy is a public and media sceptical of organizations' corporate communication function.

CONCLUSION AND FUTURE DIRECTIONS

An organization's media relations function remains important in the fast-changing digital media environment. Its working routines, tools and tactics may have changed to some degree, but for corporate communication the news media is an important channel as well as stakeholder in the dissemination of corporate messages. Corporate communication, thus, should maintain its relationship with journalism as a critical and professional counterpart in mass communication processes, even if stakeholders increasingly do not trust the media and even if it sometimes comes at the cost of critical coverage of corporate behaviour. Media relations and journalism professionals are often described and perceived as antagonists. However, as empirical and theoretical research illustrates, they may be more symbiotic or interdependent than one would expect at first glance (Bentele and Nothhaft, 2008; Macnamara, 2014; Schönhagen and Meißner, 2016).

As this chapter illustrates, the media relations function, whether for corporations, governments, NGOs or even a secretive network of professionals, is still of high value from a corporate communication perspective, despite new and seemingly more direct or efficient ways to interact with the public and stakeholder groups. Given the ongoing crisis of journalism in Western countries, it remains an open question as to how traditional media relations will continue to evolve and if it will remain important in the future (see Hutchins and Tindall, 2016; Waters et al., 2010; Young, 2021; Zerfass et al., 2016). Media relations is often looked at retrospectively and perceived as outdated as it is linked to the old world of journalism. As we show in this chapter, media relations still has relevance in the digital media environment. Research should, thus, not only investigate the development of media relations and the influence of digitalization empirically, but also further theoretically develop the idea of digital media relations and develop it into a valuable analytical concept.

Media relations literature is still dominated by a focus on for-profit organizations while neglecting other types of organizations. The Covid-19 pandemic, as well as the climate crisis, has shown that the intersection of science and journalism is a crucial element of crisis management, as the news media are still a primary source of information for many people. Media relations can contribute to the transfer of scientific knowledge to societies through the news media (Lee and Merle, 2018). Media relations research could focus on media relations of public institutions during the Covid-19 pandemic and beyond and contribute to providing

60 *Handbook on digital corporate communication*

instruments and techniques to transfer scientific knowledge or relevant information to the public through the news media. After all, this chapter shows that despite digitalization, news outlets still remain relevant information channels for the public and thus relevant for the interaction of organizations with many of their stakeholders.

REFERENCES

Allan, S. and Thorsen, E. (eds.) (2009). *Citizen journalism: Global perspectives*. New York: Peter Lang.
Anderson, C. (2006). *The long tail: Why the future of business is selling less of more*. New York: Hyperion.
Argenti, P. A. (2006). How technology has influenced the field of corporate communication. *Journal of Business and Technical Communication*, *20*(3), 357–370.
Atabek, U. and Alikilic, O. A. (2020). Online pressrooms: Journalists' expectations from public relations practitioners concerning online media relations. *Romanian Journal of Communication and Public Relations*, *22*(3), 65–83.
Badham, M. (2019). Four news media roles shaping agenda-building processes. In F. Frandsen, W. Johansen, R. Tench, and S. Romenti (eds.), *BIG IDEAS in public relations research and practice* (pp. 163–176). Bingley: Emerald Publishing.
Badham, M., Luoma-aho, V., Valentini, C., and Körkkö, L. (2022a). Digital strategic communication through digital media-arenas. In J. Falkheimer and M. Heide (eds.), *Research handbook on strategic communication* (pp. 416–430). Cheltenham, UK and Northampton, MA, USA: Edward Elgar Publishing.
Badham, M., Lievonen, M., and Luoma-aho, V. (2022b). Factors influencing crisis arena crossovers: The Apple iPhone #ChargeGate case. In L. Austin and Y. Jin (eds.), *Social media and crisis communication* (2nd edition). London: Routledge.
Badham, M. and Mykkänen, M. (2022). A relational approach to how media engage with their audiences in social media. *Media and Communication*, *10*(1), advance online publication.
Bajkiewicz, T. E., Kraus, J. J., and Hong, S. Y. (2011). The impact of newsroom changes and the rise of social media on the practice of media relations. *Public Relations Review*, *37*(3), 329–331.
Bentele, G. and Nothhaft, H. (2008). The intereffication model: Theoretical discussions and empirical research. In A. Zerfass, B. van Ruler, and K. Sriramesh (eds.), *Public relations research* (pp. 33–42). VS Verlag für Sozialwissenschaften. https://doi.org/10.1007/978-3-531-90918-9_3.
Berger, B. K. (2001). Private issues and public policy: Locating the corporate agenda in agenda-setting theory. *Journal of Public Relations Research*, *13*, 91–126.
Berkowitz, D. (1992). Who sets the media agenda? The ability of policy makers to determine news decisions. In J. D. Kennamer (ed.), *Public opinion, the press and public policy* (pp. 81–112). Westport, CT: Praeger.
Boukes, M., Jones, N. P., and Vliegenthart, R. (2022). Newsworthiness and story prominence: How the presence of news factors relates to upfront position and length of news stories. *Journalism*, *23*(1), 98–116.
Caplan, R. and boyd, d. (2018). Isomorphism through algorithms: Institutional dependencies in the case of Facebook. *Big Data & Society*, *5*(1), 1–12.
Carroll, C. E. and McCombs, M. E. (2003). Agenda-setting effects of business news on the public's images and opinions about major corporations. *Corporate Reputation Review*, *6*(1), 36–46.
Chadwick, A. (2017). *The hybrid media system* (2nd edition). Oxford: Oxford University Press.
Cook, T. E. (1998). *Governing with the news: The news media as a political institution*. Chicago: University of Chicago Press.
Currah, A. (2009). *What's happening to our news*. Reuters Institute for the Study of Journalism. https://reutersinstitute.politics.ox.ac.uk/about/news/item/article/whats-happening-to-our-news.html.
Curtin, P. A. (1999). Reevaluating public relations information subsidies: Market driven journalism and agenda-building theory and practice. *Journal of Public Relations Research*, *11*, 53–90.
Davies, N. (2009). *Flat earth news*. New York: Random House.

de Vreese, C. H. (2005). News framing: Theory and typology. *Information Design Journal + Document Design*, 13, 48–59.

Deephouse, D. L. (1996). Does isomorphism legitimate? *Academy of Management Journal*, *39*(4), 1024–1039.

Deephouse, D. and Heugens, P. (2009). Linking social issues to organizational impact: The role of infomediaries and the infomediary process. *Journal of Business Ethics*, *86*(4), 541–553.

Esser, F. (2013). Mediatization as a challenge: Media logic versus political logic. In H. Kriesi, S. Lavenex, F. Esser, J. Matthes, M. Bühlmann, and D. Bochsler (eds.), *Democracy in the age of globalization and mediatization* (pp. 155–176). Basingstoke: Palgrave Macmillan.

Etter, M., Ravasi, D., and Colleoni, E. (2019). Social media and the formation of organizational reputation. *Academy of Management Review*, *44*(1), 28–52.

Frandsen, F. and Johansen, W. (2010). Apologizing in a globalizing world: Crisis communication and apologetic ethics. *Corporate Communications: An International Journal*, *15*(4), 350–364.

Frandsen, F. and Johansen, W. (2018). Voices in conflict: The crisis communication of meta-organizations. *Management Communication Quarterly*, *32*(1), 90–120.

Gamson, W. A. (2004). Bystanders, public opinion, and the media. In D. A. Snow, S. A. Soule, and H. Kriesi (eds.), *The Blackwell companion to social movements* (pp. 242–264). Malden, MA: Blackwell Publishing.

Gans, H. (1979). *Deciding what's news: A study of CBS evening news, NBC Nightly News, Newsweek, and Time*. New York: Random House.

Grunig, J. E. (1990). Theory and practice of interactive media relations. *Public Relations Quarterly*, *35*(3), 18–23.

Harcup, T. (2009). *Journalism: Principles and practices* (2nd edition). London: Sage Publications.

Hutchins, A. L. and Tindall, N. T. (2016). New media, new media relations: Building relationships with bloggers, citizen journalists and engaged publics. In A. L. Hutchins and N. T. Tindall (eds.), *Public relations and participatory culture* (pp. 123–136). London: Routledge.

Jackson, D. and Moloney, K. (2016). Inside churnalism: PR, journalism and power relationships in flux. *Journalism Studies*, *17*(6), 763–780.

Jacobs, G. (2011). Press conferences on the internet: Technology, mediation and access in the news. Journal of Pragmatics, *47*, 1900–1911.

Jung Moon, S. and Hyun, K. D. (2014). Online media relations as an information subsidy: Quality of Fortune 500 companies' websites and relationships to media salience. *Mass Communication and Society*, *17*(2), 258–273.

Kalogeropoulos, A., Suiter, J., Udris, L., and Eisenegger, M. (2019). News media trust and news consumption: Factors related to trust in news in 35 countries. *International Journal of Communication*, *13*, 3672–3693.

Kalogeropoulos, A., Svensson, H. M., van Dalen, A., de Vreese, C., and Albæk, E. (2015). Are watchdogs doing their business? Media coverage of economic news. *Journalism*, *16*(8), 993–1009.

Kroon, A. C. and van der Meer, T. G. L. A. (2020). Who takes the lead? Investigating the reciprocal relationship between organizational and news agendas. *Communication Research*, *48*(1), 51–76.

Kus, M., Eberwein, T., Porlezza, C., and Splendore, S. (2017). Training or improvisation? Citizen journalists and their educational backgrounds—a comparative view. *Journalism Practice*, *11*(2–3), 355–372.

Lee, L., Yip, L., and Chan, K. (2018). An exploratory study to conceptualize press engagement behavior with public relations practitioners. *Public Relations Review*, *44*(4), 490–500.

Lee, N. M. and Merle, P. F. (2018). Media relations and universities: An assessment of digital newsrooms. *Journal of Marketing for Higher Education*, *28*(2), 232–246.

Lewin, K. (1943). Defining the "field at a given time". *Psychological Review*, *50*, 292–310.

Lobigs, F. (2018). Wirtschaftliche Probleme des Journalismus im Internet: Verdrängungsängste und fehlende Erlösquellen. In C. Neuberger and C. Nuernbergk (eds.), *Journalismus im Internet: Profession – Partizipation – Technisierung* (pp. 295–334). Cham: Springer.

Luoma-aho, V. and Vos, M. (2010). Towards a more dynamic stakeholder model: Acknowledging multiple issue arenas. *Corporate Communications: An International Journal*, *15*(3), 315–331.

Macnamara, J. (2014). Journalism–PR relations revisited: The good news, the bad news, and insights into tomorrow's news. *Public Relations Review*, *40*(5), 739–750.

Mashiah, I. (2021). The relationship between public-relations and journalists in WhatsApp technology. *Public Relations Review*, *47*(5).

McCombs, M. and Shaw, D. (1972). The agenda-setting function of mass media. *Public Opinion Quarterly*, *36*, 1766–1787.

McQuail, D. (2000). *McQuail's mass communication theory* (4th edition). London: Sage Publications.

Meijer, M. M. and Kleinnijenhuis, J. (2006). News and corporate reputation: Empirical findings from the Netherlands. *Public Relations Review*, *32*(4), 341–348.

Meissner, F. and Vogler, D. (2022). Kriselnder Journalismus, boomende PR? Qualitätsjournalismus als Bedingung für glaubwürdige Unternehmenskommunikation. In S. Pranz, H. Heidbrink, F. Stadel, and R. Wagner (eds.), *Journalismus und Unternehmenskommunikation* (pp. 235–249). Cham: Springer.

Moss, C. (2021). The corporate newsroom model. In C. Moss (ed.), *The corporate newsroom* (pp. 27–49). Cham: Springer.

Nee, R. C. and Santana, A. D. (2022). Podcasting the pandemic: Exploring storytelling formats and shifting journalistic norms in news podcasts related to the Coronavirus. *Journalism Practice*, *16*(6), 1559–1577.

Nikolaeva, R. and Bicho, M. (2011). The role of institutional and reputational factors in the voluntary adoption of corporate social responsibility reporting standards. *Journal of the Academy of Marketing Science*, *39*, 136–157.

Page, B. I. (1996). The mass media as political actors. *Political Science and Politics*, *29*, 20–24.

Pang, A. (2010). Mediating the media: A journalist-centric media relations model. *Corporate Communications: An International Journal*, *15*(2), 192–204.

Pettigrew, J. E. and Reber, B. H. (2010). The new dynamic in corporate media relations: How Fortune 500 companies are using virtual press rooms to engage the press. *Journal of Public Relations Research*, *22*(4), 404–428.

Picard, R. G. (2014). Twilight or new dawn of journalism? Evidence from the changing news ecosystem. *Journalism Practice*, *8*(5), 488–498.

Ragas, M. W., Kim, J., and Kiousis, S. (2011). Agenda-building in the corporate sphere: Analyzing influence in the 2008 Yahoo!–Icahn proxy contest. *Public Relations Review*, *37*(3), 257–265.

Rauchfleisch, A., Vogler, D., and Eisenegger, M. (2020). Transnational news sharing on social media: Measuring and analysing Twitter news media repertoires of domestic and foreign audience communities. *Digital Journalism*, *8*(9), 1206–1230.

Raupp, J. (2013). Krisenkommunikation und Media Relations. In A. Thießen (ed.), *Handbuch Krisenmanagement* (pp. 175–193). Cham: Springer VS. https://doi.org/10.1007/978-3-531-19367 -0_10.

Reuters Institute for the Study of Journalism (2021). *Digital news report*. https://reutersinstitute.politics .ox.ac.uk/digital-news-report/2021.

Salaverría, R. (2020). Exploring digital native news media. *Media and Communication*, *8*(2), 1–4.

Schönhagen, P. and Meißner, M. (2016). The co-evolution of public relations and journalism: A first contribution to its systematic review. *Public Relations Review*, *42*(5), 748–758.

Sherwood, M., Nicholson, M., and Marjoribanks, T. (2017). Controlling the message and the medium? The impact of sports organisations' digital and social channels on media access. *Digital Journalism*, *5*(5), 513–531.

Shoemaker, P. J. and Reese, S. D. (2014). *Mediating the message in the 21st century: A media sociology perspective*. London: Routledge.

Stephen, A. T. and Galak, J. (2012). The effects of traditional and social earned media on sales: A study of a microlending marketplace. *Journal of Marketing Research*, *49*, 624–639.

Van Der Haak, B., Parks, M., and Castells, M. (2012). The future of journalism: Networked journalism. *International Journal of Communication*, *6*, 2923–2938.

Vogler, D. and Eisenegger, M. (2020). CSR communication, corporate reputation, and the role of the news media as an agenda setter in the digital age. *Business & Society*, *60*(8), 1957–1986.

Vogler, D. and Schäfer, M. S. (2020). Growing influence of university PR on science news coverage? A longitudinal automated content analysis of university media releases and newspaper coverage in Switzerland, 2003–2017. *International Journal of Communication*, *14*, 3143–3164.

Wallace, J. (2018). Modelling contemporary gatekeeping. *Digital Journalism*, *6*(3), 274–293.

Waters, R. D., Tindall, N. T., and Morton, T. S. (2010). Media catching and the journalist–public relations practitioner relationship: How social media are changing the practice of media relations. *Journal of Public Relations Research*, *22*(3), 241–264.

Weaver, D. and Elliott, S. N. (1985). Who sets the agenda for the media? A study of local agenda-building. *Journalism Quarterly*, *62*(1), 87–94.

Wheaton, S. (2021, November 9). The climate activists stealing Big Oil's playbook: After all, someone's gotta check Greta Thunberg's email. *Politico*. https://www.politico.eu/article/the-climate-activists -stealing-big-oils-playbook/?aid=app_feed.

Wright, C. (1986). *Mass communication: A sociological perspective* (3rd edition). New York: Random House.

Young, P. (2021). Media relations in the social media age. In A. Theaker (ed.), *The public relations handbook* (pp. 267–288). London: Routledge.

Zerfass, A. and Schramm, D. M. (2014). Social media newsrooms in public relations: A conceptual framework and corporate practices in three countries. *Public Relations Review*, *40*(1), 79–91.

Zerfass, A., Verčič, D., and Wiesenberg, M. (2016). The dawn of a new golden age for media relations? *Public Relations Review*, *42*(4), 499–508.

Zoch, L. M. and Molleda, J. C. (2006). Building a theoretical model of media relations using framing, information subsidies, and agenda-building. In C. H. Botan and V. Hazleton (eds.), *Public relations theory II* (pp. 279–309). London: Routledge.

5. Digital corporate communication and corporate reputation

Elanor Colleoni, Stefania Romenti and Grazia Murtarelli

INTRODUCTION

One of a company's most important social evaluations is its corporate reputation (Gardberg et al., 2022). Corporate reputation is a trait that signals a company's likely behavior, a signal about future actions, a pledge that justifies and promotes expectations of a principal about the actions of the agent under information asymmetry (Fombrun and Shanley, 1990). These signals influence the way individuals evaluate a firm positively or negatively (Fombrun and Shanley, 1990; George et al., 2016; Rindova et al., 2005). Research has shown that reputation is a key mechanism used to signal the quality not only of corporations, but also other types of organizations, including NGOs (Gent et al., 2015), public institutions (Luoma-aho, 2007), and even individuals (Marwick and Boyd, 2011).

In a recent article on corporate reputation formation in social media, Etter et al. (2019) have argued how the new social media environment in which corporate reputation forms has dramatically changed in the last ten years. Social media enables dispersed stakeholders to easily connect and publicly exchange feelings, opinions, and experiences about a company, to the point of changing the collective judgments of the quality, competence, or character of an organization (Bundy et al., 2021). Moreover, from the company perspective, social media has enabled corporate communication professionals to be directly related with online stakeholders by enabling higher levels of interactivity, engagement, and positive behavioral impact (Allagui and Breslow, 2016). Social media has provided the opportunity to connect with like-minded stakeholders grouped around common topics of interest with minor transaction and coordination costs (Fieseler and Fleck, 2013). Finally, social media has also revolutionized the practice of gatekeeping by affecting the process of news distribution: interdependent networks of gatekeepers emerged, and also individuals participating in social media, liking news posts and sharing them can be considered as potential gatekeepers with different levels of influence (Welbers and Opgenhaffen, 2018).

But while there is growing anecdotal evidence of the impact of social media on corporate reputation, scholars are still debating whether and how social media impact companies (Barnett et al., 2020; Glozer et al., 2019; Roulet and Clemente, 2018; Wang et al., 2019). In particular, two main issues are arising from the transformation of the digital communication environment that challenge traditional assumptions about corporate reputation. These two issues are both related to how corporate reputation forms and, in particular, with the idea of corporate reputation as the result of a signaling process that exploits signals and signalers' qualities to reduce market uncertainty over the inner qualities of a company and as a credible source of selection within a field (Fombrun and Shanley, 1990). The first issue concerns the diffusion of false signals in the form of 'fake news' (Colleoni, 2021; Gardberg et al., 2022). Empirical studies on social media information and misinformation diffusion (Bradshaw and

Howard, 2018; Gorodnichenko et al., 2018) have shown the growing diffusion of fake news and manipulative communication with the goal to influence public debate and public perceptions about institutions and organizations (Luoma-aho, 2015). This trend also affects the formation of corporate reputation that is increasingly based on social media information, which is proving to be often not accurate, partisan, and coming from low prestige sources (Colleoni, 2021; Gardberg et al., 2022).

A second issue concerns the diffusion of false signalers mainly driven by Artificial Intelligence (AI) algorithms specialized in the creation and diffusion of online content. The diffusion of AI generated content and the increased quality of the content produced might decrease the impact that high prestige sources traditionally had in the creation of corporate reputation.

The goal of this chapter is threefold: first, to comprehensively describe what is changing in the field of corporate reputation as a result of digitalization and, in particular, the study of the formation of corporate reputation in light of digitalization of stakeholders' social evaluations; second, to shed some light on the theoretical issues that are arising due to these changes; and third, to outline future directions for research to successfully update our theories in light of the changes in the social evaluations process brought by social media.

This chapter is organized as follows. First, the chapter reviews established theory and highlights key aspects about corporate reputation formation. Second, key aspects of corporate reputation are evaluated in light of new communication technologies, particularly new media technologies, their functioning and affordances. The chapter highlights crucial aspects of new media technologies for stakeholders' engagement, and outlines the implications for corporate reputation formation. Finally, the chapter indicates current critical issues and open debates on the impact of new media technologies on corporate reputation formation.

DEFINITIONS OF THE TOPIC AND PREVIOUS STUDIES

A corporate reputation is an enduring collective representation of a firm's past behavior (Fombrun et al., 2000). This collective representation builds on social expectations about a company (Berens and van Riel, 2004) and represents a relatively stable, long-term, aggregated judgment of stakeholders and external parties about a firm's future behavior (Fombrun, 1996; Fombrun and Shanley, 1990). Fombrun and Shanley (1990) have argued that individuals evaluate corporate reputation on the basis of information about firms' relative positions within organizational fields: to do so they use market and accounting signals indicating performance, institutional signals indicating conformity to social norms, and strategy signals indicating strategic postures. Spence (1974) interpreted reputation as the outcome of a process in which firms signal their key characteristics to constituents to maximize their social status. Hall (1993) defines reputation as the overall estimation of a firm by customers, investors, employees, and the general public, which is expressed by combining cognitive and affective components of customers, investors, employees, and the general public. The combination of affective and cognitive components implies a conceptualization of reputation as an attitudinal construct, where attitude denotes subjective, emotional, and cognitive based mindsets (Mishina et al., 2011).

A good reputation represents a strategic resource for companies, which can generate competitive advantage (Fombrun and Shanley, 1990; Milgrom and Roberts, 1986). Corporate reputation represents a phenomenon with its own socially complex nature, tied to the specific history of an organization and, as such, it represents a barrier to imitation by competing companies (Barney, 1991). Corporate reputation helps companies build sustained performance, defined as the organization's ability to achieve persistently high performance and growth over a long period of time (Roberts and Dowling, 2002). In other words, the ability to create, manage, and exploit corporate reputation from a firm's perspective, allows it to drive markets rather than to be market-driven. Extensive research has shown that a favorable corporate reputation generates valuable organizational outcomes (Ravasi et al., 2018). A good corporate reputation can lower intra-company transition costs (Deephouse, 2000; Fombrun, 1996) and increases the likelihood that stakeholders will contract with a given firm (Deephouse, 2000; Rhee and Haunschild, 2006). A positive corporate reputation has also proven to positively impact on stock market and accounting performance (McMillan and Joshi, 1997; Roberts and Dowling, 2002; Vergin and Qoronfleh, 1998). Using Fortune's survey of America's Most Admired Corporations to measure reputation, numerous studies found the Fortune ratings had a positive effect on stock market and accounting performance (McMillan and Joshi, 1997; Roberts and Dowling, 2002; Vergin and Qoronfleh, 1998). Roberts and Dowling (2002) have shown how companies with good reputations are better positioned to sustain superior profit outcomes and financial performance over time. Rindova et al. (2005) have shown that a positive corporate reputation enables firms to charge premium prices and how this is tidily related to organizations' prominence in the minds of stakeholders. Drawing on propositions from social identity theory and signaling theory, Turban and Greening (1996) have shown how firms' corporate social performance (CSP) is positively related to corporate reputation and how these factors drive firms' attractiveness as employers, with the result of attracting the best talents. Finally, research has shown how a good prior corporate reputation buffers the negative impacts of a corporate crisis, creating a halo effect that protects a firm during a crisis. The prior reputation also works as a shield that deflects the potential reputational damage from a crisis while encouraging stakeholders to give the organization the benefit of the doubt in the crisis (Coombs and Holladay, 2008).

Extant research on corporate reputation has shown that reputation is signaled not only through market actions but also by communication, such as through press releases and advertising (e.g., Carter, 2006; Rindova et al., 2005). Most importantly, research has established that signals are sent out not only by the organization, but also by several accredited institutions and intermediaries, such as media and financial analysts (Deephouse, 2000; Deephouse et al., 2017) thanks to their recognized expertise and superior access to information (Rao, 1994; Rindova et al., 2005). In fact, extensive research has emphasized the critical role that publicly available evaluations disseminated through the media play in the formation of collective reputational judgments (Carroll and McCombs, 2003; Deephouse, 2000). The quality of the signal and the signaler are necessary conditions for corporate reputation to accurately signal the inner qualities of a company and, in so doing, to act as a credible source of selection within a field (Fombrun and Shanley, 1990).

In a recent article on corporate reputation formation in social media, Etter et al. (2019) have argued how the new digital communication environment, and, in particular, social media, in which corporate reputation forms has dramatically changed in the last ten years. They stress how peer-to-peer information in social media has become one of the sources used to make sense of a corporate reputation and how, as a result, firms have lost control over the definition and circulation of corporate signals. Moreover, the digital environment has provided visibility to two specific groups of stakeholders affecting corporate reputation formation and management: social media activists (Veil et al., 2015) and online hateholders (Luoma-aho, 2015). Within the online environment, individuals can easily join activist movements to exert pressure on organizations in order to change their policies, strategies, or activities, by sharing negative messages about the targeted organizations with dangerous consequences for their reputation (Veil et al., 2015). Similarly, online hateholders share negative evaluations about organizations. Unlike online activists who can join a movement without any direct experience with the organization, online hateholders are stakeholders who have been negatively engaged by organizations and who have experienced disaffection and disappointment towards them (Luoma-aho, 2015). The increasing use of social media by online stakeholders, activists, and hateholders force organizations to better investigate what is changing, what is remaining the same, and how to face critical issues linked to the formation and management of online reputation.

The following section reviews the key elements that have changed in the formation of corporate reputation in social media.

WHAT IS CHANGING IN CORPORATE REPUTATION?

Social media are new information and communication technologies that enable their users to connect and publicly exchange experiences, opinions, and views on the Internet (Colleoni et al., 2021). Social media now give voice to actors who previously had limited access to the public domain, and they enable these actors to bypass the gatekeeping function of traditional news media and reach wide audiences connected through online social networks. The mutating media landscape requires us to think in a new way about how increasingly diverse media evaluations, co-produced by multiple actors and disseminated through multiple channels, influence the formation of organizational reputation. In fact, traditional assumptions on corporate reputation formation have theorized corporate reputation as relatively homogeneous (Barnett et al., 2006) and mainly controlled by corporate organization (organization signals) and media organization (media signals). Etter et al. (2019) have described the changes that have occurred in the formation of corporate reputation due to this new media landscape:

From one media reputation to multiple interaction arenas. In current organization and management studies theories (Barnett et al., 2006), there is a general assumption that news media offer relatively homogeneous evaluative representations of organizations and that, in the absence of alternatives in the public domain, these representations influence collective judgments. The result is that organizational reputation comes to be closely aligned with media reputation, which, in turn, is largely based on prepackaged information supplied by organizations. The new paradigm enhances the active role of social media audiences in shaping the content of publicly available evaluations, as well as the paths and patterns of their diffusion. Social media now enable these audiences to independently exchange and disseminate evaluations in the public domain, reaching vast audiences.

A first important implication of this change is that individual evaluations may now gain wide attention, regardless of the status and structural position of the sender. By doing so, organizational audiences are now able to publicly challenge evaluations offered by the media, or even to subvert images projected by organizations themselves to highlight contradictions between communication and action. A second implication is that there is a many-to-many communication, meaning that vast audiences serve as both senders and receivers of evaluations and collectively engage in the co-production of these evaluations through direct access to content online (Klinger and Svensson, 2016). This means that the audience, from being once passive, becomes active (Etter et al., 2018). And information flows horizontally through large-scale networks of interconnected social relations. Social media enables a plurality of experiences, opinions, and topics to be made visible and potentially heard.

From a static to a dynamic view of media reputation. Recognizing that media reputation is continuously produced and reproduced through multiple acts of communication in a network of communicative actors (Christensen and Cornelissen, 2011) encourages us to shift attention from the conceptualization of media reputation as a 'thing' to the effect of communication exchanges and information technologies that shape how public evaluations are produced, disseminated, and disputed on an ongoing basis.

The nature of reputation: analytical and affective evaluations. In the new media landscape, individuals are increasingly exposed to a mix of informational and emotional content regarding the organization and its products. The former prevails, for instance, in the content disseminated by news media or in analytical assessments in product reviews, while the latter is found more frequently in narrative content disseminated by individual users or the textual comments that accompany analytical assessments. On social media, users may use humor to increase their visibility and popularity and to provoke emotional responses by often expressing criticism of corporate policies or decisions highlighting contradictions between the images they project and the reality of their actions that further stimulate seeking, discussing, and sharing information (Etter et al., 2018). With social media, there is an increasing emotional charge of evaluations about the quality or character of organizations available in the public domain.

This emotional content has important implications for evaluations' impact on collective judgments. First, emotionally charged content is preferentially processed (attended to or avoided and remembered) in comparison to content that is not affectively charged, whether truthful or not. Second, the emotional content of evaluations increases the likelihood that the evaluations will be shared and disseminated further, becoming viral. Confronted with a staggering increase in potential sources of information and heterogeneity of content, audiences preselect several sources that they automatically receive information from. Individuals naturally tend to seek information that confirms prior beliefs and to ignore dis-confirming information. This leads to an increased fragmentation of audiences.

Changes in the media landscape encourage us to reconsider this position and incorporate affect more explicitly into our understanding of reputation because they highlight the mediating role of emotional responses in the influence of media evaluations on judgment formation. If we accept the well-established idea that emotions "affect the way in which information is gathered, stored, recalled, and used to make particular attributions or judgments" (Etter et al., 2019, p. 35), then we should remain open to the possibility that emotional responses may also shape the processing and dissemination of information that current theories consider central to the formation of collective reputational judgments (Colleoni, 2021).

From a practical perspective, organizations need to consider listening as a powerful strategic tool that could enable them to monitor the multiple evaluations originating from and through social media (Pond and Lewis, 2019). Developing a strategic listening architecture by integrating and governing competences, platforms and data-driven contents could allow corporate communication practitioners to more effectively monitor social media audiences and foresee the emergence of negative evaluations (Kotras, 2020; Macnamara, 2015).

The transformation brought about by social media is also forcing researchers and practitioners to rethink the way corporate reputation is measured. Different from measures of satisfactions, such as the next promoter score which captures the overall satisfaction of a group of stakeholders, according to Ponzi et al. (2011), corporate reputation captures the emotional bond that the company is able to build with its different constituencies. Traditional corporate reputation measurement defines corporate reputation as the aggregate assessment of a company by a specific group of stakeholders (Walker, 2010). However, as pointed out by Etter et al. (2019), the fact that in social media a multiplicity of narratives coexist and are both visible, makes it more strategic for companies to analyze and monitor negative and positive evaluations distinctly.

WHAT REMAINS THE SAME?

Even if the spread of social media has revolutionized how organizations interact and relate with multiple stakeholders and manage their feedback and evaluations, it is possible to identify some aspects that have not changed in managing corporate reputation. Firstly, the need for organizations to go beyond how they would like to express themselves and to pay attention to how stakeholders interpret the signals organizations decide to send (Barnett et al., 2000). This is still true especially in the social media environment. Secondly, the acknowledgment from organizations to be one of the possible voices that convey expectations, needs, opinions, and evaluations about the organizations themselves (Taylor and Cooren, 1997). The organizations need to develop the ability to align the different voices by taking into account offline and online sources. Finally, the recognition of the role of offline and online reputation in creating competitive advantage for the organization (Miotto et al., 2020). Especially within the online environment, organizations need to be recognized by different stakeholders for how they behave in offline and online contexts. This is possible if organizations provide a coherent narrative framework to their initiatives, contents, and activities.

CRITICAL EXAMINATION

The communication dynamics exposed above are challenging well established assumptions about corporate reputation. The following section presents how the current digital communication environment challenges traditional assumptions of the formation of corporate reputation, and, in particular, assumptions about the quality of signals and signalers, posing a threat to companies.

Fake News and Corporate Reputation Signals

Corporate reputation is the result of a large number of signals that are sent out by a company and other signalers in the market. These signals represent reliable information portraying a company's inner qualities that crystallize over time into a general reputational judgment (Fombrun and Shanley, 1990), therefore allowing individuals to optimize their choices in the market operating under information asymmetry. One often unstated assumption about these signals is that they reflect the true characteristics of the company (Gardberg et al., 2022).

70 *Handbook on digital corporate communication*

At times the signal may be perceived differently or not fully aligned with the inner qualities (Connelly et al., 2011), but in the long run, corporate reputation will approximate the true characteristics of a company and acts as a credible source of selection within a field (Fombrun and Shanley, 1990).

However, in this fake news era, this assumption might no longer hold true (Gardberg et al., 2022). Fake news may be broadly defined as any type of information that has a nonfactual basis and is presented in a news format (Tandoc et al., 2018), such as misinformation and disinformation. Disinformation is particularly critical for corporate reputation formation (Colleoni, 2021) as it refers to fabricated information intended to spread misleading or biased content about an object or event (Tandoc et al., 2018). Empirical studies on social media information and disinformation (Bradshaw and Howard, 2018; Gorodnichenko et al., 2018) have shown the tremendous growth of fake news and manipulative communication with the goal to steer public debate. The most prominent example is probably that of Cambridge Analytica (Kim and Routledge, 2022), a firm that gained access to the personal data of more than 50 million Facebook users, and used the knowledge gained from their profiles to target adverts and spread fake news to trigger extreme emotional reactions so as to manipulate their voting intentions. However, fake news about companies is becoming more and more frequent (Di Domenico et al., 2021). For instance, recently, Starbucks was accused of supposedly giving out free drinks to undocumented immigrants. The Seattle-based company had to move quickly to counter seemingly legitimate social media advertisements that carried the hashtag "#borderfreecoffee" and were adorned with the company's logo, signature font, and graphics (The Washington Post, 2019).

The increased diffusion of fake news is not only related to the increasing ability of *fakeholders* (Luoma-aho, 2015) to create content that resembles real content, but also the increased number of individuals who are willing believers (Luoma-aho, 2015; Roulet, 2020) and who have little trust in corporate and institutional signals and high trust in "people like me" (Luoma-aho, 2015). In this sense, as pointed out by Luoma-aho (2015), this is also related to the challenge of trust companies increasingly face. The implication of the diffusion of untrustworthy signals about a company challenges the nature of corporate reputation, which is a strategic asset as long as it is able to convey reliable information about a company's behavior. If corporate reputation becomes the sum of fake and real signals or the result of orchestrated manipulation of signals, then it is no longer able to discriminate between good and bad companies and therefore it is no longer a corporate strategic asset worth building and maintaining. If no solutions are found to effectively contrast fake news, we might hypothesize that the nature of corporate reputation will change in two key ways. First, the role of intermediaries as strategic sources of corporate reputation will be reduced in favor of direct experience. As the most reliable source of signal about a company will be direct experience, companies will probably have to invest more in providing multiple touchpoints to prospects and customers, while decreasing the investment in touchpoints related to intermediaries' signal diffusion, such as news media and social media. Second, if the reputational signals shared by intermediaries become increasingly unreliable and increasingly driven by *fakeholders* (Luoma-aho, 2015), then corporate reputation management will become more and more a crisis management exercise of protecting the company from fake news, rather than reputation building.

Digital corporate communication and corporate reputation   71

Artificial Intelligence as Reputed Signaler

Third-party signalers, such as news media, play a key role in the formation of corporate reputation, as they represent powerful influential institutions. Thanks to their superior access to information, expertise, and strategic "structural position" (Rindova et al., 2005, p. 1034), they exert extensive control over the production of social reality in general and on the societal acceptance of organizations (Etter et al., 2019; Pollock and Rindova, 2003; Rao, 1994) and their reputation (Deephouse, 2000; Etter et al., 2019; Rindova et al., 2005). A critical assumption behind the theory of corporate reputation formation is that these third-party signalers can be trusted to report facts about companies in a balanced and neutral way, or in the case of opinionated topics, to report different viewpoints (Etter et al., 2019). This is assumed because, following strategic management and game-theory, cheating is not an efficient strategy in the long-run perspective for a news media or an accredited source, as the more an organization (or an intermediary) spreads inaccurate information, the less credible it becomes, to the point of having no impact on the receiver (Farrell and Rabin, 1996). It is in fact thanks to their credibility and high prestige that news media and intermediaries are valid reputational signalers.

However, the proliferation of unreliable signalers that goes hand in hand with the diffusion of fake news represents another challenge to the validity of the corporate reputation construct. In fact, research indicates that fake news and misinformation are increasingly spread by means of artificial intelligence (AI) agents specialized in text generation (Colleoni, 2021), which allows the spread of non-factual information that mimics the news media style with the goal of shaping individuals' perceptions about companies. In fact, research has shown how AI generated text is not only used for robot journalism (i.e., automating the generation of news stories without human-journalistic intervention), but increasingly used for fake journalism and fake content diffusion in general (Firat, 2019), with the latter having a crucial impact for the formation of corporate reputation.

The level of sophistication of AI agents seems to be so high that they are able to generate text and visuals that are perceived as completely authentic and that may represent a threat to society in general (Beer, 2017; Campolo and Crawford, 2020). AI agents have proven to be able to create highly credible news media content. An experiment conducted by *The Guardian* in September 2020 was published in an article entitled "A robot wrote this entire article: are you scared yet, human?" (The Guardian, 2020). In this article the AI agent was able to write an entire 'opinion column', writing content that was highly credible and relatable. Spreading credible information about companies with great ease and on a large scale may have an effect on the perception of a corporate reputation to the point of threatening its existence. Furthermore, the blogs, websites, and fake accounts related to these unreliable sources are generated massively and in real-time and have, in general, a short-run perspective so that they are not affected by the potential debunking of the content they produce (Wallace, 2018).

To summarize, the diffusion of fake signals and fake signalers is challenging traditional assumptions about the validity of corporate reputation as a credible asset signaling the inner qualities of a company. This demands corporate reputation scholars to rethink the traditional assumptions about corporate reputation formation and its validity as a strategic asset. However, to date, little has been done to theorize a new reputational construct (Gardberg et al., 2022).

ILLUSTRATIVE EXAMPLE: DOLCE & GABBANA IN CHINA

The illustrative example of Italian fashion house Dolce & Gabbana managing a reputational crisis in China enables a practical analysis of some theoretical insights related to the changes in forming and managing reputation due to the increasing use of social media. When, in 2018, Dolce & Gabbana (D&G) posted their advertisement campaign launching their products in the Chinese market, they did not expect to receive such a backlash (D'Arco et al., 2019). Yet, when moving from the perspective of corporate behavior to stakeholders' expectations, a social media reaction of such resonance should have been foreseen by D&G's top management. The company's leadership indeed has a long history of disregarded behaviors that resulted in corporate scandals (Friedman and Wee, 2018). In 2015 for instance, during an interview with an Italian magazine, Domenico Dolce and Stefano Gabbana claimed to be against the idea of gay parents and of 'synthetic' children. Such comments stimulated an online uproar by the general public and a number of celebrities, such as Elton John. As a response, Domenico Dolce and Stefano Gabbana decided to launch the hashtag #boycottEltonJohn, which did not gain much support and a few months later they tried to pour oil on troubled waters by promoting their support of gay adoption (Fisher, 2015). In 2016, they sold a product called 'slave sandals'. The name of this product sparked criticism amongst social media users. In 2017, the two famous designers publicly showed their support of Melania Trump and they designated her as a #DGWoman through Instagram posts. This D&G stance also received critical remarks from online stakeholders. As a result, they decided to counterattack negative comments by launching their own #BoycottDolceGabbana slogan T-shirts, by stirring up social media comments. If we consider corporate reputation as a perceptual representation of past actions and future expectations, we can claim that Domenico Dolce's and Stefano Gabbana's past actions have not positively contributed to the development of a strong reputational capital to use for overcoming potential difficulties in the digital landscape. Moreover, D&G seems to have underestimated the informative power of data and signals that could be collected through social media. By developing both a strategic listening architecture and a continuous monitoring activity, the organization could have foreseen the potential results of future campaigns in China. The organization has also overestimated the relationship with successful influencers, by believing that they could be enough to recover and gain positive feedback from digital stakeholders. As explained below, online influencers joined the group of online activists and hateholders by showing their disapproval of the organization online.

Table 5.1   *Chronological sequence of the events regarding users' backlash against D&G in 2018*

Date	Action
November 18, 2018	D&G video series showing Chinese model eating Italian food begins spreading via social media (e.g., Weibo and Instagram).
November 19, 2018	D&G removed the video from Weibo platform.
November 20, 2018	Disrespectful comments from Stefano Gabbana were spread through social media.
November 21, 2018	D&G claimed the social media account was hacked and published an official statement to apologize to Chinese stakeholders.
November 23, 2018	D&G published an official video apology including the two designers saying sorry and asking for forgiveness.

Digital corporate communication and corporate reputation 73

In 2018, for instance, D&G was forced to respond to social media users who reacted furiously, accusing the fashion house of racism in its advertisement showing a Chinese woman struggling to eat pizza and spaghetti with chopsticks. Table 5.1 synthesizes the chronological sequence of events.

D&G decided to celebrate its strong relationship with China by organizing an event with 1,400 celebrities, called 'The Great Show'. On November 18, to promote the event, the brand released a video series presenting a Chinese model who was trained to eat typical Italian foods, such as pasta, cannoli, or pizza, with chopsticks. The video was deemed as stereotypical and disrespectful of Asian women. During the video, indeed, when the Asian girl was trying to eat the *cannolo*, a voiceover said: "Is it too huge for you?". Similar questions with a double entendre were also posed. The reaction was not long in coming: the brand was accused of having released an offensive advertising video and on Weibo the term 'Boycott Dolce' spread quickly. The brand underestimated the power of social media in spreading news and affecting collective judgment towards organizational behavior. After the sharing of the video on different Instagram accounts, the crisis indeed crossed local borders by becoming an international case study with negative consequences for D&G's reputation. In less than 24 hours, the company decided to delete the post featuring the video as angry comments spread like wildfire on Weibo.

On November 20, the model Michaela Tranovo allegedly published a screenshot of messages received from Stefano Gabbana's personal account. In replying to the questions posted by the user about the critical event, Stefano allegedly answered with regrettable language by defining China in the following way: "China Ignorant Dirty Smelling Mafia". On November 21, the brand defended itself by claiming that the Instagram accounts were hacked, and Stefano Gabbana published a statement in which he declared his love for China. In the meantime, 'The Great Show' in China was canceled.

On November 23, the brand published an official video apology in which the two designers said they were sorry and asked for forgiveness. "We have always been in love with China", Dolce said. "We love your culture and we certainly have much to learn. That is why we are sorry if we made mistakes in the way we express ourselves". In the video, the two designers wore black shirts and sat at a large table with a classic red background. "We will never forget this experience and it will certainly never happen again. From the bottom of our hearts, we ask for forgiveness", Gabbana added. At the end of the video, both designers apologized in Mandarin. The video contributed to fuel negative comments from digital users who accused the company of simulating a sad attitude. Moreover, on this occasion, social media enabled dispersed users to easily connect and share feelings and opinions about the company and thus affect their judgments concerning corporate behavior.

Although this reputational crisis case study allows us to explore and discuss the real impact that social media can exert on corporations, we acknowledge that we did not measure the company's reputation through the stock market or other financial outcomes. The D&G social media crisis quickly escalated to Chinese e-commerce sites boycotting D&G products. For instance, the e-commerce site Yoox-Net-a-Porter prevented the online sale of D&G items. Similarly, other retailers such as Alibaba, JD and Lane Crawford dropped D&G from all their stores in China. Finally, the two Chinese brand ambassadors Kerry Wang Junkai and Dilraba Dilmurat decided to terminate their contracts with D&G. Other Chinese celebrities showed their aversion towards the brand and several Chinese influencers published videos of themselves destroying D&G products. A report on Luxury published by Gartner (2019) stated that in China content featuring celebrities drove 94 percent of all the engagement in the fashion and jewelry industry. Clearly, breaking off relationships with influencers could have affected the loss of sales in the Asiatic region, even though the organization did not release any official comment about this. D&G experienced negative evaluations by online activists and hateholders, who have pointed out the negative organizational behaviors and exerted pressure on D&G to change. To date, the Dolce & Gabbana brand is still struggling to shake off the fallout from this controversial advertising campaign in China.

CONCLUSION AND FUTURE DIRECTIONS

Within the digital environment, can corporate reputation remain a strategic asset for organizations? This chapter attempts to answer this question by emphasizing new ways to understand the role of fake news and AI applications in the formation of reputation. Research about corporate reputation in management studies tends to make three main theoretical assumptions about how corporate reputation is formed. First, corporate reputation is an enduring collective representation. This means that corporate reputation is based on representations that last over time and that are shared by fairly stable groups of individuals. Second, corporate reputation is formed through emotional and cognitive signals sent by organizations to their publics, signals which are presumed to be true and credible. This means that there is no space for fake, ambiguous, or incomplete signals and, moreover, for signals which are out of control of an organization. Third, corporate reputation grows thanks to the consistency of emotional and informative signals. This means that any inconsistent content can challenge and weaken the development of corporate reputation.

This chapter argues that the theoretical assumptions developed by corporate reputation scholars have been deeply challenged by social media and AI applications. Social media challenges information reported by mainstream media by diffusing conflicting views about the information without people questioning its authenticity. Within the digital communication environment, consistency decreases due to the fact that content is dispersed, fragmented, and part of a continuous flow of conversations (Barnett et al., 2020). This contributes to companies being judged on the basis of uncontrolled information. Furthermore, one might assume that some reputational dimensions will be more affected by fake news, as related to emotional elements, rather than factual knowledge.

If corporate reputation becomes the sum of fluid, emotional, fake content as well as the result of signals manipulated by AI applications, then it is no longer a strategic asset worth maintaining. Accordingly, the role of corporate communication will be more to protect the company from fake news, rather than to develop a corporate reputation.

Additional research is needed to rethink the traditional assumptions about corporate reputation formation, such as the notion of accumulation of true signals and prestigious signalers, and most importantly to understand whether corporate reputation is still a strategic asset worth building and managing for companies. Future research should also investigate whether and how the different stakeholders that have traditionally tried to exert influence over corporations, such as activists and NGOs, are taking advantage of this new media landscape, or, in contrast, can become new corporate allies in order to mitigate the impact of AI and human-generated fake news.

REFERENCES

Allagui, I. and Breslow, H. (2016). Social media for public relations: Lessons from four effective cases. *Public Relations Review*, *42*(1), 20–30.

Barnett, M. L., Boyle, E., and Gardberg, N. A. (2000). Towards one vision, one voice: A review essay of the 3rd International Conference on Corporate Reputation, Image and Competitiveness. *Corporate Reputation Review*, *3*(2), 101–111.

Barnett, M. L., Henriques, I., and Husted, B. W. (2020). The rise and stall of stakeholder influence: How the digital age limits social control. *Academy of Management Perspectives*, *34*(1), 48–64.

Barnett, M. L., Jermier, J. M., and Lafferty, B. A. (2006). Corporate reputation: The definitional landscape. *Corporate Reputation Review*, *9*(1), 26–38.

Barney, J. (1991). Firm resources and sustained competitive advantage. *Journal of Management*, *17*/1 (March). https://doi.org/10.1177/014920639101700108.

Beer, D. (2017). The social power of algorithms. *Information, Communication & Society*, *20*(1), 1–13.

Berens, G. and van Riel, C. B. M. (2004). Corporate associations in the academic literature: Three main streams of thought in the reputation measurement literature. *Corporate Reputation Review*, *7*, 161–178.

Bradshaw, S. and Howard, P. (2018). The global organization of social media disinformation campaigns *Journal of International Affairs*, *71*(1), 23–32.

Bundy, J., Iqbal, F., and Pfarrer, M. D. (2021). Reputations in flux: How a company defends its multiple reputations in response to different violations. *Strategic Management Journal*, *42*(6), 1109–1138.

Campolo, A. and Crawford, K. (2020). Enchanted determinism: Power without responsibility in artificial intelligence. *Engaging Science, Technology, and Society*, *6*, 1–19.

Carroll, C. E. and McCombs, M. (2003). Agenda-setting effects of business news on the public's images and opinions about major corporations. *Corporate Reputation Review*, *6*(1), 36–46.

Carter, S. M. (2006). The interaction of top management group, stakeholder, and situational factors on certain corporate reputation management activities. *Journal of Management Studies*, *43*, 1146–1176.

Christensen, L. T. and Cornelissen, J. P. (2011). Corporate and organizational communication in conversation. *Management Communication Quarterly*, *25*(3), 383–414.

Colleoni, E. (2021). Fake news and the formation of reputation: New avenues. *Academy of Management Conference 2021, Panel Symposium Fake News: Implications for Management, Organization and Society*, August.

Colleoni, E., Illia, L., and Zyglidopoulos, S. (2021). Beyond differences: The use of empty signifiers as an organizing device with fragmented stakeholders. *Journal of the Association for Consumer Research*, *6*(4), 491–502.

Connelly, B. L., Certo, S. T., Ireland, R. D., and Reutzel, C. R. (2011). Signaling theory: A review and assessment. *Journal of Management*, *37*(1), 39–67.

Coombs, W. T. and Holladay, S. J. (2008). Comparing apology to equivalent crisis response strategies: Clarifying apology's role and value in crisis communication. *Public Relations Review*, *34*(3), 252–257.

D'Arco, M., Marino, V., and Resciniti, R. (2019). How to (not) survive a social media firestorm: The Dolce & Gabbana's ad debacle in China. In F. Martínez-López, J. Gázquez-Abad, and A. Roggeveen (eds.), *Advances in national brand and private label marketing*. Sixth International Conference, 2019. Springer Proceedings in Business and Economics (pp. 181–189). Cham: Springer. https://doi.org/10.1007/978-3-030-18911-2_23.

Deephouse, D. L. (2000). Media reputation as a strategic resource: An integration of mass communication and resource-based theories. *Journal of Management*, *26*, 1091–1112.

Deephouse, D. L., Bundy, J., Tost, L. P., and Suchman, M. C. (2017). Organizational legitimacy: Six key questions. In R. Greenwood, C. Oliver, T. B. Lawrence, and R. E. Meyer (eds.), *The SAGE Handbook of Organizational Institutionalism* (2nd edition, pp. 27–54). London: Sage Publications.

Di Domenico, G., Sit, J., Ishizaka, A., and Nunan, D. (2021). Fake news, social media and marketing: A systematic review. *Journal of Business Research*, *124*, 329–341.

Etter, M., Colleoni, E., Illia, L., Meggiorin, K., and D'Eugenio, A. (2018). Measuring organizational legitimacy in social media: Assessing citizens' judgments with sentiment analysis. *Business & Society*, *57*(1), 60–97.

76 *Handbook on digital corporate communication*

Etter, M., Ravasi, D., and Colleoni, E. (2019). Social media and the formation of reputation. *Academy of Management Review*, *44*(1), 28–52.

Farrell, J. and Rabin, M. (1996). Cheap talk. *Journal of Economic Perspectives*, *10*, 103–118.

Fieseler, C. and Fleck, M. (2013). The pursuit of empowerment through social media: Structural social capital dynamics in CSR-blogging. *Journal of Business Ethics*, *118*(4), 759–775.

Firat, F. (2019). Robot journalism. *The International Encyclopedia of Journalism Studies*. Malden, MA: Wiley-Blackwell. https://doi. org/10.1002/9781118841570.iejs0243.

Fisher, L. (2015). Inside the Elton John-Dolce & Gabbana feud. *abcNews*. https://abcnews.go.com/Entertainment/inside-elton-john-dolce-gabbana-feud/story?id=29702355.

Fombrun, C. J. (1996). *Reputation: Realizing value from the corporate image*. Boston: Harvard Business School Press.

Fombrun, C., Gardberg, N., and Sever, J. (2000). The Reputation Quotient SM: A multi-stakeholder measure of corporate reputation. *Journal of Brand Management*, *7*, 241–255.

Fombrun, C. and Shanley, M. (1990). What's in a name? Reputation building and corporate strategy. *Academy of Management Journal*, *33*(2), 233–258.

Friedman, V. and Wee, S. L. (2018). The crash and burn of Dolce & Gabbana. *The New York Times*. https://www.nytimes.com/2018/11/23/fashion/dolce-gabbana-china-disaster-backlash.html.

Gardberg, N., Barnett, M., and Colleoni, E. (2022). Unbelievable! How fake news affects the relationship between business and society, *Special Issue Business & Society*. https://businessandsociety.org/unbelievable-how-fake-news-affects-the-relationship-between-business-and-society/.

Gartner (2019). *Luxury US & Europe: Fashion and watches and jewelry*. Digital IQ Index. https://www.gartner.com/en/marketing/research/luxury-us-europe-2019-fashion.

Gent, S., Crescenzi, M., Menninga, E., and Reid, L. (2015). The reputation trap of NGO accountability. *International Theory*, *7*(3), 426–463.

George, G., Dahlander, L., Graffin, S., and Sim, S. (2016). Reputation and status: Expanding the role of social evaluation in management research. *Academy of Management Journal*, *59*, 1–13.

Glozer, S., Caruana, R., and Hibbert, S. (2019). The never-ending story: Discursive legitimation in social media dialogue. *Organization Studies*, *40*(5), 625–650.

Gorodnichenko, Y., Pham, T., and Talavera, O. (2018). Social media, sentiment and public opinions: Evidence from #Brexit and #USElection. National Bureau of Economic Research Technical Report. http://blogs.hbr.org/2013/04/the-hidden-biases-in-big-data/.

Hall, R. (1993). A framework linking intangible resources and capabilities to sustainable competitive advantage. *Strategic Management Journal*, *14*, 607–618.

Kim, T. W. and Routledge, B. R. (2022). Why a right to an explanation of algorithmic decision-making should exist: A trust-based approach. *Business Ethics Quarterly*, *32*(1), 75–102.

Klinger, U. and Svensson, J. (2016). Network media logic: Some conceptual considerations. In A. Bruns, G. Enli, E. Skogerbø, A. O. Larsson, and C. Christensen (eds.), *The Routledge companion to social media and politics* (pp. 23–38). New York: Routledge.

Kotras, B. (2020). Opinions that matter: The hybridization of opinion and reputation measurement in social media listening software. *Media, Culture & Society*, *42*(7–8), 1495–1511.

Luoma-aho, V. (2007). Neutral reputation and public sector organizations. *Corporate Reputation Review*, *10*, 124–143.

Luoma-aho, V. (2015). Understanding stakeholder engagement: Faith-holders, hateholders & fakeholders. *RJ-IPR: Research Journal of the Institute for Public Relations*, *2*(1). http://www.instituteforpr.org/understanding-stakeholder-engagement-fai.

Macnamara, J. (2015). Breaking the measurement and evaluation deadlock: A new approach and model. *Journal of Communication Management*, *19*(4), 371–387.

Marwick, A. and Boyd, D. (2011). To see and be seen: Celebrity practice on Twitter. *Convergence*, *17*(2), 139–158.

McMillan, G. and Joshi, M. (1997). Part IV: How do reputations affect corporate performance? Sustainable competitive advantage and firm performance: The role of intangible resources. *Corporate Reputation Review*, *1*, 81–85.

Milgrom, P. and Roberts, J. (1986). Price and advertising signals of product quality. *Journal of Political Economy*, *94*(4), 796–821.

Miotto, G., Del-Castillo-Feito, C., and Blanco-González, A. (2020). Reputation and legitimacy: Key factors for higher education institutions' sustained competitive advantage. *Journal of Business Research*, *112*, 342–353.

Mishina, Y., Block, E. S., and Mannor, M. J. (2011). The path dependence of organizational reputation: How social judgment influences assessments of capability and character. *Strategic Management Journal*, *33*(5), 459–477.

Pollock, T. and Rindova, V. (2003). Media legitimation effects in the market for initial public offerings. *The Academy of Management Journal*, *46*(5), 631–642.

Pond, P. and Lewis, J. (2019). Riots and Twitter: Connective politics, social media and framing discourses in the digital public sphere. *Information, Communication & Society*, *22*(2), 213–231.

Ponzi, L., Fombrun, C., and Gardberg, N. (2011). RepTrak™ pulse: Conceptualizing and validating a short-form measure of corporate reputation. *Corporate Reputation Review*, *14*, 15–35.

Rao, H. (1994). The social construction of reputation: Certification contests, legitimation, and the survival of organizations in the American automobile industry, 1895–1912. *Strategic Management Journal*, *15*, 29–44.

Ravasi, D., Rindova, V., Etter, M., and Cornelissen, J. (2018). The formation of organizational reputation. *Academy of Management Annals*, *12*(2). https://journals.aom.org/doi/10.5465/annals.2016.0124.

Rhee, M. and Haunschild, P. (2006). The liability of good reputation: A study of product recalls in the US automobile industry. *Organization Science*, *17*(1). https://doi.org/10.1287/orsc.1050.0175.

Rindova, V. P., Williamson, I., Petovka, A., and Sever, J. (2005). Being good or being known: An empirical examination of the dimensions, antecedents and consequences of organizational reputation. *Academy of Management Journal*, *48*(6), 1033–1049.

Roberts, P. and Dowling, G. (2002). Corporate reputation and sustained superior financial performance. *Strategic Management Journal*, *23*, 1077–1093.

Roulet, T. J. (2020). *The power of being divisive: Understanding negative social evaluations*. Stanford, CA: Stanford University Press.

Roulet, T. J. and Clemente, M. (2018). Let's open the media's black box: The media as a set of heterogeneous actors and not only as a homogenous ensemble. *Academy of Management Review*, *43*(2), 327–329.

Spence, A. M. (1974). *Market signaling: Informational transfer in hiring and related screening processes*. Cambridge, MA: Harvard University Press.

Tandoc Jr., E. C., Lim, Z. W., and Ling, R. (2018). Defining "fake news": A typology of scholarly definitions. *Digital Journalism*, *6*(2), 137–153.

Taylor, J. R. and Cooren, F. (1997). What makes communication 'organizational'? How the many voices of a collectivity become the one voice of an organization. *Journal of Pragmatics*, *27*(4), 409–438.

The Guardian (2020). A robot wrote this entire article. Are you scared yet, human? https://www.theguardian.com/commentisfree/2020/sep/08/robot-wrote-this-article-gpt-3.

The Washington Post (2019). Fake news threatens our businesses, not just our politics. https://www.washingtonpost.com/outlook/fake-news-threatens-our-businesses-not-just-our-politics/2019/02/08/f669b62c-2b1f-11e9-984d-9b8fba003e81_story.html.

Turban, D. B. and Greening, D. W. (1996). Corporate social performance and organizational attractiveness to prospective employees. *Academy of Management Journal*, *40*, 658–672.

Veil, S. R., Reno, J., Freihaut, R., and Oldham, J. (2015). Online activists vs. Kraft foods: A case of social media hijacking. *Public Relations Review*, *41*(1), 103–108.

Vergin, R. C. and Qoronfleh, M. W. (1998). Corporate reputation and the stock market. *Business Horizons*, *41*(1), 19–30.

Walker, K. (2010). A systematic review of the corporate reputation literature: Definition, measurement, and theory. *Corporate Reputation Review*, *12*, 357–387.

Wallace, J. (2018). Modelling contemporary gatekeeping: The rise of individuals, algorithms and platforms in digital news dissemination. *Digital Journalism*, *6*(3), 274–293.

Wang, X., Reger, R. K., and Pfarrer, M. D. (2019). Faster, hotter, and more linked: Managing social disapproval in the social media era. *Academy of Management Review*, *46*(2). https://doi.org/10.5465/amr.2017.0375.

Welbers, K. and Opgenhaffen, M. (2018). Social media gatekeeping: An analysis of the gatekeeping influence of newspapers' public Facebook pages. *New Media & Society*, *20*(12), 4728–4747.

6. Digital corporate communication and CSR communication
Lina Gomez-Vasquez

INTRODUCTION

Digital technologies such as social media have transformed how people and organizations communicate, reshaping communication practices at different levels. The communication revolution has allowed organizations more accessibility, high efficiency, and low-cost message production (Mishra and Bakshi, 2018). This new digital environment has influenced diverse core corporate communication functions, such as Corporate Social Responsibility (CSR). Communicating CSR on social media helps companies to increase public awareness of their CSR commitments and develop authentic relationships with stakeholders (Capriotti et al., 2021; Farache et al., 2018), engaging in transparent conversations that reflect action (Hamadi, 2021). Previous studies have shown that organizations report CSR initiatives and efforts on digital platforms like blogs, Facebook, and Twitter (Gomez, 2021). However, organizations have used these tools mainly like other traditional communication media, such as to broadcast CSR information (Cho et al., 2017; Gomez, 2021).

The latest industry reports (e.g., Edelman, 2021; Hamadi, 2021) show the importance of transparent, interactive, and actionable CSR communication that can impact social change. According to Edelman's 2021 Trust Barometer (Edelman, 2021), 86 per cent of consumers expect companies to take action beyond their product and business, such as engaging in CSR. Fortune Global 500 companies spend $20 billion annually on CSR initiatives, allowing CSR efforts to become more mainstream (Sutherland Global, 2018). Consumers value companies making actionable CSR efforts communicated well; however, companies still focus on CSR aspirational talk and not CSR actionable talk (Hamadi, 2021). If CSR aspirational talk is prioritized over actionable CSR communication, it could lead to customer disengagement and even employee cynicism (Hamadi, 2021).

Social media has been a popular avenue to allow CSR conversations (CONE Communications, 2015). A recent report by DataReportal (2022) revealed that 76 per cent of global users aged 16 to 64 use social media to find information about brands and products. According to CONE Communications (2015), three in five global consumers go to social media to learn and share opinions about CSR, get informed, or interact with companies to talk about CSR. Furthermore, the 2017 US Chamber of Commerce Foundation report suggests companies can bring CSR value if they strategically communicate CSR efforts online by encouraging thoughtful and emotional responses to CSR actions from different stakeholders, which is critical for long-term success of organizations. The World Economic Forum (as cited by McCraken, 2022) identified the following three key trends for communication of CSR efforts that drive social impact. First, using data storytelling (e.g., how results are backed up with data, showing opportunities to improve). Second, CSR initiatives need to be addressed in systems, not in a silo, showing alignment with the ecosystem of companies and their culture. Third, CSR initiatives need to be understood and embraced in organizations from both top-down and bottom-up, providing opportunities for companies to grow. In sum, strategic, actionable, and purposefully connected communicative efforts are required for maximum CSR outcomes. This chapter examines how digital technologies like social media are changing CSR communication as an essential function within corporate communication and discusses challenges, opportunities, and implications for companies and practitioners to create a more strategic and actionable CSR communication.

DEFINITIONS OF THE TOPIC AND PREVIOUS STUDIES

Corporate social responsibility can be defined as the process in which organizations manage daily operations to ensure that they do not cause harm and that they positively contribute to the public and society (Gomez, 2021). CSR involves organizations assessing the needs of diverse stakeholders and developing and implementing these actions to meet (or ignore) those needs (Ihlen et al., 2011). There are many definitions of CSR in the literature (Dahlsrud, 2008), but there is still no universally accepted definition of what CSR involves (Pompper, 2015).

Today, CSR efforts are communicated through news reports, blogs, company websites, word-of-mouth, and social media platforms (Diddi and Niehm, 2016). Earlier studies of CSR communication focused on traditional media like corporate websites (e.g., Gomez, 2021), which mainly highlighted a unidirectional communication approach. By early/mid-2010, CSR social media studies began to emerge (e.g., Castelló et al., 2016; Colleoni, 2013), accelerating a more interactive communicative environment focused on honesty and transparency (Suddaby et al., 2015). Literature on CSR social media communication has reported the increasing use of different social media platforms by organizations. In the early 2010s, CSR communication studies focused on blogging platforms primarily. By mid-2010, scholars began to research social media platforms like Facebook and Twitter (Gomez, 2021), which are continually studied in the literature. A recent search on Google Scholar (filtered by any time) showed 12 publications that included the words 'CSR', 'communication' and 'Facebook' in the title, 32 CSR studies about Twitter, and one CSR study about Instagram. Eighty-nine publications included 'CSR' 'communication' and 'social media' in the title. This suggests that CSR communication on social media is still an understudied topic in the literature. Accordingly, this chapter fills a gap in the literature by discussing the changes, challenges, and opportunities of studying and practising CSR communication on social media.

WHAT IS CHANGING?

Digital technologies like social media are shifting older practices of CSR communication in terms of strategies, message framing, stakeholder power, and the use of CSR-devoted accounts. CSR communication, especially on social media, has been mainly used as a traditional channel to broadcast an informational strategy (Cho et al., 2017; Colleoni, 2013; Okazaki et al., 2020). However, recent studies have witnessed a slow shift to a more interactive approach (Abitbol and Lee, 2017; Saxton et al., 2019). Specifically, companies with a high reputation use dialogue spaces on social media to converse about CSR issues (Illia et al., 2017). These dialogic spaces promote co-learning, co-innovating, and co-deciding, which are highly valued by stakeholders (Illia et al., 2017).

80 *Handbook on digital corporate communication*

To improve CSR communication and encourage stakeholder participation, a digital corporate communication approach is needed. There are two imperatives to this approach. First, CSR motives: Organizations must address reasons regarding how CSR initiatives benefit society or the public and how these initiatives fit with the company's mission or business (Du et al., 2010; de Jong and Van der Meer, 2017); communicating this 'fit' is essential to helping consumers make sense of CSR engagement (de Jong and Van der Meer, 2017), which subsequently impacts the company's credibility (Rifon et al., 2004). Second, companies must consider how CSR messages are constructed, shared, and comprehended by stakeholders (Golob and Podnar, 2018). This also needs to include storytelling elements that encourage the inclusion of diverse publics from various backgrounds and life experiences (Wehmeier and Schultz, 2011).

A social media strategy is vital for CSR engagement, but it requires significant resourcing implications, including creating relevant content and constant monitoring and responding to stakeholders' participation (Okazaki et al., 2020). Recent studies (e.g., Ma and Bentley, 2022) have found the importance of using a credit-sharing framing approach in CSR communication since it leads customers to believe that CSR efforts are driven by values, not just a company's self-interest, even if other social media users (e.g., a stranger or a friend) question the company's motives. A self-promoting framing approach, commonly used in CSR communication, is less effective than a credit-sharing framing approach (Ma and Bentley, 2022). When motives are ambiguous (e.g., utilizing self-promoting messages) they can hurt the company's image since self-promoting motives are perceived as insincere (Yoon et al., 2006). Other recent studies (Dalla-Pria and Rodríguez-de-Dios, 2022) have revealed that a value-driven motive framing approach (i.e., society-oriented) helps to increase corporate reputation and generation of word-of-mouth. This approach motivates stakeholders to speak positively of organizations. Consequently, if companies are truly invested in socially responsible practices, the community will be more supportive (Digital Marketing Institute, 2021).

Additionally, CSR devoted accounts have been mainly used for interactive CSR communication more than generic accounts (Cho et al., 2017; Farache et al., 2018, Saxton et al., 2019, 2021). Recent studies (e.g., Saxton et al., 2021) indicated dialogic evidence between firms and stakeholders on CSR-devoted accounts on Twitter. In fact, Twitter may be a better medium than Facebook for company–stakeholder engagement since it is a platform for broadcasting and engagement simultaneously (Okazaki et al., 2020). However, firm responses to social media messages are mainly to stakeholders with more connective power (i.e., larger network size and higher network centrality). And firms with more normative power (i.e., those with more robust CSR performance) are less likely to respond to stakeholder messages. Firm and stakeholder power is an understudied area of CSR research (Saxton et al., 2021), which can bring light to organization–stakeholder response selectivity on social media platforms and how it impacts interactivity.

WHAT REMAINS THE SAME?

Although digital technologies like social media are slowly shifting older practices of CSR communication, there are still practices that remain the same in terms of communication approaches and strategies. CSR activities are still primarily communicated unidirectionally, using a broadcasting strategy (Gomez, 2021; Kent and Taylor, 2016; Okazaki et al., 2020).

A one-way communication strategy on social media commonly uses hyperlinks and hashtags, but they rarely include multimedia (e.g., video), replies, or mentions (Adi and Grigore, 2015). This high level of sharing CSR information, which contributes to shallow engagement, could be the result of company employees not having enough experience in social media management or being afraid of adopting a more interactive communication approach (Adi, 2018).

Firms communicating CSR information on social media usually do so as random posts without a clear strategy, thus missing opportunities for stakeholder engagement and relationship building (Okazaki et al., 2020). If the content posted on social media is unfocused, it could risk either reducing engagement, as users can associate the content with noise, or even potentially losing followers since they can unfollow brands that do not provide value (Okazaki et al., 2020). A company that focuses only on disseminating CSR information does not demonstrate the authenticity of the company's involvement in CSR efforts (Ramesh et al., 2018; Rawlins, 2009). However, having readily available CSR information that is trustworthy and has value for stakeholders can showcase a company's genuine commitment to CSR (Moreno and Kang, 2020).

With the popularization and widespread use of social media platforms, publics today express high expectations that organizations must behave as socially responsible citizens contributing to the economy, society, and environment (Ali et al., 2015; Moreno and Kang, 2020). The challenge for companies is that communication via social media is uncontrolled, and the information flow through these platforms is sometimes difficult to predict (Cho et al., 2017). Therefore, it remains the case that organizations and corporate communication practitioners face problems in both having a clear CSR strategy on social media and understanding how to leverage these platforms to encourage honest stakeholder engagement that builds long-term relationships. The following section examines the main challenges to digital CSR communication and discusses critical factors for communication on how those challenges can be overcome.

CRITICAL EXAMINATION

One of the most critical challenges in CSR communication is the lack of planning and resources to manage and measure it. This includes unfamiliarity with using social channels (i.e., lack of personnel capable of handling social media correctly) and managerial scepticism in using these platforms for CSR interactive communication (Adi and Grigore, 2015), which results in poorly cohesive strategies (Abitbol and Lee, 2017). Having a clear CSR strategy that considers stakeholder expectations is key. However, social media professionals make their content and activity decisions based on their perceptions rather than their analysis of public needs (Navarro et al., 2017). The lack of resources, a clear strategy, and content that drives value to stakeholders bring another challenge to the communication of CSR practices: stakeholder scepticism. Many stakeholders are sceptical of companies' motives behind CSR messages since they perceive them as controlled and mainly benefiting the companies themselves rather than the community or society at large (Illia et al., 2017). In addition, stakeholders recognize that when a company engages too much in CSR communication (e.g., self-promotion or self-congratulation messages), they are perceived as not being transparent (Coombs and Holladay, 2015; Kollat and Farache, 2017).

82   *Handbook on digital corporate communication*

To reduce stakeholder scepticism, CSR messages must include facts rather than self-promotion (Coombs and Holladay, 2015), especially for consumers unfamiliar with CSR initiatives (Kollat and Farache, 2017). Stakeholders' reaction to CSR messages is not only impacted by company motives but also by the comments of CSR sceptics, usually vented on social media platforms (Ma and Bentley, 2022). Online sceptical comments increase when company trust does not exist and ambiguity predominates (Heath et al., 2018). However, there is still scarce research on minimizing the effects of sceptical online comments regarding CSR messages (Rim and Song, 2017).

In light of the above, greenwashing is another challenge to CSR communication. With uncontrolled messaging via social media platforms, corporate statements, like environmental initiatives, can be interpreted, translated, and transmitted by stakeholders as greenwashing (Heath et al., 2018). Within each CSR message, ethical dilemmas could be associated, and multiple purposes could be served (Saxton et al., 2021). At the same time, if CSR initiatives do not provide tangible benefits, consumers could find discrepancies between expectations and perceptions regarding the CSR initiatives and the company, generating more scepticism among stakeholders (Chen, 2013). A wrong CSR communication approach (e.g., aggressive promotion) or inappropriate message can create more suspicion and decrease corporate legitimacy (Illia et al., 2017).

Another challenge when using social media for communication is data misuse and privacy issues. Companies are under pressure to guarantee trust among their customers when it comes to protecting their private data (Sutherland Global, 2018). There are many issues in CSR social media communication to include when creating guidelines, such as how to handle and assure the privacy of personal information, freedom of speech, identity theft, inaccurate information, data selling, and data leakages (Kumar and Nanda, 2019).

The following five critical factors are offered as solutions to CSR communication challenges.

1. *Interact with stakeholders using a conversational human voice.* As discussed, although social media has disrupted CSR communication by providing a more dynamic and interactive setting for stakeholders to learn and collaborate about CSR activities, organizations have primarily focused on one-way regularly scheduled annual CSR communication (Saxton et al., 2021). For companies to realize the potential of CSR for interactive communication and value co-creation (Okazaki et al., 2020), they must interact with stakeholders and provide informative and valuable experiences through a conversational human voice, which makes CSR messages more personal and relatable (Oh and Ki, 2019). A CSR gain-focused message (showing positive benefits of CSR actions) in a conversational human voice can enhance stakeholders' willingness to engage in positive word-of-mouth communication about the organization (Oh and Ki, 2019). Lastly, by responding to consumer messages about CSR on social media, organizations can encourage consumers to advocate for the company or a specific social cause (Colleoni et al., 2022).

2. *Focus on CSR interactive content aligned with the company mission (CSR fit).* CSR content using interactive language and storytelling elements (Abitbol and Lee, 2017) and an informative tone (i.e., focused on facts) (Kim and Ferguson, 2018) can impact public engagement (Kucukusta et al., 2019), especially if CSR topics are aligned with the company's mission (Abitbol and Lee, 2017). Multimedia forms like video are an excellent tool to communicate CSR to achieve higher interaction (CONE Communications,

2015; Kucukusta et al., 2019), in addition to photos, graphics, and call-to-action language (Abitbol and Lee, 2017; CONE Communications, 2015; Gomez, 2018). Video can enhance the richness of content and make it more appealing to audiences, leading to more effective communication (Kucukusta et al., 2019). Consequently, CSR interactive content could lead to countersignals (i.e., shares), reflecting how effective interactive messages resonate with stakeholders, which over the long term, could impact positive changes in reputation (Saxton et al., 2019).

3. *Leverage an actionable audience through gamification.* CSR communication on social media must involve multiple interested publics since it has the potential to co-create value (Okazaki et al., 2020). For instance, an excellent approach to co-create value is to call volunteers to help with a CSR project, request feedback on past CSR activities, or generate ideas for future efforts (Okazaki et al., 2020). Companies can also engage in gamification to request CSR activity participation, asking consumers to create content – in other words, engaging in user-generated content (UGC). A UGC strategy in CSR communication encourages interactive and authentic conversations, promoting message credibility and reputation (Illia et al., 2017; Mishra and Bakshi, 2018). UGC can use a gamification approach, which is one of the main advantages of social media for creating creative inter-active experiences. Through gamification, stakeholders are treated as drivers of the CSR efforts (Coombs and Holladay, 2015). UGC and gamification encourage the co-creation of valuable content since it is based on stakeholder participation. Therefore, dialogue spaces that enable co-learning, co-innovating, and co-deciding are the avenues most valued by stakeholders when interacting with corporations on CSR issues (Illia et al., 2017). If some of the consumers' networks (e.g., friends or contacts) are involved (e.g., through tagging), it provides a more positive and active response to messages (Crisan and Zbuchea, 2017). These co-creation efforts will likely increase company value and reputation, reducing scepticism (Okazaki et al., 2020).

4. *Seek ambassador partnerships.* To increase trust and credibility in CSR messages, having influencers or third-party information sources participate in CSR initiatives helps decrease criticism or scepticism (Cheng et al., 2021; Cho et al., 2017; Coombs and Holladay, 2015). Consumers expect organizations to partner with ambassadors or advocates in CSR endeavours (Golob and Podnar, 2018) since the public is more likely to perceive them as credible communicators than the company itself (Coombs and Holladay, 2015). With the advancement of technology to a more decentralized and user-centric web (i.e., Web3), it is imperative to create more genuine and long-term relations with third-party content creators who are building engaged communities (Quesenberry, 2022). A content creator, no matter if nano, micro, or macro, has 'connective power' since could influence and mobilize others (Saxton et al., 2021), positively affecting brand awareness and purchase intentions (Cheng et al., 2021).

5. *Monitor social media and develop social media policies.* After planning and executing a CSR content strategy on social media, organizations must assess their plans to re-evaluate the strategies and communication approaches that worked (or did not work). This also includes monitoring the online conversations of stakeholders and competitors regarding CSR. Assessment is critical to avoiding crises such as data breaches by designing secure data systems and applications, focusing on a human-centric approach, and incorporating limited third-party access to user data (Sutherland Global, 2018). Companies must be more transparent about their data practices since firms with a more substantial, trustworthy,

84 *Handbook on digital corporate communication*

and engaging CSR presence will be more effective in mitigating the effects of the breach (Du et al., 2010). Through social media policies, companies can provide guidelines to address social media communication risks regarding privacy, data security, and disclosure (Gomez, 2018). Policies provide intelligent use of social media for communicating diverse company CSR efforts (Patel and Jasani, 2010).

ILLUSTRATIVE EXAMPLE: GRUPO NUTRESA, COLOMBIA

Latin America has the second largest number of companies (after Europe) that belong to the United Nations Global Compact, one of the world's largest corporate sustainability initiatives (Balch, 2022). It is a region with a cultural predisposition towards philanthropy, influenced by strong firm-founder values but with little strategic alignment (Balch, 2022). However, some Latin American companies are excellent CSR drivers. One of those companies is Grupo Nutresa in Colombia. Grupo Nutresa is the leading processed food company in Colombia. Founded in 1920, it currently has nearly 46,000 employees and has a direct presence in 17 countries with 47 production plants (products are present in 78 countries on five continents). Grupo Nutresa runs through eight business units: Cold Cuts, Biscuits, Chocolates, Tresmontes Lucchetti (TMLUC), Coffee, Retail Food, Ice Cream, and Pasta (Grupo Nutresa, 2022b).

Grupo Nutresa was identified by the Dow Jones Sustainability Indices (DJSI) (2021) as an industry leader in the food sector, being included in the DJSI for 11 consecutive years (Grupo Nutresa, 2022b). According to a 2020 press release, Grupo Nutresa was ranked as the second most socially responsible company in Colombia, and fourth with the greatest social commitment during the Covid-19 pandemic (Grupo Nutresa, 2020a). In the last two years, Grupo Nutresa has invested more than 265 million Colombian pesos (60,000 US dollars approximately) in CSR initiatives for the economic and social recovery due to the pandemic, benefiting more than 6 million people and more than 250,000 small businesses (Grupo Nutresa, 2022a). Grupo Nutresa has adopted sustainable development as part of its strategic framework by establishing long-term goals and programmes focused on generating value for all its stakeholders. The company aligns its efforts and actions with the Sustainable Development Goals of the United Nations (SDGs) (Grupo Nutresa, 2020b). Some of the goals that have been prioritized and lined up with the SDGs are SDG 8 – Decent work and economic growth; SDG 9 – Industry, innovation, and infrastructure; SDG 12 – Responsible consumption and production; and SDG 13 – Climate action (Grupo Nutresa, 2020b).

The company has been committed to creating new ways of doing business, for instance, by transforming the social problems in Colombia, such as giving entrepreneurship training to small farmers or social investment in actions related to the Colombian post-conflict process (Grupo Nutresa, 2020a). It is committed to improving the business sector's integrity, helping companies they work with to be more accountable, improving stakeholder confidence, and promoting an environment that encourages cooperation and trust (Sustainable Development Goals Fund, n.d.).

Grupo Nutresa communicates CSR efforts through its social media accounts on Twitter and Instagram. The company publishes distinctive approaches on each platform. Twitter is focused on sharing news and acknowledgements, while Instagram is more interactive, focusing on educating people about CSR efforts (Grupo Nutresa, n.d. a). For instance, it recently developed the campaign *Todos por el planeta* (All for the planet), encouraging followers to recycle bottles, fill them with plastic (e.g., trash bags and candy packaging), and put them in bins the company has distributed in different parts of the country. The campaign was launched on 20 April 2021, for Earth Day, and it is still running.

The campaign posts on Instagram are engaging, for instance, asking people how many bottles they have put in the bins and highlighting how everyone can create a better world by recycling. The campaign developed the hashtags *#adoptaunabotella* (adopt a bottle) and *#entretodoscontribuimos* (everyone contributes) which are included in the Instagram visuals. They also posted video testimonials of customers participating in the campaign, educating followers on the importance of everyone taking part in the initiative. With compelling language, Grupo Nutresa encourages stakeholders to be part of their CSR efforts.

CSR fit is key when companies communicate their commitment to environmental issues (Chen, 2013), drawing stakeholder attention to the positive aspects of the CSR activity rather than to the company itself (Moreno and Kang, 2020). For Grupo Nutresa, preserving the planet and cooperating with stakeholders are two of the core areas of its commitment to CSR for growing value generation (Grupo Nutresa Strategic Framework, n.d. b). Grupo Nutresa has succeeded in its CSR communication by first focusing on creating valuable CSR content aligned with its mission. The *Todos por el planeta* CSR campaign fits the company's strategic objectives since Grupo Nutresa is committed to preserving the planet, by achieving 100 per cent of packaging materials to be recyclable, reusable, or compostable (Grupo Nutresa Strategic Framework, n.d. b). By December 2021, the company achieved 85.7 per cent of this goal (Grupo Nutresa, 2022a). The reduction of waste production and increasing its recovery and reuse in their operations and value chain is only one of several efforts they are making to preserve the planet. Second, Grupo Nutresa has succeeded in the campaign by interacting with stakeholders using a conversational human voice to encourage actionable responses on their Instagram account. And lastly, through ambassador partnerships, Grupo Nutresa showcases ambassadors in their campaign, including children, employees, small entrepreneurs, and customers. According to a press release by Grupo Nutresa in early 2022, all the responsible efforts performed, their flexibility during the pandemic, and their focus on productivity, have contributed to their excellent financial results.

CONCLUSION AND FUTURE DIRECTIONS

This chapter explored how social media is changing CSR communication by analysing changes, challenges, opportunities, and implications for companies and practitioners. Social media platforms are impacting older practices of CSR communication by encouraging a more interactive approach, focusing on topics that drive value and are aligned with the business goals. For instance, Grupo Nutresa (illustrative example) excelled in creating relevant content to communicate CSR value-driven motives to an actionable audience, using aesthetically pleasing visuals and videos on communication platforms like Instagram. An actionable audience is highly motivated (either by the company or by themselves) to interact and participate (and even co-create) in the developing of CSR initiatives. An actionable audience can involve working with nano or micro-influencers, ambassadors, opinion leaders, or non-profits. Grupo Nutresa built relationships with small entrepreneurs and customers, becoming ambassadors of the *Todos por el planeta* campaign and encouraging followers to participate in the cause. An actionable audience can help to enhance CSR communication processes for the better since it can generate mutual benefits for the organization and the community.

As society and technology advance, so too must companies advance in their efforts to contribute to society. More than ever, younger generations like Generation Z and Millennials feel that when they use a product of a socially responsible company, they are doing their bit for society (Digital Marketing Institute, 2021), and in so doing they also are pressuring companies to invest in improving society and identifying solutions that help in those improvements (Digital Marketing Institute, 2021). In this sense, organizations must embrace CSR as part of their core mission, involving stakeholders in the process and taking advantage of all the resources digital technologies like social media contribute to improving CSR communication. However, risks could be present in the communication no matter how much planning is involved. Stakeholder scepticism, greenwashing, online negative comments, conflicting opinions, and uncontrolled messages posted by social media users are among the main risks associated with CSR communication on social media.

Despite our acquired knowledge of best CSR communication practices in the current social media era, unanswered questions remain, thus offering suitable avenues for further research. For instance, how can companies with limited resources and staff create an effective CSR communication presence online that includes compelling and actionable content like videos? Future trends in social media indicate that for brands to succeed in emergent platforms like TikTok, they must become publishers instead of acting like advertisers (Liederman, 2022). Then, how can CSR be communicated via visually-oriented yet dialogic media like TikTok? Furthermore, how can companies nurture influencer relationships (e.g., advocates, ambassadors, and other third-party organizations) to create interactive content that appeals to their followers? And more importantly, how can companies create compelling CSR content that aligns with the corporate mission while at the same time demonstrating authenticity and fostering a human connection? Further studies can also explore how companies can ensure consumer data privacy as part of CSR efforts aligning with company values. Finally, researchers could also delve into how analytics shapes and impacts the practice of CSR communication, increasing the effectiveness of CSR communication.

There are ample studies on CSR online communication that have been published in the past ten years (Gomez, 2021); however, the practice of CSR online communication remains in its infancy (Okazaki et al., 2020). If there is no genuine commitment among firms to develop an effective online CSR strategy that communicates relevant and engaging content and involves consumers' CSR participation in these initiatives, the challenges linked to older practices in CSR communication will remain the same. With younger generations impacting and changing trends in CSR (Digital Marketing Institute, 2021), the role of genuine CSR communication that co-creates value with stakeholders is expected to be at the core of companies' responsible efforts.

REFERENCES

Abitbol, A. and Lee, S. Y. (2017). Messages on CSR-dedicated Facebook pages: What works and what doesn't. *Public Relations Review*, *43*(4), 796–808.

Adi, A (2018). #CSR on Twitter: A hashtag oversimplifying a complex practice. In A. Lindgreen, J. Vanhamme, F. Maon, and R. Mardon (eds.), *Communicating corporate social responsibility in the digital era* (pp. 340–357). New York: Routledge.

Adi, A. and Grigore, G. (2015). Communicating CSR on social media: The case of Pfizer's social media communications in Europe. In A. Adi, G. Grigore, and D. Crowther (eds.), *Developments in corporate governance and responsibility: Corporate social responsibility in the digital age* (pp. 143–163). Bingley: Emerald Group Publishing.

Ali, I., Jiménez-Zarco, A. I., and Bicho, M. (2015). Using social media for CSR communication and engaging stakeholders. In A. Adi, G. Grigore, and D. Crowther (eds.), *Developments in corporate governance and responsibility: Corporate social responsibility in the digital age* (pp. 127–142). Bingley: Emerald Group Publishing.

Balch, O. (2022, 16 May). *From philanthropy to radical new business models in Latin America*. Reuters. https://www.reuters.com/business/sustainable-business/philanthropy-radical-new-business-models -latin-america-2022-05-16/.

Capriotti, P., Zeler, I., and Camileri, M. A. (2021). Corporate communication through social networks: The identification of the key dimensions for dialogic communication. In M. A. Camilleri (ed.), *Strategic corporate communication in the digital age* (pp. 33–51). Bingley: Emerald Group Publishing.

Castelló, I., Etter, M., and Nielsen, F. A. (2016). Strategies of legitimacy through social media: The networked strategy. *Journal of Management Studies*, *53*, 402–432.

Chen, Y. (2013). Towards green loyalty: Driving from green perceived value, green satisfaction, and green trust. *Sustainable Development*, *21*(5), 294–308.

Cheng, Y., Flora Hung-Baesecke, C.-J., and Regina Chen, Y.-R. (2021). Social media influencer effects on CSR communication: The role of influencer leadership in opinion and taste. *International Journal of Business Communication*. Advance online publication. https://doi.org/10.1177/23294884211035112.

Cho, M., Furey, L., and Mohr, T. (2017). Communicating corporate social responsibility on social media: Strategies, stakeholders, and public engagement on corporate Facebook. *Business and Professional Communication Quarterly*, *80*(1), 52–69.

Colleoni, E. (2013). CSR communication strategies for organizational legitimacy in social media. *Corporate Communications: An International Journal*, *18*, 228–248.

Colleoni, E., Romenti, S., Valentini, C., Badham, M., Choi, S. I., Kim., S., and Jin, Y. (2022). Does culture matter? Measuring cross-country perceptions of CSR communication campaigns about COVID-19. *Sustainability*, *14*(2), Article e889. https://doi.org/10.3390/su14020889.

CONE Communications (2015). *2015 Cone Communications/Ebiquity Global CSR Study*. CONE. https://www.conecomm.com/research-blog/2015-cone-communications-ebiquity-global-csr-study.

Coombs, W. T. and Holladay, S. J. (2015). Two-minute drill: Video games and social media to advance CSR. In A. Adi, G. Grigore, and D. Crowther (eds.), *Developments in corporate governance and responsibility: Corporate social responsibility in the digital age* (pp. 127–142). Bingley: Emerald Group Publishing.

Crisan, C. and Zbuchea, A. (2015). CSR and social media: Could online repositories become regulatory tools for CSR related activities' reporting? In A. Adi, G. Grigore, and D. Crowther (eds.), *Developments in corporate governance and responsibility: Corporate social responsibility in the digital age* (pp. 197–219). Bingley: Emerald Group Publishing.

Dahlsrud, A. (2008). How corporate social responsibility is defined: An analysis of 37 definitions. *Corporate Social Responsibility and Environment Management*, *15*(1), 1–13.

Dalla-Pria, L. and Rodríguez-de-Dios, I. (2022). CSR communication on social media: The impact of source and framing on message credibility, corporate reputation and WOM. *Corporate Communications: An International Journal*, *27*(3), 543–557.

DataReportal (2022). *Digital 2022: Global Overview Report*. DataReportal. https://datareportal.com/reports/digital-2022-global-overview-report.

de Jong, M. D. T. and Van der Meer, M. (2017). How does it fit? Exploring the congruence between organizations and their corporate social responsibility (CSR) activities. *Journal of Business Ethics*, *143*(1), 71–83.

Diddi, S. and Niehm, L. S. (2016). Corporate social responsibility in the retail apparel context: Exploring consumers' personal and normative influences on patronage intentions. *Journal of Marketing Channels*, *23*(1–2), 60–76.

88 *Handbook on digital corporate communication*

Digital Marketing Institute (2021, 1 September). *16 Brands Doing Corporate Social Responsibility Successfully*. Digital Marketing Institute. https://digitalmarketinginstitute.com/blog/corporate-16 -brands-doing-corporate-social-responsibility-successfully.

Du, S., Bhattacharya, C. B., and Sen, S. (2010). Maximizing business returns to corporate social responsibility (CSR): The role of CSR communication. *International Journal of Management Reviews*, *12*(1), 8–19.

Edelman (2021). *Social issue-driven crisis simulation*. Edelman. https://www.edelman.com/expertise/ crisis-reputation-risk/our-work/social-issue-driven-crisis-simulation.

Farache, F., Tetchner, I., and Kollat, J. (2018). CSR communications on Twitter: An exploration into stakeholder reactions. In G. Grigore, A. Stancu, and D. McQueen (eds.), *Corporate responsibility and digital communities: An international perspective towards sustainability* (pp. 145–163). Cham: Palgrave Macmillan.

Golob, U. and Podnar, K. (2018). Exploring CSR communication patterns in social media: A review of current research. In A. Lindgreen, J. Vanhamme, F. Maon, and R. Mardon (eds.), *Communicating corporate social responsibility in the digital era* (pp. 69–84). London: Routledge.

Gomez, L. (2018). Social media concepts for effective CSR online communication. In A. Lindgreen, J. Vanhamme, F. Maon, and R. Mardon (eds.), *Communicating corporate social responsibility in the digital era* (pp. 193–215). London: Routledge.

Gomez, L. (2021). The state of social media research in CSR communication. In D. Crowther and S. Seifi (eds.), *The Palgrave handbook of corporate social responsibility* (pp. 577–598). Cham: Palgrave Macmillan.

Grupo Nutresa [@nutresaoficial] (n.d. a). *Posts* [Instagram profile]. Instagram. https://www.instagram .com/nutresaoficial/.

Grupo Nutresa (n.d. b). *Strategic Framework*. Grupo Nutresa. https://gruponutresa.com/en/inversionistas/ perfil-de-la-compania/marco-estrategico/.

Grupo Nutresa (2020a). *Grupo Nutresa, the second most socially responsible company in Colombia and is the fourth with the greatest social commitment during the pandemic*. Grupo Nutresa. https:// gruponutresa.com/en/noticias/grupo-nutresa-the-second-most-socially-responsible-company-in -colombia-and-is-the-fourth-with-the-greatest-social-commitment-during-the-pandemic/.

Grupo Nutresa (2020b). *Grupo Nutresa and its commitment to the Sustainable Development Goals*. Grupo Nutresa. https://informe2020.gruponutresa.com/pdf/Commitment-to-the-Sustainable-Development -Goals.pdf.

Grupo Nutresa (2022a). *Sostenibilidad, flexibilidad y productividad contribuyen a los resultados de Grupo Nutresa durante el primer semestre de 2022*. Grupo Nutresa. https://gruponutresa.com/ noticias/sostenibilidad-flexibilidad-y-productividad-contribuyen-a-los-resultados-de-grupo-nutresa -durante-el-primer-semestre-de-2022.

Grupo Nutresa (2022b). *We are Grupo Nutresa*. https://gruponutresa.com/en/quienes-somos/.

Hamadi, B. (2021, 26 October). *How to stop talking and start taking action on CSR*. World Economic Forum. https://www.weforum.org/agenda/2021/10/how-your-brand-can-walk-the-csr-talk/.

Heath, R. L., Saffer, A. J., and Waymer, D. (2018). "The Devil's in the details": Contested standards of corporate social responsibility in social media. In A. Lindgreen, J. Vanhamme, F. Maon, and R. Mardon (eds.), *Communicating corporate social responsibility in the digital era* (pp. 193–215). London: Routledge.

Ihlen, O., Bartlett, J. L., and May, S. (2011). Corporate social responsibility and communication. In O. Ihlen, J. L. Bartlett, and S. May (eds.), *The handbook of communication and corporate social responsibility* (pp. 3–22). Malden, MA: Wiley-Blackwell.

Illia, L., Romenti, S., Rodríguez-Cánovas, B., Murtarelli, G., and Carroll, C. E. (2017). Exploring corporations' dialogue about CSR in the digital era. *Journal of Business Ethics*, *146*, 39–58.

Kent, M. and Taylor, M. (2016). From homo economicus to homo dialogicus: Rethinking social media use in CSR communication. *Public Relations Review*, *42*(1), 60–67.

Kim, S. and Ferguson, M. A. T. (2018). Dimensions of effective CSR communication based on public expectations. *Journal of Marketing Communications*, *24*(6), 549–567.

Kollat, J. and Farache, F. (2017). Achieving consumer trust on Twitter via CSR communication. *Journal of Consumer Marketing*, *34*(6), 505–514.

Kucukusta, D., Perelygina, M., and Lam, W. (2019). CSR communication strategies and stakeholder engagement of upscale hotels in social media. *International Journal of Contemporary Hospitality Management*, *31*(5), 2129–2148.

Kumar, V. and Nanda, P. (2019). Social media to social media analytics: Ethical challenges. *International Journal of Technoethics*, *10*(2), 57–70.

Liederman, E. (2022, 22 July). *To succeed on TikTok, brands must become publishers*. Adweek. https://www.adweek.com/agencies/to-succeed-on-tiktok-brands-must-become-publishers/.

Ma, L. and Bentley, J. M. (2022). Can strategic message framing mitigate the negative effects of skeptical comments against corporate-social-responsibility communication on social networking sites? *Public Relations Review*, *48*(4), Article e102222. https://doi.org/10.1016/j.pubrev.2022.102222.

McCraken, J. (2022, 7 July). Business for good is good for business: the evolution of CSR to ESG. *PR Daily*. https://www.prdaily.com/csr-to-esg-evolution/.

Mishra, P. and Bakshi, M. (2018). Strategic imperatives of communicating CSR through digital media: An emerging market perspective. In A. Lindgreen, J. Vanhamme, F. Maon, and R. Mardon (eds.), *Communicating corporate social responsibility in the digital era* (pp. 35–49). London: Routledge.

Moreno, F. and Kang, J. (2020). How to alleviate consumer skepticism concerning corporate responsibility: The role of content and delivery in CSR communications. *Corporate Social Responsibility and Environmental Management*, *27*, 2477–2490.

Navarro, C., Moreno, Á., and Al-Sumait, F. (2017). Social media expectations between public relations professionals and their stakeholders: Results of the ComGap study in Spain. *Public Relations Review*, *43*(4), 700–708.

Oh, J. and Ki, E.-J. (2019). Factors affecting social presence and word-of-mouth in corporate social responsibility communication: Tone of voice, message framing, and online medium type. *Public Relations Review*, *45*(2).

Okazaki, S., Plangger, K., West, D., and Menéndez, H. D. (2020). Exploring digital corporate social responsibility communications on Twitter. *Journal of Business Research*, *117*, 675–682.

Patel, N. and Jasani, H. (2010). Social media security policy: Guidelines for organizations. *Issues in Information Systems*, *11*(1), 628–634.

Pompper, D. (2015). *Corporate social responsibility, sustainability and public relations: Negotiating multiple complex challenges*. London: Routledge.

Quesenberry, K. (2022, 15 July). The future of digital and social media marketing with Web3. *Post Control Marketing*. https://www.postcontrolmarketing.com/the-future-of-digital-and-social-media-marketing-with-web3/.

Ramesh, K., Saha, R., Goswami, S., Sekar, and Dahiya, R. (2018). Consumers' response to CSR activities: Mediating role of brand image and brand attitude. *Corporate Social Responsibility and Environmental Management*, *26*(2), 377–387.

Rawlins, B. (2009). Give the emperor a mirror: Toward developing a stakeholder measurement of organizational transparency. *Journal of Public Relations Research*, *21*(1), 71–99.

Rifon, N. J., Choi, S. M., Trimble, C. S., and Li, H. (2004). Congruence effects in sponsorship: The mediating role of sponsor credibility and consumer attributions of sponsor motive. *Journal of Advertising*, *33*(1), 29–42.

Rim, H. and Song, D. (2017). Corporate message strategies for global CSR campaigns: The mediating role of perceived altruism. *Corporate Communications: An International Journal*, *22*(3), 383–400.

Saxton, G., Gomez, L., Ngoh, Z., Lin, Y. P., and Dietrich, S. (2019). Do CSR messages resonate? Examining public reactions to firms' CSR efforts on social media. *Journal of Business Ethics*, *155*, 359–377.

Saxton, G., Ren, C., and Guo, C. (2021). Responding to diffused stakeholders on social media: Connective power and firm reactions to CSR-related Twitter messages. *Journal of Business Ethics*, *172*, 229–252.

Suddaby, R., Saxton, G. D., and Gunz, S. (2015). Twittering change: The institutional work of domain change in accounting expertise. *Accounting, Organizations and Society*, *45*, 52–68.

Sustainable Development Goals Fund (n.d.). *Universality and the SDGs: A business perspective*. Sustainable Development Goals Fund. https://www.sdgfund.org/universality-and-sdgs.

Sutherland Global (2018, 12 April). *Why protecting data is critical for CSR moving forward*. Sutherland Blog. https://www.sutherlandglobal.com/our-thinking/blog-protecting-user-data-critical-csr.

Wehmeier, S. and Schultz, F. (2011). Communication and corporate social responsibility: A storytelling perspective. In O. Ihlen, J. Bartlett, and S. May (eds.), *The handbook of communication and corporate social responsibility* (pp. 467–490). Malden, MA: Wiley-Blackwell.

Yoon, Y., Gurhan-Canli, Z., and Schwarz, N. (2006). The effect of corporate social responsibility (CSR) activities on companies with bad reputations. *Journal of Consumer Psychology, 16*(4), 377–390.

7. Digital corporate communication and financial communication and investor relations
Alexander V. Laskin and Christian P. Hoffmann

INTRODUCTION

There is hardly an area of corporate communication more important than investor relations. In fact, investors are often considered to be the most valuable public among all corporate stakeholders as they have the most power over corporations (Kelly et al., 2010). Thus, managing relationships with investors is an important part of the corporate agenda and an important contributor to corporate value (Laskin, 2021; Ragas et al., 2014). The process of digitalization has a significant impact on these relationships by expanding participation in investment activities, raising informational demands on corporations, and creating new channels of communication between corporations and the investment community. As society transitions to a post-information age, when information becomes a commodity and the torrents of data overwhelm people's processing abilities, digital tools become essential to also help generate insights out of all the communication generated (Laskin, 2022).

DEFINITIONS OF THE TOPIC AND PREVIOUS STUDIES

The largest professional investor relations association, the National Investor Relations Institute (NIRI), defines *investor relations* as "a strategic management responsibility that integrates finance, communication, marketing, and securities law compliance to enable the most effective two-way communication between a company, the financial community, and other constituencies, which ultimately contributes to a company's securities achieving fair valuation" (NIRI, 2016, p. 4). Effective two-way communication is at the heart of this definition. A comprehensive and fast flow of information is the basis not just of investor relations, but of the entire modern economy.

According to the Efficient Market Hypothesis, in order for markets to be efficient they must fully reflect all available information. In this case, the prices of securities in these markets will achieve their fair valuation or, in other words, will fully and accurately reflect the intrinsic value of the company. An investor relations officer (IRO) is the first step in the corporate disclosure process aimed at supporting the efficiency of markets.

Much of the information disclosed by IROs is financial information. As a result, another term, *financial communication*, is often used to describe investor relations activities. However, technically speaking, it is not correct to equate investor relations with financial communication. First of all, IROs often communicate non-financial information – the disclosure may focus on technology, legal issues, social issues, or even the personal life of the CEO. Second, financial communication may include banks communicating about interest rates, or a government talking about federal debt, or a medical non-profit organization talking about prescription

92   *Handbook on digital corporate communication*

costs. These are all financial communications outside the scope of investor relations since governments and non-profits don't even have investors to talk to. Finally, while communication, and especially financial communication, is at the heart of investor relations, investor relations is more than communications – it is about building and maintaining relationships with investors and the financial community. Relationships are about actions as much as they are about words – thus, IROs are expected to do more than just communicate (Laskin, 2022).

Nevertheless, information disclosure, whether financial or non-financial, is the most visible task of the investor relations profession. Some even equate the overall function of investor relations with disclosure and call investor relations professionals Chief Disclosure Officers (NIRI, 2016). Shareholders as pharmaceutical outsiders do not possess direct and constant knowledge about what is going on inside the company. This makes IROs a conduit of knowledge between insiders and outsiders of the corporation (Laskin, 2011).

According to NIRI (2016) disclosure is "informing investors and potential investors about a company's business and strategy, financial results, and prospects". Such disclosure is generally divided into two groups: periodic and current reporting. Although specific regulations change from country to country, periodic reporting tends to include annual reports and quarterly reports. The annual report is one of the most important documents corporations produce; its value goes beyond investor communications as it is readily consumed also by employees, customers, media and many other stakeholders (Laskin, 2022). Annual reports are usually audited; in other words, an independent third party verifies key information found in the report. This increases annual reports' validity and reliability. While quarterly reports are not usually audited and do not have as many details as annual reports, they present a more up-to-date picture of the corporation's progress.

Sometimes, however, corporations may experience a development that can significantly impact their value. For example, a pharmaceutical company may receive an approval for a promising new drug. In this case, waiting until the next quarterly or annual report will be a disservice to the financial stakeholders who would be missing a key piece of data about the company. Such important information is called material information, the events that generate such information are called material events, and in the case of material events investor relations professionals are expected to produce an emergency or current report. In the United States, for example, a dedicated form exists for such current reports: Form 8-K. This form must be filed as soon as possible after the material event happens to ensure that all current and prospective investors are properly notified and have timely access to the material information.

Regulatory agencies in different countries are monitoring all the information corporations disclose no matter what channels IROs are using for such disclosures. Recent developments in digitalization have created a variety of new channels available for the investor communications function. However, investor relations professionals may be cautious in their adoption of this new digital infrastructure (Laskin, 2017).

WHAT IS CHANGING?

Investor relations' adoption of digital communication can be characterized as pragmatic, efficient, and, at times, somewhat conservative. Since the investor relations department tends to be small and its budget largely dedicated to costly annual expenditures, such as the annual report, roadshows and the annual shareholders meeting, IROs frequently lack the resources

Digital corporate communication and financial communication and investor relations 93

necessary to experiment with new, unproven digital tools or platforms. As a result, IROs tend to carefully observe the digital services market, investor behaviour and peer investor relations teams to decide which digital tools are most likely to support core functions and, if possible, reduce costs. Investor relations tends to be quickest to embrace digital tools or services that (a) facilitate the distribution of information to capital markets, and (b) support two-way communication with analysts and investors.

Most research on digital investor relations tools has focused on websites (cf. Hoffmann et al., 2018a). Based on a content analysis of Fortune 500 company websites, Esrock and Leichty (2000) suggest that the investor relations section can be considered the most important element of the corporate website. Bollen at al. (2006) find that listed companies tend to invest more in high-quality investor relations websites depending on their (a) size, (b) international exposure, (c) free float (i.e., proportion of publicly tradable shares), and (d) regulatory requirements. Investor relations websites are usually employed for one-way investor communication (Bollen et al. 2006; Đorđević et al. 2012), and they serve as a comprehensive repository for a wide range of reports, analyses, spreadsheets, presentations and factsheets provided to financial publics. All current information, such as annual or quarterly reports, press releases and ad hoc announcements, can be found on the investor relations website (Ettredge and Gerdes, 2005). Increasingly, companies also provide recordings and transcripts of calls and presentations (such as earnings calls or presentations at investor conferences).

While it is common to provide corporate annual reports in a PDF format, some companies also provide Excel sheet downloads of key data, and some – predominantly larger – companies even offer dedicated microsites where all or parts of the annual report are presented in HTML-format. In the US and EU, XBRL (eXtensible Business Reporting Language) or iXBRL (inline XBRL) is prescribed to render HTML financial reports machine-readable. As a result, financial reporting (and increasingly sustainability reporting) is provided in digital formats that allow for seamless data use by key audiences, such as analysts and investors.

Press releases and ad hoc announcements on material events have long been distributed to capital markets digitally. Financial audiences commonly subscribe to wire services, such as Bloomberg or Reuters, for comprehensive access to financial data, analytical tools, reports, charts and more. Corporate announcements are distributed through these services to analysts and investors. While there are some studies on the rhetoric and readability of annual reports (Lehavy et al., 2011), there is scant research on digital reporting beyond the accounting literature.

Given that investor relations websites are commonly used for unidirectional communication, there is some interest in the potential benefits of social media for investor relations. Laskin (2006, 2014) points out that two-way symmetrical communication is widely employed in financial communication. However, the state of research on social media in investor relations remains ambivalent, and adoption of social media tools by IROs tends to lag behind that of public relations or marketing departments. While some argue for the importance of social media, pointing out that analysts and investors take social media data into consideration in their corporate analyses (Alexander and Gentry, 2014), it remains more likely that retail investors, journalists or other stakeholders of lesser importance to IROs are reached directly through social media (cf. Zerfaß and Köhler, 2017).

While social media are received with some reservation among IROs, digital tools that facilitate dialogue with key financial audiences (especially analysts and investors) are adopted rapidly, especially in the context of the Covid-19 pandemic that severely restricted travel and

94 *Handbook on digital corporate communication*

personal meetings. Conference calls are complemented with webcasts – which have been shown to improve understanding of financial information among participants (Brown, 2011). In 2020 there was a boom in virtual investor conferences, capital market days and roadshows. Annual shareholders meetings were conducted online – in many countries for the first time ever. The future will tell whether these innovations will stick or remain an aberration necessitated by unusual circumstances.

An important aspect of digital investor relations with little visibility and no research coverage to date is the widespread employment of tools supporting dialogue and relationship management with individual (rating and equity) analysts, portfolio managers and other key members of the investor relations audiences. IROs are quick to embrace customer relationship management (CRM) tools, shareholder ID services and similar digital instruments that facilitate regular one-on-one interaction with important decision makers and influencers. Usage of such tools tends to result in personal conversations (frequently phone calls), one-on-one meetings or invitations to conference calls or conferences, so they do not necessarily facilitate digital interactions, but they still constitute widely used digital tools supporting investor relations efforts.

Reversing the perspective and focusing on the impact of digitalization on investor relations audiences, the impact of digital technologies and tools are both dramatic and undeniable. Capital markets today *are* digital marketplaces, interfaces to investors are digital, orders are inputted and processed digitally, and assets are transferred and stored digitally. In some instances, even the investors are digital (algorithmic trading), resulting in an entirely digital ecosystem in which digital agents employ digital tools to trade digital assets.

The impact of this development on capital markets is, at least, twofold. First, capital markets have reached unprecedented levels of speed and liquidity. High-frequency trading is characterized by the processing of orders within milliseconds, allowing for tremendous trading volumes as well as the exploitation of miniscule asset price spreads. The sheer volume of high-frequency trading tends to increase market liquidity. The speed of trading is so great that even the physical distance between servers can result in speed advantages for individual investors. As a result, capital markets' hunger for current news and corporate data is tremendous. Investors that are able to receive, interpret and translate current data into trade orders the quickest tend to benefit most from new information. Some asset managers, particularly in hedge funds, engage in large-scale data scraping and big data analyses to identify trends and trade upon algorithmic analyses. Trends in reporting, such as XBRL data files, contribute to an ever-quicker processing of company data by financial audiences.

Second, pressure on listed companies to ensure transparency has never been greater. Periodic reporting and regular updates through press releases and ad hoc announcements have always rendered investor relations a quick-paced function, ensuring up-to-date information and comprehensive corporate accountability. Yet, in a digital environment, investors and analysts are actively seeking out ever more information on the state and development of businesses, scraping online data, observing social media conversations, tracking the behaviour of corporate leaders, etc. The most obscure data points can be combined to form the basis for adjustments in investors' long or short positions, without any active communication by investor relations departments. As a result, there is a constant danger for corporations to lose control of their equity story, and a need to stay in continuous dialogue with financial audiences and to provide timely information as requested. Digital capital markets provide a wealth of

Digital corporate communication and financial communication and investor relations   95

information to the financial community, allowing for rapid analyses and peer comparisons – at an international level.

Again, given the limited size and resources of the investor relations departments, the investor relations function tends to lag behind its audiences in terms of digital data flows and analyses. IROs realize the need for ever more speed and transparency, however, much of their efforts remain focused on offline interactions, and corporate IT infrastructures as well as accounting practices frequently limit the speed at which data and information can be provided. IROs tend to lack understanding of how tech-savvy investors collect and process digital data to evaluate assets. While investor relations departments do employ digital tools to analyse and track market participants and sentiment, the level of sophistication of these tools is quite limited compared to those employed by some investors. As a result, the traditional information asymmetry (cf. Fama and Jensen, 1983) between corporate insiders (agents) and investors (principals) can shrink considerably in the digital capital market environment.

WHAT REMAINS THE SAME?

As noted above, the core functions of the investor relations department remain largely unchanged by digitalization: Providing information, ensuring transparency and accountability, and fostering relationships with the financial community still shape investor relations activities (Binder-Tietz et al., 2021; Hoffmann and Binder-Tietz, 2021). Among these, the publication and transmission of current data is likeliest to be disrupted by digital innovation – up to and including increasing automatization. Conversely, maintaining and fostering relationships with analysts, investors and, to a lesser degree, journalists, retail shareholders, brokers and other intermediaries tends to remain a 'people's business'.

As a corporate audience, investors are characterized by (a) a limited size, and (b) significant power. Of course, most listed companies have a dispersed shareholder base with thousands of individual stockowners. However, numerically, most of these are retail shareholders that hold only a few shares. The bulk of shares is held by a small number of large institutional investors. These investors, as a result, hold significant sway over capital access, share prices and governance decisions. The investor relations function, therefore, tends to focus its efforts on a close, personal, and frequent exchange with these few particularly powerful members of the financial community. This, aside from regulatory requirements, is a key reason why two-way symmetrical communication is important in investor relations. In fact, several studies of IROs found that one-on-one meetings with analysts and investors is the most important communication channel in the industry (Laskin, 2006, 2014, 2022). These personal exchanges demand particular attention in the context of corporate disclosures and capital market transactions (Green et al., 2014).

Research on the rhetoric of financial communication focuses on the dynamics displayed in the personal exchanges of analysts and investors, on the one hand, and corporate management, on the other hand. Palmieri et al. (2015) show that corporate representatives (CEO or CFO) take the role of a protagonist by defending and justifying corporate perspectives (particularly in terms of evaluative and predictive concerns), whereas analysts take the role of an antagonist, challenging the assumptions put forth in corporate presentations. Roberts et al. (2006) find that power relations between investors and corporate directors tend to be asymmetrical as corporate representatives initiate meetings and travel to meet fund managers in order to present recent developments.

While travel and meeting restrictions during the Covid-19 pandemic led to a flourishing of digital meetings and exchanges in IR, it is unclear if these practices will prevail. Some IROs fear that the preponderance of digital exchanges will weaken ties between corporations and the financial community, and will ultimately make it more difficult for corporations to shape their equity story. As a result, it remains likely that investor relations will strive to maintain live formats of investor communication, such as roadshows, conferences and one-on-one meetings. A question remains as to the willingness of analysts and investors to participate in such meetings, especially in the case of asset management companies pursuing a passive investment strategy, and in the case of investors increasingly relying on automated analyses and algorithmic trading. There is an argument to be made that in-person communication will most likely remain a critical component of the investor relations arsenal in the context of capital market transactions, or extraordinary circumstances such as shareholder activist interventions (Hoffmann et al., 2016).

CRITICAL EXAMINATION

The review above highlights that the key function of investor relations – disclosure of information – still remains as important as ever. Without information, financial markets cannot function. Much of the change, however, is quantitative rather than qualitative; there is more information being disclosed, it is disclosed faster, and IROs use more of a variety of channels for the disclosure. In other words, the digitalization of investor relations did not change the essence of practitioners' day-to-day work, but increased its volume.

In some cases, however, quantity is transforming into quality. Investors and financial analysts have always demanded information that goes beyond the minimum obligatory disclosure requirements. For example, information about the management team of a corporation, the strategic vision for the future, research and development pipeline, disclosure of environmental, governance and social issues, including issues of diversity, equity and inclusion, and other intangible and non-financial indicators (Laskin and Kresic, 2021). Digitalization significantly expanded the potential bandwidth for disclosure making it possible to provide this additional information. Instead of printing and mailing a few thousand copies of the corporate report, IROs can build a website or an interactive PDF document dedicated exclusively to, for example, sustainability reporting and making it instantly available to billions of people worldwide.

This non-financial information, however, is typically not audited and typically not standardized. As a result, approaches to non-financial disclosure can vary greatly from corporation to corporation (Schramm et al., 2022). Furthermore, this lack of standardization also presents challenges for investors and financial analysts on how to process such data. The resulting uncertainty creates additional demands on IROs, who must go beyond their disclosure function and focus on helping investors understand what the disclosed information actually means. IROs cannot assume that once the information has been disseminated it will be properly understood and evaluated. Thus, on the one hand, digitalization made disclosure easier, but on the other hand, by exponentially increasing the volume and types of information disclosed, digitalization forced IROs to focus more on educating investors and explaining the meaning behind the information (Laskin, 2016).

Today, there are torrents of information generated by and about corporations. This information is also easily accessible not just by professional investors but by anybody with connection to the internet. This makes data a commodity: "The 20th century was widely considered an *information age*, when information was the most treasured asset. Today, however, we may be entering a *post-information age*, when information is widely, publicly, and freely available to everybody and, in fact, commoditized" (Laskin, 2022, p. 197). What becomes a challenge is processing all these data and generating insights based on the data. Often the demands for data processing outstrip human capabilities – therefore more and more investors use AI to assist with their decision making. It is likely that this trend will continue to grow. This also creates additional demand for investor relations practitioners who must also be knowledgeable in data science. Indeed, if investor relations disclosures will be consumed and processed by computers, IROs should understand how AI processes information to ensure it will be delivered and analysed correctly. Of course, IROs are not expected to do all this by themselves; in addition to the usual partners of investor relations departments, such as public relations, legal, treasury and so on, IROs now must work together with data scientists to prepare corporate disclosure.

As described in the previous section, although social media is changing almost every aspect of human behaviour, investor relations professionals are quite cautious about widespread adoption of social media. While corporations may be slow to utilize social media, investors, especially retail investors, have embraced social media with open hearts. In fact, several dedicated communities appeared on social media focused specifically on discussing investing in various corporations. One of these dedicated communities for discussing stocks is *StockTwits*. StockTwits, developed based on Twitter's interface, allows the sending of short messages organized around cashtags. *Cashtags* are similar to Twitter's *hashtags*, only instead of using a hash sign they use a dollar sign followed by a stock ticker symbol – for example, $FB for Facebook, Inc. Even if IROs do not formally post or otherwise engage on StockTwits or similar social media platforms, they must engage in the practice of social listening and monitor the conversation around their company's cashtag; millions of investors participating on StockTwits may be a powerful force when it comes to stock trading, and even more powerful when it comes to generating and spreading rumours. StockTwits is not just for retail investors – financial analysts and professional investment managers also frequent this social media app.

While StockTwits is designed exclusively for discussing investments, other social media platforms can also become important platforms for social media listening. Among such platforms are more established ones such as Facebook and Twitter, as well as emerging platforms such as TikTok and Discord. A powerful example of the importance of social media in the investment world is the case of GameStop. While professional hedge fund investors were short-selling the stock of GameStop in early 2021, pushing the stock price down, regular retail investors banded together on Reddit. Using the sub-reddit r/WallStreetBets, these individuals shared information about GameStop and activities surrounding its stock. Even more, they shared their own trading activities and strategies, and encouraged each other to buy and hold these shares. Since digitalization also made access to trading significantly more affordable, they were able to participate on the stock market through such apps as Robinhood (18 million accounts) and ETrade (5 million accounts). In the end, retail shareholders were able to temporarily overpower large institutional investors worth billions of dollars and pushed the stock price from less than \$1 to above \$450 in January 2021, causing significant losses to professional investment funds.

Although GameStop stock traded slightly below \$200 at the end of September 2021, Laskin (2022) proposed that digitalization can lead to a democratization of financial markets and empowerment of retail shareholders. With more diverse voices in the investment community, it can be expected that the growing numbers of retail shareholders can amplify voices arguing for social justice, wealth redistribution and improved access to corporate information, and mount pressure on companies to demonstrate environmental, social and governance (ESG) commitments. All this can result in the continued growth in shareholder activism (Hoffmann and Fieseler, 2018). As it is reasonable to expect more shareholder activism in terms of pure numbers, it is likely that shareholder activism will grow qualitatively too, involving more and more issues, especially focusing on the issues of *diversity*, *equity*, and *inclusion* (DEI), that will become more and more relevant (Laskin, 2018). Digitalization has also led to a global expansion of investment activities forcing corporations to learn to adapt to a variety of different audiences from a variety of different cultures who may impose different demands on what corporations do and say (Farias et al., 2018; Melgin et al., 2018; Westbrook, 2018).

This, of course, will add more pressure on the investor relations professionals who must become experts in managing expectations for both shareholders and corporate leaders. Some companies have started paying attention to retail shareholders and many others will likely join in on this trend soon. CarParts corporation, that saw its stock go up more than 50 per cent at the start of 2021, has begun planning to host special events specifically designed for retail shareholders. The CFO of CarParts, David Meniane, explained that after seeing how retail shareholders could move the stock price, it was important to give them a chance to talk to the management the same way as large institutional investors are used to. Retail shareholders may generate a sizeable part of the trading volume for corporations, and, as result, can have a significant effect on stock price fluctuations.

Digitalization also enables these individual investors to join forces to perform *crowdinvesting*, a phenomenon not that different from *crowdsourcing* efforts to organize knowledge on Wikipedia or *crowdfunding* efforts to support an important cause (Laskin, 2022). In crowdinvesting, hundreds, thousands, or millions of retail investors combine their financial and intellectual resources to attempt to outperform the market. If a company today has about five financial analysts covering its stock, in the future it will have thousands of individuals-turned-analysts on Reddit, discussing the corporate earnings, future potential and actions of the CEO. Some of these individuals may even be financial professionals, but even the ones who have very little knowledge of investment markets may nevertheless have a very captive audience in their social media peers and may have a chance to move the stock price as much as Wall Street professionals.

On the plus side, thousands of people focusing their attention on the stock can actually discover price irregularities and discrepancies from the stock's intrinsic value, leading to a more efficient stock market and optimizing capital allocation. The optimistic view suggests that two heads are better than one, and thus a thousand heads are better than a few. The pessimistic view, however, points to the madness of crowds and suggests that individuals may react based on emotions without any substantive fundamental reasons (Laskin, 2022). This can lead to unexpected crisis situations and stock price volatility. Thus, IROs would also be expected to become proficient in crisis management and, more importantly, crisis prevention.

Digital corporate communication and financial communication and investor relations 99

CASE STUDY: SAP SE

In a study conducted in cooperation with the German Investor Relations Association, Hoffmann et al. (2018b) differentiate four stages of investor relations digitalization, illustrated by a typology. In the first stage, called 'digital transmitters', IROs focus on fulfilling regulatory requirements, such as digital filings and announcements. Smaller listed corporations are predominantly observed in this category. In the second stage ('digital optimizers'), IROs employ digital CRM-platforms as well as digital collaboration tools to enhance efficiency. In the third stage, named 'digital positioners', these (usually large and international) investor relations departments experiment with more recent and less established digital tools, such as AI chatbots, IR smartphone apps and messenger services. These services are frequently geared towards broader publics and serve to position the company as digitally innovative in the public eye. The fourth stage, which is rarely observed, was dubbed 'digital pioneers'. Here, IROs attempt to incorporate IT know-how (akin to the ComTech concept), to expand and tailor current digital tools or develop entirely new, bespoke tools.

One corporation that was categorized as a 'digital pioneer' in the study was the multinational enterprise software corporation SAP SE. SAP is the largest non-American software company by revenue, and the largest German company by market capitalization. SAP is very active in retail shareholder communications. Aside from a comprehensive investor relations website,[1] offering all reports, press releases and announcements, a detailed overview of the investment story, share information and latest results (including sustainability data), governance data, information for fixed income investors, presentations, factbooks and recordings of webcasts and earnings calls, the company offers a digital shareholder magazine, a messaging service and a Twitter account.

Given the in-house tech expertise, SAP's investor relations team constantly challenges the digital tools sourced by service providers and expands upon their functionalities, occasionally developing entirely new, in-house solutions. One domain in which this 'IR Tech' approach has successfully been implemented, is corporate reporting. The company developed a dedicated platform to facilitate the reporting process, allowing all involved departments to input their respective data contributions and manage the publication process (including deadlines), up to and including the eventual publication of the digital report. According to the company, this new reporting platform significantly reduced resource requirements and improved the reporting quality. SAP is currently analysing improvements in the HTML-front end to facilitate flexible access to various elements of the report by providing a choice of stakeholder-specific displays of the data (filters). Again, such improvements would be developed in-house.

At the same time, the SAP investor relations team still engages heavily in personal dialogue with key analysts and investors – in countless inbound and outbound calls, webcasts, conference calls, capital market days, roadshows, etc. In fact, the improvement of digital tools, such as the reporting platform, is seen as an opportunity to free resources to invest in personal interactions with shareholders and intermediaries. Given its focus on retail investors, this includes local shareholder conferences, visits to shareholder clubs and similar outreach measures. The relatively high average age of retail investors is, in fact, considered a bottleneck on the road to a more rapid digitalization of investor relations services, as many still demand printed reports and magazines and insist on personally attending the annual shareholders meeting. As a result, even a 'digital pioneer' such as SAP illustrates the, at times, conservative approach of investor relations to digitalization, and the persistent focus on dialogic, in-person communication.

100 *Handbook on digital corporate communication*

This example demonstrates that the investor relations profession combines new digital tools with traditional communication practices: while web sites, social media and mobile apps are important, investors still value one-on-one, face-to-face time with management and retail shareholders appreciate paper reports and in-person meetings. Digitization augments the practice of investor relations by providing fast and universal access to basic information about the company, which, in turn, affords more time for deeper and more nuanced dialogue.

CONCLUSION AND FUTURE DIRECTIONS

Digitalization has a significant impact on the practice of investor relations and the day-to-day work of investor relations professionals. Yet, such impact may not always be direct. Large corporations, such as SAP, promote dialogic, in-person, one-on-one and small-group communications in their efforts to build and maintain relationships with shareholders and investors. Yet, investors themselves employ more and more digital tools in their investment practice – from AI programs to help them process data and make decisions to social media to help them discuss and share information about corporations. Thus, digitalization demands IROs become expert listeners and knowledgeable in data science. Currently, research on such aspects of the investor relations profession is virtually non-existent.

At the same time, corporations do utilize digital channels to enhance in-person communications or when in-person communications are not available. During the Covid-19 pandemic, annual shareholder meetings became virtual shareholder meetings, roadshows became virtual roadshows, and investor days became virtual investor days. It is reasonable to expect that these digital opportunities will not simply disappear after the pandemic, but instead will become an additional virtual layer on top of the face-to-face communications traditionally characterizing the investor relation practice. For example, an annual shareholder meeting, while being conducted primarily in-person, may have a Zoom access for those who would prefer to participate virtually. More research is needed to evaluate how such multi-layer access to corporate information can affect investors and the stock price.

Digitalization also significantly expanded the bandwidth of corporate disclosure; there is now more information, on more topics, that travels faster and farther across the globe. Investor relations professionals are the ones generating this information and their responsibility is to help investors understand and process this information. Future research will undoubtedly review the effects of quantitative and qualitative changes in corporate disclosure practices. More research is also needed on emergent roles of IROs in crisis communication and prevention. Overall, digitalization entails a widening of responsibilities and required competencies of investor relations professionals.

NOTE

1. See https://www.sap.com/investors/.

REFERENCES

Alexander, R. M. and Gentry, J. K. (2014). Using social media to report financial results. *Business Horizons*, *57*(2), 161–167.

Binder-Tietz, S., Hoffmann, C. P., and Reinholz, J. (2021). Integrated financial communication: Insights on the coordination and integration among investor relations and public relations departments of listed corporations in Germany, Austria and Switzerland. *Public Relations Review*, *47*(4), 102075.

Bollen, L., Hassink, H., and Bozic, G. (2006). Measuring and explaining the quality of Internet investor relations activities: A multinational empirical analysis. *International Journal of Accounting Information Systems*, *7*(4), 273–298.

Brown, W. C. (2011). Evaluating persuasion theory in financial webcasts. *Culture & Religion Review Journal*, *2011*(4), 115–148.

Đorđević, B., Đorđević, M., and Stanujkić, D. (2012). Investor relations on the internet: Analysis of companies on the Serbian stock market. *Economic Annals*, *57*(193), 113–136.

Esrock, S. L. and Leichty, G. B. (2000). Organization of corporate web pages: Publics and functions. *Public Relations Review*, *26*(3), 327–344.

Ettredge, M. and Gerdes, J. (2005). Timeliness of investor relations data at corporate web sites. *Communications of the ACM*, *48*(1), 95–100.

Fama, E. F. and Jensen, M. C. (1983). Separation of ownership and control. *Journal of Law and Economics*, *26*(2), 301–325.

Farias, L. A., Nasser, P., and Paraventi, A. C. (2018). Investor relations in Brazil: From the protection of major stakeholders to value management for concerned parties. In A. V. Laskin (ed.), *Handbook of financial communication and investor relations* (pp. 493–507). Malden, MA: Wiley-Blackwell.

Green, T. C., Jame, R., Markov, S., and Subasi, M. (2014). Broker-hosted investor conferences. *Journal of Accounting and Economics*, *58*, 142–166.

Hoffmann, C. P. and Binder-Tietz, S. (2021). Strategic investor relations management: Insights on planning and evaluation practices among German prime standard corporations. *Journal of Communication Management*, *25*(2), 142–159.

Hoffmann, C. P. and Fieseler, C. (2018). Shareholder activism and the new role of investor relations. In A. V. Laskin (ed.), *Handbook of financial communication and investor relations* (pp. 179–185). Malden, MA: Wiley-Blackwell.

Hoffmann, C. P., Simcic Bronn, P., and Fieseler, C. (2016). A good reputation: Protection against shareholder activism. *Corporate Reputation Review*, *19*(1), 35–46.

Hoffmann, C. P., Tietz, S., and Hammann, K. (2018a). Investor relations: A systematic literature review. *Corporate Communications: An International Journal*, *23*(3), 294–311.

Hoffmann, C. P., Tietz, S., Fetzer, M., and Winter, J. (2018b). *Digital leadership in investor relations: Wie digital ist die Investor Relations in Deutschland?* DIRK – Deutscher Investor Relations Verband.

Kelly, K. S., Laskin, A. V., and Rosenstein, G. A. (2010). Investor relations: Two-way symmetrical practice. *Journal of Public Relations Research*, *22*(2), 182–208.

Laskin, A. (2006). Investor relations practices at Fortune-500 companies: An exploratory study. *Public Relations Review*, *32*, 69–70.

Laskin, A. V. (2011). How investor relations contributes to the corporate bottom line. *Journal of Public Relations Research*, *23*(3), 302–324.

Laskin, A. V. (2014). Investor relations as a public relations function: A state of the profession in the United States. *Journal of Public Relations Research*, *26*(3), 200–214.

Laskin, A. V. (2016). Nonfinancial information in investor communications. *International Journal of Business Communication*, *53*(4), 375–397.

Laskin, A. V. (2017). New media in investor relations. In S. Duhe (ed.), *New media and public relations* (3rd edition) (pp. 107–116). New York: Peter Lang.

Laskin, A. V. (2018). The third-person effects in the investment decision making: A case of corporate social responsibility. *Corporate Communications: An International Journal*, *23*(3), 456–468.

Laskin, A. V. (2021). Measuring investor relations and financial communication: An empirical test of scales of public relations. *Organicom*, *18*(35), 95–115.

Laskin, A. V. (2022). *Investor relations and financial communication*. Malden, MA: Wiley-Blackwell.

Laskin, A. V. and Kresic, K. M. (2021). Inclusion as component of CSR and a brand connection strategy. In D. Pompper (ed.), *Public relations for social responsibility: Affirming DEI commitment with action.* Bingley: Emerald Group Publishing.

Lehavy, R., Li, F., and Merkley, K. (2011). The effect of annual report readability on analyst following and the properties of their earnings forecasts. *The Accounting Review, 86*(3), 1087–1115.

Melgin, E., Luoma-aho, V., Hara, M., and Melgin, J. (2018). The Nordic approach to investor relations. In A. V. Laskin (ed.), *Handbook of financial communication and investor relations* (pp. 419–428). Malden, MA: Wiley-Blackwell.

NIRI: The Association for Investor Relations (2016). *Definition of investor relations.* https://www.niri.org/about-niri.

Palmieri, R., Rocci, A., and Kudrautsava, N. (2015). Argumentation in earnings conference calls: Corporate standpoints and analysts' challenges. *Studies in Communication Sciences, 15*(1), 120–132.

Ragas, M. W., Laskin, A. V., and Brusch, M. (2014). Investor relations measurement: An industry survey. *Journal of Communication Management, 18*(2), 176–192.

Roberts, J., Sanderson, P., Barker, R., and Hendry, J. (2006). In the mirror of the market: The disciplinary effects of company/fund manager meetings. *Accounting, Organizations and Society, 31*(3), 277–294.

Schramm, M. E., Place, K. R., and Laskin, A. V. (2022). Framing the strategic R&D paradigm shift in Big Pharma: A content analysis of pharmaceutical annual reports. *Journal of Communication Management.* https://doi.org/10.1108/JCOM-05-2021-0052.

Westbrook, I. (2018). Influences and priorities in investor relations in Australia. In A. V. Laskin (ed.), *Handbook of financial communication and investor relations* (pp. 473–484). Malden, MA: Wiley-Blackwell.

Zerfaß, A. and Köhler, K. (2017). Investor relations: Online-Kommunikation mit Analysten und Anlegern. In A. Zerfaß and T. Pleil (eds.), *Handbuch Online-PR: Strategische Kommunikation in Internet und Social Web* (2nd edition) (pp. 181–196). Köln: Herbert von Halem.

8. Digital corporate communication and stakeholder relationship management

Linjuan Rita Men, Marc Vielledent, Cen April Yue and Alvin Zhou[1]

INTRODUCTION

The advancement of digital technologies has transformed the media landscape, stakeholder dynamics and the practice of corporate communication. With the digital natives from the millennial and Gen-Z generations entering the consumer space and workforce (Parker and Igielnik, 2020), it is now not a question of *whether* companies should communicate with stakeholders on digital media, but *how* to effectively engage them and build meaningful relationships capitalizing on the unique characteristics of emerging technologies.

A typical example of digital technology – social media – has been argued to process unique features of being two-way, interactive, conversational, relational, decentralized, and communal (e.g., Men and Tsai, 2014; Valentini, 2015). These characteristics aptly positioned social media as a novel tool, which can facilitate companies' and brands' two-way symmetrical and dialogic communication with stakeholders, strengthen connections, and build relationships (Kelleher and Miller, 2006). However, the viral and immediate nature of social media also poses challenges to corporate reputation and stakeholder relationship management. Around the clock and on a global scale, companies now face numerous threats and overlapping issues from an unimaginable amount of data created and exchanged across a myriad of platforms.

In other words, digital technology is a double-edged sword, which generates both enormous opportunities and unpredictable challenges for corporate communication (e.g., reputational risks, digital divide, data security, mis/dis-information, and polarization, etc.). Often used interchangeably with public relations in the communication literature (e.g., Moss et al., 2005), corporate communication is a strategic management function of the organization that entails coordination of all formal communication activities, both externally and internally (Argenti, 1996). A critical issue that is faced by companies, business leaders, and corporate communicators in today's digital era is how to utilize these digital technologies to their full potential while simultaneously mitigating risks in the practice of digital-mediated stakeholder relationship management.

This chapter takes a deep dive into the topic of digital corporate communication and stakeholder relationship management. We first provide an overview of the relationship management literature and define digital corporate communication. We then transition to digital corporate communication and its transformation of relationship management from perspectives of increased access, voice, engagement, and so on. We also discuss the flip side of the coin – that is, the risks and challenges associated with digital corporate communication and relationship management, followed by a case study. Finally, we present our concluding thoughts regarding how digital corporate communication has reshaped the theorization and practice of stakeholder relationship management and identify opportunities for future research.

DEFINITION OF THE TOPIC AND PREVIOUS STUDIES: OVERVIEW OF RELATIONSHIP MANAGEMENT LITERATURE

The study on organization-public relationships (OPRs) has been a mainstay of public relations research for almost four decades (Huang and Zhang, 2013). This perspective derives its roots from Ferguson's (1984) pioneering work, encouraging public relations scholars to advance a new paradigm. Since then, numerous scholars have investigated different aspects of OPRs, including its measurement (e.g., Huang, 2001), antecedents (e.g., Seltzer and Lee, 2018), outcomes (e.g., Kim and Rhee, 2011), and structure (e.g., Yang and Taylor, 2015). The relationship management perspective has taken hold in the field of public relations and fundamentally shifts the practice of public relations away from manipulating public opinion (Bruning and Ledingham, 2000).

According to Bruning and Ledingham (1999, p. 160), OPRs are the "state which exists between an organization and its key publics in which the actions of either entity impact the economic, social, political, and/or cultural well-being of the other entity". Similarly, Broom et al. (2000, p. 18) defined OPRs as being objective but dynamic: "patterns of interaction, transaction, exchange, and linkage between an organization and its public". On the other hand, most of the literature viewed OPRs from the perspective of individual perceptions (Ki and Hon, 2012). A widely accepted definition from Huang (1998, p. 12) highlighted the subjective nature of relationships and encapsulated key dimensions constituting OPRs: "the degree that the organization and its publics trust one another, agree on one has rightful power to influence, experience satisfaction with each other, and commit oneself to one another". Later, Hon and Grunig (1999) developed quantitative measures of the four relationship outcomes, namely, *trust* (includes dimensions of integrity, dependability, and competence), *control mutuality* (the degree to which parties agree on issues of power and control), *satisfaction* (the degree to which parties feel positive about the relationship), and *commitment* (the degree to which parties think the relationship is worth maintaining). In addition to measuring the quality of relationships, scholars also proposed to measure the status of relationships via two indicators: *exchange relationship* (both parties provide benefit to each other in the hope of return of benefits) and *communal relationship* (both parties benefit each other without expecting anything in return) (Hung, 2005). Later, Strömbäck and Kiousis (2011) proposed another categorization of relationships, noting that relationships exist along a continuum; one anchor of the spectrum is called *reputational relationships* built on publics' vicarious, indirect interaction with organizations, and the other end is *experiential relationships* based on direct interactions among parties involved. The traditional OPR model falls under experiential relationships because it assumes publics' first-hand engagement with organizations (cf. Hallahan, 2000).

More recently, scholars have proposed building organization-stakeholder relationships (OSR), a concept which is rooted in the principle of stakeholder intimacy and organizations' equal partnership with stakeholders (Badham, 2020). OSR is defined as the "management of common interests between the organization and strategic stakeholder(s) over time in order to achieve mutually beneficial goals (Slabbert and Barker, 2014, p. 72). In many ways, OSR resembles OPR with different theoretical origins (i.e., stakeholder management vs. public relations).

Antecedents, Relationship Maintenance Strategies and Outcomes

Relationship scholars have developed a process model of OPRs that includes antecedents, maintenance strategies, and relationship outcomes (Grunig and Huang, 2000) (see Table 8.1). Antecedents, such as motives, needs, norms, and value congruence, serve as reasons for the formulation of relationships (Seltzer and Lee, 2018). Maintenance strategies, known as cultivation strategies, refer to any organizational efforts to build and sustain long-term, quality relationships with strategic publics. Finally, relationship outcomes are consequences of relationships that are generated by antecedents and maintenance strategies (Grunig and Huang, 2000).

Throughout the last few decades, public relations scholars have been devoted to studying different types of relationship maintenance strategies, believing that "the more that these cultivation strategies are utilized, the more likely that OPR perceptions will be positive" (Seltzer and Lee, 2018, p. 6). One stream of research on relational maintenance strategies, developed by Hon and Grunig (1999), drew insights from the interpersonal relationship literature (Canary and Stafford, 1992). These strategies include: *access* (organizational efforts to assist publics in reaching information); *positivity* (organizational efforts to make the interaction with publics joyful); *openness* (organizational efforts to provide information of value to publics); *sharing of tasks* (organizational efforts to involve publics in performing responsibility); *networking* (organizational efforts to build affiliations with the same groups their publics do); and *assurances* (organizational efforts to ensure their publics' concerns are acknowledged). Subsequent research has verified the effectiveness of these cultivation strategies in fostering quality relationships (e.g., Seltzer and Zhang, 2010; Sung and Kim, 2018). Others emphasized the role of dialogic communication in fostering beneficial relationships and social capitals (Kent and Lane, 2017). Dialogue can be formed by following *mutuality* (i.e., collaboration and mutual equality), *propinquity* (i.e., dialogic exchange and mutual consultation), *empathy* (i.e., an atmosphere of trust and support), *risk* (taking relational risks in dialogue), and *commitment* (i.e., a commitment to conversations and interpretations) (Kent and Taylor, 2002). More recently, Badham (2020) proposed that in managing relationships with stakeholders, organizations should initiate and nurture an affective orientation of intimacy, commitment, and love toward their stakeholders.

In studying online relationship-building, Kelleher and Miller (2006) developed more parsimonious relationship maintenance measures, including *communicated relational commitment*, *conversational human voice*, *task sharing*, *responsiveness*, and *positivity/optimism*. Communicated relational commitment refers to "communication in which members of an organization work to express their commitment to building and maintaining a relationship" (Kelleher, 2009, p. 176), and conversational voice indicates "an engaging and natural style of organizational communication as perceived by an organization's publics based on interactions between individuals in the organization and individuals in publics" (Kelleher, 2009, p. 177). Task sharing refers to sharing of responsibilities between organizations and stakeholders in solving problems. Responsiveness shows an organization's willingness to respond promptly to stakeholders' inquiries, requests, or complaints. Positivity/optimism indicates that an organization interacts with its stakeholders in a cheerful, uncritical manner. This modified measure of relational maintenance strategy is positively associated with OPR dimensions (e.g., Kelleher, 2009; Sweetser and Kelleher, 2016).

106 *Handbook on digital corporate communication*

A plethora of studies have also examined the effects of quality OPRs. For instance, publics' perception of favourable OPRs leads to positive attitudes (e.g., Bruning and Ledingham, 2000) and supportive behaviours toward organizations (e.g., Kang and Yang, 2010). Internal stakeholders, such as employees, are more likely to engage in positive megaphoning and scouting (Kim and Rhee, 2011), job engagement (Kang and Sung, 2017), and extra-role behaviours (Men, 2021) when they perceive quality relationships with organizations. External stakeholders like consumers tend to show higher brand loyalty, purchase intention, and brand preferences when a strong relationship forms between brands and their customers (Cheng and Jiang, 2022). In addition, literature has shown the positive role of relationships in driving organizational reputation (e.g., Coombs and Holladay, 2001; Yang, 2007).

Table 8.1   *Relationship maintenance strategies, indicators, types, and outcomes*

Relationship maintenance strategies	Relationship indicators, types, and outcomes
Hon & Grunig (1999)	Relationship indicators:
● Access	Hon & Grunig (1999)
● Positivity	● Trust
● Openness	● Satisfaction
● Sharing of tasks	● Control mutuality
● Networking	● Commitment
● Assurances	Badham (2020)
	● Intimacy
	● Commitment
	● Love
Kent & Taylor (2002)	Relationship types:
● Mutuality	Hon & Grunig (1999)
● Propinquity	● Exchange relationship
● Empathy	● Communal relationship
● Risk	Strömbäck & Kiousis (2011)
● Commitment	● Reputational relationships
	● Experiential relationships
Kelleher & Miller (2006)	Relationship outcomes:
● Communicated relational commitment	(e.g., Bruning & Ledingham (2000); Kang & Sung (2017); Kang &
● Conversational human voice	Yang (2010); Kim & Rhee (2011); Men (2021)
● Task sharing	● Stakeholder positive attitudes
● Responsiveness	● Stakeholder supportive behaviours
● Positivity/optimism	● Organizational reputation

Relationship Management in the Digital Era

The proliferation of digital technologies has provided more opportunities for organizations and publics to build and strengthen their relationships (Men et al., 2018; Yue et al., 2021a, 2021b), but also made relationship-destroying behaviour easier (Ji et al., 2017; Samaha and Palmatier, 2015). Digital corporate communication (DCC) is defined as "an organization's strategic management of digital technologies, digital infrastructures and digitalization processes to improve communication with internal and external stakeholders and more broadly within society for the maintenance of organizational tangible and intangible assets" (Badham and Luoma-aho, Chapter 1 in this volume, p. 9). Organizations and their representatives are more likely to

Digital corporate communication and stakeholder relationship management 107

cultivate meaningful relationships with stakeholders by employing personalized, interactive, conversational, engaging, and genuine communications on digital media (e.g., Tsai and Men, 2017). In the section below, we take a deep dive into the issue of how digital technologies are transforming organization's stakeholder relationship management.

WHAT IS CHANGING?

Digital technologies are more than social media. Before every stakeholder and corporation jumped onto Facebook and Instagram, there was a period of time when digital technologies developed in the Web 1.0 era mainly accelerated information dissemination through website communication. Websites facilitated exchanges between stakeholders and organizations but did not make their two-way direct interactions as prevalent as we see today on platforms. Therefore, a more holistic view is necessary to fully consider which characteristics of digital technologies are consequential to stakeholder relationship management. We focus on three aspects here: access, voice, and engagement (see Table 8.2).

Access. First, digital technologies have democratized access to corporate information. According to Hootsuite's Global State of Digital 2021, 45 per cent of global Internet users employed social media to search for brand information in 2020 (Cooper, 2021). Long gone are the days when organizations could fully conceal their operational details and communication conduct from public scrutiny, which also sets new standards for organizational transparency and demands a more relational model of public communication that deviated from the traditional informational or persuasive approach to stakeholder management. Organizations need to tailor communication to stakeholders' information needs, making sure it is useful, relevant, and practical as a way to avoid falling into the trap of oversaturation of information. In other words, companies and brands need to embrace the mindset of stakeholder-based transparency, focusing not just on what they need to tell, but more on what stakeholders want or need to know via digital technologies (Men and Tsai, 2016). On the flip side, however, the access to digital technologies is still troubled by various forms of social inequality that have been present in our offline world for decades (DiMaggio et al., 2004). As a result, corporations are now advised to develop relational strategies that consider those who lack access or are misrepresented in the online space.

Voice. Digital technologies have also altered how voices are expressed and framed. Many would argue that this change occurred mainly during the Web 2.0 era when ordinary Internet users started creating content, and social networks emerged through various platforms as business services were launched to help organizations monitor and respond to stakeholder needs. Though scholars have questioned whether the communicative power has truly landed in the hands of stakeholders (Valentini, 2015), it is indisputable that the interactive nature of Web 2.0 has created a new landscape and presented new opportunities for stakeholders to voice their opinions, ideas, and concerns, thus facilitating organizational listening and stakeholder relationship management. Specifically, first, the amount of information related to a corporation has skyrocketed, which has necessitated the deployment of systematic online listening protocols (Macnamara, 2019). Second, digital platforms have enabled stakeholders to raise concerns and voice discontent in various issue arenas that require corporations' immediate attention and reaction to avoid risk to corporations' tangible and intangible assets (Luoma-aho and Vos, 2010). Third, relationship networks among organizations and their stakeholders

108 *Handbook on digital corporate communication*

have become increasingly intricate, in that the management of one relationship could now have important implications for another relationship (Yang and Taylor, 2015; Zhou, 2019). As a result, more and more companies and brands have devised strategic social listening tools and platforms, such as Hootsuite, BrandWatch, and Audiense, to monitor, track, analyse, and respond to online conversations. Such attention to stakeholder voice can help enhance understanding of stakeholder needs, mitigate risks, and maintain the increasingly intricate and multi-faceted stakeholder relationships (Huang et al., 2021).

Engagement. Digital technologies have also changed how corporations and stakeholders engage one another. Before the digital revolution, corporations' relational efforts were mostly carried out with face-to-face engagement. Now, most companies have embraced digital technologies as interactions are enabled by a variety of social platforms, such as social networking sites, social messengers, or even artificial-intelligence enabled applications such as chatbots. Men and Tsai (2014, 2016) conceptualized public engagement with corporate social media to include two main dimensions: reactive message consumption and proactive contributing, with the former focusing on cognitive corporate or brand message consumption (e.g., viewing pictures, videos, reading posts) and the latter emphasizing affective and behavioural engagement, (i.e., interacting with the company/brand by liking, sharing, or commenting on the companies' posts or engaging in one-on-one or group conversations). These scholars' studies have consistently shown that both reactive and proactive engagement contributes to stakeholder relational outcomes, such as trust, control mutuality, commitment, and satisfaction (Men and Tsai, 2013). In other words, companies' social media engagement can not only facilitate the reach of corporate messages; more importantly, they can encourage stakeholder interactions and two-way conversations, which, over time can enhance organization-public mutual understanding, foster stakeholder perception of organizational transparency and authenticity, build communities and collaboration, that eventually contribute to offline stakeholder relationships (Men and Tsai, 2016).

The transformation of the media landscape also called into question whether our traditional understanding of OPRs still fits the digital environment and how the online relationship cultivation strategies (should) differ from those in the offline setting. One stream of research has tested the aforementioned relationship cultivation strategies (i.e., access, positivity, openness, sharing of tasks, networking, and assurance) in the social media context. For instance, recently, Huang et al., (2021) examined how companies in China utilized relationship cultivation strategies to maintain relationships with stakeholders on social media during the Covid-19 pandemic. Their results showed that access, openness, positivity, and sharing of tasks all had significant positive effects on at least one level (cognitive, affective, and behavioural) of stakeholder engagement on social media, which showcased the relevance of the traditional offline relationship building approaches in the digital environment and abnormal crisis times. Others have established the connection of social presence and conversational human voice projected in corporate social messaging (Men et al., 2018; Yue et al., 2021a, 2021b), dialogic communication (Kent and Lane, 2017), and digital communication channels' affordances (Zhou and Xu, 2021, 2022) to stakeholder relationship outcomes. These findings reinforce the essential question of how corporations can use digital technologies to mimic their decade-old, face-to-face communication practice, while in conversation with another camp of research inquiring how digital technologies create new possibilities that were non-existent in their face-to-face storytelling (e.g., Barreda-Ángeles et al., 2021).

Digital corporate communication and stakeholder relationship management 109

Table 8.2 *Access, voice, and engagement before and after digital technologies*

	Before digital technologies	After digital technologies
Access	• Access to corporate information granted to a few • Persuasive approach to corporate messaging • Social inequality to information access	• Access to corporate information democratized to most inquiring entities • Dialogic approach to corporate messaging • Digital inequality to Internet access
Voice	• One-way communication from organizations to stakeholders with organization-created content • Selected voices amplified by media or other institutional gatekeepers • Low volume handled by a small team of corporate communication professionals	• Two-way communication between organizations and stakeholders with user-generated content • Selected voices amplified by other concerned stakeholders • High volume that demands large-scale social listening protocols
Engagement	• Face-to-face engagement limited in scale and quantity due to budget and personnel constraints • Engagement outcomes measured through surveys, interviews, and other methods	• A plethora of mediated engagement possibilities with reactive consumption and proactive contributions • Engagement outcomes aggregated to big data and quantified through digital metrics

WHAT REMAINS THE SAME?

Overall, significant changes have been observed in stakeholder relationship management practices resulting from digital technologies and their characteristics, but some practice principles remain the same. First, digital technologies facilitate mass dissemination of corporate messages but typically lack cues that convey personas or emotions. In this regard, adhering to the conversational human voice and communicating to stakeholders in a humane, personable, approachable, and empathetic way are still considered the gold standard of relationship management in this digital world (Kelleher, 2009; Men and Tsai, 2015). Furthermore, stakeholder groups, targeted intentionally or unintentionally, might have varying reactions based on their demographics and interests, similar to the offline context. All of these factors suggest that corporations should still take caution on how, when, and through which channel they communicate messages with specific stakeholder groups, using segmentation tools and by understanding the contextual environment and predicting the possible consequences of their messages.

Second, corporations have come to recognize that digital organization-public relationships are becoming more abstract and volatile than ever, which further emphasizes their parasocial nature. Studies such as Tsai and Men (2017) have shown that parasocial interactions between corporate spokespersons and stakeholders are an important antecedent of organization-public relationships. In an effort to reprogram communication management and reemphasize long-term relationship building, scholars have suggested corporations expand their listening capacities using digital technologies by implementing large-scale techniques to monitor online word-of-mouth and initiate parasocial interactions (Macnamara, 2019). It is worth noting that listening to stakeholders has been long deemed critical in understanding stakeholder needs and wants and establishing mutually beneficial relationships (Grunig et al., 2002). While digital technologies have brought new tools and platforms (e.g., social media, AI-powered chatbots) that enable large-scale organizational listening in an efficient manner, the tenets of listening, which not only entail information and feedback gathering, but more importantly, responding to and addressing stakeholder needs, remain essential.

Digital evolution has also slightly changed the goal of corporate communication and relationship management. Many prior communication program designs fulfilled marketing needs and increased consumers' purchase intentions. However, with the democratic effect of digital technologies and the rise of social media platforms in particular, corporations now position themselves as one central, ordinary actor in the broader, social system filled with multiple issues (Luoma-aho and Vos, 2010). Stakeholders expect corporations to assume their citizenship in the civil society. As such, traditional practices of communicating corporate social responsibility and purpose remain critical, or perhaps play an increasingly important role in fostering long-term stakeholder relationships (Chen et al., 2019).

CRITICAL EXAMINATION

Digital technologies now penetrate all arenas of corporate communication practices and shift the conventional one-way and organization-centred approaches to a more democratic, two-way, relationship-oriented, and public-centred communication. However, its ubiquitous existence across the corporate landscape is fraught with associated risks and potential, unintended outcomes (Gallager, 2008). Some of the risks include, but are not limited to, over-reliance, privacy, data security, social disconnect, unpredictability, and digital media manipulation, just to highlight a few (Picazo-Vela et al., 2012).

Managing Risks and Challenges in Digital Corporate Communication and Relationship Management

Some of the most prescient challenges to date in digital corporate communication and relationship management exist in cybersecurity and data risk; corporate entities must now wrestle with how to best maximize their digital technologies without disrupting their existing, core functions, interests, and service to stakeholders (Luoma-aho, 2015). Engaging stakeholders is becoming increasingly challenging when considering that organizational messages can quickly leak or be taken out of the intended context in a digital, information-rich environment (Hennig-Thurau et al., 2010). Furthermore, the effectiveness of any message in the digital space is increasingly influenced by and dependent on source credibility (Yuan and Lou, 2020). People tend to be less concerned with risks originating "from places, people, or organizations that they trust", compared with those risks communicated or originating from unknown sources (Sandman, 2006). Further complicating matters, research also shows that negative online reports have been found to be more credible than positive online reports, especially in the online environment (Chen and Lurie, 2013). This presents a real challenge with the reality and prevalence of misinformation. Visitors tend to "select and share content related to a specific narrative and then they ignore the rest; social homogeneity is a primary driver of content diffusion, which can result in the formation of homogeneous, polarized clusters" (Del Vicario et al., 2016, p. 558).

From the relationship management perspective, levels of different relationship indicators (e.g., trust, satisfaction, commitment, and control mutuality) can dictate the varying level of concern or stress of stakeholders, based on added or reduced uncertainty (Coombs, 2007). In digital corporate communication, trust correlates with risk in the sense that it is connected to uncertainty; in the absence of trust, the communicator's perceived message clarity may in fact be ambiguous and open to different interpretations in the digital space (Levenshus, 2012). Some of these relationship-centric approaches that can positively affect relationship indicators include ensuring that digital communication establishes a built-in channel for stakeholders to communicate directly with the organization (Allagui and Breslow, 2016).

Digital corporate communication should incorporate tools in environmental scanning to listen and respond to risk or crisis concerns of stakeholders and risk bearers (Hennig-Thurau et al., 2010). To offset rumours and manage relationships, successful digital communicators should segment publics on the most appropriate channel. While relationships remain vital in curbing misinformation and solidifying the organizational establishment as a credible source, at its core, digital communication is still interpersonal communication because it allows for human interactions and emotional support as a mode to influence stakeholders (Gonzalez-Herrero and Smith, 2010).

The risks and challenges can be further overcome by appropriate use of language and channel selection, to strengthen relationships over a sustained period of time and bolster trust through more precise messaging. Incorporating meaning-making and empathetic language can accentuate organizational missions, values, and purpose while simultaneously communicating empathy, compassion, care, support, and encouragement to the appropriate publics (Yue, 2021). Further, the selection of 'rich' digital channels is commonly perceived to be more instrumental in promoting authentic communication, openness, and transparency – all of which strengthens relationships (Clayton, 2015). Finally, assuring precise messaging may require additional involvement from communication and public relations professionals to ensure accuracy in both purpose and content (Grunig, 2006). These approaches may not alleviate all risks and challenges, but can contribute to increasing the probability of effective digital corporate communication.

Post-Digital Classifications of Stakeholders

In the post-digital era, the Internet and social media will have entered the lexicon of everyday English (Kelleher, 2009) and digital technology will be a ubiquitous, seamless backbone of the economy and society. The post-digital era is defined by an environment where organizations no longer explore emerging technology and almost all are implementing mobile, social, cloud, and artificial intelligence as standard practice and as a fundamental necessity. As the premier global provider of market intelligence, the International Data Corporation (IDC) identifies the post-digital era unfolding as 60 per cent of global businesses are now digitized (IDC, 2022).

This post-digital landscape now requires brands and organizations to interact with stakeholders on various issues and balance the relationship or rhetoric between stakeholders and organizations on a more level playing field (Luoma-aho and Vos, 2010). Corporate stakeholders or customers have increased power, emotion, and access into potentially publishing and sharing their experiences to much larger audiences (Luoma-aho, 2015). Massive digital misinformation is "becoming pervasive in online social media to the extent that it is now considered one of the main threats to our society (Del Vicario et al., 2016, p. 554). To counteract this trend, algorithmic-driven solutions have been proposed to develop a trustworthiness score and rank results of the queries (Del Vicario et al., 2016). Consequently, new forms of stakeholders can now be distinguished as: positively engaged authentic 'faith-holders', the negatively engaged 'hateholders', and the artificially-generated 'fakeholders', who are designed to either oppose or support a specific issue (Luoma-aho, 2015).

With the rise of fakeholders, trust has risen in "people like me" (Edelman Trust Barometer, 2012), which incurs additional risks from stakeholders relying on auto-generated or fake online reviews (Kolivos and Kuperman, 2012). Recent work by Luoma-aho (2015) identified that organizations and brands who hope to distinguish between their real stakeholders and those created through algorithms and robots find themselves increasingly curious about whether or not specific stakeholders be ignored? But even if the actual messages of fakeholders can be ignored, they still present the prospect of real damage through the reality of misinformation and the inaccurate perceptions of any unexpected new stakeholder groups (Luoma-aho and Paloviita, 2010). Thus, with increasing regularity in digital corporate communication, it appears different stakeholders can be the cause of questioned or challenged legitimacy. Such was the experience of Mondelez International in late 2020.

ILLUSTRATIVE EXAMPLE: THE 'HUMAN' MISHAP AT MONDELEZ

In November 2020, the multinational confectionary giant Mondelez kicked off a global marketing strategy called 'humaning'. Humaning was described as "a consumer-centric approach to marketing that creates real, human connections with purpose" (Mondelez International, 2020). In this instance, the intent was to transition from marketing to consumers and switch toward creating connections with humans via faithholders; yet the result of this campaign faced auto-generated critique from fakeholders, and was accompanied with mockery and ridicule from hateholders across the industry on social media. Instead of initiating a positive, fresh approach, the company was immediately managing its reputation as the result of widespread scrutiny from a misguided movement. In response, Mondelez leadership doubled down on their approach by signalling their intent to not only maintain the campaign, but to further engage in a dialogue with stakeholders to discuss "the concept of humaning" in greater detail (Hoffman, 2020). Ultimately, despite the righteousness in developing a consumer-focused approach as opposed to a financially-focused approach, stakeholders in the digital space had an opportunity to openly challenge and question its motives. In the post-digital age, critique can far outweigh openness and support. Undoubtedly, the risks and challenges that exist through digital corporate communication can negatively impact relationships and generate unintended outcomes.

In the future, digital corporate communicators must prioritize aligning their values, audiences, and messages. Mondelez's campaign failed to see its consumers as humans in the first place, and thus, the intent of their message backfired. This mantra would have been much better served as an internal memo to their employees rather than a marketing pitch to external consumers "who likely wondered how the company viewed them prior to this humaning campaign … as valuable only for the sales they could provide" (Mordecai Inc., 2020). In addition, this digital communication also did not enable a two-way conversation to encourage direct feedback; instead, it informed stakeholders, or consumers, the way in which they were previously viewed and the way in which they will be viewed moving forward. Absent this critical two-way dialogue, any misstep with digital communication incurs increased criticism in its oversight, inaccuracy, or delivery. While raising brand awareness remains an important aspect of the consumer experience (Schick, 2020), this case highlights the primacy of relationship management in the digital era.

CONCLUSION AND FUTURE DIRECTIONS

The evolution of digital technologies has transformed the media landscape and corporate communication practice in an unprecedented way. While the unique features of social media – such as being interactive, conversational, communal, democratic, and engaging – have facilitated two-way interactions, personalized communications, and relationship management with stakeholders, it also poses challenges and risks for corporate cybersecurity, credibility, and reputation management with the prevalence of mis/disinformation and the emergence of fakeholders (Luoma-aho, 2015). With digitalization becoming an inevitable trend that is facing organizations, companies and brands should embrace digital technologies, internalize digital communication best practices, capitalize on the advantageous features of technological tools, and identify methods to mitigate potential risks. To that end, companies should develop a digital corporate communication system spearheaded by communication professionals, supported by corporate leadership and related functions such as information technology, legal, marketing, and human resources. Essentially, digital technologies help elevate the role of corporate communication to the new, integrated, and strategic level, as it facilitates communication functions beyond corporate speaking and information dissemination; more importantly, the digitalization trend promotes listening, connecting, engaging, and striking a deeper bond with stakeholders, providing new opportunities for relationship management.

To inform and guide today's digital corporate communication and relationship management practice, scholars should keep pace to address the unanswered questions and emerging issues, such as (1) how to combat specific mis/disinformation online that poses challenges for corporate credibility and stakeholder relationship maintenance; (2) how to utilize emerging technologies to aid large-scale corporate social listening; (3) how artificial intelligence (AI) tools such as chatbots can be incorporated in digital corporate communication to facilitate AI-enabled relationship cultivation; and (4) how to effectively segment digital publics and evaluate the success of digital communication. The integration and investment from corporate communication scholars and professionals is necessary to help organizations fully harness the power of digital technologies for stakeholder relationship management in the Web 2.0 era and beyond.

NOTE

1.   Authors are listed in alphabetical order and contributed equally to the chapter.

REFERENCES

Allagui, I. and Breslow, H. (2016). Social media for public relations: Lessons from four effective cases. *Public Relations Review*, *42*(1), 20–30.
Argenti, P. (1996). Corporate communication as a discipline: Toward a definition. *Management Communication Quarterly*, *10*(1), 73–97.

Badham, M. (2020). Love wins: A love lens approach to cultivation of organization–stakeholder relationships. In R. Tench, A. T. Vercic, and S. Einwiller (eds.), *Joy: Using strategic communication to improve well-being and organizational success* (pp. 3–20). Bingley: Emerald Group Publishing.

Barreda-Ángeles, M., Aleix-Guillaume, S., and Pereda-Baños, A. (2021). Virtual reality storytelling as a double-edged sword: Immersive presentation of nonfiction 360°-video is associated with impaired cognitive information processing. *Communication Monographs*, *88*(2), 154–173.

Broom, G. M., Casey, S., and Ritchey, J. (2000). Concept and theory of organization-public relationships. In J. A. Ledingham and S. D. Bruning (eds.), *Public relations as relationship management: A relational approach to the study and practice of public relations* (pp. 3–22). Mahwah, NJ: Lawrence Erlbaum.

Bruning, S. D. and Ledingham, J. A. (1999). Relationships between organizations and publics: Development of a multi-dimensional organization-public relationship scale. *Public Relations Review*, *25*(2), 157–170.

Bruning, S. D. and Ledingham, J. A. (2000). Perceptions of relationships and evaluations of satisfaction: An exploration of interaction. *Public Relations Review*, *26*(1), 85–95.

Canary, D. J. and Stafford, L. (1992). Relational maintenance strategies and equity in marriage. *Communication Monographs*, *59*(3), 243–267.

Chen, Z. and Lurie, N. H. (2013). Temporal contiguity and negativity bias in the impact of online word of mouth. *Journal of Marketing Research*, *50*(4), 463–476.

Chen, Z. F., Hong, C., and Occa, A. (2019). How different CSR dimensions impact organization-employee relationships: The moderating role of CSR-culture fit. *Corporate Communications: An International Journal*, *24*(1), 63–78.

Cheng, Y. and Jiang, H. (2022). Customer–brand relationship in the era of artificial intelligence: Understanding the role of chatbot marketing efforts. *Journal of Product & Brand Management*, *31*(2), 252–264.

Clayton, S. (2015). Change management meets social media. *Harvard Business Review*, 10 November.

Coombs, W. T. (2007). Protecting organization reputations during a crisis: The development and application of situational crisis communication theory. *Corporate Reputation Review*, *10*(3), 163–176.

Coombs, W. T. and Holladay, S. J. (2001). An extended examination of the crisis situations: A fusion of the relational management and symbolic approaches. *Journal of Public Relations Research*, *13*(4), 321–340.

Cooper, P. (2021, 13 April). 140+ social media statistics that matter to marketers in 2021. Hootsuite. https://blog.hootsuite.com/social-media-statistics-for-social-media-managers/.

Del Vicario, M., Bessi, A., Zollo, F., Petroni, F., Scala, A., Caldarelli, G., Stanley, H. E. and Quattrociocchi, W. (2016). The spreading of misinformation online. *Proceedings of the National Academy of Sciences*, *113*(3), 554–559.

DiMaggio, P., Hargittai, E., Celeste, C., and Shafer, S. (2004). Digital inequality: From unequal access to differentiated use. In K. M. Neckerman (ed.), *Social inequality* (pp. 355–400). New York: Russell Sage Foundation.

Edelman Trust Barometer (2012). *2012 Edelman Trust Barometer Global Report*.

Ferguson, M. A. (1984). Building theory in public relations: Interorganizational relationships as a public relations paradigm. Paper presented to the Association for Education in Journalism and Mass Communication, Gainesville, FL, August.

Gallager, R. G. (2008). *Principles of digital communication* (Vol. 1). Cambridge: Cambridge University Press.

Gonzalez-Herrero, A. and Smith, S. (2010). Crisis communications management 2.0: Organizational principles to manage crisis in an online world. *Organization Development Journal*, *28*(1), 97–105.

Grunig, J. E. (2006). Furnishing the edifice: Ongoing research on public relations as a strategic management function. *Journal of Public Relations Research*, *18*(2), 151–176.

Grunig, L. A., Grunig, J. E., and Dozier, D. M. (2002). *Excellent public relations and effective organizations: A study of communication management in three countries*. Mahwah, NJ: Lawrence Erlbaum.

Grunig, J. E. and Huang, Y. H. (2000). From organizational effectiveness to relationship indicators: Antecedents of relationships, public relations strategies, and relationship outcomes. In J. A. Ledingham and S. D. Bruning (eds.), *Public relations as relationship management: A relational approach to the study and practice of public relations* (pp. 23–54). Mahwah, NJ: Lawrence Erlbaum.

Hallahan, K. (2000). Inactive publics: The forgotten publics in public relations. *Public Relations Review*, *26*(4), 499–515.

Hennig-Thurau, T., Malthouse, E. C., Friege, C., Gensler, S., Lobschat, L., Rangaswamy, A., and Skiera, B. (2010). The impact of new media on customer relationships. *Journal of Service Research*, *13*(3), 311–330.

Hoffman, B., (2020, 23 November), Mondelez and the self-delusion of brand purpose. *PR Week*. https://www.prweek.com/article/1702684/biggest-brand-fails-2020.

Hon, L. C. and Grunig, J. E. (1999). *Guidelines for measuring relationships in public relations*. Gainesville, FL: Institute for Public Relations.

Huang, Q., Jin, J., Lynn, B. J., and Men, L. R. (2021). Relationship cultivation and social media during the Covid-19 pandemic in China. *Public Relations Review*, *47*, 102064.

Huang, Y. H. (1998). Public relations strategies and organization-public relationships. Annual conference of the Association for Education in Journalism and Mass Communication, Baltimore, August.

Huang, Y. H. (2001). OPRA: A cross-cultural, multiple-item scale for measuring organization-public relationships. *Journal of Public Relations Research*, *13*(1), 61–90.

Huang, Y. H. and Zhang, Y. (2013). Revisiting organization-public relations research over the past decade: Theoretical concepts, measures, methodologies and challenges. *Public Relations Review*, *39*, 85–87.

Hung, C. F. (2005). Exploring types of organization–public relationships and their implications for relationship management in public relations. *Journal of Public Relations Research*, *17*(4), 383–426.

International Data Corporation (2022). *IDC Worldwide Survey 2022: Digital Force Strategies*. https://www.idc.com/getdoc.jsp?containerId=US48899122.

Ji, Y. G., Li, C., North, M., and Liu, J. (2017). Staking reputation on stakeholders: How does stakeholders' Facebook engagement help or ruin a company's reputation? *Public Relations Review*, *43*(1), 201–210.

Kang, M. and Sung, M. (2017). How symmetrical employee communication leads to employee engagement and positive employee communication behaviors: The mediation of employee-organization relationships. *Journal of Communication Management*, *21*(1), 82–102.

Kang, M. and Yang, S. U. (2010). Mediation effects of organization–public relationship outcomes on public intentions for organizational supports. *Journal of Public Relations Research*, *22*(4), 477–494.

Kelleher, T. (2009). Conversational voice, communicated commitment, and public relations outcomes in interactive online communication. *Journal of Communication*, *59*(1), 172–188.

Kelleher, T. and Miller, B. M. (2006). Organizational blogs and the human voice: Relational strategies and relational outcomes. *Journal of Computer-Mediated Communication*, *11*(2), 395–414.

Kent, M. L. and Lane, A. B. (2017). A rhizomatous metaphor for dialogic theory. *Public Relations Review*, *43*(3), 568–578.

Kent, M. L. and Taylor, M. (2002). Toward a dialogic theory of public relations. *Public Relations Review*, *28*(1), 21–37.

Ki, E. J. and Hon, L. C. (2012). Causal linkages among relationship quality perception, attitude, and behavior intention in a membership organization. *Corporate Communications: An International Journal*, *17*(2), 187–208.

Kim, J. N. and Rhee, Y. (2011). Strategic thinking about employee communication behavior (ECB) in public relations: Testing the models of megaphoning and scouting effects in Korea. *Journal of Public Relations Research*, *23*(3), 243–268.

Kolivos, E. and Kuperman, A. (2012). Consumer law: Web of lies – legal implications of astroturfing. *Keeping Good Companies*, *64*(1), 38–41.

Levenshus, A. B. (2012). The social coast guard: An ethnographic examination of the intersection of risk communication, social media, and government public relations (Doctoral dissertation).

Luoma-aho, V. (2015). Understanding stakeholder engagement: Faith-holders, hateholders & fakeholders. *RJ-IPR: Research Journal of the Institute for Public Relations*, *2*(1). http://www.instituteforpr.org/understanding-stakeholder-engagement-fai.

Luoma-aho, V. and Paloviita, A. (2010). Actor-networking stakeholder theory for today's corporate communications. *Corporate Communications: An International Journal*, *15*(1), 49–67.

Luoma-aho, V. and Vos, M. (2010). Towards a more dynamic stakeholder model: Acknowledging multiple issue arenas. *Corporate Communications: An International Journal*, *15*(3), 315–331.

116 *Handbook on digital corporate communication*

Macnamara, J. (2019). Explicating listening in organization-public communication: Theory, practices, technologies. *International Journal of Communication, 13,* 5183–5204.

Men, L. R. (2021). The impact of startup CEO communication on employee relational and behavioral outcomes: Responsiveness, assertiveness, and authenticity. *Public Relations Review, 47*(4), 102078.

Men, L. R. and Tsai, W. S. (2013). Beyond liking or following: Understanding public engagement on social networking sites in China. *Public Relations Review, 39*(1), 13–22.

Men, L. R. and Tsai, W. S. (2014). Perceptual, attitudinal, and behavioral outcomes of organization–public engagement on corporate social networking sites. *Journal of Public Relations Research, 26*(5), 417–435.

Men, L. R. and Tsai, W. S. (2015). Infusing social media with humanity: Corporate character, public engagement, and relational outcomes. *Public Relations Review, 41*(3), 395–403.

Men, L. R. and Tsai, W. S. (2016). Public engagement with CEOs on social media: Motivations and relational outcomes. *Public Relations Review, 42,* 932–942.

Men, L. R., Tsai, W. S., Chen, Z. F., and Ji, Y. G. (2018). Social presence and digital dialogic communication: Engagement lessons from top social CEOs. *Journal of Public Relations Research, 30*(3), 83–99.

Mondelez International (2020, 30 November). *Announcing Humaning.* https://www.mondelezinternational.com/News/New-Approach-to-Marketing-Humaning.

Mordecai Inc. (2020). Humaning should be an internal message, not a marketing mantra. *The Drum.* https://www.thedrum.com/opinion/2020/11/16/humaning-should-be-internal-message-not-marketing-mantra.

Moss, D., Newman, A., and DeSanto, B. (2005). What do communication managers do? Defining and refining the core elements of management in a public relations/corporate communication context. *Journalism & Mass Communication Quarterly, 82*(4), 873–890.

Parker, K. and Igielnik, R. (2020, 14 May). On the cusp of adulthood and facing an uncertain future: What we know about Gen Z so far. Pew Research Center. https://www.pewresearch.org/social-trends/2020/05/14/on-the-cusp-of-adulthood-and-facing-an-uncertain-future-what-we-know-about-gen-z-so-far-2/.

Picazo-Vela, S., Gutiérrez-Martínez, I., and Luna-Reyes, L. F. (2012). Understanding risks, benefits, and strategic alternatives of social media applications in the public sector. *Government Information Quarterly, 29*(4), 504–511.

Samaha, S. A. and Palmatier, R. W. (2015). Anti-relationship marketing: Understanding relationship-destroying behaviors. In R. Morgan, J. Turner Parish, and G. Deitz (eds.), *Handbook on research in relationship marketing* (pp. 268–300). Cheltenham, UK and Northampton, MA, USA: Edward Elgar Publishing.

Sandman, P. M. (2006). Crisis communication best practices: Some quibbles and additions. *Journal of Applied Communication Research, 34*(3), 257–262.

Schick, S. (2020). What the Mondelez 'Humaning' approach fails to achieve from a CX standpoint. *360 Magazine,* 25 November. https://360magazine.com/2020/11/25/what-the-mondelez-humaning-approach-fails-to-achieve-from-a-cx-standpoint/.

Seltzer, T. and Lee, N. (2018). The influence of distal antecedents on organization-public relationships. *Journal of Public Relations Research, 30*(5-6), 230–250.

Seltzer, T. and Zhang, W. (2010). Toward a model of political organization-public relationships: Antecedent and cultivation strategy influence on citizens' relationships with political parties. *Journal of Public Relations Research, 23*(1), 24–45.

Slabbert, Y. B. and Barker, R. (2014). Towards a new model to describe the organization-stakeholder relationship (OSR) building process: A strategic corporate communication perspective. *Communicatio: South African Journal for Communication Theory and Research, 40*(1), 69–97.

Strömbäck, J. and Kiousis, S. (2011). Political public relations: Defining and mapping an emergent field. In J. Strömbäck and S. Kiousis (eds.), *Political public relations: Principles and applications* (pp. 1–32). London: Routledge.

Sung, K. H. and Kim, S. (2018). Do organizational personification and personality matter? The effect of interaction and conversational tone on relationship quality in social media. *International Journal of Business Communication, 58*(4). https://doi.org/10.1177/2329488418796631.

Sweetser, K. D. and Kelleher, T. (2016). Communicated commitment and conversational voice: Abbreviated measures of communicative strategies for maintaining organization-public relationships. *Journal of Public Relations Research*, *28*(5–6), 217–231.

Tsai, W. S. and Men, L. R. (2017). Social CEOs: The effects of CEOs' communication styles and parasocial interaction on social networking sites. *New Media & Society*, *19*(11), 1848–1867.

Valentini, C. (2015). Is using social media "good" for the public relations profession? A critical reflection. *Public Relations Review*, *41*(2), 170–177.

Yang, A. and Taylor, M. (2015). Looking over, looking out, and moving forward: Positioning public relations in theorizing organizational network ecologies. *Communication Theory*, *25*(1), 91–115.

Yang, S. U. (2007). An integrated model for organization–public relational outcomes, organizational reputation, and their antecedents. *Journal of Public Relations Research*, *19*(2), 91–121.

Yuan, S. and Lou, C. (2020). How social media influencers foster relationships with followers: The roles of source credibility and fairness in parasocial relationship and product interest. *Journal of Interactive Advertising*, *20*(2), 133–147.

Yue, C. A. (2021). Creating organizational authenticity and identification: Effect of leaders' motivating language and impact on employee advocacy. *International Journal of Business Communication*. https://doi.org/10.1177/23294884211035116.

Yue, C. A., Chung, Y. J., Kelleher, T., Bradshaw, A. S., and Ferguson, M. A. (2021a). How CEO social media disclosure and gender affect perceived CEO attributes, relationship investment, and engagement intention. *Journalism & Mass Communication Quarterly*, *98*(4), 1157–1180.

Yue, C. A., Qin, Y. S., Vielledent, M., Men, L. R., and Zhou, A. (2021b). Leadership going social: How US nonprofit executives engage publics on Twitter. *Telematics and Informatics*, *65*. https://doi.org/10.1016/j.tele.2021.101710.

Zhou, A. (2019). Bring publics back into networked public relations research: A dual-projection approach for network ecology. *Public Relations Review*, *45*(4), 101772.

Zhou, A. and Xu, S. (2021). Digital public relations through the lens of affordances: A conceptual expansion of the dialogic principles. *Journal of Public Relations Research*, *33*(6), 445–463.

Zhou, A. and Xu, S. (2022). Computer mediation vs. dialogic communication: How media affordances affect organization-public relationship building. *Public Relations Review*, *48*(2), 102176.

9. Digital corporate communication and measurement and evaluation

Sophia C. Volk and Alexander Buhmann

INTRODUCTION

It is undisputed that digitalization and technological changes will have a lasting impact on corporate communication. Despite the evolving debates in research and practice, the question remains as to how the challenges and opportunities associated with digital transformation can be successfully implemented in corporate communication. One area where digital technologies, methods, and tools can offer significant advances is measurement and evaluation (M&E). M&E has been a cornerstone of the strategic management of corporate communication for decades (Buhmann et al., 2018; Volk, 2016). The recent rise of digital communication formats (for example, social media, virtual reality, social intranets, chat bots, or digital annual reports) continues to challenge traditional practices in the evaluation of corporate communication (Weiner and Kochhar, 2016). With advances brought by artificial intelligence and machine learning to automate M&E analyses, and a boom in technology providers, many avenues for innovation in M&E of digital corporate communication are opening up. In addition, the increase in digitalized processes in organizations, such as digital workflows, virtual collaboration, or video-conferencing, offers new approaches for the strategic management of communication, but also requires appropriate methods for evaluating efficiency and performance.

This chapter examines how digitalization is changing M&E and what remains the same. Digitalization is understood as a socio-technical process, in which digital information and communication technologies, such as software, platforms, information systems, or devices, are integrated into processes, structures, capabilities, and products and thus become part of the infrastructure (Brennen and Kreiss, 2016; Tilson et al., 2010). In the organizational context, the increasing use of disruptive digital technologies is seen as an important lever for far-reaching changes that alter, threaten, replace, or complement existing rules, values, structures, practices, or business models, often discussed under the term *digital transformation* (Nadkarni and Prügl, 2021). Digital transformation and the increase in digital platforms and social media also have consequences for the communication of organizations, which itself is becoming more digital and digitalized (Verčič et al., 2015). Digital corporate communication in this chapter is defined as "an organization's strategic management of digital technologies, digital infrastructures and digitalization processes to improve communication with internal and external stakeholders and more broadly within society for the maintenance of organizational tangible and intangible assets" (Badham and Luoma-aho, Chapter 1 in this volume, p. 9).

In addressing the question of how digitalization changes M&E of digital corporate communication, this chapter looks at two levels. First, at the *activities level* of digital corporate communication products, campaigns, or programs. Second, at the *administrative level* of the functions, departments, and individuals who develop, manage, and execute digital corporate communication activities. To systematically address M&E of corporate communication, the conceptual framework by Buhmann and Likely (2018) is adapted below, which (a) visualizes the key units and stages of M&E, (b) connects them to the basic management cycle, and (c) distinguishes three foundational forms of evaluation. Next, this chapter discusses opportunities and challenges as well as directions for reconsidering M&E practices in a digitalized world. First, the chapter examines the *M&E of digital corporate communication* (at the activities level) and posits that M&E practices experience a shift from largely summative, retrospective evaluation to the use of digital technologies for real time and 'intelligent' monitoring, which in turn enables data-based communication planning and strategizing. Second, it reflects on the *M&E of digital corporate communication management* (at the administrative level), which includes, for example, the evaluation of digitalization processes within corporate communication and aligns to an understanding of M&E as a pillar of strategic management.

Finally, the chapter discusses the societal, ethical, legal, organizational, and individual challenges related to a proliferation of digital approaches in the M&E of corporate communication and presents a case study on its implementation in practice. Directions for research and implications for M&E practice conclude this chapter.

DEFINITIONS OF M&E AND PREVIOUS RESEARCH

Basic Concepts and Terminology

Debates in the research field of M&E address the question of how the effects and impact of corporate communication can be measured and how the success of communication can be evaluated with regard to defined goals (Buhmann and Volk, 2022; Stacks, 2017; Watson and Noble, 2014). The terms measurement and evaluation are often used alongside one another and sometimes interchangeably (Macnamara and Likely, 2017). While *evaluation* is understood as the systematic assessment of the value of an object, *measurement* comprises the collection and analysis of data as an important part of such value assessments (Buhmann and Likely, 2018). To this end, quantitative and qualitative social science research methods (such as surveys, content analyses, observations) are used. This is done with *research instruments* (such as standardized questionnaires, codebooks, or semi-structured interview guides for focus groups) that generate quantitative or qualitative data which can inform communication evaluators on performance indicators to compare targets and actual results (target-performance comparison). *Indicators* that aggregate critical and strategically relevant information in a single result are called *key performance indicators* (KPIs) (Van Ruler and Körver, 2019). For the M&E of corporate communication, in addition to social science research methods, business management methods (e.g., process analysis, budget analysis, competency analysis) (Volk and Zerfass, 2020) and computational approaches (e.g., web scraping, API-based data collection, data mining, topic modelling, natural language processing, big data analytics, etc.) are used for data collection and analysis of business processes or large amounts of data.

Within the concept of evaluation, the root term *value* signals the necessity to define and explain what the value of corporate communication is, prior to any measurement and value assessments. Four generic and interrelated value dimensions can be distinguished (Zerfass and Viertmann, 2017).

Corporate communication

1. enables operations, as it raises publicity, attention, customer preferences, and employee commitment and, thus, keeps the organization running and ensures immediate success in terms of primary objectives;
2. builds intangible values, as it fosters reputation, brands, and corporate culture and, thus, creates the immaterial assets that are the basis for sustainable and long-term success;
3. ensures flexibility, as it builds relationships, trust, and legitimacy and, thus, secures the organization's license to operate and increases its room for manoeuvre;
4. adjusts strategy, as it monitors the organization's environment, thus increasing the reflective capacities of strategic management decisions. This helps secure thought leadership, innovation potential, and crisis resilience.

Further, according to the distinction between the level of *activities* on the one hand and *administration* on the other hand (cf. introduction), M&E must assess the value added both with regard to messages, channels, campaigns, etc. *as well as* with regard to the structures, practitioners, management systems, processes, etc. that the former activities are based on.

A Framework for M&E of Digital Corporate Communication

M&E in corporate communication can be conceptualized in relation to a basic cycle that consists of four core elements: situation analysis (formative research, needs assessment); planning (strategizing, objective setting, tactical planning); implementation (strategy execution), and *evaluation* to show if objectives were met (accountability) and how they were met (improvement/learning), which may provide feedback for future planning (Figure 9.1).

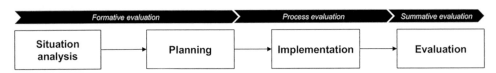

Figure 9.1   The basic management cycle and types of evaluation

Concordant with this basic management cycle, three types of evaluation can be distinguished:

1. *Formative evaluation* (sometimes: formative research) comprises elements of situation analysis and strategic planning and provides intelligence and insight for strategizing. Formative evaluation is a baseline for strategic decision-making and is provided through organizational listening and environmental scanning, e.g., using surveys, focus groups, or media content analysis to identify stakeholder attitudes or channel preferences. In the strategic planning stage, objectives for purposeful communication activities/products, campaigns, and programs are set. Later evaluations are conducted against these objectives.
2. *Process evaluation* (sometimes: monitoring) tracks ongoing activities during strategy implementation and gathers (often in real time) insights on immediate message distribution and reach, audience attention and engagement, or shifts in stakeholder attitudes. This type

focuses on an evaluation of operations and on determining whether processes are 'on track' in relation to predefined targets.

3. *Summative evaluation* determines results, looking at how communication activities or the attempts of their management have met their objectives and are contributing to realizing broader communication and organizational strategy. This type emphasizes feedback for both accountability and learning.

Management processes in practice are, of course, more disordered than this idealized cycle would suggest and usually play out in an iterative fashion. Digital technology especially is rapidly changing a formerly more sequential and stepwise dynamic between different stages of the process and the three M&E types. This is because many digital platforms used for corporate communication (take social networking sites as an example) will allow to measure and evaluate communication in real time, leading not only to more overlap between the different management phases (analysis, planning, implementation, evaluation) but also between the respective types of evaluation. Furthermore, this process can become even more reflexive and iterative in very dynamic contexts of communication such as corporate crises.

Based on the management cycle and the three types of evaluation, we can develop a framework for M&E by distinguishing different M&E stages within the implementation process. A plethora of frameworks and standards has been developed over the past decades (see, e.g., Buhmann et al., 2019; Macnamara, 2018b), partly with very dissimilar approaches and terminologies, but most of them resembling common 'logic models' (Frechtling, 2015). One seminal effort at a standard framework in recent years has been the integrated evaluation framework (IEF) developed by the International Association for the Measurement and Evaluation of Communication (AMEC, 2016), which today exists in more than 20 languages. Other models include, e.g., the British Government Communication Service's Evaluation Framework 2.0. (GCS, 2021) or the German DPRG/ICV model (DPRG/ICV, 2011). A discussion of the different models is beyond the scope of this chapter, but can be found, e.g., in Macnamara (2018a).

Buhmann and Likely (2018) have recently made an effort to align and integrate different M&E frameworks based on a review of existing approaches. Their model distinguishes between five main stages of M&E: inputs, outputs, outtakes, outcomes, and impacts (cf. also Buhmann and Volk, 2022). In the following, we explain each stage and denote alternative labels:

1. *Inputs* comprise the resources needed to prepare and produce communication (e.g., strategic objectives, budget, employee assignment; as such, the inputs stage is the bridge between planning and implementation).
2. *Outputs* comprise the communication that is published and received by the target audiences and can be further distinguished between *primary* outputs (sometimes also referred to as 'activities') (e.g., number of press releases, websites, events, etc.) and *secondary* outputs (e.g., actual media coverage, event attendance, reach, etc.).
3. *Outtakes* (sometimes also referred to as 'direct outcomes') comprise what the target audience *does* with the communication (e.g., shares, likes, recall, attention, etc.).
4. *Outcomes* comprise the effect of communication on the target audience (e.g., knowledge, attitudes, intentions, behaviour, etc.).
5. *Impact* (sometimes also referred to as 'outgrowth') comprises the long-term value created (often only in part) by communication at the organizational level (e.g., reputation, relationships, customer loyalty) or the societal level (e.g., social equity, public trust, justice).

122   *Handbook on digital corporate communication*

In digital corporate communication, especially the stages of outputs and outtakes, but to some degree also outcomes, tend to get a special emphasis due to the increased availability of data. In fact, the stage of outtakes was added to many M&E frameworks as a *consequence* of the popularity of digital platforms, such as social media, and the heightened ability to measure different forms of stakeholder interactions and engagement digitally (e.g., through likes, comments, shares, return visits to websites, etc.).

In line with the prior distinction between the level of communication *activities* on the one hand and the level of *managing and administering* such activities on the other, two basic clusters of evaluation objects can be distinguished:

- At the level of *communication activities*, units of assessment can be distinguished according to their level of aggregation, ranging from: individual products (evaluated rather in the short term according to, e.g., distribution, reach, tonality, or likes), to campaigns (evaluated in the short- and mid-term with an emphasis on campaign engagement and outcomes such as attitude change), to entire programs, i.e., 'bundles' of campaigns (evaluated across the whole range of implementation, reaching all the way to the long-term impacts on organizational or even societal value creation). As such, these units of assessment are 'nested' (communication products are elements of campaigns, which in turn are part of larger programs). The level of complexity and the time horizon (short-, medium-, and long-term) of M&E thus increases with each unit and therefore requires different levels of aggregation and combination of methods, measurements, and KPIs.
- At the level of *managing and administering* communication activities, units of assessment can be distinguished between the level of individual units (such as communication practitioners, but also processes, systems or tools) and the level of the communication function (comprising the aggregation of all the former individual units charged with managing communication across the organization, not limited to an individual department).

The above discussion can be visually summarized in an integrated framework that relates the basic management cycle to (a) the three types of evaluation (formative, process, and summative; with a tendency to move from a more sequential to a 'real-time' practice), (b) the five stages of M&E during implementation (inputs – outputs – outtakes – outcomes – impact), and (c) the five units of assessment at the level of both communication activities and their administration (Figure 9.2).

WHAT IS CHANGING?

The changes brought about by the digitalization have important implications for the field of corporate communication: On the one hand, the media usage patterns of stakeholders have changed tremendously in recent years, as mobile and digital consumption have long since overtaken traditional analogue media consumption (Newman et al., 2022), creating many more digital traces that can be analysed and used for targeting audiences. On the other hand, the number of channels, voices, and platforms has increased, and technological and methodological advances in computerized analyses of large amounts of data have occurred. This opens new opportunities for *real-time measurement* (data collection and data analysis) and *real-time use of evaluation insights* for learning and strategic planning.

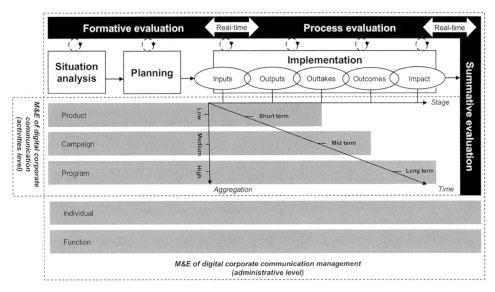

Source: Adapted from Buhmann and Likely (2018).

Figure 9.2   A framework of M&E in digital corporate communication

In what follows, we first discuss what is changing for (1) *M&E of digital corporate communication* (activities level) and then reflect on (2) the *M&E of digital corporate communication management* (administrative level).

M&E of Digital Corporate Communication

The M&E of digital corporate communication must, of course, first and foremost expand with a view to the increased variety of new communication channels and cross-platform interactions, ranging from social media, influencer communication to chat bots. Beyond this, however, there are more profound changes in the digital age that relate to data collection, data analysis, and the use of data (Wiencierz and Röttger, 2019).

First, at the level of *data collection*, there is a growing availability of free and paid tools and technologies for in-house data collection as well as a growing market of data collection vendors and third-party data brokers. A recent systematization lists more than 9,000 tools available in MarTech (Brinker, 2022), otherwise known as 'marketing technology', of which many are also applicable in corporate communication or 'CommTech' (Arthur Page Society, 2021). These tools can be used for the M&E of outputs, outtakes, and outcomes generated on corporate websites or social media channels (Weiner, 2021). What distinguishes M&E of digital communication from more traditional evaluation methods, such as media response analysis, is that data is collected in real-time and that the process is increasingly automated, for example, through scraping. Moreover, in the digital age, it is much easier to link digital data trails collected at various stakeholder touch points with the organization (e.g., search histories, web tracing data, app data, location data, likes, shares, etc.) to individual stakeholders, i.e., to capture personalized data (Mai, 2016). Collecting such real-time and networked data

124 *Handbook on digital corporate communication*

allows systematic (social) listening and intelligent monitoring (Zhang and Vos, 2014), which is increasingly important in the age of disinformation, crises and consumer-generated content, as organizations struggle to retain control over their own communication in algorithmically curated media environments (Macnamara, 2020). Of course, access to data in real-time does not improve M&E per se, but also requires new ways of analysing big data.

Second, at the level of *data analysis*, the most important advances for M&E concern recent technological and methodological developments in data sciences, computer linguistics (such as semantic analysis), and business intelligence. The increasing sophistication of computerized research methods, automation, and artificial intelligence (AI) nowadays enable organizations to analyse large amounts of data in an efficient, fast, reliable, and timely way (Vogler and Meissner, 2022). AI here refers to a machine's ability to produce results for a task that are indistinguishable from the results achieved by a human agent (Corea, 2019; Buhmann and Gregory, Chapter 20 in this volume). In corporate communication, it involves the use of supervised or unsupervised machine learning or deep learning to analyse large text corpora. Automatized text analyses based on AI can be used, for instance, to examine sentiments of user comments on corporate social media, tonality, and share of voice in online media articles, or transcripts of stakeholder interviews or focus groups. Predictive analytics or modelling, already widely used in the retail sector, enables digital corporate communication M&E to find patterns in big data and make predictions on future stakeholder behaviour based on stakeholders' personalized data collected (Gandomi and Haider, 2015). However, predictions based on such data also require new statistical approaches, since basic assumptions in the social sciences, e.g., about normal distributions and generalizability, do not hold, as data on the entire (Internet) population are impossible to collect (Lazer et al., 2021). Visual analytics help to facilitate the representation of data in graphs, heat maps, charts, etc. so that decision makers can more easily make sense of large amounts of data. Real-time dashboards are often used to make the insights of M&E accessible and visible in a 'dense' form focused on a small number of KPIs (Zerfass and Volk, 2019). A major challenge remains, however, the need to verify and scrutinize the validity and reliability of automated text analysis or sentiment detection, as well as of predictions based on data. The core problem is that the data sources that can be used for predictions are usually not created specifically for this purpose, and are in their raw or unprocessed form often messy, sometimes inaccurate, or even faked (Stieglitz et al., 2018). For example, unlike survey responses, data obtained through tracking or mobile sensing was not designed for research purposes. Therefore, intensive data cleansing and maintenance and 'data hygiene' are essential to gaining meaningful insights. Moreover, procedures must be developed to distinguish between human and computer-generated communication, e.g., to identify fake followers or bots from real social media users, which is likely to become a more important use case in the age of disinformation.

Table 9.1 presents an overview of common methods for the collection and analysis of data as well as KPIs used for the M&E of digital corporate communication. Each column lists available methods and KPIs in *alphabetical* order. Meanwhile, as mentioned, there are countless technology providers for implementation; among the most popular are Google Analytics, Hootsuite, Talkwalker, as well as social media platforms' own analytics toolkits such as Facebook Insights, Instagram Insights or LinkedIn analytics.

Third, at the level of *data usage*, the major change is that real-time data and insights can also be incorporated into ongoing campaigns and real-time digital content creation. This goes beyond the rationale of traditional summative M&E that uses such insights at the end of cam-

Digital corporate communication and measurement and evaluation   125

Table 9.1   Digital KPIs for M&E in digital corporate communication

Level	Methods	Digital KPIs
Outputs	● Observation, netnography (e.g., online events) ● Online media content analysis ● Online touchpoint analysis ● Social media tracking ● Website tracking	*Primary outputs* ● Number of activities (e.g., social media posts, digital campaigns, digital press conferences, etc.) *Secondary outputs* ● Online media coverage volume ● Online media share of voice ● Social media reach ● Click-through rate, open rate ● Virtual event attendance ● Website visits, impressions
Outtakes	● Sentiment analysis ● Social media tracking and analysis ● Surveys ● Website tracking	● Attention ● Awareness ● Downloads ● Online tonality, sentiment ● Recall (aided/unaided) ● Recognition ● Mentions (tags, brand, organization) ● Engagement (e.g., likes, shares, comments)
Outcomes	● Focus groups, interviews ● Observation, netnography ● Online surveys (e.g., customers), public opinion polls ● Social media analysis	● Attitude (e.g., trust, acceptance) ● Behaviour / conversion rate (e.g., buying, donating) ● Intention (to buy, to recommend) ● Knowledge ● Learning ● Preference (e.g., brands)

paign implementations. The process of systematically recording, classifying, and relating data to individual stakeholders and thereby creating personalized profiles is known as algorithmic *profiling* (Büchi et al., 2021). Although stakeholder mapping has been used for decades, digital data opens up new opportunities for corporate communication to (micro)segment different stakeholder groups in a very fine-grained manner and substantiate the identified segments with granular data collected in other parts of the organization (e.g., sales or CRM: stakeholders' user profiles, purchase behaviours, psychological traits, age, location, health, private interests, etc.) (Matz and Netzer, 2017). This allows the creation of content and messages tailored to very specific stakeholder groups (e.g., potential or current customers, journalists, social media followers) in near real-time. To this end, organizations make increasing use of *microtargeting*, which is a major trend in political and commercial marketing (White and Boatwright, 2020). In other words, corporate communication can target different stakeholders with unique content, rather than disseminating one-size-fits-all messages to larger stakeholder groups. This allows a more efficient allocation of budgets for digital communication according to predicted outcomes for specific stakeholders and micro segments and could be a means for more intensive stakeholder engagement and co-creation of content in the long term.

M&E of Digital Corporate Communication Management

In addition to the M&E of communication activities, a second area facing the changes of digitalization is the M&E of the management or administrative level of communication. While the former concerns primarily the output, outtake, and outcome stages, the latter particularly involves the input and impact stages. For the *M&E of digital corporate communication management*, perhaps the most pressing question is the extent to which processes, structures, and management approaches in communication teams, divisions, or entire departments have been digitalized or digitally transformed (see Zerfass and Brockhaus, Chapter 17 in this volume; see also Zerfass and Brockhaus, 2021). M&E does not have to reinvent the wheel but can adapt new evaluation methods and approaches for assessing digitalization processes from digital controlling (e.g., Keimer and Egle, 2020), information systems, business analytics, or human resources and marketing research. At the level of concrete digital processes, for example, process analyses can be used to assess whether digitalized workflows in communication units or teams are efficient and effective when creating content or responding to journalists' queries. Approaches and KPIs to evaluating the digital maturity of structures and routines can be adapted to assess and benchmark the digital transformation of entire communication departments. By doing so, new opportunities open up for institutionalizing a broader understanding of M&E not only at the level of communication activities, but as a strategic pillar of corporate management.

WHAT REMAINS THE SAME?

Against the manifold changes brought by digitalization, the question inevitably arises as to what remains the same in M&E conceptualizations, methods, and practices. While especially data collection and data analysis operate under fundamentally changed conditions through digitalization, a more stable sphere in M&E may be that of the underlying/preceding building of evaluation frameworks as well as that of data use, especially at the managerial and administrative level.

Regarding the underlying M&E framework, setting up M&E for digital corporate communication can still rely on the established best practices in terms of the core dimensions to consider, i.e., types, stages, units of analysis. Here the fundamentals of building a consistent M&E framework based on 'logic models' and established communication M&E standards still prevail – see section 'A framework for M&E of digital corporate communication' above. Such standards of remaining relevance include those developed and proposed within the Barcelona Declaration of Measurement Principles, first launched in 2010 and updated in 2015 and 2020 (AMEC, 2010; AMEC, 2020; Buhmann et al., 2019): (1) setting goals and measurable objectives, (2) identifying outputs, outcomes, and potential impact, (3) identifying outcomes and impact at the level of the organization *and* its environment, (4) including both qualitative and quantitative analyses, (5) not considering 'advertising value equivalence' (AVE) as a measure of the value of communication, (6) including all relevant online and offline channels, and (7) fostering integrity and transparency to drive learning and insights.

With its strong emphasis on the importance of setting goals and objectives derived from core organizational value drivers (see section on 'Definitions of M&E and previous research' above) M&E (digital or not) needs to centre around what an organization is trying to achieve. This means operationalizing M&E based on a consistent framework as well as upon objectives that are relevant to organizational strategy *and* can be used to evaluate in a meaningful way, i.e., SMART objectives. SMART means that objectives operationalize an organization's more abstract strategic goals and visions of success in a *specific* and *measurable* manner, and they are set to be *achievable* and *relevant* (so that they may effectively motivate and engage employees), as well as *time-bound* to state concretely by which date an outcome should be achieved. The emphasis on SMART objective-setting as a necessary prerequisite to M&E is all the more important in a digital age, where indicators (regardless of their organizational goal relevance) are relatively readily available and often less costly to collect – and this availability depends much less on distinct planning on behalf of the communicator. This goes to show that where M&E practices link up with more general strategic efforts of (communication) management, digital developments are not fundamentally changing best practices – a best practice that is all about the contribution of M&E efforts to corporate strategy and, ultimately, to organizational value creation (Gilkerson et al., 2019).

In a similar vein and before the backdrop of the permanent burgeoning of new digital measures especially at the output and outtakes stages, digital corporate communication retains a strong need to focus M&E on the outcome and impact levels that are less about communication per se and more about communication's effects on stakeholder's attitudes and behaviour or even business results. There remains a strong need for education when it comes to developing M&E capabilities in corporate communication at the outcome and impact levels (Zerfass et al., 2017), paralleled by a need to further advance professional standards that can build normative pressure among practitioners to move towards more sophisticated M&E (Buhmann and Brønn, 2018).

Further, it is exactly at this crucial junction of M&E and management that we see the remaining importance of building and securing strong in-house competencies for M&E. This is necessary to build bridges between an ever-increasing availability of data on the one hand, and the constant necessity to align communication activities with the emergent process of organizational value creation (e.g., strategy development and implementation) on the other (Volk and Zerfass, 2018). Such in-house competencies, if strong, will also build a solid basis on which to critically assess the value of ever new digital ways to collect, analyse, and use data.

Finally, some other aspects of M&E may indeed remain the same where offline communication (e.g., face-to-face stakeholder dialogues, such as town halls, or physical press conferences and other PR events) or distinctly 'physical settings' are still key to developing valid insights and driving communication value. Here, more traditional 'pre-digital' M&E approaches will keep their relevance. This applies, for instance, for the role of qualitative insights generated through face-to-face focus groups (i.e., in the situational analysis/planning phases) or interviews with physical event participants (i.e., during and after the implementation phase).

CRITICAL EXAMINATION

Digitalization brings major changes for advanced data collection, data analysis, and predictions based on data and not only presents prospects for the M&E of corporate communication, but also raises several ethical, normative, and legal issues. These are, however, still little discussed in the corporate communication and public relations literature (Bourne and Edwards, 2021; Duhé, 2015; Valentini, 2015; Yang and Kang, 2015). Empirical research of the practices of M&E in corporate communication has a long tradition (e.g., Macnamara et al., 2017; Wright et al., 2009; Zerfass et al., 2017), but only recently have scholars started to address the question of how digital innovations – such as AI, big data, or automation – reshape practices in

128   *Handbook on digital corporate communication*

corporate communication from the perspective of practitioners (e.g., Buhmann and Gregory, Chapter 20 in this volume, Bajalia, 2020; Wiencierz and Röttger, 2017; Wiesenberg et al., 2017; Zerfass et al., 2020). Although most empirical studies do not explicitly relate to M&E practices, but rather general developments in digital communication, they do offer insights into the ethical and practical challenges opening up for digital M&E. We distinguish three levels to critically reflect on M&E in the context of digital corporate communication: the societal level (macro level), the organizational level (meso level), and the individual (M&E practitioner) level (micro level).

At the macro level, corporations' use of personalized stakeholder data for profiling raises legal, societal, and ethical concerns with regard to maintaining individuals' data privacy (Gregory and Halff, 2020) and is critically discussed under such terms as dataveillance (Van Dijck, 2014) or surveillance capitalism (White and Boatwright, 2020; Zuboff, 2015). Especially the use of microtargeting, e.g., for corporate or political campaigns, and algorithm-based communication is met with fears of spurring democratic challenges related to political polarization and digital inequalities and contributing to the fragmentation of the public sphere and the creation of echo chambers (e.g., Barocas, 2012). In addition, the increasing processing of big data and related energy consumption also has ecological implications and challenges pathways to sustainable corporate practices.

At the meso level, corporations must face the question of how to use the new opportunities brought about by digitalization in a responsible, accountable, and moral way, not least because the unwitting exploitation of stakeholder data could damage the relations with customers, employees, or the public (Valentini, 2015). Corporations as a whole and their communication departments also face challenges of setting up efficient structures and routines for data management and governance (Fitzpatrick and Weissman, 2021). Building in-house architectures and intelligence could be a remedy to minimize the dependency on platforms such as Meta (Facebook), Alphabet (Google), or Microsoft and data vendors for data collection. For the positioning of corporate communication departments, there is a risk of lagging behind or being booed by developments in automated marketing and MarTech, if opportunities for innovations in M&E of digital communication are overlooked.

At the micro level, the increasing use of digital technologies and tools can pose risks for the well-being of individual M&E practitioners: Collecting, analysing, interpreting, visualizing, and making sense of data require lots of time, personnel resources, and new competencies. While practitioners do not need to become expert technologists (Galloway and Swiatek, 2018), lacking competencies may be a source of digital stress or information overload, and could be a severe barrier to the implementation of new technologies or tools for M&E.

Against this backdrop, implementing digital technologies driven by AI and machine learning for M&E of digital corporate communication (to support data collection, analysis, or use) necessitates *ethical reflections* on consequences at the micro, meso, and macro level. Recent reviews on 'ethical AI' (cf. Buhmann et al., 2020), show that AI implementation may raise three interrelated types of concerns, which also relate to the field of M&E.

First, the use of AI for M&E may raise *evidence concerns* about how systems convert vast data into 'insights' (which form the basis of a system's decisions). AI-powered tools for M&E may rely on data that is inconclusive (i.e., decisions will be based on patterns that are artefacts of data), or misguided (i.e., decisions will be based on inadequate inputs, such as data that is sensitive, incomplete, or incorrect).

Digital corporate communication and measurement and evaluation   129

Second, the use of AI in M&E may raise *outcome concerns*, meaning these systems' recommendations and decisions might be wrong and harmful. When the use of digital technologies fails their intended goals, these tools may lead to false assessments and ultimately wrong business decisions. Such harm may be direct, e.g., when tactical decisions are based on false evaluations provided by AI. They may also emerge as indirect and long-term impacts that come with the application of AI more generally, e.g., when AI-powered tools become highly embedded in the strategy building process and their false assessments influence the development of communication departments or organizations in the long-run.

Third, digital technologies powered by AI may raise *epistemic concerns* through their poor transparency (also referred to as 'AI opacity') (Burrell, 2016). The self-learning capacity and a relative autonomy of AI-powered tools for M&E can make it difficult for corporate communication practitioners to evaluate the workings of these systems themselves. For example, How are data inputs processed? How does data processing lead to particular assessments and outputs of the system? The potentially decreased ability to provide straightforward explanations about the data collection, analysis, or use of AI-powered tools, highlights the need for AI literacy of communicators – especially in a field like M&E, which will likely see a relatively swift uptake of AI and supplanting of activities that have previously been performed by professionals (Virmani and Gregory, 2021).

CASE STUDY: UNICEF'S MEASUREMENT FRAMEWORK

Against the backdrop of the changes brought about by digitalization and their critical examination, this chapter now addresses the question as to how M&E is used responsibly and purposefully in practice. An illustrative example of the successful use of digital technologies for the timely and partially automated M&E of digital corporate communication comes from UNICEF.

A global welfare organization under the umbrella of the United Nations, founded in 1946, UNICEF operates in over 190 countries to improve the well-being of children. One of its cornerstones is the use of rigorous research and thoughtful analysis about the situation of children in order to make evidence-based decisions. Driven by the conviction that analysing performance and distilling insights from listening is essential to strengthening UNICEF's communication, the highly decentralized organization developed a global M&E approach in 2017, which has been implemented in regional and local offices in more than 60 countries and all seven regional offices (AMEC, n.d.). The UNICEF communication measurement framework was developed to evaluate the local implementation of global objectives – in other words, the 'glocal impact' – of UNICEF's communication and advocacy efforts and has been featured as a best practice case study on the AMEC website. The UNICEF Division of Communication in New York centrally monitors metrics at the global level and supports country offices to adapt the M&E framework to local demands and media contexts. At the global level, the Division of Communication uses a wide range of digital technologies and tools for M&E such as LexisNexis Newsdesk as a media aggregator, Factiva for archival media searches, TVEyes for broadcast media aggregator, Talkwalker for social media listening, or TrendKite as a user-friendly dashboard. Typical KPIs include media reach, digital reach, (online) share of voice, audience engagement, or brand awareness. Data is collected in real-time and in six languages (English, French, Spanish, Arabic, Chinese, and Russian). Automated daily alerts

130　*Handbook on digital corporate communication*

help to identify, coordinate, and respond to potential issues in a timely manner. Automated analysis is combined with human analysis of a random sample of 500 clips/month to validate sentiments and tonality, for example. Insights are presented in the form of in-house snapshot reports, weekly reports, or quarterly reports, which provide senior management with the opportunity to record insights rapidly and use them to identify opportunities for improvement and to develop forward looking strategies.

In retrospect, implementation of the M&E framework has given UNICEF leadership a clearer picture of how digital communication activities resonate with the public and has strengthened its position as the leading advocate for children in terms of reach and engagement. An important prerequisite is an organizational culture that values learning, experimentation, measurement, and innovation. This was part of UNICEF's digital transformation strategy, which began with investments in staff digital skills, digital infrastructure, and technology, and expanded its intelligence gathering and capacity building for systematic listening (UNICEF, n.d.).

CONCLUSION AND FUTURE DIRECTIONS

Against the background of the critical examination, it has already become apparent that many unanswered questions remain to be tackled by scholars and practitioners in the field of M&E (cf. Volk and Buhmann, 2019). In the future, research in the field of digital corporate communication should focus primarily on the question of what conditions as well as positive and negative consequences are associated with the digitalization of M&E practices from the perspective of corporate communication departments, M&E practitioners, and society. Both empirical research, conceptual work and critical approaches are needed to better understand these aspects and to shed light on the ethical implications of M&E in the digital age. In addition, interdisciplinary approaches that link literature from fields such as data science, computer linguistics, digital marketing, and digital controlling are desirable to provide insights and cross-fertilization on the path to digitalization of M&E of corporate communication. Increased collaboration between science and practice could offer particularly fruitful insights into organizational requirements for the further digitalization of M&E at the level of structures, process, cultures, competencies, and technologies. As communication professionals face ever new challenges related to the technological innovations of digitalization, such as data security and data management, continuous learning and improvement will become key in the future. This also includes ethical training of practitioners (Bourne and Edwards, 2021) and catching up with developments in neighbouring fields such as data science.

REFERENCES

AMEC (n.d.). UNICEF's communication measurement framework – four years of 'global impact' for children. https://amecorg.com/case-study/unicefs-communication-measurement-framework-four -years-of-glocal-impact-for-children/.
AMEC (2016). *AMEC Integrated Evaluation Framework*. https://amecorg.com/amecframework/de/ framework/interactive-framework/.
AMEC (2020). *Barcelona Principles 3.0*. https://amecorg.com/barcelona-principles-3-0-translations/.

AMEC (2010). *Barcelona Declaration of Measurement Principles.* http://amecorg.com/2012/06/barcelona-declaration-of-measurement-principles.

Arthur W. Page Society (2021). *ComTech Guide.* https://commtechguide.page.org/getting-started-incommtech-from-professional-to-pathfinder/a-new-profession-emerges/.

Bajalia, A. (2020). Where are we now? Public relations professionals discuss measurement and evaluation. *Public Relations Journal, 13*(2).

Barocas, S. (2012). The price of precision: Voter micro-targeting and its potential harms to the democratic process. In *Proceedings of the first edition workshop on Politics, elections and data, Conference on Information and Knowledge Management* (pp. 31–36). https://doi.org/10.1145/2389661.2389671.

Bourne, C. and Edwards, L. (2021). Critical reflections on the field. In C. Valentini (ed.), *Public Relations* (pp. 601–614). Berlin: De Gruyter Mouton.

Brennen, J. S. and Kreiss, D. (2016). Digitalization. In K. B. Jensen, E. W. Rothenbuhler, J. D. Pooley, and R. T. Craig (eds.), *The international encyclopedia of communication theory and philosophy* (pp. 556–566). Hoboken, NJ: John Wiley & Sons.

Brinker, S. (2022). Marketing technology landscape 2022. https://chiefmartec.com/2022/05/marketing-technology-landscape-2022-search-9932-solutions-on-martechmap-com/

Büchi, M., Fosch-Villaronga, E., Lutz, C., Tamò-Larrieux, A., and Velidi, S. (2021). Making sense of algorithmic profiling: User perceptions on Facebook. *Information, Communication & Society.* https://doi.org/10.1080/1369118X.2021.1989011.

Buhmann, A. and Brønn, P. S. (2018). Applying Ajzen's theory of planned behavior to predict practitioners' intentions to measure and evaluate communication outcomes. *Corporate Communications: An International Journal, 23*(3), 377–391.

Buhmann, A. and Likely, F. (2018). Evaluation and measurement in strategic communication. In R. L. Heath and W. Johansen (eds.), *The international encyclopedia of strategic communication* (vol. 1, pp. 625–640). Malden, MA: Wiley-Blackwell.

Buhmann, A., Likely, F., and Geddes, D. (2018). Communication evaluation and measurement: Connecting research to practice. *Journal of Communication Management, 22*(1), 113–119.

Buhmann, A., Macnamara, J., and Zerfass, A. (2019). Reviewing the 'march to standards' in public relations: A comparative analysis of four seminal measurement and evaluation initiatives. *Public Relations Review, 45*(4), 101825.

Buhmann, A., Paßmann, J., and Fieseler, C. (2020). Managing algorithmic accountability: Balancing reputational concerns, engagement strategies, and the potential of rational discourse. *Journal of Business Ethics, 163*(2), 265–280.

Buhmann, A. and Volk, S. C. (2022). Measurement and evaluation: Framework, methods, and critique. In J. Falkheimer and M. Heide (eds.), *Research handbook on strategic communication* (pp. 475–489). Cheltenham, UK and Northampton, MA, USA: Edward Elgar Publishing.

Burrell, J. (2016). How the machine 'thinks': Understanding opacity in machine learning algorithms. *Big Data & Society, 3*(1), 1–12.

Corea, F. (2019). AI knowledge map: How to classify AI technologies. In *An introduction to data* (pp. 25–29). Cham: Springer.

DPRG/ICV (Deutsche Public Relations Gesellschaft/International Controller Association) (2011). *Position paper communication controlling.* DPRG/ICV.

Duhé, S. (2015). An overview of new media research in public relations journals from 1981 to 2014. *Public Relations Review, 41*(2), 153–169.

Fitzpatrick, K. R. and Weissman, P. L. (2021). Public relations in the age of data: Corporate perspectives on social media analytics (SMA). *Journal of Communication Management, 25*(4), 401–416.

Frechtling, J. A. (2015). Logic models. In *International encyclopedia of the social & behavioral sciences* (pp. 299–305). Amsterdam: Elsevier.

Galloway, C. and Swiatek, L. (2018). Public relations and artificial intelligence: It's not (just) about robots. *Public Relations Review, 44*(5), 734–740.

Gandomi, A. and Haider, M. (2015). Beyond the hype: Big data concepts, methods, and analytics. *International Journal of Information Management, 35*(2), 137–144.

Gilkerson, N. D., Swenson, R., and Likely, F. (2019). Maturity as a way forward for improving organisations' communication evaluation and measurement practices: A definition and concept explication. *Journal of Communication Management, 23*(3), 246–264.

132 *Handbook on digital corporate communication*

Government Communication Service (GCS) (2021). Evaluation Framework 2.0. https://gcs.civilservice.gov.uk/guidance/evaluation/tools-and-resources.

Gregory, A. and Halff, G. (2020). The damage done by big data-driven public relations. *Public Relations Review, 46*(2), 101902.

Keimer, I. and Egle, U. (2020). *Die Digitalisierung der Controlling-Funktion. Anwendungsbeispiele aus Theorie und Praxis*. Cham: Springer Gabler.

Lazer, D., Hargittai, E., Freelon, D., et al. (2021). Meaningful measures of human society in the twenty-first century. *Nature, 595*, 189–196.

Macnamara, J. (2018a). A review of new evaluation models for strategic communication: Progress and gaps. *International Journal of Strategic Communication, 12*(2), 180–195.

Macnamara, J. (2018b). *Evaluating public communication: Exploring new models, standards, and best practice*. London: Routledge.

Macnamara, J. (2020). *Beyond post-communication: Challenging disinformation, deception, and manipulation*. New York: Peter Lang.

Macnamara, J. and Likely, F. (2017). Revisiting the disciplinary home of evaluation: New perspectives to inform PR evaluation standards. *Research Journal of the Institute for Public Relations, 3*(2), 1–21.

Macnamara, J., Lwin, M. O., Adi, A., and Zerfass, A. (2017). *Asia-Pacific Communication Monitor 2017/18. Strategic challenges, social media and professional capabilities – Results of a survey in 22 countries*. APACD.

Mai, J.-E. (2016). Big data privacy: The datafication of personal information. *The Information Society, 32*(3), 192–199.

Matz, S. C. and Netzer, O. (2017). Using big data as a window into consumers' psychology. *Current Opinion in Behavioral Sciences, 18*, 7–12.

Nadkarni, S. and Prügl, R. (2021). Digital transformation: A review, synthesis and opportunities for future research. *Management Review Quarterly, 71*, 233–341.

Newman, N., Fletcher, R., Robertson, C. T., Eddy, K., and Nielsen, R. K. (2022). *Reuters Institute Digital News Report 2022*. Reuters Institute for the Study of Journalism.

Stacks, D. (2017). *Primer of public relations research* (3rd edition). New York: Guilford Press.

Stieglitz, S., Mirbabaie, M., Ross, B., and Neuberger, C. (2018). Social media analytics – Challenges in topic discovery, data collection, and data preparation. *International Journal of Information Management, 39*, 156–168.

Tilson, D., Lyytinen, K., and Sørensen, C. (2010). Research commentary: Digital infrastructures: The missing IS research agenda. *Information Systems Research, 21*(4), 748–759.

UNICEF (n.d.). Communicate to advocate for every child: UNICEF's Global Communication and Public Advocacy Strategy, 2014–2017. http://amecinternationalsummitstockholm.org/wp-content/uploads/2015/06/UNICEF-Global-Communication-and-Public-Advocacy-Strategy1.pdf.

Valentini, C. (2015). Is using social media 'good' for the public relations profession? A critical reflection. *Public Relations Review, 41*(2), 170–177.

Van Dijck, J. (2014). Datafication, dataism and dataveillance: Big Data between scientific paradigm and ideology. *Surveillance & Society, 12*(2), 197–208.

Van Ruler, B. and Körver, F. (2019). *The communication strategy handbook: Toolkit for creating a winning strategy*. New York: Peter Lang.

Verčič, D., Tkalac Verčič, A., and Sriramesh, K. (2015). Looking for digital in public relations. *Public Relations Review, 41*(2), 142–152.

Virmani, S. and Gregory, A. (2021). *The big data and AI readiness report*. CIPR.

Vogler, D. and Meissner, F. (2022). Tackling the information overload. In *The handbook of crisis communication* (pp. 53–65). John Wiley & Sons.

Volk, S. C. (2016). A systematic review of 40 years of public relations evaluation and measurement research: Looking into the past, the present, and future. *Public Relations Review, 42*(5), 962–977.

Volk, S. C. and Buhmann, A. (2019). New avenues in communication evaluation and measurement (E&M): Towards a research agenda for the 2020s. *Journal of Communication Management, 23*(3), 162–178.

Volk, S. C. and Zerfass, A. (2018). Alignment: Revisiting a key concept in strategic communication. *International Journal of Strategic Communication, 12*(4), 433–451.

Volk, S. C. and Zerfass, A. (2020). Management tools in corporate communications: A survey among practitioners and reflections about the relevance of academic knowledge for practice. *Journal of Communication Management*, *25*(1), 50–67.

Watson, T. and Noble, P. (2014). *Evaluating public relations* (3rd edition). London: Kogan Page.

Weiner, M. (2021). *PR technology, data and insights: Igniting a positive return on your communications investment*. London: Kogan Page.

Weiner, M. and Kochhar, S. (2016). *Irreversible: The public relations big data revolution*. IPR Measurement Commission.

White, C. and Boatwright, B. (2020). Social media ethics in the data economy: Issues of social responsibility for using Facebook for public relations. *Public Relations Review*, *46*(5). https://doi.org/10.1016/j.pubrev.2020.101980.

Wiencierz, C. and Röttger, U. (2017). The use of big data in corporate communication. *Corporate Communications: An International Journal*, *22*(3), 258–272.

Wiencierz, C. and Röttger, U. (2019). Big data in public relations: A conceptual framework. *Public Relations Journal*, *12*(3), 1–15.

Wiesenberg, M., Zerfass, A., and Moreno, A. (2017). Big data and automation in strategic communication. *International Journal of Strategic Communication*, *11*(2), 95–114.

Wright, D., Gaunt, R., Leggetter, B., Daniels, M., and Zerfass, A. (2009). *Global survey of communications measurement 2009 – final report*. AMEC.

Yang, K. C. C. and Kang, Y. (2015). Exploring big data and privacy in strategic communication campaigns: A cross-cultural study of mobile social media users' daily experiences. *International Journal of Strategic Communication*, *9*(2), 87–101.

Zerfass, A. and Brockhaus, J. (2021). Towards a research agenda for CommTech and digital infrastructure in public relations and strategic communication. In B. Birmingham, B. Yook, and Z. F. Chen (eds.), *Contributing at the top and throughout an organisation: Research and strategies that advance our understanding of public relations. Proceedings of the 24th International Public Relations Research Conference* (pp. 202–216). IPRRC.

Zerfass, A., Hagelstein, J., and Tench, R. (2020). Artificial intelligence in communication management: A cross-national study on adoption and knowledge, impact, challenges and risks. *Journal of Communication Management*, *24*, 377–389.

Zerfass, A., Verčič, D., and Volk, S. C. (2017). Communication evaluation and measurement: Skills, practices and utilisation in European organisations. *Corporate Communications: An International Journal*, *22*(1), 2–18.

Zerfass, A. and Viertmann, C. (2017). Creating business value through corporate communication: A theory-based framework and its practical application. *Journal of Communication Management*, *21*(1), 86–91.

Zerfass, A. and Volk, S. C. (2019). *Toolbox communication management: Thinking tools and methods for managing corporate communications*. Cham: Springer Gabler.

Zhang, B. and Vos, M. (2014). Social media monitoring: Aims, methods, and challenges for international companies. *Corporate Communications: An International Journal*, *19*(4), 371–383.

Zuboff, S. (2015). Big other: Surveillance capitalism and the prospects of an information civilization. *Journal of Information Technology*, *30*, 75–89.

PART II

DIGITALLY-INFLUENCED ISSUES AFFECTING ORGANIZATIONS

10. Digital corporate communication and issues management
Laura Illia and Elanor Colleoni

INTRODUCTION

Issues management (IM) has become a priority over time for organizations due to changes in the economy and society. Initially, IM was boosted with the rise of the consumers' economy; that is, when businesses had not only to understand consumers' needs but also to deal with the first consumer associations that were becoming more and more powerful in the non-market landscape. Lately, with the rise of the globalized economy, IM really became a priority for businesses at the global level, since businesses had to learn how to proactively identify and manage timely issues related to the internationalization of their business. It is, however, with the advent of the digital economy that IM has increased in organizational value because actors advocating for or against a business are multiplied, the pressure is higher, and the voices to manage are fragmented given the digital media landscape. Finally, the global Covid-19 pandemic that began in early 2020 has forced organizations to enter into a constant issues management mode.

Accordingly, IM is no longer an option, but a necessity, as it is crucial to learn to proactively and promptly respond to issues, even if the latter are unrelated to organizations. In this landscape, where economic changes and societal crisis influence IM relevance for an organization, it is crucial to understand how to best practise IM today. This chapter provides an overview of the main assumptions to IM in the pre-digital communication era and a comprehensive overview of new relevant assumptions.

DEFINITIONS OF ISSUES MANAGEMENT AND PREVIOUS STUDIES

Issues management (IM) refers to "the strategic use of issues analysis and strategic responses to help organizations make adaptations needed to achieve harmony and foster mutual interests with the communities in which they operate" (Heath, 1997, p. 3). In particular, it focuses on strategic management processes (Mahon et al., 2004) aimed at detecting and responding appropriately to emerging issues in the socio-political environment (Hainsworth and Meng, 1988). In the IM framework, issues represent any sort of social problem that may negatively influence the quality of life of any societal actor, from individuals to institutions (Young and Leonardi, 2012). It is therefore not surprising that IM has risen in importance during the closing decades of the last century, with the highest peak in the 1980s and 1990s, when communication specialists had the main objective of understanding the viewpoints of all parties involved in the organization, including civil society actors such as environmentalists and activist groups of any sort (Balmer and Soenen, 1997).

135

136 *Handbook on digital corporate communication*

Given its orientation to monitoring and mitigating negative outcomes, IM is often considered a synonym of risk management. However, IM differs from it, in that issues identified are not only important emerging risks to monitor or to control but also urgent concerns to be resolved instantly (Gaunt and Ollenburger, 1995). This is why IM, as a discipline, focuses not only on putting in place a good monitoring and control of compliance system as risk management does, but also on strategizing good action plans that help to resolve immediate issues. It therefore focuses on turning a risk into an opportunity for the organization.

Given its orientation to resolving issues in the immediate and putting in place an action plan, IM is often considered an important pre-phase for assuring good crisis management (Regester and Larkin, 2002). However, an IM plan typically focuses on crisis prevention (i.e., being proactive to avoid the crisis from emerging), whereas a crisis management plan focuses on crisis preparation (i.e., being ready for when an issue eventually evolves during a crisis).

Various disciplines (see Table 10.1) have approached questions that are key for IM – such as which issue is most critical and urgent and which stakeholder's voice to address first. Scholars in business and management (e.g., Baron, 1992; Mahon and Waddock, 1992; Zadeck, 2004) have focused on analysing the relationship between business and society, with the final goal to understand how companies can learn from their environment and become a better societal actor (Mahon and Waddock, 1992; Zadeck, 2004). The studies' main interest is to theorize on how organizations can proactively identify issues that are of societal relevance and intrinsic interest to individuals (Baron, 1992), thereby having the potential to attract media coverage and threaten the organization. These studies develop tools that allow organizations to learn from their environment – e.g., the Civil Learning Tool (Zadeck, 2004).

Reputation management scholars (e.g., Eckert, 2017; Fombrun and van Riel, 2004; Knittel and Stango, 2014) focus on developing a comprehensive assessment of what may threaten a corporate reputation (e.g., threats coming from operations, finance, marketing, HR, leadership, among others) in order to identify how weaknesses can be addressed proactively. In particular, their focus is on material issues across the business value chain and also on the identification of the gaps between who the company claims to be (strategy) vs what it actually is (reality) (Fombrun and van Riel, 2004). Reputation risks management is carried out mainly using the enterprise risk management (ERM) system traditionally used by companies to manage all different kinds of risk (Pérez-Cornejo et al., 2019). ERM is defined as "a systematic process that allows the company to identify opportunities and threats for the performance of the entire organization and manages them in a unitary way in order to achieve the objectives of the company" (Regan, 2008, p. 188), and usually comprises five steps (Regan, 2008). The first step requires the definition of a strategy and the outlying of a governance system in which the reputation goals are shared. Once the key internal stakeholders are identified and engaged in the process, the following step consists of the identification of potential threats through an internal audit. Once the risks are identified, they are ranked according to their potential severity and likelihood of occurrence, so as to prioritize them. The final step consists of implementing coherent actions to mitigate the potential damage upstream through preventive actions and downstream through communication response strategies (Coombs, 2007). However, as risks are continuously evolving, the company must continue to monitor the emergence of new risks and periodically reassess the risks.

Studies in corporate communication and public relations (PR) (e.g., Ingenhoff, 2004; Vos et al., 2014) and public affairs and activism (e.g., Heath, 1992) have instead proposed frameworks to study the evolution of issues' lifecycles (e.g., Regester and Larkin, 2002), the prioritization of issues (e.g., Heath, 1997), and the segmentation of institutionalized stakeholders (e.g., Grunig and Repper, 1992) with the final aim of avoiding corporate crises. These studies have concentrated on developing tools and frameworks to analyse issues management processes, professional roles, and management systems that allow the establishment of monitoring systems tracking influential actors around specific socio-political issues (Ingenhoff, 2004).

Table 10.1   Disciplines studying issues management

	Business and management	Reputation management	Corporate communication/affairs
Fundamental questions	Which issue is most critical and urgent for a business?		
	Which stakeholders to prioritize (and engage with) on each issue?		
Focus is on	Any sort of business socio-political issue	Business reputational issues	Any sort of business socio-political issue
Primary areas of interest	Monitoring in CSR, strategy, innovation	Controlling operations, finance, marketing, HR, leadership …	Monitoring issues and stakeholders
Final desired outcome	Organizational learning	Low gap between reality-intention – perception	No crisis
Examples of theoretical frameworks	Stakeholder theory, organization theory, neo-institutional theory	Signalling theory, resource management theory	Agenda setting theory, framing theory

Source: Authors' own elaboration.

WHAT IS CHANGING?

IM in the Digital Communication Era

Undoubtfully, the rise of communication technologies and new media platforms such as Facebook, Twitter, and TikTok have revolutionized the way IM is studied and applied in practice. Even though questions of interest remain fundamentally the same, scholars studying IM do this from the perspective of digital media (e.g., Grüblbauer and Haric, 2013; Ruggiero and Vos, 2014), artificial intelligence and computer science (Buhmann and White, 2022), and cyber-activism and hacking (e.g., Bruns and Burgess, 2011; Hearn et al., 2009; Illia, 2003; McCaughey, 2014; Schrock, 2016), among others. In the digital era, issues not only have a shorter and recursive lifecycle (Illia, 2003); new professional roles also are required (Grüblbauer and Haric, 2013), as well as new conceptual frameworks and methods to prioritize issues and stakeholders (Ruggiero and Vos, 2014). In sum, this new media landscape is forcing IM scholars to reconsider the way stakeholders and societal issues in relation to organizations are studied.

Identification of Stakeholders in the Pre-Digital Communication Era

The study of stakeholders is aimed at proactively segmenting the different groups or individuals that have an interest in the actions of the organization. As Table 10.2 highlights, this research has been dominated by the analysis of institutional actors (market or non-market related ones such as NGOs, suppliers, etc.) with the final aim to pre-emptively build a strategic

138   *Handbook on digital corporate communication*

relationship with audiences having an impact on the organization. The process of engagement and relationship with these audiences is taking place in the long term and is focused on improving the relationship considering the specific "stake" the audience has in the organization. Monitoring systems are oriented to identify each stakeholder's stake and analyse any social evaluation (i.e., reputation, legitimacy, stigma) expressed in the digital sphere, such as sentiment, tone, and interest-opinion.

But while these measures are key to mapping traditional forms of engagement and their audiences, they might not be suited to capture new forms of audiences emerging in the digital landscape. In fact, as previous research has shown (Arvidsson and Caliandro, 2016; Colleoni et al., 2021), new forms of audiences have emerged such as digital collectives (e.g., slacktivists) that are made up of multiple individuals – typically citizens – who have a light form of engagement with the organization. More than having a stake in the organization, these audiences express a temporary interest in the organization which is mainly driven by the general attention around an issue that relates to the organization. In this sense, these audiences express their evaluation and opinion of the organization online in their personal social media networks, satisfying a need for personal publicity (Arvidsson and Caliandro, 2016). As soon as the attention around the event vanishes, they no longer show interest in the organization. This implies that, even if it continues to be key to monitor evaluations by strategic stakeholders through sentiment and tone analysis, it becomes of primary importance to also monitor the communication behaviour of these audiences, investigating what is triggering their reactions, whether they are influenced by someone, or whether they influence others. In the next subsection, key concepts, processes, and practices are highlighted in detail, focusing on stakeholder segmentation before and after the advent of digital communication.

Table 10.2   Changes in stakeholders' segmentation in the digital communication era

	Pre-digital communication	Digitalcommunication
Audience	Institutional actors: NGOs, activist groups, interest groups	Digital collectives: #boycotters, slacktivists
Engagement & relationship	Institutional long term	Light form of engagement
Voices & type of stake	Stake in the company	Personal stake, personal publicity, self-enhancement, identity building
Control & mapping	Stakes of institutional actors	Communication ecosystems
Segmentation variable	Opinions:	Communication behaviour:
	• Sentiment, tone	• Dependence
	• Interests – opinions	• Influence
Expected impact	Segment stakeholders to influence their perception	Engage stakeholders to dialogue with them

Source: Authors' own elaboration.

Pre-Digital: Mapping Stakes of Institutionalized Actors

Following IM principles, an organization willing to segment audiences has to map audiences' 'stakes' and the evolution of their stakes over time. Controlling systems put in place at the IM level are first devoted to the identification of critical stakeholders of the organization (e.g., NGOs or interest groups – i.e., institutionalized actors) and, after, to the monitoring of their opinions. The identification procedure consists of three steps: first, the creation of broad maps

Digital corporate communication and issues management 139

(Freeman, 1984) which provide a classification of audiences as having primary and secondary stakes. Second, a segmentation a priori map (Esman, 1972) that highlights stakeholders' negative relationship with the organization. Third, a situational map (Grunig, 1997) that classifies stakeholders' communication behaviour as either active or inactive. These three types of segmentation provide a comprehensive overview of which audience is an ally expressing a positive opinion about the organization on a given issue, and which, instead, is an opponent expressing negative opinions.

Digital: Mapping Digital Collectives and their Communication Ecosystems

In the contemporary digital environment, individuals and groups engage and organize quite differently, making it difficult to apply traditional mapping tools as outlined above.

First, while the relevant audiences in the pre-digital communication environment were mainly institutional actors, recent research has shown how, in the contemporary digital environment, issues involving organizations are mainly driven by individuals who hold a momentary interest in the organization that together constitute temporary digital collectives (Arvidsson, 2013). In this sense, digital collectives represent a light form of civic engagement constituting fluid publics (Arvidsson, 2013) that are often driven by light forms of slacktivism (Barnett et al., 2020); namely, mild demonstrations of engagement that rarely evolve into a long-term relationship with a cause or the organization. In contrast to institutional audiences, individuals within publics communicate around an issue without needing to establish a relationship with all or any of the other participants in that group (Bruns and Burgess, 2011) and do not have to pursue a coherent collective identity – as in the case of individuals joining an NGO or activist group. Instead, publics are united around an aggregative frame (Colleoni et al., 2021) in the form of a linguistic marker (e.g., hashtag) (Arvidsson and Caliandro, 2016) which allows them to express themselves in a collective discourse (Bennett and Segerberg, 2011, 2012; Colleoni et al., 2021). This aggregative frame has the double function of connecting dispersed individuals, and, at the same time, making them express their personal opinion on the issue, and, in so doing, repurposing the frame to serve their desire for publicity (Kozinets et al., 2017). For instance, Colleoni et al. (2021) have recently shown how the #Occupy movement engaged in the creation of aggregative frames that allowed different individuals and groups to join the protest, without establishing a common identity. This study indicates that one major aggregative frame (i.e., WeAre) is able to connect different groups with different issues and goals. Its meaning is defined by the four different discursive communities that 'hook' the meaning to a specific context such as (1) minorities issues, (2) working conditions issues, (3) participation and democracy issues, and (4) justice and protest issues.

As these digital collectives are primarily communication ecosystem spaces, they can emerge and disappear at any time. This implies that mapping and monitoring systems based on the a priori identification of audiences having a stake are not as good as they used to be at predicting the emergence of potential issues, urging reconsideration of the way stakeholders can be segmented. Consequently, some scholars have proposed a shift in attention from actors to stakeholders' communication ecosystems (e.g., Mariconda and Lurati, 2015).

Indeed, given that publics are primarily communication ecosystems, it becomes crucial to learn to identify and monitor digital collectives, as well as any light form of slacktivism. In order to do so, on the one hand, it is crucial to focus on identifying who is influencing whom, and who is influenced by whom. However, most importantly, it is crucial to monitor how these

140   *Handbook on digital corporate communication*

ecosystems form and evolve discursively around aggregative frames, that function as nodal points in a conversation (Colleoni et al., 2021), allowing digital collectives to aggregate and emerge.

This implies monitoring stakeholders' 'echo chambers' (Colleoni et al., 2014) (that is, communities of individuals having similar ideologies), but also 'refracted chambers' (Rieder, 2012) (i.e., communities of discussions), where individuals with different experiences engage in a connective action (Bennet and Segerberg, 2012), regardless of a common ideology or a follower-followee relationship that derives from it. The latter constitute what other scholars call issues arenas (Badham et al., 2022), that is fluid discursive arenas where issues are debated and become visible.

In particular, in order to segment digital collectives, it is crucial to focus on two elements. First, companies should focus on the personal and emotional motivations driving the engagement in an issue, rather than focusing on the issue itself. This is because individuals have a stake in self-publicizing their own personal experiences, rather than objectively informing about an organization (Etter et al., 2019). Second, companies should focus on monitoring communication ecosystems (rather than stakes of holders), and consequently, on the communication behaviour, rather than solely on the evaluations.

Issues Prioritization before and during the Digital Communication Era

Table 10.3   Changes in issues prioritization

	Pre-digital communication era	Digital communication era
Communication flow	Two-step flow	Networked communications
Control & Monitoring	Diffusion of information, formal communications on material issues	Conversations, networked interactions on material issues
Sources	Data: Few – moderate	Big Data: Millions
Monitor – Identification of	Focused frame of a stakeholder	Aggregative frames of digital collectives and refraction within conversations (i.e., co-occurrence of messages)
Likelihood of fake news influence	Limited (as in a two-step flow): the gatekeeper is a professionalized actor following fact-checking procedures	High (as in networked communications): actors that communicate are not professionals and fact-checking is not a practice

As Table 10.3 shows, controlling and monitoring issues has always been based on the principle of the two-step communication flow theory (Katz and Lazarsfeld, 1955), according to which it is important to identify issues advocated by important stakeholders who are gatekeepers to others, providing access to information to a wide mass of individuals. In particular, such monitoring has aimed to identify which information is diffused by stakeholders through a moderate number of formal communications. In practice, the monitoring has been made around specific keywords that represent focused frames used by stakeholders to advocate for or against an issue. With the advent of digital media, however, it is also important to start monitoring issues following principles of networked communications (i.e., dialogues, interactions, conversations that occur among multiple individuals online on material issues related to the organization). While the data to analyse is vast (i.e., big data including up to millions of conversations), the monitoring is aimed at identifying aggregative frames that allow digital collectives to emerge through the analysis of the co-occurrence of messages (i.e., hashtags that are co-paired in tweets; tags that link posts in Instagram) (Etter et al., 2018). This methodology allows

Digital corporate communication and issues management 141

monitoring of all new features that an issue is acquiring each time new individuals refract the aggregative frame (i.e., twist its meaning by adding its own interpretation of it) (Rieder, 2012). In the next subsection, the key concepts, processes, and practice within issues prioritization before and after the advent of digital communication are elaborated.

Pre-Digital: Monitoring Issues of Interest of Well-Identifiable Audiences

Following IM principles, issues are monitored by identifying those that are visibly attracting the interest of specific audiences, thereby increasing the pressure toward organizations (Achtleitner, 1985; Regester and Larking, 2002). To identify an issue at a rather early stage (e.g., potential and emerging), it is important to monitor material issues related to the organizations (e.g., issues in operations) that receive the attention of institutionalized stakeholders (e.g., NGOs, interest groups, consumer associations, and news media). These stakeholders produce information that conveys a focused viewpoint on the issue, as this kind of stakeholder has a clear agenda regarding the issue and how to strategically push it at the public level (Barnett et al., 2020). Given this, this type of stakeholder diffuses information that contains an opinion on the issue through various channels following a two-step flow process, in which several intermediaries acting as gatekeepers (e.g., news media) are targeted with the goal of shaping the stakeholder's viewpoint on the issue to the masses (e.g., news media articles that present a report from the NGO). In this setting diffusion of fake news is limited as gatekeepers are professionalized actors following fact-checking procedures. The communication material to monitor is typically moderated, as it relates to official material produced by the stakeholder and mediated by the gatekeepers. Figure 10.1 shows a typical issue lifecycle and the gatekeepers who are typically monitored, which are mainly influencers (such as bloggers or consumers' associations) in the potential and emerging phase and mass news media (such as newspapers, TV, and radio) in the emerging and current phase.

In order to understand whether an issue is having a potential impact on the organization or is very likely to arise, issues managers typically map issues to identify deeds and misdeeds about the organization and grasp how these are narrated by stakeholders (Heath, 1997; Winter and Steger, 1998). Regarding concerns about the potential impact, one typically asks the following questions (rated on a scale from 1 to 10 in a grid, where the total refers to the potential impact of an issue): What is the effect of the issue on reputation? Which issue influences finances? Does an issue have an effect on the company? Are other organizations affected? Are patents, supply chain or any other internal operational processes affected? Are arguments advanced on the issue plausible? Does the issue resonate emotionally with mass audiences? Regarding what concerns the probability of development of an issue, one instead typically asks (rated on a scale from 1 to 10 in a grid, where the total refers to the probability of development): Does the issue have a link with other issues that are relevant for the business? Is our business isolated? Is there any audience already active in searching or producing information on the issue? Is the solution of the issue very difficult to put in place? The final output is an issue matrix which allows organizations to prioritize issues that are urgent.

Digital: Monitoring Refraction of Digital Collectives around Issues

In the contemporary digital environment, where digital collectives and light forms of engagements with organizations are becoming increasingly relevant, organizations need to monitor

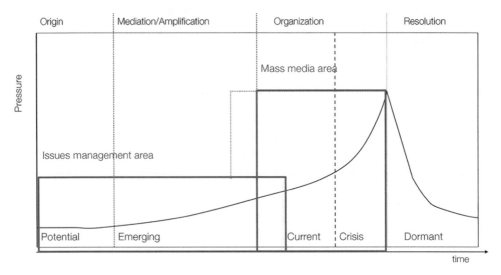

Source: Adapted from Hainsworth and Meng (1988) and Achtleitner (1985).

Figure 10.1   Issues lifecycle

not only the information spread by institutional stakeholders about issues, but also the network of conversations of dispersed individuals who are mentioning the organization in relation to different issues. However, given the high volume and fragmentation of platforms and voices (Barnett et al., 2020), big data techniques are needed (Etter et al., 2018; Hirsch, 2018), in particular, algorithms that can extract patterns from large sets of unstructured data and that can similarly predict anomalies in the conversations around a company or an issue that might signal an incoming crisis (Colleoni, 2012). This is of particular relevance, as there are no clear actors to be identified a priori, and there are multiple formats of messages to monitor.

In order to predict potential risks, the identification of relevant conversations should not be based on a priori influencers (e.g., individuals with a high number of followers). In fact, within digital collectives, content is not diffused via a two-step flow model of communication in which there are few gatekeepers, but with a networked communication model, as any individual can, in principle, publish content that becomes viral (Illia et al., 2021). Individuals who join social networks are not just passive users, but 'produsers' (Bruns, 2007); namely, users who can easily produce content (e.g., reviews or opinions) that may influence others' opinions (Dellarocas, 2003). In this setting the possibility of diffusion of fake news is potentially high, as actors that communicate are not professionals and fact-checking is not a practice.

To capture potential issues, it is also crucial to move beyond the idea of virality as simple sharing of content that can be produced by either an influencer or a simple individual. Thanks to social networks increasingly organizing content around aggregative frames, individuals can express their opinions, and at the same time co-associate their messages with the messages of others (Bruns and Burgess, 2011). Despite expressing heterogeneous viewpoints (Barros, 2014), digital collectives can converge around these 'aggregative frames' by refracting the different and yet connected voices of dispersed individuals (Colleoni et al., 2021) and impact an organization.

Figure 10.2 shows how aggregative frames can be monitored within conversations using two key indicators: the conversational broadness and the conversational volume generated by a message such as a tweet or Instagram post (Illia et al., 2021). Within this figure, conversational broadness refers to a message that has a high in-between centrality in a network, as represented by the node on the left. That node represents a message that is central to bridging two communities of conversations; that is, it indicates issues that are peripheral to one another, yet interconnected. These issues are important to keep an eye on, especially if they are bridging two communities of conversations that are dangerously attacking the company. They are, however, not urgent matters to be addressed, as extant research suggests that these do not have a direct impact on business outcomes (Illia et al., 2021). Moreover, news media cover them mainly in the post-crisis phase, which is when they are interested to know if there are many conversations that, despite not talking primarily about that issue, are related to it (Illia et al., 2021).

Conversational volume, instead, refers to a message that is high in volume and high in convergence (i.e., many hashtags aggregating around the same hashtags that function as an aggregative frame) (see node in the network in the middle, in Figure 10.2) (Illia et al., 2021). Such an indicator points out that there is a discussion that is receiving a lot of refracted attention (Illia et al., 2022a) and that is prominently and saliently emerging as a key issue to address. This type of issue may receive media coverage at any time, as media are interested to know which issue is attracting the attention of many users, even if individuals have refracted (i.e., diverse) viewpoints on the issue. There may be instances in which it is possible to find a message that is core in bridging more communities (Illia et al., 2022c) and low in convergence (see node in the network on the left, in Figure 10.2), or high in convergence (see node in the network on the right, in Figure 10.2). These issues are rare, but very dangerous, and would indicate respectively that there are either many digital collectives to address or many digital collectives that are not only bridged, but also starting to converge around one main issue. Monitoring systems focusing on conversational broadness and conversational volume need to develop an alerting system related to the combination of conversational broadness and volume, which is able to predict the exceeding of a tipping point (Illia et al., 2022a) after which the issue is impactful for the organization (Gladwell, 2000; Goel et al., 2016; Kitchin and Purcell, 2017; Van Nes et al., 2016) (i.e., a critical mass of converging conversations). When this happens "a change in the state" (Van Nes et al., 2016, p. 902) of influence between social media and news media happens, which indicates the point in which "issues evolve into a crisis" (Kitchin and Purcell, 2017, p. 662) that corresponds to "that magic moment when an idea, trend, or social behaviour crosses a threshold, tips, and spreads like wildfire" (Gladwell, 2000, p. 24).

WHAT IS CHANGING?

IM in the Digital Era: A Real Revolution?

Despite all changes illustrated, it is important to underline that concepts, frameworks, and tools presented for the digital communication era are not substitutive for those presented in the pre-digital era. Digital collectives represent new forms of audiences that communicate around issues in a different way to stakeholders, however they are not substituting them. Extant

144 *Handbook on digital corporate communication*

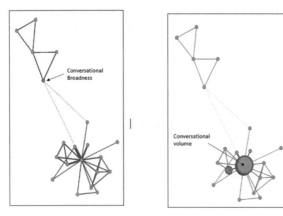
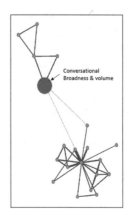

Source: Adapted from Illia et al. (2021).

Figure 10.2   Monitor broadness of issues vs convergence of issues

research suggests that social media become particularly impactful when news media pick up on their negative sentiment and amplify it (Castelló et al., 2013; Coombs and Holladay, 2012; Illia, 2003), with recent studies postulating that news media magnify their impact (Etter et al., 2019; Wang et al., 2019). This happens because news media provide credibility and visibility to evaluations posted on social media (Etter et al., 2019). Hence, in a media environment, where digital collectives' discussions may be lost in the fluidity and information overload of the digital media landscape (Barnett et al., 2020), their influence often relies on the validation through news media (Illia, 2003). This becomes even more true with the growing issue of disinformation in the digital sphere (Allcott and Gentzkow, 2017), where fakeholders (Luoma-aho, 2015) – i.e., socio-bots and stakeholders artificially generated by either individuals or persona-creating software and algorithms to either oppose or support an issue – are either misinforming or disinforming, and mass media validate what is published online by stakeholders. Furthermore, news media receive the important function of simplifying a message that otherwise seems complex (Ragas and Kiousis, 2010).

CRITICAL EXAMINATION

It is also important to underline that digitalization may imply possibly also a dark side of IM, that is, negative consequences in the way IM is implemented or managed. First, digitalization has implied that the IM industry is devoted to the gathering and exploitation of data that users disseminate online (West, 2019). Although IM in principle justifies such practice on the basis that the information is made publicly available by users, there are increasing concerns about the commercialization of data (Darmody and Zwick, 2020). Data ingested for IM purposes may constitute new forms of surveillance (West, 2019), that cannot be easily limited by current regulations (Andrew and Baker, 2021). Second, digitalization has multiplied the unethical use of monitoring systems with the final aim to do 'Dark PR' (Gold, 2020), that is, to know more about a specific target so as to spread negative stories, mostly fake, with the essential aim to discredit a target. Notable examples are campaigns that were launched by communication

Digital corporate communication and issues management   145

agencies enacting Dark PR to discredit political adversaries as demonstrated during the US and French presidential elections, respectively in 2016 and 2017 (Audigane, 2018), and the Brexit campaign in the UK in 2016 (Adams, 2018). Third, similarly, IM may also be instrumentalized toward a non-ethical use of cancel culture. Cancel culture is the "collective desire by consumers to withdraw support of those individuals and brands in power, perceived to be involved in objectionable behavior or activities through the use of social media" (Saldanha et al., 2022). Even though in principle cancel culture has enabled voice disapproval in social media, these digital collectives become mobs if the intention at the base is instrumentalized malevolently. IM practice and principles may be used in this way, fomenting further 'Dark PR' also in this setting.

CASE ILLUSTRATION: #DELETEUBER BOYCOTT

At the end of January 2017, during the Travel Ban strikes at US airports, Uber drivers continued to provide ride services (Wong, 2017a). This motivated a massive number of users to uninstall their Uber app and join the #deleteuber boycott (Lynley, 2017). A few weeks later, Uber was again in the public spotlight, when it was accused of exploitation by its drivers (Carson, 2017) and of promoting a sexist culture by one of its engineers (Carson, 2017; Hern, 2017; Horowitz, 2017). In the following weeks, the boycott became massive, inflamed by a variety of issues such as the distasteful behaviour of its CEO, intellectual property theft, attempts to defraud city regulators, and the use of the software called Greyball to avoid inspections in the states where Uber was banned (Wong, 2017b). The #deleteuber boycott shows that individuals online have started to bond as a digital collective not only because the founder's management style was reprehensible (Wong, 2017a, 2017b), but also because of a number of issues related to Uber as a sharing economy and a very successful Silicon Valley technological giant.

As Illia et al. (2022b) indicate, during the boycott there were 12 issues that were the focus of the conversations online. Only two of them expressed a positive sentiment and related to conversations on employability, mobility, and the future. All other ten issues, instead, were rather expressed with negative sentiment and refer to the following conversations, some related to Uber mismanagement practices, others with corporate behaviours that are attributed to Uber as a sharing economy company, or Uber as a tech giant, the latter being the most significant recrimination advanced against Uber (Illia et al., 2022b):

- Ethnic and Gender Discrimination: People disliked the fact that Uber did not stop its services during the travel ban manifestation and transport strikes against the immigration ban. People also debated Uber as a tech company that discriminates against women in many instances, such as sexual harassment and violence toward women clients. These conversations were not unique to Uber, as sexism episodes are typical of Silicon Valley tech start-ups.
- Anarchism and Resistance (Anti-Capitalism): The criticism, in some instances, anti-capitalist, addressed to Uber and other tech giants is of the ubiquitous character of these companies' services (i.e., one cannot function without these companies' services/ products anymore).
- Corporate America: The link between politics and tech giants in the US is controversial. People contested that corporations such as Uber could be in a position to develop social

welfare, but only pursue their own business agenda. Uber and other tech giants were contested for their support of President Trump.

- Toxic Culture: People contested the corporate culture of Uber that was considered too aggressive and, in certain instances, sexist. This is considered typical of CEOs of tech giants who are originally entrepreneurs (typically males), such as Uber's CEO, Kalanick.
- Human-based Service (Poor Quality): The business model of the sharing economy allows normal people to provide a service or good. Because of this, professionality decreases and the quality of experience for Uber mainly depends on drivers' human touch.
- Legal Infringements: Corporate behaviours that are at the limit of legality. Uber had been considered guilty of several crimes against states, companies, and even its own drivers.
- Dangerous Workers: Due to drivers' criminal records or risks of artificial intelligence (i.e., self-driving cars), Uber's drivers were perceived as potentially dangerous. People expressed the need to provide a clear regulatory framework for the shared economy.
- Privacy: Privacy of user data is a sensitive issue that is not only related to Uber but to all companies that, like Uber, extensively register clients' personal data.
- Eroding Professional Categories: The negative impacts on professional categories that companies like Uber create have been contested due to the flexible, non-regulated business.
- Exploitation of Workers: This issue expresses the lack of protection of the rights of the providers of sharing economy services; specifically, for Uber, the drivers.

Figure 10.3 shows the digital collectives that discussed these issues. As this figure highlights, the conversations around 'Ethnic and gender discrimination', 'Corporate America', and 'Anarchism and resistance' reached a conversational volume, hence were urgent in their necessity to be managed. 'Privacy' instead denotes a conversational broadness, which means that it is connecting two other communicatees of discussions: 'Legal infringement' and 'Toxic culture'. Although these last two seem unrelated, as one barely has anything to do with the other, the way Uber was managing privacy issues related to its business seemed to be dangerously bridging these two communities and themes (this is probably due to the case of Greyball that happened at the end of March that same year). Hence, it is important to keep an eye on this issue of privacy, as it may become complex over time, if it also reaches conversational volume, rather than only broadness.

CONCLUSION AND FUTURE DIRECTIONS

In conclusion, although IM does not change in terms of objectives and its core of monitoring stakeholders and issues, the digital landscape has made more complex the way the segmentation of stakeholders and the monitoring of issues is conducted. It is not sufficient to simply develop control systems to proactively engage in a relationship with formalized stakeholders, it is also important to identify new types of stakeholders' expressions that may impact the organization. For this reason, it becomes crucial to further develop concepts and frameworks that allow broadening the type of indicators that can be used to predict digital collectives or the rise of issues. In this chapter, evidence was provided of these new forms of emerging issues along with examples that have recently attracted scholarly attention on how social media are becoming impactful despite the heterogeneity of content and fragmentation of the media landscape. It is therefore imperative for corporate communication and public relations scholars to

Digital corporate communication and issues management 147

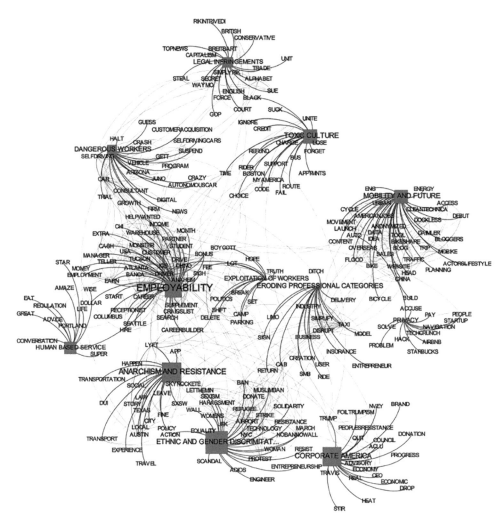

Source: Illia et al. (2022b).

Figure 10.3   Digital collectives during the #deleteuber boycott

continue pushing for IM theory and practice toward prediction rather than merely monitoring, so to be further embedded in business education and practice.

In sum, three important future research paths are worth further exploration in the area of IM. First, the study of the characteristics of discourse put forward by digital collectives that may determine the overcoming of the discursive tipping point. Second, the definition of typologies of prominent users in digital collectives. Third, the exploration of new methodologies that successfully combine volume and influence of actors with discourse characteristics.

REFERENCES

Achtleitner, P. (1985). *Sozio-politische strategien multinationaler unternehmungen: ein ansatz gezielten umweltmanagements* (vol. 13). Bern.

Adams, T. (2018). Facebook's week of shame: The Cambridge Analytica fallout. *The Guardian.* https://www.theguardian.com/technology/2018/mar/24/facebook-week-of-shame-data-breach-observer-revelations-zuckerberg-silence.

Allcott, H. and Gentzkow, M. (2017). Social media and fake news in the 2016 election. *Journal of Economic Perspectives, 31*(2), 211–236.

Andrew, J. and Baker, M. (2021). The general data protection regulation in the age of surveillance capitalism. *Journal of Business Ethics, 168*, 565–578.

Arvidsson, A. (2013). The potential of consumer publics. *Ephemera, 13*(2), 367–391.

Arvidsson, A. and Caliandro, A. (2016). Brand public. *Journal of Consumer Research, 42*(5), 727–748.

Audigane, L. (2018). *Les fake news qui ont émaillé la campagne présidentielle.* BFMTV. https://www.bfmtv.com/politique/les-fake-news-qui-ont-emaille-la-campagne-presidentielle-1466265.html.

Badham, M., Luoma-aho, V., Valentini, C., and Körkkö, L. (2022). Digital strategic communication through digital media-arenas. In J. Falkheimer and M. Heide (eds.), *Research handbook on strategic communication* (pp. 416–430). Cheltenham, UK and Northampton, MA, USA: Edward Elgar Publishing.

Balmer, J. M. T. and Soenen, G. (1997). Operationalising the concept of corporate identity: Articulating the corporate identity mix and the corporate identity management mix. *Department of Marketing Working Paper Series, 97*(8), University of Strathclyde.

Barnett, M. L., Henriques, I., and Husted, B. W. (2020). The rise and stall of stakeholder influence: How the digital age limits social control. *Academy of Management Perspectives, 34*(1), 48–64.

Baron, D. P. (1992). *Business and its environment.* Harlow: Pearson.

Barros, M. (2014). Tools of legitimacy: The case of the Petrobas corporate blog. *Organization Studies, 35*, 1211–1230.

Bennett, W. L. and Segerberg, A. (2011). Digital media and the personalization of collective action: Social technology and the organization of protests against the global economic crisis. *Information, Communication and Society, 14*(6), 770–799.

Bennett, W. L. and Segerberg, A. (2012). The logic of connective action. *Information, Communication and Society, 15*(5), 739–768.

Bruns, A. (2007), Produsage. Paper presented at the 6th ACM SIGCHI conference on Creativity and cognition, 1 June, Washington, DC. https://dl.acm.org/doi/10.1145/1254960.1254975.

Bruns A. and Burgess, J. E. (2011). The use of Twitter hashtags in the formation of ad hoc publics. Paper presented at the European Consortium for Political Research Conference, 25–27 August, Reykjavik.

Buhmann, A. and White, C. L. (2022). Artificial intelligence in public relations: Role and implications. In J. H. Lipschultz, K. Freberg, and R. Luttrell (eds.), *The Emerald handbook of computer-mediated communication and social media* (pp. 625–638). Bingley: Emerald Publishing.

Carson, B. (2017). Uber just tried to bury the hatchet with angry drivers – but it dug a deeper hole instead. *Business Insider.* https://www.businessinsider.com/uber-president-jeff-jones-holds-disastrous-qa-with-drivers-2017-2?r=US&IR=T.

Castelló, I., Morsing, M., and Schultz, F. (2013). The construction of corporate social responsibility in network societies: A communication view. *Journal of Business Ethics, 115*(4), 681–692.

Colleoni, E. (2012). New forms of digital marketing research. In R. Belk and R. Liama (eds.), *The Routledge companion to digital consumption* (pp. 124–134). London: Routledge.

Colleoni, E., Illia, L., and Zyglidopoulos, S. (2021). Exploring how publics discursively organize as digital collectives: The use of empty and floating signifiers as organizing devices in social media. *Journal of the Association for Consumer Research, 6*(4). https://www.journals.uchicago.edu/doi/abs/10.1086/716067.

Colleoni, E., Rozza, A., and Arvidsson, A. (2014). Echo chamber or public sphere: Predicting political orientation and measuring political homophily in Twitter using big data. *Journal of Communication, 64*(2), 317–332.

Coombs, W. T. (2007). Protecting organization reputations during a crisis: The development and application of situational crisis communication theory. *Corporate Reputation Review, 10*(3), 163–176.

Coombs, W. T. and Holladay, J. S. (2012). The paracrisis: The challenges created by publicly managing crisis prevention. *Public Relations Review*, *38*(3), 408–415.

Darmody, A. and Zwick, D. (2020). Manipulate to empower: Hyper-relevance and the contradictions of marketing in the age of surveillance capitalism. *Big Data & Society*, *7*(1), 1–12.

Dellarocas, C. (2003). The digitization of word of mouth: Promise and challenges of online feedback mechanisms. *Management Science*, *49*(10), 1407–1424.

Eckert, C. (2017). Corporate reputation and reputation risk: Definition and measurement from a (risk) management perspective. *The Journal of Risk Finance*, *18*(2), 145–158.

Esman, M. (1972). The elements of institution building. In J. W. Eaton (ed.), *Institution building and development* (pp. 19–40). Beverly Hills, CA: Sage Publications.

Etter, M., Colleoni, E., Illia, L., Meggiorin, K., and D'Eugenio, A. (2018). Measuring organizational legitimacy in social media: Assessing citizens' judgments with sentiment analysis. *Business and Society*, *57*(1), 60–97.

Etter, M., Ravasi, D., and Colleoni, E. (2019). Social media and the formation of reputation. *Academy of Management Review*, *44*(1), 28–52.

Fombrun, C. J. and van Riel, C. B. M. (2004). *Fame and fortune: How successful companies build winning reputations*. Upper Saddle River, NJ: Prentice Hall.

Freeman, R. E. (1984). *Strategic management: A stakeholder approach*. London: Pitman.

Gaunt, P. and Ollenburger, J. (1995). Issues management revisited: A tool that deserves another look. *Public Relations Review*, *21*(3), 199–210.

Gladwell, M. (2000). *The tipping point: How little things can make a big difference*. Boston: Little, Brown.

Goel, S., Anderson, A., Hofman, J., and Duncan, J. W. (2016). The structural virality of online diffusion. *Management Science*, *62*(1), 180–196.

Gold, B. (2020). Why PR pros should worry about 'Dark PR'. *PR Daily*. https://www.prdaily.com/why-pr-pros-should-worry-about-dark-pr/.

Grüblbauer, J. and Haric, P. (2013). Social media monitoring tools as instruments of strategic issues management. In M. Friedrichsen and W. Mühl-Benninghaus (eds.), *Handbook of social media management: Value chain and business models in changing media markets* (pp. 671–687). Cham: Springer VS.

Grunig, J. E. (1997). A situational theory of publics: Conceptual history, recent challenges and new research. In D. Moss, T. MacManus, and D. Vercic (eds.), *Public relations research: An international perspective* (pp. 3–48). London: International Thomson Business Press.

Grunig, J. E. and Repper, F. C. (1992). Strategic management, publics, and issues. In J. E. Grunig (ed.), *Excellence in public relations and communication management: Contributions to effective organizations* (pp. 117–157). Mahwah, NJ: Lawrence Erlbaum.

Hainsworth, B. E. and Meng, M. (1988). How corporations define issues management. *Public Relations Review*, *14*(4), 18–30.

Hearn, K., Mahnicke, R., and Williams, P. A. (2009). Culture jamming: From activism to haktivism. Australian information warfare and security conference. https://www.arifyildirim.com/ilt510/kay.hearn.pdf.

Heath, R. L. (1992). Critical perspectives on public relations. In R. L. Heath and E. Toth (eds.), *Rhetorical and critical approaches to public relations II* (pp. 37–62). London: Routledge.

Heath, R. L. (1997). *Strategic issues management: Organizations and public policy challenges*. London: Sage Publications.

Hern, A. (2017). Uber writes to users abandoning service over sexual harassment claims. *The Guardian*. https://www.theguardian.com/technology/2017/feb/23/deleteuber-taxi-app-writes-to-users-deleting-their-account.

Hirsch, B. (2018). Tie me to the mast: Artificial intelligence & reputation risk management. *Journal of Business Strategy*, *39*(1), 61–64.

Horowitz, J. (2017). Uber CEO orders 'urgent' investigation after sex harassment allegations. *CNNMoney's Tech*. https://money.cnn.com/2017/02/19/technology/uber-harassment-investigation/index.html.

Illia, L. (2003). Passage to cyberactivism: How dynamics of activism change. *Journal of Public Affairs*, *3*, 326–337.

150 *Handbook on digital corporate communication*

Illia, L., Colleoni, E., and Meggiorin, K. (2021). How infomediaries on Twitter influence business outcomes of a bank. *International Journal of Bank Marketing, 39*(5), 709–724.

Illia, L., Colleoni, E., Etter, M., and Meggiorin, K. (2022a). Finding the tipping point: When heterogeneous evaluations in social media converge and influence organizational legitimacy. *Business & Society.* Online first. https://doi.org/10.1177/00076503211073516.

Illia, L., Colleoni, E., Ravindran, K., and Ludovico, N. (2022b). Mens rea, wrongdoing and digital advocacy in social media: Exploring quasi-legal narratives advocated by boycotters during #deleteuber. *Journal of Public Affairs.* Online first. https://doi.org/10.1002/pa.2805.

Illia, L., Etter, M., Meggiorin, K., and Colleoni, E. (2022c). From micro-level to macro-level legitimacy: Exploring how judgments in social media create thematic broadness at meso-level. In G. Thomas, D. Logue, B. Hinings, and M. Barrett (eds.), *Digital transformation and institutional theorizing: Consequences, opportunities and challenges* (pp. 111–132). Bingley: Emerald Publishing.

Ingenhoff, D. (2004). Issues management: Das Konzept aus interdisziplinärer Perspektive. In *Corporate issues management in multinationale Unternehmen. Eine empirische Studie zu organisationalen Strukturen und Prozessen* (pp. 40–87). Cham: Springer VS.

Katz, E. and Lazarsfeld, P. F. (1955). *Personal influence: The part played by people in the flow of mass communication.* New York: Free Press.

Kitchin, P. J. and Purcell, P. A. (2017). Examining sport communications practitioners' approaches to issues management and crisis response in Northern Ireland. *Public Relations Review, 43*(4), 661–670.

Knittel, C. and Stango, V. (2014). Celebrity endorsements, firm value, and reputation risk: Evidence from the Tiger Woods scandal. *Management Science, 6*(1), 21–37.

Kozinets, R., Patterson, A., and Ashman, R. (2017). Networks of desire: How technology increases our passion to consume. *Journal of Consumer Research, 43*(5), 659–682.

Luoma-aho, V. (2015). Understanding stakeholder engagement: Faith-holders, hateholders & fakeholders. *RJ-IPR: Research Journal of the Institute for Public Relations, 2*(1). http://www.instituteforpr.org/understanding-stakeholder-engagement-fai.

Lynley, M. (2017). Uber apologizes for "confusion" at JFK during immigration protest. *Techcrunch.* https://techcrunch.com/2017/01/29/uber-apologizes-for-confusion-at-jfk-during-immigration -protest/ .

Mahon, J. F., Heugens, P. P. M. A. R., and Lamertz, K. (2004). Social networks and nonmarket strategy. *Journal of Public Affairs, 4*(2), 170–189.

Mahon, J. F. and Waddock, S. A. (1992). Strategic issues management: An integration of issue life cycle perspectives. *Business & Society, 31*(1), 19–32.

Mariconda, S. and Lurati, F. (2015). Stakeholder cross-impact analysis: A segmentation method. *Corporate Communications: An International Journal, 20*, 276–290.

McCaughey, M. (2014). *Cyberactivism on the participatory web.* New York: Routledge.

Pérez-Cornejo, C., de Quevedo-Puente, E., and Delgada-Garcia, J. B. (2019). How to manage corporate reputation? The effect of enterprise risk management systems and audit committees on corporate reputation. *European Management Journal, 37*(4), 505–515.

Ragas, M. W. and Kiousis, S. (2010). Intermedia agenda-setting and political activism: MoveOn.org and the 2008 presidential election. *Mass Communication and Society, 13*(5), 560–583.

Regan, L. (2008). A framework for integrating reputation risk into the enterprise risk management process. *Journal of Financial Transformation, 22*, 187–194.

Regester, M. and Larkin, J. (2002). *Risk issues and crisis management: A casebook of best practice* (2nd edition). London: Kogan Page.

Rieder, B. (2012). The refraction chamber: Twitter as sphere and network. *First Monday, 17*(11). https://doi.org/10.5210/fm.v17i11.4199.

Ruggiero, A. and Vos, M. (2014). Social media monitoring for crisis communication: Process, methods and trends in the scientific literature. *Online Journal of Communication and Media Technologies, 4*(1), 105–130.

Saldanha, N., Mulye, R., and Rahman, K. (2022). Cancel culture and the consumer: A strategic marketing perspective, *Journal of Strategic Marketing.* Online first. https://doi.org/10.1080/0965254X.2022 .2040577.

Schrock, A. R. (2016). Civic hacking as data activism and advocacy: A history from publicity to open government data. *New Media & Society, 18*(4), 581–599.

Van Nes, E. H., Arani, B. M. S., Staal, A., van der Bolt, B., Flores, B. M., Bathiany, S., and Scheffer, M. (2016). What do you mean, 'tipping point'? *Trends in Ecology & Evolution, 31*(12), 902–904.

Vos, M., Schoemaker, H., and Luoma-aho, V. L. (2014). Setting the agenda for research on issue arenas. *Corporate Communications: An International Journal, 19*(2), 200–215.

Wang, X., Reger, R. K., and Pfarrer, M. D. (2019). Faster, hotter, and more linked in: Managing social disapproval in the social media era. *Academy of Management Review, 46*(2). https://doi.org/10.5465/amr.2017.0375.

West, S. (2019). Data capitalism: Redefining the logics of surveillance and privacy. *Business & Society, 58*(1), 20–41.

Winter, M. and Steger, U. (1998). *Managing outside pressure: Strategies for preventing corporate disaster*. Hoboken, NJ: Wiley.

Wong, J. C. (2017a). #DeleteUber: How tech companies are taking sides in the battle over Trump. *The Guardian*. https://www.theguardian.com/technology/2017/jan/31/trump-travel-ban-tech-companies-uber-lyft-apple-google.

Wong, J. C. (2017b). Uber CEO Travis Kalanick resigns following months of chaos. *The Guardian*. https://www.theguardian.com/technology/2017/jun/20/uber-ceo-travis-kalanick-resigns.

Young, L. E. and Leonardi, P. M. (2012). Social issue emergence on the web: A dual structurational model. *Journal of Computer-Mediated Communication, 17*(2), 231–246.

Zadeck, S. (2004). The path to corporate responsibility. *Harvard Business Review, 82*(12), 125–132.

11. Digital corporate communication and activism
Maureen Taylor

INTRODUCTION

Badham and Luoma-aho define digital corporate communication (DCC) as "an organization's strategic management of digital technologies, digital infrastructures and digitalization processes to improve communication with internal and external stakeholders and more broadly within society for the maintenance of organizational tangible and intangible assets" (Chapter 1 in this volume, p. 9). Corporations are not alone in their use of digital technologies to improve communication. Public sector, non-profits and activists also use digital technology to create and change social outcomes. This chapter explores the different types of digital activists' communication that seek to influence corporations.

Activism is a "process by which groups of people exert pressure on organizations or other institutions to change policies, practices, or conditions the activists find problematic" (Smith, 2005, p. 5). McCarthy and Zald (1977) argued that groups are only as successful in their advocacy as they are in their efforts to mobilize resources and scholars have clearly established that resources matter for activist outcomes (Smith and Ferguson, 2010). There are many types of activism, including individual activists who may stand alone in their commitment to an issue. Individuals can join advocacy, social movement, and protest groups to further their interests, thus becoming involved in collective action.

Digital communication helps to amplify the voices of activists. George and Leidner (2019) showed that digital activism can influence corporations' decision making. Digital activism that targets corporations includes diverse activities such as clicktivism, hacktivis, and data activism which may include exposure of embarrassing or illegal corporate practices. Edwards et al. (2013, p. 4) defined digital activism from a political perspective as "an organized public effort, making collective claim(s) on a target authority(s), in which civic initiators or supporters use digital media". Activist and advocacy groups use digital communication to organize, inform, persuade and pressure corporations and governments to change. Activism has evolved from people standing on picket lines and public boycotts to digital tactics such as hashtag advocacy, hashtag hijacking and tweetjacking, distributed denial of service (DDOS) attacks and other online tactics that seek to pressure corporations to change their behaviour. One popular example is the platform Change.org that offers a digital petition site "where users can create or sign a petition unheeded and undirected, requiring only a signature from its participants, and a comment if they choose to share; any individual can create a petition" (Minocher, 2019, p. 626). The digital space provides opportunities for activism that can force corporations to change their behaviours.

Activists are 'canaries in the coalmine' alerting corporations of upcoming shifts in societal expectations. Activists play an important role in bringing issues into the public sphere and activist networks amplify local, regional and international advocacy efforts. Whereas many early communication scholars treated activists as an obstacle for corporations to overcome (Grunig, 1992), scholars now argue that activists play an important role in civil society

Digital corporate communication and activism   153

(Taylor, 2009). Activists raise issues that prompt people, corporations and government to rethink long-held positions and change their actions. While government is where policy and laws are changed, it is often activist organizations' communication that defines a problem and identifies a solution that initiates change.

This chapter applies the network perspective (Yang and Taylor, 2015) to digital activism and argues for a 'bird's eye' network approach for activists to diagnose weak or vulnerable members of a network. The network of interest for this chapter is a supply/value chain. A supply chain is a network of goods and services that an organization relies upon to accomplish its objectives. A supply chain includes all processes from extracting raw materials to the final products that end up on store shelves. Supply chains are often global in nature as raw materials are sourced from some countries (often in developing nations) and then are finished off as consumer products (often in wealthier nations). Farmers, natural resource companies, transportation companies and manufacturing organizations comprise the supply chain. Supply chain networks are managed to ensure that corporations have the right materials, at the right time, to meet the demand for desired products or services. Supply chains exist as

> a network of relationships within a firm and between interdependent organizations and business units consisting of material suppliers, purchasing, production facilities, logistics, marketing, and related systems that facilitate the forward and reverse flow of materials, services, finances and information from the original producer to final customer with the benefits of adding value, maximizing profitability through efficiencies, and achieving customer satisfaction. (Stock and Boyer, 2009, p. 706)

Supply chain management ensures that raw materials and products produced across the chain follow the ethical and sustainable principles stated by the corporation selling the products to consumers. Unethical or unsustainable practices at the lower ends of the supply chain can negatively affect larger corporations (Roberts, 2003). A corporation's promise of sustainable and ethical sourcing is only as good as its partners down the chain.

Covid-19 and other global events like war and conflict have shown how vulnerable global supply chains can be. A disruption in one part of the network can negatively influence others who sit further up or down on the supply chain. A supply chain can experience network vulnerabilities that are not just related to Covid-19. Supply chain networks may have other vulnerabilities that can be leveraged by activists.

Supply chains provide a useful lens to understand digital activism and network relationships. We argue that it is not the 'just in time' management strategy and the overall availability of resources that make corporations vulnerable to supply chain disruption. We also believe that activism can disrupt supply chains by encouraging network members to pressure others to change their behaviour through the threat of breaking off business relationships.

This chapter begins with a discussion of activism (Smith and Ferguson, 2010) and positions activism within a network engagement framework (Johnston and Taylor, 2018; Yang and Taylor, 2015). It explores how activists are using communication to encourage corporations to undertake changes in their supply chain networks. The chapter shows the digital interactions, networks, negotiations and evolving relationships through a case study of decades-long digital activism against the Asian Pulp and Paper Company – a long-time target of environmental activists like Greenpeace. The final section discusses future directions for digital activism and corporations.

154　*Handbook on digital corporate communication*

DEFINITIONS AND PREVIOUS RESEARCH

Engagement in Civil Society: A Network Approach

Civil society is the ground upon which diverse public spheres come together. Civil society means that there are "institutions that represent groups within the society, in broad cultural, political, and ideological senses, both in the context of society itself and in relations to the state" (Shaw, 1996, p. 13). There are many different types of partners in a civil society. Taylor (2009) identified seven civil society partners: (1) individuals, (2) social cause groups such as activists, NGOs or non-profits, (3) societal institutions including army, political process and public sector organizations, (4) media, (5) business organizations such as corporations, (6) governance, and (7) international organizations. These seven partners have the potential to create a foundation for civil society by representing different citizen and societal interests. Partners develop their own networks of like-minded organizations to pursue common interests. For instance, individuals join groups that advocate for their priorities. Groups collaborate with like-minded groups or media to amplify their voice and impact. Corporations, sometimes even competitors, come together in industry or trade groups to advocate on shared issues. Civil society exists when these partners have interrelated objectives. When the interests of two or more civil society partners converge, then there is a much greater opportunity for those groups to achieve their goals. An enduring civil society occurs when there is engagement among different combinations of the seven partners' interests.

Stakeholder Engagement

Corporations have many different stakeholders and must make strategic decisions about which stakeholders to engage at which times and on which issues. A stakeholder can be considered a person, group or party with an interest in the actions and decisions of a corporation. Stakeholder salience theory (Agle et al., 1999; Frooman, 1999; Mitchell et al., 1997) has been extensively applied in the communication management literature (Lewis, 2007). Mitchell et al. (1997, p. 853) proposed a normative theory of stakeholder identification to explain why "managers should consider certain classes of entities as stakeholders". Publics who are active in digital media can be divided into faith-holders and hateholders. Luoma-aho (2015) defined faith-holders as "positively engaged stakeholders who trust and like the organization or brand and support it via their beliefs, emotions and behaviours" (Luoma-aho, 2015, p. 9). They may defend the organization when it is targeted by activists. While faith-holders have a positive orientation to an organization, hateholders are negatively engaged stakeholders who "dislike or hate the brand or the organization and harm it via their behaviours" (Luoma-aho, 2015, p. 11).

Implicitly associated with discussions of the concept of stakeholders is the concept of engagement. The research on engagement has grown over the last decade (Johnston and Taylor, 2018) with much of it coming from the public relations discipline but making clear contributions to corporate communication. Engagement can be understood as a psychological state that comprises three dimensions: cognitive, affective and behavioural (Dhanesh, 2017; Johnston and Taylor, 2018; Karanges et al., 2015; Men, 2012; Welch, 2011). Johnston (2018, p. 22) defined the *cognitive dimension* as "an individual's investment in attention and processing to develop understanding or knowledge about a topic or an idea". There are also *affective dimensions* of engagement which include both positive and negative emotions. Cho et al.

Digital corporate communication and activism 155

(2014) noted that digital and social media engagement are generally characterized by the level of *behavioural dimension* of engagement (low, medium, high) on actions such as clicks, likes, comments, tweets, shares, views and other user-generated content or activities. Many stakeholders engage in this low-level relationship with corporations, and this is where many digital activist campaigns begin as well. This level of relationship allows the corporation to engage with publics, but some activists create closed groups, making it difficult for corporations to engage members.

There is also a social level of engagement that "can be represented in behavioural (collective action, group participation), cognitive (shared knowledge) and affective forms (orientation, intention and experience) and is an outcome of a dynamic, socially situated system" (Johnston, 2018, p. 26). The three dimensions interact to create a social level of engagement within a group. Johnston and Taylor (2018) noted that engagement has an impact on individuals and society in general, and the impact is not necessarily positive, though the positive side of engagement is what is primarily stressed by corporation communication scholarship (Johnston and Taylor, 2018). It is this level that digital activism seeks to change. Digital activists seek to change corporate and social systems. It is through engagement that meaning is co-created, relationships emerge and narratives are exchanged by individuals, groups and networks (Johnston and Taylor, 2018).

Network Theory

Network theory embodies both implicit and explicit engagement assumptions. Marin and Wellman (2011) noted that a social network is a set of relationships among related social actors. The social network perspective argues that social networks are the "primary building blocks of society. To study these networks, the social network perspective examines the patterns of relations, monitors flow of resources, and reveals how social structural factors constrain or foster the activities of networked actors" (Yang and Taylor, 2015, p. 96). All organizations operate within networks. Corporations are embedded in networks of supply/ value chains, competitors, peers, industry experts, government and supra-government organizations (UN, EU, NATA, ASEAN), consumers and activists.

Yang and Taylor (2015) offered a conceptual model of a network approach to organization– public relationships. Figure 11.1 illustrates different network building strategies for specific outcomes.

The focus of their model is to build relationships. They did not take into account that some organizations may not be working to build positive, empowering relationships but instead may use their network position and power to sanction or break ties with other organizations. It is the consideration of engagement in this different approach to network relationships that informs this chapter.

Over the past few years, communication scholars have studied how activist organizations have used social media to influence organizations (Thompson, 2018; Woods, 2019). Despite repeated calls from scholars to go beyond dyadic studies of organization–public relationships (Saffer et al., 2018), we still see a prevalence of dyadic activist–organization studies in the literature. This chapter considers a network approach to digital activism that is not dyadic in nature but is instead network based. The network of interest is the evolution of supply chains/ value chains in which network members may influence others' behaviours up and down the supply chain.

Source: Used with permission from Yang and Taylor (2015).

Figure 11.1   The grid of network building strategies and tactics

One of the most important networks influencing an organization's success is its supply chain. Over the last 20 years, business scholars have suggested that a better way to understand supply chains is to see them as 'value chains'. Feller et al. (2006, p. 1) noted that "the primary focus in value chains is on the benefits that accrue to customers, the interdependent processes that generate value, and the resulting demand and funds flows that are created". Value chains matter because the professionalism, transparency and ethics of an organization's 'down the chain' relationships influence its final product or service provided to consumers or other businesses (i.e., B2B). Feller et al. (2006, p. 4) note that "value chains focus downstream, on creating value in the eyes of the customer". Thus, in a value chain, value is created or lost in the chain based on how consumers feel and behave toward a product or service. Value is co-created and the consumer is not just the recipient of the product or service but is engaged in the entire value process.

Relationships in a value chain go beyond functional reciprocity. Relationships are built on trust, transparency, reliability and resource dependency (Pfeffer and Salancik, 1978). Many supply chains are held together by sector wide associations and trade groups. For instance, in the beef industry, there are at least 20 different governance, statutory and NGO organizations that monitor the supply chain (Friends of the Earth, 2014). Companies join these groups for both individual level and group level advantages. For example, corporate leaders may take on industry-wide leadership roles and sometimes competitors become cooperative partners around issues that affect the sector. When it comes to activism, corporations can respond as individual entities or as members of a network. The next section looks at activism in the supply chain.

Evolving Activist Engagement in Value Chains

The Internet and social media allow both activist organizations and corporations to build public support and mobilize resources. Over time, we can see that activism has evolved. Minocher (2019) provided insights into the evolution of how social media advocacy can create corporate change through case stories of Mars and Amazon, Canada. Minocher tracked how Change.org, a petition-based platform that collected signatures and supported social media advocacy, moved from petition (step one) to media coverage (step two) to corporate change (final step), concluding:

> For an activist public to be effective, it must attract and engage a large number of participants: this increases the likelihood of further participants, extensive sharing on personal social media, and the attraction of public media attention. Although critical meanings emerge from the activist public, much of the criticality is limited to the activist public itself until the media picks up the story. (Minocher, 2019, p. 634)

George and Leidner (2019) note that online activism is not always benign, but that gladiator activism, such as hacking, distributed denial of service (DDOS), and personal exposure of individuals, often creates higher impact than more passive digital approaches like clicktivism. George and Leidner (2019) concluded that diverse digital media tactics will need to be used in different circumstances.

Digital Activism and Corporate Communication

Both activists and corporations rely on and incorporate digital communication into their communication portfolios. Corporations often use digital communication in a one-way model sending out messages to social media publics. Their digital communication is often marketing focused rather than focused on building mutually beneficial relationships. However, in addition to using digital media as a tool to communicate with publics, activists use social media to pressure corporations and their stakeholders to change their behaviour.

WHAT IS CHANGING?

There are several major changes in the tools, processes and practices fomented by digital media that affect relationships between corporations and activists. First, in terms of communication tools, the rise of the Internet and online social networks has created additional mediated channels that have been utilized for social change. New channels allow people from different locations to share common understandings of problems and co-create and coordinate a shared vision of action. Technology allows them to work together on similar issues, thus amplifying the impact of the activism at both a local and global level. Digital tools allow activists to bridge and connect to others. These connections alter the flow of information in an activist network, thus allowing some organizations to gain influence in the network. Social media have a role to play in activism because they create engagement opportunities between organizations and publics. Digital communication has created activist impacts at local, national, regional and global levels.

158   *Handbook on digital corporate communication*

Second, the process of corporate engagement with stakeholders, including activists, is no longer limited to *external relationships*. In recent years, a new trend has emerged in which shareholder activists have formed networks to empower shareholders and magnify shareholder voices. Yang et al. (2017) explored the structural patterns and effectiveness of shareholder activism networks. Shareholder activists are internal stakeholders. They are the people who own corporate stock and seek to influence the organization from 'the inside'. In the United States, since 1992, the Securities and Exchange Committee has relaxed rules that had previously prohibited shareholders from communicating with one another. This change in regulation has enhanced activists' use of social media to form alliances and activism networks based on their disapproval of corporate practices (Goranova and Ryan, 2015). In recent decades, shareholder activists have formed online networks to empower themselves. They magnify their voices through social media (Yang et al., 2017). Shareholder activism networks are created when shareholders join forces to file a resolution against certain corporations. It is digital communication that creates and ties these shareholder activists together.

Third, and perhaps most important for this chapter, is the realization that corporate communication practices are changing. Corporations seem more willing to listen to activists and they are using digital media to listen (Macnamara, 2016). Heath (2006) argued that corporations need to act in enlightened self-interest by balancing corporate needs with societal expectations. Corporate managers now see activists as canaries in the coalmine and can adjust their business strategies to meet societal expectations. Managers may proactively reach out to most central shareholder activists, such as religious organizations, because they can be influential actors (Yang et al., 2017). By properly responding to these activists' demands through the engagement process and proactively enacting change in corporations, managers may mitigate the potential pressure from larger activism networks. In addition, corporations should monitor the building of online coalitions among shareholder activists to better anticipate issues that may gain considerable popularity among shareholders. Popular issues among shareholder activists give managers early warning signals of serious issues ahead. These three changes, made possible by social and digital media, signal opportunities for activists and corporations to work together.

WHAT REMAINS THE SAME?

From 'In the Streets' to 'On Your Screen'

Activism relies on the contributions of both organizations and individuals. In the past, activism required face-to-face communication or mediated communication for issues mobilization and coordination. Face-to-face communication was at the heart of activism because that was how people met others who shared similar ideas. Face-to-face interactions created collaborative action through engagement (Snow et al., 1980). Activism and social movements have generally mobilized people in large numbers to raise the visibility of their issues and rallies were often deemed effective when large numbers of people (and media) attended (Snow et al., 1980). Street protests that often confronted police or military gained lots of media attention (Kim, 2018). Thus, past activism followed an 'in the streets' approach.

Over the last two decades, research that informs corporate communication practice has moved from studying how organizations respond to or attempt to control activists to studying how activists use communication to achieve social outcomes. Dozier and Lauzen (2001) were among the first to call for scholars to study activists. Ciszek (2016), Veil et al. (2015) and Xiong et al. (2019) have provided deep insights into how digital tools can be used by activists. Activism has moved from the 'in the streets' approach to 'on your screen'. Activism is created by communication strategies such as information exchange, persuasion, network and coalition building, and publicly identifying organizations and brands that violate societal expectations. Activism outcomes are amplified from tools and tactics such as online petitions, social networks, hashtag activism, blogs, hashtag hijacking, podcasts and crowdsourcing, as discussed below.

- **Online petitions as tools.** Websites such as Change.org, ipetitions.org and Avaaz.org are hubs for online activism. Citizens and activists can communicate with others regarding their cause. Petitions show corporations that people across the world are interested in an issue. They are valuable because they articulate the exact actions that are required by corporations to address a problem. Corporations can show that they are listening to activists when they respond to petitions.
- **Social networks as tools.** Facebook, YouTube, Instagram, Tumblr, TikTok and others help to spread social and political messages. Social networks are powerful tools because people share content with friends and thus amplify message credibility. Facebook created Workplace which is an internal social networking site for corporations to share information with employees. For activists, social media are powerful tools for sharing videos, memes and news. For corporations, social networks provide direct access to people who have expressed an interest in the organization. Corporations can use social networks to build awareness and agency. They can also use social networks to correct misinformation or immediately communicate with social media followers.
- **Influencer content (such as blogs/vlogs) as tools.** Influencer content is everywhere. Blogs are one of the tools used to influence opinions and behaviours. Kent (2008) called blogs one of the most under-used tools for strategic communication. A blogger can be a citizen journalist, an activist, a corporate leader or just about anyone who wants to share their views. Blogs are not limited by space or time and often lead media content and provide valuable frames for understanding issues. Blogs are valuable to activists because they can reach followers. Knowing which bloggers are experts on which topics helps corporations and activists to identify influencers. In addition to blogs, there are video blogs/logs, sometimes shortened to vlog, which provide video. Vlogs are tools that combine embedded video with supporting text, images and other metadata. Like blogs, they are shared across social media leveraging network connections.
- **Crowdsourcing platforms as tools.** Crowdsourcing facilitates organizational interactions with publics, and it can include publics in the organization's decision-making. Park and Kang (2020) noted that crowdsourcing can help corporations build relationships through corporate social responsibility (CSR). Digital communication has made possible crowdsourcing platforms as well. Crowdsourcing brings people together for fundraising, problem-solving and advocacy. GoFundMe helps individuals and activists to mobilize a global community and create collaboration among unconnected people. Wikipedia, Kickstarter and Indiegogo also provide opportunities to grow support for an issue.
- **Podcasts and YouTube as tools.** Many activists use podcasts and YouTube to share information, fundraise and activate their base. Podcasts have a learning dimension to

160　*Handbook on digital corporate communication*

them. Ciszek (2013) studied how YouTube provided a space for LGBTQ youth in the "It Gets Better" campaign to deal with bullying, family pressure and societal expectations. The platform amplified positive messaging and showed people they were not alone. Corporations, elected officials and other influencers have used podcasts and YouTube to call for social change. The platforms can organize members of activist groups and motivate active or aware publics to action. YouTube and podcasts provide archived content that stimulates discussions and they also foster network formation.

- **Hashtag activism tactics.** Unlike blogs, micro-blogging sites such as Sina Weibo or Twitter provide short messages about an issue. Hashtags (#) allow people to have their tweets contribute to larger global conversations. Social movements have been able to organize activism around hashtags such as #metoo (sexual harassment) or #BlackLivesMatter (racial equality). Xiong et al. (2019, p. 20) view hashtag activism as a form of participatory culture which encourages the public to become involved in "civic engagement and social change".
- **Hashtag hijacking tactics.** Related to micro-blogging is the tactic of hashtag hijacking or tweetjacking. These are more aggressive forms of activist use of micro-blogs. Sanderson et al. (2016, p. 35) noted that "not only can the audience hijack the campaign, but in doing so, the media can be alerted, which can result in negative press and an inflammation of the crisis and reinforce negative perceptions of the organization". Corporations don't usually hijack others' hashtags, making this tactic more relevant for activists to use in their engagement with corporations in the value chain.
- **Cancel tactics.** Activists can also use digital media to create 'cancel' tactics and campaigns. Cancel culture has emerged as a way to ostracize people and organizations that are perceived to have violated social norms. To be cancelled means that someone or a group is shunned within society. Cancel culture 'calls out' bad behaviour and tries to stop certain people or organizations from speaking.

CRITICAL EXAMINATION

While many scholars and activists are very optimistic about the value of digital media for activist outcomes, there are some challenges that need to be acknowledged. One of the more aggressive tactics that has been used to target corporations is distributed denial of service (DDOS) attacks. Google (2020) and Amazon (2020) have been targets of large-scale attacks that shut down services. Sauter (2019, p. 1) notes that:

> DDoS actions have become a popular tactic for digital activism, due to their ability to involve many casual participants and the relative ease with which they can be deployed. Activist DoS and DDoS actions are controversial, having been simultaneously compared with respected tactics like sit-ins and denigrated as censorship or network damage.

DDOS attacks can be problematic because they affect the people who rely on those corporations for services, products or even employment.

Activists may also face problems from some of the unintended consequences of digital activism against corporations. For example, people outside of an activist movement can hijack messages, slogans and hashtags and pretend to represent the activist group. Activists who anonymously participate regularly on social media discussions could be 'outed' by companies that purchase analytics to identify those activists. Trolling and fake accounts are problems as well. However, for most corporations and activist groups, social and digital media will continue to be a part of their corporate communication strategy in the future. The next section provides some examples of both well-known and recent case studies of activists' use of social media.

ILLUSTRATIVE EXAMPLE: THE ASIA PULP AND PAPER (APP) COMPANY

A good way to understand the use of digital media and 'in the streets' activism between corporations and activists is through the case study of digital activism targeting the Asia Pulp and Paper (APP) company. APP is a Singapore-based paper manufacturing company. It operates in Indonesia and across Asia, packaging and distributing over 20 million tons of products per year to more than 150 countries across six continents. Its business relationships span the Global Fortune 500 and APP products can be found in most retailers and homes. It comprises two private, family-owned companies and two publicly traded companies.

Activists had long targeted APP for buying wood products resourced from old growth and endangered forests. Environmentalists have criticized APP for its lack of transparency in its supply chain. Environmental activists have reported that APP continues to obscure the source of pulp and is continuing illegal, unethical and unsustainable practices. In 2011, Greenpeace activists turned their attention from directly trying to stop APP from logging in Indonesia's old growth forests to pressuring its supply chain partner, US-based Mattel, makers of the popular Barbie and Ken dolls and accessories (Roosevelt, 2011). Greenpeace mobilized activists from around the world, Mattel shareholders and parents to pressure Mattel to change its sourcing relationship with suppliers who were illegally logging old growth forests in Indonesia. The activist campaign included Facebook, Twitter, petitions and other social media tactics.

Activists have learned that the supply chain of consumer product companies that buy raw materials from environmentally negligent companies can be a more productive avenue for achieving environmental objectives. Today, activists do not just target a company, they can also demand that a finished goods company better manage or break relationships in its lower value chain. Value chain activism occurs when activists or shareholders identify ethical violations in the sourcing of raw or finished materials. Kovacs (2006) noted that the supply chain and sustainable development are core CSR principles for many corporations.

A decade later, Greenpeace and the Environmental Paper Network (EPN) activists again turned their attention from directly stopping APP from logging in Indonesia's old growth forests to targeting organizations on the higher end of the supply chain that use APP products. A 2020 open letter that was disseminated widely through social media and petitions demanded:

> We, Indonesian and international organizations, encourage buyers and investors to avoid brands and papers linked to APP, Sinar Mas, Paper Excellence and their sister companies controlled by APP's owner, the Widjaya family. (Civil Society Open Letter, 2020)

In 2022, Greenpeace and the EPN used social media again to force APP's supply chain to stop using its products. Because of the social media campaigns and other activist efforts, global companies that have discontinued sourcing from APP include Adidas, Disney, Fuji,

162 *Handbook on digital corporate communication*

Gucci, Hasbro, Kraft, Lego, Levis, Marks & Spencer, Nestlé, Office Depot, Scholastic, Tesco, Tiffany & Co., United Stationers, Unilever, Volkswagen, Wal-Mart, Woolworths and Xerox.

CONCLUSION AND FUTURE DIRECTIONS

Activist groups are using digital communication to organize their members and inform, persuade and pressure corporations to change. Today's activism now includes online tactics such as hashtag advocacy, hashtag hijacking and tweetjacking, DDOS attacks, and other online tactics that seek to pressure corporations to change their behaviour. As technology evolves in the future, so too will digital activism. Corporations will have to be mindful that activists are committed to social and environmental change and that they are equal partners in civil society. Corporations need to consider the outcomes of their decisions and be aware that they are vulnerable to activists. The future likely holds more digital activism and greater demands for corporate accountability.

It is clear that activist communication can influence corporations and their supply chain. Activists play their role in civil society by providing a much-needed level of oversight of corporate behaviour. They define problems in society and identify solutions that have real tangible outcomes for society. Yet, digital media are only one tool in the activists' tool chest. There will also be a need for people to advocate in person and a mixed model of activism will continue as demands for corporate ethics and sustainability grow.

Future research should continue to explore the new and diverse ways that activists can use via digital media to create social change. We should also study how corporations respond to digital activism to identify new patterns of stakeholder engagement. Finally, future research should look for ways to match the best social media tactics and platforms with social outcomes. Such research would help corporate communicators, activists and even platform designers to better create and employ engaging digital media.

REFERENCES

Agle, B. R., Mitchell, R. K., and Sonnefeld, J. A. (1999). Who matters to CEOs? An investigation of stakeholder attributes and salience, corporate performance, and CEO values. *Academy of Management Journal, 42*, 507–525.

Cho, M., Schweickart, T., and Haase, A. (2014). Public engagement with nonprofit organizations on Facebook. *Public Relations Review, 40*(3), 565–567.

Ciszek, E. L. (2013). Advocacy and amplification: Non-profit outreach and empowerment through participatory media. *Public Relations Journal, 7*(2), 187–213.

Ciszek, E. L. (2016). Digital activism: How social media and dissensus inform theory and practice. *Public Relations Review, 42*(2), 314–321.

Civil Society Open Letter About APP's Recurrent Violation of Farmers' Land Rights in Jambi, Indonesia (2020). https://environmentalpaper.org/wp-content/uploads/2020/05/20200515-NGOs-letter-on-APP-violation.pdf.

Dhanesh, G. S. (2017). Putting engagement in its PRoper place: State of the field, definition and model of engagement in public relations. *Public Relations Review, 43*(5), 925–933.

Dozier, D. M. and Lauzen, M. M. (2000). Liberating the intellectual domain from the practice: Public relations, activism, and the role of the scholar. *Journal of Public Relations Research, 12*, 3–22.

Edwards, F., Howard, P. N., and Joyce, M. (2013). Digital activism and non-violent conflict. https://papers.ssrn.com/sol3/papers.cfm?abstract_id=2595115.

Digital corporate communication and activism   163

Feller, A., Shunk, D., and Callarman, T. (2006). Value chains versus supply chains. *BP Trends*, *1*, 1–7.

Friends of the Earth (2014). Leading NGOs slam greenwashing by meat industry, demand beefier sustainability standards. https://foe.org/news/2014-11-leading-ngos-slam-greenwashing-by-meat-industry-demand-beefier-sustainability-standards/.

Frooman, J. (1999). Stakeholder influence strategies. *Academy of Management Review*, *24*(2), 191–205.

George, J. G. and Leidner, D. E. (2019). From clicktivism to hacktivism: Understanding digital activism. *Information & Organization*, *29*(3), 1–45.

Goranova, M. and Ryan, L. V. (2015). Shareholder empowerment: An introduction. In M. Goranova and L. V. Ryan (eds), *Shareholder empowerment: A new era in corporate governance* (pp. 1–32). Basingstoke: Palgrave Macmillan.

Grunig, L. A. (1992). Activism: How it limits the effectiveness of organizations and how excellent public relations departments respond. In J. Grunig (ed.), *Excellence and public relations and communications management* (pp. 503–530). Mahwah, NJ: Lawrence Erlbaum Associates.

Heath, R. L. (2006). Onward into more fog: Thoughts on public relations' research directions. *Journal of Public Relations Research*, *18*, 93–114.

Johnston, K. A. (2018). Toward a theory of social engagement. In K. A. Johnston and M. Taylor (eds.), *The handbook of communication engagement* (pp. 19–32). Malden, MA: Wiley-Blackwell.

Johnston, K. A. and Taylor, M. (eds.) (2018). *The handbook of communication engagement*. Malden, MA: Wiley-Blackwell.

Karanges, E., Johnston, K. A., Beatson, A. T., and Lings, I. (2015). The influence of internal communication on employee engagement: A pilot study. *Public Relations Review*, *41*(1), 129–131.

Kent, M. L. (2008). Critical analysis of blogging in public relations. *Public Relations Review*, *34*(1), 32–40.

Kim, J. (2018). Why do people take to the streets? Understanding the multidimensional motivations of protesting publics. *Public Relations Review*, *44*(4), 501–513.

Kovacs, R. (2006). Interdisciplinary bar for the public interest: What CSR and NGO frameworks contribute to the public relations of British and European activists. *Public Relations Review*, *32*(4), 429–431.

Lewis, L. K. (2007). An organizational stakeholder model of change implementation communication. *Communication Theory*, *17*(2), 176–204.

Luoma-aho, V. (2015). Understanding stakeholder engagement: Faith-holders, hateholders & fakeholders. *RJ-IPR: Research Journal of the Institute for Public Relations*, *2*(1). http://www.instituteforpr.org/understanding-stakeholder-engagement-fai.

Macnamara, J. R. (2016). *Organizational listening: The missing essential in public communication*. New York: Peter Lang.

Marin, A. and Wellman, B. (2011). Social network analysis: An introduction. In J. Scott and P. J. Carrington (eds.), *The SAGE handbook of social network analysis* (pp. 11–25). London: Sage Publications.

McCarthy, J. D. and Zald, M. N. (1977). Resource mobilization and social movements: A partial theory. *American Journal of Sociology*, *82*(6), 1212–1241.

Men, L. R. (2012). CEO credibility, perceived organizational reputation, and employee engagement. *Public Relations Review*, *38*(1), 171–173.

Minocher, X. (2019). Online consumer activism: Challenging companies with Change.org. *New Media & Society*, 21(3), 620–638.

Mitchell, R. K., Agle, B. R., and Wood, D. J. (1997). Toward a theory of stakeholder identification and salience: Defining the principle of who and what really counts. *Academy of Management Review*, *22*(4), 853–886.

Park, Y. E. and Kang, M. (2020). When crowdsourcing in CSR leads to dialogic communication: The effects of trust and distrust. *Public Relations Review*, *46*(1), 101867.

Pfeffer, J. and Salancik, G. (1978). *The external control of organizations: A resource dependence perspective*. New York: Harper and Row.

Roberts, S. (2003). Supply chain specific? Understanding the patchy success of ethical sourcing initiatives. *Journal of Business Ethics*, *44*(2), 159–170.

Roosevelt, R. (2011). Greenpeace versus Mattel: A social media battle over rain forest. https://latimesblogs.latimes.com/greenspace/2011/06/mattel-rainforest-greenpeace-social-media.html.

Saffer, A. J., Yang, A., and Taylor, M. (2018). Reconsidering power in multi-stakeholder relationship management. *Management Communication Quarterly*, *32*(1), 121–139.

Sanderson, J., Barnes, K., Williamson, C., and Kian, E. T. (2016). 'How could anyone have predicted that #AskJameis would go horribly wrong?' Public relations, social media, and hashtag hijacking. *Public Relations Review*, *42*(1), 31–37.

Sauter, M. (2019). Denial of service action. In R. Hobbs, P. Mihailidis, G. Cappello, M. Ranieri, and B. Thevenin (eds.), *The international encyclopedia of media literacy* (pp. 1–9). Malden, MA: Wiley-Blackwell.

Shaw, M. (1996). *Civil society and media in global crises: Representing distinct violence*. London: Pinter.

Smith, M. (2005). Ecological citizenship and ethical responsibility: Arendt, Benjamin and political activism. *Environments*, *33*(3), 51.

Smith, M. and Ferguson, D. (2010). Activism. In R. L. Heath (ed.), *The handbook of public relations* (pp. 291–300). London: Sage Publications.

Snow, D. A., Zurcher, L. A., and Ekland-Olson, S. (1980). Social networks and social movements: A microstructural approach to differential recruitment. *American Sociological Review*, *45*(5), 787–801.

Stock, J. R. and Boyer, S. L. (2009). Developing a consensus definition of supply chain management: A qualitative study. *International Journal of Physical Distribution & Logistics Management*, *39*(8), 690–711.

Taylor, M. (2009). Civil society as a rhetorical public relations process. In R. Heath, E. L. Toth, and D. Waymer (eds.), *Rhetorical and critical approaches to public relations II* (pp. 76–91). Mahwah, NJ: Lawrence Erlbaum Associates.

Thompson, G. (2018). Social gains from the public relations voice of activist investors: The case of Herbalife and Pershing Square Capital Management. *Public Relations Review*, *44*(4), 481–489.

Veil, S., Reno, J., Jordan, J. and Oldham, R. (2015). Online activists vs. Kraft foods: A case of social media hijacking. *Public Relations Review*, *42*, 103–108.

Welch, M. (2011). The evolution of the employee engagement concept: Communication implications. *Corporate Communications: An International Journal*, *14*, 328–346.

Woods, C. L. (2019). From an "outside group" to a catalyst for corporate change: Examining activists' legitimation strategies. *Public Relations Review*, *45*(2), 332–347.

Xiong, Y., Cho, M., and Boatwright, B. (2019). Hashtag activism and message frames among social movement organizations: Semantic network analysis and thematic analysis of Twitter during the #MeToo movement. *Public Relations Review*, *45*(1), 10–23.

Yang, A. and Taylor, M. (2015). Looking over, looking out, and moving forward: A network ecology framework to position public relations in communication theory. *Communication Theory*, *25*, 91–115.

Yang, A., Uysal, N., and Taylor, M. (2017). Unleashing the power of networks: Shareholder activism, sustainable development and corporate environmental policy. *Business Strategy and the Environment*, *16*, 141–154.

12. Digital corporate communication and paracrises and AI

Timothy Coombs and Sherry Holladay

INTRODUCTION

The digital environment is causing changes to corporate communication. These changes tend to take two forms. First, simple translations shift tasks from analogue to digital such as moving from print to digital messaging. Second, evolutionary steps are significant changes in how a corporate communication function must be approached. This chapter argues for the understanding of digital corporate communication (DCC) as the strategic management of digital technologies to improve communication in organizations, in society, and with organizational stakeholders for the maintenance of organizational intangible and tangible assets. Organizational crises are threats to stakeholder relationships that can impact tangible and intangible corporate assets. In addition, crises disrupt strategy by distracting managers from organizational goals. Corporate crisis communication, with a focus on organizations in crisis, should be considered a strategic communicative response to disruption. Corporate crisis communication reflects the duality of threat and opportunity. While a crisis is a threat, the crisis response, manifest through crisis communication, is an opportunity. The performance of the crisis response can mend the damage a crisis might inflict upon an organization and its stakeholders.

Crisis communication serves to protect stakeholders and the organization from harm. Moreover, crisis communication seeks to re-establish organizational strategy by redressing the strategic disruption posed by a crisis (Coombs and Tachkova, 2023). Digital technologies have become a part of crisis communication. Unfortunately, crisis communication research often focuses on the digital channels as 'unique' without considering how these channels relate to the larger practice of crisis communication. Some researchers cannot see the forest for the trees. In this chapter, we take a holistic approach to examining how corporate crisis communication has changed with the growth of digital communication thereby illuminating the evolutionary steps of one segment of DCC.

DEFINITIONS AND PAST RESEARCH

A Crisis

Any time researchers use the term 'crisis' there is a need to clarify its use because it is such a broad concept. This chapter examines crisis within the context of a corporation, hence with a focus on organization crises. An organizational crisis can be defined as "the perceived violation of salient stakeholder expectations that can create negative outcomes for stakeholders and/ or the organization" (Coombs, 2019, p. 3). Crises are driven by the perceptions of stakehold-

165

166 *Handbook on digital corporate communication*

ers, centre on violated expectations, and pose a threat to stakeholders and/or the organization. Furthermore, crises can disrupt corporate strategy by interrupting/limiting revenue generation, damaging the social evaluations by stakeholders such as reputation (Rindova et al., 2010), and distracting managers from organizational goals by demanding that they focus on the crisis. Part of defining a situation as a crisis is identifying that the situation demands attention and resources (Billings et al., 1980).

A crisis is a process rather than just an event. Many crises are event driven, such as industrial accidents. However, many crises are driven by a realization that there is a problem, such as in product harm crises. The regenerative model of crises argues that crises have two phases: pre-crisis and post-crisis. The pre-crisis phase encompasses all action prior to a crisis, including preparation and risk mitigation efforts by the corporation. Once a crisis is recognized, it shifts to the post-crisis phase which involves efforts to redress the crisis both immediately and long-term, including the crisis responses, follow-up messages, and efforts to facilitate stakeholder resilience. The regenerative model is dynamic because it considers turning points in crises. A turning point is when the crisis situation becomes significantly redefined. An example would be when the cause of a crisis shifts from being an isolated instance to a systemic problem or from an employee mistake to management misconduct. The turning point redefines the crisis in a way that demands a change in how the corporation responds to the crisis because the redefinition alters how stakeholders fundamentally view the crisis (Coombs, 2017).

Crisis Communication: Concepts and Theories

Corporate crisis communication can be viewed as the strategic response to the crisis-induced disruption that seeks to maximize benefits for the stakeholders and the organization affected by the crisis. A variety of theories have been developed to explore crisis communication. Corporate apologia and image repair theory are descriptive theories that focus on identifying crisis response strategies and potential effects of those messages (Coombs, 2019). *Stealing thunder* examines how the organization benefits from being the first to disclose the existence of a crisis (Arpan and Pompper, 2003; Claeys, 2017). Rhetorical arena theory (RAT) takes a multi-vocal approach to understanding the array of crisis communications that emerges when a rhetorical arena emerges around a crisis (Frandsen and Johansen, 2017). Situation crisis communication theory (SCCT) is a cognitive-based, prescriptive theory that identifies the optimal and suboptimal crisis response based upon which specific cues are used to define the crisis situation (Coombs, 2018; Coombs and Holladay, 2001). Social media crisis communication (SMCC) integrates social media into the crisis communication process including a refined understanding of various social media actors (Liu et al., 2013). Contingency theory has also been applied to crisis communication with a focus on understanding the threat aspect of a crisis.

WHAT IS CHANGING?

This chapter's focus is on what is changing in DCC and therefore addresses the two most significant evolutionary steps in crisis communication created by digital communication: (1) the rise of paracrises and (2) the utilization of AI in processing risk information.

Paracrisis: Context

The context is critical to understanding how paracrises relate to crises and their increasing relevance. The wider socio-political environment in which corporations operate as well as expectations for corporate action within this environment are changing rapidly. The roles and impacts of corporations in contemporary society are scrutinized and reimagined. These types of concerns often are included in the umbrella term *corporate social responsibility* (CSR). Aware of this trend, corporations increasingly devote resources to communicating how they enact CSR. Stakeholder demands for transparency coupled with their expectations for the ability to collect desired information has led corporations to supply an increasing amount of information online. Stakeholders want to know: "What are you doing for society and the environment and how are you doing it?" Moreover, stakeholders want to know how societal concerns and values are reflected in corporate practices. What do the corporations care about and how do they act upon those concerns? When stakeholders want to know the values and purpose of a corporation they may seek to support, an additional question is: "Are you on my side?" Overall, stakeholder expectations of corporate behaviour, including potentially divisive values-driven actions, have changed and stakeholders are better able to voice concerns about corporate actions via social media. However, because the expectations of different stakeholder groups can conflict, corporations risk alienating those groups who disagree with their CSR activities. Greater stakeholder activism due to violations of stakeholders' expectations means corporations have witnessed increases in the frequencies of paracrises.

The connection between social assessments and CSR is critical for understanding the emergence and relevance of paracrises for corporate communication. Reputation is a very common and valued social assessment monitored by organizations. Managers want to protect reputational assets. Increasingly, perceptions of CSR are a critical facet of reputations. CSR assessments comprise over 40 per cent of most corporate reputations (Smith, 2012).

Engaging in CSR creates a risk for a corporation. Once a corporation publicly commits to CSR and incorporates it into its reputation, the corporation becomes vulnerable to claims of social irresponsibility (Coombs and Holladay, 2015b). Corporations that have never been considered socially responsible are much less vulnerable to charges of social irresponsibility because they have never been dependent upon that perception to create favourable social assessments (King, 2008). Stakeholders can create power by threatening perceptions of CSR.

Digital technology facilitates the ability of social irresponsibility claims to threaten social assessments. Research into boycotts, one form of presenting social irresponsibility claims, finds that media attention is a major factor in determining the success or failure of a boycott to drive corporate change. The reason media attention matters is because it increases the reputational threat posed by the boycott (King, 2008, 2011; McDonnell and King, 2013) by increasing awareness of the claims. Prior to the Internet, activists had to rely upon coverage from traditional media (what is known as media advocacy) to attract attention to their claims of social irresponsibility. Now, social media platforms and other digital channels are utilized to focus attention on and to create awareness of irresponsible corporate practices (Coombs and Holladay, 2012a, 2012b, 2015a, 2015b).

The shift to digital channels is important because activists now depend more on owned media than on earned media. Owned media allows activists to control when a message appears and how it appears. Earned media is dependent on gatekeepers who decide if a message is used and how that message will appear. Publicity is an archetype of earned media. Owned media

168 *Handbook on digital corporate communication*

can create a crossover by attracting the attention of traditional media thereby amplifying attention and awareness of a social irresponsibility claim (Coombs and Holladay, 2012b).

CSR, social assessments, and digital media are three interwoven threads used to create the tapestry that becomes the paracrisis. Social assessments become valued, intangible corporate assets. CSR is a critical element for developing favourable social assessments (positive corporate reputations). Digital channels provide a mechanism activists can employ to create perceptions of certain corporate polices/behaviours reflecting corporate irresponsibility thereby threatening social assessments. Concerns over damaged social assessments via perceptions of social irresponsibility nudge corporations towards changing the problematic practices.

Paracrisis: Definition

The term *paracrisis* was proposed by Coombs in 2012 to address problems associated with the overuse of the phrase 'social media crisis' to describe virtually any negative information about a corporation that appeared online (Coombs, 2012). As is the case with the development of any new technology, potential uses of social media were not well understood and corporations feared they were 'losing control' of their messages. The digital landscape was portrayed as the 'wild west' and fraught with danger. To sell their services, agencies and trade publications were quick to catastrophize the potential of 'social media crises' to damage reputations. Corporations were forced to adapt to an unfamiliar environment where stakeholders could post positive as well as critical posts that could be viewed by other interested stakeholders as well as the corporation. However, corporations learned that though stakeholders may post negative comments about an organization, their original comments and additional negative responses posted by other users very rarely met the criteria for defining the incident as a crisis.

The ambiguous phrase 'social media crisis' prompted Coombs to differentiate between crises and online risks, the latter of which became termed *paracrises* (Coombs and Holladay, 2012b). Crises and paracrises do share some characteristics: they are perceptual, violate at least some stakeholder expectations for responsible behaviour, and may affect both reputations and operations. Although a social construction process among the corporation and various stakeholder groups underlies both crises and paracrises, ultimately managers must decide whether they agree with stakeholder assessments (Coombs, 2012).

Coombs and Holladay (2012b, p. 409) defined a paracrisis as "a publicly visible crisis threat that charges an organization with irresponsible or unethical behavior". This definition includes three important characteristics. First, the online environment in which the paracrisis appears requires public management rather than private management of the challenge. Thus, stakeholders can see if and how the corporation manages the risk and leaves open the possibility of attracting additional stakeholders. An unsatisfactory paracrisis response may prompt further discussion and even engender a crisis. A second characteristic is the stakeholder challenge implicated in the crisis risk. The challenge seeks to redefine the corporation's actions as irresponsible (Lerbinger, 1997) and challenge reveals at least one vulnerability that may develop into a crisis. The challenge can serve as a warning sign that allows the corporation to anticipate and respond to potential problems. This enables a proactive rather than reactive response for identifying and managing risks. Thirdly, paracrises are primarily reputational risks because they signal expectation violations for responsible and ethical behaviour. The revelation of expectation gaps provides valuable information about stakeholder perceptions, knowledge, and values. Mismanagement of a paracrisis could escalate into an actual, operational crisis.

Digital corporate communication and paracrises and AI   169

For example, if a corporation fails to respond to the challenge, stakeholders could organize to disrupt its operations (see also Coombs and Holladay, 2015b).

The distinction between crisis and paracrisis is significant because a crisis poses a severe threat that can harm stakeholders and the corporation and thus necessitates a crisis management response. A crisis creates the exigency for crisis management whereas a paracrisis signals only a risk or threat that potentially requires risk management/preventative action. This makes paracrisis management akin to risk management which is part of the pre-crisis phase (Coombs, 2019). However, the fact that the corporation's response to the paracrisis may be visible and scrutinized means "the paracrisis blurs the line between pre-crisis and crisis response because addressing the paracrisis can appear to be a *crisis response* rather than *preventative action*" (Coombs, 2019, p. 6).

It also is the case that news media and others in the online environment may seek to exaggerate the risk and quickly declare the corporation is in crisis. Apt examples of hyperbole that garner attention but are not actually crises include situations where online content or critiques become "spectacles" or late-night talk show jokes through memes, parodies, and humour. Though the 'crisis' label may attract people's attention, the corporation's response(s) likely demonstrates a more nuanced, realistic appraisal of the situation and threat level.

Paracrisis: Types and Frequency of Occurrence

Various types of paracrises have been identified and refined over the years (e.g., Coombs 2012, 2017, 2019; Coombs and Holladay, 2012a, 2015b). Notably, the *challenge* implicated in the paracrisis has always been a central feature in explanations of paracrises and the challenge type of paracrisis was the first to be identified and elaborated (Coombs and Holladay, 2012a, 2015b). The idea of challenge can be traced to Lerbinger (1997) who first proposed the challenge type of crisis as a crisis that involves claims by some stakeholder group that a corporation is engaging in an action that is irresponsible or immoral. This is the heart of a CSR-based challenge paracrisis as well (Coombs and Holladay, 2012a, 2015b). The challenge type of paracrisis is linked to the rhetoric of agitation and control in which discontented stakeholders demand a response from the corporation. Challenges implicated in other types of paracrisis signal stakeholders are paying attention to the corporations' actions and develop negative perceptions of those actions.

The most comprehensive and useful study of paracrisis types was conducted by Chen (2019). Chen systematically identified and described 143 online situations from 2014 through 2017 that met the definition of a paracrisis and appeared in traditional media. She used their shared characteristics to identify six paracrisis clusters and offer more precise definitions of these paracrisis types. Chen also reported the frequencies with which these types were observed in her data set. The following paracrisis clusters were identified: (1) faux pas (two types) (39.16 per cent); (2) challenge (30.80 per cent); (3) guilt by association (22.38 per cent); (4) misinformation (3.50 per cent); (5) social media misuse (3.80 per cent); and (6) social media account hacking (0.7 per cent). The content of the faux pas paracrisis could take two forms, both of which result in online content that offends some stakeholders. In the first type, a corporation takes an action that is perceived by at least some stakeholder group as embarrassing, offensive, or insensitive. In the second type, the corporation unintentionally allows someone to create embarrassing or offensive content which is then attributed to the organization. In both types,

170   *Handbook on digital corporate communication*

at least some stakeholders criticize the organization and declare it culpable. Over one-third of the cases contained characteristics of a faux pas paracrisis.

The challenge cluster comprised less than one-third of the observed paracrises. However, as noted earlier, some form of stakeholder challenge underpins all paracrises. The challenge paracrisis cluster is consistent with past research that describes the corporation as being charged with unethical or irresponsible actions.

The last three paracrisis clusters were infrequently observed. The guilt by association cluster is characterized by the corporation's association with a negatively viewed actor. The misinformation cluster involves the circulation of false information about the corporation. In the social media misuse paracrisis cluster, the corporation's use of social media violates an 'unspoken rule' of social media to which stakeholders object. Lastly, the social media account hacking cluster involves an unauthorized entity taking control of a social media account creating content the corporation would never post.

AI, Big Data, Corporate Communication and Crisis Communication

Artificial intelligence (AI) is a broad category of software that allows computers to mimic intelligent human behaviour. AI ranges from very basic, such as a personal digital assistance like Siri or Alexa, to more advanced such as self-driving cars and machine learning. AI has been applied to corporate communication to address the analytic problems created by 'big data'. Big data is characterized by volume, velocity, and variety. Volume is the massive amount of data that exists. Velocity is the speed at which data is created. Variety refers to the types of data that are created including structured data (organized data such as information found in spreadsheets) and unstructured data (raw data such as social media posts and news stories) (Gewirtz, 2018). Big data is a potential source of actional information for corporate managers. The problem is how do managers extract actional information from a massive data set that continues to grow every minute? AI is one answer to addressing the analytic problems posed by big data.

An example of AI that has been applied to corporate communication is automated content analysis (ACA). Early ACA was simple counting and dictionaries that identified the number of specific words or co-occurring words in a data set. This is known as a visibility analysis and is used for sentiment analysis, a common metric found in corporate communication. Historically, corporations have wanted to know if traditional media coverage of the corporation is positive, negative, or neutral. Sentiment analysis can provide insights into social assessments (intangible assets). Now many corporations benefit from a sentiment analysis of social media data. However, social media data is big data that easily overwhelms the capacity of a corporate communication office to process. However, AI has more sophisticated applications beyond word counts and the co-occurrence of words.

Machine learning provides a more refined and sophisticated analysis of a data set. For instance, machine learning can be used to identify frames and themes (Boumans and Trilling, 2016), not just simple word counts and co-occurrences of words. Machine learning is the "study of computer algorithms that allow computer programs to automatically improve through experience" (Mitchell, 1997, p. 1). Machine learning examines and compares data to explore nuances and to find patterns. The algorithm is the mathematical model that helps the machine to identify patterns. Machine learning can be supervised or unsupervised. Supervised learning is predictive modelling that establishes a connection between variables X and Y.

Digital corporate communication and paracrises and AI 171

Supervised machine learning requires a classification algorithm as a starting point. Training data sets are used to help the computer 'learn' the algorithms (rules) used to identify patterns. The training data sets have been coded by humans. By processing the training data sets, the computer learns the rules the humans have used to identify the patterns. Various data sets are used to train and to validate the accuracy of the machine learning. Accuracy is determined by comparing the computer's coding to that by humans, much like identifying intercoder reliability in traditional content analysis. As the computer processes more data, the accuracy should improve, hence the idea of machine learning. Supervised learning has been used to help identify patterns in medicine and risk analysis (Baryannis et al., 2019; Park and Han, 2018).

Unsupervised learning is used to identify patterns that exist within a data set. The computer examines a large set of data for possible patterns. The problem is that it is easy to find patterns in data, but those patterns may not be relevant or useful. Data science defers to human review of the patterns to make sense of the results. If a useful pattern is found in the data, that new pattern can form the basis for future algorithms that can then be applied to supervised learning (Jiang et al., 2017).

Environmental scanning has long been a part of corporate communication through issues management and other functions (Coombs, 2019). Clever managers constantly scan for possible threats and opportunities. Proactive corporate communication is predicated upon environment scanning. Crisis communication is one of the functions of corporate communication that is driven by environmental scanning. Because environmental scanning frequently involves big data, managers are leveraging AI to combat the potential information overload. To summarize, the need to cope with big data is the reason AI has been integrated into corporate crisis communication.

AI helps to extract actionable information from the crisis scanning data by identifying risks that could escalate into crises and identifying when an organization is in a crisis (Coombs, 2019). Algorithms can be developed to identify risks. Humans can identify risks from data by looking for specific cues that suggest a risk exists. Computers can be trained to find those cues. For instance, AI has been used to locate supply chain risks (Baryannis et al., 2019). SCCT has identified cues associated with specific types of crises. Based upon SCCT, AI has been developed that can identify when an organization is in crisis and even the specific type of crisis. Moreover, AI can predict how various crisis responses will affect the time it takes for the discussion of the organization in crisis to return to pre-crisis levels (CapeStart, 2020). Crisis responses do affect tangible assets (stock valuations and purchase intentions) and intangible assets (social assessments). These two examples illustrate how DCC becomes enacted in corporate crisis communication through AI. The AI application in crisis communication is used to improve corporate communication, shape relationships with stakeholders, and does affect both intangible and tangible corporate assets.

This chapter views the application of AI to corporate crisis communication as evolutionary because it is a significant change to the communication process. Managers must learn how to integrate AI into corporate crisis communication. AI does not negate the need for human intelligence. Human intelligence must review the results and make the final decisions about whether or not a risk exists and what actions to take in regard to the risk or to determine if an organization is in crisis and how to respond to that crisis. AI provides a tool for enhancing crisis decision making by allowing crisis managers to understand the big data that now populates its environment.

WHAT REMAINS THE SAME?

Most of the effects of digital technologies on crisis communication have been simple translation. Simple translation is when digital technologies replace some existing technology but do not really change the nature of the corporate communication. Crisis management is an established function within corporate communication. Digital technologies have not altered the core components and primary tasks of communication. This chapter next focuses on the crisis communication plan (CCP), the crisis team, and crisis responses to illustrate the translation effect of digital technologies.

Crisis Communication Plan

The CCP is the element most closely associated with crisis management. A corporation is very likely to have a CCP and that might be its only crisis management effort. CCPs used to be binders or small cards, something with a physical presence the managers could hold. Now, CCPs are digital, making them easier to access. As long as you have a smart device, you have access to the digital CCP. Even in a digital form, the CCP must remain simple if it is to be usable. CCPs provide reminders of points to consider during a crisis, forms to document actions, and contact information for those who might be needed during a crisis. Digital technologies make it easier to connect the CCP with additional information, what is known as the crisis appendix (Coombs, 2019). Crisis managers often need additional information that is not in the CCP but can be helpful. An example would be links to sites with additional information such as the Centers for Disease Control if the crisis involves a foodborne illness. Such links would clutter a CCP, but the information is useful in the crisis response. CCPs and crisis appendices have always been about information storage and retrieval (Coombs, 2019). Digital technologies make the information storage and retrieval easier and faster. CCPs and crisis appendices have simply been translated from analogue to digital forms.

Crisis Communication Team and Crisis Command Centre

The crisis communication team (CCT) is an interdisciplinary team whose composition can vary by the nature of the crisis. Digital technologies mean that IT and social media personnel are now added to the mix of crisis team members. These newer positions are simply integrated in the CCT and its training (Coombs, 2019).

CCTs used to assemble in the crisis command centre, a dedicated physical space for the team to meet and to conduct its business. Some large corporations even built special spaces for the crisis command centre (Barton, 2001). Technology permits CCTs to meet remotely or be partially distributed (some in-person and some remotely) (Coombs, 2019). The nature of what the team does remains the same. The team collects information, analyses data, and makes decisions. What does change is the teams no longer have to gather in one place to begin the crisis management effort. Digital technologies allow the team to begin managing a crisis immediately through the use of stable technological connections.

Delivery of the Crisis Response

To be effective, corporations in crisis must respond to the crisis through actions and words. Much of the crisis communication research is dedicated to understanding what makes for an effective crisis response (e.g., Bundy et al., 2017). Digital technologies provide additional channels for delivering crisis responses. Crisis managers should be integrating digital channels into their crisis responses because they are a quick way to use owned channels in the crisis response and many stakeholders rely heavily upon digital channels. However, not all stakeholders utilize digital channels, hence the need for a mix of channels in any crisis response. The goal in crisis communication typically is to reach as many stakeholders as possible, especially when telling them what to do to protect themselves from the crisis and trying to help them to cope psychologically with the crisis (Coombs and Holladay, 2001; Sturges, 1994). It has never been a good idea to rely upon one channel or a limited range of channels in a crisis response. Moreover, the research into channel effects rarely shows a significant or important channel effect for crisis communication – the channel does not have a major effect on how people perceive or react to crisis communication (e.g., Coombs et al., 2017). Crisis managers should be utilizing their digital channels as part of the media mix for the crisis response.

CRITICAL EXAMINATION

In this section, the chapter moves beyond documenting the changes in digital corporate crisis communication to reflecting upon those changes. The two reflection points focus on the salience of stakeholders and the limits of using AI.

Salience of Stakeholders

People often mistake the ability of stakeholders to create and to share content through digital channels as a form of power that shifts the dynamic of the stakeholder–organization relationship. There has always been the potential to generate power through digital channels but no guarantee that controlling digital content was actual power (e.g., Coombs, 1998, 2002; Heath, 1998; Nothhaft, 2016). People make the mistake of seeing a few successful efforts by activist stakeholders as meaning any activist stakeholder will be able to bend a corporation to their will. Corporate managers still prioritize stakeholders, usually based upon the mix of legitimacy, power, and urgency (Mitchell et al., 1997). This means that many marginalized stakeholders will remain marginalized unless they can leverage digital channels to increase their power, legitimacy, and urgency. Although digital channels have the potential to increase the salience of a marginalized constituency, there is no guarantee that using digital channels will make them powerful. Yes, digital channels allow the marginalized to control and to express their own messages, but that does not mean those messages will have the desired effect upon corporations (Coombs, 2002).

Limitations of AI

Entertainment has a long history of warning us of the dangers of AI. AI has generated some fear for those involved in corporate communication that they will be replaced by AI.

174   *Handbook on digital corporate communication*

However, AI is still rather limited to more simplistic tasks. It is great at identifying 'things' but not so useful at creating 'things', especially messages. We are not talking about the simple AI-generated chat bot messages but rather the detailed responses to communicative problems faced by corporations. This holds true for crisis communication. AI can help to identify risks, recognize when a corporation is in a crisis, and recommend possible crisis response strategies. But AI does not convert the crisis response strategy into actual messages, does not verify the risk, and does not prove the organization is in crisis. The crisis managers must decide which crisis response strategy to use and how to convert that strategy into actual crisis messaging. Keep in mind that each AI program will have an element of error. That error includes false negatives and false positives. A false negative would be when the AI misses a risk or does not see that the organization is in crisis. A false positive is when AI identifies a risk that is not a relevant risk or claims the organization is in crisis when there is no crisis. That is why human intelligence must review the data created by AI and make the final decisions. AI makes recommendations; managers make decisions.

PARACRISIS CASE STUDY: VW'S RACIST ADVERTISEMENT

In March 2020, VW launched a German-market advertising campaign for its 2021 Golf. The campaign included four short videos about the romance between a white woman and a dark-skinned man. Videos were posted on 24 March but could only be viewed by select followers on Instagram. On 1 May, the ads were circulated to wide audiences on Instagram and Facebook. On 8 May, the ad in question was posted on Twitter. There were negative reactions and the ad was removed from Twitter. Following additional negative comments online, the ad was completely removed from the digital world on 20 May. When one of those ads appeared on Instagram, stakeholders were appalled by its racist tones rather than encouraged to buy a VW Golf. The video showed a giant white hand (the woman) pushing around the dark-skinned man. The hand motif was popular on TikTok at the time. The man was pushed into the Petit Colon Café, which means 'little settler', and reminded some of colonialism. The hand made the 'ok' gesture, which has been linked to white supremacy, and as letters (in German) spelled 'The New Golf', the letters first spelled out the German equivalent of a racial slur (Teague, 2020). The ad was condemned as racist by people online and by traditional media.

VW management was shocked and appalled by the advertisement, which was created by an outside agency, and quickly removed it and began apologizing for the problematic ad. VW had created a faux pas paracrisis (type 1) with the ad. Stakeholders online were defining the ad as racist rather than humorous. As is common with paracrises, digital communication channels were a driving force. The ad was digital and the initial identification of the ad as racist appeared on social media platforms. Jürgen Stackmann, Head of Sales and Marketing, and Elke Heitmüller, Head of Diversity Management of Volkswagen Group, posted apologies on Twitter and LinkedIn that included the text: "We're ashamed of it and cannot explain how it came about. All the more reason for us to make sure we clear this up. And we will make the results and consequences of the investigation public" (Ziady, 2020, para 7).

In addition to management personnel posting apologies on the two social media platforms, VW placed all the various managerial responses on its corporate web site in the corporation's digital newsroom. Here is part of the VW response:

> One thing is clear: There is no place for racism, discrimination and intolerance at Volkswagen. We fully understand the disgust and anger in response to the video. It is quite clear that this video is wrong and distasteful. We firmly distance ourselves from the video and apologize sincerely. (Volkswagen, 2020, paras 3–4)

VW acknowledged the ad was racist and offensive while arguing the corporation itself was not racist. Management was disgusted and angry at the ad that was identified as distasteful. The response included the following statement from Hiltrud Werner, Member of the Board of Management responsible for integrity and legal affairs:

> Volkswagen stands for humanity and diversity. The group is committed to the fight against any form of racism, discrimination and xenophobia – in the past and in the future. The racist and disgraceful short video on Instagram is absolutely inexcusable and I share the horror and indignation of the public as well as of our own employees. I do not understand under which circumstances this video could be produced and published. I find it particularly disappointing that the clear and unambiguous rules of our Code of Conduct, which applies throughout the group, were broken. (Volkswagen, 2020, paras 10–11)

This response noted how the ad violated VW's own policies designed to combat racism and discrimination.

VW launched an investigation into the situation and, after reviewing documents and conducting interviews, concluded that the creation and approval of the ad had no racist intent. Those who created and approved the ad simply failed to grasp its racist overtones (Riley and Ziady, 2020). As a result of the review, VW created a new checkpoint for reviewing future creative content composed of diversity experts who were not part of the creative process as well as boosting training for ethics and culture within VW. However, no one was fired over the incident (Riley and Ziady, 2020). Interest in the paracrisis began to wane after the initial response and dissipated completely following the results of the internal review – it was no longer a topic of interest online or in the traditional media. We can consider it a successful paracrisis response because the risk was de-escalated.

CONCLUSION AND FUTURE DIRECTIONS

DCC is now an established element of corporate crisis communication. Research needs to focus on how to integrate digital channels into crisis communication rather than seeking to find isolated effects of various digital channels in crisis communication. The primary effects of digital channels on corporate crisis communication are simple translations as various aspects of crisis communication become digitalized. The evolutionary effects of digital channels on corporate crisis communication include the increased need to address paracrises and the potential of AI in helping to identify crisis risks and actual crises. Future research needs to continue refining our understanding of paracrises, including understanding what factors shape effective responses to paracrises and the specific effects paracrises have on corporations. We also must examine the various ways AI can be integrated into and enhance crisis communication practices. Generally, we need to spend more time examining strategy and how to integrate digital channels and corporate crisis communication instead of simply featuring digital channels as a unique aspect of corporate crisis communication.

REFERENCES

Arpan, L. M. and Pompper, D. (2003). Stormy weather: Testing "stealing thunder" as a crisis communication strategy to improve communication flow between organizations and journalists. *Public Relations Review*, 29, 291–308.

Barton, L. (2001). *Crisis in organizations II* (2nd edition). Cincinnati, OH: College Divisions South-Western.

Baryannis, G., Validi, S., Dani, S., and Antoniou, G. (2019). Supply chain risk management and artificial intelligence: State of the art and future research directions. *International Journal of Production Research*, 57(7), 2179–2202.

Billings, R. S., Milburn, T. W., and Schaalman, M. L. (1980). A model of crisis perception: A theoretical and empirical analysis. *Administrative Science Quarterly*, 25, 300–316.

Boumans, J. W. and Trilling, D. (2016). Taking stock of the toolkit: An overview of relevant automated content analysis approaches and techniques for digital journalism scholars. *Digital Journalism*, 4(1), 8–23.

Bundy, J., Pfarrer, M. D., Short, C. E., and Coombs, W. T. (2017). Crises and crisis management: Integration, interpretation, and research development. *Journal of Management*, 43(6), 1661–1692.

CapeStart (2020). Using AI to predict public relations crises and recommend effective responses (and how CapeStart built the solution). https://www.capestart.com/resources/blog/using-ai-to-aid-crisis -communication.

Chen, F. (2019). Understanding paracrisis communication: Towards developing a framework of paracrisis typology and organizational response strategies (Doctoral dissertation, Texas A&M University). TAMU Campus. Repository. https://oaktrust.library.tamu.edu/handle/1969.1/186574.

Claeys, A. S. (2017). Better safe than sorry: Why organizations in crisis should never hesitate to steal thunder. *Business Horizons*, 60(3), 305–311.

Coombs, W. T. (1998). The internet as potential equalizer: New leverage for confronting social irresponsibility. *Public Relations Review*, 24, 289–304.

Coombs, W. T. (2002). Assessing online issue threats: Issue contagions and their effect on issue prioritisation. *Journal of Public Affairs*, 2(4), 215–229.

Coombs, W. T. (2012). The emergence of the paracrisis: Definition and implication for crisis management. In S. Duhé (ed.), *New media and public relations* (2nd edition) (pp. 267–276). New York: Peter Lang.

Coombs, W. T. (2017). Digital naturals and the rise of paracrises: The shape of modern crisis communication. In S. Duhé (ed.), *New media and public relations* (3rd edition) (pp. 281–290). New York: Peter Lang.

Coombs, W. T. (2018). Revising situational crisis communication theory: The influences of social media on crisis communication theory and practice. In L. L. Austin and Y. Jin (eds.), *Social media and crisis communication* (pp. 159–167). London: Routledge.

Coombs, W. T. (2019). *Ongoing crisis communication: Planning, managing, and responding.* Thousand Oaks, CA: Sage Publications.

Coombs, W. T., Claeys, A. S., and Holladay, S. J. (2017). Social media's value in crisis: Channel effect or stealing thunder? In L. Austin and Y. Jin (eds.), *Social media and crisis communication* (pp. 159–167). New York: Routledge.

Coombs, W. T. and Holladay, S. J. (2001). An extended examination of the crisis situations: A fusion of the relational management and symbolic approaches. *Journal of Public Relations Research*, 13(4), 321–340.

Coombs, W. T. and Holladay, S. J. (2012a). Internet contagion theory 2.0: How internet communication channels empower stakeholders. In S. Duhé (ed.), *New media and public relations* (2nd edition) (pp. 21–30). New York: Peter Lang.

Coombs, W. T. and Holladay, S. J. (2012b). The paracrisis: The challenges created by publicly managing crisis prevention. *Public Relations Review*, *38*(3), 408–415.

Coombs, W. T. and Holladay, S. J. (2015a). CSR as crisis risk: Expanding how we conceptualize the relationship. *Corporate Communications: An International Journal*, *20*(2), 144–162.

Coombs, W. T. and Holladay, S. J. (2015b). How activists shape CSR: Insights from internet contagion and contingency theories. In A. Adi, G. Grigore, and D. Crowther (eds.), *Corporate social responsibility in the digital age* (pp. 85–97). Bingley: Emerald Group Publishing.

Coombs, W. T. and Tachkova, E. R. (2023). Crisis communication theory. In C. Botan and E. Sommerfeldt (eds.), *Public relations III: In the age of publics* (pp. 173–190). New York: Routledge.

Frandsen, F. and Johansen, W. (2017). *Organizational crisis communication*. Thousand Oaks, CA: Sage Publications.

Gerwirtz, D. (2018). Volume, velocity, and variety: The three V's of big data. https://www.zdmet.com/article/volume-velocity-and-variety-understanding-the-three-vs-of-big-data/.

Heath, R. L. (1998). New communication technologies: An issues management point of view. *Public Relations Review*, *24*(3), 273–288.

Jiang, Y., Wu, D., Deng, Z., Qian, P., Wang, J., Wang, G., … Wang, S. (2017). Seizure classification from EEG signals using transfer learning, semi-supervised learning and TSK fuzzy system. *IEEE Transactions on Neural Systems and Rehabilitation Engineering*, *25*(12), 2270–2284.

King, B. G. (2008). A political mediation model of corporate response to social movement activism. *Administrative Science Quarterly*, *53*(3), 395–421.

King, B. G. (2011). The tactical disruptiveness of social movements: Sources of market and mediated disruption in corporate boycotts. *Social Problems*, *58*(4), 491–517.

Lerbinger, O. (1997). *The crisis manager: Facing risk and responsibility*. Mahwah, NJ: Lawrence Erlbaum.

Liu, B. F., Jin, Y., and Austin, L. L. (2013). The tendency to tell: Understanding publics' communicative responses to crisis information form and source. *Journal of Public Relations Research*, *25*(1), 51–67.

McDonnell, M. H. and King, B. (2013). Keeping up appearances: Reputational threat and impression management after social movement boycotts. *Administrative Science Quarterly*, *58*(3), 387–419.

Mitchell, R. K., Agle, B. R., and Wood, D. J. (1997). Toward a theory of stakeholder identification and salience: Defining the principle of who and what really counts. *Academy of Management Review*, *22*(4), 853–886.

Mitchell, T. M. (1997). Does machine learning really work? *AI Magazine*, *18*(3), 11.

Nothhaft, H. (2016). The dream of enlightenment within digital reach? Concepts of modern democracy. In W. T. Coombs, J. Falkheimer, M. Heide, and P. Young (eds.), *Strategic communication, social media and democracy: The challenge of the digital naturals* (pp. 65–82). London: Routledge.

Park, S. H. and Han, K. (2018). Methodologic guide for evaluating clinical performance and effect of artificial intelligence technology for medical diagnosis and prediction. *Radiology*, *286*(3), 800–809.

Riley, C. and Ziady, H. (2020). Volkswagen made a racist ad. https://www.cnn.com/2020/06/11/business/volkswagen-racits-ad-investigation/index.html/.

Rindova, V. P., Williamson, I. O., and Petkova, A. P. (2010). Reputation as an intangible asset: Reflections on theory and methods in two empirical studies of business school reputations. *Journal of Management*, *36*(3), 610–619.

Smith, J. (2012). The companies with the best CSR reputations. http://www.forbes.com/sites/jacquelynsmith/2012/12/10/the-companies-with-the-best-csr-reputations/.

Sturges, D. L. (1994). Communicating through crisis: A strategy for organizational survival. *Management Communication Quarterly*, *7*, 297–316.

Teague, C. (2020). Volkswagen pulls 2021 Golf ad, apologizes for racist overtones. https://www.thedrive.com/news/33601/volkswagen-pulls-2021-golf-ad-apologizes-for-racist-overtones.

VW (2020). Golf 8 Instagram spot. https://www.volkswagen-newsroom.com/en/stories/golf-8-instagram-spot-the-group-board-of-management-will-evaluate-first-findings-6084.

Ziady, H. (2020). Volkswagen apologies for racist ad. https://www.cnn.com/2020/05/21/business/volkswagen-racist-ad-instagram/index.html.

13. Digital corporate communication and crisis life cycles

Augustine Pang and Jerena C. K. Ng[1]

INTRODUCTION

No organization is immune to crises – they are, literally, battling crises of some form or other every day (Diers-Lawson and Pang, 2021). These can range from internal crises like organizational miscommunication or personality clashes to external ones, like those arising from policy mismanagement or from terrorism. Even as this chapter is written, the world is in the throes of the global Covid-19 outbreak which began in early 2020. Pinsdorf (1987) argued for the inevitability of crises affecting organizations. They are "no longer a matter of if, but when; no longer an exception, but the expected, even the inevitable" (Pinsdorf, 1987, p. 37).

While organizations recognize the probability of the occurrence of crises, studies have shown that some do not have any plan to deal with them. Deloitte's 2018 Global Crisis Management Survey, cited in *PR News*, found that of the organizations which had plans, only slightly more than a third were regularly updated. About 14 per cent of organizations surveyed had no plans. This compares with only 50 per cent that had plans in 2016 (PR crisis preparedness survey, 2019). Arenstein (2020) noted that nearly 40 per cent of respondents said their plans were not exercised.

Beyond designing crisis plans, scholars agree that crisis management must be a dynamic, ongoing process conducted through a life cycle (Coombs, 2019; Fearn-Banks, 2017; Pang, 2012; Wilcox et al., 2015). This chapter first examines how corporate communication can harness digital communication to manage a crisis across a life cycle. While the current sets of life cycles have provided foundational insights (see next section), this chapter argues that it may not be sufficient to equip organizations. Second, to equip organizations, a framework for digital communication across a crisis life cycle is proposed. Third, digital communication tactics proposed at each phase of the framework are applied to a case in Singapore to demonstrate how organizations can potentially leverage insights from the framework to equip them in digital communication. It is hoped that this revised framework can spur organizations to enhance their preparation.

DEFINITIONS OF THE TOPIC AND PREVIOUS STUDIES

Fearn-Banks (2017, p. 1) argued that a crisis is "a major occurrence with a potentially negative outcome affecting the organization, company, or industry, as well as its publics, products, services, or good name". A key to managing crises is through a life cycle. Coombs (2019, p. 8) described it as a "staged approach", where the crisis is dealt with in a segmented and orderly manner. Coombs (2019, p. 8) argued that the life cycle framework helps to organize the vast crisis management knowledge to create a "unified set of crisis management guidelines".

179

180 *Handbook on digital corporate communication*

Various scholars have their own conceptualizations and each stage of the life cycle has been consistently articulated thus far.

Diers-Lawson and Pang (2021) described how the life cycle operates in the following terms. The Proactive phase is the time before a crisis occurs. Gonzalez-Herrero and Pratt (1996) described it as the birth stage; Fink (1986) called it the prodromal stage; Meyers (1986) named it the pre-crisis stage; and Turner (1976) labelled it the normal point. Coombs (2019), Seeger et al. (2003) and George (2012) defined it as the pre-crisis stage. Fearn-Banks (2017) called it the detection stage while James et al. (2013) described it as the signal detection stage. At this phase, organizations begin scanning the environment for possible issues, track emerging ones, and crisis planning. Sturges (1994) described it as a time when the organization is actively internalizing all this information.

The Strategic phase is when issues and risks have been identified and some may be showing signs of emergence. Gonzalez-Herrero and Pratt (1996) called it the growth stage; Fink (1986) named it the acute phase; Meyers (1986) called it the pre-crisis stage; and Turner (1976) termed it the incubation phase. Coombs (2019), Seeger et al. (2003) and George (2012) defined it as the pre-crisis stage. Fearn-Banks (2017) and James et al. (2013) called it the prevention/preparation stage. At this time, organizations must engage in risk communication and activate their crisis communication plan. Sturges (1994) described it as the time when the organization is instructing and sharing with its stakeholders what needs to be done.

The Reactive phase is when the crisis explodes. Gonzalez-Herrero and Pratt (1996) called it the maturity phase; Fink (1986) termed it the chronic phase; Meyers (1986) named it the crisis phase; Turner (1976) labelled it the precipitating/rescue and salvage phase. Coombs (2019), Seeger et al. (2003) and George (2012) defined it as the crisis stage. Fearn-Banks (2017) called it the containment stage while James et al. (2013) described it as the containment/damage control stage. This is when organizations engage in crisis communication, which predominantly means managing the media; instructing and sharing with stakeholders their action plans (Sturges, 1994; Coombs and Holladay, 2011).

The Recovery phase is when the crisis has subsided. Gonzalez-Herrero and Pratt (1996) called this the decline phase; Fink (1986) labelled it the resolution phase; Meyers (1986) termed it the post-crisis phase; Turner (1976) named it the cultural readjustment phase. Coombs (2019), Seeger et al. (2003) and George (2012) called it the post-crisis stage. Fearn-Banks (2017) defined it as the recovery and learning stages while James et al. (2013) described it as the business recovery stage. This is when the organization needs to restore a battered reputation. Sturges (1994) argued this is the time when organizations adjust to the new landscape and internalize what they have learnt from the experience (see Figure 13.1).

The life cycle operates in a continuous wave. When one wave of the life cycle is completed, another begins. For instance, once an organization completes the management of a particular crisis, lessons learnt are consolidated to prepare for the next wave. This is what Pauchant and Mitroff (1992) described as organizational learning or interactive crisis management.

While these prescriptive suggestions may provide organizations with sufficient guidance before, during and after crises, this chapter argues that there are gaps that current frameworks have not addressed specifically relating to the use of digital communication. The next section discusses the changing media landscape and the challenges posed to crisis communication.

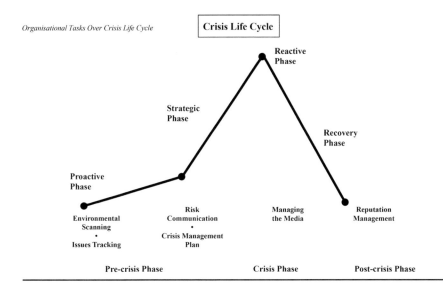

Figure 13.1   Crisis life cycle phases

WHAT IS CHANGING?

With the proliferation of social media, the speed at which information is shared and spread has soared (Wan et al., 2015). Increases in digital conversations and user- and bot-generated content have dominated the digital space (Cardoso et al., 2020). New social media platforms have emerged with sophistication. For instance, TikTok (which started in August 2018) reaches out to a youthful demographic who make up more than 80 per cent of the social media users (Coombs, 2020; Rampersad and Althiyabi, 2020). The increased volume of users generating content online, the lack of gatekeeping and the growing number of social media platforms make the digital space susceptible to crises that could be triggered online (Pang et al., 2014).

Siah et al. (2010) argued that the new environment is a double-edged sword. On one hand, it provides new platforms and means for organizations to communicate with stakeholders. On the other hand, the same platforms and means can be used to escalate the crisis. Besides focusing on generating their own online content (Shin et al., 2015), Diers-Lawson and Pang (2021) suggested four phenomena which social media has contributed to organizational crises.

First, a paracrisis is unique to the social media age. A paracrisis is a "publicly visible crisis threat that charges an organization with irresponsible or unethical behaviour" (Coombs and Holladay, 2012, p. 409). While not full scale, it can potentially develop into a crisis. Given that social media is widely used and publicly visible, Coombs and Holladay (2012, p. 409) argued that a paracrisis started on social media would be difficult for an organization to cover up.

Second, Pang et al. (2014) found that not only is social media a platform for the public to participate in events, it has also emboldened them to speak up, and forces mainstream news media to report such events, which further fuels the crisis.

Whipping up public sentiment online is the third phenomenon. Known as social media hype, netizens converge online to discuss an issue of interest. Pang (2013b) described this as a netizen-generated hype that creates huge interest and is defined by (1) an event that the public obsesses over; (2) public interest that continues to mount within 24 hours of an event occurring; (3) "ebbs and falls in user interest" of the primary event; (4) a spread that is visible and sustained across other mediums and other social media platforms.

A fourth phenomenon is the parody of organizations' official online accounts. Termed parody social media, Wan et al. (2015) suggested three ways it can appear: (1) the crisis or paracrisis forces organizations to create an account; (2) when organizations botch the handling of a crisis/paracrisis, an unhappy public would create the account; (3) when the organization fails to act and an information vacuum ensues (Pang, 2013a), and a parody social media account appears to fill the void.

Two additional phenomena are also observed. First, fake news. Waisbord (2018, p. 1866) described fake news as a fabrication that "astutely mimics news and taps into existing public beliefs" to deliberately misinform. The proliferation of social media has meant that the speed and scale of false information consumption has grown massively. Verstraete et al. (2017) classified fake news into four distinct types based on the intent and motivation/payoff: hoax, propaganda, trolling and satire. Organizations need to know how to discern, detect and counter fake news appropriately. Understanding the intent (to deceive or not) and motivation/payoff (financial or non-financial) behind possible fake news linked to an organization allows them to focus their resources on monitoring and listening in the right space. Verstraete et al. (2017) proposed that organizations automate and review the robustness of their processes to detect and counter these malicious narratives.

Last but not least, there is the rise of social media influencers (SMIs). Many organizations employ advocates to amplify their brand. Sng et al. (2019, p. 302) described SMIs as independent parties who are passionate in creating content around a niche area of interest on social media and have the ability to shape audiences' attitudes. Beyond viral and social media marketing, SMIs have great influence on strategic communications which organizations are increasingly leveraging as third-party advocates. SMIs, however, also pose threats to organizations as they are constantly under public scrutiny, and any misdemeanours from SMIs can threaten organizational reputation due to guilt by association (Sng et al., 2019).

WHAT REMAINS THE SAME?

Just before the world spiralled into the Covid-19 pandemic at the start of 2020, an online survey urged corporate communicators to use social media to enhance organizational communication and "drive business forward" (Gutman, 2021; Sprout Social, 2021). Organizations increased their social media presence by 67 per cent; about 57 per cent of them changed their "digital platforms to better meet consumer needs" (Gutman, 2021), and some posted gains of 24 per cent in investment as compared to the preceding years when investment returns had plateaued (Moorman and McCarthy, 2021). Although social media has enabled consumers to "engage, feedback, review and report product" (Cover, 2021), it remains a fertile ground for crises to be triggered (Pang et al., 2014).

While external media environments have evolved, the best practices in crisis communication remain the same and continue to be relevant. The following five insights which specifically address the use of digital corporate communication are integrated from best practices in crisis communication proposed by Seeger (2006) and best practices in social media crisis communication by Lin et al. (2016).

First, align policy with communication. Seeger (2006) argued that communication strategies should be integrated into the decision-making process so that communication issues are brought to bear more immediately. Lin et al. (2016, p. 602) proposed that organizations "fully integrate social media into decision making and policy development". As the publics are increasingly using social media for information, it is critical for organizations to ensure that all relevant decision makers are kept informed.

Second, relate to the publics and listen to their concerns. Seeger (2006) contended that organizations should do so, and respond accordingly. Lin et al. (2016) suggested that "active engagement in online dialogue" should be practised. Social media has empowered the public to participate in conversations on many issues, including misinformation. Engaging with them would help the public "make sense of the overflow of information" (Lin et al., 2016, p. 602). An organization in crisis would have the means of protecting its beleaguered image if it is able to engage its publics and wrest control of the conversation in the social sphere.

Third, leverage mainstream news media to provide credible information. Seeger (2006) argued that rather than viewing the media as a liability, organizations should engage the media openly and honestly and use them as a strategic resource. Lin et al. (2016, p. 602) suggested using "media affordances to provide credible sources of information". In a dynamic social mediascape, where both real and fake news prevail, organizations must provide authentic information that the public can trust, and even sway their opinions in the event the organization itself is mired deep in crisis. Lin et al. (2016, p. 3) proposed that organizations work with experts to "set up official social media accounts with official identities" to provide credibility in presenting its side of the story to the public.

Fourth, collaborate with credible partners. Seeger (2006) argued for the development of a network of third-party advocates. This study argues that social media influencers could be in this network. Lin et al. (2016, p. 604) suggested that organizations "cooperate with the public and similar organisations". Doing so allows relevant parties and experts to join the conversation, share information and also secure their support. The authors also advised organizations to identify "gatewatchers" – concerned publics who actively process and disseminate information – and work with them as they "can add to, promote and comment on the information" (Lin et al., 2016, p. 4).

Fifth, engage in deliberate communication. Seeger (2006) argued for honest and open communication. Lin et al. (2016, p. 603) contended that organizations need to be "cautious about message update speed". The 24-hour news cycle is dynamic and information is constantly updated. In the event of a crisis, an information vacuum is generated (Pang, 2013a). "Owning the hashtag" (Lin et al., 2016, p. 603) to track disseminated information and monitoring misinformation and rumours are ways for organizations to control the narrative.

The Digital Crisis Life Cycle Framework

To be in the driver's seat, organizations should engage in proactive planning. Seeger (2006) argued that having a plan serves as a reminder of potential problems and provides checkpoints to follow. Olaniran and Williams (2012) described this as the anticipatory perspective (i.e., how organizations anticipate and pre-plan for crises before they occur). Siah et al. (2010, p. 153) argued that in examining the use of digital tools across the crisis life cycle, organiza-

184 *Handbook on digital corporate communication*

tions could establish corporate communication online "to monitor (mis)information online and conduct environmental scanning so that prompt responses could be made". This chapter proposes a revised framework that harnesses digital communication across a crisis life cycle by integrating Siah et al.'s (2010) new media crisis communication model with Tan and Pang's (2020) crisis social media organizational communication model frameworks. The framework does not replace current frameworks; instead, the tasks recommended add to them.

This Digital Crisis Life Cycle framework uses Wilcox et al.'s (2015) framework as a theoretical lens, anchored in the key tasks of Programming, Preparing, Responding and Reviewing. In the Proactive phase, where organizations begin scanning the environment for possible issues and tracking emerging issues (Wilcox et al., 2015), the anchor task is Programming. Siah et al. (2010) argued that while organizations are active in online news monitoring and environmental scanning, they should keep their online presence relevant and updated. This would mean tactical work like the updating of important emailing lists and contact databases; enrolling a vigilant online media monitoring service; the registering of all possible domain names; and getting the corporate communication team to gain familiarity with the threats that can pose as challenges for the organization.

In the Strategic phase where organizations engage in risk communication and activate the crisis communication plan (Wilcox et al., 2015), the anchor task is Preparing. Here, Siah et al. (2010) argued that organizations should be more active digitally, identifying and responding to potential threats. This involves forming relationships with prominent online influencers/ opinion leaders; using platforms such as Instagram and TikTok, and technology such as AI to establish an online monitoring alert system; creating a hidden website – a site that could be used externally in the event of a crisis to update all constituencies about the issue (Gonzalez-Herrero and Smith 2008, p.149); and developing, testing and refining an online crisis manual.

In the Reactive phase, where organizations engage in crisis communication, the anchor task is Responding, online and offline. Siah et al. (2010) proposed for organizations to respond as expeditiously as possible; involving the CEO or member from the dominant coalition to personally address stakeholders through owned and earned media; using transparent coverage of the crisis on the homepage with a feedback feature; utilizing links to third-party endorsements; and activating the hidden site if necessary.

In the Recovery phase, while organizations engage in restoring a battered reputation, the anchor task is Reviewing what has worked and what could be improved on. Siah et al. (2010) argued for the continuous tracking of how the issues had left their mark online and offline; evaluation of the crisis and a thorough review of how the company responded; and defining the strategies to rebuild the company's reputation (see Figure 13.2).

CRITICAL EXAMINATION

Based on this Digital Crisis Life Cycle framework, the tasks are clearly set out in each phase of the life cycle. However, threats like fake news can emerge at any juncture of the life cycle. Organizations need to actively identify them at each phase. Jahng et al. (2020) argued that practitioners can manage dubious information in several ways. First, verify information with mainstream media. Second, verify information through crowdsourcing and interpersonal sources. Practitioners should, throughout the life cycle, maintain control of information

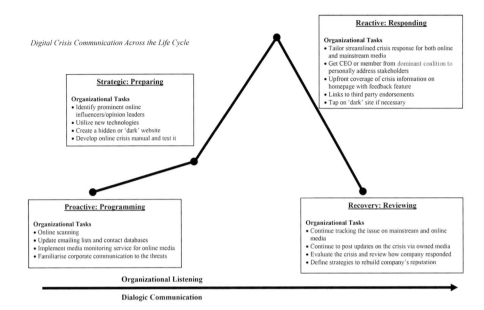

Figure 13.2   Digital crisis life cycle framework

relating to the organization and direct users to the organizations' owned platforms for official information and to address fake news transparently, accurately and in a proactive manner.

While this life cycle approach provides a framework for analysis, or what Frandsen and Johansen (2011, p. 351) described as a "heuristic method", there are limitations. Three are suggested here. First, even though Coombs (2019) argued that crisis managers need to understand how the life cycle works, some still adopt the "seat-of-the-pants" thinking (Heath and Coombs, 2006, p. 197), reacting to every emerging threat without thinking holistically. Second, one reason why crisis managers may not engage in "reasoned action" (Heath and Coombs, 2006, p. 197), or understanding how such a framework can enhance their capabilities, is possible exposure to crisis training. Some may be thrust into the role, others may not have the benefit of undergoing crisis education or exposure to studies. Crandall et al. (2014) argued that one can be exposed to crisis management education through books, cases and best practices. Third, Coombs (2019) argued that organizational memory must be archived and shared. Even if a previous crisis has been managed well and frameworks employed, institutional knowledge and experiences from previous crises may not be passed down to succeeding generations of crisis managers. New managers may have to learn from scratch and they tend to rely on what has been done before, rightly or wrongly, instead of what needs to be done.

Managers who want a framework to help them deal with crises can consider the one proposed in this chapter. For organizations that have embarked on some of the tasks, this framework serves to affirm and validate their efforts. Additionally, the authors propose that organizations consider two overarching approaches as they enhance their efforts.

186   *Handbook on digital corporate communication*

Approach 1: Organizational Listening

Organizational listening is the "culture, policies, structure, processes, resources, skills, technologies and practices" that pay heed to what stakeholders and publics are saying (Macnamara, 2015, p. 19). Tan and Pang (2020) suggested that the potential of organizational listening in grooming advocates could change the way organizations communicate during crisis. Macnamara (2018) argued for an architecture of listening to achieve two-way communication and engagement, and listed eight elements: (1) building an organizational culture to listen – recognizing rights, paying attention, understanding views and responding with respect and acknowledgement; (2) addressing the politics of listening, avoiding selective listening; (3) incorporating policies that address issues of power differentials to specify and require listening; (4) establishing systems that are open and interactive to welcome feedback, comments and questions; (5) using technologies to aid listening, automate responses, sensing and analyses; (6) doing the "work of listening" (Macnamara, 2018, p. 12) to establish forums for more channels to listen; (7) developing the skills to listen; and (8) articulating the voices of stakeholders and publics in policy and decision making.

There are "seven canons of listening" (Macnamara, 2015): (1) give recognition; (2) acknowledge to show attention; (3) pay attention to empathize better; (4) interpret fairly and receptively as much as possible; (5) understand views, perspectives and feelings; (6) give consideration to what is said; and (7) respond appropriately.

In listening, Macnamara (2015) highlighted the use of natural language programming to automate listening on social media. Such systemic organizational listening extends two-way communication further as differentiated monitoring and approach for different stakeholder groups online can be programmed to allow better acknowledgement, and timely and appropriate responses.

Approach 2: Dialogic Communication

Since corporate communication is premised on relationship building, organizations' dialogic communication with stakeholders is crucial. Dialogic communication refers to "any negotiated exchange of ideas and opinions" (Kent and Taylor, 1998, p. 325). It encompasses an organization's efforts to engage in an open, honest and ethical relationship with its publics (Bortree and Seltzer, 2009), to hear from them and to adapt to their needs (Hong et al., 2010).

Although many organizations have some social media presence, research suggests that they do not fully utilize the interactive capabilities of online media to foster their image. Vernuccio (2014) found that global organizations are hesitant in encouraging active stakeholder participation when communicating their brands and image. Research also shows that organizational representatives tend to rely on one-way communication to control messages, and therefore do not truly interact with stakeholders online (Lovejoy et al., 2012; Shin et al., 2015).

Taylor et al. (2001) argued that an organization's use of dialogic communication to build relationships with publics shares the same quality of an individual's dialogues in interpersonal relationships. Admittedly, dialogic communication may be difficult to execute. Shin et al. (2015), citing studies, argued that organizations appear reticent in committing resources to this endeavour. They find they have no control over the messaging; they are not able to connect directly with their target audiences to generate profits. Second, organizations may be concerned that they would be overwhelmed by the inordinate number of messages from stakeholders, especially so when there is an issue that has dominated media coverage or in times of crises. Third, Lock (2019) argued that for a dialogue to take place, both the organization and stakeholders need to recognize that there is a relationship to begin with.

This leads to the question: how do organizations utilize online media to engage in dialogic communication? Pang et al. (2018) proposed the model in Figure 13.3, which includes (a) the articulation of the specific approach(es) to dialogic communication processes; (b) the application of media resources that can support dialogic efforts; (c) the application of computer-mediated communication (CMC) strategies in various stages of relational development; (d) CMC tactics that further advance dialogic goals; (e) potential outcomes that may result from these applications; and finally, (f) implications for the solicitation and evaluation of feedback to further improve processes and outcomes.

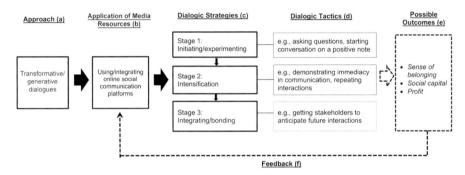

Source: Pang et al. (2018).

Figure 13.3 Trajectory in dialogic communication

ILLUSTRATIVE EXAMPLE: OPERATIONALIZING THE DIGITAL CRISIS LIFE CYCLE FRAMEWORK

In July 2019, NETS, an electronic payment service provider in Singapore, was appointed to start a new electronic payment service (e-pay) that unified cashless payments in retail outlets. NETS, through its advertising agency Havas Worldwide Singapore, had engaged local celebrity Dennis Chew for a series of marketing visuals. Chew, a radio DJ and actor with local broadcaster Mediacorp, had made his name playing a female character called Aunty Lucy. His portrayal of her was so well-loved that it brought him fame and numerous endorsement deals. He was voted one of the Top 10 Most Popular Male Artistes at a local programme called Star Awards 2009 and has since made it to this list ten times (Mediacorp, n.d.).

In the NETS campaign, Chew acted out different ethnic characters with the message that "everyone can e-pay" (Balakrishnan, 2019). The campaign was flagged when a journalist tweeted how distasteful the advertisements were – a Chinese man in darkened skin acting first as a Malay woman and then as an Indian man (Menon, 2019). Public criticism ensued. Analysing the case through the Digital Crisis Life Cycle framework, this section examines what NETS could have done to pre-empt and manage the public outcry.

188 *Handbook on digital corporate communication*

Proactive: Programming Phase

The corporate communication team at NETS played an important role in scanning the online space and familiarizing itself with possible threats when orchestrating a campaign. The multi-ethnic society in Singapore presents opportunities, and threats to organizations especially when marketing campaigns are not planned with ethnic sensitivity in mind, and with nuanced messaging for diverse audiences.

NETS would have done better if it had conducted a detailed analysis of the local digital communication environment and planned the possible trajectories and threats. They could have learnt from a similar incident in 2016, where Mediacorp had removed a drama series after a Chinese actor in black face make-up was perceived as perpetuating racial stereotypes (Yee, 2016).

Strategic: Preparing Phase

During the strategic phase, organizations should identify prominent online influencers or opinion leaders, and utilize technologies like sentiment and trend analysis dashboards to detect and prepare for potential issues. If NETS and Havas Worldwide Singapore had had most of the organizational tasks prepared, their monitoring and sensing tools would have prevented a crisis from developing.

Reactive: Responding Phase

With better monitoring and online sentiment sensing, NETS could have averted the crisis which escalated when a parody rap video by a local comedian created another social media hype (Lim, 2019a). The video by local YouTuber Preeti Nair and her brother, rapper Subhas Nair was uploaded on 29 July 2019, and removed the next day by the authorities on grounds of upholding national harmony (Ong, 2020). As Singapore is a multi-racial and multi-religious society, the government is concerned that any discord among the ethnic groups could squander the progress it had made on race issues since independence (Ang and Chew, 2021), and destabilize a peaceful environment that has thus far been attractive in driving businesses and investors into Singapore (MCCY, 2020). The timing of responses by NETS and Havas Worldwide Singapore was also testament to the lack of preparation in the earlier phases – it took five days for NETS to apologize for the campaign (Lim, 2019b) although Mediacorp and Havas Worldwide Singapore had apologized within the first two days of the incident erupting on social media. NETS and Havas Worldwide Singapore did, however, remove images of Dennis Chew and replaced them on the campaign website.

Recovery: Reviewing Phase

Despite the late apology and lack of a crisis spokesperson, NETS appeared to have charted its recovery tasks systematically. It had worked with authorities to review its strategies and messaging, removing the visuals in question, and refocusing on messages that reinforced the convenience and efficiency of e-payments. Additionally, it showed that even though a celebrity known for his witty portrayal of locals is used for marketing campaigns, sensitive issues like race should be carefully considered in a context like Singapore. If the organization had

CONCLUSION AND FUTURE DIRECTIONS

Digital corporate communication is the way forward as organizations make their marks in the marketplace. A key role in digital corporate communication is to manage threats across the life cycle. Coombs (2019, p. 8) argued that the life cycle provides "an overarching framework" that "organises the scattered crisis management insights and permits crisis managers to easily envision their best options during any stage of the process". For effective crisis management, corporate communication should integrate the life cycle into "normal operations of the organisation" (Coombs, 2019, p. 8). Managing the life cycle is "ongoing" (Coombs, 2019, p. 8) as opposed to reactive and tactical. An experience in managing crisis should be looped back to learning, making it a continuous process of Programming, Preparing, Responding and Reviewing. While some organizations have dedicated personnel in the Crisis Management Teams (CMT), communication professionals should be actively involved at each stage.

With the tasks proposed at each stage of the cycle in place, organizations should deepen and automate their organizational listening abilities (Macnamara, 2018) beyond the usual media and social media monitoring routines. Listening involves processing, analysing and reaching out (Macnamara, 2016). Organizations should also reach out via dialogic communication, which many have been reticent in doing (Shin et al., 2015). If organizations enlarge these capabilities, managing and pre-empting threats across the life cycle would be more effective.

Pang et al.'s (2014, p. 112) statement that "The axiom, the best way to manage a crisis is to prevent one, rings ever so true in this era where organisations can be so empowered when embracing technology to reach out to stakeholders, yet can be rendered disempowered when it does not sufficiently harness the very tools available to them", remains true today. To wit: digital corporate communication should be at the forefront of all organizational imperatives.

NOTE

1. This research was supported by the Singapore Ministry of Education (MOE) Academic Research Fund (AcRF) Tier 1 grant. This chapter was derived in part from an article published in the *Journal of Marketing Communications* (2018) (copyright Taylor & Francis), available at http:www.tandfonline.com (DOI: 10.1080/13527266.2016.1269019); and from an article published in *Corporate Communications: An International Journal* (2010) (copyright Emerald Group Publishing) (DOI: 10.1108/13563281011037919). The authors thank the journal for the use of the figure as well as the co-authors of the article, Joanna Siah Ann Mei and Namrata Bansal.

REFERENCES

Ang, H. M. and Chew, H. M. (2021). Singapore right to be concerned about racist incidents as there is 'always a risk' of regression on race issues: Lawrence Wong. *Channel News Asia*. https://www.channelnewsasia.com/singapore/racism-singapore-forum-ips-rsis-lawrence-wong-incidents-1942276.

190 *Handbook on digital corporate communication*

Arenstein, S. (2020). 62% have crisis plans, but few update them or practice scenarios. https://www.prnewsonline.com/crisis-survey-CSA-practice.

Balakrishnan, R. (2019). Singapore-based E-Pay takes down controversial ad following alleged racism row. *Mumbrella Asia*. https://www.mumbrella.asia/2019/07/singapore-based-e-pay-takes-down-controversial-ad-following-alleged-racism-row.

Bortree, D. S. and Seltzer, T. (2009). Dialogic strategies and outcomes: An analysis of environmental advocacy groups' Facebook profiles. *Public Relations Review*, *35*(3), 317–319.

Cardoso, F., Luceri, L., and Giordano, S. (2020). Digital weapons in social media manipulation campaigns. Workshop Proceedings of the 14th International AAAI Conference on Web and Social Media, 3.

Coombs, W. T. (2019). *Ongoing crisis communication* (5th edition). Thousand Oaks, CA: Sage Publications.

Coombs, W. T. (2020). Public sector crises: Realizations from Covid-19 for crisis communication (1.0) [Data set]. University of Salento. https://doi.org/10.1285/I20356609V13I2P990.

Coombs, W. T. and Holladay, S. J. (eds.). (2011). *The handbook of crisis communication* (Vol. 22). United Kingdom: Wiley-Blackwell.

Coombs, W. T. and Holladay, J. (2012). The paracrisis: The challenges created by publicly managing crisis prevention. *Public Relations Review*, *38*(3), 408–415.

Cover, L. (2021). 7 statistics that prove the importance of social media marketing in business. Sprout Social.com. https://sproutsocial.com/insights/importance-of-social-media-marketing-in-business/.

Crandall, W. R., Parnell, J. A., and Spillan, J. E. (2014). *Crisis management: Leading in the new strategy landscape*. London: Sage Publications.

Diers-Lawson, A. and Pang, A. (2021). Strategic crisis management: State of the field, challenges and opportunities. In C. Valentini (ed.), *Public relations* (pp. 195–215). Berlin: De Gruyter Mouton.

Fearn-Banks, K. (2017). *Crisis communications* (5th edition) New York: Routledge.

Fink, S. (1986). *Crisis management: Planning for the inevitable*. New York: AMACOM.

Frandsen, F. and Johansen, W. (2011). The study of internal crisis communication: Towards an integrative framework. *Corporate Communications: An International Journal*, *16*(4) 347–361.

George, A. M. (2012). The phases of crisis communication. In A. M. George and C. B. Pratt (eds.), *Case studies in crisis communication: International perspectives on hits and misses* (pp. 31–50). New York: Routledge.

Gonzalez-Herrero, A. and Pratt, C. B. (1996). An integrated symmetrical model for crisis-communications management. *Journal of Public Relations Research*, *8*(2) 79–105.

Gonzelez-Herrero, A. and Smith, S. (2008). Crisis communications management on the Web: How Internet-based technologies are changing the way public relations professionals handle business crises. *Journal of Contingencies and Crisis Management*, *16*(3), 143–153.

Gutman, A. (2021). Most influential communication platforms according to global PR professionals 2019. https://www.statista.com/statistics/1057871/influential-communications-platforms-for-pr-world/.

Heath, R. L. and Coombs, W. T. (2006). *Today's public relations: An introduction*. Thousand Oaks, CA: Sage Publications.

Hong, S. Y., Yang, S.-U., and Rim, H. (2010). The influence of corporate social responsibility and customer-company identification on publics' dialogic communication intentions. *Public Relations Review*, *36*(2), 196–198.

Jahng, M. R., Lee, H., and Rochadiat A. (2020). Public relations practitioners' management of fake news: Exploring key elements and acts of information authentication. *Public Relations Review*, *46*(2), 101907.

James, E. H., Crane, B., and Wooten, L. P. (2013). Managing the crisis lifecycle in the information age. In A. J. Du Brin (ed.), *Handbook of research on crisis leadership in organizations* (pp. 177–192). Cheltenham, UK and Northampton, MA, USA: Edward Elgar Publishing.

Kent, M. L. and Taylor, M. (1998). Building dialogic relationships through the World Wide Web. *Public Relations Review*, *24*(3), 321–334.

Lim, A. (2019a). Rap video by local YouTube star Preetipls on "brownface" ad crosses the line, not acceptable: Shanmugam. *The Straits Times*. https://www.straitstimes.com/politics/rap-video-by-local-youtube-star-preetipls-on-brownface-ad-crosses-the-line-not-acceptable.

Lim, A. (2019b). Nets and Havas apologise for hurt caused by "brownface" ad, advertising authority says it did not breach guidelines. *The Straits Times.* https://www.straitstimes.com/politics/nets-apologises-for-hurt-caused-by-brownface-advertising-campaign.

Lin, X. L., Spence, P. R., Sellnow, T. L., and Lachlan, K. A. (2016). Crisis communication, learning and responding: Best practices in social media. *Computers in Human Behavior, 65,* 601–605.

Lock, I. (2019). Explicating communicative organization-stakeholder relationships in the digital age: A systematic review and research agenda. *Public Relations Review, 45*(4), 101829.

Lovejoy, K., Waters, R. D., and Saxton, G. D. (2012). Engaging stakeholders through Twitter: How non-profit organizations are getting more out of the 140 characters or less. *Public Relations Review, 38*(2), 313–318.

Macnamara, J. (2015). Creating an 'architecture of listening' in organizations: The basis of engagement, trust, healthy democracy, social equity, and business sustainability. University of Technology, Sydney.

Macnamara, J. (2016). Organizational listening: Addressing a major gap in public relations theory and practice. *Journal of Public Relations Research, 28*(3–4), 146–169.

Macnamara, J. (2018). Toward a theory and practice of organizational listening. *International Journal of Listening, 32*(1), 1–23.

Menon, M. (2019). I feel terrible: Dennis Chew apologises for e-pay "brownface" advertisement. *The Straits Times.* https://www.straitstimes.com/singapore/actor-and-dj-dennis-chew-apologises-for-e-pay-brownface-advertisement.

Mediacorp (n.d.). *Dennis Chew. The Celebrity Agency.* https://www.mediacorp.sg/business/tca/male-djs/dennis-chew-12357578#:~:text=Dennis%20started%20in%20 radio%20broadcast,and%20Milan%20changed%20his%20life.

Meyers, G. C. (1986). *When it hits the fan: Managing the nine crises of business.* New York: Mentor.

Ministry of Culture, Community, and Youth (MCCY) (2020). Fostering racial and religious harmony in Singapore across the generations. https://www.mccy.gov.sg/about-us/news-and-resources/speeches/2020/dec/fostering-racial-religious-harmony-in-singapore-across-generations.

Moorman, C. and McCarthy, T. (2021). CMOs: Adapt your social media strategy for a post-pandemic world. *Harvard Business Review,* 19 January. https://hbr.org/2021/01/cmos-adapt-your-social-media-strategy-for-a-post-pandemic-world.

Olaniran, B. and Williams, D. (2012). The need for an anticipatory perspective in crisis communication. In B. Olaniran, D. Williams, and W. T. Coombs (eds.), *Pre-crisis planning, communication, and management: Preparing for the inevitable* (pp. 3–16). New York: Peter Lang.

Ong, J. (2020). When race made the news in Singapore. *The Straits Times,* 5 December. https://www.straitstimes.com/singapore/politics/when-race-made-the-news-in-singapore.

Pang, A. (2012). Towards a crisis pre-emptive image management model. *Corporate Communications: An International Journal, 17*(3), 358–378.

Pang, A. (2013a). Dealing with external stakeholders during the crisis: Managing the information vacuum. In A. J. Du Brin (ed.), *Handbook of research on crisis leadership in organizations* (pp. 209–229). Cheltenham, UK and Northampton, MA, USA: Edward Elgar Publishing.

Pang, A. (2013b). Social media hype in times of crises: Nature, characteristics, and pact on organizations. *Asia Pacific Media Educator, 23*(2), 313–340.

Pang, A., Nasrath, B., and Chong, A. (2014). Negotiating crisis in the social media environment: Evolution of crises online, gaining credibility offline. *Corporate Communications: An International Journal, 19*(1), 96–118.

Pang, A., Shin, W., Lew, Z., and Walther, J. B. (2018). Building relationships through dialogic communication: Organizations, stakeholders, and computer-mediated communication. *Journal of Marketing Communications, 24*(1), 68–82.

Pauchant, T. C. and Mitroff, I. I. (1992). *Transforming the crisis-prone organization.* San Francisco: Jossey-Bass.

Pinsdorf, M. K. (1987). *Communicating when your company is under siege: Surviving public crises.* Lexington, MA: D. C. Heath.

PR crisis preparedness survey: Responding to crises in the digital age (2019). *PR News & Crisp.*

Rampersad, G. and Althiyabi, T. (2020). Fake news: Acceptance by demographics and culture on social media. *Journal of Information Technology & Politics, 17*(1), 1–11.

Seeger, M. W. (2006). Best practices in crisis communication: An expert panel process. *Journal of Applied Communication Research*, *34*(3), 232–244.

Seeger, M. W., Sellnow, T. L., and Ulmer, R. R. (2003). *Communication and organizational crisis*. Westport, CT: Praeger.

Shin, W. S., Pang, A., and Kim, H. J. (2015). Building relationships through integrated online media: Global organizations' use of brand web sites, Facebook, and Twitter. *Journal of Business and Technical Communication*, *29*(2), 184–220.

Siah, J., Bansal, M., and Pang, A. (2010). New media and crises: New media – a new medium in escalating crises? *Corporate Communications: An International Journal*, *15*(2), 143–155.

Sng, K., Au, T. Y., and Pang, A. (2019). Social media influencers as a crisis risk in strategic communication: Impact of indiscretions on professional endorsements. *International Journal of Strategic Communication*, *13*(4), 301–320.

Sprout Social (2021). The state of social media: After a year of transformation, executives are all-in on social. https://sproutsocial.com/insights/data/social-media-future-of-business-intelligence/.

Sturges, D. L. (1994). Communication through crisis: A strategy for organizational survival. *Management Communication Quarterly*, *7*(3), 297–316.

Tan, K. Y. and Pang, A. (2020). Operationalising crisis communication from within: Toward the crisis organisational communication framework in the social mediated environment. *Asia Pacific Public Relations Journal*, *22*(1), 1–20.

Taylor, M., Kent, M., and White, W. (2001). How activist organizations are using the internet to build relationships. *Public Relations Review*, *27*, 263–284.

Turner, B. (1976). The organizational and interorganizational development of disasters. *Administrative Science Quarterly*, *21*(3), 378–397.

Vernuccio, M. (2014). Communicating corporate brands through social media: An exploratory study. *International Journal of Business Communication*, *51*, 211–233.

Verstraete, M., Bambauer, D. E., and Bambauer, J. R. (2017). Identifying and countering fake news. *SSRN Electronic Journal*. https://doi.org/10.2139/ssrn.3007971.

Waisbord, S. (2018). Truth is what happens to news: On journalism, fake news, and post-truth. *Journalism Studies*, *19*(13), 1866–1878.

Wan, S., Koh, R., Ong, A., and Pang, A. (2015). Parody social media accounts: Influence and impact on organizations during crisis. *Public Relations Review*, *41*(3), 381–385.

Wilcox, D. L., Cameron, G. T., and Reber, B. H. (2015). *Public relations strategies and tactics* (11th edition). Boston: Pearson Allyn & Bacon.

Yee, Y. W. (2016). Mediacorp's Toggle removes Shane Pow's "blackface" episode following outcry. *The Straits Times*, 26 October. https://www.straitstimes.com/lifestyle/entertainment/ mediacorp s-toggle-removes-shane-pows-blackface-episode-following-outcry.

14. Digital corporate communication and complaint management

Sabine Einwiller and Wolfgang Weitzl

INTRODUCTION

Consumers regularly experience *corporate failures*, which describe situations in which a company's performance falls below a person's consumption expectations (Hoffman and Bateson, 1997). This includes service failures such as unfriendly staff, late delivery and product failures, such as when an ordered good is delivered damaged or in poor quality. Corporate stakeholders sometimes also perceive *corporate misconduct*, which is an unacceptable or improper behaviour by a company (Davies and Olmedo-Cifuentes, 2016). This happens when a company violates social norms like, for example, discriminating against employees or other members of society, corruption or misuse of power by corporate executives. The perception of such corporate failures or misconduct generally results in consumers' and stakeholders' dissatisfaction and negative emotions. According to Hirschman (1970), dissatisfaction leads to various coping behaviours, which range from passiveness (i.e., remaining loyal) to voicing discontent directly to the involved company. In the digital era, this negative voice behaviour is no longer restricted to traditional complaint channels like a company's telephone hotline. Anyone who is dissatisfied can go online (e.g., on a company's Facebook page, Instagram or TikTok account) and share his or her negative experience with the company and – more importantly – with many interested others by voicing an *online complaint*. These company-critic comments are a form of negative electronic word-of-mouth; that is, written online statements from dissatisfied persons which denigrate a brand or company in public (Laczniak et al., 2001).

The Internet offers a plethora of possibilities for consumers and other stakeholders to express their opinions as online complaints (e.g., by writing unfavourable reviews or publishing brand-critical videos on YouTube). This carries the risk of harming the involved company by triggering dissatisfaction and negative emotions also in others who observe the online complaint (i.e., bystanders), which can even lead to collective outrage and boycotting. Take, for example, the case of Gucci. In their fall/winter 2018 collection, the luxury brand released a black balaclava-style sweater featuring a pull-up neck with a cut-out around the lips that was surrounded by a big red circle. The sweater was considered racist as it resembled a pejorative caricature of dark-skinned children and thus blackfacing. A cynical tweet by a Twitter user with a picture of a woman wearing the sweater ignited negative emotions in many and caused a flood of complaints and calls for a boycott (Wekwerth, 2019), which was also taken up by the mainstream media (e.g., Griffith, 2019).

Thus, handling complaints voiced online in a way that calms and ideally satisfies the complainants and complaint observers is important for the successful management of corporate reputation and for preventing a paracrisis that may even turn into a full-blown crisis (Coombs and Holladay, 2012). Online complaint management is an important element of *digital corporate communication* (DCC), which is defined as "an organization's strategic management of

194   *Handbook on digital corporate communication*

digital technologies, digital infrastructures and digitalization processes to improve communication with internal and external stakeholders and more broadly within society for the maintenance of organizational tangible and intangible assets" (Badham and Luoma-aho, Chapter 1 in this volume, p. 9). This chapter addresses the phenomenon of complaining via online media and discusses companies' complaint management in digital environments.

This chapter first develops a model of consumer complaining, before outlining what is changing and what stays the same in the digital sphere. The chapter next elaborates on how to handle online complaints by means of complaint management and discusses the case example of Gucci. The chapter ends by discussing open questions and future directions in the area of online complaining.

DEFINITIONS OF COMPLAINING AND PREVIOUS RESEARCH

When individuals experience corporate failures or misconduct they typically become dissatisfied. Following the affect theory (e.g., Scherer, 1984; Shaver et al., 1987; Weiner, 1986), dissatisfaction is a distress emotion that develops when an event is perceived as unpleasant or as obstructing a person's (or group's) goals or needs. Dissatisfaction is a relatively undifferentiated, unfavourable emotion in reaction to a disadvantageous event (Bougie et al., 2003; Li and Stacks, 2017). It is accompanied by a diffuse feeling of unfulfilment and disappointment (Bougie et al., 2003; Hastie, 1984; Weiner, 1986). Thus, *dissatisfaction* can be conceptualized as the transient negative feeling by individuals after experiencing corporate failures or misconduct. It is the basic emotion that energizes individuals' subsequent reactions (MacDowell and Mandler, 1989; Mandler, 1990; Reeve, 2009).

Appraisal theory claims that when people are dissatisfied, they try to make causal inferences about the negative event. Hence, cognitions of appraisal enter the emotion process and elicit more specific discrete emotions, which can be classified into inward- and outward-directed emotions (Lazarus, 1991; Smith and Lazarus, 1993; Smith et al., 1993). The attribution of agency (i.e., the attribution to self vs. others) is a key element when experiencing different types of emotions. On the one hand, inward-directed negative emotions (e.g., sadness, guilt, embarrassment) are activated when persons hold themselves responsible for a failure (Lazarus, 1991; Tangney and Dearing, 2002). In this case, the individual will not turn against the company, but rather internalize the problem by remaining silent. On the other hand, when individuals attribute a harmful action to an external source (e.g., a company) and hence blame the other party for the incident, they are likely to feel outward-directed negative emotions (Lazarus, 1991). Anger is a classic example for such an emotion. People regularly get angry, for instance, after a service failure, when they almost automatically make external attributions to protect their self (Blaine and Crocker, 1993).

Angry individuals feel a strong emotional imbalance, which urges them to restore their mental state by means of *coping*, which describes persons' efforts to master or minimize a stressful situation (Lazarus and Folkman, 1984). Individuals' coping behaviours in the case of corporate failures and misconduct can take different forms. These range from staying loyal to the company or brand because of a positive reinterpretation of the situation, inertia or lock-in, to exiting the relationship, to negative acts like confrontation and revenge taking by voicing negative and sometimes aggressive comments and complaints (Hirschman, 1970; Yi and Baumgartner, 2004). Although some authors consider attitude change or forgiveness as non-behavioural forms of complaining (Day and Landon, 1977; Singh, 1988), we follow Kowalski (1996, p. 192), who describes complaining as a behavioural expression and a "potent form of interpersonal communication" that allows individuals to achieve certain goals.

Complaints are a specific form of *voice* (Hirschman, 1970) and a type of negative word-of-mouth. Yet, while negative word-of-mouth comprises any form of negative comment, the motivational element, that is wishing to achieve certain goals, is central to complaining (Kowalski, 1996). For the definition of complaining, we draw on Einwiller and Steilen (2015) and define *complaining* in the case of corporate failures or misconduct as an expression of dissatisfaction for the purpose of drawing attention to a corporate failure or perceived misconduct and for achieving personal or collective goals. The goals consumers possibly aim to achieve through complaining are manifold. They can be either personal or collective.

Personal goals address the individual needs of the complainant. For example, *redress seeking* has been identified as one of the major complaint motives (e.g., Bearden and Teel, 1983; Blodgett et al., 1997). The motive refers to the rectification of a problem (e.g., a product failure) or 'righting a wrong' (Mattila and Wirtz, 2004). Redress seeking complainants desire restitution in an amount equivalent to the imbalance which they attach to the dissatisfactory event (Adams, 1965; Wirtz and Mattila, 2004). The perceived imbalance is affected by suffered monetary losses, lost resources (e.g., time) and unpleasant emotions. Depending on the context, the restoration of the balance can take place with some kind of monetary compensation, including product replacement, a full or partial refund of the expenses, or a repair. But complainants regularly also demand non-monetary measures such as an apology or an explanation; that is, social benefits (Cambra-Fierro et al., 2015). While the desire for redress is fundamentally corrective, it is also constructive as the complainant regards the involved company as being capable to resolve the problem with a compensatory act.

Complaints can also stem from vindictive personal motives. *Venting* is a very common motive for complaint behaviour allowing people to release their frustration, anxiety and other unpleasant emotions by means of a complaint (Hennig-Thurau et al., 2004; Willemsen et al., 2013). By venting, people communicate their negative emotions to the company and to sympathetic others in order to obtain emotional relief for the dissatisfactory experience (Hennig-Thurau et al., 2004). Complaints are also used as a way to *take revenge* and to punish the party responsible for the failure with negative public statements (Grégoire et al., 2009; Ward and Ostrom, 2006).

Aside from these personal goals, complaints can also help to achieve *collective goals*. Public complaints are often the result of an act of *altruism* (Bronner and De Hoog, 2011), when complainants wish to warn others about unsatisfactory experiences. They are concerned about the well-being of their fellow consumers and want to help them to avoid the negative experience they have encountered (Willemsen et al., 2013). The goal is to *help other individuals* by warning them and by calling for collective retaliation against, for example, a company.

Nowadays, consumers have a plethora of possibilities to voice their complaints to a wider social circle, and many turn to digital platforms by filing an *online complaint*. Here, to share their negative experiences, they can use either (a) a *direct* digital channel provided by the involved company like its Facebook page or its Twitter channel or (b) an *indirect* one like a consumer interest group or a complaint site or review platform provided by a third party. These two channel types, direct vs. indirect, differ with respect to the prime recipients of the complaint (i.e., company vs. others). With an indirect complaint, the sender primarily targets non-corporate interest groups such as fellow shoppers or consumer protection agencies. In

196 *Handbook on digital corporate communication*

both cases, the complaining behaviour can occur in a *private* setting, where complainants inform only a very limited number of other persons about their dissatisfying experience (e.g., via email to the involved company or the consumer interest group), or in a *public* setting. When complaints are voiced publicly, complainants address a much broader audience, for example, by a posting on a company's Twitter channel or on a complaint site like Pissed Consumer or Complaints Board. Figure 14.1 summarizes these optional complaining behaviours. The way dissatisfied consumers complain opens different opportunities for companies to recover complainants and to reduce the chances that, for example, a public complaint becomes viral. This can happen when injustice is identified by interested others, which can trigger an online firestorm where suddenly "large quantities of messages containing negative WOM and complaint behaviour against a person, company, or group in social media networks" (Pfeffer et al., 2014, p. 118) are discharged.

WHAT IS CHANGING?

Because negative comments in the form of *public online complaints* (POCs) are voiced publicly they can reach a much larger number of people than complaints voiced privately or in the offline environment. Thus, they bear the risk of harming the involved company by triggering unfavourable attitudes and behaviours not just in the complainant and a few of his or her acquaintances, but also in a potentially very large number of bystanders who observe the complaint. The public nature of the POC, and of the corporate response, enhances the power of the complainant. Thus, in the online environment *empowerment* is considered another motive for complaining (Bronner and De Hoog, 2011; Hennig-Thurau et al., 2004). Aware of the impact a POC can have on a company, people voice their complaint online to draw the attention of others to the corporate failure or misconduct and to exert power and pressure on the company to act in order to protect its reputation (Willemsen et al., 2013).

If the problem raised in the POC confirms others' own experiences or meets with their approval, yet uninvolved bystanders become engaged by sharing the negative comment with others which can even lead to collective outrage or calls for a boycott (Grégoire et al., 2009; Lee and Song, 2010). This can lead to *negative engagement online*, that is "an experience-based series of participative actions in online environments where negative issues concerning an organization or brand are publicly discussed" (Lievonen and Luoma-aho, 2015, p. 288). When this discussion contains large quantities of POCs which are discharged rapidly and suddenly, the organization under fire experiences an *online firestorm* (Pfeffer et al., 2014). Johnen et al. (2018) consider online firestorms a specific form of moral panic, yet with certain differences due to the online context: First, their formation is facilitated by online platforms where users can easily find many like-minded people who share the indignation about a certain issue; second, factors such as invisibility, anonymity, asynchronicity and the lack of non-verbal cues are supposed to lead to more uncivil behaviour of participants than in traditional moral panics; and third, online firestorms are faster but more short-term in nature than traditional moral panics.

Participation in online firestorms is influenced by multiple factors including people's involvement in the issue, their perception of being collective actors and their approval of slacktivism behaviours (Gruber et al., 2020), that is "low-risk, low-cost activity via social media, whose purpose is to raise awareness, produce change, or grant satisfaction to the person

Digital corporate communication and complaint management 197

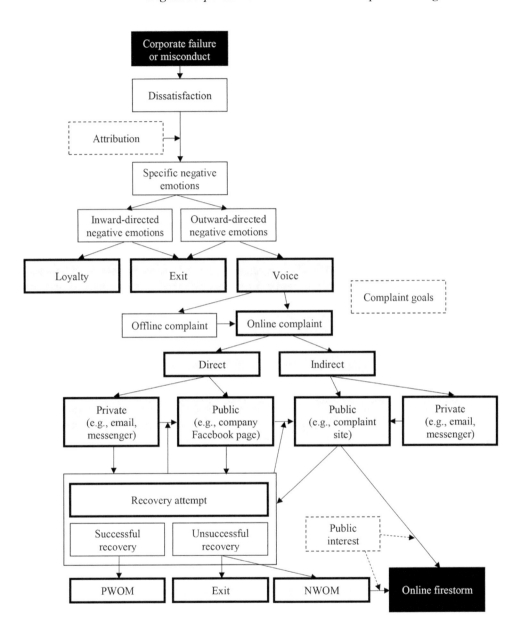

Figure 14.1 Process model of complaining behaviour

engaged in the activity" (Rotman et al., 2011, p. 821). Other contributing factors triggering individuals' engagement in online firestorms range from situational elements (e.g., emotions) to stable personality characteristics (e.g., Frischlich et al., 2021). When the mainstream media pick up the firestorm and report about it the negative situation is amplified by a boost of public attention (Einwiller et al., 2017). This may lead to a *paracrisis* or even a full-fledged crisis

198   *Handbook on digital corporate communication*

(Coombs and Holladay, 2012). In the online sphere, the issue associated with the complaint can spread across several *crisis arenas*, which are "dynamic online communicative spaces where stakeholders participate in the formation and expression of mostly negative assessments about issues and which contribute to the social construction and spread of crises" (Badham et al., 2022, p. 227). Hence, POCs – in contrast to traditional, private complaints – should be regarded as possible triggers of far-reaching consequences stimulated by the power of social media.

WHAT REMAINS THE SAME?

Despite the changes caused by the public and online nature of POCs, some elements still stay the same. Corporate failures and misconduct lead to dissatisfaction, which elicits the experience of inward- or outward-directed negative emotions. Also, the goals of dissatisfied individuals remain the same and may be personal, like seeking redress, or collective, like helping others not to become victims of a corporate failure. Yet, with the use of public online channels empowered complainants can exert more pressure on the involved company and generate support by – possibly many – others for achieving their goal. As before, companies are well advised to implement a sound cross-channel complaint management system, nowadays also including digital channels, which can identify and react to complaints in their early stages. Research shows that dissatisfied consumers often first try to solve a problem offline by directly addressing the involved company. Yet, when this attempt remains unsuccessful (i.e., consumers experience a *double deviation*), they go online, where they voice a POC to put pressure on the company and to escalate the situation (Weitzl and Hutzinger, 2019).

CRITICAL EXAMINATION: COMPLAINT MANAGEMENT IN DIGITAL ENVIRONMENTS

Handling POCs in a way that calms or ideally satisfies the complainants and complaint observers is important for protecting the corporate reputation and for preventing a paracrisis that may turn into a full-blown crisis (Coombs and Holladay, 2012). Research shows that both complainants and bystanders evaluate a company's response in terms of three notions of justice: procedural, distributive and interactional (e.g., Smith et al., 1999; Smith and Bolton, 2002).

Procedural justice focuses on the perceived fairness in the procedures and criteria used by the company to arrive at the outcome of a dispute (Blodgett et al., 1997). Here, the individual evaluates the extent to which consumer-centric standards and procedures to settle the conflict are carried out during the service recovery process (Goodwin and Ross, 1992). In the online environment, timing and speed of response are critical elements of procedural justice (Istanbulluoglu, 2017) as they indicate the extent to which the company is concerned about the complaint. *Interactional justice* refers to the communication between the complainant and the company's representatives. Providing an explanation for the failure (Tax and Brown, 1998) and communicating politely and respectfully (Patterson et al., 2006) are ways to enhance the perception of interactional justice. Both empathy (Johnston and Fern, 1999) and apology (Kelley and Davis, 1994) can help to appease complainants – especially if the company is not offering any tangible compensation (Goodwin and Ross, 1992). In social media, using a conversational human voice has been proven particularly useful to enhance interactional justice (Javornik et al., 2020). Lastly, *distributive justice* refers to perceived fairness derived from a compensatory or reparative act. This justice type has the greatest impact on complainants' satisfaction (Mattila, 2001). All three justice perceptions are responsible for the post-complaint judgement of satisfaction (Gelbrich and Roschk, 2011).

Companies try to recover complainants and influence bystanders by offering what van Noort and Willemsen (2012, p. 115) call *webcare*, which is "the act of engaging in online interactions with (complaining) consumers, by actively searching the web to address consumer feedback". Here, the company's intention is to restore customer satisfaction and to limit the potential damage that online complaints could have on others observing the situation (Weitzl and Hutzinger, 2017; Willemsen et al., 2013), and to mitigate complainants' failure attributions (Weitzl et al., 2018). By analysing how large companies handle complaints on their Facebook and Twitter pages, Einwiller and Steilen (2015) found that responding to a complaint compared to not responding at all is associated with more complaint satisfaction. Specific responses that were associated with more complaint satisfaction are offering a corrective action, transferring the complainant to an authority that can resolve the problem as well as expressing gratitude. Overall, the study shows that accommodative responses are positively related to complaint satisfaction, while defensive strategies are not. However, if accommodative responses are interpreted as a confession of guilt they can backfire on the company and stimulate even more POCs (Weitzl and Hutzinger, 2019).

Sophisticated webcare strategies should, however, take several factors into account, including the prior relationship between customer and complainant, the type of POC (Grégoire et al., 2015) or the goal pursued by the complainant (Weitzl, 2019). Research shows that customers who had a strong relationship with the company before the negative incident are even more demanding than those with only a weak relationship. That's because they think that they deserve better than regular customers (Wolter et al., 2021). There is some evidence that a strong prior relationship leads to more annoyance – even after minor failures (Craighead et al., 2004; Mattila, 2004). These individuals feel especially disappointed, harmed and unfairly treated which leads to a sense of betrayal that triggers destructive, retaliatory desires. Such reactions have been discussed as the betrayal hypothesis (Singh and Sirdeshmukh, 2000) or the love-becomes-hate effect (Grégoire and Fisher, 2006). Therefore, companies must be very careful when addressing these complaints and be sure to keep the promises they make in their webcare communication.

When the POC is voiced directly to a company, for which the complainant initially often uses a private online channel, he or she generally pursues a personal, constructive goal (e.g., redress seeking). In this case, an accommodative response strategy covering all three types of perceived justice is most effective. The problem encountered by the complainant should be quickly acknowledged and fixed, if possible, to avoid a *double deviation* (Grégoire et al., 2015). If the problems are addressed satisfactorily, yielding a successful recovery, complainants may forgive and remain loyal to the company or brand. They may even voice positive word-of-mouth, which shows that POCs can also generate beneficial effects for a company at the end (*service recovery paradox*). However, not responding enhances passive negative brand-related reactions (e.g., an unfavourable corporate image) and defensive responses – due to their higher perceived unfairness – trigger active company-aversive reactions like more POCs (Weitzl, 2019).

200   *Handbook on digital corporate communication*

If a POC is voiced on a platform of a third party, literature suggests that the aggrieved company should contact the complainant (van Noort and Willemsen, 2012) after identifying the complaint by means of social media monitoring. Grégoire et al. (2015) suggest to publicly acknowledge the situation, show a sense of caring and good faith, and invite the complainant to engage in a private discussion about the matter. After solving the problem, the company is advised to communicate the outcome, positive or negative, on the same social media site to show their efforts also to bystanders.

An ugly situation arises after a complainant has experienced a double – or more – deviation. This is the case when prior complaints were unsuccessful, which enhances the complainants' dissatisfaction and negative emotions. These types of complainants may seek revenge against the firm by trying to share their dissatisfying and frustrating experience with a large online audience as a means to restore justice (Grégoire and Fisher, 2008). They often try to create an attention-grabbing post to spread it widely. Such "[s]pite driven complaints are the most likely to go viral, in part because customers will do whatever it takes to tarnish the firm's reputation and credibility in order to fulfil their desire for revenge" (Grégoire et al., 2015, p. 178). Webcare in such a situation is very reactive and mainly damage control (van Noort and Willemsen, 2012). Grégoire et al. (2015) suggest two different types of actions: First, the complainant should be contacted privately in order to find a reasonable solution for him or her. However, at this stage, this may not be accepted as vindictive complainants are often indifferent to any type of webcare (Weitzl, 2019). This is because the act of complaining itself helps them to achieve their personal (e.g., venting, seeking revenge) or collective (e.g., helping fellow consumers) goals. Nonetheless, when the complaint goes viral, a second type of action is necessary in form of public communication. "[T]the firm needs to directly address the public at large, describing all the actions it took" to fix the problem and recover the situation (Grégoire et al., 2015, p. 181). Yet, once a post went viral, it is almost impossible to stop. Therefore, it is vital to have an effective complaint management in place in order to prevent double deviations from happening.

Online firestorms are an extreme form of such an ugly social media situation. Aside from emerging from a double deviation experienced by a single customer, they are often triggered by perceived corporate misconduct or irresponsibility when companies violate social norms. Einwiller et al. (2017) found that perceived moral misconduct (e.g., sexism, racism, misuse of power, animal rights) was the main reason for online firestorms which were taken up by the mainstream media, followed by perceptions of market misconduct (e.g., unreasonable pricing, bad product or service). Identifying the conduct that may be perceived as moral or market misconduct is critical to preventing online firestorms. Coming back to the introductory example of Gucci, attentive and sensitive marketers should have been able to identify the potential for outrage in the black balaclava-style sweater. Similar cases abound. In 2017, for example, H&M sold a T-shirt with the slogan "Unemployed" on it and in 2018, the Swedish fashion retailer used an advert featuring a black boy modelling a hoodie with the slogan "Coolest Monkey in the Jungle", which led to the appointment of a diversity division at H&M (Blanchard, 2019). However, if even good issues management cannot prevent a firestorm from erupting, companies need to react and try to extinguish the fire. The primary goals pursued by firestorm participants identified in the study by Einwiller et al. (2017) were achieving short-term corrective actions, that is restoring distributive justice, followed by vilification of the firestorm object and venting. Thus, reparative actions should be effective in appeasing at least those participants in an online firestorm who aim for a change in corporate behaviour. Yet, because vilification

Digital corporate communication and complaint management 201

and venting are also central goals of firestorm participants and because "[t]he messages in a firestorm are predominantly opinion, not fact, thus having a high affective nature" (Pfeffer et al., 2014, p. 118), calming down the outrage can be highly challenging. The following case of Gucci exemplifies this challenge.

CASE STUDY: GUCCI'S HANDLING OF THE BALACLAVA SWEATER FIRESTORM

On 6 February 2019, Gucci experienced the start of a severe online firestorm, after posts showing the picture of a white model wearing a black balaclava-style Gucci sweater with a pull-up neck covering half of her face and featuring a thick red line around the mouth opening started circulating on social media. Many called the garment's design racist, because the sweater's design and the way it was modelled created an image that resembled the title character of a nineteenth-century children's book called "The Story of Little Black Sambo", which has been used as a racist trope (Chiu, 2019). People also pointed to the fact that the timing of the sweater's release was especially unfortunate, because February is black history month in the United States. The fashion activist Cocolo Chanel, for example, commented: "Balaclava knit top by *Gucci*. Happy Black History Month y'all."[1] Another user tweeted: "someone obviously didnt let gucci know its Black HISTORY Month and NOT BLACKFACE Month."[2] Many users were outraged by the sweater and calls for boycott were not long in coming.

Gucci reacted within a few hours. The company had removed the product and published an apology on its Twitter account on 7 February early in the morning (Ferrier, 2019). The statement read: "Gucci deeply apologizes for the offense caused by the wool balaclava jumper. We can confirm that the item has been immediately removed from our online store and all physical stores." The statement continued: "We consider diversity to be a fundamental value to be fully upheld, respected, and at the forefront of every decision we make. We are fully committed to increasing the diversity throughout our organization and turning this incident into a powerful learning moment for the Gucci team and beyond."[3] Thus, in this first response, Gucci applied several accommodative response strategies, namely apology, accepting responsibility and two types of corrective actions (removing the product and the commitment to increase diversity) as well as one bolstering message, when stating that the firm considers diversity a fundamental value. Yet, the post was rather ineffective in calming down users' anger as the reactions to it were mainly negative (Wekwerth, 2019). In the days to come, the firestorm gained speed when many celebrities such as Lil Pump, Russell Simmons, Spike Lee and rapper T.I. joined in and announced that they would boycott Gucci (Griffith, 2019). Rapper 50 Cent posted a drastic statement by publishing a video of him burning a Gucci shirt on Instagram (Ritschel, 2019).

Nine days after the first tweet, Gucci communicated a second response on Twitter[4] and Instagram which began with a personal quote by Gucci's CEO Marco Bizzarri: "We accept full accountability for this incident which has exposed shortfalls in our ongoing strategic approach to embedding diversity and inclusion in both our organization and in our activities. I am particularly grateful to Dapper Dan for the role he has played in bringing community leaders together to offer us their counsel at this time." Dapper Dan is a black Harlem designer who had previously worked with Gucci. He had harshly criticized the firm for the incident, but also agreed to meet with Bizzarri to help Gucci learn.[5] In the post, Gucci furthermore introduced four initiatives for increasing cultural diversity and awareness in the company, e.g.,

202 *Handbook on digital corporate communication*

the newly created role of Global Director of Diversity and Inclusion. Gucci also announced a Multi-Cultural Design Scholarship Program for college students at fashion schools to "amplify opportunities for underrepresented groups of talents leading to full-time employment". This second response featured several important elements: an accommodative response by demonstrating personal accountability and sincerity from the very top, which reinforced the acknowledgement of mistakes, and showed openness to learn from a prominent person affected by the offence. It furthermore stated very concrete corrective actions that have the potential to not just foster diversity and inclusion at the firm but also throughout the whole industry. This second post was much more effective than the first one. A majority of 83 per cent of users on Twitter and Instagram reacted positively and only 12 per cent of the comments were negative (Wekwerth, 2019).

One month later, on 15 March, Gucci published a long-term diversity and inclusion action plan on Twitter,[6] Instagram and Facebook where it announced Gucci Changemakers, a global programme to support industry change including a Changemakers Fund of $5 million and a $1.5 million scholarship programme in North America, alongside a global employee-volunteering framework to fuel the company's commitment to creating lasting social impact in communities and within the fashion industry. The post again included a quote from Gucci's CEO Bizzarri: "I believe in dialogue, building bridges and taking quick actions." Dapper Dan was also quoted expressing his pride to work with Gucci and stating that "it is imperative that we have a seat at the table to say how we should be represented and reimagined". A Changemaker Council made up of community leaders and social change experts was also mentioned. With this third post, Gucci demonstrated the fulfilment of its promises and the progress made. The responses were again not just largely positive but also much smaller in number.

The case of Gucci demonstrates the challenge of handling POCs in the situation of an online firestorm. To restore justice, a single post or tweet, even if it is accommodative including an apology and quick corrective actions and promises for betterment, is not sufficient. Outrage of the dimension experienced by Gucci requires sincere and credible communication by the firm's top management, the inclusion of the affected party, and – most importantly – very concrete corrective actions to tackle the issue and to restore justice for those affected. The activities undertaken by Gucci were not just encompassing but also quickly implemented so that the company was able to demonstrate results after a few weeks.

CONCLUSION AND FUTURE DIRECTIONS

Complaining and complaint management have become more challenging in the online environment. The public nature of POCs puts pressure on companies, and the velocity of communication on online platforms requires fast responses. However, responding quickly is just one requirement in online complaint management. Choosing the right response strategy that meets the goals of the complainants without unreasonably compromising corporate goals is essential. While complaint management was previously mainly a marketing communication task, as complaints were largely about product or service failures, complaints about perceived corporate misconduct and irresponsibility have become more prevalent and also dangerous in the online environment. The moralization of markets, where notions of fairness, solidarity, environment, health and political considerations are increasing (Stehr, 2008), calls upon digital corporate communication for the maintenance of organizational intangible and tangible assets (Badham and Luoma-aho, Chapter 1 in this volume). Companies need to invest in sufficient personnel who are knowledgeable about the dynamics of online complaining in general and online firestorms in particular.

Yet, several questions remain with regards to online complaining behaviour, which should be addressed in future research. First, there is still limited understanding of the differences between the effects of webcare on online complainants and complaint bystanders. Extant research shows that trustworthy and accommodative responses including apology, promise and compensation have a positive effect on bystanders, when many complaints were voiced (Dens et al., 2015), yet research also shows that sometimes even defensive responses can have positive effects on bystanders (Weitzl and Hutzinger, 2017). Furthermore, identifying the motives of bystanders to read POCs and corporate responses and analysing the effects on their attitudes as well as behavioural intentions to like, share or comment will help improve online complaint management. It will also enhance our knowledge on the role of bystanders turning into active communicators, who can either support the complainant or the company in their webcare activities.

Second, more research is needed to understand which factors stimulate different coping strategies – exit, voice or loyalty – of people experiencing a corporate failure or misconduct. Particularly, why do some people voice their complaint publicly online, and why do others remain silent? Research in the area of traditional complaining behaviour shows, for example, the influence of personality characteristics. Risk-taking was shown to exert an influence on the propensity to complain, while self-efficacy, Machiavellianism and perceived control only influence people's attitude toward complaining (Bodey and Grace, 2007). Yet, which personality characteristics differentiate online complainants from those not complaining online? Cultural differences can also play an important role for voicing POCs or not. People from cultures that value harmony, like those in the Confucian Asia cluster, may be less inclined to complain online than people in other cultures, where direct language and individualism prevails, like countries in the Germanic Europe cluster.

Third, technology can help to identify which webcare responses lead to more satisfaction and less sharing of negative emotions. With the application of artificial intelligence, it may be possible to develop a predictive system that helps to choose the most suitable response to specific POCs. Based on this knowledge a webcare or service recovery bot could be developed, which can be applied to generate answers in standard complaining situations. Yet, when the situation escalates and turns into an online firestorm, humans will most likely be better communicators than technology.

Fourth, more research is needed in the area of online firestorms. Once triggered, often by perceptions of moral misconduct (Einwiller et al., 2017), they are very hard to stop. Research needs to shed more light on the triggers of online firestorms. This knowledge can then be used in issues and complaint management to sensitize communication and marketing representatives. Through studying the dynamics of firestorm cases (e.g., Badham et al., 2022; Wekwerth, 2019), the diffusion of issues in different crisis arenas and the effects of different response strategies on those dynamics can be analysed, while considering the typicality of the issue and cultural context. When and how do complaints reach a tipping point, where simple webcare strategies are no longer sufficient? In this case the company has to switch to crisis mode, which means also involving corporate management and other affected departments aside from communications and/or the complaint management unit.

204 *Handbook on digital corporate communication*

Finally, on an organizational level, complaint management in digital environments needs to be well integrated in the complaint management unit that handles complaints on traditional channels. This is essential, as POCs are often not the first utterance of dissatisfaction, but are resorted to after traditional private complaints were unsuccessful. Furthermore, especially with regards to corporate issues, online complaint management has to be closely aligned with corporate issues management, which is also responsible for detecting critical issues at an early stage before they turn into a firestorm, a paracrisis or possibly even a full-fledged crisis. Having the right organizational structure in place, where information flows easily and coordination happens smoothly between units, is a sine qua non for effective complaint management in digital as well as analogue environments.

NOTES

1. See https://twitter.com/evilrashida/status/1093213729603239936.
2. See https://twitter.com/cosmicdonutt/status/1093268733739614218.
3. See https://twitter.com/gucci/status/1093345744080306176.
4. See https://twitter.com/gucci/status/1096559663452176384.
5. See https://www.instagram.com/p/BttpJA7gCIy/?utm_source=ig_embed.
6. See https://twitter.com/gucci/status/1107719685171236864?lang=de.

REFERENCES

Adams, J. S. (1965). Inequity in social exchange. In L. Berkowitz (ed.), *Advances in experimental social psychology* (vol. 2, pp. 267–299). New York: Academic Press.

Badham, M., Lievonen, M., and Luoma-aho, V. (2022). Factors influencing crisis arena crossovers: The Apple iPhone #ChargeGate case. In L. Austin and Y. Jin (eds.), *Social media and crisis communication* (2nd edition). London: Routledge.

Badham, M. and Luoma-aho, V. (2023). Introduction to the Handbook on digital corporate communication. In V. Luoma-aho and M. Badham (eds.), *Handbook on digital corporate communication* (pp. 1–16). Cheltenham, UK and Northampton, MA: Edward Elgar Publishing.

Bearden, W. O. and Teel, J. E. (1983). Selected determinants of consumer satisfaction and complaint reports. *Journal of Marketing Research*, 20(1), 21–28.

Blaine, B. and Crocker, J. (1993). Self-esteem and self-serving biases in reactions to positive and negative events: An integrative review. In R. Baumeister (ed.), Self-esteem: The puzzle of low self-regard (pp. 55–85). New York: Plenum Press.

Blanchard, T. (2019). Courting controversy: From H&M's 'coolest monkey' to Gucci's blackface jumper. *The Guardian*, 8 February. https://www.theguardian.com/fashion/2019/feb/08/courting-controversy-from-hms-coolest-monkey-to-guccis-blackface-jumper.

Blodgett, J. G., Hill, D. J., and Tax, S. S. (1997). The effects of distributive, procedural, and interactional justice on postcomplaint behavior. *Journal of Retailing*, 73(2), 185–210.

Bodey, K. and Grace, D. (2007). Contrasting "complainers" with "non-complainers" on attitude toward complaining, propensity to complain, and key personality characteristics: A nomological look. *Psychology & Marketing*, 24(7), 579–594.

Bougie, R., Pieters, R., and Zeelenberg, M. (2003). Angry customers don't come back, they get back: The experience and behavioral implications of anger and dissatisfaction in services. *Journal of the Academy of Marketing Science*, 31(4), 377–393.

Bronner, F. and De Hoog, R. (2011). Vacationers and eWOM: Who posts, and why, where, and what? *Journal of Travel Research*, 50(1), 15–26.

Cambra-Fierro, J., Melero, I., and Sese, F. J. (2015). Managing complaints to improve customer profitability. *Journal of Retailing*, 91(1), 109–124.

Chiu, A. (2019). 'Haute Couture Blackface': Gucci apologizes and pulls 'racist' sweater. *The Washington Post*, 7 February. https://www.washingtonpost.com/nation/2019/02/07/haute-couture-blackface-gucci-apologizes-pulls-racist-sweater/.

Coombs, W. T. and Holladay, J. S. (2012). The paracrisis: The challenges created by publicly managing crisis prevention. *Public Relations Review*, *38*(3), 408–415.

Craighead, C. W., Karwan, K. R., and Miller, J. L. (2004). The effects of severity of failure and customer loyalty on service recovery strategies. *Production and Operations Management*, *13*(4), 307–321.

Davies, G. and Olmedo-Cifuentes, I. (2016). Corporate misconduct and the loss of trust. *European Journal of Marketing*, *50*(7–8), 1426–1447.

Day, R. L. and Landon, E. L. Jr. (1977). Towards a theory of consumer complaining behaviour. In A. Woodside, J. Sheth, and P. Bennett (eds.), *Consumer and industrial buying behaviour* (pp. 425–437). Amsterdam: North Holland Publishing Company.

Dens, N., De Pelsmacker, P., and Purnawirawan, N. (2015). "We(b)care": How review set balance moderates the appropriate response strategy to negative online reviews. *Journal of Service Management*, *26*(3), 486–515.

Einwiller, S. A. and Steilen, S. (2015). Handling complaints on social network sites: An analysis of complaints and complaint responses on Facebook and Twitter pages of large US companies. *Public Relations Review*, *41*(2), 195–204.

Einwiller, S., Viererbl, B., and Himmelreich, S. (2017). Journalists' coverage of online firestorms in German-language news media. *Journalism Practice*, *11*(9), 1178–1197.

Ferrier, M. (2019). Gucci withdraws $890 jumper after blackface backlash. *The Guardian*, 7 February. https://www.theguardian.com/fashion/2019/feb/07/gucci-withdraws-jumper-blackface-balaclava.

Frischlich, L., Schatto-Eckrodt, T., Bogerg, S., and Wintterlin, F. (2021). Roots of incivility: How personality, media use, and online experiences shape uncivil participation. *Media and Communication*, *9*(1), 195–208.

Gelbrich, K. and Roschk, H. (2011). A meta-analysis of organizational complaint handling and customer responses. *Journal of Service Research*, *14*(1), 24–43.

Goodwin, C. and Ross, I. (1992). Consumer responses to service failures: Influence of procedural and interactional fairness perceptions. *Journal of Business Research*, *25*(2), 149–163.

Grégoire, Y. and Fisher, R. J. (2006). The effects of relationship quality on customer retaliation. *Marketing Letters*, *17*(1), 31–46.

Grégoire, Y. and Fisher, R. J. (2008). Customer betrayal and retaliation: When your best customers become your worst enemies. *Journal of the Academy of Marketing Science*, *36*(2), 247–261.

Grégoire, Y., Salle, A., and Tripp, T. M. (2015). Managing social media crises with your customers: The good, the bad, and the ugly. *Business Horizons*, *58*(2), 173–182.

Grégoire, Y., Tripp, T. M., and Legoux, R. (2009). When customer love turns into lasting hate: The effects of relationship strength and time on customer revenge and avoidance. *Journal of Marketing*, *73*(6), 18–32.

Griffith, J. (2019). Spike Lee, T.I. boycott Gucci, Prada over 'blackface' fashion. *NBCnews*, 10 February. https://www.nbcnews.com/news/us-news/spike-lee-t-i-boycott-gucci-prada-over-blackface-fashion-n969821.

Gruber, M., Mayer, C., and Einwiller, S. (2020). What drives people to participate in online firestorms? *Online Information Review*, *44*(3), 563–581.

Hastie, R. (1984). Causes and effects of causal attribution. *Journal of Personality and Social Psychology*, *46*(1), 44–56.

Hennig-Thurau, T., Gwinner, K. P., Walsh, G., and Gremler, D. D. (2004). Electronic word-of-mouth via consumer-opinion platforms: What motivates consumers to articulate themselves on the internet? *Journal of Interactive Marketing*, *18*(1), 38–52.

Hirschman, A. O. (1970). *Exit, voice, and loyalty: Responses to decline in firms, organizations, and states*. Cambridge, MA: Harvard University Press.

Hoffman, K. D. and Bateson, J. E. (1997). *Essentials of services marketing: Concepts, strategies & cases*. Nashville, TN: South-Western.

Istanbulluoglu, D. (2017). Complaint handling on social media: The impact of multiple response times on consumer satisfaction. *Computers in Human Behavior*, *74*, 72–82.

206 *Handbook on digital corporate communication*

Javornik, A., Filieri, R., and Gumann, R. (2020). "Don't forget that others are watching, too!" The effect of conversational human voice and reply length on observers' perceptions of complaint handling in social media. *Journal of Interactive Marketing, 50*, 100–119.

Johnen, M., Jungblut, M., and Ziegele, M. (2018). The digital outcry: What incites participation behavior in an online firestorm? *New Media & Society, 20*(9), 3140–3160.

Johnston, R. and Fern, A. (1999). Service recovery strategies for single and double deviation scenarios. *Service Industries Journal, 19*(2), 69–82.

Kelley, S. W. and Davis, M. A. (1994). Antecedents to customer expectations for service recovery. *Journal of the Academy of Marketing Science, 22*(1), 52–61.

Kowalski, R. M. (1996). Complaints and complaining: Functions, antecedents, and consequences. *Psychological Bulletin, 119*(2), 179–196.

Laczniak, R. N., DeCarlo, T. E., and Ramaswami, S. N. (2001). Consumers' responses to negative word-of-mouth communication: An attribution theory perspective. *Journal of Consumer Psychology, 11*(1), 57–73.

Lazarus, R. S. (1991). Cognition and motivation in emotion. *American Psychologist, 46*(4), 352–367.

Lazarus, R. S. and Folkman, S. (1984). *Stress, appraisal, and coping.* Dordrecht: Springer.

Lee, Y. L. and Song, S. (2010). An empirical investigation of electronic word-of-mouth: Informational motive and corporate response strategy. *Computers in Human Behavior, 26*(5), 1073–1080.

Li, Z. C. and Stacks, D. (2017). When the relationships fail: A microperspective on consumer responses to service failure. *Journal of Public Relations Research, 29*(4), 158–175.

Lievonen, M. and Luoma-aho, V. (2015). Ethical hateholders and negative engagement: A challenge for organizational communication. In A. Catellani, A. Zerfass, and R. Tench (eds.), *Communication ethics in a connected world* (pp. 285–303). New York: Peter Lang.

MacDowell, K. and Mandler, G. (1989). Constructions of emotion: Discrepancy, arousal, and mood. *Motivation and Emotion, 13*(2), 105–124.

Mandler, G. (1990). A constructivity theory of emotion. In N. L. Stein (ed.), *Psychological and biological approaches to emotion* (2nd edition, pp. 211–238). Mahwah, NJ: Lawrence Erlbaum.

Mattila, A. S. (2001). Emotional bonding and restaurant loyalty. *Cornell Hotel and Restaurant Administration Quarterly, 42*(6), 73–79.

Mattila, A. S. (2004). The impact of service failures on customer loyalty: The moderating role of affective commitment. *International Journal of Service Industry Management, 15*(2), 150–166.

Mattila, A. S. and Wirtz, J. (2004). Consumer complaining to firms: The determinants of channel choice. *Journal of Services Marketing, 18*(2), 147–155.

Patterson, P. G., Cowley, E., and Prasongsukarn, K. (2006). Service failure recovery: The moderating impact of individual-level cultural value orientation on perceptions of justice. *International Journal of Research in Marketing, 23*(3), 263–277.

Pfeffer, J., Zorbach, T., and Carley, K. (2014). Understanding online firestorms: Negative word of mouth dynamics in social media networks. *Journal of Marketing Communications, 20*(1–2), 117–128.

Reeve, J. (2009). *Understanding motivation and emotion* (5th edition). Hoboken, NJ: Wiley.

Ritschel, C. (2019). 50 Cent burns Gucci shirt following blackface controversy. *The Independent*, 14 February. https://www.independent.co.uk/life-style/50-cent-gucci-blackface-instagram-burn-shirt-katy-perry-boycott-a8779611.html.

Rotman, D., Vieweg, S., Yardi, S., Chi, E. H., Preece, J., Shneiderman, B., Pirolli, P., and Glaisyer, T. (2011). From slacktivism to activism: Participatory culture in the age of social media. *CHI'11 Extended Abstracts on Human Factors in Computing Systems* (pp. 819–822). http://yardi.people.si.umich.edu/pubs/Yardi_CHI11_SIG.pdf.

Scherer, K. R. (1984). On the nature and function of emotion: A component process approach. In K. R. Scherer and P. Ekman (eds.), *Approaches to emotion* (pp. 293–317). Mahwah, NJ: Erlbaum.

Shaver, P., Schwartz, J., Kirson, D., and O'Connor, C. (1987). Emotion knowledge: Further exploration of a prototype approach. *Journal of Personality and Social Psychology, 52*(6), 1061–1086.

Singh, J. (1988). Consumer complaint intentions and behavior: Definitional and taxonomical issues. *Journal of Marketing, 52*(1), 93–107.

Singh, J. and Sirdeshmukh, D. (2000). Agency and trust mechanisms in consumer satisfaction and loyalty judgments. *Journal of the Academy of Marketing Science, 28*(1), 150–167.

Smith, A. K. and Bolton, R. N. (2002). The effect of customers' emotional responses to service failures on their recovery effort evaluations and satisfaction judgments. *Journal of the Academy of Marketing Science*, *30*(1), 5–23.

Smith, A. K., Bolton, R. N., and Wagner, J. (1999). A model of customer satisfaction with service encounters involving failure and recovery. *Journal of Marketing Research*, *36*(3), 356–372.

Smith, C. A., Haynes, K. N., Lazarus, R. S., and Pope, L. K. (1993). In search of the "hot" cognitions: Attributions, appraisals, and their relation to emotion. *Journal of Personality and Social Psychology*, *65*(5), 916–929.

Smith, C. A. and Lazarus, R. S. (1993). Appraisal components, core relational themes, and the emotions. *Cognition & Emotion*, 7(3–4), 233–269.

Stehr, N. (2008). The moralization of the markets in Europe. *Society*, *45*(1), 62–67.

Tangney, J. P. and Dearing, R. L. (2002). Gender differences in morality. In R. F. Bornstein and J. M. Masling (eds.), *The psychodynamics of gender and gender role* (pp. 251–269). Washington, DC: American Psychological Association.

Tax, S. S. and Brown, S. W. (1998). Recovering and learning from service failure. *MIT Sloan Management Review*, *40*(1), 75–88.

Van Noort, G. and Willemsen, L. M. (2012). Online damage control: The effects of proactive versus reactive webcare interventions in consumer-generated and brand-generated platforms. *Journal of Interactive Marketing*, *26*(3), 131–140.

Ward, J. C. and Ostrom, A. L. (2006). Complaining to the masses: The role of protest framing in customer-created complaint web sites. *Journal of Consumer Research*, *33*(2), 220–230.

Weiner, B. (1986). Attribution, emotion, and action. In R. M. Sorrentino and E. T. Higgins (eds.), *Handbook of motivation and cognition: Foundations of social behavior* (pp. 281–312). New York: Guilford Press.

Weitzl, W. J. (2019). Webcare's effect on constructive and vindictive complaints. *Journal of Product & Brand Management*, *28*(3), 330–347.

Weitzl, W. J. and Hutzinger, C. (2017). The effects of marketer- and advocate-initiated online service recovery responses on silent bystanders. *Journal of Business Research*, *80*, 164–175.

Weitzl, W. J. and Hutzinger, C. (2019). Rise and fall of complainants' desires: The role of pre-failure brand commitment and online service recovery satisfaction. *Computers in Human Behavior*, *97*, 116–129.

Weitzl, W. J., Hutzinger, C., and Einwiller, S. (2018). An empirical study on how webcare mitigates complainants' failure attributions and negative word-of-mouth. *Computers in Human Behavior*, *89*, 316–327.

Wekwerth, Z. M. (2019). Responding to online firestorms on social media: An analysis of the two company cases Dolce & Gabbana and Gucci (Master's thesis, University of Twente). http://essay.utwente.nl/79702/.

Willemsen, L., Neijens, P. C., and Bronner, F. A. (2013). Webcare as customer relationship and reputation management? Motives for negative electronic word of mouth and their effect on webcare receptiveness. In S. Rosengren, M. Dahlén, and S. Okazaki (eds.), *Advances in advertising research* (vol. 4, pp. 55–69). Cham: Springer Gabler.

Wirtz, J. and Mattila, A. S. (2004). Consumer responses to compensation, speed of recovery and apology after a service failure. *International Journal of Service Industry Management*, *15*(2), 150–166.

Wolter, J. S., Donavan, D. T., and Giebelhausen, M. (2021). The corporate reputation and consumer-company identification link as a sensemaking process: A cross-level interaction analysis. *Journal of Business Research*, *132*, 289–300.

Yi, S. and Baumgartner, H. (2004). Coping with negative emotions in purchase-related situations. *Journal of Consumer Psychology*, *14*(3), 303–317.

15. Digital corporate communication and hostile hijacking of organizational crises

Sofia Johansson, Howard Nothhaft and Alicia Fjällhed

INTRODUCTION

Andrew Chadwick (2013) argues that we live in a hybrid media system – in a constant 'in-betweenness' of old and new technology, with one foot in the past and the other in the future. While the hybridization of the current media system and the transition to a high-choice media environment (Van Aelst et al., 2017) have democratized content production and increased connectivity (Bennett and Segerberg, 2012), these developments have also opened a historically unprecedented Pandora's box of disinformation techniques that can harm organizations in significant ways.

Today, disinformation operators make use of various automated and algorithmic tools to spread false and misleading information on social media platforms (Tsyrenzhapova and Woolley, 2021). Blaming the technology in isolation, however, would be misleading. What is exploited through the platforms are cognitive and affective mechanisms in the human mind (Nisbet and Kamenchuck, 2019; Pamment et al., 2018). In most cases, disinformation operators take advantage of technological developments to amplify pre-existing concerns, emotions, and prejudice.

As disinformation campaigns often aim to disrupt public debate and decrease levels of institutional trust, they pose a threat to democracy (Bennett and Livingstone, 2018; Pamment et al., 2018). That said, disinformation rarely targets democracy in general. Instead, disinformation campaigns attack concrete institutions as well as organizations and their representatives (i.e., politicians, officials, and experts). Organizations are particularly vulnerable to disinformation attacks during crises when their leadership is under scrutiny and pressure. In such situations, crises can be hijacked by disinformation operators with no interest in a constructive solution. *Hostile hijacking* of organizational crises occurs when operators driven by ideological interests amplify public outrage to make a point about the organization's country of origin or countries that are similar culturally and/or politically. For instance, by attacking IKEA or The Swedish National Board of Health and Welfare, disinformation operators do not primarily aim to taint the organization but seek to undermine the Swedish political system (Johansson, 2020).

Although disinformation is gaining increased attention from crisis communication scholars (see, for example, Jahng, 2021; Vafeiadis et al., 2020; Coombs et al., 2020), practice and research largely remain wedded to traditional assumptions. Conventional crisis communication theory rests on assumptions that are well suited to the majority of 'regular' crises but become problematic in the small number of hostile crisis hijacks. Therefore, the purpose of this chapter is to make digital communication practitioners and scholars more aware of hostile hijacks. It starts by defining hostile hijacking and introducing studies on disinformation. After that, a discussion of changes and continuities is provided, followed by a critical examination of the potential consequences of identifying hostile hijacks. The chapter then presents a selection

Digital corporate communication and hostile hijacking of crises   209

of cases suspiciously constituting hostile hijacks. It concludes with diagnostic criteria that digital corporate communicators can employ and a roadmap of future directions for the topic.

DEFINITIONS OF THE TOPIC AND PREVIOUS STUDIES

The key observation in this chapter is that disinformation operators can exploit organizational crises in cases of hostile hijacking. To understand what a hostile hijack entails, it is helpful to compare it to three other crisis scenarios. Imagine, for instance, that an oil spill gives rise to protests among climate activists who argue that oil companies should be shut down due to their effect on the climate. In this scenario, the crisis remains within the arena in which it was initially triggered (effects on the climate). During a hijack, on the other hand, the crisis scenario is transferred to a different arena. Consider instead that a group of stakeholders note that the statements made on behalf of the oil company and other parties involved are made solely by males, demonstrating the lack of females in leadership positions in the industry. In this example, the crisis is transferred to a different arena (gender) where it is used to promote a political agenda (although based on legitimate concerns). In the third case, the hijack is additionally considered hostile. Not only is the crisis transferred to a different arena, it is hijacked by disinformation operators with the goal to generate distrust and undermine democracy. If the oil spill were used as evidence of a corrupt government who allegedly covered it up (although no evidence of such behaviour exists), the crisis scenario is not only transferred to a different arena (corruption) but connected to a _hostile narrative._ Such a narrative resembles a conspiracy theory at the same time as it positions the elites against the people. _Hostile hijacks_ thus cover situations where the organizational crisis is instrumentalized to spread disinformation in order to further destructive political agendas.

Hostile hijacks, to be clear, do not require that disinformation operators 'take over' the conversation in its entirety. More often, their efforts prolong and exacerbate the crisis. Digital corporate communication practitioners need to understand that disinformation operators act differently, although posing as concerned stakeholders. As 'fakeholders' (Luoma-aho, 2015), they do not have an interest in 'settling the matter' or the organization. By applying the conventional strategy of two-way communication and unreserved acknowledgement of grievances, communication managers not only dig a deeper hole for their employer but play into the hands of operators who aim to disrupt the public debate.

Hostile Narratives and Conspiracy Theories

The _hostile narratives_ employed by disinformation operators vary from culture to culture, depending on what is perceived as a sensitive societal trigger topic. For this chapter's case study, the analysis is based on the list of hostile narratives identified by the EU's European External Action Service (EEAS). According to their taskforce EUvsDisinfo, Russia deploys five recurring narratives against Western democracies (European External Action Service Task Force, 2019).

The first narrative, _The Elites vs. the People_, propagates the view that the evil elite does not care about the needs of ordinary citizens. Very similar to populist rhetoric, it is effective since it provides a scapegoat for social and political dysfunctionalities. The second narrative, _Threatened Values_, includes questioning and challenging Western attitudes towards ethnic

210 *Handbook on digital corporate communication*

and religious minorities or women's rights. It suggests that tradition, decency, and common sense are threatened and that the West is falling apart due to extensive feminism and political correctness. The third narrative, *Lost Sovereignty/Lost National Identity*, laments the loss of people's democratic rights and cultural identity to supranational bureaucracies. NATO and the EU, for instance, are portrayed as pursuing bureaucratic and militaristic aims. The fourth narrative, *Imminent Collapse*, suggests that European member states are "on the verge of civil war" (European External Action Service Task Force, 2019). The fifth and final narrative, the *Hahaganda* narrative, includes the use of different "derogatory words to belittle" concepts such as "democracy, democratic procedures, and candidates" (European External Action Service Task Force, 2019).

Citizens can, of course, be legitimately concerned about these issues. In many cases, however, the narratives identified by EUvsDisinfo take constructive concern to the point of *conspiracy theory*. Not only are Western societies experiencing troubles, but their collapse is imminent and orchestrated by a powerful yet invisible elite. Conspiracy theories are usually part of a monological belief system (Goertzel, 1994), where one conspiracy theory engenders belief in another. This gives rise to so-called 'closed epistemologies' (Goertzel, 1994; Sutton and Douglas, 2014), where beliefs are assessed primarily by their compatibility with other beliefs within the system rather than verifiable facts. Attempts to disprove the core assertion thus only serve to prove how deeply-rooted the conspiracy is. Due to their circular structure, conspiracy theories are excellent carriers of dis- and misinformation (Önnerfors, 2021).

Disinformation and Hostile Hijacking

Disinformation is defined as content that is false or misleading and intended to harm. The intention to deceive separates disinformation from misinformation, which is the unintentional spreading of false or misleading information (Humprecht et al., 2020; Lazer et al., 2018; Wardle, 2018). As this chapter focuses on hostile narratives with the overriding goal to undermine democracy, it is mainly concerned with disinformation activities conducted by state actors (such as intelligence agencies), state-controlled actors (such as troll factories), or proxies (domestic groups or individuals in one country, often the target country) controlled by a foreign state actor (Pamment et al., 2018; Wanless and Pamment, 2019). Disinformation can, of course, be spread by other actors as well, including competitors and single individuals.

Attention is often drawn to the appearance of disinformation on digital media. Here, focus has been put on content mimicking news, i.e., content which appears to conform to the standards and conventions of professional journalism. 'Fake news' has become a buzzword scrutinized by both professional media and the scholarly community (Tandoc et al., 2017; Wanless and Pamment, 2019). Yet, as Wardle puts it (2018, p. 951), "the ecosystem of polluted information extends far beyond content that mimics news". For example, disinformation masquerading as satire and parody is a subtle way of making unacceptable arguments appear acceptable. Attaching organizations' logos or journalists' names to unrelated content makes fabrications appear more trustworthy. Scholars therefore argue for a more 'fluid' understanding of information pollution, ranging from obviously faked content to grey zones, including satire, forgeries, and impostor content (Wardle, 2018).

Irrespective of the narratives propagated, the overriding goal of disinformation spread by the actors of interest in this chapter is often to create a "climate of distrust between a state and citizens" (Swedish Civil Contingencies Agency, 2018, p. 11). These types of disinformation activities are therefore particularly problematic for political orders which rely on the consent of the governed, i.e., democracies. Liberal democracy is committed to the idea "that those affected by a collective decision have the right, opportunity, and capacity to participate in consequential deliberation about the content of decisions" (Ercan et al., 2019, p. 23). Democratic decision-making is, in other words, not solely about voting but encompasses the active participation of citizens in political debates (McKay and Tenove, 2021). It is consequently not surprising that social media platforms have become an important political arena. At the same time, the centrality of civil society and free and open debate makes democracies vulnerable to disinformation campaigns.

Because consent of the governed is vital for democracies, disinformation operators often target the institutions at the interface of state and society, such as journalism, political leaders, and democratic institutions and processes (Bradshaw and Howard, 2018; Swedish Civil Contingencies Agency, 2018). In attempts to generate distrust, public organizations and high-profile corporations are also becoming targets of disinformation campaigns (Berthon et al., 2018; Jin et al., 2020; Pamment et al., 2018). As stated before, they are especially vulnerable to disinformation attacks during crises when public leadership is under pressure (Swedish Civil Contingencies Agency, 2018). In such instances, the event can be used to showcase a general trend, such as the decay of traditional values or the immoral and self-serving nature of the elites. While the strategy is not new, technological advancements have made hostile hijacks easier to carry out. Using trolls (Paavola et al., 2016) and bots (Gorwa and Guilbeault, 2020; Grimme et al., 2017), disinformation operators take advantage of vulnerabilities in the opinion formation process. Hostile hijackers can, for instance, amplify debates about the crisis to give the impression of widespread 'real' concern, or target stakeholders based on cognitive and affective vulnerabilities (Pamment et al., 2018). As Pamment et al. (2018, p. 9) put it, disinformation operators "exploit the open system of opinion formation in Western democracies, turning its greatest asset, free and open debate, into a vulnerability".

Hostile Hijacking and Crisis Communication

In general, disinformation and illegitimate actors have received little attention from crisis communication scholars. Conventional crisis communication research tends to assume that the interests of actors engaged in a crisis are legitimate by default. Scholars frequently stress "the need to develop dialogue and to choose the right message, source and timing" (Eriksson, 2018, p. 531). Here, "effective dialogue seems mainly to be about taking actions in social media that demonstrate that the organization is listening to affected or critical citizens and consumers during crisis situations" (Eriksson, 2018, p. 531). In other words, communication managers should acknowledge the legitimacy of grievances, and by doing so, adapt the organization to its environment (Diers-Lawson, 2019). According to crisis communication research, the preferred way is by applying honest and transparent communication strategies engaging stakeholders in two-way communication (see, for example, Maal and Wilson-North, 2019; Ngai and Falkheimer, 2016; Sellnow and Seeger, 2013).

The situation is, however, changing. Corporate communication research has recognized the presence of troll stakeholders or 'fakeholders' (see, for example, Lievonen et al., 2018; Luoma-aho, 2015) and disinformation has gained increased attention among crisis communication scholars in the last years (see, for example, Coombs et al., 2020; Jahng, 2021; Vafeiadis et al., 2020). Despite the growing interest, crisis communication remains ill-adapted to face the

212   *Handbook on digital corporate communication*

complexity of a media environment where genuine and legitimate stakeholders coexist with malicious fakeholders. Empirical research and case studies analysing disinformation targeting organizations during crises and potential responses remain scarce.

WHAT IS CHANGING?

The instrumentalization of crises for political purposes is not new. Politicians, activists, and journalists have always conducted crisis hijacks in order to spread their political agenda. However, digital transformation has restructured the public sphere and given rise to new ways to influence public opinion covertly. In the modern information system, it is thus easier to conduct hostile hijacks benefiting disruptive and potentially harmful agendas or foreign actors (i.e., as part of disinformation campaigns).

Several overlapping macro-trends explain the media system's vulnerability to disinformation and, by extension, hostile hijacks. While these trends have made the system more democratic and dynamic, they might have eroded what Habermas termed the 'epistemic' or 'truth-tracking function' of the public sphere (2006). Some scholars even argue that we live in a post-truth era (Lewandowsky et al., 2017), where 'alternative facts' replace verifiable ones, and feelings outweigh arguments.

Hybridization and the Attention Economy

According to Chadwick (2013), the current information eco-system is characterized by hybridity. The core challenge of hybridity does not only lie in the coexistence of old media on one side (i.e., newspapers and television) and new media on the other (i.e., social media). Hybridity is characterized by a constant 'in-betweenness', where new developments are quickly superseded by even newer ones. A constantly changing media system with blurred boundaries between different types of content makes it increasingly difficult to analyse news sources and triangulate facts (Chadwick, 2013; Pamment et al., 2018).

Hybridity is closely connected to commercial reconfiguration and the development of a high-choice media environment (Van Aelst et al., 2017). In the high-choice media environment, content fights for audiences' attention on a market where the devotion of time and cognitive capacity serves as the most sought-after commodity (see, for example, Franck, 2019; Lanham, 2007; Venturini, 2019). The attention economy thus provides an incentive to spread content irrespective of its truth or utility to make a profit (Bakir and McStay, 2018; Tandoc et al., 2017) – a dynamic that facilitated the circulation of clickbait and highly emotional content online. During a crisis, disinformation operators are thus provided with the opportunity to harness strong emotions in order to further a hostile narrative.

Connectivity

The new digital landscape has not only enabled collective action but also connective action (Bennett and Segerberg 2012, Luoma-aho, 2015), putting civil society in a much stronger position vis-à-vis organizations and the state. Before, stakeholders needed to attract media attention about organizational misconduct by putting forward an interesting story to journalists. Today, claims about organizational misconduct are made online "in full view of other

Digital corporate communication and hostile hijacking of crises 213

stakeholders" (Coombs and Holladay, 2012, p. 408), making it easier to raise awareness about organizational wrongdoing. While positive in principle, the new digital environment not only makes it easier for stakeholders to identify each other and group against the organization (Luoma-aho, 2015). It also makes it easier for disinformation operators to identify concerned stakeholders during a crisis, determine their interests, and ultimately exploit their networks.

Another result of increased connectivity is the integration of the private and the public sphere, being one of the most significant challenges for countering disinformation. Disinformation reaches audiences not only through obscure sources but via 'sharing' by friends and family (Asmolov, 2018; Tandoc et al., 2017, p. 148). The success of disinformation activities, and by extension hostile hijacks, largely depends on their ability to "penetrate social spheres" (Tandoc et al., 2017, p. 149). As emphasized by Tsyrenzhapova and Woolley (2021, pp. 161–162), bots and other amplifying entities "do not work to communicate directly with people on social media – they are constructed to trick trending algorithms and journalists into re-curating content to users via existing 'trusted' sources". On a concrete level, individuals with similar interests and opinions can be targeted during a crisis, increasing the likelihood that a hostile narrative related to the event spreads to others within the network.

Democratization: Reduction of the Filter Function, Anonymization

Besides increasing connectivity, technological advancements have democratized media access. While again positive in principle, access to social media and the rise of 'citizen journalism' (Tandoc et al., 2017) have weakened the public sphere's filter function. In addition, anonymity and the central role of algorithms have further undermined the public sphere's 'truth tracking' function. Taken together, these transformations make it easier for hostile hijackers to give the impression of concerned stakeholders with legitimate grievances, while simultaneously boosting engagement and visibility through organized (covert) activity.

Before the development of social media, the news agenda was determined mainly by professional journalists and editors. While this system offered limited opportunity for the public to impact the agenda, it guaranteed a minimal degree of filtering. As a result of journalistic standards, facts were counter-checked, opinion (ideally) separated from reporting, and the other side of the story heard. Although turning audiences into news 'prosumers' empowered citizens (Asmolov, 2018; Weeks et al., 2017), it also diminished the truth-tracking function. As long as established media outlets acted as the news agenda's gatekeepers, journalists had to disclose their identities. Actors' track records determined their credibility and substantially impacted whether they would gain access to the debate again. Today, actors can participate without disclosing their identity, either by remaining anonymous or by setting up fake personas or accounts (through, for example, spam accounts, fake accounts, compromised accounts, or phishing – see distinctions outlined by Adewole et al., 2017). Needless to say, unidentifiable actors do not care if their credibility is destroyed by being caught spreading false information.

In addition to weakening the public sphere's filter function, anonymity contributed in other ways to the transformation of the public sphere. The online disinhibition effect suggests that users feel less restrained in front of their screens, making them act in more vile and emotional ways (referred to as *toxic inhibition*) (Suler, 2004, 2016). Bakir and McStay (2018, p. 159) argue that these emotionally charged interactions create a "fertile ground for the rise of targeted media content and news contexts (such as filter bubbles in the form of Facebook news feeds) that elicit affective reactions" (p. 159) – feeding a vicious cycle of vile and emotional

214 *Handbook on digital corporate communication*

responses. During a hostile crisis hijack, disinformation operators harness such affective reactions and consequently 'feed' the cycle of emotional responses.

Finally, access to today's social media sphere is not as unrestricted as it appears. Gatekeeping by journalistic professionals has been replaced by algorithmic gatekeeping. Although content is available in principle, algorithms controlled by tech giants determine what users read in their Facebook stream or what results are returned by a Google search. The difference between journalistic and algorithmic gatekeeping is that the companies controlling algorithms are not motivated by epistemic concerns but by keeping users engaged on the platform (Bakir and McStay, 2018; Venturini, 2019). As algorithms generally promote sensational content, a crisis provides an opportunity to further hostile hijacks by spreading disinformation disguised as sensational news about the crisis to a large number of users.

WHAT REMAINS THE SAME?

Despite the fundamental changes outlined, platforms and technological advancements remain surface phenomena. The success (i.e., large spread) of disinformation campaigns hinges on exploiting cognitive and affective vulnerabilities (Pamment et al., 2018). In most cases, disinformation efforts take advantage of historically well-known prejudices, such as xenophobic tendencies. As emphasized by Nisbet and Kamenchuck (2019), it is not surprising that the large spread of disinformation campaigns coincides with political trends, including immigration flows, economic inequality, populism, and political polarization.

To exploit existing concerns and anxieties, disinformation campaigns often take the shape of what Nisbet and Kamenchuck (2019) refer to as 'identity-grievance' campaigns. Identity grievance campaigns activate "polarised social identities (political, ethnic, national, racial and religious, etc.)" and exploit "real or perceived political, economic, religious, or cultural wrongs and/or leveraging low institutional trust" (Nisbet and Kamenchuck, 2019, p. 67). When a claim threatens beliefs closely connected to our identity, it elicits aversive emotions, influencing our judgement and assessment of new information. Dislike and distrust towards an out-group increase our tendency to believe in messages targeting that specific group (Nisbet and Kamenchuck, 2019). Identity-grievance campaigns thus exploit two fundamental human principles: motivated reasoning (the desire to avoid dissonant information) and affective polarization (polarization based on increased disliking of the out-group and liking of the in-group) (Nisbet and Kamenchuck, 2019). Similar to disinformation campaigns, hostile hijacks are successful not because they factually convince audiences, but because they exploit human tendencies.

CRITICAL EXAMINATION

Although there can be little doubt that disinformation operations are being conducted against Western democracies, the specifics remain extremely difficult to prove. Disinformation is covert and obscure. Without access to classified intelligence, there rarely is clear and definite proof of disinformation. Consequently, our cases are *presumably* cases of hostile hijacks. They have been selected because they display similar, theoretically identified traits (see, for example, the diagnosis criteria outlined by the Swedish Civil Contingencies Agency, 2018 or

Digital corporate communication and hostile hijacking of crises   215

Pamment et al., 2018 and the narratives outlined by the EEAS Task Force 2019). Although disinformation operations tend to be characterized by a vitriolic tone, malicious rhetoric is not a sufficient criterion on its own. Scholars and authorities argue for a holistic perspective that considers the potential strategic narratives, target groups, and intent.

Given the identification difficulties, how can one be sure that one is, indeed, in the middle of a hostile hijack? Is it advisable that communicators, as the front-line operators, should make that call? When heavily involved and under pressure, it can be tempting to disregard inconvenient concerns or arguments as disinformation. Yet, it is crucial to guard against paranoia. After all, hostile hijacks are relatively few and far between. Adopting a benevolent disposition towards stakeholders and a transparent communication strategy is, in principle, a sound stance. What makes crisis communication managers vulnerable to exploitation is unawareness coupled with *unconditional* benevolence. While vigilance is imperative, communicators must not identify stakeholders as malevolent simply because they push for controversial or inconvenient agendas.

CASE STUDY: HOSTILE HIJACKING AT FOUR SWEDISH ORGANIZATIONS

Imagine yourself a communicator arriving at the office one morning. Yesterday was a hectic day as one of your employees tweeted something highly inappropriate that quickly went viral, soon picked up by the tabloids. You left the office satisfied though, having issued an impromptu and apologetic statement that seemed to have done the trick. But just before entering the board's morning meeting, you notice that the story is trending once again. Taking a nasty political turn, the organization has become a battering-ram in an infected political debate. A couple of tweets gleefully point to your statement as unwittingly exposing your company's ties to the 'deep state' network of powerful elites manipulating the public. The statement is an example of how you hide The Truth about what is *really* going on. On the way back to your office, you decide that the situation warrants a response. Soon, a press release, a string of posts on social media, and a list of FAQs to be distributed among the spokespersons is ready. But just before it all goes live, your social media manager recognizes one of the Twitter-handles. Digging deeper, you realize that hashtags are driven by fishy online profiles that post multiple entries within seconds, gaining unprecedented amounts of engagement. Something is definitely suspicious.

As illustrated above, a hostile hijack is notoriously difficult to comprehend and detect as it unfolds in real-life. In order to aid practitioners and researchers trying to navigate and identify such an attack, the following section takes a closer look at the narrative techniques used during likely cases of hostile hijacks in Sweden (see Johansson, 2020). By analysing discourse on Twitter during the acute phases of corporate crises, the qualitative case study presented shows how decentralized networks amplify corporate wrongdoing to gain leverage for a specific political agenda and undermine a political system. The analysis rests on four in-depth qualitative case studies that emerged as 'highly suspicious' after carefully examining 15 recent organizational crises in Sweden.[1] The cases discussed are:

- The SAS crisis related to the commercial "What is truly Scandinavian?"[2]

216 *Handbook on digital corporate communication*

- The Swedish National Board of Health and Welfare's crisis related to the brochure "Information to you who is married to a child."[3]
- PostNord's delayed votes during the general election.[4]
- The Confederation of Swedish Enterprises' crisis in the wake of Leif Östling's statement, "What the hell do I get for my money?"[5]

The four cases were identified as suspicious because they featured four of the five hostile narratives identified by EUvsDisinfo (the exception was Lost Sovereignty). In every case, the organizational crisis was utilized to construct a broader, destructive narrative about Sweden. In some instances, several hostile narratives were combined in a metanarrative or 'grand narrative'. Here, the organizations were framed as part of an evil elite enforcing 'political correctness', threatening traditional values, ultimately paving the way for societal collapse or civil war (Johansson, 2020). The analysis taken together with theory led to the formulation of four diagnostic criteria which can be used to identify an ongoing hostile hijack. While contribution to one of the typical hostile narratives is the strongest indicator, there are three other tell-tale patterns: (1) link by association; (2) rhetoric manoeuvres like victimization and accusations of mask-slipping; (3) conspiracy logic and sustained futility of response.

Link by Association

One tell-tale sign of hostile hijacking is link by association. Link by association means that the organizational crisis is construed as being a 'telling' piece in a larger puzzle, although the logical connection between the specific event and the general trend is, on closer inspection, spurious. Links by association are typically not argued out but remain on the level of insinuation. The agent, in other words, does not offer a coherent argument but leaves the readers to fill in the blanks themselves (Johansson, 2020).

In most of the cases investigated by us, there were attempts to associate the organizational crisis with issues of immigration and crime. For example, several accounts linked the tagline "Travelers bring great ideas home" from SAS's (2020) commercial with news about increasing levels of crime, immigration, and terrorist attacks. Any connection between terrorist attacks or violent crimes and SAS is highly spurious, but the aim was, presumably, to insinuate that the ruin of Swedish society is sanctioned by internationalist elites (Johansson, 2020).

Similarly, in the case of the Swedish National Board of Health and Welfare, the brochure "Information for you who is married to a child" was portrayed as giving child marriage advice. In fact, the brochure explains the legal situation and strongly suggests that the spouses should not live together until partners are of legal age. However, by portraying the brochure as normalizing child marriage and linking it to news about Social Democrats voting against stricter legislation (Johansson, 2020), the posts suggested that the governing elites pursue a covert agenda of accommodating the Islamization of Swedish society. To further underline this point, several accounts used taglines such as "latest insanity from Sweden", "This is Sweden 2018" and "PC[6] gone mad" together with information about the brochure (Johansson, 2020).

Link by association requires users to engage with the discourse actively. In the analysed cases, the technique seemed to work. The posts generated high amounts of likes and shares by associating the crisis with issues users have strong feelings about (Johansson, 2020). In several cases, a considerable number of likes without any comment suggested that engagement levels were boosted by organized bot activity.

Victimization and Mask-Slipping

Victimization and mask-slipping become evident when corporate crises are exploited to reinforce a discourse of 'us vs. them'. Organizational actors are portrayed as representatives of a repressive elite ('them'), which exploits and silences the minority ('us'). Victimization often goes hand in hand with mask-slipping. Crises are construed as inadvertent events which reveal the true extent of corruption and discrimination against the victims (Johansson, 2020).

In our case, supporters of the Swedish Democrats were portrayed as victims of an election fraud aided by PostNord. Users claimed that the left-oriented elite betrayed the Swedish Democrats of election victory, with PostNord part of the betrayal. Delayed postal votes proved the conspiracy. Similarly, Östling's statement "What the hell do I get for my money?" has been used to demonstrate how certain political voices are silenced in public debate. Twitter accounts stated, for instance, that Swedish media institutions frequently engage in systematic efforts to silence opposing opinions. That the public service broadcasters condemned Östling's statement served as evidence of the conspiracy (Johansson, 2020).

SAS's commercial also illustrates victimization and mask-slipping. In an attempt at celebrating open-mindedness, SAS's commercial pointed out that most good things in Swedish society are, in fact, foreign inventions. Several actors responded by claiming that SAS's commercial was reverse-racist against Swedes and constituted another attempt by the elite to enforce 'politically correct' values. Several accounts emphasized how Swedish people were marginalized by a left-oriented elite only interested in furthering the interests of minority groups. It was argued that this type of racism is relatively common, but the debate about it was silenced. The commercial thus became proof of a larger conspiracy betraying and oppressing the people (Johansson, 2020).

By communicating that the group is subjected to injustice, actors aim to gather public support by highlighting the complainant's victimhood together with information about what actions people can take against the experienced injustice. For example, Östling's statement has been used to urge people to stand up for their values and be more critical of the tax system. Likewise, PostNord's incident is mentioned together with information on how people can take action by joining demonstrations or demanding re-election. In a similar vein, SAS's stakeholders were encouraged to sign a petition demanding an apology from SAS and boycott the company until they had apologized properly (Johansson, 2020). Taken together, victimization and mask-slipping suggest metanarratives indistinguishable from conspiracy theory. Organizations are portrayed as part of a corrupt elite conspiring against the common good; crises are mask-slipping events proving the existence of the conspiracy.

Conspiracy Logic and Sustained Futility of Response

Conspiracy logic and the use of circular arguments is another tell-tale sign of a hostile hijack. The circular nature of conspiracy logic makes it impossible to defend the organization with rational arguments and empirical evidence. Counterarguments provided by the organization only prove the depth and sophistication of the conspiracy. As a result, conspiracy logic often goes hand in hand with sustained futility of response (Johansson, 2020).

Except for SAS, all cases were characterized by a very low engagement with organizational responses among those previously outraged. PostNord's explanation for the delayed postal votes – that it was due to an unexpectedly high number of advance votes and understaffing

218　*Handbook on digital corporate communication*

– generated only a very limited amount of engagement (Johansson, 2020). One account suggested that PostNord only covered up for organized, systematic fraud. Similarly, engagement after the withdrawal of the brochure "Information to you who is married to a child" was surprisingly low among previously outraged users. Predictably, a few responses were sarcastic, ridiculing the National Board of Health and Welfare. One account suggested that the 'real' reason the brochure was withdrawn was to add a section about 'care of sick child wife' (Johansson, 2020).

Although SAS responded to the criticism by underlining pride in its Scandinavian heritage, it did not receive positive feedback. However, the situation was complicated because SAS actively suggested that the criticism constituted an online attack, i.e., a campaign hijack or troll takeover (SAS, 2020). After that, several actors criticized SAS for blaming trolls, ridiculing the response with the 'Damn Putin' meme (a meme where everyday mishaps are blamed on Vladimir Putin's machinations). Together with other claims, SAS's response was taken as proof that the company was part of a left-oriented elite with a hidden agenda (Johansson, 2020).

Conspiracy logic and sustained futility of response serve as a reminder that disinformation operators do not have an interest in a constructive solution. If responding to grievances does not help despite continued efforts, the explanation might be that seemingly concerned stakeholders are, in fact, not concerned. Hostile hijacks thus seem to require a different mindset and approach. How that approach should look, however, remains unclear.

CONCLUSION AND FUTURE DIRECTIONS

There is currently a growing body of knowledge on potential diagnostic criteria, i.e., ways of detecting disinformation through observable characteristics. Practitioners and theorists of digital communication can make use of a substantial body of knowledge. Important sources include the EUvsDisinfo collection (as used in this chapter), debunked stories from fact-checkers, or the platform's takedown-databases (see, e.g., Twitter's and Facebook's transparency centre) available on their webpages.

Concerning hostile hijacking, our chapter outlined four potential patterns which could be used to aid the identification of such attacks: (1) contribution to one of the typical hostile narratives and sensitive trigger topics; (2) incoherence and link by association; (3) victimization and suggestions of mask-slipping; (4) conspiracy logic and sustained futility of response. It should be noted, however, that the presented study is qualitative, meaning that additional studies are needed to analyse whether the patterns hold true across cases and settings. Nevertheless, if the outlined tell-tale signs are evident, communicators should consider whether the textbook approach – two-way dialogue and acknowledgement of grievances – is the best option. Although posing as concerned stakeholders, 'fakeholders' (Luoma-aho, 2015) do not have an interest in the organization per se.

Despite a growing body of literature on how to debunk and build resilience against disinformation (see, for instance, Compton et al., 2021; Humprecht et al., 2020; Lewandowsky et al., 2020; Lewandowsky and van der Linden, 2021), the question regarding the most effective response remains unanswered. There is currently no 'best practice' response to disinformation operations, and it remains doubtful whether there ever will be. However, awareness and a constructive, stakeholder-oriented narrative are crucial. Communicators need to build

Digital corporate communication and hostile hijacking of crises   219

vigilance within the organization while, at the same time, guarding against paranoia. Not every controversy is a hostile hijack. It is important to keep in mind, furthermore, that the aim of counter-activities is not to expose or outmanoeuvre the source but to protect the organization's reputation and reaffirm democratic values (Pamment et al., 2018). Since disinformation operators' main goal is to create a climate of distrust, they are likely to turn anything the organization does against it. If the organization does nothing, it betrays that it does not care. If it cracks down, it shows that the concerns were justified. Communicators are, in other words, not fighting to win *against* the disinformation operators but *for* the trust and acceptance of genuine stakeholders. A compelling counternarrative or brand story (Levinger, 2018; Mills and Robson, 2019) should therefore figure in the strategy, regardless of other actions taken.

NOTES

1. Posts, retweets and answers to posts in both English and Swedish published on Twitter during the first two months of the crises were collected as primary data. Two separate searches were carried out. First, the organizations' names were used as key search word. After that, a phrase related to the organizational crisis was used, including: "Information to you who is married to a child", "What the hell do I get for my money?", "Delayed votes" and "Travelers bring great ideas home". In total, 146 tweets were gathered.
2. Scandinavian Airlines.
3. The Swedish National Board of Health and Welfare (Socialstyrelsen) is a Swedish government agency dealing with health-related services.
4. PostNord AB is a Swedish/Danish holding company which provides communications and logistics solutions in the Nordic region. Forty per cent is held by the Danish state while 60 per cent is held by the Swedish state.
5. The Confederation of Swedish Enterprise (Svenskt Näringsliv) is a large employers' organization for private sector companies in Sweden.
6. Short for political correctness.

REFERENCES

Adewole, K. S., Anuar, N. B., Kamsin, A., Varathan, K. D., and Razak, S. A. (2017). Malicious accounts: dark of the social networks. *Journal of Network and Computer Applications*, *79*, 41–67.
Asmolov, G. (2018). The disconnective power of disinformation campaigns. *Journal of International Affairs*, *71*, 69–75.
Bakir, V. and McStay, A. (2018). Fake news and the economy of emotions: Problems, causes, solutions. *Digital Journalism*, *6*(2), 154–175.
Bennett, W. L. and Livingstone, S. (2018). The disinformation order: Disruptive communication and the decline of democratic institutions. *European Journal of Communication*, *33*(2), 122–139.
Bennett, W. L. and Segerberg, A. (2012). The logic of connective action. *Information, Communication & Society*, *15*(5), 739–768.
Berthon, P., Treen, E., and Pitt, L. (2018). How truthiness, fake news and post-fact endanger brands and what to do about it. *NIM Marketing Intelligence Review*, *10*(1), 18–23.
Bradshaw, S. and Howard, P. (2018). The global organization of social media disinformation campaigns. *Journal of International Affairs*, *71*(1.5), 23–30.
Chadwick, A. (2013). *The hybrid media system: Politics and power*. Oxford: Oxford University Press.
Compton, J., Linden, S., Cook, J., and Basol, M. (2021). Inoculation theory in the post-truth era: Extant findings and new frontiers for contested science, misinformation, and conspiracy theories. *Social And Personality Psychology Compass*, *15*(6).

Coombs, W. T. and Holladay, S. J. (2012). The paracrisis: The challenges created by publicity managing crisis prevention. *Public Relations Review*, *38*(3), 408–415.

Coombs, W. T., Holladay, S., and White, R. (2020). Corporate crises, sticky crises and corporations. In Y. Jin, B. Reber, and G. Nowak (eds.), *Advancing crisis communication effectiveness* (pp. 35–51). New York: Routledge.

Diers-Lawson, A. (2019). *Crisis communication: Managing stakeholder relationships*. London: Routledge.

Ercan, S. A., Hendriks, C. M., and Dryzek J. S. (2019). Public deliberation in an era of communicative plenty. *Policy & Politics*, *47*(1), 19–36.

Eriksson, M. (2018). Lessons for crisis communication on social media: A systematic review of what research tells the practice. *International Journal of Strategic Communication*, *12*(5), 526–551.

European External Action Service's East StratCom Task Force (2019). *5 common pro-Kremlin disinformation narratives*. https://euvsdisinfo.eu/5-common-pro-kremlin-disinformation-narratives/.

Franck, G. (2019). The economy of attention. *Journal of Sociology*, *55*(1), 8–19.

Goertzel, T. (1994). Belief in conspiracy theories. *Political Psychology*, *15*(4), 731–742.

Gorwa, R. and Guilbeault, D. (2020). Unpacking the social media bot: A typology to guide research and policy. *Policy & Internet*, *12*(2), 225–248.

Grimme, C., Preuss, M., Adam, L., and Trautmann, H. (2017). Social bots: Human-like by means of human control? *Big Data*, *5*(4), 279–293.

Habermas, J. (2006). Political communication in media society: Does democracy still enjoy an epistemic dimension? The impact of normative theory on empirical research. *Communication Theory*, *16*(4), 411–426.

Humprecht, E., Esser, F., and Van Aelst, P. (2020). Resilience to online disinformation: A framework for cross-national comparative research. *International Journal of Press/Politics*, *25*(3), 493–516.

Jahng, M. R. (2021). Is fake news the new social media crisis? Examining the public evaluation of crisis management for corporate organizations targeted in fake news. *International Journal of Strategic Communication*, *15*(1), 18–36.

Jin, Y., Van der Meer, G. L. A., Lee, Y., and Lu, X. (2020). The effects of corrective communication and employee backup on the effectiveness of fighting crisis misinformation. *Public Relations Review*, *46*(3), 1–9.

Johansson, S. (2020). Hijacking an organizational crisis: A multiple case study on how organizational crises can be used to highlight narratives about Sweden (Master's thesis, Lund University). http://lup.lub.lu.se/student-papers/record/9016454.

Lanham, R. (2007). *The economics of attention*. Chicago, IL: University of Chicago Press.

Lazer, D., Baum, M., Benkler, Y., et al. (2018). The science of fake news. *Science*, *359*(6380), 1094–1096.

Levinger, M. (2018). Master narratives of disinformation campaigns. *Journal of International Affairs*, *71*, 125–134.

Lewandowsky, S., Cook, J., Ecker, U. K. H., et al. (2020). *The debunking handbook 2020*. https://sks.to/db2020.

Lewandowsky, S., Ecker, U., and Cook, J. (2017). Beyond misinformation: Understanding and coping with the "post-truth" era. *Journal of Applied Research in Memory and Cognition*, *6*(4), 353–369.

Lewandowsky, S. and van der Linden, S. (2021). Countering misinformation and fake news through inoculation and prebunking. *European Review of Social Psychology*, *32*(2), 348–384.

Lievonen, M., Luoma-aho, V., and Bowden, J. (2018). Negative engagement. In K. Johnston and M. Taylor (eds.), *The handbook of communication engagement* (pp. 531–548). Hoboken, NJ: Wiley.

Luoma-aho, V. (2015). Understanding stakeholder engagement: Faith-holders, hateholders & fakeholders. *RJ-IPR: Research Journal of the Institute for Public Relations*, *2*(1). http://www.instituteforpr.org/understanding-stakeholder-engagement-fai.

Maal, M. and Wilson-North, M. (2019). Social media in crisis communication: The "do's" and "don'ts." *International Journal of Disaster Resilience in the Built Environment*, *10*(5), 379–391.

McKay, S. and Tenove, C. (2021). Disinformation as a threat to deliberative democracy. *Political Research Quarterly*, *74*(3), 703–717.

Mills, A. J. and Robson, K. (2019). Brand management in the era of fake news: Narrative response as a strategy to insulate brand value. *Journal of Product & Brand Management*, *29*(2), 159–167.

Ngai, S. B. and Falkheimer, J. (2016). How IKEA turned a crisis into an opportunity. *Public Relations Review*, *43*, 246–248.

Nisbet, E. and Kamenchuk, O. (2019). The psychology of state-sponsored disinformation campaigns and implications for public diplomacy. *The Hague Journal of Diplomacy*, *14*(1–2), 65–82.

Önnerfors, A. (2021). *Konspirationsteorier och covid-19: mekanismerna bakom en snabbväxande samhällsutmaning*. Myndigheten för Samhällsskydd och Beredskap. https://www.diva-portal.org/smash/get/diva2:1706013/FULLTEXT01.pdf.

Paavola, J., Helo, T., Jalonen, H., Sartonen, M., and Huhtinen, A.-M. (2016). Understanding the trolling phenomenon: The automated detection of bots and cyborgs in the social media. *Journal of Information Warfare*, *15*(4), 100–111.

Pamment, J., Nothhaft, H., Agardh-Twetman, H., and Fjällhed, A. (2018). *Countering information influence activities: The state of the art*. Swedish Civil Contingencies Agency. https://rib.msb.se/filer/pdf/28697.pdf.

SAS (2020, 12 February). SAS' commercial: What is truly Scandinavian? https://www.sasgroup.net/newsroom/press-releases/2020/sascommercial-what-is-truly-scandinavian/.

Sellnow, T. L. and Seeger, M. W. (2013). *Theorizing crisis communication*. Hoboken, NJ: Wiley.

Suler, J. (2004). The online disinhibition effect. *Cyberpsychology & Behavior*, *7*(3), 321–326.

Suler, J. (2016). *Psychology of the digital age: Humans become electric*. New York: Cambridge University Press.

Sutton, R. and Douglas, K. (2014). Examining the monological nature of conspiracy theories. In J. van Prooijen and P. Lange (eds.), *Power, politics, and paranoia: Why people are suspicious of their leaders* (pp. 254–272). Cambridge: Cambridge University Press.

Swedish Civil Contingencies Agency (2018). *Countering information influence activities: A handbook for communicators*. https://rib.msb.se/filer/pdf/28698.pdf.

Tandoc, E. C., Lim, Z. W., and Ling, R. (2017). Defining "fake news": A typology of scholarly definitions. *Digital Journalism*, *6*(2), 137–153.

Tsyrenzhapova, D. and Woolley, S. (2021). The evolution of computational propaganda: Theories, debates and innovation of the Russian model. In H. Tumber and S. Waisbord (eds.), *The Routledge companion to media disinformation and populism* (pp. 158–164). London: Routledge.

Vafeiadis, M., Bortree, D., Buckley, C., Diddi, P., and Xiao, A. (2020). Refuting fake news on social media: Nonprofits, crisis response strategies and issue involvement. *Journal of Product & Brand Management*, *29*(2), 209–222.

Van Aelst, P., Strömbäck, J., Aalberg, T., et al. (2017). Political communication in a high-choice media environment: A challenge for democracy? *Annals of the International Communication Association*, *41*(1), 3–27.

Venturini, T. (2019). From fake to junk news: The data politics of online virality. In D. Bigo, E. Isin, and E. Ruppert (eds.), *Data politics: Worlds, subjects, rights* (pp. 123–144). London: Routledge.

Wanless, A. and Pamment, J. (2019). How do you define a problem like influence? *Journal of Information Warfare*, *18*(3), 1–14.

Wardle, C. (2018). The need for smarter definitions and practical, timely empirical research on information disorder. *Digital Journalism*, *6*(8), 951–963.

Weeks, B., Ardèvol-Abreu, A., and Gil de Zúñiga, H. (2017). Online influence? Social media use, opinion leadership, and political persuasion. *International Journal of Public Opinion Research*, *29*(2), 214–239.

16. Digital corporate communication and brandjacking and character assassination

Sergei A. Samoilenko and Quentin Langley

INTRODUCTION

The strategic management of digital corporate technologies, with a view to maintaining a company's intangible and tangible assets, necessitates an understanding of emergent reputational challenges. The evolution of digital communication has created new forms of visibility and the conditions for permanent scandal (Haller et al., 2021). Today, cause-driven campaigns and social movements use the strategies of disruption and subversion to exert pressure on organizations and influence public opinion (Jasper and King, 2020). This chapter focuses on two related practices, *brandjacking* and *character assassination*, advocating for their applied relevance and conceptual worth when studying digital corporate communication (DCC).

Brandjacking is typically associated with the disruption of a brand's narrative and the appropriation of corporate identity by third parties (Langley, 2014; Luoma-aho et al., 2018). This practice goes hand in hand with subversive campaigns using manipulated media or doppelgängers (Samoilenko and Suvorova, 2023). Brandjacks promoting fake corporate statements are especially harmful, as they can affect brand trust when perceived as credible (Chan-Olmsted and Qin, 2021).

Character assassination (CA) is a strategic effort to discredit an individual or group target via subversive communication (Samoilenko, 2021a). CA is prevalent in politicized contexts and considered instrumental to goal achievement in power struggles (Shiraev et al., 2022). Character attacks are persuasive attempts (Benoit, 2020) that take various forms, ranging from an offensive caricature in a newspaper to a virulent conspiracy theory in an online community.

This chapter provides a comprehensive discussion of brandjacking and CA in the corporate context of digital communications. It argues that both practices have burgeoned in association with new technologies used for manipulation and misinformation. In addition, brandjacking and CA have been weaponized by digital activists to put pressure on individuals and companies in the context of cancel culture. To illustrate this point, the chapter examines two case studies: a series of brandjacks targeting McDonald's and a scandal with a Boeing CEO that features his CA and subsequent disassociation from the brand. The implications of both concepts are mainly discussed through the lens of issues management and crisis communication theories. The chapter concludes by discussing implications for DCC research and offering ideas for future investigations.

Digital corporate communication and brandjacking and character assassination 223

DEFINITIONS OF BRANDJACKING AND PREVIOUS STUDIES

Brandjacking: Strategic Interception of Corporate Narratives

Brandjacking is typically associated with unauthorized use of a brand by impersonators and fraudsters who take over campaigns and hashtags, pretending to be brand marketers (Luoma-aho et al., 2018; Siano et al., 2021). In corporate contests, brandjacking can complement *obstructive marketing* that seeks to reduce the operational capacity of competitors through activities designed to prevent the distribution of a product by making it less valuable or damaging it in some way (Hyslop, 2014).

Conceptually, brandjacking is linked to a body of literature studying the effects of *negative engagement*. Lievonen and Luoma-aho (2015, p. 288) define negative engagement as an "experience-based series of participative actions where negative issues concerning an organization or brand are publicly discussed" (see also Lievonen et al., 2018). Scholars have established the relationship between negative engagement disposition and negative word-of-mouth (Li et al., 2021; Naumann et al., 2017). A number of negative engagement practices have been identified, including anger-driven activism (McColl-Kennedy et al., 2011; Romani et al., 2015), online brand sabotage (Kähr et al., 2016), and anti-brand sites promoting negative brand experiences (Krishnamurthy and Kucuk, 2009; Popp et al., 2016).

Brandjacking occurs when an organization loses control of the conversation around its reputation due to an external attempt to take over its narratives. Like humans, companies construct their identities through narration (Törmälä and Gyrd-Jones, 2017). It takes time to establish a seamless *narrative strand* through strategic storytelling. According to Cobb (2013, p. 12), a narrative strand is not only "a foundation for identity", but also a bully pulpit for agenda-setting. It involves coherent plot sequencing and interpretation of world events, the positioning of a protagonist, and the statement of an infallible value system, among other things.

Positions are moral locations. We locate ourselves and others through first-order positioning (Harré and van Langenhove, 1991). Every actor strives to position himself/herself within a storyline as positive and legitimate in relation to his/her audience while depicting other actors as less perfect. In some cases, the original narrative is not taken at face value; instead, it is challenged by counter-narratives (second-order positioning) advanced by another actor. The goal is to disrupt the narrative strand, promote another storyline, and eventually hijack the narrative agenda. This negative projection of a brand is intended to negatively affect the relationship between a target organization and its stakeholders, thus enabling a subsequent crisis of reputation.

CASE STUDY: BRANDJACKING AT MCDONALD'S

McDonald's was one of the top ten most valuable US brands in 2021. In 2020, the McDonald's brand was worth over $46 billion, according to *Forbes* (Swant, 2020). The assessed value of the brand was thus far greater than that of Starbucks, Pepsi, Walmart, and many other companies. Using a different methodology, Interbrand placed it ninth globally and valued the McDonald's brand slightly lower, at almost $43 billion. Some commentators have even linked the McDonald's brand to conflict prevention. According to Friedman (2012), "No two

224 *Handbook on digital corporate communication*

countries that both had McDonald's had fought a war against each other since each got its McDonald's."[1] Unsurprisingly, the value of the McDonald's brand attracts many invested hijackers, who seek to profit from its conquest.

Langley's (2014) typology demonstrates that brandjacks can be accidental, driven by third parties, or even built on a brand deliberately surrendering control. The most common type, however, is an *aggregation brandjack*, which occurs when an organization faces an organized group of unrelated stakeholders who unite in anti-brand efforts due to some shared issue with the brand. Corporate inaction or slow action on internal issues caused by employee misconduct or wrongdoing can easily be exploited by activists and critics seeking to provoke negative responses from publics (Romani et al., 2015). Reputational attacks prove especially harmful when motivated actors with malicious intent seek to cause large-scale reputational crises and damage brands. The following cases are used to illustrate this point.

The first case focuses on a 2010 advertisement produced by the Physicians' Committee for Responsible Medicine (PCRM). The ad, which linked McDonald's to heart disease, soon became popular on YouTube, garnering over 1 million views in the first two months. Langley (2014) describes the conflict between McDonald's and PCRM as an ethics brandjack. This type of brandjacking attempt centres on a clear conflict of ethical codes, in this case between a burger restaurant and an organization that advocates for a vegan diet.

The McDonald's corporation's initial reaction to the ad was rather weak, calling it "unfair" and "outrageous". Then a franchise owner for the Tristate area hit back by establishing the McDonald's Nutrition Network (MNN), which engaged 'mommy bloggers' in an initiative with a dietician advising on healthy diet choices. He offered usable guidance for how parents could resort to fast food without feeling guilty. McDonald's enhanced the power of the network by organizing a meet-up of mommy bloggers to get them engaging with each other's content. MNN also provided seed money for local initiatives providing information about nutrition. Applications for these grants reached almost 600 percent of the initial target, while the launch of the initiative appeared in nearly 100 news items.

The second case is a June 2011 Twitter campaign that showed a photoshopped sign in a McDonald's window announcing that African American customers were to be charged more. People tweeted the picture with the associated hashtag #SeriouslyMcDonalds, whether because they believed it was real or because they found it amusing. McDonald's responded quickly, but with a light touch. It immediately tweeted that the photograph was a hoax, but sent personal messages to only two of those retweeting the image. For several days, the #SeriouslyMcDonalds hashtag trended on Twitter—and the issue persisted even after McDonald's had firmly responded that the sign was a hoax.

The third case focuses on the McDonald's #MeetTheFarmers campaign. Following the #SeriouslyMcDonalds hoax, McDonald's wanted to reinforce the strengths of the brand through storytelling. Specifically, it planned to solidify its base by inviting its customers to tell their positive stories of visiting the fast food chain at #McDStories. While a large majority of initial contributions were (apparently) positive, it was the negative ones that were more likely to be shared and that therefore reached a wider audience. Critics were motivated to share their negative experiences and promote related agendas around environmental issues, animal welfare, nutrition, and a general rejection of capitalism.

The above examples demonstrate that a valuable brand is naturally a target for brandjacking. The first case shows that these attempts can be handled with proper crisis management. PCRM continues to target McDonald's, but most of its YouTube videos have gained little to moderate

Digital corporate communication and brandjacking and character assassination 225

traction. For example, two PCRM videos produced in 2018 and 2019 linking the McDonald's "Bacon Hour" promotion to colorectal cancer have only a few thousand views between them (Physicians Committee, 2019). The second case suggests that a negative campaign goes viral when the target is disliked by a significant group of people. Importantly, it keeps trending when the target chooses an inadequate crisis response (Coombs, 2019). Finally, the third case indicates that when an organization invites motivated customers to share their stories about their brand, stakeholders with negative experiences are likely to hijack the media agenda (BBC, 2014). This supports previous research stating that crowdsourcing campaigns are vulnerable to brandjacking at times when negativity drives social media conversations (Gross and Johnson, 2016). Interestingly, many McDonald's customers did not see any need to share positive content about the brand. This illustrates that McDonald's has a transactional relationship with its customers, not an aspirational one. In contrast to those who purchase expensive cars, people who eat at McDonald's are not purchasing a product with which they will have a long-lasting relationship or about which they want to boast to their social networks.

The #SeriouslyMcDonalds hoax in the second case demonstrates that some brandjacks are based on a smear effort to provoke social media outrage against the corporation. Next, we address these deliberate efforts to destroy individual and corporate reputations.

DEFINITIONS OF CHARACTER ASSASSINATION AND PREVIOUS STUDIES

Character Assassination: Strategic Subversion of Corporate Reputation

Character assassination (CA) is both a process of communication (e.g., a smear campaign) and the outcome of this process (e.g., a damaged reputation) (Samoilenko et al., 2020). Originally, it was studied as a deliberate effort to destroy an individual's reputation (Icks and Shiraev, 2014). Coombs and Holladay (2020) argued for a more inclusive view of CA by linking it in a broader way to larger collectives such as corporations, since the latter's credibility and reputation can suffer the consequences of character attacks.

Contemporary CA scholars consider *character* a matter of public perception and a public image of accepted ethical standards and social functions assigned to a public figure by various publics at a given point of time (Shiraev et al., 2022). Character-based reputation is intrinsically contestable and can be depleted through misuse or offensive transgressions (Thompson, 2000). According to Benoit (2020), an attack on character asserts that the target possesses a certain trait and argues that this trait is offensive. An accusation questioning the moral standing of a politician or a corporate leader is likely to trigger social evaluation and judgement of his/her reputation.

A character assassin is an individual or a group of people who commit a character attack with the goal of delegitimizing the target in the court of public opinion and undermining his/her social standing. The attacker may be motivated by sheer malice, envy, revenge, or more strategic goals, such as removing competitors. A politician attacks his/her rivals to make them expend time, energy, and resources on a long-term power contest (Shiraev et al., 2022). A corporation dealing with a whistle-blower issue may elect to torpedo the messenger's credibility. For example, cigarette maker Brown and Williamson retaliated against whistle-blower Jeffrey

226 *Handbook on digital corporate communication*

Wigand with a ruthless smear campaign painting him as a raging alcoholic, a wife-beater, and a pathological liar (Brenner, 1996)

Three cardinal CA media strategies are provocation, contamination, and obliteration attempts (Shiraev et al., 2022). *Provocation strategies* aim to intercept the media agenda and create highly mediated scandals. They seek to amplify a hot-button issue to further activate intense negative reactions from active publics toward the target. *Contamination strategies* involve spreading falsehoods, rumours, and conspiracy theories. The idea is to insert a small dose of misinformation about the target into a public consensus and gradually poison the well in an attempt to prime the public to change their opinion of the target's moral profile. Attackers may infiltrate online communities or create echo chambers through algorithms in order to incubate conspiracy theories or fake news stories (Wanless and Berk, 2020). Finally, *obliteration strategies* aim to purge public memory of the target's positive achievements and accomplishments. Wikipedia has become a convenient place to edit out or falsify a person's early biography, as well as to forge evidence of an individual's inappropriate social and political ties (Burrell, 2013). These strategies often overlap when used in complicated scenarios, triggering cascading network activation (Entman and Usher, 2018).

In their analysis of corporate CA, Coombs and Holladay (2020) see a CA event as a *challenge crisis*, which begins as a crisis threat manifested in public. They discuss two different goals of invested audiences. *Activist stakeholders* mainly seek to change organizational practices. *Angry stakeholders*, on the other hand, seek revenge on an organization and sometimes its complete reputational and even physical termination. If handled improperly, a challenge crisis can easily escalate into a full-blown reputational crisis, with multiple negative implications for the entire organization.

The success or failure of a subversive activist campaign depends upon the material cost of the requested changes and the fit between requested changes and the organization's strategy. It also depends on what is considered appropriate in a given society (legitimacy), the ability to affect the behaviour of others (power), commitment to the issue, and time pressure (urgency) (Mitchell et al., 1997). Research shows that a positive perception of CEOs' character traits and personal values could shield their organization from character attacks (Seiffert-Brockmann et al., 2018). Conversely, CEOs who receive negative press coverage may contaminate a corporate reputation (Love et al., 2017).

Corporate issues are not static because they change characteristics and develop throughout a business life cycle. A matter that was not an issue for a public at one point in time may become a problem for the same public at another point. When "a public has an issue with an organization, that organization has a problem" (Botan, 2018, p. 104). It can impact individuals and organizations in many negative ways and eventually bring about a crisis of legitimacy for them. The next case study illustrates this point.

CASE STUDY: CHARACTER ASSASSINATION AT BOEING

In July 2020, Niel Golightly resigned as Senior Vice President of Communications at the Boeing Company after an employee complained about an article Golightly had written more than 30 years earlier as a 29-year-old Navy pilot. Golightly's article had appeared in the December 1987 issue of *Proceedings*, a monthly publication of the United States Naval Institute. The piece argued against women fighting in combat, a position supported by 56 per

Digital corporate communication and brandjacking and character assassination 227

cent of Americans as recently as 1991 (Davis, 2013). The Department of Defense's 1994 ban on women serving in combat was lifted only in 2013.

Golightly responded to the complaint, saying that people should have room to mature as their careers progressed without being judged on opinions they had held decades earlier (Gross, 2020). One of his former colleagues spoke highly of his exemplary character and applauded Boeing's former communications chief for promoting female talent within the team. In an email to his colleagues, Golightly stated that his former views did not reflect his current opinions:

> The article I wrote—with arguments I disowned soon after—makes for painful reading. Painful because it is wrong. Painful because it is offensive to women. Painful because it reminds me of the sharp and embarrassing education the uninformed and unformed 'me' of that time received as soon as the piece appeared.

The situation with Golightly followed two other corporate crises at Boeing. The first was a scandal after the company had dismissed several employees for racist behaviour (Gross, 2020). The second was backlash following the crashes, within five months, of two of Boeing 737 Max jets, killing 346 people and resulting in the planes' subsequent grounding. This cost Boeing $18 billion on top of the downturn in air travel caused by the Covid-19 pandemic (Johnsson, 2020). Commenting on Golightly's resignation, Boeing President and CEO Dave Calhoun endorsed his decision to step down in the interest of the company and emphasized the company's "unrelenting commitment to diversity and inclusion in all its dimensions, and to ensuring that all of our employees have an equal opportunity to contribute and excel".

The public accusation of Niel Golightly and his subsequent resignation is an example of character assassination via disgracing. When someone is disgraced, their good name is publicly dragged through the mud and their distinguishing markers of honour and authority taken away (Shiraev et al., 2022). The sociocultural approach to character assassination puts heavy emphasis on cultural norms, conventions, and context (Samoilenko, 2021a). Golightly was dismissed in the aftermath of the #MeToo movement, when public opinion began to impose stricter sanctions on those individuals who have contravened current social norms and values. Boeing President Dave Calhoun wrote to his employees that the company would "have zero tolerance for bigotry of any kind" and would "redouble our determination to drive out behaviours that violate our values and injure our colleagues".

The Golightly case is a *scansis* situation. Scansis represents the intersection of a scandal and a crisis (Coombs and Tachkova, 2019). Its key characteristic is moral outrage, which derives from the perceived violation of moral norms and feelings of injustice and exploitation. The documented proof that a high-level management executive had once held misogynistic views was out of step with current corporate interests and declared values. The moral outrage in scansis situations creates a felt need for punishment. Golightly's resignation fulfilled that need. It was an appropriate crisis response that was expected to be reinforced with strategies focused on bringing about structural changes in the company.

WHAT REMAINS THE SAME?

Social media create both opportunities and risks in crisis communication (Austin and Jin, 2018; Wendling et al., 2013). According to Luoma-aho (2015), the digital environment makes it easier for stakeholders to find each other and either rally behind or coalesce against organizations. However, the dispersive nature of digital communication amplifies the initial challenges posed by brandjacks and CA transgressions.

The McDonald's cases teach us valuable lessons about the role of social media in brandjacking scenarios. In its response to the PCRM campaign, McDonald's recognized the critical importance of mommy bloggers as a channel to communicate with families. Social media create opportunities when organizational messages support the implementation of core branding strategies. The McDonald's corporation's first VP of Sustainability, Bob Langert, advocated that businesses should engage with their strongest critics to find solutions that are good for both business and society (Langert, 2019). As a result, there are now vegan options at many McDonald's franchises.

Another social media campaign run by McDonald's engaged suppliers in talking about their businesses. Flagship Farmers posted videos about McDonald's farmers from all over the world (Farmers Guide, 2020). In the videos, the farmers talk about the value to a small business of being a McDonald's supplier and how the corporation maintains rigorous standards that suppliers have to meet. Quality and sustainability – values that perhaps few people would spontaneously associate with the brand – are built into the narratives.

Social media can also create reputational risks when original campaign messages are taken over by negative sentiments. Crowdsourcing and viral campaigns therefore run a continual risk of backfiring. As the #MeetTheFarmers campaign demonstrates, having many customers does not necessarily translate into positive advocacy for the brand. While customers may not be ashamed to eat at McDonald's, they are not especially motivated to talk on social media about their fast-food habits.

The Boeing case supports the view of corporate CA as a *challenge crisis* that is associated with multiple challenges to organizational legitimacy and social responsibility (Coombs and Holladay, 2020). Ultimately, it creates situations in which stakeholders claim that an organization is acting in an irresponsible or immoral manner (Lerbinger, 1997). Repeated exposure to negative issues associated with a brand may lead various publics to scrutinize the company and its policies more closely (Coombs, 2019).

Boeing's crisis response is typical for corporations. Boeing was running the risk of its stakeholders deeming the company guilty by association for its relationship with a person with toxic views. Organizations at risk of being held responsible commonly generate discourses that attribute responsibility to the tainted employee and disassociate that individual from the organization to avoid reputational penalties (Coombs, 2019). In some cases, organizations may even lay the blame on members who are not directly responsible for the cause of moral outrage if the latter are nonessential for corporate operations and their dismissal might help deflect blame from the organization (Hargie et al., 2010; Roulet and Pichler, 2020).

Today, subversive social media campaigns are *cocreational* strategic enterprises that consider the opinions and attitudes of members representing various groups and communities on a range of different social issues, as well as their capacity for moral outrage (Samoilenko, 2021b). These campaigns also appeal to invested stakeholders (e.g., journalists, bloggers, and competitors) who profit from the downfall of reputations. Lately, the digital corporate environment has been facing reputational challenges associated with digital activism, cancel culture, and new misinformation production methods.

WHAT IS CHANGING?

Digital activism is the trademark of our time. Highly networked activists use social media to promote causes and put pressure on policymakers and industry leaders. Activist groups organize protests, boycotts, and social movement campaigns to enforce justice in the form of a public apology, legal proceedings, or revised policies (Boyd, 2012; Jasper and King, 2020). Some social media platforms, like Twitter, have proved especially effective at this, being used to build support groups around a hashtag, organize flash mobs, or call public figures to account (Carney, 2016).

Social media is the vehicle of cancel culture (CC) (Bouvier and Machin, 2021). The process of cancelling can be seen as an extreme form of CA where efforts are made not only to criticize and stigmatize the target, but also to exclude them from public media arenas (Samoilenko and Jasper, 2023). CC emerged in the context of deep ideological conflict and changing moral standards that divided progressive liberals from social conservatives (Dimock and Wike, 2020). Accordingly, in the United States, there are two popular views of CC: it is perceived either as a way to promote social justice or as a social media mobbing practice used to censor and punish dissenting voices (Vogels et al., 2021).

Brought to prominence by #MeToo and #BlackLivesMatter activists, CC put a spotlight on multiple organizational issues associated with individuals and organizations deemed to represent sexist, racist, patriarchal, or hegemonic values (Mishan, 2020). Norris (2021) refers to CC as "collective strategies by activists using social pressures to achieve cultural ostracism of targets (someone or something) accused of offensive words or deeds". Importantly, cancelling is used by both left-wing and right-wing groups to bring pressure to bear on public figures and corporate brands for actions perceived as morally offensive or dangerous (Miller-Idriss, 2021).

The #MeToo movement prompted thousands of organizations to adopt harassment policies and enhance employee training (Boyle and Cucchiara, 2018). The prominence of the #MeToo campaign and its global impact have made it more difficult for organizations dealing with sex scandals to maintain control around the brand narrative. McDonald's was just one of the many companies to find itself caught up in the massive reckoning on sexual harassment triggered by the movement. In 2019, Steve Easterbrook was fired as President and CEO of McDonald's over a consensual affair with a subordinate (Gelles and Creswell, 2021).

Activist groups that advocate boycotting countries on human rights grounds are raising clear ethical issues for corporations. Pressure from public opinion and shaming strategies applied by digital activists have prompted many Western companies to suspend operations in Russia (Kulikov, 2022). In March 2022, Yale University published a widely circulated list of companies that had pulled out of trading in Russia in response to the Ukraine invasion and a second list of companies that continued to trade there. McDonald's was on the original list of companies trading in Russia, but announced within days that it was suspending its operations throughout the country.[2]

Brandjacks and reputational attacks have further proliferated with the development of automated systems circulating misinformation and synthetic media technologies used for smear campaigns. Social bots spread materials from low-credibility sources and target users with many followers through replies and mentions (Shao et al., 2018). Machine learning frameworks can generate multiple synthetic instances of data, including fake photos, which now appear in product reviews, on fake social media accounts, and on fake personal profiles (Vaccari and Chadwick, 2020).

230 *Handbook on digital corporate communication*

Misinformation campaigns generated by artificial intelligence (AI) have become notorious for their use of manipulated media of humans. Like traditional compromising videos, deepfakes exploit the topics of sex (cheating), drug use, inappropriate behaviour, and age-related incompetency (Diakopoulos and Johnson, 2021; Samoilenko and Suvorova, 2023). There are at least four major types of deepfake producers: legitimate actors (e.g., television companies), communities of hobbyists, political players (e.g., foreign governments and activists), and fraudsters (Westerlund, 2019). In 2021, a fake video featuring a doppelgänger of entrepreneur and businessman Oleg Tinkov was posted on the fake Tinkoff Bonus website, which featured a fake registration link. Fake Tinkov promised his clients to increase by 50 per cent whatever amount a customer deposited in a newly opened investment account. This generous offer aroused suspicion and was soon refuted by Tinkov's press office (DFC, 2021).

In the context of digital activism and cancel culture, corporations are expected to constantly change with the zeitgeist of a generation, new norms of social behaviour, and the technological innovations embraced by their stakeholders (Schaeffer, 2019). These imperatives are critically assessed next.

CRITICAL EXAMINATION

Emerging social trends are perceived as especially critical indicators of developing issues that corporations need to watch for. According to Edelman's Earned Brand Study (2018), most consumers worldwide are "belief-driven buyers" who will not buy a product or go to a movie if a company or a celebrity is silent on an issue of concern. In other words, 57 per cent of consumers will buy a product line because of its political position. Most Americans believe that corporations have a responsibility to support social movements related to the environment, human rights, gender, and politics, among others (George-Parkin, 2019). Following this trend, corporate CEOs endorse social causes to make their marketing efforts relevant to the defining spirit of the time and appeal to their base and new stakeholders (Lagorio-Chafkin, 2018).

Consulting cultural intelligence experts and digital anthropologists helps organizations understand explosive and immediate cultural shifts. This concerns new social trends challenging traditional norms and perceptions of gender, ethnicity, and sexuality and shaping cultural tastes and attitudes over time (Powers, 2019). Continuously monitoring online conversations helps DCC professionals gauge the volume and intensity of conversations about a topic and align their strategies with public sentiment. Some Internet memes provide insights into critical social issues (Seiffert-Brockmann et al., 2019). In 2021, the name "Karen" went viral as a meme portraying an irritating white woman who uses her privilege to get her way by speaking to police or a restaurant manager (Edwards, 2022). In 2020, the overall number of new babies named Karen dropped nearly 26 per cent compared to the previous year (Ewing and Banfield, 2021). The name also became a pejorative slang term for angry, entitled, and often racist behaviour.

A corporate statement responding to current controversial issues presents an opportunity to engage in an important social conversation and boost consumer loyalty (Cox, 2019). Conversely, remaining quiet can be misconstrued by some stakeholders as a sign of conservatism and a lack of courage. Equally, however, a corporate response that misses the mark can tarnish a company's image. In 2017, the Papa John's brand took a massive hit during the NFL Boycott scandal when CEO John Schnatter blamed its declining pizza sales on the league,

Digital corporate communication and brandjacking and character assassination 231

saying the NFL was failing to handle the ongoing protests by football players who knelt during the national anthem to protest racial injustice (Swan, 2018). Following massive outrage on social media, Papa John's stock lost nearly a third of its value.

In times of changing social standards, a corporate focus on issues management and social corporate responsibility (CSR) is critical. *Issues management* involves proactive attempts by corporations to identify and resolve high-priority issues that present immanent challenges to organizations or their CEOs (Botan, 2018; Heath and Palenchar, 2008). The main goal is to find and execute the strategy that will turn an identified issue from a reputational risk into a managed issue before many people and groups have established their views and staked out their positions (Coombs, 2019). Historical precedents teach us that failure to identify an issue, as well as to listen to and timely respond to public concerns, leads to long-term financial and reputational losses. In the 1990s, efforts led by Monsanto to bring genetically modified (GM) foods to Europe encountered backlash from European publics, who accused GM companies of 'playing God' with nature and profiting from creating 'Frankenstein foods'.

Corporate CSR programmes have become a strong criterion of corporate ethics. Research has shown that companies that have effective CSR programmes are more profitable than those that do not (Byus et al., 2010; Hategan et al., 2018). However, corporate CSR has also been criticized for doing very little, being a PR tool subservient to the company's main business, and lacking sincerity and authenticity (Alhouti et al., 2016; Freitag, 2008; Skarmeas and Leonidou, 2013). Indeed, some companies have demonstrated a disparity between their CSR efforts and other actions. For example, many corporations show support for LGBTQ+ communities and at the same time donate to politicians who vote against gay rights (Spencer, 2021). Hence, there is an emerging trend to embrace social corporate justice (SCJ) that focuses on the lived experiences of groups perceived to be harmed or disadvantaged by society (Zheng, 2020).

Unfortunately, social movements and CSR programmes are not immune to brandjacking. Social media campaigns become a recognizable brand when propelled by online communities that help build a support base for the cause. The stronger the brand equity, the more it attracts camp followers who see popular social causes as an opportunity to advance personal agendas on the pretence of serving the cause (Béchet, 2022). The #MeToo campaign has faced criticism for selectivity and witch-hunt tendencies. Some #MeToo critics said the campaign's original mission was being weaponized, trivialized, and refocused on matters of individual accountability (Gessen, 2017; Willsher, 2018). Female survey respondents believed the campaign caused new difficulties for men in workplace interactions while having little effect on women's career opportunities (Graf, 2018; North, 2018). When punishing scapegoats is generally seen as the solution to a complex issue, the concern is that there is less urgency to promote real structural changes that would enhance women's autonomy, fix broken legal systems, and address institutionalized harassment.

CONCLUSION AND FUTURE DIRECTIONS

This chapter discusses two related concepts: brandjacking and character assassination. Both practices have become pervasive in corporate digital communication and have had a tremendous impact on organizations and their stakeholders. In the context of digital activism, cancel culture, and manipulated media, these practices are functional tools in the hands of subversive

232 Handbook on digital corporate communication

actors who seek to achieve goals ranging from settling personal scores to changing societal power dynamics.

Brandjacking and CA campaigns are subversive in nature and cocreated strategically together with multiple invested publics. Brandjacking and CA overlap in situations where deceptive stratagems are employed in an effort to damage corporate reputations. The desired outcome is the unfolding, in real time, of a scandal on social media. This type of reputational crisis is known for its speed and complexity, which impede risk prevention and crisis management.

Staying in tune with developing social trends that challenge traditional norms of gender, ethnicity, and sexuality allows corporate leaders to associate themselves with stakeholders during crucial periods of social change. Internet memes poking fun at public characters often provide critical insight into the importance of a social issue. This chapter calls for more cultural synergy between corporations and various communities of interest, which are vocal and uncompromising about their social identities.

The theoretical frameworks introduced in this chapter make a strong contribution to the body of knowledge on digital corporate communication. The discussion of both concepts through the lens of issues management and crisis communication theories reveals multiple directions for further scholarly efforts. These conceptual frameworks have implications for developing a new understanding of the causes and effects of moral outrage in response to issues created by different interpretations of changing social norms. Another strong theoretical marriage is that between the aforementioned concepts and situational crisis communication theory (Coombs, 2019), which can provide valuable information on responding to reputational crises and scandals caused by subversive campaigns. Future research should also address the sociocultural issues that moderate the effects of brandjacking and character assassination.

NOTES

1. Though Friedman's (2012) "Golden Arches Theory of Conflict Prevention" had previously been criticized, including some examples predating 2012, Russia's invasion of Ukraine was possibly its most dramatic refutation.
2. See https://som.yale.edu/story/2022/over-600-companies-have-withdrawn-russia-some-remain.

REFERENCES

Alhouti, S., Johnson, C. M., and Holloway, B. B. (2016). Corporate social responsibility authenticity: Investigating its antecedents and outcomes. *Journal of Business Research, 69*(3), 1242–1249.

Austin, L. and Jin, Y. (2018). *Social media and crisis communication*. London: Routledge.

BBC (2014). NYPD Twitter campaign 'backfires' after hashtag hijacked. *BBC*, 23 April. https://www.bbc.com/news/technology-27126041.

Béchet, N. (2022). The hashtag masquerade: Hijacking online social movement codes. *L'Atelier*, 20 January. https://bit.ly/3kNd8Z7.

Benoit, W. L. (2020). Character assassination and persuasive attack on CBS's *Face the Nation*. In S. A. Samoilenko, M. Icks, J. Keohane, and E. Shiraev (eds.), *The Routledge handbook of character assassination and reputation management* (pp. 295–306). New York: Routledge.

Botan, C. H. (2018). *Strategic communication: Theory and practice*. Hoboken, NJ: Wiley-Blackwell.

Bouvier, G. and Machin, D. (2021). What gets lost in Twitter "cancel culture" hashtags? *Discourse and Society, 32*(3), 307–327.

Digital corporate communication and brandjacking and character assassination   233

Boyd, A. (2012). *Beautiful trouble: A toolbox for revolution*. New York: OR Books.

Boyle, D. and Cucchiara, A. (2018). *Social movements and HR: The impact of #MeToo* [White Paper]. Cornell Center for Advanced Human Resource Studies. https://bit.ly/31TbTRX.

Brenner, M. (1996). The man who knew too much. *Vanity Fair*, May. https://bit.ly/3kYVzFv.

Burrell, I. (2013). Wikipedia names Texas PR firm over false manipulation of site entries. *Independent*, 20 November. https://bit.ly/3aDwKHz.

Byus, K., Deis, D., and Ouyang, B. (2010). Doing well by doing good: Corporate social responsibility and profitability. *SAM – Advanced Management Journal*, *75*(1), 44–55.

Carney, N. (2016). All lives matter, but so does race: Black Lives Matter and the evolving role of social media. *Humanity & Society*, *40*(2), 180–199.

Chan-Olmsted, S. M. and Qin, Y. S. (2021). The impact of fake news on its sponsor's brand trust. *Journal of Brand Strategy*, *9*(4), 446–465.

Cobb, S. (2013). Narrative braiding and the role of public officials in transforming the publics conflicts. *Narrative and Conflict: Explorations in Theory and Practice*, *1*(1), 4–30.

Coombs, W. T. (2019). *Ongoing crisis communication: Planning, managing, and responding* (5th edition). Thousand Oaks, CA: Sage Publications.

Coombs, W. T. and Holladay, S. (2020). Corporate character assassination and crisis communication. In S. A. Samoilenko, M. Icks, J. Keohane, and E. Shiraev (eds.), *The Routledge handbook of character assassination and reputation management* (pp. 225–235). New York: Routledge.

Coombs, W. T. and Tachkova, E. R. (2019). Scansis as a unique crisis type: Theoretical and practical implications. *Journal of Communication Management*, *23*(1), 72–88.

Cox, T. A. (2019). Corporate social responsibility in 2019: Social issues people expect businesses to support. *Clutch*, 3 April. https://bit.ly/3FafUji.

Davis, A. (2013). Americans favor allowing women in combat. *Gallop*, 25 January. https://bit.ly/3nhAsjT.

DFC (2021). Tinkov's doppelganger invites to a fake site. Deepfake Challenge Association, 15 November. https://deepfakechallenge.com/gb/2021/09/16/11906/.

Diakopoulos, N. and Johnson, D. (2021). Anticipating and addressing the ethical implications of deepfakes in the context of elections. *New Media & Society*, *23*(7), 2072–2098.

Dimock, M. and Wike, R. (2020). *America is exceptional in the nature of its political divide*. Pew Research Center, 13 November. https://pewrsr.ch/3CpSaWR.

Edelman (2018). *Edelman earned brand* [Report]. https://bit.ly/3wcazW3.

Edwards, S. B. (2022). *Cancel culture* (Special reports). Minneapolis, MN: Abdo Publishing.

Entman, R. M. and Usher, N. (2018). Framing in a fractured democracy: Impacts of digital technology on ideology, power and cascading network activation. *Journal of Communication*, *68*(2), 298–308.

Ewing, M. and Banfield, A. (2021). 'Bye, Karen': Popularity of naming babies 'Karen' plummets in 2020 after moniker becomes a meme. *NewsNation*, 4 June. https://bit.ly/37U1I31.

Farmers Guide (2020). McDonald's extends commitment to local farming with new partnerships. *Farmers Guide*, 6 October. https://bit.ly/39KcDgp.

Freitag, A. R. (2008). Staking claim: Public relations lenders needed to shape CSR policy. *Public Relations Quarterly*, *52*(1), 37–40.

Friedman, T. L. (2012). *The Lexus and the olive tree: Understanding globalization*. London: Picador.

Gelles, D. and Creswell, J. (2021). Former McDonald's C.E.O. repays company $105 million. *The New York Times*, 16 December. https://nyti.ms/3F7ZkSw.

George-Parkin, H. (2019). Why companies need to get comfortable with taking a stand on social issues. *FN*, 5 February. https://bit.ly/3C7gdti.

Gessen, M. (2017). Al Franken's resignation and the selective force of #MeToo. *The New Yorker*, 7 December. https://bit.ly/3yk4zNh.

Graf, N. (2018). *Sexual harassment at work in the era of #MeToo*. Pew Research Center. https://pewrsr.ch/3w8A3TV.

Gross, J. (2020). Boeing communications chief resigns over 33-year-old article. *The New York Times*, 8 July. https://nyti.ms/3H8Mi8z.

Gross, J. H. and Johnson, K. T. (2016). Twitter taunts and tirades: Negative campaigning in the age of Trump. *Political Science and Politics*, *49*(4), 748–754.

234 *Handbook on digital corporate communication*

Haller, A., Michael, H., and Seeber, L. (eds.) (2021). *Scandology 3: Scandals in new media*. Cham: Springer.

Hargie, O., Stapleton, K., and Tourish, D. (2010). Interpretations of CEO public apologies for the banking crisis: Attributions of blame and avoidance of responsibility. *Organization, 17*, 721–742.

Harré, R. and van Langenhove, L. (1991). Varieties of positioning. *Journal for the Theory of Social Behaviour, 21*(4), 393–407.

Hategan, C.-D., Sirghi, N., Curea-Pitorac, R.-I., and Hategan, V.-P. (2018). Doing well or doing good: The relationship between corporate social responsibility and profit in Romanian companies. *Sustainability, 10*(4). https://doi.org/10.3390/su10041041.

Heath, R. L. and Palenchar, M. J. (2008). *Strategic issues management: Organizations and public policy challenges*. Thousand Oaks, CA: Sage Publications.

Hyslop, M. (2014). *Obstructive marketing: Restricting distribution of products and services in the age of asymmetric warfare*. Farnham: Ashgate.

Icks, M. and Shiraev, E. (2014). Introduction. In M. Icks and E. Shiraev (eds.), *Character assassination throughout the ages* (pp. 1–13). New York: Palgrave Macmillan.

Jasper, J. and King, B. (2020). *Protestors and their targets*. Philadelphia, PA: Temple University Press.

Johnsson, J. (2020). Boeing says total costs for 737 Max will surpass $18 billion. *Bloomberg*, 29 January. https://bloom.bg/3HAG4Or.

Kähr, A., Nyffenegger, B., Krohmer, H., and Hoyer, W. D. (2016). When hostile consumers wreak havoc on your brand: The phenomenon of consumer brand sabotage. *Journal of Marketing, 80*(3), 25–41.

Krishnamurthy, S. and Kucuk, S. U. (2009). Anti-branding on the Internet. *Journal of Business Research, 62*, 1119–1126.

Kulikov, V. (2022). *#BUSINESS: "Stand on the right side of history" – Enterprises and society in the Russia-Ukraine war.* The Leibniz Institute for East and Southeast European Studies. https://ukraine2022.ios-regensburg.de/business01/.

Lagorio-Chafkin, C. (2018). This billion-dollar founder says hiring refugees isn't a political act. *INC*. https://bit.ly/3qH7LPm.

Langert, B. (2019). *The business case for working with your toughest critics* [Video]. TED Summit 2019. https://bit.ly/3Luw5vz.

Langley, Q. (2014). *Brandjack: How your reputation is at risk from brand pirates and what to do about it*. New York: Palgrave Macmillan.

Lerbinger, O. (1997). *The crisis manager: Facing risk and responsibility*. Mahwah, NJ: Lawrence Erlbaum.

Li, L. P., Frethey-Bentham, C., Juric, B., and Brodie, R. J. (2021). A negative actor engagement scale for online knowledge-sharing platforms. *Australasian Marketing Journal*. https://doi.org/10.1177/18393349211022044.

Lievonen, M. and Luoma-aho, V. (2015). Ethical hateholders and negative engagement: A challenge for organizational communication. In A. Catellani, A. Zerfass, and R. Tench (eds.), *Communication ethics in a connected world* (pp. 285–304). Brussels: Peter Lang.

Lievonen, M., Luoma-aho, V., and Bowden, J. (2018). Negative engagement. In K. Johnston and M. Taylor (eds.), *The handbook of communication engagement* (pp. 531–548). New York: Wiley.

Love, G. E., Lim, J., and Bednar, M. K. (2017). The face of the firm: The influence of CEOs on corporate reputation. *American Management Journal, 60*, 1462–1481.

Luoma-aho, V. (2015). Understanding stakeholder engagement: Faith-holders, hateholders & fakeholders. *RJ-IPR: Research Journal of the Institute for Public Relations, 2*(1). http://www.instituteforpr.org/understanding-stakeholder-engagement-fai.

Luoma-aho, V., Virolainen, M., Lievonen, M., and Halff, G. (2018). Brand hijacked: Why campaigns and hashtags are taken over by audiences. In A. V. Laskin (ed.), *Social, mobile, and emerging media around the world: Communication case studies* (pp. 57–68). Lanham, MD: Lexington Books.

McColl-Kennedy, J. R., Sparks, B. A., and Nguyen, D. T. (2011). Customer's angry voice: Targeting employees or the organization? *Journal of Business Research, 64*(7), 707–713.

Miller-Idriss, C. (2021). *Hate in the homeland: The new global far right*. Hoboken, NJ. Wiley.

Mishan, L. (2020). The long and tortured history of cancel culture. *The New York Times*, 3 December. https://nyti.ms/3FyWmGD.

Mitchell, R. K., Agle, B. R., and Wood, D. J. (1997). Toward a theory of stakeholder identification and salience: Defining the principle of who and what really counts. *Academy of Management Review*, *22*(4), 853–886.

Naumann, K., Bowden, J., and Gabbott, M. (2017). A multi-valenced perspective on consumer engagement within a social service. *Journal of Marketing Theory and Practice*, *25*(2), 171–188.

Norris, P. (2021). Cancel culture: Myth or reality? *Political Studies*. https://doi.org/10.1177/00323217211037023.

North, A. (2018). Why women are worried about #MeToo. *Vox*, 5 April. https://bit.ly/3sgz0A8.

Physicians Committee (2019). *Doctors against McDonald's Bacon Hour* [Video]. YouTube. https://www.youtube.com/watch?v=Td3T573yW88.

Popp, B., Germelmann, C. C., and Jung, B. (2016). We love to hate them! Social media-based anti-brand communities in professional football. *International Journal of Sports Marketing and Sponsorship*, *17*(4), 349–367.

Powers, D. (2019). *On trend: The business of forecasting the future*. Champaign, IL: University of Illinois Press.

Romani, S., Grappi, S., Zarantonello, L., and Bagozzi, R. P. (2015). The revenge of the consumer! How brand moral violations lead to consumer anti-brand activism. *Journal of Brand Management*, *22*, 658–672.

Roulet, T. J. and Pichler, R. (2020). Blame game theory: Scapegoating, whistleblowing and discursive struggles following accusations of organizational misconduct. *Organization Theory*. https://doi.org/10.1177/263178772097519.

Samoilenko, S. A. (2021a). Character assassination: The sociocultural perspective. *Journal of Applied Social Theory*, *1*(3), 186–205.

Samoilenko, S. A. (2021b). The cocreational view of character assassination. In C. H. Botan (ed.), *The handbook of strategic communication* (pp. 76–90). Hoboken, NJ: Wiley.

Samoilenko, S. A., Icks, M., Keohane, J., and Shiraev, E. (eds.) (2020). *The Routledge handbook of character assassination and reputation management*. New York: Routledge.

Samoilenko, S. A. and Jasper, J. M. (2023). The implications of character assassination and cancel culture for public relations theory. In C. Botan and E. J. Sommerfeldt (eds.), *Public relations theory III* (pp. 452–469). New York: Routledge.

Samoilenko, S. A. and Suvorova, I. (2023). Artificial intelligence and deepfakes in strategic deception campaigns: The U.S. and Russian experiences. In E. Pashentsev (ed.), *The Palgrave handbook of malicious use of AI and psychological security*. Cham: Palgrave Macmillan.

Schaeffer, L. (2019). Consumers expect the brands they support to be socially responsible. *Business Wire*, 2 October. https://bwnews.pr/3ncNbV2.

Seiffert-Brockmann, J., Diehl, T., and Dobusch, L. (2019). Memes as games: The evolution of a digital discourse online. *New Media & Society*, *20*(8), 2862–2879.

Seiffert-Brockmann, J., Einwiller, S., and Stranzl, J. (2018). Character assassination of CEOs in crises: Questioning CEOs' character and values in corporate crises. *European Journal of Communication*, *33*(4), 413–429.

Shao, C., Ciampaglia, G. L., Varol, O., Yang, K., Flammini, A., and Menczer, F. (2018). The spread of low-credibility content by social bots. *Nature Communications*, *9*, 4787. https://doi.org/10.1038/s41467-018-06930-7.

Shiraev, E., Keohane, J., Icks, M., and Samoilenko, S. A. (2022). *Character assassination and reputation management: Theory and applications*. London: Routledge.

Siano, A., Confetto, M. G., Vollero, A., and Covucci, C. (2021). Redefining brand hijacking from a non-collaborative brand co-creation perspective. *Journal of Product & Brand Management*, *31*(1), 110–126.

Skarmeas, D. and Leonidou, C. N. (2013). When consumers doubt, watch out! The role of CSR skepticism. *Journal of Business Research*, *66*(10), 1831–1838.

Spencer, C. (2021). CVS, AT&T, Comcast and others donated to anti-LGBTQ+ politicians, new study finds. *The Hill*, 15 June. https://bit.ly/3R8G25d.

Swan, A. (2018). The numbers behind Papa John's brand devastation. *Forbes*, 25 July. https://bit.ly/3nkYlHj.

Swant, M. (2020). The world's most valuable brands. *Forbes*. https://bit.ly/3xYTrFH.

236 *Handbook on digital corporate communication*

Thompson, J. B. (2000). *Political scandal: Power and visibility in the media age*. Cambridge: Polity Press.

Törmälä, M. and Gyrd-Jones, R. I. (2017). Development of new B2B venture corporate brand identity: A narrative performance approach. *Industrial Marketing Management, 65*, 76–85.

Vaccari, C. and Chadwick, A. (2020). Deepfakes and disinformation: Exploring the impact of synthetic political video on deception, uncertainty, and trust in news. *Social Media & Society*. https://doi.org/10.1177/205630512090340.

Vogels, E. A., Anderson, M., Porteus, M., et al. (2021). *Americans and 'cancel culture': Where some see calls for accountability, others see censorship, punishment*. Pew Research Center. https://pewrsr.ch/3Dh4YiZ.

Wanless, A. and Berk, M. (2020). The audience is the amplifier: Participatory propaganda. In P. Baines, N. O'Shaughnessy, and N. Snow (eds.), *The SAGE handbook of propaganda* (pp. 85–104). Thousand Oaks, CA: Sage Publications.

Wendling, C., Radisch, J., and Jacobzone, S. (2013). The use of social media in risk and crisis communication. *OECD Working Papers on Public Governance, 24*, 1–42. https://doi.org/10.1787/5k3v01fskp9s-en.

Westerlund, M. (2019). The emergence of deepfake technology: A review. *Technology Innovation Management Review, 9*(11), 40–53.

Willsher, K. (2018). Catherine Deneuve's claim of #MeToo witch-hunt sparks backlash. *The Guardian*, 10 January. https://bit.ly/3KKP97y.

Zheng, L. (2020). We're entering the age of corporate social justice. *Harvard Business Review*, 15 June. https://bit.ly/3vlUXzH.

PART III

CORPORATE COMMUNICATION'S ADOPTION OF DIGITAL TECHNOLOGIES

17. Digital corporate communication and digital transformation of communication functions and organizations

Ansgar Zerfass and Jana Brockhaus

INTRODUCTION

The digital transformation of businesses and other organizations impacts corporate communication in many ways. First and foremost, communication departments transform themselves. They adapt their structures, processes, and practices for delivering their key contributions to organizational success: stakeholder communications and internal advising. A deeply mediatized world with a 24/7 information flow requires different approaches than those established in previous decades. Moving administrative, creative, and managerial tasks to digital solutions changes the way corporate communication is practised. Second, communication departments and professionals can use their expertise to support the digital transformation of the overall organization and other functions or departments. Digitalization is a change process that involves people and culture as much as technologies, tasks, and structures. Corporate communication plays an important role in this process. It can be used to promote understanding, provide orientation, motivate participation, and foster acceptance among employees. Communication is also necessary to monitor topical debates and relevant stakeholders, to advise those responsible for transformation projects, and to position the organization or its representatives as digital pioneers in issues arenas (Luoma-Aho and Vos, 2010) and newly formed public spheres (Habermas, 2021).

This chapter outlines the dual challenge for corporate communication and those who are in charge of it by discussing (1) key concepts and terms, (2) the digital transformation of communication functions and departments, and (3) the contribution of the communication function to the digital transformation of organizations by (4) critically reflecting these developments, and (5) by illustrating the relevance for corporate practice based on an illustrative example as well as (6) for research by outlining potential areas for future investigation.

DEFINITIONS OF THE TOPIC AND PREVIOUS STUDIES

Digital corporate communication can be interpreted as the utilization of digital technologies to improve communication in organizations, in society, and with organizational stakeholders (Badham and Luoma-aho, Chapter 1 in this volume). This implies a momentum of change. Previously established patterns for the communication function (the totality of tasks that are directed towards communication activities in an organization), communication departments (organizational units responsible for the management and execution of communication activities within a defined area of responsibility), and the daily work of communication profession-

Digital corporate communication and digital transformation of communication 239

als (individuals mandated to assume tasks in this field) will differ from those in an analogue world. Generally, *digitalization* can be defined as "a sociotechnical process of applying digitizing techniques to broader social and institutional contexts that render digital technologies infrastructural" (Tilson et al., 2010, p. 749). This means that it is not only about introducing powerful software, services, and hardware. Tasks, workflows, mindsets, and competencies have to be modified as well. Some authors even argue that digitalization is primarily a cultural issue, since it is the people who have to reposition, change practices, and redefine themselves (Kirf et al., 2020, p. 56). In fact, digitalization is both externally driven and actively promoted by organizations to leverage competitive advantage. This notion has been widely discussed and highlighted with the concept of *digital transformation* as

> the intercept of the adoption of disruptive digital technologies on the one side and actor-guided organisational transformation of capabilities, structures, processes and business model components on the other side. (Nadkarni and Prügl, 2021, p. 236)

The digital transformation is one of the most important challenges for organizations of any kind in the past and coming decades (Hess et al., 2016; Nadkarni and Prügl, 2021). It forces almost all industries and organizations to adjust strategies, structures, product development, and service delivery (Dühring and Zerfass, 2021). "Organisations seeking to deploy digital technologies to garner greater competitive advantages must also ensure their respective business models are aligned" (Loonam et al., 2018, p. 102). Hence, the digital transformation is an organization-wide endeavour (Hess et al., 2016, p. 137) that encompasses profound change taking place (Orlikowski, 2000; Vial, 2019).

To remain competitive, organizations must find ways to innovate with digital technology by developing strategies "that embrace the impact of digital transformation and drive better operational performance" (Hess et al., 2016, p. 123). Such *digital transformation strategies* seek to coordinate, prioritize, and implement the transformation of products and processes (Matt et al., 2015, p. 339). Matt et al. (2015, p. 340) describe four elements of digital transformation strategies that need to be aligned to ensure successful digitalization: the use of technologies, changes in value creation, structural changes, and financial aspects. The *use of technologies* embodies the strategic role of IT for an organization and its attitude towards new technologies. New digital activities, products or services may imply *changes in value creation* by deviating from the core business. While *structural changes* refer to variations in an organization's setup, *financial aspects* are "both a driver and a bounding force for the transformation" (Matt et al., 2015, p. 341). These four elements support organizations in formulating a digital transformation strategy. Other authors argue that apart from using technologies and reconfiguring processes and structures, it is important to build up new resources and capabilities, adjust leadership routines, and establish a digital culture (Nadkarni and Prügl, 2021, pp. 235–236; Vial, 2019, pp. 127–129). This means that the digital transformation is not only about interfering with the objective world of information processing and data handling, but as much about the social world of shared interpretations and acceptance in organizations and among stakeholders, and about the individual cognitions and mindsets of individuals involved, especially of leaders and employees in organizations. Socio-technical systems theory, a classical concept from management information systems, posits that *technology, tasks, structure, and people* have to be addressed simultaneously to change work systems. The technical requirements of an organization or department are jointly optimized with its social aspects (Bostrom and

240 *Handbook on digital corporate communication*

Heinen, 1977; Pasmore et al., 2019). Empirical research proves that strategies for all four dimensions have a positive impact on the digital maturity of communication departments and agencies; with people approaches showing the highest significance in regression models (Zerfass et al., 2021, p. 29).

WHAT IS CHANGING?

What does the digital transformation mean for corporate communication? From a managerial perspective, *corporate communication* involves communication activities

> enacted by or on behalf of a business that support the internal and external coordination of action as well as the clarification of interests between the company and its stakeholders, and thus contribute to the definition or achievement of corporate goals. These communication activities are symbolic actions through which organizational members (especially senior management, communication officers, other employees) or agents (e.g., communication agencies) participate in or initiate conversations in various public spheres to create understanding and influence the knowledge, attitudes, and actions of stakeholders or the company itself. (Zerfass and Link, 2022, p. 239)

This implies that the key deliverables of actively managed communications on the meso level of organizations are (a) stakeholder communications, mainly building on messaging and listening activities with all types of media and platforms, and (b) internal advising of decision-makers in the organization, mainly based on monitoring and interpreting opinion building, stakeholder action, and other important developments in relevant public spheres.

Digitalization impacts this in two ways. On the one hand, the communication activities (corporate communication) and the processes of steering and shaping them by means of planning, organizing, leading, and control (communication management) can be digitally transformed. Here, communication departments and professionals are both *objects* and *actors* of the change process. On the other hand, supporting the digital transformation of the whole organization or of specific functions and departments (e.g., the digitalization of accounting and manufacturing) can be an objective for corporate communication. In this case, communication departments and professionals are *actors* within the change process, irrespective of whether their way of managing and executing communications has been digitalized or not. This conceptual differentiation helps to analyze the practice: digitalized means of communication management and stakeholder communications might be instrumental for any kind of topics and goals, while all kind of corporate communication activities – even traditional press releases and employee events – can promote digitalization and thus foster the digital transformation of organizations. Of course, the potential of digitalization for communications is exploited even more by combining both aspects.

Digital Transformation of Communication Functions and Departments

The digitalization of the communication function in general and communication departments specifically have been continuously discussed by communication scholars and practitioners since the 1990s. The main focus, however, was on how new media and technologies change communication activities (Duhé, 2017; Zerfass and Pleil, 2015). New concepts like CommTech or digital infrastructure have only been introduced recently in the second decade

Digital corporate communication and digital transformation of communication   241

of the twenty-first century. Overall, digitalization was discussed in three successive phases, each of the latter extending and including the earlier phases.

Digitalizing stakeholder communications: the first phase
As relationships between organizations and stakeholders have changed fundamentally in the digital age (Lock, 2019), most debates focus on using *digital technologies for stakeholder communications.* Channels and instruments like social media, websites and intranets, and their adoption by organizations have become a major research topic under umbrella terms like online communication or digital public relations (e.g., Etter et al., 2021; Ewing et al., 2019; Freberg, 2022; Lutrell et al., 2021; Valentini, 2015; Verčič et al., 2015; Wilson et al., 2020; Wright and Hinson, 2017). Newer debates focus on big data, automation, and artificial intelligence in corporate communication, and how analytical tools help practitioners to evaluate online behavioural patterns of key stakeholders (e.g., Galloway and Swiatek, 2018; Moore and Hübscher, 2022; Weiner, 2021; Weiner and Kochhar, 2016; Wiencierz and Röttger, 2019). Although such digital technologies and services can be used to generate insights for business decisions, researchers have not explicitly linked these potentials to internal advising as another key contribution of communication departments to organizational success. Management aspects have also rarely been discussed here.

Digitalizing the stakeholder journey: the second phase
In an attempt to widen the perspective, the term *CommTech* (Communication Technology) was introduced in the profession at the beginning of the second decade of the twenty-first century (Arthur W. Page Society, 2019, 2021). The concept has quickly become popular without being clearly defined. Practitioners use it to describe the intersection of communication and technology in a broad sense by widening the previously discussed view and asking how digital technologies can modify communication processes along the whole stakeholder journey: "CommTech teams use data and digital tools to target and nurture audiences from belief to action to advocacy. CommTech can engage diverse stakeholders – customers, employees, influencers, investors, citizens" (Arthur W. Page Society, 2019, p. 16; see also Weiner, 2021). Four building blocks of CommTech are proposed for developing a stakeholder-centric journey and a holistic data-driven communication approach: digital tools, methods, analytics, and agility (Arthur W. Page Society, 2021). A concise link to the existing research in managing and transforming organizational functions, however, has not been made in this debate.

It has to be noted that this practice-based notion of CommTech was stimulated by a similar, but already more advanced debate in marketing called *MarTech* (e.g., Brinker, 2022; Chaffey and Smith, 2017; Doughty, 2019). The so-called MarTech landscape, illustrated by Scott Brinker since 2011, categorizes more than 10,000 digital solutions into distinct groups (Brinker, 2022). This has been reflected in the marketing literature which discusses the adoption of marketing automation technology as well as approaches for managing the growing volume and variety of data (e.g., Berghofer et al., 2018; Mero et al., 2020). Digital marketing involves getting closer to customers, identifying, anticipating, and satisfying their needs efficiently and creating a constant dialogue with them via digital technologies (Chaffey and Smith, 2017, pp. 13–14).

242 Handbook on digital corporate communication

Digitalizing communication functions and departments: the third phase
In an attempt to clarify the fuzzy understanding of CommTech and to link the debate in communication science to elaborated theories in information systems and management research, Zerfass and colleagues (Zerfass et al., 2021; Zerfass and Brockhaus, 2021; Brockhaus et al., 2023) have expanded the debate even further by pointing out the relevance of digitalizing the infrastructure for corporate communication. A digital infrastructure is the backbone of digital corporate communication as "the strategic management of digital technologies ... to improve communication with internal and external stakeholders and more broadly within society for the maintenance of organizational tangible and intangible assets" (Badham and Luoma-aho, Chapter 1 in this volume, p. 9). It allows communication departments and professionals to manage their workflows with digital means and to execute digital communication activities. The importance of building a digital infrastructure is emphasized by empirical findings. Almost 84 per cent of communication practitioners across Europe stress the relevance of a digital infrastructure for communications (Zerfass et al., 2021, p. 18).

In information systems research, digital infrastructures are defined as "computing and network resources that allow multiple stakeholders to orchestrate their service and content needs" (Constantinides et al., 2018, p. 381). Digital infrastructure comprises two layers: 'heavyweight' and 'lightweight' (Bygstad, 2017; Constantinides et al., 2018). *Heavyweight infrastructure* is considered mainstream IT, which includes back-end solutions like the Internet and enterprise resource planning systems (e.g., SAP) and is usually owned by specialized IT departments. *Lightweight IT* is driven by immediate needs of users and directly supports activities, e.g., through front-end solutions like digital tools, apps, software, and consumer devices (Ludvigsen and Steier, 2019, p. 417). Lightweight IT may be seen as complementary to heavyweight IT. Both are governed by different development cultures and imply diverse problems. As needs of users in organizations change fast, the development culture of lightweight IT is mostly shaped by innovation and experimentation. Due to poor integration, lightweight IT can easily become isolated gadgets, and security issues may arise quickly. In contrast, heavyweight IT can handle scaling and cross-functional integration, which may result in complexity and rising costs. Its development culture is driven by systematics, quality, and security (Bygstad, 2017, p. 182). Which approach is more appropriate depends mainly on the kind of workflow within an organization which will be supported by digital infrastructure.

Linking this understanding of digital infrastructure to the debate about digital technologies in corporate communication made it possible to clarify the digital transformation of managing and executing corporate communication. Zerfass and Brockhaus (2021) combined business process analyzes (Jeston, 2018) and the value chain concept (Porter, 1985) to differentiate layers of digital infrastructure for communications. The key idea is to analyze all workstreams and activities and their relations, in order to identify options for conceptual improvement as well as for technological support, and to distinguish those processes according to their contribution to value creation into primary and support activities (Simatupang et al., 2017): Primary activities create value for organizations through communications, and supportive activities allow the primary activities take place.

Corporate communication creates value for organizations by listening, creating and conveying messages, co-creating meaning, framing debates, etc., and in the end by stimulating cognitive, affective, and behavioural effects on stakeholders which impact organizational goals. Moreover, communications creates value by advising top executives and (internal) clients on public opinion building and strategic issues (Zerfass and Link, 2022). Therefore, managing and executing communication processes with external and internal stakeholders (stakeholder communications) and internal advising can be characterized as primary activities. However, communication professionals and departments spend only part of their worktime with messaging, listening, and advising. They are engaged in managing and executing many support activities as well. These functional support activities are necessary to make primary activities happen – for example, aligning communication and business goals, monitoring and handling digital assets like logos, templates and videos. Against this background, CommTech can be defined as follows:

> CommTech are digital technologies provided or used by communications functions or departments to manage and perform primary activities, particularly stakeholder communications and internal advising, or functional support activities such as managing internal workflows for monitoring, content planning, or evaluation.

In addition to such functional digital technologies (CommTech), communication functions and departments are also using overarching software and services that support collaborative work and the division of labour. These organization-wide digital technologies (OrgTech) are another important part of the digital infrastructure.

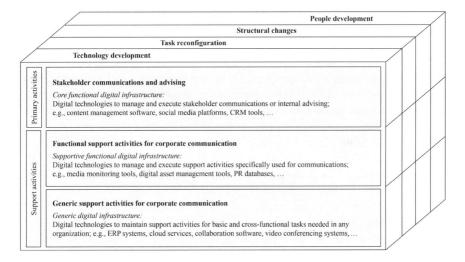

Figure 17.1 Dimensions of the digital transformation of communication functions and departments

The distinction of different dimensions helps to prioritize processes which can be supported by digital technologies, and thus guides digital transformation in practice. The framework shown in Figure 17.1 extends a systematization by Zerfass and Brockhaus (2021, p. 209) by adding the four dimensions of transformation (technology, tasks, structures, people) that have to be taken into account when upgrading the key layers of digital tools and services in corporate communication:

(a) *Core functional digital infrastructure:* Digital technologies to create, manage, and execute stakeholder communications or internal advising, which are needed to prepare and maintain primary activities. These activities are directly linked to value creation through communications. They include preparing, creating, and executing as well as adjusting stakeholder communications, e.g., content management, crisis communication, stakeholder relationship management, etc. Other processes such as analyzing and preparing insights, delivering presentations, and considering and discussing relevant issues are part of advisory activities, which are another key contribution of communications to corporate success. Core functional digital infrastructure consists of industry-specific software and service solutions for communications, i.e., content management software (e.g., Drupal), social media management tools (e.g., Hootsuite), and relationship management and distribution tools (e.g., Cision Communications Cloud). It mostly comprises lightweight IT solutions driven by the immediate needs of communication practitioners.

(b) *Supportive functional digital infrastructure:* Digital technologies for functional support activities, which are specific for corporate communication and needed to maintain secondary activities and run the department. These activities relate to specific tasks in communications, but include workflows that are necessary to manage communications in organizations professionally without being part of stakeholder communications or advisory processes. They include overall planning (aligning communication and business goals) and monitoring, handling digital assets (logos, templates, pictures, videos), and tracking staff hours and resources for projects. Supportive functional digital infrastructure consists of specific software for the communications profession (e.g., media monitoring tools like Meltwater) or customizable digital tools used for multiple functions (e.g., Adobe Experience Cloud for digital asset management; TSheets for timesheets).

(c) *Generic digital infrastructure:* Digital tools for generic support activities for communications, which are relevant for any department or organization for task fulfilment based on a division of labour. Digital infrastructure for these basic workflows, especially for collaboration and workplace needs, is usually provided by IT departments or providers and not specifically developed for communications. Lightweight as well as heavyweight IT might be used. Examples are enterprise resource systems for budgeting and sourcing (e.g., SAP), video conferencing tools (e.g., MS Teams, Zoom), and also hardware and software solutions for mobile work with remote access to internal databases.

The framework helps communication leaders to develop digital transformation strategies focusing on technologies, tasks, processes, and people (see above). Typical steps needed are (1) analyzing processes and the current use of digital tools within the communications function or department, (2) identifying and prioritizing management and execution processes which should be transformed by digital technologies, (3) decision-making for digital investments and resources allocated to people development and other initiatives.

Supporting the Digital Transformation of Organizations

Since the 1980s, there has been a vast body of literature discussing the successful management of change processes. Organizational change is mostly portrayed as a specific process with different stages; in contrast to approaches that understand change as "ongoing modifications in everyday work" (Johansson and Heide, 2008, p. 290). Since the digital transformation of organizations affects people, the role of leadership and communication is key to its success. All organization-wide measures call for communicative support (Elving, 2005; Lewis, 2019,

Digital corporate communication and digital transformation of communication 245

p. 49; Vuuren and Elving, 2008) or even for initiating moves of the communication department (Pleil and Helferich, 2022).

Thus, corporate communication can make an important contribution by moderating the digital transformation of the whole organization or other focal entities (business units, functions, departments, etc.) as change processes with various steps and interim results. Research reveals that organizational change initiatives cannot succeed if there are shortcomings in internal communication (Johansson and Heide, 2008, p. 289). A core task of corporate communication is to inform internal and external stakeholders about changes and explain their necessity. Internal communication helps to create orientation, motivation, and understanding among employees. Likewise, external stakeholders like customers and regulators are key for the success of organization-wide transformation processes. In this context, professional communication is also indispensable (Pleil and Helferich, 2022).

Recent research suggests the four main tasks for corporate communication to support an organization-wide digital transformation (Niederhäuser and Rosenberger, 2018; Pleil and Helferich, 2022):

1. participating in organizational strategy development;
2. consulting management, executives and other departments in organizational culture;
3. enabling employees and promoting knowledge sharing;
4. positioning the organization as digital leader internally and externally.

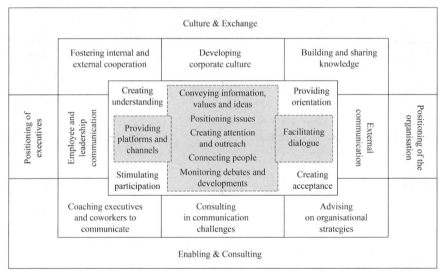

Source: Framework modified and translated from Ostermeier (2019, p. 120).

Figure 17.2 *Action fields for corporate communication supporting organizational change*

These overarching tasks are also reflected in a more detailed framework by Ostermeier (2019), who outlines the role of corporate communication in digital transformation based on an extensive literature review and qualitative interviews. Figure 17.2 shows the framework and depicts

246 *Handbook on digital corporate communication*

the different tasks and contributions of communication departments for the overall digital transformation of organizations.

Ostermeier (2019) identified various fields of action to support an organization-wide digital transformation: establishing a corporate transformation culture, fostering internal and external cooperation as well as knowledge building and sharing, advising in organizational strategies and decision-making, consulting and coaching in communicative issues, as well as internal and external communication focusing on the transformation activities. The arrangement of action fields does not imply any kind of hierarchy, as the importance of activities must be decided on a case-by-case basis.

In its centre, the framework depicts core activities of communication departments that contribute to the implementation of the digital transformation across all fields of action, such as conveying information, values, and ideas; positioning issues; creating attention and outreach; connecting people; or monitoring relevant public spheres and stakeholders. These core activities make a contribution independently of the fields of action and are aimed at creating an understanding of the transformation measures and their necessity, providing orientation in the transformation process, creating acceptance among employees, and actively motivating them to participate (Ostermeier, 2019, p. 121).

However, as the outer frame illustrates, the central contributions of corporate communication to shaping and supporting an organization-wide digital transformation are activities aimed at culture and exchange as well as enabling and consulting activities based on communication-based expertise. This indicates that communication departments and professionals do not have to take on fundamentally new tasks when contributing to the digital transformation of the organization. On the contrary, many of the listed activities and services are part of routine tasks today. Rather, established patterns of thinking and acting among organizational members must be reconsidered in order to allow and support organization-wide change processes in a comprehensive way (addressing technology, tasks, structure, and people). A digital mindset and digital competencies of communication professionals are vital to support such endeavours, i.e., skills and knowledge in data management and analytics, technology literacy, and in sensemaking for the digital transformation (Lee and Meng, 2021).

WHAT REMAINS THE SAME?

While CommTech allows (and forces) communicators to optimize their processes, the core contributions of corporate communication will not change. Generally, communication functions and departments have to align with overarching organizational goals (Volk and Zerfass, 2018) and ensure that they combine resources of all kinds in the best possible way. As a consequence, it is important to understand that technology has to be integrated into existing approaches to manage corporate communication (Zerfass and Link, 2022).

CRITICAL EXAMINATION

This chapter posits that it is necessary to consider the dual role of corporate communication within the digital transformation. Without having a digital transformation strategy and clear processes, digital technologies can neither create value for communication functions or depart-

Digital corporate communication and digital transformation of communication   247

ments nor for the whole organization. For communication departments, it is challenging to find a balance between new and tailored software applications, and to connect digital technology to their established digital infrastructure. Some digital tools are specific for communications, while others are relevant for many functions. In the latter case, decisions for digital investments will be taken by the IT department or other departments. Therefore, a holistic view of managing digitalization processes is important to avoid double effort. As no 'one fits it all' solution is available, communication departments need to build their own digital infrastructure and CommTech stack based on their objectives, processes, and resources.

Following the thoughts of Orlikowski (2000), digital transformation should assure that "people interact with technology in their day-to-day activities – not the mere presence of the technology on the desktop or factory floor – that influences performance outcomes and consequences" (Orlikowski, 2000, p. 425). To this end, it is necessary to overcome barriers such as inertia and resistance that can affect digital transformation processes (Vial, 2019, pp. 129–130). Lewis (2019, pp. 191–226) describes resistance in its varied forms in the context of organizational change and takes the view that opportunities for participation and empowerment to engage with decision-makers can turn resistance into input for improvement. Furthermore, Just and Rasmussen (2019) outline a continuum that ranges from techno-optimism to techno-pessimism: "While the optimists focus on the constructive potential of online phenomena like big data, interconnectedness, spreadability and stakeholders-as-prosumers, sceptics highlight the pitfalls of exactly the same features" (pp. 28–29).

Hence, the obstacles of any digital transformation are first and foremost in the minds of the people involved. These are not only based on individual concerns or expectations, but also grounded in corporate culture, leadership and, in many respects, in a lack of professional corporate communication. It is likely that "reactions to changes will be rooted in complex social systems, organisational structures, power relations, and other ongoing organisational dynamics" (Lewis, 2019, p. 49) including relationships between stakeholders.

The insights presented here challenge much of the traditional thinking on digitalizing corporate communication focused on interactive media, channels, and other aspects of stakeholder communications. We do not suggest that communication practitioners need to become technology or transformation experts. But they should develop a sufficient understanding of differing attainments of digital technologies, which in turn requires a process-oriented thinking and a concise understanding of change in socio-technical systems.

ILLUSTRATIVE EXAMPLE: SIEMENS HEALTHINEERS

The different challenges of the digital transformation can be illustrated using the example of Siemens Healthineers, a global medical technology company which supports hospitals and healthcare providers with medical imaging (e.g., computed tomography scanners), laboratory diagnostics, and advanced therapies equipment. The stock-listed company with over 66,000 employees, headquartered in Germany, is active in more than 70 countries. Due to the successful and rapid growth of the company since its IPO in 2018, Siemens Healthineers issued a digital transformation initiative throughout the whole organization. The organizational change was driven by external forces and eventually initiated by the CEO. The company identified six external drivers for organizational change (Table 17.1).

248 *Handbook on digital corporate communication*

Table 17.1   *Drivers for the organization-wide digital transformation*

External drivers for the digital transformation of the company	
Speed	Digitalization of mass media is leading to a 24/7 information flow and short reaction times become a crucial success factor.
Relevance	The competition for attention is becoming increasingly fierce. This makes it even more important to place the right topics at the right time for the right target group.
Consistency	In the era of digitalization, only those who tell a consistent story across all channels can be successful. Content has to be suitable for the stakeholder journey.
Agility	The dynamics of the media landscape can only be managed if content creators act transparently and collaboratively.
Efficiency	In a fast-paced content overloaded world, no one can afford to waste resources – instead of tedious duplication of work, smart content planning and recycling is needed.
Digitality	The Covid-19 pandemic is forcing organizations to rethink their way of working. Digital is the new normal.

Source: Siemens Healthineers.

The corporate communication department – a unit with almost 200 staff – launched two initiatives to contribute: (1) the 'Content Lab' project to transform internal workflows and processes, and (2) a set of communication measures to promote the company-wide digital transformation journey.

A new and holistic content management process was introduced in 2020 to become faster, more consistent, and efficient as a communication department. The Chief Communication Officer defined the Content Lab project as "the game-changing accelerator for the implementation of our digital roadmap" (Personal communication, 2021). The newly-formed Content Lab team plans, creates and publishes relevant content globally for all stakeholders and corporate channels across all business units with the aim of ensuring consistent messaging and safeguarding reputation. This required a reconfiguration of processes and digital infrastructure on various levels, including the selection and implementation of new software and services. This was done 'bottom-up' by different project teams in an agile environment. This, however, proved quite difficult as a structured overview of digital tools and how they can support different workstreams in corporate communication was missing. The same was true for transformation strategies and routines for software selection. A better understanding of these differences, as outlined in the first framework shown above (Figure 17.1), would have been helpful according to the communication leader in charge of the process.

Parallel to this initiative, the communication department identified various possibilities to support the digitalization journey of the whole company through internal and external communication and through advising executives based on insights from social media monitoring. 'Digitalization of healthcare' was a corporate theme promoted through specific topics of relevance and campaigns across multiple platforms. This helped to raise attention and build reputation among key stakeholders in short time.

CONCLUSION AND FUTURE DIRECTIONS

The ideas and frameworks presented in this chapter illustrate how communication leaders and professionals can approach the twofold challenges of digital transformation in a structured way. More exchange about successful and failed projects in the profession is needed to build

Digital corporate communication and digital transformation of communication   249

up solid knowledge about CommTech and catch up with the marketing community and the MarTech debate.

In terms of future research, there is a need for more investigations into future realities shaped by digital transformation. Table 17.2 outlines several aspects on a macro, meso, and micro level that might be addressed by the academic community. The list builds upon insights identified in the literature (e.g., Weiner, 2021; Zerfass and Brockhaus, 2021) and empirical studies (IMWF, 2021; Zerfass et al., 2021). It is not comprehensive but can be used as a starting point for debating the future of the field.

Table 17.2   Potential agenda for research on the digital transformation of corporate communication

Macro level: Digital evolution of the communication profession and industry	Meso level: Digital transformation of organizations and communication departments	Micro level: Digital upskilling of communication practitioners
Social, legal and economic barriers and drivers for digitalizing corporate communication	Concepts and practices for supporting digital transformation through internal and external communication	Adoption of CommTech stack by practitioners
Development, availability, performance and market share of CommTech solutions (software, services)	Impact of communications on transformation success	Individual competencies and mindset for digitalization and transformation
Competency development and ethical reflection on CommTech and digitalization in the profession	Digitalization strategies for communication functions and departments	Task-oriented and reflective (ethical) experiences of practitioners using CommTech

Engaging in these various areas of investigation requires interdisciplinary approaches. The digital transformation can only be analyzed by combining theories and knowledge from management, information systems, organizational and social theory, and communications. Future phases of the debate will address opportunities and challenges for corporate communication that are unknown today – which underlines the importance of this field for research and practice alike.

REFERENCES

Arthur W. Page Society (2019). *The CCO as pacesetter: What it means, why it matters, how to get there.* 2019 Page Research Report. Arthur W. Page Society.

Arthur W. Page Society (2021). *CommTech quickstart guide.* https://knowledge.page.org/report/commtech-quickstart-guide/.

Berghofer, F., Hofbauer, G., and Sangl, A. (2018). Indicators to choose a suitable marketing automation platform. *International Journal of Management Science and Business Administration, 4*(3), 52–60.

Bostrom, R. P. and Heinen, J. S. (1977). MIS problems and failures: A socio-technical perspective. Part I: The causes. *MIS Quarterly, 1*(3), 17–32.

Brinker, S. (2022). *You can now filter the 10,000+ martech landscape by revenue, size, age and G2 ratings.* https://chiefmartec.com/2022/12/you-can-now-filter-the-10000-martech-landscape-by-revenue-size-age-and-g2-ratings/.

Brockhaus, J., Buhmann, A., and Zerfass, A. (2023). Digitalization in corporate communications: Understanding the emergence and consequences of CommTech and digital infrastructure. *Corporate Communications: An International Journal, 28*(2), 274–292. https://doi.org/10.1108/CCIJ-03-2022-0035.

Bygstad, B. (2017). Generative innovation: A comparison of lightweight and heavyweight IT. *Journal of Information Technology*, *32*(2), 180–193.

Chaffey, D. and Smith, P. R. (2017). *Digital marketing excellence: Planning, optimizing and integrating online marketing* (5th edition). London: Routledge.

Constantinides, P., Henfridsson, O., and Parker, G. B. (2018). Platforms and infrastructures in the digital age. *Information Systems Research*, *29*(2), 381–400.

Doughty, C. (2019). *The what, why, who, how of Martech: Marketing technology made simple(r)*. https://www.martechalliance.com/what-why-how-martech-marketing-technology.

Duhé, S. C. (ed.) (2017). *New media and public relations* (3rd edition). New York: Peter Lang.

Dühring, L. and Zerfass, A. (2021). The triple role of communications in agile organizations. *International Journal of Strategic Communication*, *15*(2), 93–112.

Elving, W. J. L. (2005). The role of communication in organisational change. *Corporate Communication: An International Journal*, *10*(2), 129–138.

Etter, M., Winkler, P., and Pleil, T. (2021). Public relations and social media. In C. Valentini (ed.), *Public relations* (pp. 159–174). Berlin: De Gruyter Mouton.

Ewing, M., Men, L. R., and O'Neil, J. (2019). Using social media to engage employees: Insights from internal communication managers. *International Journal of Strategic Communication*, *13*(2), 110–132.

Freberg, K. (2022). *Social media for strategic communication: Creative strategies and research-based applications* (2nd edition). London: Sage Publications.

Galloway, C. and Swiatek, L. (2018). Public relations and artificial intelligence: It's not (just) about robots. *Public Relations Review*, *44*(5), 734–740.

Habermas, J. (2021). Überlegungen und Hypothesen zu einem erneuten Strukturwandel der politischen Öffentlichkeit. *Leviathan*, *49*(37), 470–500.

Hess, T., Matt, C., Benlian, A., and Wiesboeck, F. (2016). Options for formulating a digital transformation strategy. *MIS Quarterly Executive*, *15*(2), 123–139.

IMWF (2021). *Self Assessment CommTech*. IMWF Institut für Management- und Wirtschaftsforschung.

Jeston, J. (2018). *Business process management* (4th edition). London: Routledge.

Johansson, C. and Heide, M. (2008). Speaking of change: Three communication approaches in studies of organizational change. *Corporate Communication: An International Journal*, *13*(3), 288–305.

Just, S. N. and Rasmussen, R. K. (2019). When data is the issue: Re-conceptualizing public relations for the platform economy. In F. Frandsen, W. Johansen, R. Tench, and S. Romenti (eds.), *Big ideas in public relations research and practice* (pp. 25–38). Bingley: Emerald Publishing.

Kirf, B., Eicke, K. N., and Schömburg, S. (2020). *Unternehmenskommunikation im Zeitalter der digitalen Transformation* (2nd edition). Berlin: Springer Gabler.

Lee, J. J. and Meng, J. (2021). Digital competencies in communication management: A conceptual framework of readiness for Industry 4.0 for communication professionals in the workplace. *Journal of Communication Management*, *25*(4), 417–436.

Lewis, L. (2019). *Organizational change: Creating change through strategic communication* (2nd edition). Malden, MA: Wiley-Blackwell.

Lock, I. (2019). Explicating communicative organization-stakeholder relationships in the digital age: A systematic review and research agenda. *Public Relations Review*, *45*(4), 101829.

Loonam, J., Eaves, S., Kumar, V., and Parry, G. (2018). Towards digital transformation: Lessons learned from traditional organizations. *Strategic Change*, *27*(2), 101–109.

Ludvigsen, S. and Steier, R. (2019). Reflections and looking ahead for CSCL: Digital infrastructures, digital tools, and collaborative learning. *International Journal of Computer-Supported Collaborative Learning*, *14*(4), 415–423.

Luoma-aho, V. and Vos, M. (2010). Towards a more dynamic stakeholder model: Acknowledging multiple issue arenas. *Corporate Communication: An International Journal*, *15*(3), 315–331.

Lutrell, R., Emerick, S., and Wallace, A. (2021). *Digital strategies: Data-driven public relations, marketing, and advertising*. Oxford: Oxford University Press.

Matt, C., Hess, T., and Benlian, A. (2015). Digital transformation strategies. *Business & Information Systems Engineering*, *57*(4), 339–343.

Mero (Järvinen), J., Tarkiainen, A., and Tobon, J. (2020). Effectual and causal reasoning in the adoption of marketing automation. *Industrial Marketing Management*, *86*, 212–222.

Digital corporate communication and digital transformation of communication 251

Moore, S. and Hübscher, R. (2022). *Strategic communication and AI: Public relations with intelligent user interfaces*. London: Routledge.

Nadkarni, S. and Prügl, R. (2021). Digital transformation: A review, synthesis and opportunities for future research. *Management Review Quarterly, 71*(2), 233–341.

Niederhäuser, M. and Rosenberger, N. (2018). *Kommunikation in der digitalen Transformation.* ZHAW Zürcher Hochschule für Angewandte Wissenschaften.

Orlikowski, W. J. (2000). Using technology and constituting structures: A practice lens for studying technology in organizations. *Organization Science, 11*(4), 404–428.

Ostermeier, M. (2019). *Der Beitrag von Kommunikationsabteilungen zur digitalen Transformation in Unternehmen. Handlungsfelder und Unterstützungsmöglichkeiten der Unternehmenskommunikation in Zeiten des digitalen Wandels*. Berlin: Quadriga.

Pasmore, W., Winby, S., Mohrman, S. A., and Vanasse, R. (2019). Reflections: Sociotechnical systems design and organization change. *Journal of Change Management, 19*(2), 67–85.

Pleil, T. and Helferich, P. S. (2022). Unternehmenskommunikation in der digitalen Transformation. In A. Zerfass, M. Piwinger, and U. Röttger (eds.), *Handbuch Unternehmenskommunikation* (3rd edition, pp. 779–796). Berlin: Springer Gabler.

Porter, M. E. (1985). *Competitive advantage: Creating and sustaining superior performance*. New York: Simon & Schuster.

Simatupang, T. M., Piboonrungroj, P., and Williams, S. J. (2017). The emergence of value chain thinking. *International Journal of Value Chain Management, 8*(1), 40–57.

Tilson, D., Lyytinen, K., and Sorensen, C. (2010). Digital infrastructures: The missing IS research agenda. *Information Systems Research, 21*(4), 748–759.

Valentini, C. (2015). Is using social media "good" for the public relations profession? A critical reflection. *Public Relations Review, 41*(2), 170–177.

Verčič, D., Tkalac Verčič, A., and Sriramesh, K. (2015). Looking for digital in public relations. *Public Relations Review, 41*(2), 142–152.

Vial, G. (2019). Understanding digital transformation: A review and a research agenda. *Journal of Strategic Information Systems, 28*(2), 118–144.

Volk, S. C. and Zerfass, A. (2018). Alignment: Explicating a key concept in strategic communication. *International Journal of Strategic Communication, 12*(4), 433–451.

Vuuren, M. van and Elving, W. J. L. (2008). Practical implications and a research agenda for communicating organizational change. *Corporate Communication: An International Journal, 13*(3), 349–359.

Weiner, M. (2021). *PR technology, data and insights: Igniting a positive return on your communications investment*. London: Kogan Page.

Weiner, M. and Kochhar, S. (2016). *Irreversible: The public relations big data revolution*. IPR Institute for Public Relations.

Wiencierz, C. and Röttger, U. (2019). Big data in public relations: A conceptual framework. *Public Relations Journal, 12*(3), 1–15.

Wilson, C., Brubaker, P., and Smith, B. (2020). Cracking the snapcode: Understanding the organizational and technological influences of strategic social media adoption. *International Journal of Strategic Communication, 14*(1), 41–59.

Wright, D. K. and Hinson, M. D. (2017). Tracking how social and other digital media are being used in public relations practice: A twelve-year study. *Public Relations Journal, 11*(1), 1–30.

Zerfass, A. and Brockhaus, J. (2021). Towards a research agenda for CommTech and digital infrastructure in public relations and strategic communication. In B. Birmingham, B. Yook, and Z. F. Chen (eds.), *Contributing at the top and throughout an organization: Research and strategies that advance our understanding of public relations. Proceedings of the 24th International Public Relations Research Conference* (pp. 202–216). IPRRC.

Zerfass, A., Buhmann, A., Tench, R., Verčič, D., and Moreno, A. (2021). *European Communication Monitor 2021. CommTech and digital infrastructure, video-conferencing, and future roles for communication professionals. Results of a survey in 46 countries*. EUPRERA/EACD.

Zerfass, A. and Link, J. (2022). Communication management: Structures, processes, and business models for value creation through corporate communications. In J. Falkheimer and M. Heide (eds.), *Research handbook on strategic communication* (pp. 237–258). Cheltenham, UK and Northampton, MA, USA: Edward Elgar Publishing.

252 *Handbook on digital corporate communication*

Zerfass, A. and Pleil, T. (eds.) (2015). *Handbuch Online-PR. Strategische Kommunikation in Internet und Social Web* (2nd edition). UVK.

18. Digital corporate communication and social media influencers
Nils S. Borchers

INTRODUCTION

In conversations with influencer agency practitioners in the earlier days of influencer communication – days that are effectively not long gone – these practitioners regularly expressed their surprise and, increasingly, bewilderment about the main motivation of many of their prospective clients. Rather than having an idea what they wanted to achieve with endorsing social media influencers (hereafter: influencers) and whether strategic influencer communication was an apt enhancement of their communication strategy, they simply wanted to get a piece of the pie. Word was out that influencer marketing was the magic bullet and that influencers would help organizations in navigating the new digital environment. And even if some corporate communicators did not subscribe to reports of magic powers, they were at least aware that they would have to answer to their superiors at some point if they were mistaken. It can be argued that these dynamics played no small part in the rapid growth of strategic influencer communications in the late 2010s. In 2021, the global influencer marketing market was valued at 13.8 billion US dollars (Santora, 2021). With this establishment of strategic influencer communication, also the contours of what corporate communication can and cannot achieve in collaborating with influencers become clearer. It therefore seems a good time to take a critical-distanced look at this relatively new domain of digital corporate communications in this chapter.

DEFINITIONS OF THE TOPIC AND PREVIOUS STUDIES

Corporate communication collaborates with influencers to pursue both marketing and public relations goals (Borchers and Enke, 2021b). This is why this chapter refers to "strategic influencer communication": this term is more precise than the widely spread but inherently limited term "influencer marketing" that excludes the public relations rationale.

What Makes an Influencer?

From a corporate communication perspective, social media influencers can be defined as "third-party actors that have established a significant number of relevant relationships with a specific quality to and influence on organizational stakeholders through content production, content distribution, interaction, and personal appearance on the social web" (Enke and Borchers, 2019, p. 267) This definition points out the inputs that influencers can contribute to collaborations. The following paragraphs will break down the definition into its components to explain the essence of social media influencing.

253

254 *Handbook on digital corporate communication*

Influencers contribute to collaborations by adopting specific roles. As content creators, influencers produce content such as blog posts, videos, and stories. As multiplicators, they distribute content via their social media channels on platforms such as YouTube, Instagram, TikTok, and Twitch or via their personal blogs. As moderators, they interact with their audiences, for example, through private messages and comment sections on social media platforms, but also face-to-face during conventions and other live events. Finally, as protagonists, they curate a public persona, using methods of self-branding (Khamis et al., 2017), with which they appear in content and, more seldomly, in live events.

In addition to these roles, the definition considers further inputs. Influencers establish relationships with other social media users, specifically with their followers. From the perspective of corporate communication, these relationships become relevant if followers belong to the target group of the organization ('net reach'). Influencers therefore usually serve the role of secondary stakeholders who enable organizations to address their primary stakeholders. The number of relevant relationships becomes significant if the number of primary stakeholders among the influencers' followership passes a specific threshold. Where this threshold lies in absolute numbers depends on the objectives of an organization. Typically, it is higher for more general expertise such as lifestyle, fashion, and travelling than in more specialized fields such as coffee, planting, and cleaning in which a few hundred followers might suffice to consider influencers relevant. In focusing on relevant relationships rather than on absolute follower numbers, this definition departs from standard industry categorizations that sort influencers into nano (0–10k followers), micro (10–100k followers), macro (100k–1m followers), and mega (1m+ followers) categories (Campbell and Farrell, 2020). This categorization is partly misleading in that it draws on a criterion that is pertinent only for a few campaign goals such as reaching a general population. For many other goals, other criteria such as interaction rates, net reach, impression duration, or content quality become more pertinent.

The relationships that influencers establish with their audiences have a specific quality, and it has been argued that it is this quality that lies at the core of the influencer phenomenon (Farivar et al., 2021; Lou, 2021). These relationships rely on mechanisms such as intimacy, accessibility, relatability, spontaneity, and, essentially, authenticity (e.g., Duffy, 2017; Jerslev, 2016; Luoma-aho et al., 2019; van Driel and Dumitrica, 2021). Influencers and their followers establish this quality throughout interaction histories that span months and often years. The length of these relationships also explains both their robustness and the trust that followers put into influencers. The ways in which followers relate to influencers have been described in different terms: as sisters (Berryman and Kavka, 2017; Reinikainen et al., 2020), as friends (Colliander and Dahlèn, 2011; García-Rapp, 2017), or as the girl next door (Lee, 2016). Drilling deeper into the relationships, other commentators emphasize that influencers are 'regular people' who (happened to) have grown a digital following (Cocker et al., 2021; Lou, 2021). To get hold of these relationships in more conceptual terms, it is possible to theorize the influencer–follower relationship as a peer-to-peer (P2P) relationship. P2P implies that communication partners perceive themselves as structurally equal. Starting with Web 2.0, this structural equality became built into many platform designs. Platforms that depend on user-generated content (UGC) considerably lowered the access barriers for publishing content. These platforms provide an easy-to-use infrastructure for sharing content (John, 2016). Even more importantly, they democratize the publisher role by making the creation of a user profile (including the compliance with platform rules) their sole entrance barrier. Internet users were quick to seize this opportunity on platforms such as Wikipedia, TripAdvisor, or Reddit.

Digital corporate communication and social media influencers 255

On influencer-prone platforms such as YouTube and Instagram, the same mechanism applies as in the case of Wikipedia etc. Both the production role and the consumption role are equally open to all users. This implies that followers of an influencer can and usually do post content, even if it might receive less attention than the influencer's content. At the same time, influencers also can and usually do consume content on the platform. This structural role flexibility – the possibility to switch between producer and consumer roles – establishes the grounds for a peer relationship. It implies that every platform user could at least potentially gain a large following and the observation that influencers are 'regular people' (Cocker et al., 2021; Lou, 2021), including the air of 'ordinariness' (Berryman and Kavka, 2017) that comes with it, only adds to this impression. This is not to say, however, that influencers and followers are effectively equal. Influencers have established a microcelebrity status (Senft, 2008) that easily translates into an idol status at least for younger followers. This status gives them advantages over non-celebrity users in the microcosms of social media platforms. For example, algorithms prefer microcelebrity content and microcelebrities have greater opportunities for monetizing their content. Delisle and Parmentier (2016) condense these observations in the Bourdieu-inspired concept of "person-brand capital". According to Delisle and Parmentier (2016, p. 213), person-brand capital is "a combination of accumulated status and audience". From the perspective of followers, one can thus conclude that influencers oscillate between peer status and idol status.

Influencers operate in the social web. Many influencers maintain profiles on various platforms such as Instagram, YouTube, TikTok, Twitch, or LinkedIn, which is becoming increasingly popular for business-to-business influencing. However, influencers usually have a core platform whose logics they have embraced (Borchers and Enke, 2021b). These logics differ from platform to platform and manifest themselves in different ways, for example, in the reference mechanisms of platforms, in the content their algorithms favour, in their terms of service, or, maybe most obviously, in the content formats they allow. These differences bear relevance also from the perspective of corporate communication. Even before selecting influencers for cooperation, corporate communicators have to decide which platform(s) to cover with their campaigns.

Finally, influencers have established some sort of influence over their followers. Ultimately, the term 'influencer' is one that follows from a corporate communication perspective because it emphasizes a function that influencers fulfil for an organization: they can influence its primary stakeholders. In contrast, many influencers, at least influencers of the first generation, prefer less functionalistic identifiers such as content creator, blogger, gamer, or photographer. The influence of influencers extends to attitudes, knowledge, and behaviours (Freberg et al., 2011). It is becoming apparent that this influence does not end with purchasing decisions but also extends to other spheres of social life. Accordingly, strategic influencer communication is increasingly used by, for example, political parties, state bodies, and NGOs.

State of Research

Influencer research has gained in traction since the late 2010s (Borchers, 2019; Hudders et al., 2021). An important line of research explores the effects of sponsored influencer postings. Studies in this line have demonstrated that strategic influencer communication can have positive impact on various outcomes such as purchase intentions (Li and Peng, 2021), brand evaluations (Breves et al., 2021), brand trust (Reinikainen et al., 2020), and consumers' corporate social responsibility (CSR) communication engagement (Cheng et al., 2021). Remarkably, influencers' brand endorsements provoke less defensive coping behaviours in consumers than most other persuasive formats (e.g., Boerman, 2020; De Jans and Hudders, 2020; Lou et al., 2019; Lou, 2021). Rather, followers tolerate or even appreciate many brand endorsements (Lou, 2021; Sweeney et al., 2022). Some researchers have pointed to the importance of follower–influencer relationships for explaining such effects. The concept of choice to capture these relationships is parasocial relationships (PSR). Following Horton and Wohl (1956), PSR refer to intimate relationships between media audiences and media personae. Research shows that high PSR with influencers leads to more positive persuasion outcomes (Breves et al., 2021; Farivar et al., 2021; Reinikainen et al., 2020). Besides PSR, another issue that has received much attention in influencer effects research is sponsorship disclosures. Such disclosures may have a negative effect on persuasion success (Evans et al., 2017; De Jans et al., 2018), but this effect, unsurprisingly, is moderated by PSR (Boerman and van Reijmersdal, 2020). Moreover, research has demonstrated that impartiality claims – when influencers explicitly state that they voice their own opinion without or even despite compensations – can magnify persuasion effects (Hwang and Jeong, 2016; Lee et al., 2021).

In contrast to effects research, studies that investigate the corporation's perspective on strategic influencer communication are somewhat rare (Ye et al., 2021). On a basic level, existing studies confirm that strategic influencer communication has become an important domain for corporate communication (e.g., Coll and Micó, 2019; Navarro et al., 2020; Wolf and Archer, 2018). More particularly, Lin et al. (2018) developed a five-stage strategy for setting up influencer campaigns. This model can be used for organizing the state of research on the management of strategic influencer communication.

In its first stage, *planning*, corporate communicators define the objectives of the campaign and determine the role of influencers. Influencer campaigns often represent isolated initiatives rather than sitting firmly in an integrated communication strategy (Borchers and Enke, 2021b; Leung et al., 2022). While some commentators have called for holistic approaches to influencer marketing (e.g., Voorveld, 2019), research on this issue is scarce (Coll and Micó, 2019).

In the second stage, *recognition*, corporate communicators identify relevant influencers. In this process, reach plays an important, albeit at times overrated role. Corporate communicators also emphasize the importance of other metrics such as engagement rates or rely on less quantifiable criteria such as the fit between influencer and brand, the experience of influencers, or the quality of their content (Borchers and Enke, 2021b; Childers et al., 2019).

In stage three, *alignment*, corporate communicators match their products with influencers and platforms. This step acknowledges findings that fit plays a crucial role in achieving desired persuasion outcomes (Breves et al., 2019; Mettenheim and Wiedmann, 2021).

In the fourth step, *motivation*, corporate communicators negotiate financial compensations or other forms of recognition for the services of influencers. Usually, influencers are willing to enter in collaborations only if they profit from doing so. Since influencer business models heavily rely on revenues from sponsorships, financial compensations are the major motivator (Archer and Harrigan, 2016). However, influencers can also benefit from other compensations such as exclusive opportunities for content creation or administrative assistance (Borchers and Enke, 2021b).

In the fifth step, *coordination*, corporate communicators negotiate, monitor, and support influencers in their conducts. In this step, the issue of controlling influencer conduct comes into play. As discussed in the next section, control options are severely limited in strategic influencer communication due to a logic of authenticity. Monitoring also includes the evaluation of influencer campaigns. Default key performance indicators (KPIs) are reach and number of interactions, but corporate communicators feel that these KPIs are inadequate (Gräve, 2019). In unclear settings, they therefore rather rely on comment sentiment. Besides, the relevance of less standardized KPIs such as valance analysis and content documentations and finally, gut feelings should not be underestimated (Borchers and Enke, 2021b).

WHAT IS CHANGING?

The Disruptive Nature of Influencer Communication

Social media influencers are indigenous to digital environments. As such, they occupy a newly created place in the communicative environments of corporations and this novelty, by nature, causes many changes. A first change concerns communication flows. Influencers' position as nodes in communication networks redirects such flows specifically for younger audiences. Corporate communicators have to decide how to react to this redirection, and the options range from ignoring to listening to actively interfering in these flows (Godes et al., 2005). Second and as elaborated in more detail above, influencers are included into these networks as peers. This status distinguishes them from other secondary stakeholders such as mainstream celebrities and journalists and puts their content in line with peer-based phenomena such as online reviews, forum posts, or brand communities. When taking this peer status seriously, influencer communication can be regarded as another manifestation of consumer empowerment (sensu Labrecque et al., 2013). Influencers are peer consumers, peer voters, peer patients and the like who share their experience with other consumers, voters, and patients. Their activities can thus increase information-based power (via content creation) and network-based power (via content distribution and moderation), and this increase in power challenges traditional structures that gave advantage to corporative actors. Third, influencer communication rests on a logic of authenticity (Duffy, 2017; Wellman et al., 2020), and this logic makes controlling influencer conduct a tricky business even within collaborations (Childers et al., 2019; Davies and Hobbs, 2020). Authenticity requires that influencers obtain greater degrees of freedom in collaborations than, for example, traditional communication agencies. Corporate interference with the influencer's content creation and distribution process threatens authenticity. Therefore, corporate communicators are challenged to let go of control (Borchers and Enke, 2021b) – an imperative that exists also with other types of peer-based UGC and that presents difficulties for control-expecting corporate communicators (Christodoulides, 2009).

Influencer Relations

As a reaction to these specific features of influencer communication, the adoption of an *influencer relations* approach (Borchers and Enke, 2021b) has been suggested. Influencer relations can be thought of as a counterpart to media relations. Just like influencers, journalists constitute an important secondary stakeholder group. While media relations seeks to establish good relations with media organizations and individual journalists, influencer relations focuses on relevant influencers.

258 *Handbook on digital corporate communication*

An independent influencer relations function pays tribute to failures at integrating influencers into media relations structures (Pang et al., 2016). These failures result from differences in work patterns of influencers and journalists. First, influencers work under different structural conditions than journalists (Pang et al., 2016; Stoldt et al., 2019). For example, journalists are usually associated with a larger media organization and can thus tap the organization's resources. Influencers, in contrast, work as a one-person media organization or with only small teams. This explains why influencers easily feel overwhelmed when organizations include them into their press mailing list – and why they oppose such a practice (Borchers and Enke, 2022). Second, the status of influencers depends on other activities than that of journalists, and this is why influencers contribute other inputs to collaborations than journalists. Third, collaborations with influencers rest on different control mechanisms because they are characterized by compensations, contractual relationships, and control and approval processes. These three differences explain why influencers should be addressed differently than journalists and why influencer relations deserves the status of an independent instrument.

Corporate Influencers

Another leverage point for organizations to benefit from influencer potential is the implementation of structures for corporate or in-house influencers (Brockhaus et al., 2020). In their attempt to harvest the person-brand capital of their employees, corporate communicators have started to conflate social media influencing with approaches to enable employees to communicate professionally (Mazzei, 2014). Corporate influencers resemble influencers in that they perform the same four activities in social media to establish an influencer status. Their crucial difference lies in the fact that corporate influencers are employees of the organization, while influencers are independent third-party actors. Following the definition of influencers presented earlier, corporate influencers can hence be defined as employees of an organization who have established a significant number of relevant relationships with a specific quality to and influence on organizational stakeholders through organization-related content production, content distribution, interaction, and personal appearance on the social web. As such, corporate influencers open valuable opportunities for corporate communication to communicate authentically while at the same time handling its control dilemma.

WHAT REMAINS THE SAME?

Despite the genuine novelty of the influencer phenomenon, some things remain the same for corporate communication. The logic behind strategic influencer communication resembles the well-known two-step-flow of communication (Katz and Lazarsfeld, 1955). As secondary stakeholders, influencers fulfil the function of disseminating corporation-specific information into their networks. This logic has motivated some researchers to identify influencers as opinion leaders (e.g. Casaló et al., 2020; Farivar et al., 2021). While this approach has some face validity, the clothes of opinion leadership fit only partly because opinion leaders contribute fewer resources to a corporation. Specifically, their input is limited to their ability to influence secondary stakeholders and the quality and number of their relationships (Enke and Borchers, 2018).

Digital corporate communication and social media influencers 259

Another aspect that remains the same is corporate communication's failure to engage in dialogue with stakeholders. Dialogic theory (Kent and Taylor, 2002) has since long identified dialogue as a basic principle of public relations, but research has repeatedly illustrated how corporate communication fails at adopting the dialogic features of Web 2.0 and beyond (Kent, 2013). The same is true for strategic influencer communication (Borchers and Enke, 2021b; Davies and Hobbs, 2020). For influencers, engaging in dialogue with their audiences is fundamental because their status as a microcelebrity depends on building ties with their followers. This should be a gateway for corporate communication to enter the dialogue. However, with the prevalence of the "advertising-led model to influencer engagement" (Wolf and Archer, 2018) that relies on short-term collaborations with influencers, most corporate communicators have chosen to outsource the dialogue to influencers rather than taking advantage of this gateway.

CRITICAL EXAMINATION

Strategic influencer communication has strengths but also weaknesses. In an early study on the management of influencer campaigns, Nadja Enke and I (Enke and Borchers, 2018) explored its capability from the perspective of communication managers (see Table 18.1).

Table 18.1 *Advantages of and challenges in strategic influencer communication as described by corporate communicators*

	Advantages	Challenges
Input	● Intrinsic motivation of influencers to post about products and brands ● Social media competencies of influencers ● Comparably cheap prices	● Lack of professionalism in some influencers ● Limited possibilities for control ● Incorrect metrics due to fake followers ● No systematic data on individual followerships ● Large investment of time/personnel in preparation and implementation
Output	● Reach of specific stakeholder groups (e.g. younger consumers) ● Attractiveness and quality of content ● Possibilities to present products in real life setting ● Higher flexibility in brand presentations ● Possibilities for storytelling	● Difficulties in predicting content quality ● Danger of critical statements by influencers
Outcome	● Authenticity and credibility of influencers and their content ● Possibilities for evaluation via tracking links, landing pages etc.	● Brand image associated with influencer image ● Possible decrease in effectiveness due to habituation effects ● No standardized controlling processes

Advantages of Collaborating with Influencers

Some advantages that corporate communicators see in strategic influencer communication are well known in the debate. It is common industry wisdom that strategic influencer communication allows addressing younger target audiences that are increasingly hard to reach via traditional mass media (Haenlein et al., 2020). Another key advantage lies in the authenticity

260 *Handbook on digital corporate communication*

of influencers and their content (Campbell and Farrell, 2020). Whereas corporations have difficulty in being perceived as authentic, they can leverage influencers' authenticity through collaborations

Yet the list of advantages is more multifaceted and includes also advantages that have received less attention in the debate. For instance, the costs for engaging influencers are comparably low. Although corporations pay large sums for securing the services of some (mega) influencers (Childers et al., 2019), the bulk of influencers charge prices that are lower than prices for advertisements in traditional mass media. Additionally, sponsored posts remain available on influencers' channels so that they can unfold their effect also at later points in time. Another advantage lies in a certain flexibility in brand presentations. Influencer followerships are usually younger than mass media audiences, and corporations take advantage of this by adding a younger image to their brand. Finally, many corporations struggle with building social media expertise in general and platform-specific expertise in particular. Collaborating with influencers offers a quick fix. Successful influencers have developed an understanding of platform logics as the foundation for their own success. Corporations can either outsource social media activities to influencers or, provided that appropriate learning structures exist, bring social media expertise in-house.

Challenges in Collaborating with Influencers

These advantages are contrasted by considerable challenges, and given the popularity of strategic influencer communication, it sometimes seems that these disadvantages are readily overlooked. A considerable challenge that is mentioned already above is the lack of control in influencer collaborations. Even if this lack only rarely results in undesired outcomes (Reinikainen et al., 2021) or even crises (Singh et al., 2020; Sng et al., 2019), it nevertheless requires extra effort of corporate communicators to coordinate collaborations and deal with mutual irritations.

Professionalism constitutes a more structural challenge. Although standards have been raised in many national industries so that, unlike in the early years, collaborating with influencers is much less of a gamble, complaints about a lack of professionalism are still prevalent when deadlines are broken, agreements ignored, and insufficient content quality delivered. While many influencers, sometimes with the help of a talent agency, undergo a professionalization process, the current stream of new and often underaged influencers who enter the industry provides persistent irritation. Moreover, even established influencers operate with rather limited resources so that mis-planning but also illnesses or private incidents (e.g., the often heard story about the boyfriend who broke up) quickly have an impact on agreements.

Professionalism relates to an even broader issue: influencer ethics. As a relatively young industry, the influencer industry still has to debate and define its ethics. At the same time, it is becoming apparent that simply transferring the ethics of other domains such as public relations, advertising, and journalism finds its limits in the peculiarities of influencer communication such as the relationships between followers and influencers and the constant border-crossing between organic and sponsored content. In many countries, the national industry has already managed to agree on some ethical foundations such as handling endorsements transparently and refraining from buying fake followers. Many other aspects, however, are less clear. For example, autonomy, sincerity, and loyalty remain debated issues. The lack of established ethical guidelines causes insecurities in corporate communicators because they do

Digital corporate communication and social media influencers 261

not know if their expectations are shared by other actors in the industry. Developing a code of ethics, as Wellman et al. (2020) advocate, might improve the situation. However, initiatives to this effect are rare, with Croatia, Czech Republic, and Germany (Borchers and Enke, 2021a) being some notable exceptions.

ILLUSTRATIVE EXAMPLE: UNILEVER INFLUENCER CAMPAIGN IN GERMANY

Strategic influencer communication requires corporate communication to revise some of its default approaches in managing campaigns to adjust them to the peculiarities of this new instrument. The following example illustrates what may happen if corporate communication fails to let go of control.

In 2017, Unilever booked a first influencer campaign for its detergent brand Coral in Germany. Using the hashtag #coralliebtdeinekleidung (#corallovesyourapparel), approximately 40 influencers and (minor) mainstream celebrities endorsed the brand on their Instagram profiles. The campaign gained broad attention that quickly turned to ridicule because of the settings in which the influencers presented the product. The plastic bottle with the detergent popped up in episodes from the influencers' everyday lives, in line with the air of ordinariness that surrounds influencers. The problem was, however, that these were episodes in which you do not usually have a bottle of detergent on hand. For example, posts showed influencers and Coral bottles, among others, on the steps leading towards an ancient stone building, leaning against a graffiti-covered wall, going for a bike ride, and in bed with the influencer's boyfriend. In the associated texts, influencers established a relationship between the episode and the brand. For example, the bed post text read: "Ad: This morning with him having coffee. The best days start with a cup of coffee and the most beautiful person by your side, right? Snuggle up under the bright white blanket again and snooze for a few minutes – lovely! #coralloveyourclothes #advertising". The campaign earned Unilever the attention of mainstream media, a debate in the trade press and jeering comments and parody posts on social media (most pointedly: the Coral bottle next to a pizza on the table of an Italian restaurant or wrapped around the neck as a woman's handbag). The general tenor was that the campaign posts appear unnatural and posed – in a word: inauthentic.

The campaign serves as a graphic lesson on how strategic influencer communication can go off the rails when applying traditional approaches too rigidly to campaign management. The crucial shortcoming here lies in the failure to let go of control. Unilever drew the boundaries too narrowly within which influencers were allowed to be creative. The campaign specifications prevented influencers from contributing their knowledge of what content works with their audiences. Rather, they pushed them into presentations that conflict with the authenticity demand of the genre. Followers willingly accept the integration of brands into influencer content because brands are an integral part of life in consumption societies. However, followers possess a keen sense of which portrayals are authentic.

While authenticity has many facets, in the Coral campaign the mismatch between setting and product broke the illusion that influencer content emerges from the influencer's everyday experiences. For instance, an Instagram user commented on the bed post: "Nice picture but so inappropriate with the detergent. You do not have to advertise everything just for money. Does not fit at all to your Instagram". This comment illustrates that genre conventions and thus audience expectations toward influencer communication differ from more traditional corporate formats of mass media communication such as advertising that do not follow a logic of authenticity. First, social media users do tolerate the commercial motivation of influencer posts, but only to a certain extent. The Coral posts are criticized for making their commercial motivation all too salient. This way, they also break the illusion that influencers act as peers. Second, the tolerance for exaggerations and pointed emphases that are characteristic for advertising is also limited. Authenticity in itself is a 'serious' concept that leaves little room for such playful and sometimes winking strategies.

This analysis of the Coral case discusses only one, albeit pointed, example of a failure in letting go of control. Examples are, however, legion. Collections of authenticity failure can be found all over the Internet, at times emerging from anti-fan communities (McRae, 2017). Sharing insights from the industry side, agency representatives offer many stories on the effort they put into convincing their clients to grant autonomy to influencers – sometimes successful, sometimes fruitless (Borchers and Enke, 2021b). Apparently, the control expectations that corporate communication has cultivated throughout decennia of engaging with mainstream media are hard to overcome.

CONCLUSION AND FUTURE DIRECTIONS

Within only a few years, strategic influencer communication has become a well-established domain in corporate communication. Although it is no magic bullet, it offers solutions to some pressing issues in corporate communication, such as addressing younger stakeholder groups, obtaining social media expertise, and creating content that stakeholders perceive as authentic.

As this chapter showed, research on strategic influencer communication has gained traction and many facets such as follower–influencer relationships, influencer–product fit, and influencer selection criteria have received considerable attention. At the same time, research has paid less attention to integrating strategic influencer communication into the body of established conceptual approaches in corporate communication. What needs to be clarified is how strategic influencer communication sits within approaches such as stakeholder relationship management, issues management, and organizational listening.

From a more practical perspective, one may suggest three promising directions for future research. First, the field would benefit from insights on how to integrate strategic influencer communication into wider communication strategies to make the best use of its strengths. Second, it seems instructive to explore how corporate communicators attempt to balance their need for control and influencers' need for creative freedom. Third, despite their considerable potentials, research on corporate influencers is sparse and requires further efforts.

REFERENCES

Archer, C. and Harrigan, P. (2016). Show me the money: How bloggers as stakeholders are challenging theories of relationship building in public relations. *Media International Australia*, *160*(1), 1–11.
Berryman, R. and Kavka, M. (2017). 'I guess a lot of people see me as a big sister or a friend': The role of intimacy in the celebrification of beauty vloggers. *Journal of Gender Studies*, *26*(3), 307–320.
Boerman, S. C. (2020). The effects of the standardized Instagram disclosure for micro- and meso-influencers. *Computers in Human Behavior*, *103*, 199–207.

Digital corporate communication and social media influencers 263

Boerman, S. C. and van Reijmersdal, E. A. (2020). Disclosing influencer marketing on YouTube to children: The moderating role of para-social relationship. *Frontiers in Psychology*, *10*, 3042.

Borchers, N. S. (2019). Editorial: Social media influencers in strategic communication. *International Journal of Strategic Communication*, *13*(4), 255–260.

Borchers, N. S. and Enke, N. (2021a). Influencer-Kommunikation benötigt ethische Regeln. Ein Ethikkodex für die Branche. *Communicatio Socialis*, *54*(4), 537–547.

Borchers, N. S. and Enke, N. (2021b). Managing strategic influencer communication: A systematic overview on emerging planning, organization, and evaluation routines. *Public Relations Review*, *47*(3), 102041.

Borchers, N. S. and Enke, N. (2022). "I've never seen a client say: 'Tell the influencer not to label this as sponsored'": An exploration into influencer industry ethics. *Public Relations Review*, *48*(5), 102235.

Breves, P., Amrehn, J., Heidenreich, A., Liebers, N., and Schramm, H. (2021). Blind trust? The importance and interplay of parasocial relationships and advertising disclosures in explaining influencers' persuasive effects on their followers. *International Journal of Advertising*, *40*(7), 1209–1229.

Breves, P., Liebers, N., Abt, M., and Kunze, A. (2019). The perceived fit between Instagram influencers and the endorsed brand: How influencer–brand fit affects source credibility and persuasive effectiveness. *Journal of Advertising Research*, *59*(4), 440–454.

Brockhaus, J., Dicke, L., Hauck, P., and Volk, S. C. (2020). Employees as corporate ambassadors: A qualitative study exploring the perceived benefits and challenges from three perspectives. In A. T. Verčič, R. Tench, and S. Einwiller (eds.), *Joy: Using strategic communication to improve well-being and organizational success* (pp. 115–134). Bingley: Emerald Publishing.

Campbell, C. and Farrell, J. R. (2020). More than meets the eye: The functional components underlying influencer marketing. *Business Horizons*, *63*(4), 469–479.

Casaló, L. V., Flavián, C., and Ibáñez-Sánchez, S. (2020). Influencers on Instagram: Antecedents and consequences of opinion leadership. *Journal of Business Research*, *117*, 510–519.

Cheng, Y., Hung-Baesecke, C.-J. F., and Chen, Y.-R. R. (2021). Social media influencer effects on CSR communication: The role of influencer leadership in opinion and taste. *International Journal of Business Communication*. https://doi.org/10.1177/23294884211035112.

Childers, C. C., Lemon, L. L., and Hoy, M. G. (2019). #Sponsored #ad: Agency perspective on influencer marketing campaigns. *Journal of Current Issues & Research in Advertising*, *40*(3), 258–274.

Christodoulides, G. (2009). Branding in the post-internet era. *Marketing Theory*, *9*(1), 141–144.

Cocker, H., Mardon, R., and Daunt, K. L. (2021). Social media influencers and transgressive celebrity endorsement in consumption community contexts. *European Journal of Marketing*, *55*(7), 1841–1872.

Coll, P. and Micó, J. L. (2019). Influencer marketing in the growth hacking strategy of digital brands. *Observatorio (OBS*)*, *13*(2). https://doi.org/10.15847/obsOBS13220191409.

Colliander, J. and Dahlèn, M. (2011). Following the fashionable friend: The power of social media. *Journal of Advertising Research*, *51*(1), 313–320.

Davies, C. and Hobbs, M. (2020). Irresistible possibilities: Examining the uses and consequences of social media influencers for contemporary public relations. *Public Relations Review*, *46*(5), 101983.

De Jans, S., Cauberghe, V., and Hudders, L. (2018). How an advertising disclosure alerts young adolescents to sponsored vlogs: The moderating role of a peer-based advertising literacy intervention through an informational vlog. *Journal of Advertising*, *47*(4), 309–325.

De Jans, S. and Hudders, L. (2020). Disclosure of vlog advertising targeted to children. *Journal of Interactive Marketing*, *52*, 1–19.

Delisle, M.-P. and Parmentier, M.-A. (2016). Navigating person-branding in the fashion blogosphere. *Journal of Global Fashion Marketing*, *7*(3), 211–224.

Duffy, B. E. (2017). *(Not) getting paid to do what you love: Gender, social media, and aspirational work*. New Haven: Yale University Press.

Enke, N. and Borchers, N. S. (2018). *Management strategischer Influencer-Kommunikation: Projektbericht*. Leipzig. https://www.slideshare.net/communicationmanagement/management-strategischer-influencer-kommunikation-ergebnisbericht-2018.

Enke, N. and Borchers, N. S. (2019). Social media influencers in strategic communication: A conceptual framework of strategic social media influencer communication. *International Journal of Strategic Communication*, *13*(4), 261–277.

Evans, N. J., Phua, J., Lim, J., and Jun, H. (2017). Disclosing Instagram influencer advertising: The effects of disclosure language on advertising recognition, attitudes, and behavioral intent. *Journal of Interactive Advertising, 17*(2), 138–149.

Farivar, S., Wang, F., and Yuan, Y. (2021). Opinion leadership vs. para-social relationship: Key factors in influencer marketing. *Journal of Retailing and Consumer Services, 59*, 102371.

Freberg, K., Graham, K., McGaughey, K., and Freberg, L. A. (2011). Who are the social media influencers? A study of public perceptions of personality. *Public Relations Review, 37*(1), 90–92.

García-Rapp, F. (2017). Popularity markers on YouTube's attention economy: The case of Bubzbeauty. *Celebrity Studies, 8*(2), 228–245.

Godes, D., Mayzlin, D., Chen, Y., Das, S., Dellarocas, C., Pfeiffer, B., Libai, B., Sen, S., Shi, M., and Verlegh, P. (2005). The firm's management of social interactions. *Marketing Letters, 16*(3–4), 415–428.

Gräve, J.-F. (2019). What KPIs are key? Evaluating performance metrics for social media influencers. *Social Media + Society, 5*(3). https://doi.org/10.1177/2056305119865475.

Haenlein, M., Anadol, E., Farnsworth, T., Hugo, H., Hunichen, J., and Welte, D. (2020). Navigating the new era of influencer marketing: How to be successful on Instagram, TikTok, & co. *California Management Review, 63*(1), 5–25.

Horton, D. and Wohl, R. (1956). Mass communication and para-social interaction. *Psychiatry, 19*(3), 215–229.

Hudders, L., De Jans, S., and De Veirman, M. (2021). The commercialization of social media stars: A literature review and conceptual framework on the strategic use of social media influencers. *International Journal of Advertising, 40*(3), 327–375.

Hwang, Y. and Jeong, S.-H. (2016). "This is a sponsored blog post, but all opinions are my own": The effects of sponsorship disclosure on responses to sponsored blog posts. *Computers in Human Behavior, 62*, 528–535.

Jerslev, A. (2016). In the time of the microcelebrity: Celebrification and the YouTuber Zoella. *International Journal of Communication, 10*, article 19. http://ijoc.org/index.php/ijoc/article/view/5078/1822.

John, N. A. (2016). *The age of sharing.* Cambridge: Polity Press.

Katz, E. and Lazarsfeld, P. F. (1955). *Personal influence: The part played by people in the flow of mass communications.* London: Routledge.

Kent, M. L. (2013). Using social media dialogically: Public relations role in reviving democracy. *Public Relations Review, 39*(4), 337–345.

Kent, M. L. and Taylor, M. (2002). Toward a dialogic theory of public relations. *Public Relations Review, 28*(1), 21–37.

Khamis, S., Ang, L., and Welling, R. (2017). Self-branding, 'micro-celebrity' and the rise of Social Media Influencers. *Celebrity Studies, 8*(2), 191–208.

Labrecque, L. I., vor dem Esche, J., Mathwick, C., Novak, T. P., and Hofacker, C. F. (2013). Consumer power: Evolution in the digital age. *Journal of Interactive Marketing, 27*(4), 257–269.

Lee, H.-H. M. (2016). Making of celebrities: A comparative analysis of Taiwanese and American fashion bloggers. In P. Moreau and S. Puntoni (eds.), *Advances in consumer research* (pp. 319–323). Association for Consumer Research.

Lee, S. S., Vollmer, B. T., Yue, C. A., and Johnson, B. K. (2021). Impartial endorsements: Influencer and celebrity declarations of non-sponsorship and honesty. *Computers in Human Behavior, 122*, 106858.

Leung, F. F., Gu, F. F., and Palmatier, R. W. (2022). Online influencer marketing. *Journal of the Academy of Marketing Science, 50*(2), 226–251.

Li, Y. and Peng, Y. (2021). Influencer marketing: Purchase intention and its antecedents. *Marketing Intelligence & Planning, 39*(7), 960–978.

Lin, H.-C., Bruning, P. F., and Swarna, H. (2018). Using online opinion leaders to promote the hedonic and utilitarian value of products and services. *Business Horizons, 61*(3), 431–442.

Lou, C. (2021). Social media influencers and followers: Theorization of a trans-parasocial relation and explication of its implications for influencer advertising. *Journal of Advertising, 51*(1). https://doi.org/10.1080/00913367.2021.1880345.

Lou, C., Tan, S.-S., and Chen, X. (2019). Investigating consumer engagement with influencer- vs. brand-promoted ads: The roles of source and disclosure. *Journal of Interactive Advertising*, *19*(3), 169–186.

Luoma-aho, V., Pirttimäki, T., Maity, D., Munnukka, J., and Reinikainen, H. (2019). Primed authenticity: How priming impacts authenticity perception of social media influencers. *International Journal of Strategic Communication*, *13*(4), 352–365.

Mazzei, A. (2014). Internal communication for employee enablement: Strategies in American and Italian companies. *Corporate Communications: An International Journal*, *19*(1), 82–95.

McRae, S. (2017). "Get off my internets": How anti-fans deconstruct lifestyle bloggers' authenticity work. *Persona Studies*, *3*(1), 13–27.

Mettenheim, W. von, and Wiedmann, K.-P. (2021). The complex triad of congruence issues in influencer marketing. *Journal of Consumer Behaviour*, *20*(5), 1277–1296.

Navarro, C., Moreno, A., Molleda, J. C., Khalil, N., and Verhoeven, P. (2020). The challenge of new gatekeepers for public relations. A comparative analysis of the role of social media influencers for European and Latin American professionals. *Public Relations Review*, *46*(2), 101881.

Pang, A., Tan, E. Y., Lim, R. S.-Q., Kwan, T. Y.-M., and Lakhanpal, P. B. (2016). Building effective relations with social media influencers in Singapore. *Media Asia*, *43*(1), 56–68.

Reinikainen, H., Munnukka, J., Maity, D., and Luoma-aho, V. (2020). 'You really are a great big sister': Parasocial relationships, credibility, and the moderating role of audience comments in influencer marketing. *Journal of Marketing Management*, *32*(1), 1–20.

Reinikainen, H., Tan, T. M., Luoma-aho, V., and Salo, J. (2021). Making and breaking relationships on social media: The impacts of brand and influencer betrayals. *Technological Forecasting and Social Change*, *171*, 120990.

Santora, J. (2021). *100 Influencer marketing statistics for 2021.* Influencer Marketing Hub. https://in fluencermarketinghub.com/influencer-marketing-statistics/.

Senft, T. M. (2008). *Camgirls: Celebrity and community in the age of social networks.* New York: Peter Lang.

Singh, J., Crisafulli, B., La Quamina, T., and Xue, M. T. (2020). 'To trust or not to trust': The impact of social media influencers on the reputation of corporate brands in crisis. *Journal of Business Research*, *119*, 464–480.

Sng, K., Au, T. Y., and Pang, A. (2019). Social media influencers as a crisis risk in strategic communication: Impact of indiscretions on professional endorsements. *International Journal of Strategic Communication*, *13*(4), 301–320.

Stoldt, R., Wellman, M., Ekdale, B., and Tully, M. (2019). Professionalizing and profiting: The rise of intermediaries in the social media influencer industry. *Social Media + Society*, *5*(1). https://doi.org/10 .1177/2056305119832587.

Sweeney, E., Lawlor, M.-A., and Brady, M. (2022). Teenagers' moral advertising literacy in an influencer marketing context. *International Journal of Advertising*, *41*(1), 1–24.

van Driel, L. and Dumitrica, D. (2021). Selling brands while staying "authentic": The professionalization of Instagram influencers. *Convergence: The Journal of Research into New Media Technologies*, *27*(1), 66–84.

Voorveld, H. A. (2019). Brand communication in social media: A research agenda. *Journal of Advertising*, *48*(1), 14–26.

Wellman, M. L., Stoldt, R., Tully, M., and Ekdale, B. (2020). Ethics of authenticity: Social media influencers and the production of sponsored content. *Journal of Media Ethics*, *35*(2), 68–82.

Wolf, K. and Archer, C. (2018). Public relations at the crossroads: The need to reclaim core public relations competencies in digital communication. *Journal of Communication Management*, *22*(4), 494–509.

Ye, G., Hudders, L., De Jans, S., and De Veirman, M. (2021). The value of influencer marketing for business: A bibliometric analysis and managerial implications. *Journal of Advertising*, *50*(2), 160–178.

19. Digital corporate communication and gamification

Jens Seiffert-Brockmann and Ariadne Neureiter

INTRODUCTION

With the emergence of digital technologies, corporate communication has changed fundamentally (Argenti, 2006). In light of saturated markets and stakeholders' perceptions of information overload regarding corporations, products or services, stakeholders increasingly tend to show signs of resistance toward the huge amount of communication from corporations with which they are confronted every day (Lindsey, 2005). Instead of unidirectional messages from corporations, stakeholders increasingly seek unique corporate experiences including adventures and fun (Huotari and Hamari, 2017). As a consequence, corporate communication has changed from traditional one-directional to two-way communication, characterized not only by more dynamic approaches like dialogical communication, but also by adding elements that lead to superior experiences with the corporation (Argenti, 2006; Verhoef et al., 2009). One way to generate fun experiences and engage stakeholders is using gamification (Nobre and Ferreira, 2017). Gamified communication seems like a promising strategy to engage stakeholders by applying game elements and mechanics in non-game contexts (Deterding et al., 2011a), to raise motivation and change attitudes and influence behaviour of said stakeholders (Hamari et al., 2014).

Gamification in the communication context refers to either the use of individual game elements introduced into the communication context (Deterding et al., 2011a), or the use of the expressive power of games as narrative media (Bogost, 2007) to try to convey ideas and create community by applying gamification as a form of corporate storytelling. In that reading, gamification channels collective organizational storytelling to foster sense making in the relationships between a company and its relevant stakeholder groups (Lundqvist et al., 2013). The potential for corporate communication is apparent. Instead of writing long and uninspiring reports on a company's mission, its corporate social responsibility (CSR) initiatives or its merits as an employer, gamification can convey these issues through a digital, gamified simulation and engage stakeholders in a playful way. This seems like a great new possibility to communicate if we think of problems such as information overload (Edmunds and Morris, 2000) and psychological reactance (Brehm and Brehm, 1981), which are inherent to more mainstream tools of corporate communication.

While storytelling has long been deeply intertwined with corporate communication (Gill, 2015), nothing of the sort can be said about video games, which have been widely neglected as an object worthy of study (Seiffert and Nothhaft, 2015). But with the global revenues in mobile gaming, and gaming in general, ever rising (Wijman, 2018), gamification in the external as well internal communication context has been paid more and more attention by scholars of human resources (Gerdenitsch et al., 2020; Silic et al., 2019) and marketing (Hofacker et al., 2016; Hsu and Chen, 2018). Although recently, several companies have implemented game elements in their internal and external communication strategies, far too little scrutiny has been applied to gamification practice and research in corporate communication (Nobre and Ferreira, 2017). It is thus pertinent to ask: What is the contribution of gamification to corporate communication beyond the realm of marketing and human resources communication? Badham and Luoma-aho define digital corporate communication (DCC) in general as "An organization's strategic management of digital technologies, digital infrastructures and digitalization processes to improve communication with internal and external stakeholders and more broadly within society for the maintenance of organizational tangible and intangible assets" (Chapter 1 in this volume, p. 9).

Against this background, this chapter will explore gamification, and digital games in general, along two different avenues: First, as a corporate communication *tool* that is applied to influence attitudes, opinions and decisions of key stakeholder groups. Second, as a *strategy* that uses the narrative and expressive power of game and play to convey ideas important to the company through corporate storytelling – the linchpin being the building and maintenance of organization–public relationships in gamified communities. Following Badham and Luoma-aho's account of DCC in this volume, if applied strategically and managed properly, gamification can very much contribute to the creation and maintenance of organizational intangible assets.

DEFINITIONS OF THE TOPIC AND PREVIOUS STUDIES

Gamification as a Buzzword

With the rise of information and communication technologies (ICT), gamification has become one of the buzzwords in strategic communication industries such as corporate communication and marketing. Gamification is defined as the implementation of game principles in non-gaming environments (Deterding et al., 2011a) to achieve a wide range of attitudinal and behavioural change. The term *gamification* encompasses two developments: the introduction of games in everyday life and the transfer of positive game effects such as entertainment and engagement to non-game products or services (Deterding et al., 2011a). The goal is to make use of the motivational potential of games by incorporating game elements into non-game contexts (Sailer et al., 2017).

Gamification has been applied within a variety of different fields such as health communication, engineering, learning, human resources and, of course, marketing and management (Boyle et al., 2016). Whenever incentive structures are involved, gamification is one of the driving principles behind the application. Gamification is at the core of nudging concepts (Thaler and Sunstein, 2009) – that is, from an organizational point of view, decision structures that make it easy for individuals to make decisions the company desires. In that regard, gamification is present whenever customers rate their experience, and users then perceive it, when companies install bonus systems or dole out customer status ladders. They try to engage users to contribute to their cause by generating (positive) content about their brands and services, and thus aim at influencing others who are not yet in the company's orbit. Generally, gamification can be classified based on the gamified design that is used, including game elements and mechanics addressing achievement needs, immersion needs and social interaction needs (Ryan and Deci, 2000; Xi and Hamari, 2020).

Gamification as a Tool or as a Strategy

In light of corporate communication, gamification can be applied in two general ways: as a corporate communication *tool* or as a *strategy* through corporate storytelling. The first option describes achievement-related game features including various game elements and mechanics. For instance, points, badges, leaderboards, progression bars, challenges, stories, teams, avatars and goals are used as a corporate communication *tool* (Xi and Hamari, 2020).

The latter option describes gamification and digital games as a systematic approach to community-building and highlights the chance of tightening the relationships between stakeholders and company. Bogost (2007) argues that the unique feature of gaming is its expressive power, which is unleashed on the basis of the concept of *procedural rhetoric*. As Bogost defines it, procedural rhetoric is "a technique for making arguments with computational systems and for unpacking computational arguments others have created" (2007, p. 3). Whereas classical mass media need to rely on verbal and visual arguments to make a point, games can convey ideas through their code, ideas that can be experienced by users virtually as they are programmed into the software. Here, immersion-related features of gamification based on the immersion of users in "self-directed inquisitive activity" (Xi and Hamari, 2020, p. 450) possibly lead to feelings of flow (Csikszentmihalyi, 2008) and are used to create unique user experiences and adventures.

However, it needs to be stressed that gamification is at this point a conceptual idea that has not yet realized its full potential. As the next section shows, there is ample evidence that gamification can have positive effects on important variables such as motivation, engagement or attitude. But many of these insights stem from experimental studies outside the realm of corporate communication. Thus, gamification still has to prove its practicality in the real world of business.

Effects of Gamification

Generally, previous empirical research in the gamification context is characterized by positive effects of gamification on various outcomes in different disciplines (Hamari et al., 2014). Overall, gamification is positively associated with persuasive effects on users' motivation, attitudes, engagement and enjoyment (Hamari et al., 2014; Hamari and Koivisto, 2015). While gamification seems to be popular in the education context, showing positive effects on students' engagement with educational content (Gatti et al., 2019), learning (Legaki et al., 2020), and knowledge retention (Putz et al., 2020), in the commercial context, gamification has not been thoroughly researched yet (Hamari et al., 2014).

In the context of corporate communication, two branches of effect studies are interesting as they shed light on internal and external communication processes related to gamification in communication addressing different stakeholder groups. Although these effect studies are conducted in disciplines other than strategic communication and thus do not consider previous public relations or strategic communication research and stakeholder engagement nor derive implications for strategic communication practices, they give important insights into effects of corporate gamified communication on stakeholders (Seiffert-Brockmann et al., 2017).

Gamified Internal Communication

The first branch is anchored in human resources research where gamification is seen as a management tool inside corporations to address employees (Mollick and Werbach, 2015). Scholars in this field have investigated internal communication processes addressing the question of how gamified communication and work systems can keep employees motivated for work tasks and engaged in work processes. More precisely, within the field of human resources, gamification is seen as a tool with which organizational messages can be spread in an engaging way among employees (Cardador et al., 2017). Consequently, gamification is included in recruitment, training and development processes (Deterding et al., 2011a). Overall, positive effects of gamification on work-related factors such as employees' work satisfaction, performance, goal achievement, and loyalty toward the corporation are reported (for an overview, see Mollick and Werbach, 2015; Larson, 2020; Oprescu et al., 2014). In line with this, Silic and colleagues (2019) who see gamification as "a communication method" (p. 273) demonstrated that employees' job satisfaction as well as engagement is increased by integrating game elements and mechanics into existing human resources management procedures and practices (Silic et al., 2019). Similarly, Gerdenitsch and colleagues (2020) suggested that organizational gamification positively influences affective and informational pathways enhancing both employees' work enjoyment and productivity.

Gamified External Communication

The second stream is characterized by research questioning how gamification affects consumers and their perceptions of corporations and brands (Smith and Just, 2009). Studies in marketing communication are concerned with communication about the corporation, or the offered product or service in a game-oriented way, for instance, by including elements of storytelling (Xi and Hamari, 2020). Drawing on marketing research, gamification is seen as an "effective technique for brand management" as it is positively associated with consumers' brand engagement and, in turn, with brand equity (Xi and Hamari, 2020, p. 1) or self-brand connections (Berger et al., 2018). Moreover, gamification in marketing communication increases positive brand attitudes (Yang et al., 2017), satisfaction with the brand, brand love and, in turn, brand loyalty, positive word-of-mouth and resistance to negative information about the brand (Hsu and Chen, 2018).

Although human resources and marketing research have showed promising effects of gamified internal and external communication processes in corporate environments, researchers in the corporate communication, public relations and strategic communication fields have not examined gamification in much detail yet (Seiffert and Nothhaft, 2015). Only a few of these studies showed that gamification can positively influence stakeholder engagement (Seiffert-Brockmann et al., 2017) or attitude change (Ruggiero, 2015). In general, so far there has been little inquiry into the contribution of gamification to stakeholder engagement – that is, "practices the organization undertakes to involve stakeholders in a positive manner in organizational activities" (Greenwood, 2007, p. 318) – let alone its effects.

270 *Handbook on digital corporate communication*

Elements of Gamification

To differentiate gamification from related concepts like playfulness and toys, we draw on the concept of *paida* and *ludus* (Caillois, 2001; see also Deterding et al., 2011a). According to Caillois (2001), *paida* ('playing') is characterized by free choice of how to play. In contrast, *ludus* ('gaming') refers to structured, rule-based and goal-driven play. In other words, gaming and games have a different underlying *mode* of playful behaviour based on stricter rules and defined goals than playful designs and toys (Groh, 2012). Thus, when we look at gamification in corporate communication, we focus on game designs with defined rules and goals rather than freedom of choice characterized by explorative playing techniques (Deterding et al., 2011a).

Another distinction of the concept of gamification has to be made regarding serious games. Serious games, first introduced by the US military and nowadays used in various fields like education and business, offer users the possibility to play a game that goes beyond entertainment by including educational material (Laamarti et al., 2014). While gamification uses individual game elements, serious games are described as 'fully-developed' games including all conditions (i.e., mechanisms and elements) of a 'normal' game (Deterding et al., 2011a; Sailer et al., 2017, p. 372). In the strategic communication context, serious games like advergames that incorporate the promotion of a brand, product or service in a game are popular (Laamarti et al., 2014).

According to the "elemental definition" of Deterding and colleagues (2011a), the term gamification refers to the usage of single game elements independently of users' perceptions of the gamified environment (Sailer et al., 2017, p. 372). Following the authors, game elements are "a set of building blocks" that are characteristic of games such as points, badges, leaderboards, performance graphs (progress bars), avatars, meaningful stories or teammates (Deterding et al., 2011a, p. 12; Sailer et al., 2017; Werbach and Hunter, 2012). While points are a basic element of gamification that provide feedback about users' progress in games, badges additionally visually represent this progress and function as status symbols (Werbach and Hunter, 2012). Leaderboards show which player is the best in a game by accordingly ranking players regarding their success (Sailer et al., 2017). Performance graphs give graphic feedback based on the achievement of the individual player compared to players' past performance in the gamified environment (Sailer et al., 2013). Meaningful stories, which provide an immersive digital environment, form the framework within which a game takes place (Sailer et al., 2017). Moreover, avatars represent the players in the gamification setting (Werbach and Hunter, 2012) as a means to express one's identity digitally. Usually, users are actively involved in the selection of avatars or in the creation of their individual avatar (Kapp, 2012). Lastly, teammates are other real or fictional players with whom players can decide to cooperate or compete (Kapp, 2012).

However, besides the elemental perspective, gamification can be also understood as practices that evoke game-like experiences by users independently of the use of certain game elements (Werbach, 2014). According to Werbach (2014, p. 6), from a users' perspective, gamification can be described as "the process of making activities more game-like" (Leclercq et al., 2018). With this understanding, Werbach (2014) highlights a procedural perspective pointing to the underlying mechanisms that gamification entails and that are experienced by users (Werbach, 2014).

By extending the elemental definition of gamification with the procedural one, gamification could have several potential contributions to the various fields of corporate communication. With game-like interactions, corporations can offer stakeholders unique experiences that could positively influence value creation (Huotari and Hamari, 2017). More precisely, with its procedural rhetoric (Bogost, 2007) involving corporate storytelling (Lundqvist et al., 2013) and corporate communities (Nobre and Ferreira, 2017), gamification could contribute to corporate communication by engaging stakeholders based on corporate values (Seiffert-Brockmann et al., 2017).

Procedural Rhetoric and Gamification

Bogost (2007) suggested that games inherit a persuasive power by employing a procedural rhetoric. More precisely, representations and interactions (in games) can initiate persuasion processes renouncing words or pictures (Bogost, 2007). Due to this procedural rhetoric of gamification, messages are not necessarily shown in written or visual form in games; rather they arise from the story and its rhetoric by showing "how things work" (Bogost, 2007, p. 29). In other words, by following the procedure of the game, the message is indirectly conveyed to users as they "enact the meaning of the game rather than to perceive it passively" (Smith and Just, 2009, p. 57). In this framework, the active user holds a special role: While playing, s/he interactively constructs the arguments in line with their own persuasive messages and in turn, experiences sense making of these messages (Aristotle's enthymeme; Bogost, 2007). Drawing on these assumptions, Bogost (2007) comes to the conclusion that if users actively create their arguments of persuasive messages, effects based on these messages might be stronger and provide more intriguing and relatable representations of these messages than more common persuasive attempts such as traditional advertising can offer (Bogost, 2007). In the same vein, to build corporate relationships, marketing scholars and practitioners suggest familiarizing stakeholders with (1) corporate narratives by directly integrating them into gamified corporate stories, and with (2) corporate activities (i.e., development or promotion processes) by building communities around their interests (Healy and McDonagh, 2013). A pioneer in this genre was the US Army with its first person shooter *America's Army* (2002). Unlike most commercial shooters, *America's Army* incorporates the rules and regulations from the army handbook into the programming, and thus creates a more realistic representation of a special ops experience. As a recruitment tool, *America's Army* is designed to convey its idea of team play into the digital realm to attract talent and build an active community of gamers.

Gamification as Corporate Storytelling

Nowadays, corporations not only promote the advantages and benefits of their products or services, they also communicate underlying values and ideas that brought them to launch their products or to offer their services in the form of stories (Costa Sanchez, 2014). Corporate storytelling addresses different aspects of corporations giving them a 'face' (Ertemel, 2021) and guides the pattern-seeking processes of its recipients by presenting relevant content in a narrative form (Seiffert-Brockmann et al., 2021). For instance, corporate storytelling explains corporate activities, differentiating their work and character from other similar corporations, and emotionally connecting their stakeholders to the organization (Costa Sanchez, 2014). With storytelling, corporations aim at creating a discourse that is influenced by the corporations' ideology and identity. From the corporations' perspective, the best-case scenario is to persuade stakeholders with stories that trigger emotions, which then influence stakeholders' positive attitudes toward the corporation, and, in turn, increase future support (e.g., purchase intentions) (Lundqvist et al., 2013).

Gamification, which incorporates fictional realms and emotional stories with interactive game elements, is as a new corporate communication *strategy* to engage stakeholders, not only on a cognitive level, but also on an emotional one. Thus, gamification, known to evoke engagement (Seiffert-Brockmann et al., 2017), seems like a promising strategy for corporations to foster engagement by building upon storytelling. In fact, corporations increasingly use gamified storytelling elements to reach their goal to create unique corporate experiences for stakeholders (Huotari and Hamari, 2012). However, at this point, gamification as a means to materialize strategic storytelling is largely just a potential of what could be. The occasional implementation of gamified applications as gimmicks is the norm and a thorough implementation in alignment with corporate strategy is the exception.

Relationship Building: Creating Gamified Communities

One way to build corporate relationships with stakeholders is the development of communities around the interests of stakeholders to enhance their engagement (Brodie et al., 2011; Healy and McDonagh, 2013). In line with this, several studies have shown the importance of corporations' interactive platforms in engaging stakeholders and developing value co-creation experiences – that is, reciprocal value creation for the corporation as well as its stakeholders (Aarikka-Stenroos and Jaakkola, 2012; Nobre and Ferreira, 2017).

Social interaction-related features of gamification that are characterized by teams and groups can be used by corporations as a communication *tool* to evoke social interaction between users (Kovisto and Hamari, 2019; Xi and Hamari, 2020). Game elements such as teammates and leaderboards can induce and foster cooperation or competition (Malone, 1981). Leclercq and colleagues (2018) empirically supported this idea by showing that during a gamified contest, community-related game mechanics like cooperation and competition positively influenced consumer engagement by improving customer experience. Additionally, Seiffert-Brockmann and colleagues (2017) showed that besides achievement motivation, stakeholders' social motivation, that might be induced by gamified teams and groups, influenced stakeholders' engagement with corporations.

WHAT IS CHANGING?

Although gamification existed before the advent of ICT, the use of gamification within corporate communication changed with the emergence of these digital technologies, because corporations needed to look for new strategies to adapt to the new digital logic (Nobre and Ferreira, 2017; Payne et al., 2008). Since ICTs are much more strongly characterized by two-way communication than traditional mass media (e.g., newspapers, television, radio), corporations needed to rethink their communication strategies that were traditionally more reliant on unidirectional communication activities (e.g., Costa Sanchez, 2014). Also from stakeholders' perspectives, changes took place due to the emergence of ICT. Thanks to the Internet, stakeholders can and want to play a more active role in communication processes

Digital corporate communication and gamification 273

with corporations (e.g., co-creators). They are no longer satisfied with traditional one-way communication (i.e., traditional advertising), and generally have formed new patterns of media consumption tending to ignore traditional media and communication approaches (Costa Sanchez, 2014; Ertemel, 2021). As a result, instead of traditional channels (advertising on TV, etc.), stakeholders prefer immersive adventures and emotional experiences that co-create value with corporations in a collaborative gamified environment (Hollebeek et al., 2014).

Gamification, which enables these experiences, could positively contribute to new forms of corporate communication, building upon the new digital logic of communication. Further, due to the worldwide outbreak of Covid-19 beginning in early 2020, and the subsequent increase in out-of-home media and home office work, the use of digital communication technologies increased as well and gamification could become an indispensable part of internal and external digital communication processes in corporations (Gupta et al., 2022). The decrease in personal contact among employees and with key stakeholder groups has left a void that could be filled with gamified experiences on digital platforms. Instead of meeting people via physical touchpoints such as in the office, corporate communication could largely work through avatar-based communication in cyberspace (Davis and Moscato, 2018), a concept that has existed at least since the invention of the game *Second Life* in 2003, and which has recently been reintroduced by Facebook as the metaverse.

WHAT REMAINS THE SAME?

Games and gamification did not only just emerge with digital technologies (Deterding et al., 2011b). Generally, game and play are universal features of humans (Huizinga, 1949) – their origins lie deep in our species' history, and are present today in all societies and cultures across the globe. Playing is an integral part of growing up and fundamental for individuals to learn to cope with their social environments. In other words, gaming and playing are socially constitutive processes (Tomasello, 2000). Long before digital technologies became ubiquitous in our daily social and professional lives, game elements were used to create fun and engagement in different non-game situations in offline contexts (Deterding et al., 2011b).

CRITICAL EXAMINATION

Although there are advantages of implementing game elements in non-game contexts, gamification also can have negative effects, especially from the users' perspective. Although much research of gamification has focused on positive effects, some scholars draw attention to the possibility that gamification might be a 'double edged sword' if not introduced well (Mollick and Rothbard, 2014, p. 35). Together, these studies outline a critical role for users' consent to the inclusion of game elements into non-game contexts. As soon as games become mandatory, the positive effects of playing could be mitigated (Mollick and Rothbard, 2014). 'Top-down' decisions to have fun without the individuals' consent could lead to boomerang effects resulting in reduced positive effects from gameplay (Mollick and Rothbard, 2014).

In the context of corporate communication, this indicates that gamification should be coordinated with stakeholders and they should generally agree with the implementation of game elements and mechanics into communication strategies. If possible, stakeholders should even be consulted and integrated into the process of creating the gamified digital community. If legitimacy of gaming in the communication context is not given and stakeholders' choice about what they want to play is restricted, corporations could end up with practices that lead to unintended stakeholder effects (Mollick and Rothbard, 2014). Developing gamified environments and integrating serious game content is hard enough as it is. Unlike entertainment games, which are played for the sake of playing, strategically positioned business content has to be integrated without overly disturbing the flow of the gamified experience. Therefore, gamified content has to be fine-tuned to the stakeholder group in question. Equivalent to the phenomenon of gamer rage in video games, poorly applied gamification could result in user frustration when the application provides no apparent value to the stakeholder.

The decision of which game elements to include in corporate communication strategies can be decisive, not only with stakeholder participation in mind, but also in light of communication ethics. Procedural rhetoric is no apparent mode of persuasion, since the source code cannot be read and understood like a verbal or visual argument. In an immersive gamified environment, users might be totally oblivious of the underlying process, and thus might not recognize that a corporate idea is being conveyed to them through the gamification experience. Furthermore, gamification often includes competitive game elements, such as ranking lists and leaderboards (Deterding et al., 2011a). Although competition might motivate high performing individuals, low performing individuals might feel demotivated or even stressed by it (Preist et al., 2014) and it could reduce individuals' altruism (Duffy and Kornienko, 2010).

Another downside of gamification is the potential for addiction (Kim and Werbach, 2016). Addiction due to gamification can impair self-control of users that may lead to difficulties in disengaging from gamified content. Although addiction based on gamified content can be comparable to addiction to casino games, gamification in its various contexts could be more ethically questionable than the former. In the best-case scenario, casino players are aware of the seductive character of casino games. For gamification, it is often not so apparent that points, badges and other game elements could have addiction potential. Thus, companies should take ethical responsibility for preventing gamification techniques that foster addiction (Kim and Werbach, 2016). In other words, they have to be careful that their communication practices do not lead to negative effects for the social and mental well-being of stakeholders (Shahri et al., 2014). In order to prevent stakeholders from being exposed to unwanted stress situations, including pressure and tension, it is recommended that corporate communication should be attentive to individual needs of stakeholders and adapt game elements accordingly. To avoid ethical issues, businesses might focus on "normification as an engagement strategy", inducing collective engagement instead of competition mechanics (Preist et al., 2014, p. 1).

Since gamification is a persuasive communication strategy (Shahri et al., 2014), gamification in corporate communication has the inherent danger to exploit stakeholders by manipulation and persuasion (Kim and Werbach, 2016). Not surprisingly, some scholars suggest that gamification, like other persuasive or deceptive strategies, should be regulated to a stronger degree by law. However, no such regulations exist (Thorpe and Roper, 2019). Hence, drawing on normative ethics approaches, best practice examples of ethical gamification in the field of corporate communication and ethical discussions around it should be encouraged.

ILLUSTRATIVE EXAMPLES OF GAMIFICATION: NISSAN, DELOITTE AND GOOGLE

In recent years, gamification has been increasingly included into corporate communication and corporate processes (Mitchell et al., 2018; Yang et al., 2017). Since various types of gamified corporate communication exist, three examples have been chosen showing vicariously the variety of application areas of gamification within corporate communication (Larson, 2020).

Nissan's 'Leaf' Car

First, corporations use gamification to build brand–consumer relationships, loyalty, commitment and a positive image (Costa Sanchez, 2014). For instance, when Nissan introduced the electric car 'Leaf', the company simultaneously introduced a corresponding app 'Carwings' with which functions of the car could be regulated via smartphone (battery charging process, air conditioner, etc.). To engage consumers with Nissan, the corporation collected user data to provide users with feedback via regional and global rankings that compared user performances to see which user has the best average value for energy savings. Additionally, consumers could collect 'eco trees' signalling the amount of CO_2 saved by driving the Nissan electric vehicle. With the app, a comparison of the amount of 'eco trees' between countries was observable for consumers based on current figures (Nissan, 2021). With gamification mechanisms such as feedback informing users how economically they behave in comparison to other users, points (eco trees), and rewards like medals signalling users that they can achieve ecologically friendly driving behaviour, Nissan tried to engage consumers with their brand in a fun way by communicating an eco-friendly image (Nissan, 2021).

Deloitte's 'Leadership Academy'

Second, corporations tend to apply game elements into corporate communication to motivate or educate their employees. For example, Deloitte, a UK-based company that offers auditing and consulting services, communicated the corporation's values and employee training content in a gamified way to motivate employees to stay engaged with the 'Deloitte Leadership Academy' training programme. By including challenges in the form of missions, badges and leaderboards into their online training programme, employees tended to spend more time with educational content (Meister, 2013). Content on the website included educational videos, 'in-depth content' such as PDFs to a specific topic, and self-assessments in the form of quizzes and tests. The platform provided the possibility for users to interact with other users and to personalize their status update as well as their profiles (Meister, 2013).

'Google Code Jam'

Third, gamified communication strategies are implemented by corporations to address potential future employees for recruitment. 'Recruitainment' – that is, recruitment including entertaining game elements – can increase job attractiveness and thus the number of applicants (Korn et al., 2018). Since future employees' impressions about a corporation are very important for recruitment effectiveness, corporate communication's use of game elements could be a way to persuade possible future employees to engage in job application processes (Chow and

Chapman, 2013). To illustrate gamification in recruitment communication, the international programming competition 'Google Code Jam' serves as an example. By starting an online competition where possible future employees have a limited amount of time to solve algorithmic problems with programming language, Google tries to connect with the best programmers across the world in an entertaining way to make them job offers. Additionally, by including competitions with different skill levels, challenges, regional and international leaderboards, as well as prizes, Google creates a corporate image characterized by fun and challenges (Code Jam, 2021).

However, while there are plenty of examples of gamification in corporate communication, none of them have reached the level of strategic application as mentioned above. All of the three examples show rather sporadically implemented tools to engage stakeholders in a playful way, but with a limited scope (e.g., in recruitment or executive training). None of these applications are designed to create gamified communities that enable stakeholders to co-create relationships. Therefore, the full potential of gamification as a strategy has yet to materialize.

CONCLUSION AND FUTURE DIRECTIONS

Game and play are core features of the human condition. While playing, humans process information more easily and bond with those with whom they play. Building relationships on behalf of the organization (Bruning and Ledingham, 1999) is one of the central functions of corporate communication.

In today's media society, where attention of stakeholder groups is a scarce resource, where cognitive resistance toward persuasive communication attempts continues to grow, and where more and more communication channels fragment the public discourse, innovative concepts of community-building are seriously needed. As a simple tool, gamification is a means to an end when it comes to conveying corporate ideas, images or messages, ultimately to create or change attitudes and opinions of relevant stakeholder groups. In any case, gamification needs to be adapted carefully to the purpose it is intended to serve. But as an underlying strategy of relationship-building through communication, gamification has so much more potential. Digital platforms like *Second Life*, or Massively Multiplayer Online Games like *World of Warcraft*, are more than just virtual worlds that one can explore for the fun of it. They are communities of like-minded people who gather to have fun *and* socialize. Corporate communication does not need to recreate entire virtual worlds to achieve something similar. It just needs to harness the innovate potential of procedural rhetoric through gamification. Unlike other tools of digital communication, gamified communities enable stakeholders to virtually *experience* what it actually means to be part of a stakeholder–company relationship. Organizational identity can be conveyed by becoming a part of its co-construction in the digital realm.

The Covid-19 pandemic has demonstrated that organizational cohesion and connectivity is dependent on social, personal interactions. Communicating merely via visual and verbal representations is equal to using just a limited bandwidth of corporate communications' available cognitive, emotional and social capacity. Gamification can help to bring this relationship-building and maintenance onto a new level, freed from its spatial restrictions, where people interact with each other through digital interfaces. The stories that corporate communications tell will not merely be read, heard and seen by a largely anonymous audience – storytelling through gamification will become a matter of actually living them as a participant.

Although generally, several studies have shown that corporate gamification is a profitable strategy contributing to a positive brand-value connection by engaging consumers or employees with corporate storytelling or online communities, investigations of how long positive effects of gamification on brand outcomes last have been practically neglected in research. Future studies, which take a longitudinal approach into account are recommended to be undertaken (e.g., Merhabi et al., 2021). Moreover, with further progress of digitalization, corporate gamification will become increasingly popular for various companies. However, not all employees or consumers may have positive experiences with corporate gamification. Therefore, to prevent negative effects on the users' well-being and satisfaction, it is particularly important to investigate the consequences for users with negative experiences who, for instance, cannot deal with gamification due to gaming addiction or poor handling of competition. Lastly, due to progress in technology, new gaming features will emerge that could be of great use for gamified corporate communication. For instance, augmented reality or virtual reality hold a lot of potential for companies for innovative corporate storytelling. Experimental research is needed to test the effects of such innovations for corporate communication (Merhabi et al., 2021). In sum due to advancing digitalization, new forms of corporate gamification will emerge. Potentials and also challenges in this growing field are important issues for future research.

Given all the apparent potential, one should nevertheless be cautious about the future of gamification in corporate communication. The great enthusiasm that accompanied the emergence of social media in the first decade of the twenty-first century has all but disappeared and many promises have simply failed to materialize. Techno-utopian discourses tend to oversell the possibilities of digital solutions to real-world problems. The expressive power of gamified communication has yet to materialize and to realize its potential, thus more research and empirical evidence is needed. Only then can the concept be taken from the drawing board and be applied in the real world of corporate communication.

REFERENCES

Aarikka-Stenroos, L. and Jaakkola, E. (2012). Value co-creation in knowledge intensive business services: A dyadic perspective on the joint problem solving process. *Industrial Marketing Management*, *41*(1), 15–26.

Argenti, P. A. (2006). How technology has influenced the field of corporate communication. *Journal of Business and Technical Communication*, *20*(3), 357–370.

Berger, A., Schlager, T., Sprott, D. E., and Herrmann, A. (2018). Gamified interactions: Whether, when, and how games facilitate self–brand connections. *Journal of the Academy of Marketing Science*, *46*, 652–673.

Bogost, I. (2007). *Persuasive games: The expressive power of videogames*. Cambridge, MA: MIT Press.

Boyle, E. A., Hainey, T., Connolly, T. M., Gray, G., Earp, J., Ott, M., Lim, T., Ninaus, M., Ribeiro, C., and Pereira, J. (2016). An update to the systematic literature review of empirical evidence of the impacts and outcomes of computer games and serious games. *Computers & Education*, *94*, 178–192.

Brehm, S. S. and Brehm, J. W. (1981). *Psychological reactance: A theory of freedom and control*. New York: Academic Press.

Brodie, R. J., Hollebeek, L. D., Juric, B., and Ilic, A. (2011). Customer engagement: Conceptual domain, fundamental propositions, and implications for research. *Journal of Service Research*, *14*(3), 252–271.

278 *Handbook on digital corporate communication*

Bruning, S. D. and Ledingham, J. A. (1999). *Public relations as relationship management: A relational approach to the study and practice of public relations.* Mahwah, NJ: Lawrence Erlbaum Associates.

Caillois, R. (2001). *Man, play, and games.* Champaign: University of Illinois Press.

Cardador, M. T., Northcraft, G. B., and Whicker, J. (2017). A theory of work gamification: Something old, something new, something borrowed, something cool? *Human Resource Management Review, 27*(2), 353–365.

Chow, S. and Chapman, D. (2013). Gamifying the employee recruitment process. *Gamification 2013, Proceedings, Gamification '13.* http://dx.doi.org/10.1145/2583008.2583022.

Code Jam (2021). *What is Code Jam?* https://codingcompetitions.withgoogle.com/codejam/about.

Costa Sanchez, C. (2014). Transmedia storytelling, an ally of corporate communication: #Dropped by Heineken case study. *Communication & Society, 27*(3), 127–150.

Csikszentmihalyi, M. (2008). *Flow: The psychology of optimal experience.* New York: HarperCollins.

Davis, D. Z. and Moscato, D. (2018). The philanthropic avatar: An analysis of fundraising in virtual worlds through the lens of social capital. *International Journal of Strategic Communication, 12*(3), 269–287.

Deterding, S., Dixon, D., Khaled, R., and Nacke, L. (2011a). From game design elements to gamefulness: Defining "gamification". *Proceedings of the 15th International Academic MindTrek Conference: Envisioning Future Media Environments* (pp. 9–15). ACM. https://doi.org/10.1145/2181037.2181040.

Deterding, S., Sicart, M., Nacke, L., O'Hara, K., and Dixon, D. (2011b). Gamification: Using game design elements in non-gaming contexts. *ACM CHI Conference on Human Factors in Computing Systems.* https://doi.org/10.1145/1979742.1979575.

Duffy, J. and Kornienko, T. (2010). Does competition affect giving? *Journal of Economic Behavior & Organization, 74*(1–2), 82–103.

Edmunds, A. and Morris, A. (2000). The problem of information overload in business organisations: A review of the literature. *International Journal of Information Management, 20*(1), 17–28.

Ertemel, A. V. (2021). *Illusional marketing: The use of storytelling, user experience, and gamification in business.* Zea E-Books.

Gatti, L., Ulrich, M., and Seele, P. (2019). Education for sustainable development through business simulation games: An exploratory study of sustainability gamification and its effects on students' learning outcomes. *Journal of Cleaner Production, 207*, 667–678.

Gerdenitsch, C., Sellitsch, D., Besser, M., Burger, S., Stegmann, C., Tscheligi, M., and Kriglstein, S. (2020). Work gamification: Effects on enjoyment, productivity and the role of leadership. *Electronic Commerce Research and Applications, 43.* https://doi.org/10.1016/j.elerap.2020.100994.

Gill, R. (2015). Why the PR strategy of storytelling improves employee engagement and adds value to CSR: An integrated literature review. *Public Relations Review, 41*(5), 662–674.

Greenwood, M. (2007). Stakeholder engagement: Beyond the myth of corporate responsibility. *Journal of Business Ethics, 74*(4), 315–327.

Groh, F. (2012). Gamification: State of the art definition and utilization. In N. Asaj, B. Könings, M. Poguntke, F. Schaub, B. Wiedersheim, and M. Weber (eds.), *Proceedings of the 4th Seminar on Research Trends in Media Informatics* (pp. 39–46). https://d-nb.info/1020022604/34#page=39.

Gupta, M., Behl, A., and Kumar Y. L. N. (2022). Prevention is better than cure: Challenges in engaging employees through gamification. *International Journal of Manpower, 43*(2), 380–394.

Hamari, J. and Koivisto, J. (2015). Why do people use gamification services? *International Journal of Information Management, 35*, 419–431.

Hamari, J., Koivisto, J., and Pakkanen, T. (2014). Do persuasive technologies persuade? A review of empirical studies. In A. Spagnolli, L. Chittaro, and L. Gamberini (eds.), *Persuasive technology. PERSUASIVE 2014. Lecture Notes in Computer Science,* 8462 (pp. 118–136). https://doi.org/10.1007/978-3-319-07127-5_11.

Healy, J. C. and McDonagh, P. (2013). Consumer roles in brand culture and value co-creation in virtual communities. *Journal of Business Research, 66*(9), 1528–1540.

Hofacker, C. F., de Ruyter, K., Lurie, N. H., Manchanda, P., and Donaldson, J. (2016). Gamification and mobile marketing effectiveness. *Journal of Interactive Marketing, 34*, 25–36.

Hollebeek, L. D., Glynn, M. S., and Brodie, R. J. (2014). Consumer brand engagement in social media: Conceptualization, scale development and validation. *Journal of Interactive Marketing, 28*(2), 149–165.

Hsu, C.-L. and Chen, M.-C. (2018). How gamification marketing activities motivate desirable consumer behaviors: Focusing on the role of brand love. *Computers in Human Behavior, 88*, 121–133.

Huizinga, J. (1949). *Homo ludens: A study of the play-element in culture*. London: Routledge & Kegan Paul.

Huotari, K. and Hamari, J. (2017). A definition for gamification: Anchoring gamification in the service marketing literature. *Electronic Markets, 27*(1), 21–31.

Kapp, K. M. (2012). *The gamification of learning and instruction: Game-based methods and strategies for training and education*. San Francisco: Pfeiffer.

Kim, T. and Werbach, K. (2016). More than just a game: Ethical issues in gamification. *Ethics and Information Technology, 18*(2), 157–173.

Korn, O., Brenner, F., Börsig, J., Lalli, F., Mattmüller, M., and Müller, A. (2018). Defining recrutainment: A model and a survey on the gamification of recruiting and human resources. In L. E. Freund and W. Cellary (eds.), *Advances in the human side of service engineering*. Advances in intelligent systems and computing, 601 (pp. 37–49). http://dx.doi.org/10.1007/978-3-319-60486-2_4.

Kovisto, J. and Hamari, J. (2019). The rise of motivational information systems: A review of gamification research. *International Journal of Information Management, 45*, 191–210.

Laamarti, F., Eid, M., and El Saddik, A. (2014). An overview of serious games. *International Journal of Computer Games Technology, 11*, 1–15.

Larson, K. (2020). Serious games and gamification in the corporate training environment: A literature review. *Tech Trends, 64*, 319–328.

Leclercq, T., Hammedi, W., and Poncin, I. (2018). The boundaries of gamification for engaging customers: Effects of losing a contest in online co-creation communities. *Journal of Interactive Marketing, 44*, 82–101.

Legaki, N.-Z., Xi, N., Hamari, J., Karpouzis, K., and Assimakopoulos, V. (2020). The effect of challenge-based gamification on learning: An experiment in the context of statistics education. *International Journal of Human-Computer Studies, 144*, 102496. https://doi.org/10.1016/j.ijhcs.2020.102496.

Lindsey, L. L. M. (2005). Anticipated guilt as behavioral motivation: An examination of appeals to help unknown others through bone marrow donation. *Human Communication Research, 31*(4), 453–481.

Lundqvist, A., Liljander, V., Gummerus, J., and van Riel, A. (2013). The impact of storytelling on the consumer brand experience: The case of a firm-originated story. *Journal of Brand Management, 20*(4), 283–297.

Malone, T. W. (1981). Toward a theory of intrinsically motivating instruction. *Cognitive Science, 5*(4), 333–369.

Meister, J. C. (2013). *How Deloitte made learning a game*. https://hbr.org/2013/01/how-deloitte-made-learning-a-g.

Merhabi, M. A., Petridis, P., and Khusainova, R. (2021). Gamification for brand value co-creation: A systematic literature review. *Information, 12*, 345.

Mitchell, R., Schuster, L., and Jin, H. S. (2018). Gamification and the impact of extrinsic motivation on needs satisfaction: Making work fun? *Journal of Business Research, 31*(2), 82–90.

Mollick, E. and Rothbard, N. (2014). Mandatory fun: Consent, gamification and the impact of games at work. *The Wharton School Research Paper Series*. http://dx.doi.org/10.2139/ssrn.2277103.

Mollick, E. and Werbach, K. (2015). Gamification and the enterprise. In S. Deterding and S. Waltz (eds.), *The gameful world: Approaches, issues, applications* (pp. 439–458). Cambridge, MA: MIT Press.

Nissan (2021). *Carwings*. https://youplus.nissan.at/AT/de/YouPlus/welcome_pack_leaf/eco_virtual_trees.html.

Nobre, H. and Ferreira, A. (2017). Gamification as a platform for brand co-creation experiences. *Journal of Brand Management, 24*(4), 349–361.

Oprescu, F., Jones, C., and Katsikitis, M. (2014). I play at work: Ten principles for transforming work processes through gamification. *Frontiers in Psychology, 5*, 1–5.

Payne, A. F., Storback, K., and Frow, P. (2008). Managing the cocreation of value. *Journal of the Academy of Marketing Science, 36*(1), 83–96.

280 *Handbook on digital corporate communication*

Preist, C., Massung, E., and Coyle, D. (2014). Competing or aiming to be average? Normification as a means of engaging digital volunteers. *CSCW '14 Volunteering and Doing Good.* http://dx.doi.org/10.1145/2531602.2531615.

Putz, L.-M., Hofbauer, F., and Treiblmaier, H. (2020). Can gamification help to improve education? Findings from a longitudinal study. *Computers in Human Behavior, 110,* 106392. https://doi.org/10.1016/j.chb.2020.106392.

Ruggiero, D. (2015). The effect of a persuasive social impact game on affective learning and attitude. *Computers in Human Behavior, 45,* 213–221.

Ryan, R. M. and Deci, E. L. (2000). Intrinsic and extrinsic motivations: Classic definitions and new directions. *Contemporary Educational Psychology, 25*(1), 54–67.

Sailer, M., Hense, J., Mandl, H., and Klevers, M. (2013). Psychological perspectives on motivation through gamification. *Interaction Design and Architecture(s) Journal, 19,* 28–37.

Sailer, M., Hense, J. U., Mayr, S. K., and Mandl, H. (2017). How gamification motivates: An experimental study of the effects of specific game design elements on psychological need satisfaction. *Computers in Human Behavior, 69,* 371–380.

Seiffert-Brockmann, J., Einwiller, S., Ninova-Solovykh, N., and Wolfgruber, D. (2021). Agile content management: Strategic communication in corporate newsrooms. *International Journal of Strategic Communication, 15*(2), 126–143.

Seiffert, J. and Nothhaft, H. (2015). The missing media: The procedural rhetoric of computer games. *Public Relations Review, 41*(2), 254–263.

Seiffert-Brockmann, J., Weitzl, W., and Henriks, M. (2017). Stakeholder engagement through gamification: Effects of user motivation on psychological and behavioral stakeholder reactions. *Journal of Communication Management, 22*(1), 67–78.

Shahri, A., Hosseini, M., Phalp, K., Taylor, J., and Ali, R. (2014). Towards a code of ethics for gamification at enterprise. In U. Frank, P. Loucopoulos, Ó. Pastor, and I. Petrounias (eds.), *The practice of enterprise modeling.* PoEM 2014. Lecture Notes in Business Information Processing, 197. https://doi.org/10.1007/978-3-662-45501-2_17.

Silic, M., Marzi, G., Caputo, A., and Bal, M. P. (2019). The effects of a gamified human resource management system on job satisfaction and engagement. *Human Resources Management, 30,* 260–277.

Smith, J. H. and Just, S. N. (2009). Playful persuasion. The rhetorical potential of advergames. *Nordicom Review, 30*(2), 53–68.

Thaler, R. H. and Sunstein, C. R. (2009). *Nudge: Improving decisions about health, wealth and happiness.* New York: Penguin Books.

Thorpe, A. S. and Roper, S. (2019). The ethics of gamification in a marketing context. *Journal of Business Ethics, 155,* 597–609.

Tomasello, M. (2000). *The cultural origins of human cognition.* Cambridge, MA: Harvard University Press.

US Army (2002). *America's Army* (Version 1) [Computer Game]. Washington, DC.

Verhoef, P. C., Lemon, K. N., Parasuraman, A., Roggeveen, A., Tsiros, M., and Schlesinger, L. A. (2009). Customer experience creation: Determinants, dynamics and management strategies. *Journal of Retailing, 85*(1), 31–41.

Werbach, K. (2014). (Re)defining gamification: A process approach. In D. Hutchison, T. Kanade, J. Kittler, et al. (eds.), *Persuasive Technology: 9th International Conference, PERSUASIVE 2014 Padua, Italy, May 21–23, 2014, Proceedings* (pp. 266–272). Cham: Springer International.

Werbach, K. and Hunter, D. (2012). *For the win: How game thinking can revolutionize your business.* Wharton Digital Press.

Wijman, T. (2018). Mobile revenues account for more than 50% of the global games market as it reaches $137.9 billion in 2018. https://newzoo.com/insights/articles/global-games-market-reaches-137-9-billion-in-2018-mobile-games-take-half/.

Xi, N. and Hamari, J. (2020). Does gamification affect brand engagement and equity? A study in online brand communities. *Journal of Business Research, 109,* 449–460.

Yang, Y., Asaad, Y., and Dwivedi, Y. (2017). Examining the impact of gamification on intention of engagement and brand attitude in the marketing context. *Computers in Human Behavior, 73,* 459–469.

20. Digital corporate communication and artificial intelligence and future roles

Alexander Buhmann and Anne Gregory

INTRODUCTION

Artificial intelligence (AI) has been defined in many ways. One of the most widely used definitions goes back to the original coining of the term in the 1950s, as a machine's ability to produce results for a task comparable to the results achieved by a human agent (Corea, 2019). Today, computerized algorithms and the availability and collation of vast and distributed data enables AI systems to increasingly automate operations and decisions that have previously been left to human actors – for example, based on Computer Vision, Neural Networks, or Natural Language Processing (Chui et al., 2018). The ability of AI systems to identify undiscovered patterns in big data and in real time is an enhancement that adds new dimensions to aid human decision-making.

There have been copious papers on the development of interactive websites and specifically on social media related topics, but relatively little on the specific topic of AI and its implications for corporate communication. Recent surveys suggest that most communication professionals believe they need more education about and guidance on the use of AI for communication practices (Gregory and Virmani, 2020; Virmani and Gregory, 2021) and a majority also agree that AI will have great impact in the very near future – for communication practices and beyond (Zerfass et al., 2020). In addition to grappling with the ever-evolving technologies that are used for corporate communication tasks, it is thus important to consider the impacts and implications of the use of AI not just 'within' communications but more generally by the organizations for which communicators work.

This chapter presents the state of discussion on the implications of AI for professional roles and responsibilities in corporate communication. It provides context and defines AI and other relevant terms in use, gives a brief overview of how AI is currently being used in practice, and characterizes new 'horizons' of application. Further, it explores what these developments mean for the structure of the profession and, within this, focuses on issues of governance and the ethical guardian role for corporate communicators, serving as the conscience of the wider organization.

DEFINITIONS OF THE TOPIC AND PREVIOUS STUDIES

Artificial intelligence: Key Terms and Concepts

AI embraces a variety of computing technologies resembling human intelligence (Wang, 2019). It can range from expert systems, which are applications that make decisions based on complex rules or if/then logic, to applications that can emulate the common sense, free will and emotions of human beings. Machine learning is a subset of AI. Programs learn by reprograming themselves as they assimilate more data and can then perform specified tasks with increasing accuracy. Machine learning technologies include natural language processing which can process text and speech in real time, machine vision that can comprehend and differentiate visual inputs, predictive systems that can discern from patterns in data what is likely to happen, and search and information retrieval optimization. Most machine learning based AI requires human intervention to correct the algorithms used, for example, if a calculation or input mistake is discovered.

Deep learning is a subset and more sophisticated version of machine learning where a computer teaches itself to perform a specific task with increasing accuracy, but it requires no human intervention. It picks up its own inconsistencies and corrects them and builds on the new information it has created. For example, with self-driving cars, deep learning is used to understand what an obstacle looks like without the algorithm having to be constantly re-programmed to recognize every possible obstacle.

Typical AI systems can involve relatively simple automation such as robots assembling dishwashers and running administrative systems, for example, customer-ordering requests. More sophisticated AI includes chatbots which can learn to engage in 'conversations', through to facial recognition systems to fulfil hotel check-in, to writing content along with selecting additional media, such as the appropriate sounds and images, to go with it.

AI and big data often go together. Big data are data sets of a size or type that are beyond the capacity of traditional databases to capture, handle and process (De Mauro et al., 2016). Big data have three distinct characteristics: high volume, high velocity and high variety. Data can be structured (such as a log of all journeys made on a country's railway network) or unstructured (for example, the content of all TikTok posts). Sources of data are becoming more complex and varied and include mobile devices, sensors, social media, the Internet of Things, video/audio, networks, log files, transactional applications and the output of AI itself. The *variety* of data from these sources can be extensive and much of it generated in real time (*velocity*) and at a very large scale (*volume*). AI applications often use big data to inform the algorithms that program them. For example, by analysing thousands of hours of video footage, a driverless car can learn to recognize a dog or a cat and use that data to take decisions about evasive action in real time while taking other factors into account such as speed, safety of humans in and outside the car, road conditions, proximity of other traffic and so on.

Artificial Intelligence: Its Reach and Impact on Corporate Life

The topic of big data and AI is a relatively new area of enquiry in the social sciences and humanities and therefore previous studies are limited. However, what has been recognized is that business (indeed all aspects of) life is not only being enabled by AI, but also enacted through it (Zuboff, 2019). All kinds of transactions are being conducted online using AI-based systems or informing AI applications by providing data. In many instances, there is no choice: from booking and buying airline seats to donating to charities or submitting tax returns, online is often the sole method of transaction. Life online entails engaging with big data platforms such as Google, Amazon and Facebook or other proprietary platforms owned by corporate organizations. The companies operating such platforms realized many years ago that their primary business was not the provision of services, but the collection of data (West, 2019). The data, analytics and AI sectors are huge. Big data and business analytics revenues are forecast

Digital corporate communication and artificial intelligence and future roles   283

to reach US$512 billion in 2026, increasing from US$171 billion in 2018 (Bloomberg, 2020) and the global AI market will be worth US$228.3 billion by 2026 (Global Industry Analysts, 2021). AI enabled data platforms are highly efficient in providing goods and services since they not only enact transactions effectively, efficiently and at speed with minimal human intervention hence reducing costs, but they can predict and prompt likely and future needs and thereby generate business. Traditional businesses have seen their own share of their market significantly impacted by the platform business, for example, hotels by Airbnb and transport by Uber. The Covid-19 pandemic has speeded up traditional businesses' adoption of AI and many now are going through a transformation into AI, data driven organizations.

There is, however, a darker side to the advance of AI that has also been noted (West, 2019). Individuals have limited choice to opt out of using platforms if they wish to obtain the services and products they need. They have to accept the attendant relentless data collection that transactions involve, including of the highly personal, so that data collectors can identify interests and motivations and predict current and future choices (Nunan and DiDomenico, 2013). At the same time, individuals' ability to deny the aggregation of their data with that of others is limited and, in many instances, they are powerless in preventing that data being used for other purposes that they would object to if they had knowledge of that use. Human agency is being profoundly affected by the apparently unstoppable march of these technologies (Bourne, 2019).

At the corporate level, as hinted at above, the use of AI is profoundly affecting working practices with automation and AI now beginning to take over the more repetitive tasks and the disintermediation of the supply chain means that many of the 'middle man' businesses, such as high street shops are being squeezed. In a report covering the acceleration to AI driven by the need to review working practices during the 2020/2021 Covid pandemic, McKinsey (2021) foresee that over 100 million workers in the eight countries in their study, that is 1 in 16 workers, may need to switch to a different occupation to remain employed.

The State of AI in Digital Corporate Communication

Within corporate communication research and related fields, studies on AI are again limited, yet their number is quickly increasing. A few works explore the overall reach and potential impacts of AI on corporate communication (Buhmann and White, 2022; Galloway and Swiatek, 2018; Zerfass et al., 2020), big data and AI ethical concerns (Bourne, 2019; Buhmann et al., 2020; Gregory and Halff, 2020; White and Boatwright, 2020), and tools enabled by advanced machine learning, for example, chatbots (Murtarelli et al., 2020). In contrast, there is an active discussion about AI in the professional literature, i.e., from the corporate communication think tanks and professional associations. The Page Society, based in the US and representing board-level corporate communication practitioners, produced a report in 2019 (Page Society, 2019) which made a plea for the profession to upskill in digital technologies as it was falling behind other communicative disciplines such as marketing. The Institute for Public Relations, also US-based, has produced several articles on AI and has a specialist digital media research centre producing a range of resources and commentaries. Most active has been the UK-based Chartered Institute of Public Relations (CIPR), which constituted its 'AIinPR' expert panel in 2018 and who have produced numerous research reports, guides and practical implementation toolkits (see https://cipr.co.uk/CIPR/Our_work/Policy/AI_in_PR.aspx).

284 *Handbook on digital corporate communication*

The CIPR commissioned *The AI and Big Data Readiness Report* which explores the state of 'readiness' in the public relations profession (Virmani and Gregory, 2021). It shows a varied picture: some advanced practice and senior practitioners are involved in decision-making on AI in the practice and more widely in organizations, while others are not yet on the 'AI journey' and believe it is not relevant or do not know where to start. The greatest fear revealed by the survey is about loss of jobs and the supplanting of corporate communications activities by AI, particularly at the tactical level (writing, audience selection and targeting, monitoring and evaluation, etc.). Also noted in the survey underpinning the research was the general lack of knowledge about technical aspects of AI with 43 per cent of respondents believing they had limited knowledge and lacked confidence in using AI in their work. It is understandable therefore that the CIPR (2020) claimed "the profession is sleep-walking into AI". Very little is articulated on an 'expanded role' related to AI, particularly in governance, but awareness of ethical issues is apparent. Only 5 per cent thought governance was a skill believed to be most relevant as a communication practitioner currently, but 18 per cent thought ethics was the top challenge for professionals when it comes to implementing AI across an enterprise. This suggests an increasing appreciation that AI governance is relevant to corporate communications and organizationally, but practitioners are not yet clear about what is involved or how to undertake it.

Other research commissioned by the CIPR (Valin, 2018) examined the level of permeation of AI in the profession and predicted that by 2023, two thirds of activities would be AI assisted (see Figure 20.1). Recent consideration of this by its 'AIinPR' panel has concluded that this process was accelerated by the Covid-19 pandemic, which began in early 2020, and that this position has already been achieved.

The research concluded that the majority of the 'doing' parts of the public relations role were susceptible to automation and AI tools. However, Valin (2018, p. 11) asserted that, "Regardless of the tasks and skills that can be automated or benefit from AI, human intervention in editing, sensitivity, emotional intelligence, applying good judgement and ethics will always be needed."

A look at some of the industry leader commentary and propriety commercial offerings demonstrates how AI has infused every aspect of corporate communication work (see, for example, the PR tool stack proposed by Wadds Inc., 2021). From research to stakeholder identification and selection, to identifying stakeholder channel use and optimizing channel selection; content design and creation, including writing, image and audio generation; monitoring (including social listening) and evaluation; programme implementation and management and workflow optimization – there are automation and AI tools that will do the task faster and more accurately than humans. Even the most human part – the actual engagement – is now beginning to be handled well and intelligently (and with permanent collection, storage, analysis and aggregation of data) by AI-based systems such as chatbots and virtual reality applications.

WHAT IS CHANGING?

New applications and innovations are emerging on a daily basis, but one area that is developing rapidly is Intelligent User Interfaces (IUIs) which have AI at their core. IUIs seek to make the interface between machines (computers) and humans as easy as possible, and their main feature is that they attempt to emulate a human-to-human experience, including the sensory.

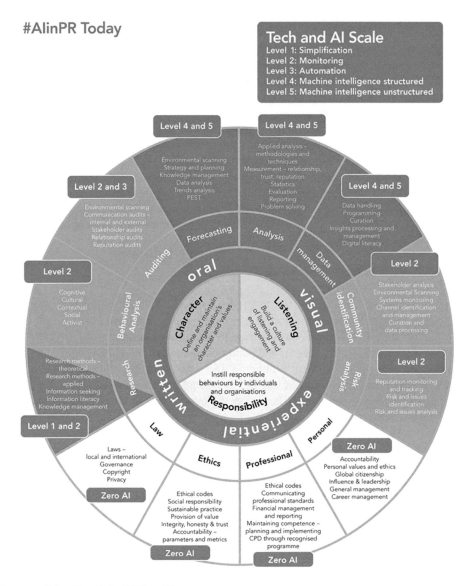

Source: Taken from Valin (2018, p. 10).

Figure 20.1 Predicted level of AI penetration into the profession by 2023: mapping the 50 skills identified in Global Alliance's Global Body of Knowledge (GBOK) with AI

Moore and Hübscher (2021) have written specifically on the uses and impact of these devices on corporate communication and they are far reaching. They claim that these intelligent interfaces "become interpreters and then arbiters of content, choices, and identities because they will be the faces of organisations" (Moore and Hübscher, 2021, p. 4). IUI technology includes

286   *Handbook on digital corporate communication*

virtual and augmented reality, chatbots, virtual assistants, avatars, indeed, all applications that incorporate at least one sensory element, such as sight, sound (speech) or touch. In AR and VR applications, sight is a key element, either providing a visual experience or engaging the sight of the user. Eye-tracking devices represent a particularly powerful technology, opening up opportunities to help the visually impaired, but also giving new insight into visual preferences, behaviours and obsessions. Touch technologies can be integrated into just about any object from tables and walls to clothes and skin. In their book, Moore recounts shaking the hand of a dead trades unionist virtually and having a tactile experience.

The potency of these technologies for corporate communication cannot be overestimated in three ways: first gaining insight into people's ways of thinking – both rational and emotional – their motivations, preferences, choices, and ways of communicating (they provide access to the 'deepest' private thinking of individuals); second, this information opens up the potential for manipulation, without the individual realizing it; and third the further blurring of reality and the unreal. These issues are already apparent in the realm of social media: they will become even more apparent in IUI.

The Impact of IUIs in Digital Corporate Communication

There are a number of features of IUIs that merit further examination. For example, these devices can be brought home and incorporated into the fabric of life, where they can see, listen and physically interact. They can enhance lives by taking on mundane tasks and predicting needs. They also constantly collect data and build rich pictures of individuals' and community lives. They can offer hyper-personalization and drill down to deliver messages and engage in conversations. These conversations will be increasingly nuanced, emotionally intelligent, extended, particular and unscripted. They offer the opportunity of data-collecting dialogue at the granular level of one-to-one for those who have the resources to harness their power – namely, corporate communicators.

IUIs will gain increasingly sophisticated emotional attributes and be able to gauge, respond to and even show it: they already have to some extent – note the use of robot comfort dogs for the lonely and people with emotional and dementia conditions. The car industry is working on user interfaces that detect driver anger. There is potential for corporate communications to build emotionally resonant brands or to generate close emotional affinity with products using these interfaces. There are even suggestions that these IUIs will, in time, integrate with the human nervous system. As Moore and Hübscher (2021) point out, emotional engagement and affinity has close connections with trust-building, a core tenet of corporate communication and a key aspect of intangible asset building. Emotions, trust and loyalty also drive consumption, thus having a direct link to the bottom-line.

Two further characteristics of IUIs merit consideration. First the increasing naturalness of their language. As Murtarelli et al. (2020) point out, there is a qualitative difference between a 'conversation' or what they call 'para conversations' with an AI agent, and reading text. In conversations meaning is created, relationships develop and trust is cultivated in a deep way, especially if these conversations are re-enforced by other sensory elements such as touch and vision. However, these are not conversations. AI agents are programmed to be purposive and data gathering whether that be for altruistic or instrumental reasons. They listen and record as well as speak, and as they become more sophisticated and able to be more human-like, they will be able to elicit more and more personal information, knowing more about their human counterparts than the latter know about themselves. This prompts questions about boundaries and power. Should there be limits put on the amount of information AI communication devices should be allowed to know about individuals? Should there be boundaries put on how they can use the information they gather? These are pertinent questions for corporate communication because with this knowledge comes a power that can be used for collaboration and complementary activities, or to lead, persuade and manipulate without the subjects' informed consent.

Second, the humanization of AI is progressing apace. Robots are mirroring human movement, have skin-like coverings, and can mimic human physical and emotional reactions: eventually they will walk like humans, talk like humans, look like humans, act like humans. They will be able to supplant even the human presence of corporate communication professionals at meetings, events, in off- and online conversations as well as helping them (or replacing them) in every activity they undertake. If AI is permeating every area of corporate communications by providing tools for *operational* activity, what is its impact on the more strategic elements of work? These may include, as the research by Valin (2018) noted, understanding context, aligning organizations with societal expectations and securing legitimacy, developing purpose and brand, negotiating values, creating meaning with stakeholders, making judgements about their reasonable and unreasonable expectations and how to deal with these, and developing organizational culture and character. It is clear that AI will be embedded in decision-making, providing the data upon which decisions can be made and in many cases, offering options based on the data. AI processes will undertake and analyse the research on all the areas outlined above, predict outcomes based on a range of scenarios, advise on best choices (on parameters set by corporate communication) and monitor progress, advising on any adjustment along the way.

WHAT REMAINS THE SAME?

The question about what remains the same is a moot one. In many ways, nothing remains the same. It was Klaus Schwab of the World Economic Forum who coined the phrase 'the fourth industrial revolution' (Schwab, 2016), and as Weiner and Kochar (2016) claim, the advance of big data and AI is irreversible. The introduction of big data and AI is, to use the much used and abused phrase, a paradigm shift. Its introduction to corporate communication is no less seismic; it will change society, organizations, the nature of work – including that in corporate communication and the potential outcomes.

The Valin (2018) research and the foregoing discussion hint at the fact that the most human elements – of understanding context, nuance, what creating meaning entails, empathy, sympathy, judgement, integrity and the self-limitations of power – will remain. Questions on the boundaries of AI and big data use and its governance will become more important, but it was ever thus. Humans have always struggled with the nature of machine/human interfaces and what this means for the human condition – right from the invention of primitive tools to the printing press, industrial machines and the introduction of modern computers. The core challenge is 'just because we can, should we?' This then leads to deeper considerations of the concerns that these new technologies raise.

CRITICAL EXAMINATION

The above discussion poses a number of crucial questions: What is known about AI? How transparent are the programming parameters and the algorithms? What can be done about potential mistakes and biases in algorithms? What about the imbalances in power between the owners, users and targets of AI? How much data should be collected and how should it be used? What voluntary and regulatory boundaries should be in place? These questions lead to a discussion about the emergent concerns that AI raises for corporate reputation and responsibility.

Both for AI developers as well as organizations applying these systems, AI may raise three interrelated ethical and reputational concerns (see Buhmann et al., 2020, and Buhmann and Fieseler, 2022, for a deeper discussion of these). First, AI may raise *evidence concerns*, i.e., concerns about how systems turn vast data into 'insights' as the basis for (potentially flawed) decisions, recommendations, etc. The 'insights' a system applies for guiding its actions may be based on inconclusive evidence from patterns that are artefacts of vast data or from inferences based simply on correlations in big datasets. Further, evidence can be misguided through inadequate inputs, such as incomplete, sensitive, or incorrect data. In sum, evidence concerns can arise through unintended or intended flaws in data and or in the way data are processed.

Second, AI can raise *outcome concerns* (i.e., about systems decisions causing harm, potentially because of incomplete or inconclusive evidence). Such harm can come in the forms of immediate and direct effects or as latent and long-term consequences of AI application. Among immediate unfair outcomes are, for example, bias and discrimination against race or gender to the detriment of diversity and inclusion. Indirect and long-term impacts can include technological unemployment or reinforcing people's socialization within closed epistemic networks on social media, such as 'filter bubbles' (Nguyen, 2020).

Third, and most importantly for communicators, AI may raise *epistemic concerns*. These concerns are also discussed under labels such as 'AI as black box', 'AI opacity' or 'AI explicability'. This refers not only to deliberate efforts to keep algorithms secret (often out of strategic necessity around proprietary systems and data), but to the often inevitable difficulty of forecasting or reconstructing how a system processes data inputs for decision-making or how these decisions affect a domain of AI application in the long term. The potentially inscrutable inputs and opaque algorithmic data processing, as well as often untraceable harmful impacts, are a significant concern. The vast sets of data used by AI, their fluid way of processing data and their ability to evolve their own algorithms may not allow for any explainable relationship between data and a system's decisions or actions. This can make it impossible to trace if and how a system may pick up 'ethically relevant' information from their training data and incorporate them within their own design. Such epistemic concerns raise significant challenges for communicators charged with explaining the conduct of organizations that develop or employ AI.

The Pivotal Role of 'Epistemic Concerns' with AI and How They Challenge Organizational Legitimation

The above discussion shows that the proliferation of AI matters to communicators way beyond the level of new tools for communication. Significant challenges also emerge though increased AI use in organizational processes more generally. Epistemic challenges in particular raise issues for communicators' efforts to explain organizational conduct and position the organization as an appropriate and socially responsible actor. Some epistemic concerns – for instance, those that come with a strategic necessity to obfuscate (e.g., for reasons of functionality, competitiveness or data privacy) – can be addressed through standard accountability frameworks to align organizational conduct with social expectations. Other epistemic concerns, however, cause fundamental issues for explainability, e.g., those related to traceable long-term negative social consequences. The ability of standard regulation to address these challenges is limited, as evidenced in the discussion around the General Data Protection Regulation, GDPR, and 'fair AI' (Butterworth, 2018). The accountable AI and AI governance discussion goes beyond the scope of GDPR and other standard frameworks for data production and use. Throughout the iterative AI development process, even software engineers, who may reuse and repurpose code from libraries, often refer to parts of their work as 'black boxes' (Mittelstadt et al., 2016). With this comes uncertainty – not just for everyday users, but also for experts and the organizations that develop and apply AI systems – about the use of potentially sensitive variables such as race and gender; latent and long-term impacts including for those who work and those who do not; responsibility for decisions across vast networks of human and non-human agents; and the embodied norms and values within systems on, for example, ethical issues. Such concerns, which are not easily solved by standardized forms of explanation and accountability (such as in reporting guidelines), call for the special attention of communication practitioners, who are charged with explaining organizational conduct and managing an organization's legitimacy and reputation.

In principle, organizational legitimation, which is the process of keeping an organization accountable and positioning it as an accepted and responsible social actor (Boyd, 2000), can happen based on three strategic options (Scherer et al., 2013): via a *manipulative approach* (where communicators make an active attempt to shape external expectations in favour and support of organizational conduct); via an *adaptive approach* (where organizations monitor external expectations, rules and regulations in their environment and work towards compliance); or via a *discursive approach* (where organizations and stakeholders engage in moral discourse to jointly develop an understanding of challenges as well as desirable solutions). The first two strategic options necessitate a relative degree of certainty, either on the side of the organization (as a basis for successful manipulation) or on the side of stakeholders (as a basis for successful adaptation). For achieving legitimation around highly fluid and poorly transparent systems, however, where certainty on both sides is low (i.e., to both expert AI developers and ordinary end users), corporate communicators need to support the facilitation of discursive engagement processes between all parties to jointly deliberate and decide on good practices for responsible and accountable AI.

Tackling 'Epistemic Concerns': Facilitating Discursive Engagement for Responsible AI

To enable engagement processes for responsible AI, communicators can follow a framework of three basic strategies that help facilitate stakeholder discourse (cf. Buhmann et al., 2020). First, communicators can focus on providing *access* to an inclusive and continuous debate where all those potentially affected by the processes and decisions of an AI system have equal opportunity to participate and spotlight potential issues and concerns. For instance, news organizations, such as BuzzFeed, maintain repositories in which data and code used for data-driven articles are at least partially published. Media outlets, such as *The New York*

290 *Handbook on digital corporate communication*

Times, upload the datasets they use to feed their machine learning algorithms to GitHub. These platforms, through commenting functions and forums, may offer opportunities for stakeholders to engage.

However, merely providing access does not ensure that discourse participants understand a relevant issue and are able to deliberate. As a second strategy, communicators can make efforts to go beyond merely providing information about systems to helping facilitate real *comprehension*. This may be supported through experiment databases that enable comparisons between different algorithms, methods of simplifying machine-learning models by visualizing their actions, or by developing alternative explanations for AI based on insights gathered through reverse engineering. Finally, as an alternative to reverse engineering whole systems, there are approaches available for generating information by focusing on actual use scenarios in algorithm audits (cf. Sandvig et al., 2014). Here communicators can help tell relatable stories via a realistic case that simulate or follow actual algorithm users to trace, for example, how AI may discriminate.

Finally, communicators can play a role in ensuring that efforts to facilitate access and comprehension can form the basis for an open debate and *deliberation* where participants get the opportunity to see issues from all relevant points of view and can jointly develop acceptable and legitimate solutions for AI systems. To facilitate such open argumentation, communicators should include and empower diverse voices, even of those parties who may not be aware that they are suffering negative outcomes. This is, of course, also important because if stakeholders become aware that proprietors of AI systems have made no efforts to reveal critical 'unknowns' about their approaches, this can yield adverse reputational ramifications.

In sum, the above strategies compel corporate communicators to place a strong emphasis on involving and empowering stakeholders. This is especially important where there are strong epistemic concerns and AI developers and applicants of AI may themselves not have all the information necessary to validly assess a system and its potential issues – and hence all parties involved may profit from open and mutual discourse to help make sound decisions and avoid harm. True discursive stakeholder engagement, however, is a challenging task. But it does not have to mean involving everyone in the same way and at the same time. Recent work on stakeholder discourse shows how such engagement may be approached as a 'distributed process' made up of several instances and venues with different stakeholders (experts, policy makers, laypersons, etc.) that may have different needs and demands for comprehending and discussing AI (cf. Buhmann and Fieseler, 2022).

IMPLICATIONS

The level at which AI is now embedded in the practice of corporate communication means there will be significant changes and challenges in the operational and strategic role of corporate communicators. At the operational level, in theory at least, most of the routine tasks, of which there are many in corporate communication (planning, audience identification and selection, content design and delivery, monitoring and evaluation) are amenable to automation and AI applications (see Figure 20.1). There are new knowledge and skills sets that need to be learned, such as knowledge of the various AI applications and their deployment, including the best combination of AI tools to use; acquisition of new technical skills to operate these applications; familiarity with the use and interpretation of data, and knowledge of the best

Digital corporate communication and artificial intelligence and future roles 291

combination of human and AI resources and their respective roles. This will demand a level of data and technical literacy far above that which has been typically required of practitioners in a profession where creativity has often been the most prized attribute.

Beyond these knowledge and skills requirements needed for the operational practice, corporate communication as a specialist function will face the same sets of questions which apply to organizations as laid out above. As the operational is increasingly taken over by AI, the role of corporate communicators will shift much more into the governance of their own communication AI systems, processes and tools. This starts with an understanding of the technology and algorithms that go into them, including issues of explainability, bias and privacy and moves on to their uses and impacts. The precision of profiling and micro-targeting derived from big and personal data and the ability for precise and potentially manipulative messaging and content delivered in ever more sensory and emotionally resonant ways, requires careful reflection by individual practitioners and the wider profession. Agreement about the ethical boundaries of the practice and formal training in AI governance and ethics to maintain trust and confidence in communication work appears to be an imperative. Hence, monitoring and governance, knowing what AI is doing, how it is doing it and making the right interventions to ensure ethical practice, is essential to the future role.

The central role that corporate communication plays in stakeholder relationships and the preservation of the tangible and intangible assets of the organization points to a potential wider contribution that the function could play in AI governance. There is a huge amount in the public relations literature about the roles and responsibilities of practitioners (for example, Dozier and Broom, 1995; Gregory, 2008; Moss et al., 2005; Tench et al., 2013) usually wrapped up in discussions about the scope and remit of public relations work and arguments about its jurisdictional boundaries.

At the centre of all these discussions are claims about the roles of practitioners beyond the functional, particularly regarding broader organizational responsibilities to society. This academic literature and professional publications point to the need for ethical practice and many refer to the role of the practitioner as 'ethical guardian': someone who serves as the conscience of the wider organization. That this role is actually practised is disputed (L'Etang, 2003), nonetheless, this chapter makes an argument for an expanded governance role for corporate communication as organizations are increasingly infused, driven and constituted by and through AI. This role requires 'ethical guardian' interventions in a whole range of areas.

As noted in the introduction, organizations are transforming and the incorporation of AI into the whole organization requires a holistic, non-technical perspective on the impact of this on intangible as well as tangible assets. This falls naturally within the board advisory role of the corporate communication function.

AI and big data gives organizations choices about their physical location and over who, how and how many employees they recruit, retain and re-train. These are moral as well as economic choices and have reputational effects. There are also issues about the interface between humans and AI and the nature of work. These can be posed as a moral question: Who drives what? Do machines drive humans and human decision-making, or do humans place protocols and structures around machines to ensure that AI and big data assisted decision-making is controlled?

Then there are concerns around the nature of decision-making; when provided with what looks like compelling AI produced evidence it is important to ask questions about the integrity of the data, the transparency and programming of the algorithms that have interrogated

292   *Handbook on digital corporate communication*

it and the implications of decisions made. That challenge is legitimately made by corporate communication professionals since they bear responsibility for communicating and defending these decisions. Crucial to this is their contribution to the understanding of context, including timing. Context is a factor that AI systems, as they currently stand, find difficult to appreciate. As options, opportunities and decisions are increasingly informed by AI systems, there is a crucial need for 'someone' to understand and interpret how they should be viewed in the light of wider societal trends, stakeholder needs and expectations and the more immediate contextual issues such as time, tone and place. Judgements need to be made not solely on the basis of logic. While contextual intelligence has always been within the remit of corporate communication, it becomes even more important when faced with AI informed, 'scientific' decisions.

The ethical guardian role extends to questions about how AI and big data systems are commissioned, implemented, and monitored. These include not just technical, but ethical questions about whether there are systems and processes in place to guarantee the privacy of user/customer data, proper control over how data is used and stored and transparency over what data is being collected, its use, with whom it is shared and aggregated in systems where AI is involved. The corporate communicator is the person often charged with communicating this information to interested stakeholders.

While there is guidance from some large transnational intuitions such as the European Union (2019) on how to implement AI organizationally in a responsible way, leaving these important questions to IT and technology specialists is not satisfactory. Corporate communication professionals need to be part of AI commissioning and build teams to pose tough ethical questions that may affect stakeholders and reputation, but may not occur to technical specialists who are focused on operational issues. To discharge this ethical guardian role requires corporate communicators to acquire a robust understanding of AI, how these systems are designed and their uses and applications. It also requires courage to resist the relentless logic of AI and 'scientific' decision-making. These decisions are based on data, and this data is often from and about people and affects them: people and society are more than atomized data parts and more than objects and targets.

CASE STUDY: CORPORATE COMMUNICATION AND AI GOVERNANCE AT VODAFONE

This case study on AI governance is based on interviews with two senior policy and corporate communication executives from Vodafone and publicly available documents from the company and Global System for Mobile Communications (GSM Association, 2021). Vodafone is a leading telecommunications company in Europe and Africa. It has mobile and fixed operations in 21 countries and partner networks in 52 more (as at 30 September 2021). Vodafone's purpose is to connect for a better future and that has underpinned its approach to AI. Vodafone has worked for the last few years to develop its own approach to managing the potential ethical issues with AI and now also partners in that approach with mobile industry body, the GSMA. At the time of writing, the GSMA AI for Impact taskforce is finalizing its strategy on how AI can be used for positive impact, both commercially and socially. Vodafone is a significant player in shaping that strategy and believes it will be a 'playbook' for all members of the Association.

AI Governance at Vodafone

Vodafone openly recognizes that AI governance is evolving and will develop and improve as the technology itself develops. As a member of GSMA, Vodafone is pushing for international legislation to ensure that issues such as privacy, human rights and diversity, and the principles of transparency and accountability are properly regulated, with those using AI systems being held to account. Since 2019, Vodafone has had a publicly available Artificial Intelligence Framework (see https://www.vodafone.com/about-vodafone/how-we-operate/public-policy/policy-positions/artificial-intelligence-framework) which sets out its principles for deploying AI in an ethical manner. Its key elements are:

- Transparency and accountability: customers and employees are informed when they communicate directly with AI systems.
- Ethics and fairness: a commitment to the ethical development of AI.
- Preservation of privacy and security: of all individuals who use their AI systems.
- Human rights, diversity and inclusivity: respecting international human rights standards and best practice to ensure diversity, accessibility and inclusivity.
- Maximizing the benefits of AI while managing the disruption of its implementation: being a responsible employer and ensuring AI systems are human-centric.

Vodafone uses AI systems extensively, particularly in ensuring the smooth running of its networks, including traffic management. The approach to governance is that the AI Framework principles should be embedded throughout the company's processes and operations. Thus, within the company itself, the principles are, for example, embedded in product and service development teams so that privacy and security are designed in from the beginning, with any individual being able to raise concerns at any point. This allows issues to be resolved early and for initiatives to be able to progress smoothly. As one of the senior policy and communication advisers stated: "What we want to avoid is go/no go decisions on products or services having to be constantly referred up to higher levels which creates bottlenecks and is disempowering." To facilitate this, there is systematic, mandatory training on AI and related topics such as inclusion and diversity from the point of employee induction onwards.

For complex and unique ethical cases (for example, questions/decisions about policy or principles and decisions with significant reputational implications), Vodafone has a number of steering committees that adjudicate according to the topic under consideration. These committees include executive directors and contributors from a range of backgrounds including legal counsel, subject matter experts and external affairs. The variety of views and the different types of expertise they bring means any issues are considered from a range of standpoints and it is human beings who make the decisions. For the senior policy and communication advisers this was crucial: "The important point here is that they are diverse teams and there is significant and sufficient human oversight of AI systems so that they are human-centric; the machines serve human beings, not the other way round."

Vodafone is mainly a user of AI and procures services from developers. Throughout its supply chain it seeks to assure itself that its own ethical standards are adhered to. The company's human rights team undertakes due diligence checks and suppliers report on, for example, the principles of privacy and transparency and again, human oversight of the performance of procured systems is regarded as crucial.

AI and Corporate Communication

For corporate communication, the AI Framework is regarded as a significant piece of work that seeks to position the company as purpose-driven and taking its corporate digital responsibilities seriously. Vodafone wants to be seen as unashamedly committed to being an architect of a digital society, and as seeking to do this for the benefit of society, not just for commercial gain. Hence, being seen to be at the forefront of the push for regulation and being an exemplar of good practice in explaining how and what its AI systems do and what this implies for its stakeholders, is seen to be a key part of reputational safeguarding and enhancement. As the senior policy and communication advisers said, "We want people to trust us on issues like privacy and data security. We need to get better on using tools like social listening so that we can get a better handle on what they are concerned about, then we can set about addressing those concerns."

On a day-to-day basis Vodafone also uses AI assistants such as chatbots and alerts customers to the fact that they are speaking to a robot, offering a human alternative if that is preferred.

Further, the company flags up a number of issues that they believe will move up the public agenda in the near and medium future. Some of this emanates from the public affairs arena where, in a European context, there is new EU legislation. The Artificial Intelligence Act (EU, 2021) is affirmative of a values-based approach which is strong on human rights; enhances governance of AI systems and insists on their safety; and provides for a "single market for lawful, safe and trustworthy AI applications" (para 7). This Act is a major step towards regulation and categorizes levels of risk in a pyramid that makes its assessment of danger explicit. At the top of the pyramid are items that are of importance to digital corporate communication such as subliminal messaging and social scoring by public authorities. Applying the risk criteria to digital corporate communication could help with a categorization of concerns around micro-targeting and the kinds of audience analysis and content that is permissible. Certainly, there are now significant questions around facial (and by implication, other forms of) recognition.

In terms of the three areas of ethical concern outlined in this chapter, Vodafone appears to be moving towards addressing them all. To address evidence concerns it has made a public declaration that it will be inclusive in the way it collects data and has put checks in place within its supply chain to assure itself that correct interpretations of data can be made (not simple correlations) and that the data itself is adequate. Outcome concerns are tackled in its policies to ensure human rights are respected and that its decisions do not impact unfairly on certain groups because of bias or inbuilt algorithmic discrimination. Epistemic concerns appear to be confronted by openly declaring when and how AI systems are being used by any stakeholder groups.

CONCLUSION AND FUTURE DIRECTIONS

We have argued that the use of AI-based tools is profoundly affecting the *operational practice* of corporate communication. In addition, we have highlighted that there are wider issues at stake, namely the *governance* of the practice and organizational governance more generally. While much of the current research effort is focusing on operational practice – on the application and implications of AI-based tools for communication as well as on practitioners'

Digital corporate communication and artificial intelligence and future roles 295

views and concerns with AI-based communication practice – less attention is being paid to the more fundamental shifts that AI brings to organizations as a whole, and how this creates new challenges for communicators. With organizations increasingly relying on AI to manage operations and make decisions, corporate communication will be expected to develop a nuanced understanding of these AI applications across all organizational spheres and the way they affect organizations and stakeholder relationships. The proliferation of AI in organizations brings about a new set of concerns with organizational conduct that corporate communicators will have to address. The implications this has for the reach, roles and responsibilities of corporate communication need to be a key focus of future research in this field.

REFERENCES

Bloomberg (2020). Big data and business analytics market size is projected to reach USD 512.04 billion by 2026. https://www.bloomberg.com/press-releases/2020-02-11/big-data-and-business-analytics-market-size-is-projected-to-reach-usd-512-04-billion-by-2026-valuates-reports.

Bourne, C. (2019). AI cheerleaders: Public relations, neo-liberalism and artificial intelligence. *Public Relations Inquiry*, *8*(2), 109–125.

Boyd, J. (2000). Actional legitimation: No crisis necessary. *Journal of Public Relations Research*, *12*(4), 341–353.

Buhmann, A. and Fieseler, C. (2022). Deep learning meets deep democracy: Deliberative governance and responsible innovation in artificial intelligence. *Business Ethics Quarterly*. https://doi.org/10.1017/beq.2021.42.

Buhmann, A., Paßmann, J., and Fieseler, C. (2020). Managing algorithmic accountability: Balancing reputational concerns, engagement strategies, and the potential of rational discourse. *Journal of Business Ethics*, *163*(2), 265–280.

Buhmann, A. and White, C. (2022). Artificial intelligence in public relations: Role and implications. In J. Lipschultz, K. Freberg, and R. Luttrell (eds.), *The Emerald handbook of computer-mediated communication and social media* (pp. 625–638). Bingley: Emerald Publishing.

Butterworth, M. (2018). The ICO and artificial intelligence: The role of fairness in the GDPR framework. *Computer Law & Security Review*, *34*(2), 257–268.

Chui, M., Manyika, J., Miremadi, M., Henke, N., Chung, R., Nel, P., and Malhotra, S. (2018). *Notes from the AI frontier: Insights from hundreds of use cases*. McKinsey Global Institute.

CIPR [Chartered Institute of Public Relations] (2020). *PR is "sleepwalking into AI" new CIPR #aiinpr report finds.* News release 16 January. https://newsroom.cipr.co.uk/pr-is-sleepwalking-into-ai-new-cipr-aiinpr-report-finds/.

Corea, F. (2019). AI knowledge map: How to classify AI technologies. In F. Corea, *An introduction to data: Everything you need to know about AI, big data and data science* (pp. 25–29). Cham: Springer.

De Mauro, A., Greco, M., and Grimaldi, M. (2016). A formal definition of Big Data based on its essential features. *Library Review*, *65*(3), 122–135.

Dozier, D. M. and Broom, G. M. (1995). Evolution of the manager role in public relations practice. *Journal of Public Relations Research*, *7*(1), 3–26.

EU (European Union) (2019). *Ethics guidelines for trustworthy AI.* https://ec.europa.eu/digital-single-market/en/news/ethics-guidelines-trustworthy-ai.

EU (European Union) (2021). Artificial Intelligence Act. https://eur-lex.europa.eu/legal-content/EN/TXT/?uri=CELEX%3A52021PC0206.

Galloway, C. and Swiatek, L. (2018). Public relations and artificial intelligence: It's not (just) about robots. *Public Relations Review*, *44*(5), 734–740.

Global Industry Analysts (2021). *Artificial Intelligence (AI) - Global Market Trajectory & Analytics.* https://www.strategyr.com/market-report-artificial-intelligence-ai-forecasts-global-industry-analysts-inc.asp.

GSMA (2021). About us. https://www.gsma.com/aboutus/.

Gregory, A. (2008). The competencies of senior practitioners in the UK: An initial study. *Public Relations Review, 34*(3), 215–223.

Gregory, A. and Halff, G. (2020). The damage done by big data-driven public relations. *Public Relations Review, 46*(2), article 101902.

Gregory, A. and Virmani, S. (2020). *The effects of AI on the professions.* https://cipr.co.uk/CIPR/Our _work/Policy/AI_in_PR_/AI_in_PR_guides.aspx.

L'Etang, J. (2003). The myth of the 'ethical guardian': An examination of its origins, potency and illusions. *Journal of Communication Management, 8*(1), 53–67.

McKinsey (2021). *The future of work after Covid 19.* McKinsey Global Institute. https://www.mckinsey .com/featured-insights/future-of-work/the-future-of-work-after-covd-19.

Mittelstadt, B. D., Allo, P., Taddeo, M., Wachter, S., and Floridi, L. (2016). The ethics of algorithms: Mapping the debate. *Big Data & Society, 3*(2), 1–21.

Moore, S. and Hübscher, R. (2021). *Strategic communication and AI: Public relations with intelligent user interfaces.* London: Routledge.

Moss, D. A., Newman, A., and DeSanto, B. (2005). What do communications managers do? Defining and refining the core elements of management in a public relations/communication context. *Journalism and Mass Communication Quarterly, 82*(4), 873–890.

Murtarelli, G., Gregory, A., and Romenti, S. (2020). A conversation-based perspective for shaping ethical human-machine interactions: The particular challenge of chatbots. *Journal of Business Research, 129,* 927–935.

Nguyen, C. T. (2020). Echo chambers and epistemic bubbles. *Episteme, 17*(2), 141–161.

Nunan, D. and DiDomenico, M. (2013). Market research and the ethics of big data. *International Journal of Market Research, 55*(1), 2–13.

Page Society (2019). *The CCO as pacesetter.* https://knowledge.page.org/wp-content/uploads/2019/09/ CCO_as_Pacesetter_2019_Page_Research_Report_Interactive.pdf.

Sandvig, C., Hamilton, K., Karahalios, K., and Langbort, C. (2014). An algorithm audit. In S. P. Gangadharan (ed.), *Data and discrimination: Collected essays* (pp. 6–10). Washington, DC: New America Foundation.

Scherer, A. G., Palazzo, G., and Seidl, D. (2013). Managing legitimacy in complex and heterogeneous environments: Sustainable development in a globalized world. *Journal of Management Studies, 50*(2), 259–284.

Schwab, K. (2016). *The fourth industrial revolution: What it means, how to respond.* Geneva: World Economic Forum. https://www.weforum.org/agenda/2016/01/the-fourth-industrial-revolution-what-it -means-and-how-to-respond/.

Tench, R., Zerfass, A., Verhoeven, P., Verčič, D., Moreno, A., and Okay, A. (2013). *Competencies and role requirements of communication professionals in Europe: Insights from quantitative and qualitative studies.* ECOPSI Research Report. Leeds: Leeds Metropolitan University.

Valin, J. (2018). *Humans still needed: An analysis of tools and skills in public relations.* London: CIPR.

Virmani, S. and Gregory, A. (2021). *The AI and big data readiness report.* London: CIPR.

Wadds Inc. (2021). *How to build your PR toolstack.* https://wadds.co.uk/blog/2020/11/26/how-to-build -your-pr-tool-stack.

Wang, P. (2019). On defining artificial intelligence. *Journal of Artificial General Intelligence, 10*(2), 1–37.

Weiner, M. and Kochar, S. (2016). *Irreversible: The public relations big data revolution.* Gainesville, FL: Institute for Public Relations.

West, S. M. (2019). Data capitalism: redefining the logics of surveillance and privacy. *Business & Society, 58*(1), 20–41.

White, C. and Boatwright, B. (2020). Social media ethics in the data economy: Issues of social responsibility for using Facebook for public relations. *Public Relations Review, 46*(5), 101980.

Zerfass, A., Hagelstein, J., and Tench, R. (2020). Artificial intelligence in communication management: A cross-national study on adoption and knowledge, impact, challenges and risks. *Journal of Communication Management, 24*(4), 377–389.

Zuboff, S. (2019). *The age of surveillance capitalism.* London: Profile Books.

21. Digital corporate communication and extended intelligence

Chris Galloway and Lukasz Swiatek

INTRODUCTION

Scholars and other commentators have much to say about Artificial Intelligence (AI), but considerably less on the emerging concept of Extended Intelligence (EI) developed by – and still evolving in the work of – the MIT Media Lab (Karachalios and Ito, n.d.). This chapter argues that practitioners of digital corporate communication should engage with both AI-driven system implementations and the concept of EI not only to enhance their own work but also to enable them to offer sound counsel, in the broader context of ubiquitous digital transformations. Such engagement should not assume that AI and EI are neutral from an ethical perspective. Rather, considering ethical implications is crucial, and should be approached acknowledging that some are genuinely new, requiring fresh thinking. This is a non-trivial pursuit; referring to AI algorithms (the "extended subset[s] of machine learning that [tell] the computer how to learn to operate on its own" [rockcontent, 2021, para. 22]), Buhmann et al. (2020, p. 265) contend that "the notion of algorithmic accountability remains an elusive ideal due to the opacity and fluidity of algorithms".

Neither practitioners nor clients and employers should view this dilemma from the viewpoint of AI eventually entirely supplanting human capability. Rather, the chapter asserts, they can adopt the more useful perspective of EI as enabling communicators to build new capacities to meet the demands of the shape-shifting environment they face. There is, therefore, an imperative to learn, even if only at a foundation level, what is happening in digital environments and to assess how it can reconfigure approaches to corporate communication not merely in the present but also, potentially, in the future.

This chapter, therefore, argues that communicators should aim to become proficient in grasping both the trajectory of digital transformations (including AI) and also their implications for present and future practice. This expertise should include how best to communicate both risks and benefits – a vital aptitude because both these aspects are freighted with professionally-relevant consequences. Such capability needs to be added to the seven categories of 'core competency' in communication management outlined by the Centre for Strategic Communication Excellence. These range from adoption of standards in ethics, law, and governance to effective strategic thinking (Papageorgiou, n.d.). It needs also to be founded on clear working understandings of the relevant terminology, as there is a confusing plethora of proposed terms and definitions.

The chapter opens by addressing definitional dilemmas, before recommending 'Extended' Intelligence as a more appropriate framework than mere 'Artificial' Intelligence within which to consider digital developments. The chapter then turns to considering corporate communication as such, and previous salient studies. It locates the discussion in the context of a closer examination of what is changing in the operating landscape for communicators – and what

298　*Handbook on digital corporate communication*

is *not* changing. A critical examination of AI and EI and their ramifications follows and is applied to a case study of the operations of the local government in Sydney, Australia. The conclusion both brings together the threads of the chapter's arguments and proposes directions for future research.

Expanded Capability

EI offers promise for enhanced digital corporate communication by expanding human communicative capability: a promise the accelerating trend of AI adoptions underscores. The idea of Extended Intelligence also aligns with the notion of digital corporate communication directed at a diversity of audiences, as Ito explained in 2016 in the context of a discussion at the MIT Media Lab about intelligence and AI:

> We propose a kind of Extended Intelligence (EI), understanding intelligence as a fundamentally distributed phenomenon. As we develop increasingly powerful tools to process information and network that processing, aren't we just adding new pieces to the EI that every actor in the network is part of? (Ito, 2016, para. 2)

EI also focuses on "finding uses for AI that support and integrate with human abilities … blurring the lines between machines and humans" (ThinkAutomation, n.d., paras. 5, 7, 10).

EI, therefore, is understood in at least two ways: first as involving better interfaces between humans and machines so that humans can enhance their performance, and second, as a network-centric concept encompassing the sharing of digitally processed material through webs of connection. Both these views are contingent on the tools, powered by AI, that Ito mentions. Artificial Intelligence itself is everywhere – from smartphones to smart systems, driving advances in fields as diverse as marketing, medicine, criminal justice, and journalism. Arguably, its ubiquity means that AI will help determine the future of human–human (not to mention human–machine) communication. However, this chapter advocates an even wider perspective on digital transformations, including those in corporate communication: a perspective that should help communicators to offer sound counsel to employers and clients while also facilitating adjustment to the new. In line with this broader view, we agree with Badham and Luoma-aho (in Chapter 1 in this volume, p. 9) that digital corporate communication (DCC) is "an organization's strategic management of digital technologies, digital infrastructures and digitalization processes to improve communication with internal and external stakeholders and more broadly within society for the maintenance of organizational tangible and intangible assets". However, although that description sounds appealing, it is also important to acknowledge that "digital transformations are even more difficult than traditional change efforts to pull off" and that effectively "communicating a change story" can make success "more than three times likely" (de la Boutetière et al., 2018).

How, then, are we to understand Extended Intelligence and AI? Attempts to define AI abound. According to Wang (2009, pp. 1–2), while "Human beings differ from animals and machine mainly in their mental, or cognitive, ability, which is commonly called 'intelligence' … AI is the attempt to reproduce this ability in computer systems". Wang distinguishes no fewer than "five typical ways to define AI" (2009, p. 2), indicating that the definitional challenge is non-trivial. Schuett (2019, p. 1) agrees that "the term 'artificial intelligence' is used for many different systems" and that "the term is highly ambiguous". For the purposes of this chapter, we understand AI as being "about building machines that can think and act intelligently" (Marr, 2018); this, in turn, enables intelligent behaviour "performing a broad variety of cognitive tasks, e.g., sensing, processing oral language, reasoning, learning, making decisions and demonstrating an ability to move and manipulate objects accordingly" (OECD, n.d.). Nevertheless, AI research and implementations continue to advance at a rapid rate, given added impetus by the Covid-19 pandemic. A four-nation annual study reported by the international PwC consulting group in India (2020) found that 94 per cent of the respondents claimed they had already implemented or were planning to implement AI in their organizations; the rate of adoption had risen from 62 per cent to 70 per cent. Based on its survey in the US, the UK, Japan, and India, PwC asserted that, "Enterprises are now more aware than earlier that AI is no longer a 'nice to have' technology but a 'must have'" (2021, p. 8). However, while digital developments include Artificial Intelligence, they are not limited to it. As Apsland and Hills (n.d., para. 17) argue, what we face "is bigger than just AI. The changes we are beginning to see around us stem as much from a long list of 'dumb' technologies as they do from AI". And more than technologies alone, as Frankiewicz and Chamorro-Premuzik (2020, para. 2) assert:

> Contrary to popular belief, digital transformation is less about technology and more about people. You can pretty much buy any technology, but your ability to adapt to an even more digital future depends on developing the next generation of skills.

Those skills, this chapter contends, must include communicating both benefits and risks of technological advances. Encouragingly, the scholarly literature about AI and EI in relation to corporate communication has been steadily growing, moving beyond the brief notes and overviews of the technology initially presented in the field.

Big Data

Offering a summary of AI and its likely roles in corporate communication, Lerbinger (2018, p. 199) describes the technology as a "major next step", especially in relation to Big Data, commenting that AI-enabled deep learning offers many benefits, from activating commands spoken into mobile devices to boosting the quality of Web search results. At the same time, he notes that firms promoting AI often face public opposition and that many categories of jobs become vulnerable: a situation "less likely", though, he suggests, to affect occupations involving human interaction and empathy.

More recently, scholars (e.g., Gregory and Halff, 2020) have focused in greater depth on the different ways in which AI and other technologies have begun to change corporate communication, including digital corporate communication.

Some of the most 'valuable' companies in the world (such as Amazon, Microsoft, Alphabet, and Apple, among others) are working on technology integration to achieve a "more interactive and immersive experience when communicating to their internal and external stakeholders" (Lalić et al., 2020, p. 378). Other researchers, such as Bowen (2019), and Troise and Camilleri (2021), have noted various similar developments. To the list of those technologies provided by Lalić et al. (2020), Troise and Camilleri (2021) add: the Internet of Things (IoT), big data analytics, mobile applications, cloud computing, blockchain (and other Fintech or financial technologies, such as initial coin offering), and crowdfunding technologies. All these "can have a disruptive impact on today's corporate communication processes" (Troise and Camilleri, 2021, p. 164). Bowen notes that "dramatic challenges" have also arisen for internal

300 *Handbook on digital corporate communication*

relations specifically, drawing on Men and Bowen's (2017) work to contend that "changes [to internal corporate communication] will dramatically escalate" (Bowen, 2019, p. 406) with developments in AI, nanotechnology, and the digital control of the physical world.

Regardless of how we think about it, AI and its various conceptualizations will likely play a major role in future communication, especially in and on behalf of corporations. A comprehensive survey of Asia-Pacific communicators has found this topic to be increasingly important (Macnamara et al., 2020). Yet, while trends can be identified, as the survey shows, even near-term outcomes are difficult to forecast, so rapid is the evolution of AI technologies.

Capable as they are, these technologies are unlikely to entirely displace human design and participation in digital corporate communication – as the "robots are coming" fear-mongers might suggest. Towers-Clark (2020, para. 8) argues that "AI and the future of work are not necessarily compatible. Definitely not in the collaboration and communication market or in the future of work 2.0".

His point is arguable, but it seems more plausible that EI will produce new and more efficient means of communicating with both employees and other stakeholders – where 'efficient' is defined as 'generating greater engagement'. Communicators need not fall prey to "technological myths [associated with] the rise of artificial intelligence" (Natale and Ballatore, 2020, p. 3): rather, they need to discern where augmenting their own capabilities with those of AI-enabled systems will produce the desired outcome. In doing so, they would be aligning themselves with the work of the Global Council on Extended Intelligence, which "aims to steer more of the talent and money being spent on AI towards projects aimed at improving the lot of everyone" (Simonite, 2018, para. 4).

That discernment calls for at least a foundation-level understanding not only of what can be considered as Artificial Intelligence but also a balanced view of both the benefits and the risks when it is applied to digital corporate communication. An interesting study conducted in New Zealand about the use of AI in reading digital eye scans found that many patients were receptive to this application when used as a clinical tool – as a support for, rather than an autonomous replacement of, human doctors (Personal communication, 29 September 2021). In a different field, this is what EI looks like: AI technologies (the leaders of the eye research call their system "a suite of AI engines") extending human capability without erasing the need for human judgement.

One cannot, however, rule out a role for machine-to-machine communication: as Petrucci (2018, para. 15) envisages,

> AI will make it possible for corporate communications to communicate directly with machines as part of daily routine work. It is somewhat radical to think of distributing information to robots, but it is coming, perhaps sooner than you think – and the robots will not be like R2-D2 from Star Wars.

DEFINITIONS OF THE TOPIC AND PREVIOUS STUDIES

According to Cornelissen (2020, p. 5) corporate communication is a management function that coordinates all internal and external communication to build and maintain favourable reputations with stakeholders. Digital corporate communication (DCC) is, therefore, the digitally based operation of this function.

We extend this definition (below) by including AI, and the concept of Extended Intelligence. AI itself is variously defined, as Marr (2018, para. 1) noted: "We're not all operating from the same definition of the term and while the foundation is generally the same, the focus of artificial intelligence shifts depending on the entity that provides the definition." Therefore, we add that

> DCC includes communication enabled by AI technologies either in part or in whole. When used to augment human communication capability, these applications can better be described as 'Extended Intelligence'.

The big challenge is implementation: according to a 2019 report by market research company Gartner:

> Although 87% of surveyed executives agree that 'digital' is a big priority, digitalization can have very different meanings to different leaders. When that organizational priority trickles down into communications, the meaning of 'digitalization' can seem even less clear. (Bryan, 2019, para. 2)

One of the roles professional communicators might well take on is helping organizational leaders to create and communicate consistent, clear messaging around what 'digital' means for their organization, now and for the future.

WHAT IS CHANGING?

It is not so much a matter of what is changing within digital corporate communication as what is shifting in the operating landscape for corporations – and that's plenty. AI's pervasive presence makes individual developments hard to track. Does this indicate AI should be a 'must have' for digital corporate communication? The question is no longer "can it be done" but "should it be done" (the ethical issues) and "what's the return if we do it"? (see PwC, 2021). While it might not be considered a 'must have', digital corporate communication could adapt AI content personalization to deliver more engaging content to both employees and other stakeholders, a concept known as identity-based corporate communication (Leeman, 2019). According to Kaput (2020, para. 5) "AI content personalization is software that uses artificial intelligence to serve up the right content at the right time for individual site visitors, based on what they've consumed in the past."

Noting AI's ability to extract insights from datasets, Kaput (2020, para. 13) comments that "given the right data, the right AI model can predict what type of content a returning site visitor is most likely to engage with, based on that visitor's historical content consumption". An employee interacting with an intranet might well be better disposed to one that sends him or her material directly aligned to his or her job needs and personal interests rather than one that broadcasts information in an undifferentiated fashion.

Similarly, stakeholders might feel more closely connected to an organization if they consider that it is taking their needs and interests into account. Extended Intelligence could use such a recommendation system to complement data gathered informally, through everything from team meetings to customer complaints; humans also have a role in providing the training material that guides the AI underlying the application. Morel (2004) examined the use of virtual adaptive and personalized agents in corporate communication, describing the extent to which exchanges of all kinds were increasingly being delegated to virtual support.

302 *Handbook on digital corporate communication*

However, specifics are elusive: even as AI implementations surge in an ever-widening range of fields, a lively prediction industry has emerged, ranging from doom-casters trying to guess when humanity will be subservient to smart machines, to those who seek to assure the worried that all will be well. However, as one research project showed, experts can be "horrific forecasters" (Epstein, 2019) although that doesn't stop people trying. For example, in 2019, the New Zealand Government Department of Internal Affairs created a 20-year chart of new and emerging technologies, focusing on those that could enable digital public services (O'Neill, 2019).

However, the temptation to focus on technology can obscure the needs of the humans it is meant to serve: *techne*, the Greek derivation of the word 'technology', means "the principles or methods employed in making something or attaining an objective" (Merriam-Webster, n.d.); it is primarily (but not exclusively) humans who make things for an intended use and are goal-seeking.

Therefore, we support Ito's (2019, para. 16) argument that

> Instead of thinking about machine intelligence in terms of humans vs machines, we should consider the system that integrates humans and machines – not artificial intelligence but extended intelligence. Instead of trying to control or design or even understand systems, it is more important to design systems that participate as responsible, aware and robust elements of even more complex systems.

The integration Ito (2019) envisages need not be sinister: as Aristotle is notably recorded as saying, the whole can be "beyond its parts" (*Metaphysics* 8.6) or, as the Collins Dictionary (n.d.) has it, "better than you would expect from the individual parts, because the way they combine adds a different quality". Perhaps for this reason, professional communicators' attitudes towards the ever-greater integration of AI into digital corporate communication are generally optimistic, although many professionals may also simply be grappling with the speed of unfolding developments. Petrucci (2018, para. 1) is one of the optimists:

> I have seen a glimpse of the future impact of artificial intelligence on corporate communications – and it is good. AI will bring a new level of trust to information, improve the way information is delivered (i.e., via augmented reality and virtual reality apps) and provide better insights and predictive analytics for decision making by corporate communications professionals.

Leeman's (2019) comment that: "This intelligence is meant to make your job easier, not to replace you" also typifies bullish practitioner commentary about AI and corporate communication. Indeed, Leeman notes that AI is able, among other things, to assist in promotion, help resolve crises, and facilitate 'identity-based corporate communication' (with specific individuals) to be undertaken with much greater precision.

These tasks are, themselves, enabled by more effective and efficient AI- and Big Data-enhanced analyses. The four key levels of analysis – descriptive (examining particular variables), diagnostic (focusing on patterns, reasons, and contexts), predictive (providing forecasts about future events), and prescriptive (generating recommendations for action) – are strengthening some corporate communicators' practices and outputs (Weichert Mehner, n.d.). At the same time, many practitioners are still coming to grips with AI developments.

For example, Macnamara et al. (2020) note that a key finding in the 2020–2021 *Asia-Pacific Communications Report* is corporate communicators' and public relations professionals' assessment that "coping with the digital evolution", "dealing with the speed and volume of information" and "using big data and algorithms for communication" have been their top three issues between 2018 and 2020. These dilemmas are likely to continue; as a Danish proverb (supposedly – there are different attributions) says, "prediction is difficult, especially about the future". Yet in what often seems like peak uncertainty for business, there are some constants for digital corporate communication.

WHAT REMAINS THE SAME?

Even though machines often need to communicate with each other to achieve a design purpose, digital developments do not make obsolete corporations' need for communication both internally and with outside human stakeholders. Rather, this need assumes new forms as the environment changes: for example, the fast uptake of the Zoom video-conferencing platform during the Covid-19 pandemic.

However, face-to-face communication still commands a special place: the *Forbes* business magazine expert panel (2020) came up with 13 cases in which direct interpersonal communication was considered better than electronic communication. For example, the panel asserted that, "When a situation requires trust-building, free ideas exchange, instant clarification and validating emotions, in-person communication is more effective" (2020, para. 4).

There's a cultural aspect to consider, too: "some cultures still honour the personalized meeting more than a remote one and find it difficult to integrate into a remote community" (Inside Telecom, 2020, para. 4). It's also true that no matter what means are used, corporations will continue to need to persuade and influence: to build employee and stakeholder engagement; to keep investors and stock analysts briefed; and to reach international partners with mutually beneficial communication.

When it comes to media, 'digital' is not the beginning and end of effective channels: Nelson (2020, p. 40) analysed "a year's worth of U.S.-based online news consumption data to show that, even in a media environment increasingly saturated with digital native news outlets, legacy news brands continue to comprise a majority of the most popular news sites". Nelson suggests that his findings may "reflect audience preferences for familiar, established brands, as well as structural advantages these brands maintain due to their size and capital" – a function of habit (2020, p. 40). On this basis, while AI and EI offer communicators fresh opportunities to create and distribute content quickly (see jasper.ai, for one AI-driven content creation engine), persuasion remains the stubborn challenge it always has been.

CRITICAL EXAMINATION

AI and EI are neither unalloyed public goods nor existential risks to humankind – especially, in this case, to those who serve as communicators. Rather, AI-related technologies are creating new communicative landscapes open to digital corporate communicators to navigate, but the territory is not without rough roads. Oliver (1997) observed that the AI-supported cognitive managerial approach that had begun to be used in the 1990s had resulted in organizations having to learn lessons through costly mistakes. Perhaps as an outcome, the literature includes a more critical approach to the implications of AI's growth for corporate communication. In relation to crisis communication, Prahl and Goh (2021, p. 1) have observed that AI failures are becoming increasingly common as organizations race to implement AI solutions, and that these "inevitable malfunctions" present an "unprecedented type of crisis" for communication professionals.

In particular, corporate communication professionals face particularly grave challenges when AI actions go awry, with the authors asking:

> who can companies blame when it is AI that is involved: can a machine really be blamed? Or, from a human perspective, can an AI designer or department head truly "know" and be held accountable for how AI performs when it is launched into the world? (Prahl and Goh, 2021, p. 1)

The authors note that without doubt, the most serious (and tragic) impact of malfunctioning AI is the loss of human life. Recent crises such as the Boeing 737 MAX 2018 and 2019 airplane crashes, followed by problematic delayed apologies and conflicting messages from Boeing, are emblematic of the problems facing corporate communication professionals. Beger (2018) has pointed out that Generation-Z will be the generation that will have to grapple with these sorts of challenges most extensively; in terms of corporate communication, he suggests, this will mean dealing with the ways in which AI often problematically integrates with human activities. That problematic includes ethical questions: according to Bryson, the ethical importance of AI is now "glaringly obvious" (2021, p. 3); the point is that AI "only occurs by and with design ... intentionally, for a purpose, by one or more members of human society" (2021, p. 6). It is that human design element that leads to debate about where the locus of accountability is to be found in networks comprising both human actors and systems supporting Extended Intelligence: a debate to which corporate communication professionals can and should contribute.

AI also poses challenges for corporate communication (and public relations; Galloway and Swiatek, 2018) practitioners' assessments of message effects and their consequent impacts on reputation; Salmon et al. (2019) have highlighted the need for practitioners to understand whether social media metrics are genuine or driven by bots, and to determine whether AI has played a role in generating messages. These two issues underscore the ways in which AI can interfere with message interpretation, with further issues being likely to appear in the coming years.

The scholarly research in communication areas that cross over into corporate communication is also highlighting the extensive impacts of the technology not just on various areas of practice, but also on professionals themselves. For instance, Zerfass et al.'s (2020, p. 377) cross-national (Europe-focused) study about AI in communication management identified a "[l]ack of individual competencies, and organisations struggling with different levels of competency and unclear responsibilities".

To counter these "key challenges and risks", the authors recommend that communication managers educate themselves and their teams about AI; additionally, they also advise transforming the implementation of AI into a leadership issue. In a different vein, focusing on chatbots in connection with communication management, Syvänen and Valentini (2020) have noted that the current research has focused on the micro-level nature of chatbots, with more research being needed about the meso (organizational) and macro (societal) levels of conversational agents. In their automation of online conversations, chatbots pose a "particular challenge" from an ethical perspective (Murtarelli et al., 2021), including the fact that tech-

Digital corporate communication and extended intelligence

nology is now available "that enables anyone to create human-like Virtual Agents" (Cognigy. com, n.d.), potentially opening the door to misuse as well as constructive purposes.

CASE STUDY: CITY OF SYDNEY'S INTEGRATION OF AI AND EI INTO CORPORATE COMMUNICATION

This chapter's case study, the digital corporate communications for the local government authority for central Sydney, Australia, offers a range of insights into the different ways in which AI is impacting digital corporate communications, including the varied ways in which it is enabling Extended Intelligence. The local government authority (officially, the City of Sydney), established in 1842, is responsible for an urban area of 26.15 square kilometres that is one of the densest and fastest growing in Australia (Morris, 2021). Before the Covid-19 pandemic, the city was Australia's economic powerhouse, representing around 8 per cent of Australia's GDP (Jones, 2020). The authority not only oversees "a vast flow of people and activities", but also helps to project "the global image of Australia to the world" (Kornberger and Clegg, 2011, p. 142). The organization's corporate communications team contributes significantly to projecting this national image, as well as overseeing other aspects of communication with internal and external publics in Sydney and further afield. Specifically, the team engages in the "development, implementation and evaluation of corporate and internal communications services for the organisation" that help to build strong relationships and keep the City's diverse communities well informed (Walsh, 2020, p. 3).

In recent years, the City of Sydney has increasingly been integrating AI into its corporate communication, and enabling Extended Intelligence more broadly, through the implementation of its Digital Strategy, as well as its Smart City Strategic Framework, both published in 2020. These two plans, in turn, build on the major 2017 Sustainable Sydney strategic plan, with its vision of making the city more "green, global and connected" (City of Sydney, 2017). The Digital Strategy focuses particularly on the digital changes set out for the local government area and the organization. The Smart City Strategic Framework outlines the more technical approaches that the organization is taking.

A key aspect of the framework is a connection between an "enabling environment" and smart infrastructure that, together, help to underpin the strategic outcomes supporting a vision of "a dynamic, responsive city, harnessing technology and data to enable collaborative innovation and create a thriving, inclusive and resilient future for all" (City of Sydney, 2020a, p. 16). The enabling environment consists of elements such as leadership, culture, funding, and partnerships; the smart infrastructure comprises components such as user interfaces, data integration and analytics platforms, sensors, and connectivity networks. The framework also includes seven "guiding principles" that articulate the ethics and fundamental values underpinning the city's ongoing digital transformation as being: community-first, collaborative, innovative, problem-driven, and evidence-based, flexible and adaptive, secure and ethical by design, and inclusive (City of Sydney, 2020a).

Increasingly AI-driven digital corporate communications have been used to bring the framework to life; more broadly, these AI-enhanced communications have been prioritized by the organization in recent years. For the Sydney authority, the digital communications approach has become so important that: "Much of the City's communication is done online, through a range of websites, social media channels, apps and platforms" (City of Sydney, 2020b).

306 *Handbook on digital corporate communication*

These AI-rich digital communication tools provide multiple Extended Intelligence opportunities that enable the organization to develop, implement, and evaluate programs for communities more effectively, as well as undertake stronger communication activities. In many respects, AI has integrated itself into communications activities in much the same way that it has simply integrated itself deeply into everyday life; this phenomenon is captured in Elliott's (2019) notion of 'the culture of AI' and its interplay of digital systems and day-to-day living.

The organization has also been actively developing its suite of AI-powered digital communications to offer more integrated and seamless experiences for communities. For instance, it is implementing a wider range of customer service management systems, offering a smart ePlanning service to make it easier to work with the organization, undertaking online collective storytelling with communities (enabling individuals and groups to share their accounts of living in the city), collecting feedback and using data analytics to undertake improvements to customers' experiences, and mapping customer journeys through all touchpoints related to particular programmes. It has also developed a content strategy to provide a coherent framework for communication through its digital channels (City of Sydney, 2020b).

One of the areas in which Extended Intelligence is being used most visibly is the area of understanding, and enhancing, community well-being. As the Council on Extended Intelligence (2019) points out, the City of Sydney is part of a small set of cities – including Santa Monica in the US, and Winnipeg in Canada – that has made community well-being indicators a central driver of its city planning framework. This situation reflects the notion that the benefits of Extended Intelligence "must be measured in worth not exclusively limited to material wealth" (Council on Extended Intelligence, 2019, p. 1). New technology-enabled approaches to gathering and instrumentalizing data – including, crucially, the analysis of patterns of communication – are generating more effective insights about the community well-being indicators (Council on Extended Intelligence, 2019, p. 31). In Sydney's case, a range of data are being gathered and analysed to understand progress in five key 'domains' of community well-being: (1) healthy, safe and inclusive communities; (2) culturally rich and vibrant communities; (3) democratic and engaged communities; (4) dynamic, resilient local economies; and (5) sustainable environments. The organization has reported that around half of its targets have now been achieved, though ongoing work is required in multiple areas; nevertheless, it is pleased with the favourable social progress being made, for example, in community safety, trust, life expectancy, education, and employment (City of Sydney, 2019, p. 5). It also has a positive view of the wealth of data being collected that is "providing the City with a strong basis for the formulation of evidence-based policy and for ongoing planning" (City of Sydney, 2019, p. 5).

A key driver in the push for the organization and its operations, including its digital corporate communications activities, to become more AI-rich was the growing number of expert voices outlining the benefits of AI and EI for the city. For instance, Wallace argued that AI, particularly an ecosystem of AI providers and capabilities, would help to improve work stability, sustainability, and overall liveability in Sydney; Williams contended that AI would help enable space across the city to be used in more flexible ways; and Drury noted that it would enhance the health and well-being of workers (in Cain et al., 2019).

The city also realizes that it has many further opportunities for integrating AI into its operations and enhancing Extended Intelligence. For example, in relation to its objective to operate as "a connected organisation to optimise the customer experience and maximise efficiencies" (City of Sydney, 2020a, p. 39), the organization is aware that it can further "[u]se machine learning and advanced analytics … for actionable insights, informing the collaborative design and delivery of services" (City of Sydney, 2020a, p. 40). In this respect, a range of questions can now be answered for which, previously, responses could not be obtained (or could not be obtained with ease); for example, questions can be answered about citizens' more minor habits (relating to day-to-day activities), and their preferences for the usage of civic infrastructure (such as public amenities). At the same time, various risks present themselves (as they always do when new technologies are involved); for instance, risks connected to privacy violations through data breaches, the unethical or incorrect use (as well as misapplication) of data, and the malfunctioning of technology, are all potential risks implicated in the further development and growth of Extended Intelligence.

The ever-deepening use of increasingly sophisticated AI-powered corporate communication will only continue because of the Covid-19 pandemic. The disruptions to daily life in Sydney that it brought (including two city-wide lockdowns in 2020 and 2021 that lasted several months), only increased the importance of, and reliance on, AI-driven digital communication. The organization found that Sydney's business leaders, in particular, "told us to use this moment to support them to respond to this new environment" (City of Sydney, 2020c). Increasingly AI-intensive communications are sure to figure ever more prominently in this response, and to further the growth of ever-more sophisticated Extended Intelligence more broadly.

CONCLUSION AND FUTURE DIRECTIONS

Corporate communicators are going to have to contend with AI either replacing or extending their capabilities for years to come. Whether that is a good thing can depend on whether one is a technological determinist or an optimist about AI's upsides, present and potential. The Council on Extended Intelligence set out its vision in a report (2019) called "The Case for Extended Intelligence". It asserted that

> One of the most powerful narratives of modern times is the story of scientific and technological progress. While our future will undoubtedly be shaped by the use of existing and emerging technologies – in particular, of autonomous and intelligent systems (A/IS) – there is no guarantee that progress defined by "the next" is beneficial. (para. 2)

The Council argues that

> Our future practices will be shaped by our individual and collective imaginations and by the stories we tell about who we are and what we desire, for ourselves and the societies in which we live. These stories must move beyond the "us versus them" media mentality pitting humans against machines. (para. 3)

On this basis, EI is a viable path ahead for digital corporate communication, as practitioners learn how to recruit AI technologies to serve the needs of corporations wishing to enhance both employee and stakeholder engagement and the communities within which the live and work.

REFERENCES

Apsland, W. and Hills, M. (n.d.). What is AI? https://www.cropleycomms.com/insights/articles/what-is-ai.

Beger, R. (2018). *Planning for corporate communication*. Singapore: Springer.

Bowen, S. A. (2019). Corporate communication. In D. W. Stacks, M. B. Salwen, and K. C. Eichhorn (eds.), *An integrated approach to communication theory and research* (pp. 399–413). London: Routledge.

Bryan, J. (2019). What digitalization means for corporate communications. https://www.gartner.com/smarterwithgartner/digitalization-means-corporate-communications.

Bryson, J. L. (2021). The artificial intelligence of the ethics of artificial intelligence: An introductory overview for law and regulation. In M. D. Dubber, F. Pasquale, and S. Das (eds.), *The Oxford handbook of ethics of AI* (pp. 3–51). Oxford: Oxford University Press.

Buhmann, A., Paßmann, J., and Fieseler, C. (2020). Managing algorithmic accountability: Balancing reputational concerns, engagement strategies, and the potential of rational discourse. *Journal of Business Ethics*, 163(2), 265–280.

Cain, I. H., Cairo, A., Duffy, M., Meli, L., Rye, M. S., Worthington Jr., E. L. (2019). Measuring gratitude at work. *The Journal of Positive Psychology*, 14(4), 440–451.

City of Sydney (2017). *Sustainable Sydney 2030: Community strategic plan*. The City of Sydney. https://www.cityofsydney.nsw.gov.au/strategies-action-plans/community-strategic-plan.

City of Sydney (2019). *Community wellbeing indicators 2019*. The City of Sydney. https://www.cityofsydney.nsw.gov.au/-/media/corporate/files/2020-07-migrated/files_c-1/community-wellbeing-indicators-2019-final-27sep2019.pdf?download=true.

City of Sydney (2020a). *Smart city strategic framework*. The City of Sydney. https://www.cityofsydney.nsw.gov.au/strategies-action-plans/smart-city-strategic-framework.

City of Sydney (2020b). *Digital strategy*. The City of Sydney. https://www.cityofsydney.nsw.gov.au/strategies-action-plans/digital-strategy.

City of Sydney (2020c). *Rebuild and recover: The priorities in our Covid-19 community recovery plan*. The City of Sydney. https://news.cityofsydney.nsw.gov.au/articles/rebuild-and-recover-the-priorities-in-our-covid-19-community-recovery-plan.

Cognigy.com (n.d.). POWER UP Amazon Connect with Cognigy.AI. https://www.cognigy.com/solutions/cognigy-for-amazon-connect.

Collins Dictionary (n.d). *More/greater than the sum of its parts.* .https://www.collinsdictionary.com/dictionary/english/more-greater-than-the-sum-of-its-parts.

Cornelissen, J. (2020). *Corporate communication: A guide to theory and practice* (6th edition). London: Sage Publications.

Council on Extended Intelligence (CXI) (2019). The case for extended intelligence: Technological advancement in service of people and planet. https://engagestandards.ieee.org/rs/211-FYL-955/images/CXI%20report.pdf.

de la Boutetière, H., Montagner, A., and Reich, A. (2018). Unlocking success in digital transformations. McKinsey & Company. https://www.mckinsey.com/capabilities/people-and-organizational-performance/our-insights/unlocking-success-in-digital-transformations.

Epstein, D. (2019, June). The peculiar blindness of experts. *The Atlantic*. https://www.theatlantic.com/magazine/archive/2019/06/how-to-predict-the-future/588040/.

Forbes expert panel (2020). 13 times in-person communication is better than electronic exchanges. *Forbes*, 17 July. https://www.forbes.com/sites/forbescoachescouncil/2020/07/17/13-times-in-person-communication-is-better-than-electronic-exchanges/?sh=2fd7219b2eb7.

Frankiewicz, B. and Chamorro-Premuzik, T. (2020). Digital transformation is about talent, not technology. *Harvard Business Review*, 6 May. https://hbr.org/2020/05/digital-transformation-is-about-talent-not-technology.

Galloway, C. and Swiatek, L. (2018). Public relations and artificial intelligence: It's not (just) about robots. *Public Relations Review*, 44(5), 734–740.

Gregory, A. and Halff, G. (2020). The damage done by big data-driven public relations. *Public Relations Review*, 46(2), 101902.

Inside Telecom Staff (2020). Can digital communication compete with f2f interactions in business? https://www.insidetelecom.com/can-digital-communication-compete-with-f2f-interactions-in-business/.

Ito, J. (2016). *Extended intelligence*. https://pubpub.ito.com/pub/extended-intelligence/release/1.

Ito, J. (2019). Forget about artificial intelligence, extended intelligence is the future. *Wired*, 24 April. https://www.wired.co.uk/article/artificial-intelligence-extended-intelligence.

Jones, A. (2020). City of Sydney decentralised renewable energy master plan. In A. Sayigh (ed.), *Renewable energy and sustainable buildings* (pp. 449–460). Cham: Springer.

Kaput, M. (2020). How AI content personalization works. Marketing Artificial Intelligence Institute. https://www.marketingaiinstitute.com/blog/how-ai-content-personalization-works#:~:text=AI%20content%20personalization%20is%20software,on%20what%20to%20consume%20next.

Karachalios, K. and Ito, J. (n.d.). Human intelligence and autonomy in the age of 'extended intelligence'. Council on Extended Intelligence. https://globalcxi.org/wp-content/uploads/CXI_Essay.pdf.

Kornberger, M. and Clegg, S. (2011). Strategy as performative practice: The case of Sydney 2030. *Strategic Organization*, 9(2), 136–162.

Lalić, D., Stanković, J., Gračanin, D., and Milić, B. (2020). New technologies in corporate communications. In Z. Anisic, B. Lalić, and D. Gracanin (eds.), *Proceedings of the 25th International Joint Conference on Industrial Engineering and Operations Management – IJCIEOM* (pp. 374–380). Cham: Springer.

Leeman, M. (2019). The impact of AI on corporate communication. *Textmetrics*, 15 July. https://www.textmetrics.com/the-impact-of-ai-on-corporate-communication.

Lerbinger, O. (2018). *Corporate communication: An international and management perspective*. Malden, MA: Wiley-Blackwell.

Macnamara, J., Lwin, M. O., Hung-Baesecke, C.-J., and Zerfass, A. (2020). *Asia-Pacific communication monitor 2020/21*. http://www.communicationmonitor.asia/media/APCM-2020-21-Report.pdf.

Marr, B. (2018). The key definitions of Artificial Intelligence (AI) that explain its importance. *Forbes*. https://www.forbes.com/sites/bernardmarr/2018/02/14/the-key-definitions-of-artificial-intelligence-ai-that-explain-its-importance/?sh=251f5a834f5d.

Men, R. L. and Bowen, S. A. (2017). *Excellence in internal communication management*. New York: Business Expert Press.

Merriam-Webster (n.d.). *Techne*. https://www.merriam-webster.com/dictionary/techne.

Morel, B. (2004). Recruiting a virtual employee: Adaptive and personalized agents in corporate communication. In S. Payr and R. Trappl (eds.), *Agent culture: Human-agent interaction in a multicultural world* (pp. 177–196). Mahwah, NJ: Lawrence Erlbaum.

Morris, A. (2021). An impossible task? Neoliberalism, the financialisation of housing and the City of Sydney's endeavours to address its housing affordability crisis. *International Journal of Housing Policy*, 21(1), 23–47.

Murtarelli, G., Gregory, A., and Romenti, S. (2021). A conversation-based perspective for shaping ethical human–machine interactions: The particular challenge of chatbots. *Journal of Business Research*, 129, 927–935.

Natale, S. and Ballatore, A. (2020). Imagining the thinking machine: Technological myths and the rise of artificial intelligence. *Convergence: The International Journal of Research into New Media Technologies*, 26(1), 3–18.

Nelson, J. L. (2020). The enduring popularity of legacy journalism: An analysis of online audience data. *Media and Communication*, 8(2), 40–50.

OECD (n.d.). Definition of artificial intelligence. http://dx.doi.org/10.1787/9789264232440-en.

Oliver, S. (1997). *Corporate communication: Principles, techniques and strategies*. London: Kogan Page.

O'Neill, R. (2019). Future tech: NZ government digital lab charts 20-year landscape. *Reseller News*. https://www.reseller.co.nz/article/666972/future-tech-nz-government-digital-lab-charts-20-year-landscape/?fp=2&fpid=1.

Papageorgiou, S. (n.d.). *Core competencies for strategic communication management*. Centre for Strategic Communication Management. https://www.thecsce.com/resources/insights/articles/core_comp_strategic_comms_mgt_art.

310 *Handbook on digital corporate communication*

Petrucci, A. (2018). How artificial intelligence will impact corporate communications. *Forbes*, 20 April. https://www.forbes.com/sites/forbescommunicationscouncil/2018/04/20/how-artificial-intelligence-will-impact-corporate-communications/?sh=38762ecd1dc6.

Prahl, A. and Goh, W. W. P. (2021). "Rogue machines" and crisis communication: When AI fails, how do companies publicly respond? *Public Relations Review*, *47*(4). https://doi.org/10.1016/j.pubrev.2021.102077.

PwC India (2020). *AI: An opportunity amidst a crisis.* https://www.pwc.in/consulting/technology/data-and-analytics/ai-an-opportunity-amidst-a-crisis.html.

rockcontent.com (2021). *Artificial Intelligence algorithm: Everything you need to know about it.* https://rockcontent.com/blog/artificial-intelligence-algorithm/#:~:text=Essentially%2C%20an%20AI%20algorithm%20is,and%20run%20tasks%20more%20efficiently.

Salmon, C. T., Poorisat, T., and Kim, S. H. (2019). Third-person effect in the context of public relations and corporate communication. *Public Relations Review*, *45*(4).

Schuett, J. (2019). A legal definition of AI. https://www.researchgate.net/profile/Jonas-Schuett/publication/336198524_A_Legal_Definition_of_AI/links/5e20599a458515ba208b9e4c/A-Legal-Definition-of-AI.pdf.

Simonite, T. (2018). A plea for AI that serves humanity instead of replacing it. *Wired*, 22 June. https://www.wired.com/story/a-plea-for-ai-that-serves-humanity-instead-of-replacing-it/.

Syvänen, S. and Valentini, C. (2020). Conversational agents in online organization–stakeholder interactions: A state-of-the-art analysis and implications for further research. *Journal of Communication Management*, *24*(4), 339–362.

ThinkAutomation (n.d.). Is extended intelligence the answer to AI uncertainty? https://www.thinkautomation.com/bots-and-ai/is-extended-intelligence-the-answer-to-ai-uncertainty/.

Towers-Clark, C. (2020). Artificial intelligence is incompatible with the future of communication – here's why. *Forbes*, 25 May. https://www.forbes.com/sites/charlestowersclark/2020/05/25/artificial-intelligence-is-incompatible-with-the-future-of-communication--heres-why/?sh=4b84a49926b2.

Troise, C. and Camilleri, M. A. (2021). The use of digital media for marketing, CSR communication and stakeholder engagement. In M. A. Camilleri (ed.), *Strategic corporate communication in the digital age* (pp. 161–174). Bingley: Emerald Publishing.

Walsh, D. (2020). *Position description.* City of Sydney. https://s3-ap-southeast-2.amazonaws.com/cdn.hr.cityofsydney.nsw.gov.au/January+2020/Communications+Manager+-+Position+Description.pdf.

Wang, P. (2009). What do you mean by "AI"? https://linas.org/mirrors/nars.wang.googlepages.com/2007.06.27/wang.AI_Definitions.pdf.

Weichert Mehner (n.d.). Big Data and AI in corporate communications. https://www.weichertmehner.com/en/insights/big-data-and-ai-in-corporate-communications/.

Zerfass, A., Hagelstein, J., and Tench, R. (2020). Artificial intelligence in communication management: A cross-national study on adoption and knowledge, impact, challenges and risks. *Journal of Communication Management*, *24*(4), 377–389.

22. Digital corporate communication and algorithmic leadership and management

Polina Feshchenko, Niilo Noponen, Vilma Luoma-aho and Tommi Auvinen

INTRODUCTION

In the era when software algorithms are controlling, organizing and monitoring millions of workers around the world, algorithmic management and leadership have gained attention in both academia and practice. Theory about communicatively constituted organizations (CCO) explains how organizations exist due to the management of different flows of communication. In fact, organizations are formed from communication that integrates, structures, contextualizes and positions the organization in a larger social system (McPhee et al., 2014). Thus, management and leadership of these flows are what essentially determines an organization's success. The new forms of gig work, app-work and platform work, which are often led fully by algorithmic systems, are changing how information flows, but not necessarily improving the leadership function or the well-being of the workers included in the new digital economy.

In the last century, many changes have happened to traditional management and leadership due to the new technologies. To better understand their effects, the two organizational practices should be distinguished first. For many critics, leadership has been simply a new word to describe management, mainly as leadership 'best practice' is often hard to find in the real world and is increasingly difficult to adopt (Edgell et al., 2016). Management is usually considered more tactical, focusing on administering and controlling functions, while leadership represents more strategic contemporary approaches that lead organizations by 'visions and values', rather than by rules and control. However, Koontz (1980, p. 183) considered leading and motivating as one of the management functions, beside controlling, planning and organizing, and he was also among the first to argue that technologies have an impact on organizational management (Cole and Kelly, 2020, pp. 112–113). To be more precise with terminology, leadership is viewed as a form of *managerialism* – the generalized ideology of management (Edgell et al., 2016). Klikauer (2013, p. 2) provides the following explanation: "managerialism combines management knowledge and ideology to establish itself systematically in organisations and society while depriving owners, employees ... and civil society ... of all decision-making powers". This suggests that both management and leadership are forms of a managerialist ideology that remains dominant across organizational work and life (Edgell et al., 2016). Taking that into account and distinct from management, leadership can been summarized here as *a social process aiming to fulfil organizational goals* (Auvinen et al., 2017). Since these functions are built around various communication processes, the effect of technological development on them has brought a new digital perspective to corporate communication.

Until recently, such tools have been used *by* human managers *to support* human managers in decision-making, controlling, supervising, planning and organizing through information systems and data collection across organization and beyond. This, however, is undergoing

312 *Handbook on digital corporate communication*

a radical change today. With the progress in Artificial Intelligence (AI) and automation technologies, computer systems are not here to just assist any more. "One of the characteristics of digital labor platforms is their reliance on algorithms that perform many management functions previously conducted by human managers in traditional work organizations" (Jarrahi and Sutherland, 2019). As numerous examples show, these tools can now mediate middle management through the direct execution of control, supervision, workforce organization, task assignment, feedback and even motivation of employees (e.g., Lee et al., 2015; Martin et al., 2016; Schildt, 2017; Derrick and Elson, 2018). Building an understanding of algorithmic technologies used for organizational management will help to shed light on the digital element of DCC.

DEFINITIONS OF THE TOPIC AND PREVIOUS STUDIES

'Algorithm' is defined as "a set of instructions that are followed in a fixed order and used for solving a mathematical problem, making a computer program, etc." (Longman Dictionary, 2020). This definition shows that algorithms can represent both theory (describing the logic behind certain phenomena; guiding) and something more complex, like computer programs that perform computation. The latter are algorithmic systems, which are well-known for their ability to learn, develop and reinforce own logic. Such attributes make them in a way intelligent, as they are designed to imitate human cognition (Mitchell, 1997; Ertel, 2011). Two directions appear to be emerging when it comes to how these technologies are applied for organizational management: one focusing on management by algorithms and the other on leadership by algorithms.

There are certain differences between algorithmic management and leadership practices. *Algorithmic management* can be perceived as a 'big brother', which is, basically, forced on workers (they *have to* comply with its rules), is in charge of control and distribution of work, not interested in any feedback and is utilizing very simple monetary non-personal incentives in a gamified manner to motivate subordinates to continue working. The origin of *algorithmic leadership* seems to be more humanistic, as the practice is aimed at helping either a human user, worker or a whole company (depending on the use case). In this context, it is more like a 'companion' than a 'big brother'. In terms of present definitions of the phenomenon, as with algorithmic management, they are not agreed and often the same term is used to describe different applications.

A significant amount of research has been done on organizations with automated middle management functions (e.g., Uber, Lyft: Lee et al., 2015; Upwork: Jarrahi et al., 2019; Airbnb: Cheng and Foley, 2019). However, the communication element has rarely been a focus of the studies. As management and leadership are executed through some form of communication, it is communication that determines how people perceive their organization's management and leadership. Therefore, digital corporate communication (DCC) is defined as "an organization's strategic management of digital technologies, digital infrastructures and digitalization processes to improve communication with internal and external stakeholders and more broadly within society for the maintenance of organizational tangible and intangible assets" (Badham and Luoma-aho, Chapter 1 in this volume, p. 9). In this context, algorithmic leadership and management represent a major shift in organizations, because they mitigate interactions between organizational stakeholders and key management players, while attempting to make organizations more cost efficient and fast.

When communication is conducted by algorithms, it has different dynamics compared to human communication. Algorithms might be perceived as less natural as they only do what they are coded to do. In addition, they seldom communicate the logic behind the coded choices, making their communication even more obscure for anyone interacting with them inside or outside the organization (Buhmann et al., 2020). Despite the lack of clarity on how algorithms communicate, there are speculations on their potential involvement in leadership activities and even top management of organizations, due to their quite powerful analytical capabilities. For example, Wesche and Sonderegger (2019, p. 200) have introduced the concept of Computer-Human Leadership (CHL), which they defined as "a process whereby purposeful influence is exerted by a computer agent over human agents to guide, structure, and facilitate activities and relationships in a group or organization". Looking even further into the past, Avolio et al. (2000, p. 617) suggested the concept of e-leadership, defining it as "a social influence process mediated by Information Technology (IT) to produce a change in attitudes, feelings, thinking, behavior, and/or performance with individuals, groups, and/or organizations". Assuming that at some point in the future algorithms will improve their communication abilities, these might be not mere speculations.

As a separate phenomenon, the study of DCC will bring clarity to communication design, execution and attributes in algorithmic management and similar digital contexts. This is important especially because Jarrahi and Sutherland (2019) emphasize that to understand the emerging role of algorithms in organizations, one should take a sociotechnical perspective and move from questions of replacement or substitution towards questions of balance, coordination, contestation and negotiation.

Wesche and Sonderegger (2019) emphasize that the acceptance from subordinates will be of crucial importance in computer–human leadership, as the user will have to obey and/or follow the system in the context of the task completion process. Their research, however, did not focus on the fully automated leadership process and nor did it focus on what specific leadership functions can be automated and what cannot. In e-leadership, the potential mediation of leadership by technology is viewed from the perspective of robots leading human subordinates (Avolio et al., 2014, p. 117). The researchers note that even if the robots are developed to the point where they are able to recognize human emotions and psychological states, assigning them as leaders may pose threats, as robots themselves will not have their own emotions, or act from moral and ethical considerations, acting only from the directives or algorithms embedded into them (2014, p. 117).

Lee et al. (2015) were pioneers in this field, introducing the term 'algorithmic management' and defining it as a practice, where software algorithms supplemented by technology devices undertake the functions normally executed by human managers. Algorithmic management should be understood as a sociotechnical process emerging from the continuous interaction of organizational members and the algorithms that mediate their work (Jarrahi and Sutherland, 2019). The boundaries between the responsibilities of managers, workers and algorithms are not fixed, but constantly negotiated and enacted in the novel management approaches. Lee et al. (2015) used the term in the context of platforms like Uber and Lyft. Schildt (2017) based his conceptualization on Lee et al.'s (2015) definition, but he was the first one to address it as 'scientific management 2.0'. With such labelling, Schildt emphasized that management has become a process executed by technology and not by human beings, referring to Taylor's

314 *Handbook on digital corporate communication*

theory of management, in which the management process is described as having strict rules and aiming at maximum efficiency of operations. In his article, the author also postulates that "algorithmic management, or Scientific Management 2.0, shifts power from a hierarchy of managers to larger cadres of professionals who master analytics, programming, and business", pointing out that there are still people in charge, but they are no longer managers and are out of sight of the workers (Schildt, 2017).

WHAT IS CHANGING?

Corporate communication is a complex multi-layered practice, which differs a lot depending on one's role in an organization, as well as on the purpose and target audience of communication. For example, managers at different levels influence the top-down transmission of corporate messages to employees, communicating their opinions back to top management (Men, 2011; Whitworth, 2011). Even though employees prefer to receive information from their immediate supervisors rather than from senior executives, the communication quality does not play a big role in this type of communication. On the contrary, communication quality, styles, competence and channels become extremely important when it comes to leadership (Men and Stacks, 2013). Leadership, as an ability to influence the attitude and behaviour of employees, is performed largely through communication (Men, 2014). Therefore, to holistically explore and form an understanding of digital corporate communication in the new emerging algorithmic leadership context, the established theoretical principles of both leadership and CCO will be reviewed in the following.

Though digitalization of organizational processes has made many management tasks (e.g., controlling, organizing) easier and more transparent, the same enablement has not happened in leadership. During recent decades leadership practice and communication have faced several fundamental changes due to digitalization (Auvinen et al., 2019). The recent epoch of digital transformation (boosted by the Covid-19 pandemic) has made interactions faster and traceable, making some of the management practices easier. Meanwhile, the leadership nature and execution has faced many challenges in the virtual context, as it is deeply rooted in communication (Holladay and Coombs, 1993; De Vries et al., 2010). Due to the varying extent of digitalization, leadership evolution has been illustrated in comparison with the industrial revolution. Is it, after all, a question of full leadership automation or of a simple distribution of leadership influence and its functions (e.g., managerial) between humans and algorithms?

The automation of leadership is not a straightforward concept. It can relate to the automation of the whole *corporate leadership process* (part of organizational governance) or to just *one of the management functions* (as it is an inherent part of any management practice – mentioned in the introduction). Harms and Han (2019) suggested that algorithmic leadership consists of elements of e-leadership, distributed or shared leadership and substitutes for leadership. From the *e-leadership* perspective, Stokols et al. already in 2009 mentioned that the use of technologies has led to constant contact between managers and employees, often resulting in higher stress, lack of socialization and sense of belonging, as well as a lack of mutual understanding between subordinates. In the present management-by-algorithms (e.g., in Uber), we can also observe a constant contact and interaction between workers and digital system (as known as 'algorithmic management') (Möhlmann and Zalmanson, 2017). This is something

Digital corporate communication and algorithmic leadership and management 315

not common for human-to-human leadership and management, as people simply cannot be in constant contact time- and resources-wise.

According to the *shared or distributed leadership* theory, there is no single leader. Instead, the leadership is distributed within the team. Each member can take the lead and influence others, when he or she has more situational expertise, and then stepping aside when the situation changes (Northouse, 2016, p. 365). Most of the present evidence shows that in algorithmic leadership there is, however, only one leader, which is the digital system. Nevertheless, in rare (and, so far, mostly conceptual) cases, the algorithmic leadership can have elements of shared leadership. In such a case, an AI-leader can act as a team member, assisting with, for example, decision-making, or as a coach, helping with activities alignment and assignment based on individual skills of each member (Wesche and Sonderegger, 2019). Considering the *substitutes for leadership* theory, though one could think that substitution is almost technically impossible in algorithmic leadership as workers must always report to the system, most of its principles are not changing in the algorithmic context and, thus, are discussed in the next section.

As corporate communication is viewed here as a major leadership enabler, it is important to explore how its processes change in the digital environment and the role and effects of algorithms in this. When technology mediates social processes in organization, it directly affects interaction, communication and power dynamics of those involved. Jarrahi et al. (2021) call this a sociotechnical phenomenon, demonstrating that algorithms coordinate the organizational choices and shift organizational roles (Figure 22.1). Their diagram demonstrates the role and place of algorithms in the communication process between management and employees in the algorithm-driven organization. Practically, there is no direct communication between human managers and workers, but rather all organizational messages and decisions go through algorithms and are mediated and/or augmented by them. Next, the existing principles of corporate communication will be overviewed and mapped on to the research evidence of algorithmic systems.

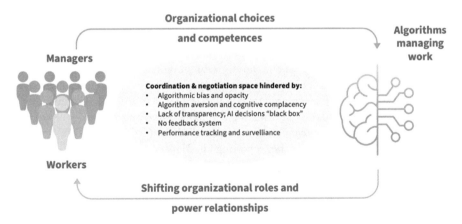

Source: Jarrahi et al. (2021).

Figure 22.1   *Sociotechnical dynamics in algorithmically mediated organizational context*

From the CCO perspective, there are ten principles of communication, as outlined by Bishop (2006): *being clear* (appropriate and understandable use of language, organization of information), *relevant* (consideration and connection with interests of involved parties), *timely* (allowing response and interaction with information), *consistent* (not opposing or contradicting the organization's discourse and actions), *truthful* (accurate and factually correct), *fundamental* (disclosing the core issues and central facts; avoiding 'spinning' – giving the positive side only, twisting information to alter impression or disregarding the truth), *comprehensive* (holistic, providing the context and meaning), *accessible* (information is available to all parties to see, hear and discuss), *caring* (showing respect and compassion for circumstances, attitudes, beliefs and feelings of those involved), *responsiveness to feedback* (organization seeks and responds to feedback and encourages mutual adaptation). The study has confirmed that these principles support the value and use of corporate communication process, with the basis that the communication is symmetric and based on dialogue, as this way it is considered to be effective (Bishop, 2006).

Do these principles persist when the communication processes are absorbed by digitalization and performed by algorithmic entities? The latest evidence shows that most of them become lost, with a slight variance and difference, depending on system and organizational contexts. When it comes to fully automated algorithmic systems, like in platform or gig work, there is a possibility that they are not even initially designed to be dialogic by humans, who program them, as most of the evidence shows lack of any open communication, support and feedback functionalities (Rosenblat and Stark, 2016). Another possibility is that organizations that deploy such systems want to deliberately avoid two-way communication with workers. In particular, Mateescu and Nguyen (2019) report lack of transparency on how the algorithms operate, creating additional challenges for the workers to figure out the logic behind decisions, even regarding their salary calculation. Transparency here is defined as a feature of the system, which gives users opportunities to see how decisions are made, to evaluate decisions' outcomes and the decision-maker (Lee, 2018), which is reflected in such CCO principles as being clear, relevant, fundamental, comprehensive and accessible. A couple of real-life examples are introduced later in the chapter to demonstrate the dynamics of how the violation of these and other principles of CCO happens in the fully digital context and under algorithmic communication.

Even though one could argue about the algorithmic communication being comprehensive, based on Cheney and Dionisopoulos's (1989) view that understanding the context is a responsibility of publics, the researchers emphasize that it is still the responsibility of an organization to provide contextual information and *to facilitate understanding as an inherent requirement of symmetrical communication.* Hond and Moser (2022) in their study on the role of algorithms in corporate sustainability reporting cite Hansen and Flyverbom (2015, p. 883): "access to reality is mediated by algorithmically coded soft and hardware devices, which afford particular kinds of knowledge and insights, *but never the full picture of anything*". The researchers note that the material agency of AI technology transforms sustainability reporting to an algorithmically mediated managerial technology that alters how corporate sustainability practices are understood and appraised by the public (Hond and Moser, 2022). According to Bishop (2006), this also violates the fundamental principle of CCO, as he mentions that not communicating the real or core issues represents an intent to mislead. Möhlmann and Zalmanson (2017) offer interesting insights on how the communication processes are organized within these algorithmic systems and affect workers. The researchers note that the com-

Digital corporate communication and algorithmic leadership and management   317

munications are one-sided and not open, which makes it impossible to deliver any suggestions or complaints, or discuss management decisions. This absence of a feedback loop and dialogue with algorithms contradicts the responsiveness to feedback, accessible and caring CCO principles, as they both are important for facilitating two-way communication, which is, in turn, an enabler of leadership (Men, 2014). Another demonstrative example is how the CCO principle of consistency is undermined in platform-mediated work environment – even though platform owners (e.g., Uber, Lyft, Deliveroo) claim this will give them more freedom and autonomy, in reality, workers face constant surveillance (e.g., Möhlmann and Zalmanson, 2017; Chan and Humphreys, 2018; Mateescu and Nguyen, 2019; Mengay, 2020).

WHAT REMAINS THE SAME?

We may approach leadership in the digital revolution from *e-leadership* (Avolio et al., 2000; Darics, 2020), *remote, distance or virtual leadership* (Watkins et al., 2007; Schmidt, 2014) conceptual frameworks. Despite the additional conceptual layer, the core of leadership – *a social process aiming to fulfil organizational goals* – remains the same (Auvinen et al., 2017). However, the comparison between a human leader and an artificial or, namely, an algorithmic (Noponen, 2019) leader, may offer an interesting perspective. Therefore, the following narrative will focus on the features and attributes of human leadership that can or could be relevant for *an algorithmic leader*, meaning that they would act the same way and produce the same effects, when applied to the algorithmic context.

Among various leadership types, transformational leadership is considered to be one of the most significant by scholars (Men, 2014). The rich amount of empirical evidence confirms its positive influence on employee attitudes and behaviour, noting that transformational leaders are usually more communicative than transactional (task-oriented) ones (De Vries et al., 2010). Such leadership style has a relationship- and people-oriented nature, while its execution happens through communication. The positive influence of transformational leaders is often reflected in the increased levels of commitment, motivation and encouragement of workers (Edgell et al., 2016).

In an algorithmic, digitally mediated, context, Rosenblat and Stark (2016) found that behavioural engagement happens merely through the promises of higher pay rates in certain areas and at specific times, resembling gambling or a gaming form of emotional experience. It is used by platform companies, such as Uber, to facilitate the relationships between supply and demand, rather than to establish relationships with employees. This example demonstrates that *leadership does not exist in the algorithmic context of platform companies*. Instead, they utilize algorithms and digital systems to empower them and maximize workers' efficiency – holding control over information, monitoring workers closely and reducing all motivational practices to standardized gamification, nudges and financial incentives (Rosenblat and Stark, 2016). The second industrial revolution gave birth to the idea that work could and should be managed (Edgell et al., 2016). Scientific management, introduced by Frederick Taylor in 1909, was based on the, at the time, novel idea that optimizing the organization of work leads to higher efficiency. Scientific management was based on dividing tasks and responsibilities between workers, as well as standardizing and measuring everything, rewarding high-performing workers with higher pay. Division of labour and standardization were also the key ideas behind the birth of mass production with assembly lines in the early 1900s, often

318 *Handbook on digital corporate communication*

referred to as Fordism (Edgell et al., 2016). Even though during the past century both of these approaches to treating employees have been criticized and recognized as less ethical (Gal et al., 2020), today, in the 2020s, algorithms have given them a second birth, offering new ways to execute them, the so-called *Digital Taylorism* or *Scientific Management 2.0* (Schildt, 2017; Günsel and Yamen, 2020).

Substitutes-for-leadership theory postulates that a leader's behaviour (or some of his/her functions) can be substituted for, neutralized or reinforced by situational factors (Kessler, 2013, p. 810). Among these factors are, for instance, the subordinates themselves (their knowledge, experience, amount of training, degree of autonomy needed, etc.), the nature of the task (its meaningfulness and intrinsic satisfaction it provides, degree of monotony and routine, feedback) and organizational characteristics (e.g., degree of formalization, flexibility of rules, amount of staff and support, etc.). There are several categories of these situational factors.

Substitutes decrease the influence of a leader over subordinates and can eventually replace him or her. One such factor is technology that can substitute a human leader or decrease the degree of the leader's influence. Another possible substitute can be the advanced training of workers, when the leader has not enough or the right competences and, thus, cannot effectively lead, guide and supervise the subordinates (e.g., leader – administrator, subordinate – surgeon) (Howell et al., 1990; Kessler, 2013). In the algorithmic context, where the leader *is* a form of technology, the latter option of substitutes is observed: human workers educate themselves and find ways to trick algorithms, avoid punishments by the system, as well as figure out how to improve their own work to maximize profit (e.g., Rosenblat and Stark, 2016; Chan and Humphreys, 2018).

Neutralizers are factors that prevent or counteract a leader's actions and encumber his or her ability to make a difference. An example of such factors can be seen when a leader is separated from subordinates and communicates virtually, since many leadership techniques become ineffective. Another possibility of neutralization is when a leader loses control over the rewarding system and, as a result, the ability to motivate employees. This is something that sometimes happens in the algorithmic context – workers simply lose interest in the financial rewards offered by the system; due to the lack of two-way communication with their algorithmic leader they fail to understand its decisions and start to question its expertise. As a result, the algorithmic leader loses influence over subordinates. To take over this leadership, algorithmic management workers have established online communities, where those with more expertise share their knowledge and guide others (Chan and Humphreys, 2018; Jarrahi and Sutherland, 2019).

When it comes to *enhancers* – factors that positively affect a leader's influence – it is controversial how they appear in the digitally mediated leadership context. For example, the human leader's influence can be enhanced with access to more information, relationship networks, organizational culture and ethics (Kessler, 2013, p. 811). An algorithmic leader can process and access more information by default, what can raise its credibility in certain situations (e.g., as explored by Lee, 2018). Nevertheless, most of the factors that positively affect a leader's influence – culture, ethics, communication and relationship networks – are not yet technically possible and/or leveraged to reinforce the digital leader's influence (Gal et al., 2020).

To sum up, it is negotiable whether there should be a line between the traditional or digital (e.g., algorithmic) leadership, yet it seems that it might be more fruitful to focus on the actual leader, disregarding its nature or origin. The long-established human leadership research shows that there is a variety of roles and functions that a leader needs to fulfil to achieve

Digital corporate communication and algorithmic leadership and management 319

organizational goals. Even though it remains obscure as to which of these roles and functions will transfer to algorithmic leadership, communication remains the only inseparable function of a leader.

What is the Role of Communication in Algorithmic Management and Leadership?

Rosenblat and Stark (2016) are among the pioneers in research on algorithmic management and the problematic issues of labour conditions and experience of work under this system. The researchers dedicated much of their focus to problems within communication processes between the company, its workers and customers. There were several issues that they discovered and discussed in their paper. First, workers are usually unable to reach company representatives. Uber, as an example, outsources its support and it is handled only by means of email. The typical replies are lacking situational understanding and are often templated (Rosenblat and Stark, 2016).

Communication often serves the central function of motivating in organizations. Jabagi et al. (2019) explored the motivation of workers in the gig or platform economy, where information technology (IT) plays a central role in organizational design and enables the connection between workers and customers. This context is generally known for the lack of social interactions (with colleagues and supervisors), because even human managers, who are traditionally in charge of maintaining and supporting workers' self-motivation, are now mediated by technology. In order to tackle this issue, Jabagi et al. (2019) proposed to the platform labour providers to integrate Enterprise Social Media (ESM) – "an organizational web-based platform that facilitates internally facing communication, social interaction and collaboration among users within an enterprise through the creation, sharing and indexing of content" (Leonardi et al., 2013, as cited in Jabagi et al., 2019). Implementation of ESM should increase motivation and work satisfaction, fulfilling the psychological needs of employees. ESM platforms resemble the well-known mass social-media platforms (e.g., LinkedIn), but also have unique functionalities (e.g., wikis, document sharing). They are considered to be very effective for a digital transformation of an organization, because of their ability to facilitate collaboration and knowledge sharing and to enable workers' social interaction, communication, self-expression and better identification of skills and knowledge (Jabagi et al., 2019). In the enterprise version, the researchers suggest introducing practices of *social networking* (e.g., having a profile, sharing status updates, expressing opinions, commenting) and *social badging* (awards for certain achievements). According to their research and background study on self-determination theory and job design, these features can increase workers' sense of belonging and competence, motivating them to commit and contribute more to their work and organization.

Communication is the means to make sense and build meaning into organizational practices. Toyoda et al. (2020) carried out an experiment, where participants (MTurk workers) had to find parasites in a blood sample with malaria, and found that when workers were provided the meaning of the task and when an Artificial Intelligence-powered system was framed as a supportive tool (used supportive messages), workers' engagement significantly increased. In fact, the results revealed the value of communication: when the workers knew the task's rationale and what was expected from it, they tried to frame their actions to be more desirable. This is also in line with CCO principles discussed in the previous chapter. Interestingly, workers were

320 *Handbook on digital corporate communication*

more engaged (though not more accurate) when the AI system was framed as a supervisor (used controlling language) and when the task was meaningless (Toyoda et al., 2020).

Another central role of communication in the context of AI is sensemaking through informal communication networks. Chan and Humphreys (2018) looked at workers' interpretations of the algorithms (i.e., messages received) and data, communication networks created and the guidance by workers among each other on forums, and the attempts at normalizing the production of social space at work. Focusing on Uber, they discovered that certain tensions emerge between the company and its workers – while Uber claimed that the rating systems and navigation were 'objective knowledge', the drivers relied on tacit knowledge and informal communication networks to make sense of the logic much like in traditional organizations. They had to develop an understanding of how the system works in order to tackle its imperfections and avoid situationally unnecessary punishments (Chan and Humphreys, 2018).

Such experiences of workers show that they expect clear communication of how ratings are comprised and how they should interact with customers and also the platform, which makes it a necessary missing element in the present management-by-algorithms work context. Chan and Humphreys suggested the term 'digitally-enabled service workers' to demonstrate better how the data influences the emergence of expectations towards social interactions and how the power dynamics are mediated through various digital processes, leading to the peer-to-peer exchange of information and building an algorithmic imaginary by the workers (Chan and Humphreys, 2018).

Jarrahi and Sutherland (2019) called this development of understanding of the platform's behaviour *sensemaking*, which they have also found to be a shared activity, since most of the research subjects used *online forums* to exchange their knowledge of the platform and its policies, seek advice, and help and support each other. Continuing this line of research, Kaine and Josserand (2019) were among those who pointed out the importance of *social media* for gig work. They discovered that it was useful for community building and for the direct facilitation of gig work (in the context of knowledge-intensive work), because workers were able to carry out self-branding and display their skills and competences better. Moreover, workers used social media not only for exchanging their knowledge, but also for collective activism and for expressing their resistance towards the platform work conditions.

These examples demonstrate that, even though in the digital context, where communication processes are automated by algorithms, most of the CCO principles are not embedded into communication, yet the social aspect of work only maximizes its importance. What happens as a result is that human workers take the lead over communication, substituting the algorithmic leadership and building their own dialogic ways to communicate between each other, educate each other and share best practice and knowledge.

CRITICAL EXAMINATION

From the organizational point of view, despite the central role of communication for work morale and sensemaking, social connectivity among workers remains unimportant to platform providers (Möhlmann and Zalmanson, 2017). Mediated by the platform, lacking human managers or co-workers, there is no direct support (only through chatbots or email) and no opportunity for social exchange for AI-led workers. As a result of the lack of interactions and sociality, workers are unable to build either negative or positive social ties and might feel isolated, as

Digital corporate communication and algorithmic leadership and management   321

if they were working for an abstract system, rather than an organization comprising people. Besides, platform communication remains one-way and closed off, disabling improvements through suggestions, complaints or discussions on decisions. Platform companies explain how they do not 'employ' people but provide them an opportunity to work independently (i.e., the Uber app) (Möhlmann and Zalmanson, 2017).

In fact, even though such functions of human resource management (HRM) as work assignment, performance management and employment relationship building are present in app-work, they are totally different from the established known models of HRM, from both their strategic planning and implementation perspectives (Duggan et al., 2020). Taking, for example, the *employment relations* in algorithmic management context, they are of a purely transactional nature, as no effort is put into the development of trust and commitment of workers. Besides, the training and competence development opportunities are non-existent in app-work, as well as social interactions and networking opportunities (Duggan et al., 2020). In app-work, platforms regulate workers based on certain rules and affordances, making them both dependent and limited in their work, which also makes it clear that the power dynamics are not balanced, but shifted towards the platform (constant control and complete authority over decisions) and customers (anonymous ratings), creating a *digital Taylorism experience.*

Additionally, the well-being of workers is significantly damaged, as no social or security benefits are provided (Duggan et al., 2020). When it comes to the *work assignment* practice itself, it is very opaque and, as the evidence shows, usually works in favour of more efficient and fast workers. Besides, the autonomy of workers to choose whether to pick a task (or to work in general), which is claimed to be one of the benefits, is highly debatable, because all their rejections and delays are monitored, recorded and affect (negatively) any further task proposals for an individual worker, thus, limiting his or her autonomy. Lastly, the *performance management* is also associated with a *lack of transparency* and relies purely on quantitative measures, not taking into account any behavioural nuances and controversial situations, even though multiple parties are involved and affect the final ratings (Duggan et al., 2020).

Another critical HRM review was conducted by Connelly et al. (2021), who identified several challenges of the traditional human HRM practices within the context of gig economy. They pointed out that, for example, workers' retention and engagement normally involve such practices as the establishment of qualified relationship with supervisors, meaningfulness of work from which the benefit for society and others is visible for the worker, team spirit and activities, training and professional development. However, they are hardly present (and not likely to appear any time soon) within algorithmic management, as already mentioned in the context of the discussion of CCO principles. Many of these kinds of practices are not present on digital labour platforms, because workers are not officially considered as employees, but are, instead, independent contractors (Connelly et al., 2021).

Having such employment status and freedom over the schedule and completion of the tasks, prevents HR departments from employing activities targeted at increasing the engagement of workers, in order to achieve higher productivity and performance quality rates. Thus, in gig work, HRM could be (and often is at present) focusing only on transactions management and accounting, general monitoring of workers, their status and differences, matching the supply and demand, recruitment, as well as suggesting when the full-time employee would be a better choice than a gig worker. In terms of performance management, the researchers note that if algorithms are used instead of the HR managers, then transparency of the data usage is required, so that employees are able to know how their personal data is used and can argue

322 *Handbook on digital corporate communication*

with that. Besides, the HR department should be the one accountable for the technology usage. However, as in the gig economy workers are not employees, these practices are not in place either (Connelly et al., 2021). Considering the compensation and benefits side, it is normally managed though the "gamification" of the system in gig work and is relatively effective. The overall design of the platform work is targeted to be motivating, because the workers' engagement cannot be encouraged by human managers within the algorithmic management setting and the communication with them or any other company representatives is not established (Connelly et al., 2021).

ILLUSTRATIVE EXAMPLE: DELIVEROO FRANCE

Generally, managerial tasks appear more prone to automation than leadership tasks. The case of Deliveroo illustrates how even a company with an extensive algorithmic management system still needs the human touch in many leadership and communication tasks. Deliveroo is an online food delivery company that operates in numerous countries from the United Kingdom to Kuwait, enabled by crowds of self-employed bicycle and motorcycle couriers. The case of Deliveroo illustrates communication's crucial role in algorithmic management. Similar to other platform companies, Deliveroo combines *algorithmic control* with *entrepreneurial rhetoric* in governing workers. As Galière (2020, p. 366) found, in France, Deliveroo promotes an atmosphere of self-entrepreneurship by promising newly registering food delivery riders flexibility, independence and an attractive income. Whereas workers in other platforms may contest these claims, Deliveroo riders in France have bought into it to a greater extent, as they believe that algorithmic management facilitates a hyper-meritocratic work setting. This is partly due to Deliveroo riders engaging in a sporting competition: those cycling fastest deliver most meals and therefore receive most assignments from the algorithmic system.

According to Galière, disciplinary mechanisms of rational control do not fully explain workers consenting to algorithmic management, as building normative control through communication is also crucial. While the promotion of an entrepreneurial atmosphere is present from the start, operational managers further reinforce the entrepreneurial identity in events organized by the company. However, whether algorithms really facilitate hyper-meritocratic work conditions seems questionable, as a ride-hailing simulation by Bokányi and Hannák (2020) shows that the system may distribute widely different incomes to identically performing drivers.

The case of Deliveroo in France displays how communication that positions an organization in its larger social system may affect the way its everyday work is organized, as well as workers' perceptions. Deliveroo's recruitment advertisements, tempting them to 'be their own boss', have contributed to building an organizational culture where algorithmic management is somewhat accepted as the facilitator in a race to deliver meals as fast as possible. This conversation is part of the larger political discourse of self-entrepreneurship that includes the contested question of whether platform workers are individual entrepreneurs or contractual employees.

CONCLUSION AND FUTURE DIRECTIONS

As we have many expectations from leaders, be they human or algorithmic, our expectations related to communication are among the most important, as this is the heart of leadership and organizing, as many examples from theory and practice have shown. Communication is a unique, complex social process that involves emotions, reasoning, negotiation and situational thinking, especially if it is supposed to lead and engage others. Digital communication and algorithmic management terrains are not yet well-known or understood, since they are continuously expanding and changing as we explore them. On the other hand, how we communicate and operate with emotions is hardly understood by the most advanced algorithms, which appears to be their stumbling block for achieving the status of a leader and acting independently. Therefore, the main question is: Do we want to take advantage of technology to improve our practices and create better ones or do we want the technology to use its advantage, disregarding the ethical side of the issues?

In this chapter, we have demonstrated that there are examples of both applications of technology and one characteristic that distinguishes one from the other is the presence and quality of communication. Future research and more detailed studies on such leadership aspects as motivation, engagement and influence in the digital context would contribute to better understanding of how we should shape our own practices and will direct the development of the algorithmic ones. What would be the characteristics and requirements for the digital communication processes led by humans to be effective? Can algorithmic leadership ever be ethical? How can we make it ethical and what role would the communication processes play in this? To what extent should organizations utilize technology in their communication processes and are there better digital tools available to facilitate the creation of organizational culture?

REFERENCES

Auvinen, T., Riivari, E., and Sajasalo, P. (2017). Lessons learned from traditional and "new-age" leadership. In A. Eskola (ed.), *Navigating through changing times: Knowledge work in complex environments* (pp. 95–112). New York: Routledge.

Auvinen, T., Sajasalo, P., Sintonen, T., Pekkala, K., Takala, T., and Luoma-aho, V. (2019). Evolution of strategy narration and leadership work in the digital era. *Leadership*, *15*(2), 205–225.

Avolio, B. J., Kahai, S., and Dodge, G. E. (2000). E-leadership. *The Leadership Quarterly*, *11*(4), 615–668.

Avolio, B. J., Sosik, J. J., Kahai, S. S., and Baker, B. (2014). E-leadership: Re-examining transformations in leadership source and transmission. *The Leadership Quarterly*, *25*(1), 105–131.

Bishop, B. (2006). Theory and practice converge: A proposed set of corporate communication principles. *Corporate Communications: An International Journal*, 11(3), 214–231.

Bokányi, E. and Hannák, A. (2020). Understanding inequalities in ride-hailing services through simulations. *Scientific Reports*, *10*(1).

Buhmann, A., Paßmann, J., and Fieseler, C. (2020). Managing algorithmic accountability: Balancing reputational concerns, engagement strategies, and the potential of rational discourse. *Journal of Business Ethics*, *163*(2), S265–S280.

Chan, N. K. and Humphreys, L. (2018). Mediatization of social space and the case of Uber drivers. *Journal of Media and Communication*, *6*(2), 29–38.

Cheney, G. and Dionisopoulos, G. N. (1989). Public relations? No, relations with publics: A rhetorical-organizational approach to contemporary corporate communications. In C. H. Botan and V. Hazelton, Jr (eds.), *Public relations theory* (pp. 135–157). Mahwah, NJ: Lawrence Erlbaum.

324 *Handbook on digital corporate communication*

Cheng, M. and Foley, C. (2019). Algorithmic management: The case of Airbnb. *International Journal of Hospitality Management*, *83*, 33–36.

Cole, G. A. and Kelly, P. (2020). *Management theory and practice* (9th edition.). Belmont, CA: Cengage Learning.

Connelly, C. E., Fieseler, C., Černe, M., Giessner, S. R., and Wong, S. I. (2021). Working in the digitized economy: HRM theory & practice. *Human Resource Management Review*, *31*(1), 100762.

Darics, E. (2020). E-leadership or "how to be boss in instant messaging?" The role of nonverbal communication. *International Journal of Business Communication*, *57*(1), 3–29.

De Vries, R. E., Bakker-Pieper, A., and Oostenveld, W. (2010). Leadership = communication? The relations of leaders' communication styles with leadership styles, knowledge sharing and leadership outcomes. *Journal of Business Psychology*, *25*, 367–380.

Derrick, D. C. and Elson, J. S. (2018). Automated leadership: Influence from embodied agents. In F. Nah and B. Xiao (eds.), *HCI in business, government, and organizations* (pp. 51–66). Cham: Springer.

Duggan, J., Sherman, U., Carbery, R., and McDonnell, A. (2020). Algorithmic management and app-work in the gig economy: A research agenda for employment relations and HRM. *Human Resource Management Journal*, *30*(1), 114–132.

Edgell, S., Gottfried, H., and Granter, E. (eds.) (2016). *The SAGE handbook of the sociology of work and employment*. Thousand Oaks, CA: Sage Publications.

Ertel, W. (2011). *Introduction to artificial intelligence*. London: Springer.

Gal, U., Jensen, T. B., and Stein, M.-K. (2020). Breaking the vicious cycle of algorithmic management: A virtue ethics approach to people analytics. *Information and Organization*, *30*(2), 100301.

Galière, S. (2020). When food-delivery platform workers consent to algorithmic management: A Foucauldian perspective. *New Technology, Work and Employment*, *35*(3), 357–370.

Günsel, A. and Yamen, M. (2020). Digital Taylorism as an answer to the requirements of the new era. In B. Akkaya (ed.), *Agile business leadership methods for Industry 4.0* (pp. 103–119). Bingley: Emerald Publishing.

Hansen, H. K. and Flyverbom, M. (2015). The politics of transparency and the calibration of knowledge in the digital age. *Organization*, *22*, 872–889.

Harms, P. D. and Han, G. (2019). Algorithmic leadership: The future is now. *Journal of Leadership Studies*, *12*(4), 74–75.

Holladay, S. J. and Coombs, W. T. (1993). Communication visions: An exploration of the role of delivery in the creation of leader charisma. *Management Communication Quarterly*, *6*, 405–427.

Hond, F. den and Moser, C. (2022). Useful servant or dangerous master? Technology in business and society debates. *Business & Society*, *62*(1).

Howell, J. P., Bowen, D. E., Dorfman, P. W., Kerr, S., and Podsakoff, P. M. (1990). Substitutes for leadership: Effective alternatives to ineffective leadership. *Organizational Dynamics*, *19*(1), 20–38.

Jabagi, N., Croteau, A.-M., Audebrand, L. K., and Marsan, J. (2019). Gig-workers' motivation: Thinking beyond carrots and sticks. *Journal of Managerial Psychology*, *34*(4), 192–213.

Jarrahi, M. H., Newlands, G., Kyung Lee, M. K., Wolf, C. T., Kinder, E., and Sutherland, W. (2021). Algorithmic management in a work context. *Big Data & Society*, *8*(2). https://doi.org/10.1177/20539517211020332.

Jarrahi, M. H. and Sutherland, W. (2019). Algorithmic management and algorithmic competencies: Understanding and appropriating algorithms in gig work. In N. Taylor, C. Christian-Lamb, M. Martin, and B. Nardi (eds.), *Information in contemporary society*. iConference 2019. Lecture Notes in Computer Science vol. 11420 (pp. 578–589). Cham: Springer.

Jarrahi, M. H., Sutherland, W., Nelson, S. B., and Sawyer, S. (2019). Platformic management, boundary resources for gig work, and worker autonomy. *Computer Supported Cooperative Work (CSCW)*, *29*(1–2), 153–189.

Kaine, S. and Josserand, E. (2019). The organisation and experience of work in the gig economy. *Journal of Industrial Relations*, *61*(4), 479–501.

Kessler, E. H. (ed.) (2013). *Encyclopedia of management theory*. London: Sage Publications.

Klikauer, T. (2013). *Managerialism: A critique of an ideology*. Basingstoke: Palgrave Macmillan.

Koontz, H. (1980). The management theory jungle revisited. *The Academy of Management Review*, *5*(2), 175–187.

Lee, M. K. (2018). Understanding perception of algorithmic decisions: Fairness, trust, and emotion in response to algorithmic management. *Big Data & Society*, *5*(1).

Lee, M. K., Kusbit, D., Metsky, E., and Dabbish, L. (2015). Working with machines. In *Proceedings of the 33rd Annual ACM Conference on Human Factors in Computing Systems* (pp. 1602–1612). New York: ACM.

Leonardi, P. M., Huysman, M., and Steinfield, C. (2013). Enterprise social media: Definition, history, and prospects for the study of social technologies in organizations. *Journal of Computer-Mediated Communication*, *19*(1), 1–19.

Longman Dictionary Online (2020). https://www.ldoceonline.com/.

Martin, R., Guillaume, Y., Thomas, G., Lee, A., and Epitropaki, O. (2016). Leader–member exchange (LMX) and performance: A meta-analytic review. *Journal of Applied Psychology*, *101*(2), 230–251.

Mateescu, A. and Nguyen, A. (2019). Explainer: Algorithmic management in the workplace. *Data & Society* (February)

McPhee, R. D., Poole, M. S., and Iverson, J. (2014). Structuration theory. In L. L. Putnam and D. K. Mumby (eds.), *The SAGE handbook of organizational communication* (3rd edition, pp. 75–100). Thousand Oaks, CA: Sage Publications.

Men, L. R. (2011). Exploring the impact of employee empowerment on organization–employee relationship. *Public Relations Review*, *37*, 435–437.

Men, L. R. (2014). Strategic internal communication: Transformational leadership, communication channels, and employee satisfaction. *Management Communication Quarterly*, *28*(2), 264–284.

Men, L. R. and Stacks, D. W. (2013). The impact of leadership style and employee empowerment on perceived organizational reputation. *Journal of Communication Management*, *17*, 171–192.

Mengay, A. (2020). Digitalization of work and heteronomy. *Capital & Class*, *44*(2), 273–285.

Mitchell, T. (1997). *Machine learning*. New York: McGraw Hill.

Möhlmann, M. and Zalmanson, L. (2017). Hands on the wheel: Navigating algorithmic management and Uber drivers. *38th International Conference on Information Systems (ICIS 2017)*.

Noponen, N. (2019). Impact of artificial intelligence on management. *Electronic Journal of Business Ethics and Organization Studies*, *24*, 43–50.

Northouse, P. G. (2016). *Leadership: Theory and practice* (7th edition). London: Sage Publications.

Rosenblat, A. and Stark, L. (2016). Algorithmic labor and information asymmetries: A case study of Uber's drivers. *International Journal of Communication*, *10*, 3758–3784.

Schildt, H. (2017). Big data and organizational design: The brave new world of algorithmic management and computer augmented transparency. *Innovation*, *19*(1), 23–30.

Schmidt, G. B. (2014). Virtual leadership: An important leadership context. *Industrial and Organizational Psychology*, *7*(2), 182–187.

Stokols, D., Mishra, S., Gould-Runnerstrom, M., and Hipp, J. (2009). Psychology in an age of ecological crisis: From personal angst to collective action. *American Psychologist*, *64*(3), 181–193.

Toyoda, Y., Lucas, G., and Gratch, J. (2020). The effects of autonomy and task meaning in algorithmic management of crowdwork. In B. An, N. Yorke-Smith, A. El Fallah Seghrouchni, and G. Sukthankar (eds.). *Proceedings of the 19th International Conference on Autonomous Agents and Multiagent Systems (AAMAS 2020)*.

Watkins, A., Myria, S. J., Coopman, J. L. H., and Kasey, L. W. (2007). Workplace surveillance and managing privacy boundaries. *Management Communication Quarterly*, *21*(2), 172–200.

Wesche, J. S. and Sonderegger, A. (2019). When computers take the lead: The automation of leadership. *Computers in Human Behavior*, *101*, 197–209.

Whitworth, B. (2011). Internal communication. In T. Gillis (ed.), *The IABC handbook of organizational communication* (2nd edition, pp. 195–206). San Francisco: Jossey-Bass.

23. Digital corporate communication and visual communication

Chiara Valentini and Grazia Murtarelli

INTRODUCTION

Especially over the past decade, information and communication technology (ICT) advancements have brought a number of opportunities to people and organizations, including possibilities to utilize other forms of communicative expressions beyond words. A 'visual turn' (Machin, 2014), which essentially underlines the increasing role of images and visual elements in people's daily lives, has taken place thanks to the development of visual apps and high-definition cameras installed on smartphones, ready to capture the world around the phone's owner. Visual communication – that is, communication based on images – is currently the preferred form of communication among young adults and teenagers who use visual content to convey stories, emotions and ideas to others (Baron, 2019; Pew Research Center, 2018). Organizations have exponentially increased their offering of digital visual contents beyond traditional product advertisements as a way to convey stories and emotions that can be easily shared via digital devices. Effective visual communication can create a competitive position for organizations and companies in their digital corporate communications. While opportunities to leverage digital visual content for corporate communication have increased, professionals are still faced with challenges related to the planning of visual content production (Zerfass et al., 2017).

This chapter deals with the phenomenon of the 'visual turn' (Machin, 2014) in digital corporate communication, and offers an overview of the most important findings related to digital visual communication research. The chapter also introduces the reader to a newly developed theoretical framework: the *Four Realms of Digital Visual Experience*. This theoretical framework is an interdisciplinary theoretical effort addressing the changes in the digital media ecosystem and in digital consumer behaviours and expectations. The framework integrates elements of visual content production with existing knowledge about visual communication and experiential marketing. The chapter also discusses drawbacks and challenges related to organizational efforts in addressing the visual turn. It then concludes with an illustrative example of the applicability of the proposed framework and includes the authors' reflections on its limits and suggestions for further research avenues.

DEFINITIONS OF THE TOPIC AND PREVIOUS STUDIES

Visual communication is defined as a form of communication which is conveyed through the use of visual aids and contents, such as photographs, drawings, charts, figures and symbols (Thelander, 2018). Much of visual communication today is about moving images, which can include a broad variety of media (e.g., film, television, games) and genres (e.g., documentary or fiction, real life or animation). Primarily, research on visual communication has focused on the aesthetics of static and moving images, their impact on consumers (e.g., in the form of emotions, attitudes, opinions, values, beliefs, knowledge and behaviours), and their potential for application in conveying different messages. Together with verbal and non-verbal communications, visual communication is commonly used in corporate communication for different purposes such as enhancing an organization's identity or culture by using visual symbols, marketing and advertising products and brands (Wiesenberg and Verčič, 2021), and in public advocacy campaigns for social causes (Chouliaraki, 2012).

Images are a very powerful means to convey a message as they do not require a person to know any specific language or to read text. They enhance comprehensibility and clarity of a message, thus increasing the informative power of the written or verbal content. Images are strong memory devices. For this, viewers can easily recall them and experience emotional reactions that are held in a person's brain (Domke et al., 2002). They can convey organizational messages in an engaging and informative manner, as they help publics to develop a deep elaboration of the communication content (Philips, 2017), allowing for a story to emerge as a result of "an on-going sense-making effort through which identities, relations and actions assume shape and significance" (Gabriel, 2012, p. 4). In certain ways, visual contents speak multiple voices to multiple people, and can thus be very powerful devices for corporate communication.

Despite the relevance of visual contents in corporate communication, the field has lagged behind other disciplines' theorizing efforts on visual communication (Göransson and Fagerholm, 2018; Wiesenberg and Verčič, 2021). Overall, four major perspectives have emerged in the study of visual communication: (a) a rhetorical perspective focusing on studying visual content production as well as the meaning-making process; (b) a semantic perspective focusing on the features of images and the cultural elements they represent; (c) a pragmatic perspective focusing on investigating the features of images and how these communicate messages in implicit and symbolic ways; and (d) a visual strategy perspective focusing on the strategies of the organizations' visual communication (Göransson and Fagerholm, 2018; Wiesenberg and Verčič, 2021).

While there is already a wide body of literature on visual communication from linguistics, semiotics and cultural studies, primarily focusing on the consumption, perception and recipients' co-creation of meanings (Wiesenberg and Verčič, 2021), the studies addressing visual content production are limited, and, according to Fahmy et al. (2014), most of our stock of knowledge in this area is based on visual journalism (photojournalism, citizen journalism, bloggers) and mass communication in general.

In digital corporate communication research, visual social semiotics functions of images have gained traction among researchers interested in identifying those elements that can increase engagement and overall experience with digital content (Maier et al., 2019). Research shows that high-quality visual content can increase social media visibility and stimulate consumers' engagement (Kujur and Singh, 2020) and that both high-quality content and image purposes (informative, entertaining and remunerative) impact on consumer engagement and affect consumer–brand relationships. Online images positively or negatively affect the level of digital engagement in terms of users' liking and sharing processes (Domke et al., 2002). The presence of image-based content with specific visual features such as colourfulness, the presence of a human face, the image source, resolution and professional quality, and the image-text fit have a positive effect on users' engagement in both Facebook and Twitter (Li

328 *Handbook on digital corporate communication*

and Xie, 2020). Similarly, Romney and Johnson (2020) investigated what types of images could affect audience engagement by analysing nearly 2000 images shared by Sports Network on Instagram. They found that images, including narrative or meta-communicative messages using graphics and multimedia elements, generated higher engagement shown by an increasing number of likes and shares. Users' intention to purchase and to share visual content with their own network of friends is also affected by the presence of human beings and salient brands and products in the digital images (Valentini et al., 2018). Focusing on the use of visual metaphor, Peterson (2019) found that visual structure, object intimacy, informational loci and illustration style positively impacted the participation and engagement of consumers, as these visual features reinforce digital experiences of games like puzzles to be solved by viewers. Image narrativity, intended as the ability of an image to tell a story, and dynamism, which is related to the degree of movement an image can evoke, were also found to positively affect digital users' emotions and their digital visual engagement attitude (Murtarelli et al., 2021).

WHAT IS CHANGING?

Images have historically been used in corporate communication via traditional owned media (internal magazine, newsletter, poster) or paid media (commercial advertisements in newspapers, television, billboards, etc.). With the increasing digitalization of media and the increasing use and consumption of digital content, today most images circulate virally on the web. Not only that, the type, form and genre of content circulating in the digital media ecosystem have dramatically changed and are continuously changing as ICT evolves. In 2021, 70 per cent of digital content was made of visual elements, such as photos, images, drawings, sketches, etc. (Khoja, 2021). This trend is reflected in the growing popularity of visual social media such as Instagram, Pinterest, TikTok, YouTube and Tumblr and has been intensified by the increasing use of visual elements in digital communications by both people and organizations.

Digitalization has also impacted consumer and stakeholder expectations and their digital behaviours, inducing scholars to speak about a visual turn in communication. Consumers and stakeholders communicate more and more via images, and new visual cultures are emerging as well as new ways of using visual content to digitally communicate with networks of friends, fans and followers (Machin, 2014). Phone memes have become common visual elements of written messages in the digital sphere, often ridiculing, satirizing or overly emphasizing some characteristics of an image and transposing those from one context to another. To these, emoticons, or textual portrayals of someone's mood, have emerged as new visual symbols communicating personal feelings. Additionally, stakeholders expect to receive visual content from organizations that is engaging, meaningful and tells a relevant story. Experiencing it is now equal to seeing it. People do not need to travel anymore to see the *La Gioconda* painting by Leonardo da Vinci, they can experience it online, and via digital media they can have a whole tour of The Louvre Museum in Paris. Similarly, many once live experiences are now virtually possible through the powerful use of digital visual contents that enhance virtual realities (Cho et al., 2002; Yung et al., 2021). All in all, digital images have altered the dynamics of people's relationships and how they experience and memorialize social and organizational lives (Davison et al., 2012).

Müller (2008) speaks about three major communication shifts driven by technological developments: the rise of amateur visual productions, the global dissemination of visuals and their de-contextualization. He states: "While visual production structures were once confined to professionals, and reception processes happened more or less in the private sphere, today the inverse is true – production is privatised, while dissemination is globalised" (Müller, 2008, p. 102). Visual content production, once primarily an activity carried out by professionals, is now more and more a user-generated activity. The spread of smartphone cameras, drawing apps and digital media have empowered digital publics' creativity and interest in creating, publishing and distributing visual content. Digital media have become thus the *loci* of visual content production and distribution, and above all, they have empowered digital publics to easily access information and exert their power by making their voices heard and to obtain control and influence over content and market processes (Li, 2018), including those related to visual content. The digital media ecosystem is thus populated by many visual stories that are transcended by mass-produced images, some of which assume iconic status. Yet, because there are as many consumers as producers, it is not always simple to judge the authenticity of visual content circulating on the web, recognizing the source of the digital visual content, and understanding if alterations or manipulations of the original content were made.

Because anyone technically can be a producer, disseminator and consumer of digital images, individuals are continuously experiencing a stable stream of visual stimulations coming from different sources and media (Fausing, 2013; Rigutto, 2017). The challenge for communication professionals is, thus, 'standing out' from the crowd of digital images by creating authentic digital experiences that are engaging (Valentini et al., 2018). This means understanding what features of images suggest specific meanings and consequently how to create an architecture (Cohn, 2014; Schöning and Heidemann, 2018) of visual content that can enhance stakeholder engagement and generate some form of return on investment at the level of intangible and tangible assets.

WHAT REMAINS THE SAME?

As a practice of communicating, visual communication is not new. Using images to tell a story and explain an event is the very essence of human communication. From the dawn of human beings, cavemen created visual content by drawing stories, animals and situations that they wanted to pass on to others as a learning lesson (Novak, 1975). Today, the production, dissemination and consumption of visual images have become more sophisticated, yet effortless, also due to ICT developments and an increased digitalization of our communication means.

Despite digitalization, much of the knowledge on visual aesthetics is still relevant for visual content circulating in digital media. Literature on visual semiotics has heavily contributed to the development of an architecture of visual content that can be applied to *digital* visual content. This architecture essentially contributes to a better understanding of images and their "semiotic resources, what can be said and done with images (and other visual means of communication) and how the things people say and do with images can be interpreted" (Jewitt and Oyama, 2001, p. 136), thus answering the question: How can organizations stand out visually from the large amount of digital content currently available in the digital media ecosystem?

The large, well-established body of visual semiotics work studying and classifying image-based features and their communicative functions offers relevant knowledge on the three main functions of images for digital visual content production too. Developed for analysing images in general, the *representational/ideational, interpersonal* and *compositional/*

330 *Handbook on digital corporate communication*

textual functions (Harrison, 2003; Jewitt and Oyama, 2001; Kress and Van Leeuwen, 1996) have been specifically applied to analyse online and digital visual content as well, including moving images (e.g., Alkateeb, 2020; Elhamy, 2022; Maier, 2012; Maier et al., 2019; Murtarelli et al., 2021; Valentini et al., 2018). Briefly, the representational/ideational function is linked to the illustrated narrative with a specific emphasis on the sequential order of the represented objects and subjects and how they are presented in the image (Harrison, 2003; Jewitt and Oyama, 2001; Kress and Van Leeuwen, 1996). To recognize the representational function of an image, it is necessary to detect the presence of eventual vectors of motions or the relationship distance between what is represented. According to Kress and Van Leeuwen (1996, pp. 56–57), "when participants are connected by a vector, they are represented as doing something to or for each other". This function supports viewers in developing a better understanding of the meaning of a specific image (Aiello, 2006; Jewitt and Oyama, 2001; Kress and Van Leeuwen, 1996). The interpersonal function is about the relationship that an image enables between viewers and what is depicted. It refers to the presence of specific elements such as the direct or indirect gaze or the social distance between the represented subjects and the viewers (Harrison, 2003; Jewitt and Oyama, 2001; Kress and Van Leeuwen, 1996). This function offers a specific understanding of how an image can engage the viewers (Aiello, 2006; Harrison, 2003; Jewitt and Oyama, 2001; Kress and Van Leeuwen, 1996). The compositional/textual function is about the images' layout (Aiello, 2006; Jewitt and Oyama, 2001) and describes the compositional arrangement of visual elements such as the informational value, salience or resolution of the image. It shows which elements contribute to help a viewer make sense of a visual message (Harrison, 2003). Composition in visual content "is the equivalent of syntax in language—a set of rules that enable the signs of language (that is, words) to be arranged grammatically so that they make sense to the reader" (Harrison, 2003, p. 55). Each function requires the use of specific features for structuring the visual content and that are synthesized in Table 23.1. Table 23.1 also illustrates what aspects need to be prioritized by communication managers in order to enhance specific image elements.

In the next section, we move one step forward and present a theoretical framework which combines and integrates existing knowledge in visual semiotics, digital communication and experiential marketing into something that professionals can use to develop engaging digital experiences via digital visual content. The theoretical framework specifically addresses the following questions: What kind of experiences can visual content convey in digital media? What features of digital visual content can enhance these experiences?

THE FOUR REALMS OF DIGITAL VISUAL EXPERIENCE: A THEORETICAL FRAMEWORK

Drawing on the literature of social semiotics and that of experiential marketing (Pine and Gilmore, 1998; Schmitt, 1999; Schmitt and Zarantonello, 2013) we postulate that the most engaging images are those which can develop an imaginary around one or more experiences, which in our theoretical framework are called 'realms of digital visual experiences'. The *Four Realms of Digital Visual Experience* (4ReDiVE) framework can be considered a micro-range theory as it starts by observing and analysing the phenomenon of digital images and stakeholder engagement to develop specific propositions addressing visual content production aimed at virtual, online experiences that can be tested. The 4ReDiVE framework is

Table 23.1   Visual social semiotics functions of images, key features and implications for communication managers

Visual functions	Visual features	Description	How to apply
Representational/ideational	Narrativity	The image tells a story	To increase narrativity power, images should be constructed to include the presence of one or more actors, preferably while these are doing an action.
	Dynamism	The image evokes a perception of movement	To increase dynamism, images should stimulate an idea of change and/or movement by depicting, for example, individuals interacting with objects, or elements that communicates mobility or flow.
Interpersonal	Demand gaze	Subject represented in the picture is looking directly at the viewer	To have a person's face looking directly towards the viewer's eyes can create an effect of demand gaze.
	Offer gaze	Actor represented in the picture is looking outside the picture or at someone or something within the image	The individual in the picture should look towards someone/something depicted in the image or else have its gaze not directed to the viewer.
	Intimate distance	Head and face are only represented in the picture	Intimacy is created by portraying image elements that communicate closeness and proximity, such as a face or some facial elements.
	Far personal distance	Actor is represented in the picture from the waist up (as a unit or in parts)	Images where individuals are represented from the waist up tend to communicate a less intimate, and yet still personal, feeling.
	Close social distance	The whole figure of the actor is represented in the picture	Full body representation of people communicates a less intimate feeling and more of a social/group level distance.
	Frontal angle	Objects or subjects are presented frontally to the viewer	Individuals or objects should be shown frontally in the image.
	Oblique angle	Objects or subjects are presented obliquely to the viewer	Individuals or objects should be shown diagonally or else be positioned so as to represent an imaginary diagonal line from one corner of the image to another.
	Vertical angle	Objects or subjects are presented from above to the viewer	Individuals or objects should be positioned in the image so as to create an imaginary vertical line from top down.

Visual functions	Visual features	Description	How to apply
Compositional/Textual	Salience (Object/Subject)	Size of the objects or subjects represented within the image (quantity of portion of the image occupied by them)	Elements that are big compared to the rest of the image elements communicate salience. Salience is also increased when there are logos, products or other recognizable organizational elements (high salience situation) in the image.
	Modality	Resolution level of the image (if high or low)	Modality is modified by the image resolution. High resolution images are credible and are assimilated as a true photo depicting the reality as it is; if the resolution is low, the credibility and reliability of the image decreases as the image is perceived more as an illustration, a painting, or a drawing.
	Informative value	Where the object/subject is located in the picture (left, right, at the margin, at centre, in multiple positions within the same image)	The location or disposition of image elements, such as objects, logos, individuals and others affect the informative value of the image. Deciding if the presence of textual elements within the visual content should follow a left/right system, a top/bottom system or a centre/margin system is dependent on the culture of viewers: For cultures characterized by a left-to-right reading system, the positioning of the main object/subject should be on the left. For cultures characterized by a right-to-left reading system, it is better to locate the object/subject on the right side of the image. Normally, elements located at the top of an image provide higher informative value as viewers tend to give more attention to this area compared to those at the bottom of the image. A central position of subjects/objects occupying a wider space including margins can offer higher informative value.

Source: Own elaboration from Harrison (2003); Kress and Van Leeuwen (1996); Jewitt and Oyama (2001).

Digital corporate communication and visual communication   333

theory-driven and substantiated by meta-empirical research. The 4ReDiVE main premises are adopted from those developed by Pine and Gilmore (1998) and integrated with recent findings from social semiotics image-based features studies. Similarly, as in the original conceptualization of experiences (Pine and Gilmore, 1998), we propose to conceptualize digital visual experiences across two dimensions: participation and connection. Participation is one of the forms of online engagement; it is represented by a continuum from active to passive. At one end, active participation requires stakeholders to actively participate in content creation by providing their own visual content, for example, by posting their online photos of the experience with the product/service or their own artcraft. At the other end, there is passive participation in which stakeholders are not involved in the co-creation or even creation of the visual content, but consume and share it with others in their social networks. Even if stakeholders are not participating in the content creation, they are not completely passive as they can still contribute to the success of visual content by engaging with the content in the form of liking, sharing and commenting. The second dimension is connection with the experience and the storyline illustrated by the image. This is essentially a mental relationship that is formed during the process of constructing, decoding and interpreting the message(s) of the image. On the one side of the dimension is absorption, and on the other side is immersion. Being part of the visual content, as a testimonial, for example, or being the staging director behind the image, is a more immersing experience than watching, sharing or using others' images for own digital communication. These latter experiences belong to an absorbing engagement with the visual content, as viewers are connected with the image by its inner message.

Across these two dimensions, there are several middle points. A stakeholder experience with visual content is always a personal experience, thus the same image can technically produce different types of experiences. Yet, one type of experience may become dominant, representing one of the four realms in the 4ReDiVE framework. Digital corporate communicators can play around with image-based features to suggest specific experiences by also considering the level of participation and connection that they want to offer to their stakeholders. The four possible realms that are formed crossing participation with connections are: entertainment, aesthetic, educational and escapist (see Figure 23.1).

The *Entertainment* realm is defined by visual contents whose experience is characterized by generating amusement among those who experience the image. Here, stakeholders are rather passive and absorbed with the visual content. Digital visual engagement is manifested in viewing, liking, sharing and re-posting visual content that has amused the viewer. An example is represented by online memes, images with humorous features, parodying real situations. The image of Bernie Sanders wearing mittens during the inauguration ceremony for the 46th President of the United States and shared in the digital environment is an example of an entertainment visual experience (Glenday, 2021). Memes are visual content with a primary function of entertainment, especially when they are used without any hidden intentions, but for conveying humorous vignettes and providing digital stakeholders the opportunity for escape from reality and living a fun moment (Milosavljević, 2020). This is what happened with the Bernie Sanders meme: the picture of the senator donning mittens and a brown coat has been transposed and dropped into diverse situations, moments and contexts such as historical events, famous paintings, and movie and TV series scenes.

According to the visual social semiotics perspective, this realm is characterized by low narrativity and dynamism: visual elements are de-contextualized and made static to create an effect of hilarity in the digital users (Holm, 2021). They have low resolution and low informative

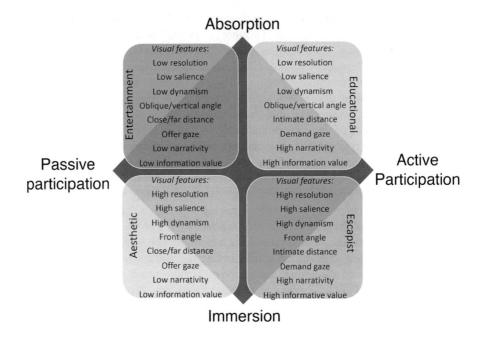

Figure 23.1   The four realms of digital visual experience

value. Memes need to include simple and realistic visual elements to be easily interpreted by digital users (Barnes et al., 2021). In this realm, the represented object should occupy a large portion of the image to suggest an entertaining objective for digital viewers. The salience of the object should be high; objects should be in the foreground to attract the attention of the viewer and create a contrast between single visual elements and the background (Dancygier and Vandelanotte, 2017). If subjects are included in the image, they are usually used in combination with objects and textual elements. The idea is to convey funny messages and keep the viewer detached from the visual content (Shifman, 2013). To plan visual content including a subject, three main features should be considered: (a) the human gaze, (b) the far distance between the subjects, and (c) the perspective angle. As for the human gaze, this can be an 'offer gaze', when a human subject is used for emphasizing other elements in the images. Here the subject does not look directly at the viewer. As the aim of this realm is to entertain and surprise the viewer, the most effective perspective to represent an image is with oblique or vertical angles as these suggest different observing viewpoints of what is represented in the visual content without being directly immersed in the image.

The *Aesthetic* realm suggests an immersive experience, with a rather passive participation. Here digital publics can immerse themselves in a situation by the simple act of mentally visualizing the scene/action through the help of visual content, without being physically part of it. An example could be participation in a virtual tour of a museum, or playing the part of an archaeologist discovering new historical artefacts digitally. To enhance an aesthetic experience, high dynamism is key, and this can be expressed, for example, by using virtual reality technologies. The aesthetic realm requires high resolution-based visual content and a frontal angle perspective, as the involvement of digital publics is crucial and so are their feelings of living the experience first-hand. The digital experience organizer does not provide a defined story, but visual elements are instrumental to suggest a specific task/experience. For this reason, narrativity is quite low, and visual content production should be less concerned about directing attention to specific visual elements and more about the overall visual experience. Single subjects, objects or textual elements are preferred visual elements. The visual content in this realm is characterized by low salience related to the objects; low informative value in relation to textual elements; far distance and 'offer gaze' when including human beings in the image. The success of this specific visual experience is obtained by harmonizing different elements (graphics, humans, texts) in a unique visual experience.

The *Educational* realm represents a form of experience that can generate some learning/ new understanding for those involved. Digital publics become active and are absorbed with the visual content, for instance, when the image tells a story prompting the viewer's actions or informing the viewer about something that is not well known. Social advocacy campaigns that depict strong images illustrating, for example, women's genital mutilation or poor living conditions in some parts of the world can be very informative and generate an absorbing experience to some viewers. By imagining the experience of being a woman under those circumstances, stakeholders develop mental and even emotional participation with the subject depicted in the image.

This realm is characterized by the following visual social semiotics features: high informative value, high narrativity and high salience. Here the visual experience intends to convey a message, a story with a meaning that can become remarkable for the viewers and consequently needs to be evidenced in the visual content. Furthermore, low dynamism, as the message or meaning are more easily understood if illustrated and presented in a static way; intimate distance and 'demand gaze' if human beings are included in the visual experience, are preferred features when helping viewers to better understand the message presented in the visual content. Finally, an educational realm is characterized by visual elements with low resolution, as the content should be more relevant than the form or graphical elements, and oblique and vertical angles to provide alternative viewpoints for attracting the attention of digital viewers.

The fourth realm is the *Escapist* one and this is characterized by a viewer's high immersion in the visual content and active participation. Experiences where the viewer creates visual content and shares this with an online community, or even with companies if allowed, are examples of escapist experiences. Fashion companies such as the Finnish brand Marimekko have prompted their customers to showcase their creativity, for example, with Marimekko products and textiles through the sharing of their own images on Instagram and Twitter (Pakarinen, 2018). This realm is created with visual features such as high narrativity and high dynamism, as digital publics are totally immersed in the digital setting of the story and are able to create a hypothetical development path for the story; high resolution, as the realm should be perceived as real by the digital users; frontal angle, which allows viewers to live the experience first-hand; intimate distance and 'demand gaze' of subjects involved in the content; high informative value, as the viewers should receive all the necessary visual clues for contributing to the creation of the digital experience; low salience of objects, to reduce the viewer's attention to single objects and prompt a whole scenario visual experience.

Between the four realms of experiences proposed, there can be several middle points, in part because the way images are interpreted is still a personal matter. Furthermore, as much of the current visual experiences are digital, supported by digital media and technologies that can augment a reality, image-related features must take into consideration the evolving char-

336 *Handbook on digital corporate communication*

acteristics of the digital environment. As this chapter is being written, Facebook's Metaverse is an under-construction project of advanced virtual realities where images of all kinds are used to enhance a user's experience to a high level. Other emerging digital technologies and environments may offer different opportunities to enhance these experiences. Yet, we argue, the central image-based features proposed in 4ReDiVE are still relevant in the production and construction of visual content behind each digital experience. Adaptation of the visual content to the channel is a key because digital media affordances and technicalities are different, and can lead to different types of experiences. For instance, if the message is crafted with moving images, like in a TikTok video, or with a simple image, like a photo in Instagram, certain image characteristics are more suitable than others. In the next section, some of the critical aspects related to visual communication are discussed before presenting an illustrative example of effective use of digital visual contents.

CRITICAL EXAMINATION

Along with the opportunities offered by digital visual communication, there are a number of drawbacks and challenges that must be accounted for. As more and more content is now produced and consumed by amateur publics through the use of digital apps, the credibility, authenticity and reliability of visual content circulating in the digital media ecosystem is questionable. Considering that visual content speaks to everyone and beyond any possible language barrier, thus rapidly impacting people's opinions, attitudes and behaviours, the presence and circulation of manipulated images in the digital media ecosystem can negatively impact how people think, feel and act upon issues, events, and even products, brands and organizations. The phenomenon of fake news and deepfake videos are, in fact, also enhanced by the spread of altered images. Deepfake videos are essentially hyper-realistic videos using face swaps that leave little trace of manipulation (Chawla, 2019). The technology behind deepfake thus makes it increasingly difficult to distinguish between real and fake digital content (Westerlund, 2019). Coupled with the reach and speed of social media, convincing deepfake videos can quickly reach millions of people and have negative impacts on their perceptions and even decisions.

Similarly, when images are de-contextualized and used to construct a new, altered scenario, they can become vehicles for misinformation and malinformation. As a case in point, widely used spoofs are essentially consumers' reinterpretation of iconic brands in an ironic manner (Fournier and Avery, 2011). If most spoofs are simply new expressions of consumer culture, at times they can turn into laudatory ways for branding an organization, but in others they can turn into subversive attempts by fakeholders (Luoma-aho, 2015). Sharing misappropriate brand identities or user-manipulated images not only confuses digital publics but also satirizes the original meanings of the visual content (Vicari et al., 2020). Even digital visual content is today more and more out of the control of organizations' message production (Berthon et al., 2008), and this is something that organizations cannot do much about.

Research has also emphasized the dark side of digital visual communication, meaning the ethical implications of suggesting questionable meanings via powerful images. Visual contents have historically been used by the propaganda machine in authoritarian nation-states, for instance during Soviet Union and Marxist times (Mignemi, 1996; Ventrone, 2005), but today cyber attempts to attack public understanding and images of prominent leaders (Buscemi,

Digital corporate communication and visual communication 337

2017; Vaccari and Chadwick, 2020) as well as the use of images by terrorist organizations (Matusitz, 2021) are other distorted communication practices exploiting the power of images. Furthermore, visual content shared online has a certain impact on younger generations and when this promotes wrong, false or distorted myths, the implications for social relations and personal identity can be devastating. Visual contents often promoted in advertisements dealing with body image and body icon representations (Hargreaves and Tiggemann, 2004), sexuality (Charteris et al., 2018) and depression or anxiety (Keles et al., 2020) can be highly controversial. Being aware of what kind of visual features can affect individuals' attitudes and behaviours such as liking, commenting on and sharing visual content in social media can help communication managers to avoid the production of content that negatively affects people's beliefs. Knowing how to identify deepfake videos and fake, manipulated images is also a very important skill set that organizations and communication professionals must learn so as to be able to detect and respond to them in order to protect the image of their own organization from cyberattacks. Knowing the basics of the visual social semiotics architecture in part can help in distinguishing real from manipulated images, for instance, by looking at image resolution inconsistency in digitally manipulated faces (also known as affined face warpings) (Güera and Delp, 2018).

In the next section, an illustrative example of a case company addressing its consumers' visual needs by offering digital visual experiences across different digital media is presented and discussed. The case is analysed through the lens of the 4ReDiVE framework.

ILLUSTRATIVE EXAMPLE: HEINEKEN®

Heineken Lager Beer, commonly known as Heineken®, is a 150-year-old Dutch brewery company specializing in beer and cider production. The company has over 300 brands and sells across over 190 countries (Heineken, 2021). The company has a massive presence in social media with 89 accounts including 19 Facebook pages, 42 Twitter handles, 17 Instagram accounts, 10 YouTube channels and one LinkedIn account (Unmetric.com, 2021). Since 2009, the company has decided to invest in experiential communication and marketing in different digital media, including its official social media accounts for interacting with digital consumers and developing engaging online relationships with them. Heineken® has creatively employed different types and forms of visual contents that generate high levels of content engagement, which is why it has been chosen as an illustrative example to explore the applicability of the 4ReDiVE framework. In its social media pages, the company has repeatedly tried to create a realm of entertainment, as most of the visual imaginary proposed to its consumers and fans is heavily rooted in irony and humour. The company has widely used memes in its digital visual communication as some examples from its Twitter corporate international account show.

An example is the image posted on 7 January 2022, that contains 30 single squares.[1] Taking inspiration from the Wordless game, Heineken utilized a similar visual structure to communicate its product in a funny manner. The top line of the image has a row of white squares, whereas the rest of the squares are yellow gold, reflecting the colour and shape of a glass of beer. No human being is included in the image; no text is present to enrich the informative value of the image. The image is totally abstract and there is no visual element offering an idea of movement or that narrates a scene. Similarly, in another Twitter image posted on 7 October 2021, depicting the neck of a Heineken beer bottle,[2] there is no movement and no

338   *Handbook on digital corporate communication*

human subject playing a narrative scene. Green is the dominant colour, and a vertical angle is suggested. The image also includes four symbols – a square, a triangle, a star and an umbrella – recalling the television show *Squid Game*. Text is minimal. The words "Easy choice" appear at the left bottom corner of the image, whereas the company logo is visible at the right bottom corner.

In these two examples from Heineken's® Twitter account, the entertainment experience is conveyed through the use of visual content characterized by specific features such as low narrativity and dynamism, the absence of human beings, the use of oblique or vertical angles, and low informative value. Both images have been appreciated by digital viewers and generated an engaging effect as testified by the above-average number of likes and retweets and some of the users' comments (e.g., "Send six packs my way👍", "Genius", "Best beer. In the world").

The company has also used the realm of aesthetics in some specific initiatives, for instance in the Heineken® Experience. The Heineken® Experience is an attraction located at Heineken's® first built brewery in Amsterdam's city centre. In 1988 the brewery closed down, and the historical building was transformed into an exhibition venue where visitors can learn more about the company, the brewing process, its innovations, projects and so on. During the Covid-19 pandemic, the attraction became virtual, offering an opportunity for people to experience a virtual self-guided tour of the Heineken® Experience. Looking at the visual elements employed in this virtual experience, it is possible to identify specific visual features, such as: high resolution for a satisfying overview of the location; high dynamism, as the digital viewer can actively move through the venue; low narrativity, as the tour is self-guided and there is no narrated story during the experience; low informative value, as textual elements are not included in the visual experience; and the absence of human beings during the tour, indicating a passive immersion. All these visual features contribute to increase a perception of an aesthetic experience while learning about Heineken®.

Heineken® has also been attentive in offering an educational experiential realm. The Legendary 7 campaign about sustainability via social media accompanied by user's participation via augmented reality is an example of an educational experience. The goal of this experience is to make digital users aware of the company's sustainability strategy to buy 50 per cent of its main raw materials from sustainable resources (TheHeinekenCompany.com, 2015). Strategically this was done by developing a virtual experience where consumers and fans can meet the farmers via an augmented reality smartphone app and hear the farmers' stories about producing high quality ingredients from different countries for Heineken® 3. By scanning the Heineken® label with their smartphones, viewers have access to visual content suggesting an educational experience. This experience requires active participation and absorption of participants, since they have to take concrete action – scanning through the use of their smartphones – to live the experience. By accessing the augmented reality platform, individuals can access content from different perspectives (oblique or vertical angles). They can visualize the farmers' stories and these are characterized by high informative value and high salience, and the company's logo and products on evidence. The Amsterdam experience has been communicated and promoted by using visual content also via Twitter.[3]

Another example from the company's pool of digital experiential activities related to the last realm, the escapist one, is the use of virtual reality for internal communication and organizational matters. Since 2019 the company has been using virtual reality developed by the University of Beer located in Italy (https://www.universitadellabirra.it) for training and teaching purposes for its employees. Visual content are accessible via virtual reality, showing the production cycle of different beers, including the diverse phases and materials of production. The visual imaginary suggested in this experience prompts a deep immersion with the content and the use of gaming via a visual sensor increases employee engagement. Through these, employees are virtually able to live all the production processes as protagonists. The visual features of this experience are characterized by high dynamism, high resolution and high narrativity, as employees actively participate in the story narrated by the organization.

CONCLUSION AND FUTURE DIRECTIONS

This chapter offers an overview of most of the significant changes in the way digital visual corporate communication is and will be performed in the future. As more and more communication is mediated, digitized and augmented, the role of visual elements has become more important than ever. The increasing preoccupation and interest in visibility and visual elements in societies in general has radically changed the interest of scholars in humanities and social sciences who have increasingly focused on analysing the use of visuals for organizational meaning construction (Meyer et al., 2013). A 'visual turn' has been reported occurring even in corporate communication. Professionals across the world are calling for more theoretical knowledge in understanding the architecture of visual content in order to better strategize their digital corporate communication. As argued in this chapter, successful digital visual communications are those capable of creating memorable digital visual experiences that provide economic value in the form of intangible and tangible assets, such as reputation, brand loyalty, trust, increased sales and investments. Far from knowing whether this phase of visual turn will pass, this chapter calls for an increased understanding of visual features for the planning and management of digital visual communication.

After reviewing the main literature on social semiotics addressing image-based features, and borrowing from experiential marketing literature, we proposed a theoretical framework, 4ReDiVE, explaining what features of visual content can enhance digital experiences and what these may be. 4ReDiVE offers a theoretical framework to help professionals to create a specific architecture of images around one or more realms of experiencing visual content. Hence, 4ReDiVE addresses the call for more theory-driven work on visual content production specifically addressing corporate communication professionals' needs. The framework was developed inductively from the literature and used to analyse a posteriori the content production of a business company engaging with different visual content efforts. The illustrative example of Heineken® shows that 4ReDiVE is far from being a normative framework; companies are already engaging consciously or otherwise in the construction of memorable digital experiences through the use of visual content. Yet, to validate the framework further, empirical studies are needed. Future studies should, for example, measure the concrete effects of 4ReDiVE in relation to indicators such as engagement, reputation, customer satisfaction, word-of-mouth and organization–stakeholder relationships across industries, contexts and situations. Likewise, understanding when and how negative experiences with digital visual content form is another underdeveloped area and which deserves academic attention. In an increasingly visual society, we argue, understanding what experiences can be offered and what visual elements may enhance those experiences can help communication managers not just in their planning and execution of digital corporate communication but also in measuring the effects (positive or negative) they are able to create digitally.

NOTES

1. The image is retrievable from https://twitter.com/heineken/status/1479582879982268421?s=46&t=OOnoIbf2rkdTDO6qRF_Shw; image 2.
2. The image is retrievable from https://mobile.twitter.com/Heineken/status/1446145794172653568; image 2.
3. See for example, https://twitter.com/Heineken/status/1488105061431627785.

REFERENCES

Aiello, G. (2006). Theoretical advances in critical visual analysis: Perception, ideology, mythologies, and social semiotics. *Journal of Visual Literacy*, *26*(2), 89–102.

Alkateeb, H. A. (2020). The British Council's role in nourishing the English language teaching industry in the Gulf Cooperation Council region: A visual social semiotic perspective. *Social Semiotics*. https://doi.org/10.1080/10350330.2020.1833686.

Barnes, K., Riesenmy, T., Trinh, M. D., Lleshi, E., Balogh, N., and Molontay, R. (2021). Dank or not? Analyzing and predicting the popularity of memes on Reddit. *Applied Network Science*, *6*(1), 1–24.

Baron, J. (2019). *The key to gen Z is video content*. https://www.forbes.com/sites/jessicabaron/2019/07/03/the-key-to-gen-z-is-video-content/?sh=2e6e35313484.

Berthon, P., Pitt, L., and Campbell, C. (2008). Ad lib: When customers create the ad. *California Management Review*, *50*(6), 6–30.

Buscemi, F. (2017). Linear or digital, they are, however, lies: Fake news in a Nazi newspaper and on today's social media. *Journal of Visual Political Communication*, *5*(1), 9–28.

Charteris, J., Gregory, S., and Masters, Y. (2018). 'Snapchat', youth subjectivities and sexuality: Disappearing media and the discourse of youth innocence. *Gender and Education*, *30*(2), 205–222.

Chawla, R. (2019). Deepfakes: How a pervert shook the world. *International Journal of Advance Research and Development*, *4*(6), 4–8.

Cho, Y.-H., Wang, Y., and Fesenmaier, D. R. (2002). Searching for experiences. *Journal of Travel & Tourism Marketing*, *12*(4), 1–17.

Chouliaraki, L. (2012). *The ironic spectator: Solidarity in the age of post-humanitarianism*. Cambridge: Polity Press.

Cohn, N. (2014). The architecture of visual narrative comprehension: The interaction of narrative structure and page layout in understanding comics. *Frontiers in Psychology*, *5*, article 680. https://dx.doi.org/10.3389%2Ffpsyg.2014.00680.

Dancygier, B. and Vandelanotte, L. (2017). Internet memes as multimodal constructions. *Cognitive Linguistics*, *28*(3), 565–598.

Davison, J., McLean, C., and Warren, S. (2012). Exploring the visual in organisations and management. *Qualitative Research in Organizations and Management: An International Journal*, *7*(1), 5–15.

Domke, D., Perlmutter, D., and Spratt, M. (2002). The primes of our times? An examination of the 'power' of visual images. *Journalism*, *3*(2), 131–159.

Elhamy, H. M. (2022). Social semiotics for social media visuals: A framework for analysis and interpretation. In G. Punziano and A. Delli Paoli (eds.), *Handbook of research on advanced research methodologies for a digital society* (pp. 548–570). Hershey, PA: IGI Global.

Fahmy, S., Bock, M., and Wanta, W. (2014). *Visual communication theory and research: A mass communication perspective*. Cham: Springer.

Fausing, B. (2013). Become an image: On selfies, visuality and the visual turn in social medias. *Digital Visuality*. Paper presented at Digital Visuality conference, Rome, Italy.

Fournier, S. and Avery, J. (2011). The uninvited brand. *Business Horizons*, *54*(3), 193–207.

Gabriel, Y. (2012). A picture tells more than a thousand words: Losing the plot in the era of the image. In F.-R. Puyou, P. Quattrone. C. McLean, and N. Thrift (eds.), *Imagining organizations: Performative imagery in business and beyond* (pp. 230–248). New York: Routledge.

Glenday, J. (2021). Ikea muscles in on the Bernie Sanders meme with a 'get the look' ad. *The Drum*. https://www.thedrum.com/news/2021/01/25/ikea-muscles-the-bernie-sanders-meme-with-get-the-look-ad.

Göransson, K. and Fagerholm, A.-S. (2018). Towards visual strategic communications: An innovative interdisciplinary perspective on visual dimensions within the strategic communications field. *Journal of Communication Management*, *22*(1), 46–66.

Güera, D. and Delp, E. J. (2018). Deepfake video detection using recurrent neural networks. *2018 15th IEEE International Conference on Advanced Video and Signal Based Surveillance (AVSS)*, 2018 (pp. 1–6). https://doi.org/10.1109/AVSS.2018.8639163.

Hargreaves, D. A. and Tiggemann, M. (2004). Idealized media images and adolescent body image: "Comparing" boys and girls. *Body Image*, *1*(4), 351–361.

Harrison, C. (2003). Visual social semiotics: Understanding how still images make meaning. *Technical Communication*, *50*(1), 46–60.

Heineken (2021). *Who we are*. Heineken official website. https://www.theheinekencompany.com/our-company/who-we-are.

Holm, N. (2021). Deadpan humour, the comic disposition and the interpretation of ironic ambiguity online. *New Media & Society*. https://doi.org/10.1177%2F14614448211054011.

Jewitt, C. and Oyama, R. (2001). Visual meaning: A social semiotic approach. In T. van Leeuwen and C. Jewitt (eds.), *Handbook of visual analysis* (pp. 134–157). London: Sage Publications.

Keles, B., McCrae, N., and Grealish, A. (2020). A systematic review: The influence of social media on depression, anxiety and psychological distress in adolescents. *International Journal of Adolescence and Youth*, *25*(1), 79–93.

Khoja, N. (2021). *15 visual content marketing statistics to know for 2021* [Infographic]. https://venngage.com/blog/visual-content-marketing-statistics/.

Kress, G. and van Leeuwen, T. (1996). *Reading images: The grammar of visual design*. New York: Routledge.

Kujur, F. and Singh, S. (2020). Visual communication and consumer-brand relationship on social networking sites: Uses and gratifications theory perspective. *Journal of Theoretical and Applied Electronic Commerce Research*, *15*(1), 30–47.

Li, Q. (2018). Data visualization as creative art practice. *Visual Communication*, *17*(3), 299–312.

Li, Y. and Xie, Y. (2020). Is a picture worth a thousand words? An empirical study of image content and social media engagement. *Journal of Marketing Research*, *57*(1), 1–19.

Luoma-aho, V. (2015). Understanding stakeholder engagement: Faith-holders, hateholders & fakeholders. *RJ-IPR: Research Journal of the Institute for Public Relations*, *2*(1). http://www.instituteforpr.org/understanding-stakeholder-engagement-fai.

Machin, D. (ed.) (2014). *Visual communication*. Handbooks of Communication Science Vol. 4. Berlin: De Gruyter.

Maier, C. D. (2012). Closer to nature: A case study of the multifunctional selection of moving images in an environmental corporate video. *Journal of Multimodal Communication*, *1*(3), 233–250.

Maier, C. D., Frandsen, F., and Johansen, W. (2019). Visual crisis communication in the Scandinavian press. *Nordicom Review*, *40*(2), 91–109.

Matusitz, J. (2021). Understanding Hezbollah symbolism through symbolic convergence theory. *Journal of Visual Political Communication*, *7*(1), 43–60.

Meyer, R. E., Höllerer, M. A., Jancsary, D., and Van Leeuwen, T. (2013). The visual dimension in organizing, organization, and organization research: Core ideas, current developments, and promising avenues. *Academy of Management Annals*, *7*(1), 489–555.

Mignemi, A. (1996). *Propaganda politica e mezzi di comunicazione di massa: tra fascismo e democrazia* (3rd edition). Turin: Ed. Gruppo Abele.

Milosavljević, I. (2020). The phenomenon of the Internet memes as a manifestation of communication of visual society-research of the most popular and the most common types. *Media Studies and Applied Ethics*, *1*, 9–27.

Müller, M. G. (2008). Visual competence: A new paradigm for studying visuals in the social sciences? *Visual Studies*, *23*(2), 101–112.

342 *Handbook on digital corporate communication*

Murtarelli, G., Romenti, S., and Valentini, C. (2021). The impact of digital image-based features on users' emotions and online behaviours in the food industry. *British Food Journal*, 129, 927–935. https://doi.org/10.1108/BFJ-12-2020-1099.

Novak, M. (1975). Story and experience. In J. B. Wiggins (ed.), *Religion as story* (pp. 175–200). Lanham, MD: University Press of America.

Pakarinen, S. (2018). Marimekko as a building block of online identity: Representations of the self and Marimekko in Instagram users' posts (Master's thesis, University of Tampere). https://urn.fi/URN: NBN:fi:uta-201811012758.

Peterson, M. O. (2019). Aspects of visual metaphor: An operational typology of visual rhetoric for research in advertising. *International Journal of Advertising*, 38(1), 67–96.

Pew Research Center (2018). *YouTube, Instagram and Snapchat are the most popular online platforms among teens.* https://www.pewresearch.org/internet/2018/05/31/teens-social-media-technology -2018/pi_2018-05-31_teenstech_0-01/.

Philips, B. J. (2017). Consumer imagination in marketing: A theoretical framework. *European Journal of Marketing*, 51(11–12), 2138–2155.

Pine, I. I. and Gilmore, J. H. (1998). Welcome to the experience economy. *Harvard Business Review*, 76(4), 97–105.

Rigutto, C. (2017). The landscape of online visual communication of science. *Journal of Science Communication*, 16(2), 1–9.

Romney, M. and Johnson, R. G. (2020). Show me a story: Narrative, image, and audience engagement on sports network Instagram accounts. *Information, Communication & Society*, 23(1), 94–109.

Schmitt, B. (1999). Experiential marketing. *Journal of Marketing Management*, 15(1–3), 53–67.

Schmitt, B. and Zarantonello, L. (2013). Consumer experience and experiential marketing: A critical review. *Review of Marketing Research*, 10, 25–61.

Schöning, J. and Heidemann, G. (2018). Visual video analytics for interactive video content analysis. *Future of Information and Communication Conference Proceedings* (pp. 346–360). Cham: Springer.

Shifman, L. (2013). Memes in a digital world: Reconciling with a conceptual troublemaker. *Journal of Computer-Mediated Communication*, 18(3), 362–377.

TheHeinekenCompany.com (2015). New Heineken campaign brings sustainability message closer to consumers. https://www.theheinekencompany.com/newsroom/new-heineken-campaign-brings -sustainability-message-closer-to-consumers/.

Thelander, A. (2018), Visual communication. In R. L. Heath and W. Johansen (eds.), *The international encyclopedia of strategic communication* (pp. 1–13). Hoboken, NJ: John Wiley & Sons.

Unmetric.com (2021). A deep dive into the social media habits and performance of Heineken. https:// unmetric.com/brands/heineken.

Vaccari, C. and Chadwick, A. (2020). Deepfakes and disinformation: Exploring the impact of synthetic political video on deception, uncertainty, and trust in news. *Social Media + Society*, 6(1), 1–13.

Valentini, C., Romenti, S., Murtarelli, G., and Pizzetti, M. (2018). Digital visual engagement: Influencing purchase intentions on Instagram. *Journal of Communication Management*, 22(4), 362–381.

Ventrone, A. (2005). *Il nemico interno. Immagini, parole e simboli della lotta politica nell'Italia del Novecento*. Rome: Donzelli editore.

Vicari, S., Iannelli, L., and Zurovac, E. (2020). Political hashtag publics and counter-visuality: A case study of #fertilityday in Italy. *Information, Communication & Society*, 23(9), 1235–1254.

Westerlund, M. (2019). The emergence of deepfake technology: A review. *Technology Innovation & Management Review*, 9(11), 40–53.

Wiesenberg, M. and Verčič, D. (2021). The status quo of the visual turn in public relations practice. *Communications*, 46(2), 229–252.

Yung, R., Khoo-Lattimore, C., and Potter, L. E. (2021). Virtual reality and tourism marketing: Conceptualizing a framework on presence, emotion, and intention. *Current Issues in Tourism*, 24(11), 1505–1525.

Zerfass, A., Moreno, Á., Tench, R., Verčič, D., and Verhoeven, P. (2017). *European Communication Monitor 2017. How strategic communication deals with the challenges of visualisation, social bots and hypermodernity. Results of a survey in 50 Countries*. Berlin: EACD/EUPRERA, Quadriga Media.

24. Digital corporate communication and voice communication

Alex Mari, Andreina Mandelli and René Algesheimer

INTRODUCTION

AI-enabled smart devices are becoming a common interface between organizations and stakeholders (Syvänen and Valentini, 2020). Apple, Microsoft, Amazon, Alphabet, Meta and Tesla, along with the China-based platforms Tencent and Alibaba, represent eight of the ten most valuable firms globally (Statista, 2021a, 2021b). Over the past decade, these tech giants have all developed proprietary voice technology based on AI natural language processing techniques such as automatic speech recognition and text-to-speech. Some of the most prominent commercially available AI-based Voice Assistants (VAs) are Amazon Alexa, Google Home and Apple HomePod. VAs are best understood as artificially enabled agents that utilize human language to engage in dialogues while elaborating requests in context and expanding their knowledge (Mari and Algesheimer, 2022). These digital technology artefacts have the capacity to empower organizations to engage in two-way communication of unprecedented speed and automation (Argenti, 2015). This can be attributed to VAs' ability to monitor human behaviour, utilize algorithms to identify patterns and predict future needs.

VAs affect the fundamental information processing capabilities of the organization as they contribute to boundary-breaking, communication extension and data storage (Carley, 2002; Sproull and Kiesler, 1991). Technology providers like Amazon utilize open technological interfaces to facilitate the implementation of new third-party services with the aid of application programming interfaces (APIs), software development kits and templates. For instance, in a similar manner to smartphones, Amazon Alexa can host applications from third-party organizations that extend the value and functional use of VAs. Organizations can provide stakeholders with a broad range of searchable services for either internal (e.g., employees) or external (e.g., consumers) use. Thus, VAs facilitate interactions among multiple stakeholders, simultaneously performing the dual roles of intermediaries and data aggregators. Driven by the fast adoption of VAs, the field of digital voice communication (DVC) represents a disruptive advancement in the digital corporate communication (DCC) discipline for two main reasons.

First, vocal characteristics provide socially relevant cues. Speech generates physiological and affective arousal because the voice incorporates rich non-verbal cues through varying tones, intonation, speed and emphasis. This helps people make inferences regarding emotions, attitudes, social status and personality (Nass and Brave, 2005). Users perceive a conversation more favourably than text-only interaction because it allows for more natural and effective dialogue (Nass and Brave, 2005). Consequently, individuals consider VAs a social entity even where there may be minimal indices of similarity with humans and scarce automation capabilities. Reeves and Nass (1996) argue that the human brain did not evolve fast enough to elaborate on the ontological nature of an agent. In that sense, when a machine is involved in real-time, unstructured language production, users adopt the same social rules and heuris-

344 *Handbook on digital corporate communication*

tics used in their interpersonal relationships (Nass and Moon, 2000). Furthermore, studies on human–machine interaction suggest that voice is a powerful indicator of the presence of another person (Lester et al., 1997). As such, the perceived automated social presence, defined as the "extent to which technology makes customers feel the presence of another social entity" (van Doorn et al., 2017, p. 43), is higher in spoken communication than in written (Qiu and Benbasat, 2009).

Second, voice helps maximize the realism of machines and authenticity of interactions. Agents that primarily interact with humans using voice convey more robust human-like mental capacities such as intelligence and memory (Nass and Moon, 2000). This effect is most potent when the voice sounds more human-like (Schroeder et al., 2017). Thus, VA manufacturers increasingly deploy features to maximize the realism of voice-based conversations and increase users' perceptions, beliefs and behavioural intentions with empathic VAs (Mari et al., 2022). For instance, Alexa uses modern text-to-speech technology to respond in a happy tone to a correctly answered trivia question or in a disappointed manner when the answer is wrong. The increase of empathetic cues powered by AI technologies contributes to strengthening the perceived usefulness, trusting competence and empathy of VAs, making them more human-like social exchange partners (Guzman and Lewis, 2020; Mari et al., 2022). Thus, researchers largely agree that software-based voices can significantly alter the interpersonal nature of human–machine interactions and potentially the organization–stakeholder relationship (e.g., Mari et al., 2020).

However, the use of VAs for managing stakeholder relations has introduced new challenges for corporate communication professionals. Galloway and Swiatek (2018) posit that these smart agents do not currently handle complex relational tasks and are incapable of developing or maintaining trustworthy relationships. At the same time, DVC differs in nature to human-to-human interactions. Because of their assistive nature, VAs increasingly exhibit independent and unique behaviours (Rahwan et al., 2019). Thus, organizations may experience negativity in stakeholder engagement due to a loss of message control (Lievonen et al., 2018). Furthermore, organizations often struggle to effectively use digital technologies for communication (Gartner, 2018). Consequently, it is essential to examine the opportunities and threats that VAs offer concerning corporate communication goals, such as building and maintaining stakeholder relationships (Grunig and Huang, 2000).

Corporate communication experts are called to decide if and how to implement voice-based initiatives. This study explores how VAs are changing interactions between stakeholders and organizations in the context of DCC. The first section of this chapter introduces an overarching framework of the current organizations' best practices in voice-based corporate communication. Next, the threats and opportunities associated with VAs in the context of DCC are explored. The chapter concludes with illustrative examples and final remarks.

DEFINITIONS OF THE TOPIC AND PREVIOUS STUDIES

Following the definition of DCC by Badham and Luoma-aho (Chapter 1 in this volume), DVC is defined as the strategic management of voice-based communication channels to improve communication in organizations, society and with organizational stakeholders. Adobe (2019) suggests that 20 per cent of organizations are using voice-activated services to improve experience and engagement with strategic audiences. It follows from this diffusion of VAs that corporate communication professionals can employ a growing variety of push and pull DVC initiatives shaped around the unique bi-directional characteristics of the voice touchpoint. To understand the environment in which DVC takes place, it is necessary to reflect upon the function of VAs in an organizational context.

In the digital environment, VAs can be conceptualized as both spaces of interactions (arenas) and vehicles of communication (media) (Badham et al., 2022). From a corporate function perspective, organizations can leverage voice-based initiatives for corporate communication with stakeholders, marketing and commerce. The framework in Figure 24.1 addresses the diverse needs of professionals in terms of understanding how to use VAs for effective corporate communication. The framework takes inspiration from the PESO model of Paid, Earned, Shared, and Owned media use (Macnamara et al., 2016) and emerging forms of communication presented in the digital media-arenas (DMA) framework, such as Searched media (Badham et al., 2022). The DVC framework recognizes the importance of engaging with stakeholders critical to the organization, such as employees, influencers and customers. Thus, this work revolves around the universality of DCC, which includes communications within and between organizations and also in society at large (Badham and Luoma-aho, Chapter 1 in this volume).

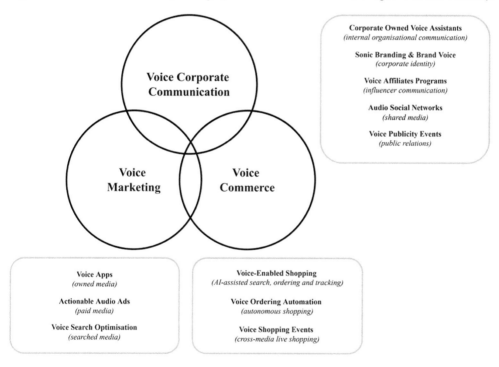

Figure 24.1 Digital voice communication (DVC) framework

The DVC framework represents a research outcome of semi-structured and open-ended interviews with (a) industry executives (internal) and (b) suppliers (external) and is supplemented with (c) secondary archival material. Purposeful random sampling was used to select groups of executives in the consumer goods packaged industry in the process of considering, implementing or deploying voice-based initiatives. Data were triangulated with interviews from suppliers, such as voice-specialized agencies and VA manufacturers (e.g., Amazon). All 94 interviews, lasting an average of 40 minutes, were recorded, transcribed verbatim and checked for accuracy. The final sample for the in-depth archival was composed of 99 documents which included 15 videos and podcasts (transcribed), 36 press articles, 28 blog entries, and 20 analyst reports.

Following an iterative and inductive content analysis approach, the findings describe how VAs may impact the organization–stakeholder relationship (Corley and Gioia, 2004). The DVC arenas and media are discussed in connection to three functional areas born by the rise of VAs: voice corporate communication, voice marketing and voice commerce.

Voice Corporate Communication

Voice corporate communication (VCC) defines the strategic usage and management of voice-based agents to improve communication within organizations and with stakeholders. Five best practices describe the current use of VAs in the VCC context: corporate-owned VAs (i.e., internal corporate communication), sonic branding and brand voice (i.e., corporate identity), voice affiliate programs (i.e., influencer communication), audio social networks (i.e., shared media), and voice publicity events (i.e., public relations).

Corporate-owned voice assistants. DVC is increasingly relevant for an organization's internal communication with employees, with managers finding them useful in quickly retrieving business information. For example, during meetings, managers can ask a corporate-owned VA (OVA) for information from a company database. For example: "What was our market share in the segment SUV in Japan during Q4-2021?" OVAs are also becoming a popular tool to support the frontline workforce. For instance, Walmart has created a mobile-based VA called 'Ask Sam' to help 5,000 employees in the US perform their duties. The VA answers questions and supports customer requests about prices and product placements, including maps. In addition, Walmart's OVA enables important updates about policies to be promptly communicated to managers from company headquarters. These internal tools are compelling during a corporate crisis (Mandelli and Mari, 2012). VAs have offered exceptional support to employees during the pandemic health crisis, and associates use Ask Sam for information related to Covid-19. VAs are also able to promote work productivity; for example, Alexa helps with meeting (re)scheduling or reading and sending emails through simple voice commands.

Sonic branding and brand voice. The expression of a brand through clear auditory association with an organization, often referred to as sonic or audio branding, is now widespread. Organizations have engaged in this through auditory components such as music jingles. As a result, corporate identity consisting of design, architecture, culture, etc., has expanded to include corporate sound. A sound identity is fundamental for brands due to human beings' fast reaction to sound (160 ms) in comparison to other senses such as sight (190 ms) (Jain et al., 2015). Examples include the 'Intel Inside' jingle and the McDonald's 'I'm Lovin' it' audio signature, which contribute to a more immersive brand experience. However, the association of sound to a brand represents just an initial step towards a more immersive corporate identity. It is likely that brand voice and tone of voice will soon become both a component of the corporate identity and a functional aspect of a brand. Using VAs, brands will speak to stakeholders using a set of authentic speech characteristics such as intonation, pauses and emphasis that will make them unique to the ears of interlocutors, using personas ranging from sounding

Digital corporate communication and voice communication 347

either similar to a TV news anchor or less formal, like a friend. Furthermore, Amazon has partnered with several companies to develop a unique voice for Alexa apps. The neural text-to-speech technology service turns text into human-like speech which enables companies to design a custom voice for their brand utilizing a spokesperson like Samuel L. Jackson. Another example is KFC's voice brand designed to sound like Colonel Sanders (founder of the company), following the same style used in other official communications such as TV or radio commercials.

Voice affiliate programs. Affiliate programs allow influencers to create content such as podcasts to promote third-party products and earn referral commissions. The Amazon Associates Program is an affiliate marketing program in which associates, often media companies, direct their audience to their recommendations and earn from qualifying purchases. Affiliates share millions of products with their audience and earn up to 10 per cent in associate commissions. A similar situation exists with influencers through the Amazon Influencer Program where influencers curate a personalized page on Amazon with live streams, shoppable photos, and videos. This gives communication managers the opportunity to leverage a wide array of influencers to inspire customers to shop their products on Amazon. Voice-based affiliate programs on Alexa also make it easier for organizations to connect with strategic influencers and content creators (independent or media companies) to disseminate company messages to Amazon's customer base.

Audio social networks. Like other social media platforms, VAs are expected to function as a social platform that enables social connections where people exchange opinions and information. Since the rise of Clubhouse, a voice-only social network where users communicate in audio chat rooms, several organizations are reconsidering the importance of being part of their brand-related conversations. Although initially launched or moderated by influencers, audio chat rooms on Clubhouse or similar apps are increasingly used by strategic stakeholders interested in sustainability, gender equality or cryptocurrency investment. From here, corporate communicators can decide to what extent they want to be at the centre of a conversation or take a marginal role as listeners. For instance, organizations can sponsor rooms and guest speakers but not actively engage in conversations; in contrast, they can organize an open event in which corporate managers or spokespersons present or moderate discussions. Regular users will proactively produce user-generated audio content more actively as they become accustomed to it. Because of the flat hierarchy on this channel, it is often possible to hear public figures like Elon Musk, CEO of SpaceX and Tesla, participating in talks.

Voice publicity events. Organizations may seek publicity by staging newsworthy voice-related events that attract media coverage. Burger King and Nike designed voice publicity events with remarkable results (see 'Illustrative examples').

Voice Marketing

Voice marketing utilizes a mix of push and pull communication mechanisms to create immersive, convenient and relevant brand experiences that strengthen the relationship with consumers (Mari and Algesheimer, 2022). A steep adoption of voice marketing is connected to the rise of voice apps (i.e., owned media), actionable audio ads (i.e., paid media), and voice search optimization (i.e., searched media).

Voice apps. Branded voice apps, called 'skills' by Amazon and 'actions' by Google, are developed by organizations around four main service objectives: utility, entertainment,

348 *Handbook on digital corporate communication*

information and education (Mari and Algesheimer, 2021). Like smartphone apps, third-party voice apps are available in different markets and languages and offer infinite possibilities to strengthen strategic relationships. Some companies have swiftly established a prominent voice presence. For instance, Nestlé has launched over 20 Alexa skills for several brands and in various languages (e.g., Ask Purina and BabyService). The British alcohol beverage company Diageo was the first to build an Alexa skill to enrich the customer tasting experience. The 'Talisker Tasting Experience' app by the scotch brand Talisker replicates a guided tasting that the brand offers in its distillery. It provides a step-by-step audio guide to help the listener enjoy and appreciate their whisky. A tasting experience usually takes place in a living room and during intimate conversations, so the VA user can impress family and friends while interacting with the brand in a social setting. Users can gather insights, suggestions and stories while the DVC experience enhances properties of a physical product. Participating in unique DVC experiences is expected to lead to deeper emotional connections with the brand (Mari et al., 2020).

Audio ads. Actionable audio-based ads are in-stream advertisements that encourage listeners to interact with their VAs to complete a campaign goal such as engaging with a brand or purchasing a product. Recently, Amazon launched a service that allows advertisers to play audio-based ads periodically during breaks between songs and helps drive brand awareness through the default music service on Alexa devices. Beyond the classic ads placement, the vitamin tablet brand Berocca (Bayer Consumer Health) has launched the first actionable audio ads. Using voice commands, digital radio listeners can respond to an ad requesting more information about the product or order it directly through Amazon Alexa. Another example is Spotify, which suggests buying tickets for the closest concert venue of the user's favourite artist. Similar examples of hybrid organic and paid formats that leverage AI personalization and the growing trust towards VAs are emerging on Google where, for example, books might be recommended in a proactive form of assistance that is individualized, personalized and contextualized.

Voice search. The algorithms that rank information and products on VAs are constantly scrutinized by managers. Voice search optimization (VSO) optimizes content to increase the likelihood of appearing in related voice searches. These practices consider how people conduct verbal searches and optimize the content against them. A recent industry study shows that, despite the importance of VSO for DCC, only 3.8 per cent of businesses are adapting their content for voice searches (Uberall, 2019). Voice searches differ from screen-based searches in that they include key phrases and long-tail keywords, which have filler words such as 'the' or 'for' (e.g., 'benefits of voice' versus 'what are the benefits of voice'). Companies like P&G update their product information according to concise and simple conversational queries. For instance, a page on Amazon.com under the title 'Gillette Sensor3 men's disposable razor, eight counts, men's blades' on Alexa will be simplified to 'Gillette men's razor, blades, eight counts' (Onespace, 2018). Thus, managers' understanding of voice search best practices may affect their organization's performance in the digital environment.

Voice Commerce

Voice commerce refers to the transaction of placing an order using voice, directly or through third-party marketplaces (Mari, 2019). This definition includes technical capabilities and communication activities that allow users to search for a product, listen to reviews, add items to a list, track the order and so on. Voice-enabled shopping (i.e., AI-assisted search, ordering

Digital corporate communication and voice communication 349

and tracking), voice ordering automation (i.e., autonomous shopping) and voice shopping events (i.e., cross-media live shopping) are some of the commerce practices organizations are employing in the DVC context.

Voice-enabled shopping. With a simple 'yes' requiring no additional information such as address or credit card details, repeat users can buy physical products or services from third-party voice apps such as Domino's Pizza or Sony games. Additionally, organizations can sell directly through native voice shopping capabilities (e.g., Amazon Alexa, Google Shopping) or indirectly via the platform's approved brick-and-mortar retailers (e.g., Whole Foods for Alexa, Walmart for Google Home). In the US, VA users can receive delivery of a large set of household products and fresh produce within two hours. Currently, voice commerce is characterized by high penetration in the 18- to 34-year-old user group; in this segment, 17 per cent of US VA owners have purchased at least one product or service (eMarketer, 2020). These users appreciate the convenience of seamlessly shopping for products using payment options associated with their accounts (e.g., Amazon Pay).

For instance, Domino's Pizza developed one of the early custom skills for Amazon Alexa that directly involves a commercial transaction. By saying, "Alexa, ask Domino's to feed me!" users can build a new pizza order, repurchase the most recent one or track each stage of the delivery process. Concurrently, Nespresso launched a dedicated app for Google Home, allowing ordering, reordering or order tracking by simply saying "Hey Google, ask Nespresso where is my order?" Customers can also carry out other tasks; for example, by saying "Okay, Google, Talk to Nespresso", the VA can provide background information on a specific coffee or indicate the closest recycling point.

Voice ordering automation. VAs represent the initial step towards autonomous shopping as they have the potential to significantly reduce (or even eliminate) the need for human decision-making (de Bellis and Johar, 2020). Organizations can generate repeated revenue through a subscription-like business model called in-skill purchasing (ISP). Using ISP, organizations can charge users for premium services, such as interactive stories or exclusive features, as part of their voice experiences. For instance, Jeopardy!, produced by Sony Pictures Television, was the first Alexa skill to offer an ISP option. For a payment of $1.99 per month, users can access premium features like participating in previous episodes they have missed.

Voice shopping events. Cross-media live shopping events represent a new frontier of digital commerce. They combine the users' need for discovery with the time-limited availability of products, thus creating a sense of urgency in the shopper. They often involve several media, such as being prompted while watching TV to ask Alexa to buy your favourite cereal brand in a limited edition only available for purchase during the football match time (see 'Illustrative examples').

The archival data in this study show that nearly half of the top 100 global consumer goods companies have launched voice-based initiatives in some form. The mentioned examples further reinforce the strategic importance of VAs in delivering the right message to specific audiences at the optimal time via the most productive digital media and arenas. While automating and hyper-personalizing DCC, these devices drive efficiencies and build relationships at scale. However, novel technologies like VAs pose new challenges and opportunities for organizations seeking to integrate them into DVC practices.

WHAT IS CHANGING?

The rapid growth of VAs has resulted in voice being seen as an essential communication channel capable of influencing individual and organizational perceptions and decisions. DVC characteristics differ from human-to-human interactions. Unlike traditional mass media, VAs are always-on devices with a proactive and bidirectional nature (e.g., Holtzhausen and Zerfass, 2015). Managers and consumers can leverage VAs to process or automate tasks with a simple voice command. Like other AI-based conversational agents (e.g., chatbots), VAs can assume a persona and recall relevant facts from previous conversations, giving continuity to subsequent interactions. Like in human–human relationships, the ability of VAs to display emotions through voice and engage in casual jokes makes them more human-like conversational partners. A foundational characteristic of VA is the contextualization of interactions to particular cues such as location and purchase history, increasing the overall personalization level. Additionally, using unsupervised systems, which operate without manual human annotation, VAs can detect unsatisfactory utterances and automatically self-learn how to recover from these errors.

Like other transformational technologies such as social media, DVC is now omnipresent in our private and professional lives, allowing for repeated, ongoing interactions that fulfil functional and social needs. VAs are increasingly present in our daily environments to connect the various nodes of our lives into one experience. These agents can take one of three primary forms depending on whether it is integrated into a voice-enabled product (e.g., coffee machine), built to work with a VA (e.g., thermostat) or deployed as an additional service app (e.g., pay at a gas station). For example, the 'Lavazza Voicy' coffee machine has a built-in Alexa providing entertainment during daily coffee routines. Users can customize their coffee experiences and start the machine using voice commands. Capsules can also be ordered directly from the VA-enabled coffee machine. VAs can also perform tasks such as temperature control, where a simple voice command could adjust the room's thermostat as with Nest Thermostat via Google. Examples such as these highlight the capacity of these VA-enabled devices to simplify ordinary aspects of daily routines.

These unique features position VAs as our personal and professional advisers while influencing both short- and long-term individual and collective decisions. However, voice-only communications present several limitations compared to screen-based interactions (Mari et al., 2020). For instance, VAs are designed to process one request at a time and on a turn-by-turn basis, which avoids voice overlap necessary to decrease speech recognition errors. However, it does not favour multi-tasking activities found in sensorially richer devices like computers or smartphones, thus simultaneously presenting multiple pieces of information on a screen. In addition, auditory cues demand high working memory effort not affected in screen-based interactions.

WHAT REMAINS THE SAME?

Scholars posit that DCC objectives and goals are fundamentally unchanged as the basis for human and organizational communication remains the same (Camilleri, 2021). However, given the fast rise and the variety of digital media arenas, organizations are tempted to swiftly introduce novel DVC initiatives without a clear understanding of their consequences for all stakeholders involved in the adoption process (Galloway and Swiatek, 2018). As such, corporate communicators must reflect on why they are actually using VAs. Ultimately, the findings of this study show that an organization's decision to adopt VAs is centred around two different business objectives: (i) establishing and defending a strategic market position and (ii) building social and digital legitimacy.

First, organizations may seek to build a strong DVC presence, growing the ability to establish and defend a strategic market position in the voice-based channels (Cusumano et al., 2019). Launching services on VAs can be a way to differentiate communication, marketing and distribution. Differentiation represents an increasingly strategic objective in a competitive environment affected by product commoditization and communication touchpoints explosion (Porter, 1996). Furthermore, organizations seek to interact with stakeholders in a multichannel setting offering unique and holistic experiences (Lock, 2019) at the same time as reaping the first-mover advantages associated with early entrance into DVC.

Second, establishing a partnership with VA manufacturers like Amazon that have a sizeable installed base allows traditional organizations to demonstrate their social (Hearit, 1995) and digital legitimacy (Mandelli, 2018). Simultaneously, partnerships show the organization's commitment to adopting transformative and innovative technologies. Extant research shows that alliance partners and media coverage can affect impression formation and impart legitimacy while increasing visibility, reputation and prestige (Stuart et al., 1999). Third parties such as investors will be more willing to engage in exchange relationships when the organization shows the ability to innovate by leveraging the latest technologies, also in the area of DVC (Pollock and Rindova, 2003).

In order to avoid impulsive adoption decisions, managers should clarify why and how VAs are necessary for their DCC strategy as their implementation does not come without relational, communicational and reputational risks.

CRITICAL EXAMINATION

Digital technologies are a game-changer for communication between organizations and stakeholders (Lock, 2019). However, given the recent implementation of AI-powered features, it is not yet possible to reach definitive conclusions about the holistic impact that smart agents may have on DCC (Syvänen and Valentini, 2020). Current predictions see VAs assuming a mediator role acting as suppliers of the content, information and services in the organizational context (Frandsen and Johansen, 2015). Thus, VAs appear to be a powerful digital tool for supporting relationship formation and maintenance. However, most use cases are today related to just one strategic stakeholder: consumers. Here, little is known about the dark side of VAs for corporate communication and the new challenges for professional communicators.

Extant studies anticipate some limitations organizations may experience when adopting VAs to manage stakeholder relations in the digital environment. First, human-like agents can operate for extended periods without human intervention, exhibiting independent behaviour and making their own decisions (Rahwan et al., 2019). Thus, organizations may experience negative stakeholder engagement due to a loss of message control (Lievonen et al., 2018). AI-based agents are expected to augment human communication rather than completely replace it through automation, at least in the foreseeable future (Wilson and Daugherty, 2018). However, questions pertaining to accountability for the outcomes of communication remain

352   *Handbook on digital corporate communication*

unanswered when automated systems essentially perform the activity (Galloway and Swiatek, 2018). Second, besides autonomy, corporate communicators may underestimate the role of trust in the human–machine relationship-building process. DCC is inherently connected with trust, credibility and reputation (Badham and Luoma-aho, Chapter 1 in this volume). For instance, the question of whether VAs can build direct relationships with strategic audiences functioning as mediators between organizations and stakeholders has not been specifically addressed by academic research. Furthermore, voice-based agents will be increasingly required to handle complex relational tasks with substantial consequences for developing or maintaining organizational relationships. Thus, the absence of emotional intelligence, critical thinking and creativity may result in lower perceptions of VA transparency, integrity and authenticity (Christensen, 2002; Galloway and Swiatek, 2018).

ILLUSTRATIVE EXAMPLES

The following illustrative examples show the applicability of the DVC framework to an actual digital communicative situation and the convergence of corporate communication, marketing and commerce goals.

(a) Convergence of corporate communication and marketing. Burger King's 'Google Home of the Whopper' was awarded campaign of the year at Cannes Lions in 2017. During a TV commercial, Burger King hacked all the homes where a Google Home was active. The initial 15 seconds of the ad featured a Burger King employee explaining that he cannot provide the details of what makes the Whopper so great in such a short time. The commercial closes, saying, "Okay, Google, what is the Whopper burger?" This question activates Google Home in people's homes, which reads the Wikipedia entry for the signature menu item. The campaign bridging the TV creative with voice search generated 9.3 billion ad impressions globally and $135 million in free media coverage for the Whopper, becoming the company's most talked-about TV commercial. This case reveals a convergence between corporate communication and searched media goals in the context of DVC.

(b) Convergence of corporate communication and commerce. Nike launched an award-winning campaign leveraging the diffusion of VAs to, directly and indirectly, reach relevant stakeholders. In 2019, during half-time of an NBA game, 2.6 million viewers were invited to use Google Assistant to 'Ask Nike' to buy the pre-release Nike Adapt BB shoes worn by two top players. The voice-activated drop gave fans an exclusive pre-release opportunity to purchase the shoes. This first-ever live in-game shopping experience was powered entirely by voice. More than 15,000 viewers asked to buy a pair of the $350 shoes, and, within six minutes, the shoes were gone. Following this publicity event, broad media coverage generated several million dollars in media exposure. This case reveals a convergence between corporate communication and live shopping goals in the context of DVC.

(c) Convergence of corporate communication, marketing and commerce. Alibaba created a customized version of its VA 'Tmall Genie' for Starbucks. In China, people can arrange to have their Starbucks order delivered to their office or private home while paying with their Starbucks account and receiving loyalty rewards. At the same time, the voice app enables users to listen to Starbucks' well-known music playlists, recreating the coffee shop experience wherever they are. The music break enables delivery of messages that reinforce its corporate identity. In the future, the VA is expected to converse naturally with consumers making use

of the newest sonic branding features. This case reveals a convergence of corporate identity, owned media and assisted shopping goals in the context of DVC.

Overall, these examples show that DVC can play an impactful role in driving real-time and autonomous organization-stakeholder interactions combining different functional objectives.

CONCLUSION AND FUTURE DIRECTIONS

The diffusion of voice technologies through AI-enabled devices like VAs is changing traditional forms of corporate communication. This chapter has explored the impact of emerging VAs in the context of DCC. In particular, it discussed how DVC enables organizations to interact and build relationships with relevant stakeholders. The authors posit that VAs represent a novel medium for organizations through which they can technically initiate a variety of DVC initiatives in different but goal-converging digital arenas. The research outcome is observable in the DVC framework, which combines internal and external, push and pull, organic and paid communication mechanisms. At the same time, it shows the convergence of voice-based activities centred around corporate communication, marketing and commerce objectives. Although DVC represents an increasingly critical opportunity for organizations in the DCC context, they pose new challenges for corporate communicators through the unique characteristics of autonomy and agency that might lead to a loss of control of corporate messages and negative digital experiences.

Organizations have often struggled to effectively use digital technologies with corporate communication goals such as nurturing stakeholder relationships. Future studies in DCC should investigate more closely how AI assistive technologies like VAs affect organizational stakeholders' perceptions and decisions. At the same time, the swift evolution of DVC requires researchers to review real-life and in-context case studies that can further shed light on the effect of agent-led voice channels on communicative relationships between organizations and their stakeholders. While doing so, it is recommended to view digital arenas in the context of DVC as operationally linked to multiple and converging functional areas, rather than in isolation.

REFERENCES

Adobe (2019). *State of voice technology for brands: Industry report presentation*. http://www.slideshare .net/slideshow/embed_code/key/v76vHDbO0WLnWw.
Argenti, P. A. (2015). *Corporate communication*. New York: McGraw-Hill.
Badham, M., Luoma-aho, V., Valentini, C., and Körkkö, L. (2022). Digital strategic communication through digital media-arenas. In J. Falkheimer and M. Heide (eds.), *Research handbook on strategic communication* (pp. 416–430). Cheltenham, UK and Northampton, MA, USA: Edward Elgar Publishing.
Camilleri, M. A. (2021). Strategic dialogic communication through digital media during COVID-19 crisis. In M. A. Camilleri (ed.), *Strategic corporate communication in the digital age* (pp. 1–18). Bingley: Emerald Publishing.
Carley, K. M. (2002). Smart agents and organisations of the future. In L. Lievrouw and S. Livingstone (eds.), *The handbook of new media* (pp. 206-220). Thousand Oaks, CA: Sage Publications.
Christensen, L. T. (2002). Corporate communication: The challenge of transparency. *Corporate Communications: An International Journal, 7*(3), 162–168.

Corley, K. G. and Gioia, D. A. (2004). Identity ambiguity and change in the wake of a corporate spin-off. *Administrative Science Quarterly, 49*(2), 173–208.

Cusumano, M. A., Gawer, A., and Yoffie, D. B. (2019). *The business of platforms: Strategy in the age of digital competition, innovation, and power*. New York: Harper Business.

De Bellis, E. and Johar, G. V. (2020). Autonomous shopping systems: Identifying and overcoming barriers to consumer adoption. *Journal of Retailing, 96*(1), 74–87.

eMarketer (2020). *There's still lackluster enthusiasm for shopping and buying via voice*. https://www.emarketer.com/content/there-s-still-lackluster-enthusiasm-shopping-buying-via-voice.

Frandsen, F. and Johansen, W. (2015). The role of communication executives in strategy and strategizing. In D. R. Holtzhausen and A. Zerfass (eds.), *The Routledge handbook of strategic communication* (pp. 229–243). London: Routledge.

Galloway, C. and Swiatek, L. (2018). Public relations and artificial intelligence: It's not (just) about robots. *Public Relations Review, 44*(5), 734–740.

Gartner (2018). *What digitalization means for corporate communications*. https://www.gartner.com/smarterwithgartner/digitalization-means-corporate-communications.

Grunig, J. E. and Huang, Y. H. (2000). From organisational effectiveness to relationship indicators: Antecedents of relationships, public relations strategies, and relationship outcomes. In J. A. Ledingham and S. D. Bruning (eds.), *Public relations as relationship management* (pp. 23–58). Mahwah, NJ: Lawrence Erlbaum.

Guzman, A. L. and Lewis, S. C. (2020). Artificial intelligence and communication: A human–machine communication research agenda. *New Media & Society, 22*(1), 70–86.

Hearit, K. M. (1995). "Mistakes were made": Organisations, apologia, and crises of social legitimacy. *Communication Studies, 46*(1–2), 1–17.

Holtzhausen, D. and Zerfass, A. (2015). Strategic communication. In D. Holtzhausen and A. Zerfass (eds.), *The Routledge handbook of strategic communication* (pp. 3–17). London: Routledge.

Jain, A., Bansal, R., Kumar, A., and Singh, K. D. (2015). A comparative study of visual and auditory reaction times on the basis of gender and physical activity levels of medical first year students. *International Journal of Applied & Basic Medical Research, 5*(2), 124–127.

Lester, J. C., Converse, S. A., Kahler, S. E., Barlow, S. T., Stone, B. A., and Bhogal, R. S. (1997). The persona effect: Affective impact of animated pedagogical agents. In *Proceedings of the ACM SIGCHI Conference on human factors in computing systems* (pp. 359–366).

Lievonen, M., Luoma-aho, V., and Bowden, J. (2018). Negative engagement. In K. Johnston and M. Taylor (eds.), *The handbook of communication engagement* (pp. 531–548). New York: Wiley.

Lock, I. (2019). Explicating communicative organisation-stakeholder relationships in the digital age: A systematic review and research agenda. *Public Relations Review, 45*(4), 101829.

Macnamara, J., Lwin, M., Adi, A., and Zerfass, A. (2016). 'PESO' media strategy shifts to 'SOEP': Opportunities and ethical dilemmas. *Public Relations Review, 42*(3), 377–385.

Mandelli, A. (2018). *Intelligenza artificiale e marketing: Agenti invisibili, esperienza, valore e business*. Milan: EGEA spa.

Mandelli, A. and Mari, A. (2012). The relationship between social media conversations and reputation during a crisis: The Toyota case. *International Journal of Management Cases, 14*(1), 456–489.

Mari, A. (2019). Voice commerce: Understanding shopping-related voice assistants and their effect on brands. Paper presented at IMMAA Annual Conference, Northwestern University in Doha, Qatar.

Mari, A. and Algesheimer, R. (2021). The role of trusting beliefs in voice assistants during voice shopping. In *Proceedings of the 54th Hawaii International Conference on System Sciences (HICSS)*. Manoa, Hawaii, USA.

Mari, A. and Algesheimer, R. (2022). AI-based voice assistants for digital marketing: Preparing for voice marketing and commerce. In O. Niininen (ed.), *Contemporary issues in digital marketing* (pp. 72–82). London: Routledge.

Mari, A., Mandelli, A., and Algesheimer, R. (2020). The evolution of marketing in the context of voice commerce: A managerial perspective. In F.-H. Nah and K. Siau (eds.), *HCI in business, government and organizations* (pp. 405–425). Cham: Springer International.

Mari, A., Mandelli, A., and Algesheimer, R. (2022). Shopping with voice assistants: How empathy affects decision-making outcomes. University of Zurich, Institute of Business Administration, UZH Business Working Paper (399).

Digital corporate communication and voice communication   355

Nass, C. I. and Brave, S. (2005). *Wired for speech: How voice activates and advances the human-computer relationship*. Cambridge, MA: MIT Press.

Nass, C. and Moon, Y. (2000). Machines and mindlessness: Social responses to computers. *Journal of Social Issues*, *56*(1), 81–103.

OneSpace (2018). *What is Amazon's choice, and what does it mean for brands?* https://www.onespace .com/blog/2018/05/what-is-amazons-choice-what-does-it-mean-brands.

Pollock, T. G. and Rindova, V. P. (2003). Media legitimation effects in the market for initial public offerings. *Academy of Management Journal*, *46*(5), 631–642.

Porter, M. E. (1996). Competitive advantage, agglomeration economies, and regional policy. *International Regional Science Review*, *19*(1–2), 85–90.

Qiu, L. and Benbasat, I. (2009). Evaluating anthropomorphic product recommendation agents: A social relationship perspective to designing information systems. *Journal of Management Information Systems*, *25*(4), 145–182.

Rahwan, I., Cebrian, M., Obradovich, N., Bongard, J., Bonnefon, J. F., Breazeal, C., … Wellman, M. (2019). Machine behaviour. *Nature*, *568*(7753), 477–486.

Reeves, B. and Nass, C. (1996). *The media equation: How people treat computers, television, and new media like real people*. Cambridge: Cambridge University Press.

Schroeder, J., Kardas, M., and Epley, N. (2017). The humanising voice: Speech reveals, and text conceals, a more thoughtful mind in the midst of disagreement. *Psychological Science*, *28*(12), 1745–1762

Sproull, L. and Kiesler, S. (1991). Computers, networks and work. *Scientific American*, *265*(3), 116–127.

Statista (2021a). *The 100 largest companies in the world by market capitalisation in 2021*. https://www .statista.com/statistics/263264/top-companies-in-the-world-by-market-capitalization.

Statista (2021b). *Installed base of smart speakers worldwide in 2020 and 2024*. https://www.statista .com/statistics/878650/worldwide-smart-speaker-installed-base-by-country.

Stuart, T. E., Hoang, H., and Hybels, R. C. (1999). Interorganizational endorsements and the performance of entrepreneurial ventures. *Administrative Science Quarterly*, *44*(2), 315–349.

Syvänen, S. and Valentini, C. (2020). Conversational agents in online organisation–stakeholder interactions: A state-of-the-art analysis and implications for further research. *Journal of Communication Management*, *24*(4), 339–362.

Uberall (2019). *Voice search readiness report 2019*. https://m.uberall.com/ uberall-report-voice-searc h-readiness-uk-2019.

Van Doorn, J., Mende, M., Noble, S. M., Hulland, J., Ostrom, A. L., Grewal, D., and Petersen, J. A. (2017). Domo arigato Mr. Roboto: Emergence of automated social presence in organisational frontlines and customers' service experiences. *Journal of Service Research*, *20*(1), 43–58.

Wilson, H. J. and Daugherty, P. R. (2018). Collaborative intelligence: Humans and AI are joining forces. *Harvard Business Review*, *96*(4), 114–123.

PART IV

CORPORATE COMMUNICATION'S RESPONSE TO DIGITALLY-INFLUENCED EFFECTS IN SOCIETY

25. Digital corporate communication and organizational listening

Jim Macnamara

INTRODUCTION

As sociologist John Dewey remarked, society *is* communication, arguing that human society cannot exist without communication. Communication is the 'glue' that binds groups of people, and organizations, together. CCO theory, variously expressed as *communication constitutes organization* and the *communicative constitution of organizations* (Schoeneborn et al., 2019; Vásquez and Schoeneborn, 2018) specifically recognizes the fundamental role of communication in the establishment and operation of organizations, as well as in the general function of human organizing.

The centrality of communication in human society is not to say that communication is easy, or that it always works to the satisfaction of the parties involved. As John Durham Peters says poetically, drawing on William James: "That we can never communicate like the angels is a tragic fact, but also a blessed one" (Peters, 1999, p. 29). He says communication, in all its fractures and mediations, is what makes us human. Interestingly, Peters also says that, despite the potential for misunderstanding in human communication, "most of the time we understand each other quite well; we just do not agree" (Peters, 1999, p. 269). This is an important point in the context of this chapter that specifically discusses listening as part of digital corporate communication.

A number of communication scholars label humans as *Homo narrans* (story tellers), referring to humankind's development of advanced languages and capacity for speaking, talking, and telling (Fisher, 1984). This reflects a broad philosophical focus on speech and rhetoric from the time of ancient civilizations in Greece, Egypt, and China. In Book 1 of his *Politics*, Aristotle wrote that "Nature ... has endowed man[1] alone among the animals with the power of speech" and he identified speaking as a key attribute that defines humans (as cited in Haworth, 2004, p. 43). Renaissance philosopher Thomas Hobbes echoed Aristotle's trope in *Leviathan*, saying "the most noble and profitable invention of all others was that of speech" (Hobbes, 1946, p. 18).

However, contemporary communication studies scholar Robert Craig (2006, p. 39) succinctly reminds us that communication requires "talking and listening". In writing about voice, sociologist Nick Couldry (2009, p. 580) describes voice as "the implicitly linked practices of speaking and listening". It is significant that Couldry notes that listening is implicit, not explicit. Despite attempts by some such as Back (2007) to highlight the importance of listening, Fiumara noted that listening is often "a secondary issue" in discussion of communication (1995, p. 6).

Furthermore, a review of the literature on listening, summarized in the following sections, shows that most of the literature focuses on interpersonal communication in dyads and small groups in which listening is performed aurally. While aural listening is possible in

357

358 *Handbook on digital corporate communication*

organizational settings such as face-to-face meetings, telephone calls, and teleconferencing applications, corporate communication commonly seeks to engage with stakeholders who are distanced in time and space and who may number in the thousands, hundreds of thousands, or even millions in the case of large multinational corporations and other corporate bodies. In this chapter, the broad definition of 'corporate' based on *corpus*, meaning body and *corpora* (plural), is used to include government agencies, non-government organizations (NGOs), and non-profit organizations (NPOs), as well as the incorporated companies.

This chapter addresses a significant gap in the literature by examining (1) principles and approaches that need to be applied for effective listening in and by organizations; (2) methods for organizational listening, particularly how digital communication technologies can be applied; and (3) the substantial benefits, as well as potential risks, that can result for organizations as well as their stakeholders.

DEFINITIONS OF CORE CONCEPTS

Corporate communication is described as "a management function that offers a framework for the effective coordination of all internal and external communication with the overall purpose of establishing and maintaining favourable reputations with stakeholder groups upon which the organization is dependent (Cornelissen, 2017, p. 5). Cornelissen adds that the function of corporate communication has developed to "incorporate a whole range of specialised disciplines, including corporate design, corporate advertising, internal communication to employees, issues and crisis management, media relations, investor relations, change communication and public affairs" (Cornelissen, 2017, p. 4). This broad view is supported by other corporate communication scholars such as Argenti (2016), and indicates that corporate communication is closely aligned, overlapping, or synonymous with the practices of public relations, organizational communication, some aspects of marketing communication, and evolving notions of strategic communication. This holistic view is taken in discussing how organizational listening can be applied as part of corporate communication.

Digital Corporate Communication

Since the development of computers, and particularly since the creation of the internet and the World Wide Web, digital forms of communication have permeated almost every corner of society. It is unsurprising, and eminently logical, that corporate communication has embraced digital communication for engaging both internal and external stakeholders. As outlined in this *Handbook*, digital corporate communication includes media such as websites, social media platforms, online publications and videos, videoconferencing, and emerging communications technologies such as bots including chatbots, and other uses of algorithms and artificial intelligence (AI).

Before examining how listening can be undertaken as part of digital corporate communication, we need to return for a moment to define the foundational concept being addressed: communication. The term 'communication' is largely used as an ideograph – a concept that is invoked as if it has a precise, unambiguous, and shared meaning, but which in reality is often not understood, equivocal, and even antithetical. A lack of clarity in relation to what communication involves muddies understanding of the role, importance, and benefits of listening.

Communication vs. Information

While the term 'communication' and its common abbreviation 'comms' are used widely to denote the creation and distribution of information such as through publications, website content, videos, and social media posts, the English term is derived from the Latin root *communis* meaning common or public, and from the related noun *commūnicātiō*, which denotes "sharing or imparting", and from the verb *communicare*, which means to "share or make common" (Peters, 2015, p. 78). Thus, while imparting information is one element in the process of human communication, it is not complete without sharing information and achieving some common understanding with others. Contemporary scholars therefore associate communication with meaning making and sharing meaning. Dictionaries define 'communication' as "exchange" ("Communication", 2021a) and refer to "discussing, debating", and "conferring" ("Communication", 2021b).

Communication is therefore a *two-way* dialogic process. However, even dialogue is commonly misunderstood, with many assuming that the Greek term *dia* means 'two'. In fact, *dia* means 'through' or 'between' ("Dia", 2021), with *logos* meaning 'speech', 'logic', and 'reasoning or argument'. In practice, dialogue can be no more than two or more parties speaking, with each paying little attention or giving little consideration to others.

Listening vs. Hearing

Recent studies of communication and dialogue draw attention to the importance of listening while others speak, rather than what Jacqueline Bussie calls "re-loading our verbal gun" (2011, p. 31). Author of *The Seven Habits of Highly Effective People*, Stephen Covey, similarly warns that even when they do listen, "most people do not listen to understand; they listen with the intent to reply. They're either speaking or preparing to speak" (1989, p. 251).

It is important to recognize that hearing is not the same thing as listening. Hearing in humans involves intelligible sound waves striking the ear drum. The organizational equivalent is the receipt of correspondence, telephone calls, research data, and so on. It is well known that much of what people hear receives little attention, or is even ignored – and the same occurs in the case of information, requests, and reports received by organizations (see Case study 1).

Listening requires openness to others. While being 'open-minded' slips easily off the tongue, the concept is spelled out in quite specific terms by philosopher Hans-Georg Gadamer (1989) in his *magnum opus* in which he said that openness requires not only passive listening, but asking questions and allowing others to "say something to us", even to the point of "recognizing that I myself must accept some things that are against me" (Gadamer, 1989, p. 361). Listening is also informed by the *dialogism* of Mikhail Bakhtin (1981, 1986) and particularly Martin Buber's description of dialogue contrasted with monologue and "monologue disguised as dialogue" (Buber, 2002, p. 22).

Glenn (1989) identified 50 definitions of listening in a literature review published in the *International Journal of Listening*. However, these focus predominantly on interpersonal listening as applied in human resource (HR) management, leadership, and therapeutic contexts. Drawing on this literature, as well as communication studies, political science, psychology, psychotherapy, and ethics, "seven canons" of listening were identified in an extensive study of organizational listening (Macnamara 2016, pp. 41–43). These are:

360 *Handbook on digital corporate communication*

- *Recognition* of others as having a right to speak and be treated with respect (Honneth, 2007; Husband, 2009);
- *Acknowledgement* (Schmid, 2001);
- Giving *attention* to what is said (Bickford, 1996; Honneth, 2007; Husband, 2009);
- *Interpreting* what others say fairly and receptively, such as avoiding stereotyping and overcoming reactance and cognitive dissonance;
- Trying as far as possible to achieve *understanding* of others' views and context (Bodie and Crick, 2014; Husband, 1996, 2000);
- Giving *consideration* to what others say (Honneth, 2007; Husband, 2009); and
- *Responding* in an appropriate way (Lundsteen, 1979; Purdy and Borisoff, 1997).

At no point does the literature identify agreement or compliance with all requests, suggestions, or recommendations as a requirement of listening. Studies in relation to human communication, democratic politics, and ethics note that listening requires an active and authentic attempt to reach a shared or common position. But sociology, cultural studies, and democratic political science also advocate acceptance of difference and even dissent. In many cases, there are good reasons that people and organizations cannot agree or comply with requests or recommendations. In such cases, an appropriate response is an explanation. Response is essential to close the 'communication cycle'. William James (1952), the founder of American pragmatism, stated that ignoring someone is the most "fiendish" way to deal with another.

Organizational Listening

Judy Burnside-Lawry (2011) was one of the first to offer a definition of what is commonly referred to as *organizational listening*. In her study of listening competency of employees, she drew on the listening competency research of Cooper (1997) and Wolvin and Coakley (1994), and the research of Flynn et al. (2008) in relation to listening in business, to say:

> Organisational listening is defined as a combination of an employee's listening skills and the environment in which listening occurs, which is shaped by the organisation and is then one of the characteristics of the organisational image. (Burnside-Lawry, 2011, p. 149)

The term 'organizational listening' is not a misguided attempt to anthropomorphize organizations. It recognizes that, ultimately, it is people in organizations who listen, or don't listen. However, there are three key characteristics that distinguish organizations in terms of how listening to stakeholders can occur. First is the issue of *scale* – what Andrew Dobson (2014, pp. 75, 124) refers to as the problem of "scaling up" from interpersonal and small group communication. As noted previously, a corporation may have hundreds of thousands or even millions of customers with whom it seeks to engage, and vice versa. Many organizations have thousands of employees with whom communication is important, and government agencies, NGOs, and institutions often have very large and diverse groups of stakeholders whose views, concerns, complaints, suggestions, and requests need to be listened to in order to maintain relationships.

The challenge of scale leads to the second key characteristic of organizational listening: *delegation*. To engage with a large number and range of stakeholders, organizations typically delegate listening to functional units such as customer or member relations; call centres,

Digital corporate communication and organizational listening 361

research departments, social media monitoring teams, public relations; and HR for listening to employees.

Scale, in addition to distance in space and time that occurs in the case of organizations operating in multiple locations and even internationally, leads to the third key factor to be addressed in organizational listening: *mediation*. The 'voice' of stakeholders is commonly expressed to organizations through correspondence such as letters and emails, written complaints, online comments, submissions to consultations, phone calls to call centres, and other mediated means.

These factors indicate that we need to go beyond Burnside-Lawry's identification of the listening skills of organizational employees, which were formulated based on study of face-to-face communication at stakeholder engagement events. Listening to potentially large volumes of delegated and mediated communication requires the application of technologies, as discussed in this chapter.

The characteristics of organizational listening, the 'seven canons' of listening drawn from the literature, and empirical research conducted as part of the Organizational Listening Project, which involved in-depth qualitative research into relations between a total of 60 organizations and their stakeholders over five years, led to the following definition of organizational listening:

> Organisational listening comprises the creation and ethical implementation of scaled processes and systems that enable decision makers and policy makers in organisations to actively and effectively access, acknowledge, understand, consider and appropriately respond to all those who wish to communicate with the organisation or with whom the organisation wishes to communicate interpersonally or through delegated, mediated means. (Macnamara, 2019, p. 5191)

This supports the definition of digital corporate communication (DCC) as "the strategic management of digital technologies, digital infrastructures and digitalization processes to improve communication with internal and external stakeholders and more broadly within society for the maintenance of organizational tangible and intangible assets" (Badham and Luoma-aho, Chapter 1 in this volume, p. 9).

In order to operationalize this definition of organizational listening, the Organizational Listening Project and studies by a number of other researchers (see Table 25.1) proposed that organizations need to adopt what is conceptualized as an *architecture of listening* (Macnamara, 2013, 2015, 2016, 2019). Rather than ad hoc attempts at listening such as periodic 'listening tours' or 'listening posts', or relying on monitoring services, listening needs to be designed into an organization to be effective. The architecture of listening proposed for organizations is based on eight key principles and elements as shown in Table 25.1.

WHAT IS CHANGING?

Organizational listening which, as explained, is often required at large scale, delegated, and applied to mediated messages, is substantially aided by a range of digital systems and technologies as well as advanced research methods. While organizations typically have sophisticated systems for speaking, such as website development teams, media production departments, and advertising and public relations units or agencies, they often lack specific methods and tools for listening.

362 *Handbook on digital corporate communication*

Table 25.1 Elements of an 'architecture of listening' in an organization

Element	Description	References
Culture	Open to listening as defined – that is, one that *recognizes* others as having something to say, pays *attention* to them, and tries to *understand* their views and context	Gadamer (1989); Honneth (2007); Husband (1996, 2009)
Politics of listening	Avoid or address organizational politics, such as selective listening to certain individuals or groups, while others are ignored or marginalized	Bassel (2017); Dreher (2009, 2010)
Policies	Developing and applying policies that require listening	Macnamara (2013, 2015, 2016)
Systems	Open and interactive, such as websites that allow visitors to post comments and questions (see 'What is changing?')	Macnamara (2019)
Technologies	Monitoring tools or services for tracking media and online comment; automated acknowledgement systems; and data analysis tools (see 'What is changing?')	Dreher (2012); Karpf (2016); Macnamara (2013, 2016, 2019)
Resources	Including staff to operate listening systems and do the "work of listening", such as establishing forums and consultations, inviting comment, and monitoring, analysing, and responding to comments and questions	Macnamara (2013, 2015, 2016)
Skills/competencies	E.g., ability to conduct textual analysis; social media analysis; as well as statistical data analytics	Burnside-Lawry (2011); Cooper (1997); Wolvin and Coakley (1994).
Articulation	Presenting what is said to an organization to policy-makers and decision-makers honestly and clearly, without which voice has no value	Macnamara (2013, 2015, 2016)

For organizational listening to be effectively applied at scale to large numbers of stakeholders such as customers, employees, and communities as part of digital corporate communication, advanced software applications and internal systems and processes for acknowledging, giving attention, interpreting, and responding are required. A number of examples are outlined in Table 25.2 and the following case studies.

Table 25.2 Methods for digital organizational listening

Listening methods	Digitalization
Surveys (including open-ended as well as closed-ended questions)	• Use of e-surveys (online) • Statistical analysis of quantitative data (e.g., SPSS, Excel) • Textual analysis of open-ended responses using natural language processing (NLP) software with machine learning capabilities
Interviews	• Digital recording • Automated transcripts using speech recognition software (e.g., Otter.ai; Temi; Microsoft Stream) • Textual analysis using NLP machine learning applications
Focus groups	• Textual analysis using NLP machine learning applications
Media content analysis	• Automated algorithmic-based content analysis applications (quantitative and qualitative)
Social media analysis	• Automated algorithmic-based content analysis applications (qualitative) • Google Analytics (quantitative)
Website content review	• Google Analytics to track views, duration, bounces, conversions/clickthroughs
Website feedback	• Use of web page plug-ins such as Usabilla that record user feedback

Digital corporate communication and organizational listening 363

Listening methods	Digitalization
Public consultations	● Online public consultation sites (proprietary or using applications such as Citizen Space)
	● Textual analysis of submissions using NLP machine learning applications
Call centre telephone calls	● Digital recording
	● Automated transcripts using speech recognition software (e.g., Otter.ai; Temi; Microsoft Stream)
	● Textual analysis using NLP machine learning applications
Customer feedback	● Customer satisfaction e-surveys
	● NPS surveys
Customer experience (CX) study	● Customer journey mapping (a wide range of software applications is available)
Forums and public meetings	● Digital recording
	● Automated transcripts using speech recognition software (e.g., Otter.ai; Temi; Microsoft Stream)
	● Textual analysis using NLP machine learning applications
Employee satisfaction/feedback	● E-surveys
	● Intranet feedback site
	● Internal social media (e.g., Workplace by Facebook; Yammer; Socialcast)

As shown in Table 25.2, organizational listening requires and depends on systematic *analysis* of data, not simply collection of data such as research reports, submissions, and feedback. Too often vast quantities of information from stakeholders such as submissions to consultations, online feedback, and call centre recordings remain unread and unused, as evidenced in Case study 1.

Table 25.2 also shows that organizational listening needs to extend beyond quantitative methodologies that focus on statistics. People speak and write in words, not numbers. Therefore, textual analysis and related analysis methods such as content analysis are essential skills for a listening organization. Specialist software applications are available and often needed as part of listening systems.

In addition, organizational listening can be implemented through a number of in-depth research and engagement methods including *deliberative polling* (Fishkin, 2011); *participatory action research* (PAR); *sensemaking methodology* (Dervin and Foreman-Wernet, 2013); *behavioural insights* (Thaler and Sunstein, 2008); and *customer journey mapping* (Court et al., 2009).

Digital technologies such as voice to text (VTT) software enables recorded phone calls to be transferred to text for textual analysis that can identify common messages, themes, and patterns to inform decision-making and policy-making.

Organizations are also adopting artificial intelligence (AI) tools such as *chat bots* to 'listen' to users of web pages and respond with relevant information, as well as learning algorithms based on NLP and machine learning code that responds to users' data entry and selections (Macnamara, 2019).

364   *Handbook on digital corporate communication*

CASE STUDIES

The following case studies illustrate how digital technologies can be applied as part of digital corporate communication, leading to significant insights. The first involved a large government agency, noting that in some countries the term 'corporate communication' refers to communication by all types of organizations based on the Latin *corpus* meaning body, while the second case study reports on the application of listening using digital tools in a multinational corporation.

CASE STUDY 1

The second stage of the Organizational Listening Project, which focused on listening by government organizations, reviewed the 2015 National Health Service (NHS) Mandate consultation in the UK which invites submissions from health professionals, patients, and the general public. This discovered that 127,400 submissions had been received, some involving 10 or more pages. Neither the NHS nor the UK Department of Health and Social Care had natural language processing (NLP) textual analysis software, or staff with the necessary training to undertake such a task, so their response was based on manual reading of a sample. Thus, many thousands of people were not listened to on important health issues and concerns in which they had lived experience (Macnamara, 2017, pp. 26–27). Such situations occur despite research that shows listening can improve health policy and services (Matthews and Sunderland, 2017) and policy generally in cases of deliberative engagement (Collingwood and Reedy, 2012, pp. 233–259).

As part of the Organizational Listening Project, a specialized machine learning textual analysis application was licensed (Method52), two analysts were trained in coding using the system, and the submissions were analysed, resulting in discovery of seven major findings that were highly relevant to government policy making (Macnamara, 2017, pp. 27–28).

CASE STUDY 2

Achmea is a multinational insurance and financial services corporation headquartered in the Netherlands, with operating companies in a number of European countries as well as Australia. In total, the group has more than 10 million customers and almost 14,000 staff. In 2018–19, Achmea committed to a participatory action research (PAR) project to improve listening to its key stakeholders (customers and employees) and evaluate the results. The project involved Achmea International in the Netherlands and two of its major operating companies – Interamerican in Greece and Union poisťovňa in Slovakia.

The project tested a wide range of listening activities. One is reported here as an example of the benefits that can accrue from effective organizational listening as part of corporate communication.

Achmea International and its operating companies conduct regular Net Promoter Score (NPS) surveys of their customers, which primarily focus on identifying a 0–10 score in which ratings of 9–10 are regarded as 'promoters', ratings of 7–8 are considered 'passive', and ratings of 0–6 are described as 'detractors'. Marketing research shows that 'promoters' are highly likely to remain customers, while 'detractors' are highly likely to be lost customers.

As part of improving its listening to customers, Achmea added open-ended questions to its NPS surveys to gain insights into why customers gave the ratings they did. Then, to pay attention to, understand, and give consideration to NPS customer feedback, operating companies such as Interamerican employed text analysts and textual analysis software (SAS Text Analytics in this case) to identify key concerns of 'detractors' as well as the views of 'passives' and 'promoters' stated in response to open-ended questions.

Following this, the group introduced what it calls a 'closed loop' methodology in which well-trained staff in its call centres proactively called 'detractors' to discuss and try to resolve their concerns.

The group expected that the call-backs might change 'detractors' to be at least 'passive'. However, follow-up NPS surveys found that 21.5 per cent converted to 'passives'; 29.9 per cent remained 'detractors'; and, surprisingly, 48.6 per cent converted directly to being 'promoters'.

If this trend is maintained across the group, which in 2018 had 17,000 'detractors' – just 0.17 per cent of its customer base, but a substantial number nevertheless – the group calculated that, based on a conservative average customer lifetime value (CLV) of €5,000, this listening activity would generate more than €20 million in revenue that otherwise was likely to be lost (Macnamara, 2020).

WHAT REMAINS THE SAME?

Listening systems do not replace face-to-face and other forms of interpersonal communication such as meetings, telephone calls, and video conferencing, which are emphasized by many researchers (e.g., Bassel, 2017; Bodie and Crick, 2014). As Hargie (2021) says in the latest edition of his text on interpersonal communication, people have a deep-seated and universal need to interact with others on a personal level. This is particularly the case in communication with employees, major customers, and business partners who can be engaged one-on-one (dyads) or in small groups. As noted previously, organizational listening using digital methods is applicable and becomes essential when engagement is required at scale and through delegated and mediated methods.

Also, research shows that respect (similar to what Honneth calls recognition) and empathy remain essential elements in digital corporate communication, just as they are in interpersonal communication. For example, in a study of how corporations respond to complaints on social networks, Einwiller and Steilen (2015, p. 197) found that "respect, empathy, and a willingness to listen and learn about the complainant's concern" positively contribute to complainants' satisfaction.

Furthermore, as noted in the definition of organizational listening, it is ultimately humans in organizations who listen, or don't listen, particularly CEOs and senior managers. Digital media and applications simply aid the process.

366 *Handbook on digital corporate communication*

CRITICAL EXAMINATION

The field of organizational listening research is continuing to expand. Reinikainen et al. (2020) have noted that, as young people have turned to social media to interact, build relationships, and discuss issues of concern, organizations have similarly turned to social media as platforms to address and engage young people. However, they note that many reports show that these attempts fail and that young people's trust in institutions, brands, and organizations continues to decline. Nevertheless, they found in a study of more than 1,500 young people aged 15–24 that listening by organizations is connected to higher levels of trust. They concluded: "The results highlight the role of competent listening on social media" (Reinikainen et al., 2020, p. 185).

Brandt (2020, p. 156) has studied how organizations listen to the "voice of the consumer (VOC)" and found that, while a majority of organizations capture consumer feedback, they are not effectively analysing, disseminating, or utilizing findings to improve products, services, and consumer experiences. This validates the focus on analysis in Table 25.2. Brandt concludes by pointing to the benefits, but also challenges, of processing both structured and unstructured data and the need to consider both "inbound" voice and outbound calls for feedback (2020, p. 174).

A study in the USA by Neill and Bowen (2021) found that employees, particularly non-managers and women, continue to be dissatisfied with their organization's listening efforts. So much remains to be done.

In studying organizational listening during organizational change, Sahay (2021) has confirmed that organizations struggle to incorporate effective listening due to lack of systems, processes, structures, resources, and skill sets. He noted a prevalence of "inauthentic listening" (2021, p. 2), which has negative consequences for organizations and input providers. He also calls for organizations to develop comprehensive analysis, as well as empathetic skills among those soliciting or receiving input (p. 10), and using "culturally sensitive and relevant technologies" (2021, p. 11). This last point links to a related area of critique.

It needs to be recognized that advanced digital listening systems bring with them risks and concerns about privacy and ethics. For example, critical scholars warn of dangers in *digital surveillance* (e.g., Gillespie, 2018; Landau, 2017; Napoli, 2014) and *algorithmic filtering* (Caplan, 2018). As Caplan says, in many if not most online platforms, algorithms decide "the inclusion or exclusion of information" (Caplan, 2018, p. 564). In a recent book Lewis (2020) devotes a chapter to what she calls the "dark side of organisational listening". Exploitive and manipulative applications or espionage are not what is proposed in organizational listening as part of digital corporate communication. An architecture of listening should be guided by ethics as well as regulations in relation privacy and data security.

Nevertheless, active, open, ethical listening by organizations offers many benefits to individuals, organizations, and society. Commercial organizations are shown to gain benefits such as increased customer loyalty; increased employee morale, motivation, productivity; and increased insights into market needs (Jenkins et al., 2013; Leite, 2015). Ultimately, Sheila Bentley (2010) and others contend that effective listening by commercial organizations can increase profitability. Research also shows that all types of organizations can gain increased trust and reputation through listening to their stakeholders (Leite, 2015; Tomlinson and Mayer, 2009). Increased and effective listening by government and political parties is cited as a key step to address the concerning "democratic deficit" identified in a number of countries

Digital corporate communication and organizational listening   367

(Coleman, 2013; Couldry, 2010, p. 49; Dobson, 2014; Norris, 2011) and what some even refer to as a "crisis of democracy" (Przeworski, 2019; Van der Meer, 2017).

CONCLUSION AND FUTURE DIRECTIONS

This chapter has drawn attention to a major gap in corporate communication in which organizations deploy substantial resources, time, systems, and processes to disseminating information and their messages (i.e., speaking), but apply comparatively little resources, time, systems, and processes to listening to their stakeholders.

To address this gap, key principles and definitions of organizational listening have been advanced based on recent research and an 'architecture of listening' is described and advocated to embed two-way communication in an organization. The elements identified are referred to as an *architecture* because they establish a framework that informs the design of specific listening activities to suit different types of organizations and varying circumstances. These concepts contribute to both the theory and practice of corporate communication.

Looking to the future, digital corporate communication will continue to apply an ever-expanding array of digital technologies. Future research is needed to maintain currency, particularly with developments in data analytics, the use of so-called 'big data', and AI that can afford insights through digital listening and two-way communication. Also, further research is required to understand and develop strategies for ensuring organizational listening is conducted ethically and, ideally, for mutual benefits. This must include keeping a critical eye on digital surveillance techniques that compromise privacy and listening tools for collecting 'intelligence' that is used for manipulative targeting of people for commercial or political objectives. However, the benefits identified show that balancing the 'architecture of speaking' that shapes most digital and traditional corporate communication with a digitally enhanced architecture of listening offers productive directions for digital corporate communication.

NOTE

1.   Gendered term in original text.

REFERENCES

Argenti, P. (2016). *Corporate communication* (7th edition). New York: McGraw-Hill.
Back, L. (2007). *The art of listening*. Oxford: Berg.
Bakhtin, M. (1981). *The dialogic imagination: Four essays*, ed. M. Holquist, trans. C. Emerson and M. Holquist. Austin: University of Texas Press.
Bakhtin, M. (1986). *Speech genres and other late essays*, ed. C. Emerson and M. Holquist, trans. V. McGee. Austin: University of Texas Press. (Original work published 1979)
Bassel, L. (2017). *The politics of listening: Possibilities and challenges for democratic life*. Cham: Palgrave Macmillan.
Bentley, S. (2010). Listening practices: Are we getting any better? In A. Wolvin (ed.), *Listening and human communication in the 21st century* (pp. 181–192). Malden, MA: Wiley-Blackwell.
Bickford, S. (1996). *The dissonance of democracy: Listening, conflict and citizenship*. Ithaca, NY: Cornell University Press.

368 *Handbook on digital corporate communication*

Bodie, G. and Crick, N. (2014). Listening, hearing, sensing: Three modes of being and the phenomenology of Charles Sanders Peirce. *Communication Theory, 24*(2), 105–123.

Brandt, D. (2020). The current state of corporate voice of the consumer programs: A study of organizational listening practices and effectiveness. *International Journal of Listening, 34*(3), 156–177.

Buber, M. (2002). *Between man and man*, trans. R. Smith. London: Kegan Paul. (Original work published 1947)

Burnside-Lawry, J. (2011). The dark side of stakeholder communication: Stakeholder perceptions of ineffective organisational listening. *Australian Journal of Communication, 38*(1), 147–173.

Bussie, J. (2011). Reconciled diversity: Reflections on our calling to embrace our religious neighbours. *Intersections, 33*, 30–35.

Caplan, R. (2018). Algorithmic filtering. In P. Napoli (ed.), *Mediated communication* (pp. 561–583). Berlin: De Gruyter.

Coleman, S. (2013). *How voters feel.* Cambridge: Cambridge University Press.

Collingwood, L. and Reedy, J. (2012). Listening and responding to criticisms of deliberative civic engagement. In T. Nabatchi, J. Gastil, M. Leighninger, and G. Weiksner (eds.), *Democracy in motion: Evaluating the practice and impact of deliberative civic engagement* (pp. 233–259). Oxford: Oxford University Press.

Communication (2021a). In *Merriam-Webster Dictionary.* https://www.merriam-webster.com/dictionary/communication.

Communication (2021b). In *Online Etymology Dictionary.* https://www.etymonline.com/word/communication.

Cooper, L. (1997). Listening competency in the workplace: A model for training. *Business Communication Quarterly, 60*(4), 7–85.

Cornelissen, J. (2017). *Corporate communication: A guide to theory and practice* (5th edition). London: Sage Publications.

Couldry, N. (2009). Commentary: Rethinking the politics of voice. *Continuum: Journal of Media & Cultural Studies, 23*(4), 579–582.

Couldry, N. (2010). *Why voice matters: Culture and politics after neoliberalism.* London: Sage Publications.

Court, D., Elzinga, D., Mulder, S., and Vetvik, O. (2009, June). The consumer decision journey. *McKinsey Quarterly.* https://www.mckinsey.com/business-functions/marketing-and-sales/our-insights/the-consumer-decision-journey.

Covey, S. (1989). *The seven habits of highly effective people: Powerful lessons in person change.* New York: Free Press.

Craig, R. (2006). Communication as a practice. In G. Shepherd, G. St John, and T. Striphas (eds.), *Communication as ... Perspectives on theory* (pp. 38–49). London: Sage Publications.

Dervin, B. and Foreman-Wernet, L. (2013). Sense-making methodology as an approach to understanding and designing for campaign audiences. In R. Rice and C. Atkin (eds.), *Public communication campaigns* (4th edition, pp. 147–162). London: Sage Publications.

Dia (2021). In *Online Etymology Dictionary.* https://www.etymonline.com/word/dia-.

Dobson, A. (2014). *Listening for democracy: Recognition, representation, reconciliation.* Oxford: Oxford University Press.

Dreher, T. (2009). Listening across difference: Media and multiculturalism beyond the politics of voice. *Continuum: Journal of Media & Cultural Studies, 23*(4), 445–458.

Dreher, T. (2010). Speaking up or being heard? Community media interventions and the politics of listening. *Media, Culture and Society, 32*(1), 85–103.

Dreher, T. (2012). A partial promise of voice: Digital storytelling and the limits of listening. *Media International Australia, 142*(1), 157–166.

Einwiller, S. and Steilen, S. (2015). Handling complaints on social network sites: An analysis of complaints and complaint responses on Facebook and Twitter pages of large US companies. *Public Relations Review, 41*, 195–204.

Fisher, W. (1984). Narration as a human communication paradigm: The case of public moral argument. *Communication Monographs, 51*(1), 1–22.

Fishkin, J. (2011). *When the people speak: Deliberative democracy and public consultation.* Oxford: Oxford University Press.

Fiumara, G. (1995). *The other side of language: A philosophy of listening*. London: Routledge.

Flynn, J., Valikoski, T., and Grau, J. (2008). Listening in the business context: Reviewing the state of research. *International Journal of Listening*, 22(2), 141–151.

Gadamer, H. (1989). *Truth and method*, trans. J. Weinsheimer and D. Marshal (2nd edition). New York: Crossroad. (Original work published 1960)

Gillespie, T. (2018). *Custodians of the internet: Platforms, content moderation, and the hidden decisions that shape social media*. New Haven, CT: Yale University Press.

Glenn, E. (1989). A content analysis of fifty definitions of listening. *International Journal of Listening*, 3(1), 21–31.

Hargie, O. (2021). *Skilled interpersonal communication: Research, theory and practice* (7th edition). London: Routledge.

Haworth, A. (2004). *Understanding the political philosophers: From ancient to modern times*. London: Routledge.

Hobbes, T. (1946). *Leviathan*. Oxford: Basil Blackwell. (Original work published 1651)

Honneth, A. (2007). *Disrespect*. Cambridge: Polity Press.

Husband, C. (1996). The right to be understood: Conceiving the multi-ethnic public sphere. *Innovation: The European Journal of Social Sciences*, 9(2), 205–215.

Husband, C. (2000). Media and the public sphere in multi-ethnic societies. In S. Cottle (ed.), *Ethnic minorities and the media* (pp. 199–214). Maidenhead: Open University Press.

Husband, C. (2009). Commentary: Between listening and understanding. *Continuum: Journal of Media & Cultural Studies*, 23(4), 441–443.

James, W. (1952). *The principles of psychology*. Chicago: William Benton.

Jenkins, H., Ford, S., and Green, J. (2013). *Spreadable media: Creating value and meaning in a networked culture*. New York: New York University Press.

Karpf, D. (2016). *Analytic activism: Digital listening and the new political strategy*. Oxford: Oxford University Press.

Landau, S. (2017). *Listening in*. New Haven, CT: Yale University Press.

Leite, E. (2015). Why trust matters in business. Address to the World Economic Forum, Davos-Klosters, Switzerland, 19 January. https://agenda.weforum.org/2015/01/why-trust-matters-in-business.

Lewis, L. (2020). *The power of strategic listening*. Lanham, MD: Rowman &Littlefield.

Lundsteen, S. (1979). *Listening: Its impact on language and the other language arts*. ERIC Clearing House on Reading and Communication Skills.

Macnamara, J. (2013). Beyond voice: Audience-making and the work and architecture of listening. *Continuum: Journal of Media and Cultural Studies*, 27(1), 160–175.

Macnamara, J. (2015). The work and 'architecture of listening': Requisites for ethical organization-public communication. *Ethical Space: Journal of the Institute of Communication Ethics*, 12(2), 29–37.

Macnamara, J. (2016). *Organizational listening: The missing essential in public communication*. New York: Peter Lang.

Macnamara, J. (2017). Creating a 'democracy for everyone': Strategies for increasing listening and engagement by government. London School of Economics and Political Science. https://www.lse.ac.uk/media-and-communications/assets/documents/research/2017/MacnamaraReport2017.pdf.

Macnamara, J. (2019). Explicating listening in organization-public communication: Theory, practices, technologies. *International Journal of Communication*, 13, 5183–5204.

Macnamara, J. (2020). Corporate listening: Unlocking insights from VOC, VOE and VOS. *Corporate Communications: An International Journal*, 25(3), 377–393.

Matthews, M. and Sunderland, N. (2017). *Digital story telling in health and social policy: Listening to marginalised voices*. London: Routledge.

Napoli, P. (2014). Automated media: An institutional theory perspective on algorithmic media production and consumption. *Communication Theory*, 24(3), 340–360.

Neill, M. and Bowen, S. (2021). Employee perceptions of ethical listening in US organizations. *Public Relations Review*, 47(5). Advance online publication. https://doi.org/10.1016/j.pubrev.2021.102123.

Norris, P. (2011). *Democratic deficit: Critical citizens revisited*. Cambridge: Cambridge University Press.

Peters, J. (1999). *Speaking into the air: A history of the idea of communication*. Chicago: University of Chicago Press.

370 *Handbook on digital corporate communication*

Peters, J. (2015). Communication: History of the idea. In W. Donsbach (ed.), *The concise encyclopedia of communication* (pp. 78–79). Malden, MA: Wiley-Blackwell.

Przeworski, A. (2019). *Crisis of democracy*. Cambridge: Cambridge University Press.

Purdy, M. and Borisoff, D. (1997). *Listening in everyday life: A personal and professional approach* (2nd edition). Lanham, MD: University Press of America.

Reinikainen, H., Kari, J., and Luoma-aho, V. (2020). Generation Z and organizational listening on social media. *Media and Communication*, 8(2), 185–196.

Sahay, S. (2021). Organizational listening during organizational change: Perspectives of employees and executives. *International Journal of Listening*. Advance online publication. https://doi.org/10.1080/10904018.2021.1941029.

Schmid, P. (2001). Acknowledgement: The art of responding: Dialogical and ethical perspectives on the challenges of unconditional relationships in therapy and beyond. In J. Bozarth and P. Wilkins (eds.), *Rogers' therapeutic conditions: Evolution, theory and practice* (Vol. 3, pp. 155–171). Monmouth: PCCS Books.

Schoeneborn, D., Kuhn, T., and Kärreman, D. (2019). The communicative constitution of organization: Organizing and organizationality. *Organization Studies*, 40(4), 475–496.

Thaler, R. and Sunstein, C. (2008). *Nudge: Improving decisions about health, wealth, and happiness*. New Haven, CT: Yale University Press.

Tomlinson, E. and Mayer, R. (2009). The role of causal attribution dimensions in trust repair. *Academy of Management Review*, 34, 85–104.

Van der Meer, T. (2017). Political trust and the crisis of democracy. *Oxford research encyclopedia of politics*. Oxford: Oxford University Press.

Vásquez, C. and Schoeneborn, D. (2018). Communication as constitutive of organization. In R. Heath and W. Johansen (eds.), *The international encyclopedia of strategic communication* (pp. 1–12). Hoboken, NJ: Wiley & Sons.

Wolvin, A. and Coakley, G. (1994). Listening competency. *International Journal of Listening*, 8(1), 148–160.

26. Digital corporate communication and the market for big data

Gregor Halff and Anne Gregory

INTRODUCTION

The definition of digital corporate communication provided by Badham and Luoma-aho in Chapter 1 of this *Handbook* is as follows:

> An organization's strategic management of digital technologies, digital infrastructures and digitalization processes to improve communication with internal and external stakeholders and more broadly within society for the maintenance of organizational tangible and intangible assets. (p. 9)

The purpose of this conceptual chapter is to take a step back from the immediate management of digital technologies and to look at the broader context in which they are set. Underpinning corporate digital communication is the large market in digital technology. Since the Covid-19 pandemic which began in 2020, there has been a steep change in digital transformation and this market – which includes Cloud Computing, Big Data and Analytics, Mobility/Social Media, Cybersecurity, Artificial Intelligence (AI) and the Internet of Things (IoT) – is projected to grow from US$521.5 billion in 2021 to US$1247.5 billion by 2026, at a compound annual growth rate (CAGR) of 19.1 per cent (Marketsandmarkets, 2021).

To put some boundaries around the area for consideration, this chapter looks specifically at the Big Data and Analytics part of this market. Digital corporate communication is both a producer and beneficiary of the big data market, but missing from the corporate communication academy's inquiry is a perspective in which the detrimental societal changes in its operation can be explained. There are several perspectives that can be taken to consider the digital transformation phenomenon (see, for example, Chapter 20 by Buhmann and Gregory in this volume), but given the discussion here is about markets, this chapter draws on economic theory to describe the implications of digital corporate communication's use of big data. These detrimental impacts affect not only organizational stakeholders, but markets and societies as a whole.

DEFINITIONS OF THE TOPIC AND PREVIOUS STUDIES

The corporate communication academy is rich with inquiry about the use of online transactions and big data (Annenberg Center for Public Relations, 2019; Buhmann et al., 2020; Galloway and Swiatek, 2018; Gregory and Halff, 2020; Weiner and Kochar, 2016; Wiesenberg et al., 2017). Missing from that inquiry, however, is a macroscopic (as opposed to organizational) perspective in which the vertical links between digital corporate communication, organizational stakeholders, the market for big data and societies can be explained and critiqued. This chapter fills that gap by drawing on economic theory. Specifically, the concept of 'external-

372 *Handbook on digital corporate communication*

ities' is drawn from economics and applied to understand the costs to society of big data in digital corporate communication. The chapter focuses on the three economic theories that are often proposed as remedies to negative externalities, but posits that they provide only partial solutions. Differences and extensions to these economic responses are identified and proposed, which in aggregate help in conceptualizing a taxonomy of responses. These responses have specific, practical implications for digital corporate communication, particularly at the highest level, defined as being 'deliberative', which calls for a society-wide discussion on how the risks and opportunities presented by big data can be handled.

Digital corporate communication with an organization's stakeholders involves the transfer of data, often via a data-enabled platform, to that organization in exchange for its products, services or purely to engage in dialogue. The data-enabled platform can be owned by the organization or by a service-provider, but in either case, it is a third party in the transaction which is more than a simple transfer mechanism. The platform subsequently commodifies the data and frequently aggregates it with data supplied by others, in ways mostly unknown to the individual. This technically-enabled three-way market exchange has become a regular subject of media attention, political awareness and published research (Bambauer, 2014; Bateman et al., 2013; DeGeorge 2003; Hong and Thong, 2013; Nunan and Di Domenico, 2013, 2017).

'Big data' is an indistinct and controversial label that has numerous alternative definitions. Sivarajah et al. (2017) posit that the term captures not just a change in quantity, but also in kind in that through analytics, additional and marketable value is created. As described by Nunan and Di Domenico (2017, p. 483), the "large scale analysis of data, not just collection, and the combination of multiple datasets" creates the market for big data.

In common with many business functions, corporate communication conducts its business increasingly online. From social listening, to identifying and profiling stakeholders, developing content that resonates, and tracking and evaluating responses, data collection, aggregation and analysis – big data and artificial intelligence has infused the practice (CIPR, 2021). Although there is "an ever-growing discourse about [big data] offering both Big Opportunities and Big Challenges through the plethora of sources through different domains" (Sivarajah et al., 2017, p. 264), the latter are typically studied as negative impacts on businesses' strategy, efficiency and/or competitiveness. Conversely, critics with a more abstract perspective often do not go much beyond urgent metaphors to point to the damage done by commercial purveyors of big data: an 'internet-industrial complex' (Flyverbom et al., 2017) is using 'weapons of math destruction' (O'Neil, 2016) to create 'surveillance capitalism' (Zuboff, 2019) within a 'black box society' (Pasquale, 2015). Popular media speak of "the new capitalist mutant rampaging through our societies" (Naughton, 2019).

In this chapter, we contend that additional analysis, critique and recommendations about the societal impact of big data should be developed with a nuanced understanding of big data as economy.

WHAT IS CHANGING?

The market in big data and analytics alone is set to grow to reach US$512 billion in 2026, increasing from US$171 in 2018 (Bloomberg, 2020). This growth is fuelled by the negligible cost of its input production: it rests on provision of data that is given for free by individuals. Moreover, even the cost of storing, replicating and exchanging that data is fast approaching zero. Thus, while organizations incur negligible input and storage production costs, they generate significant economic value from analysis, interpretation and trade. As a participant in that market, the collection and aggregation of data creates new value for corporate communication and the organizations it serves, but it does so based on data-contributing individuals who are progressively unable to exercise choice on how and when that data is used (West, 2017; Zwitter, 2014). With aggregate data being owned by the data collector and analyst, it becomes exceedingly hard – if not impossible – for individuals to exert their capacity of choice in the marketplace. This limitation of choice – which begins with a first data transaction and is amplified as that data is aggregated with the next transactions of an individual and possibly with the data of others – fulfils the basic requirements for the economic definition of an externality. An externality is a positive or negative consequence that is produced by a specific transaction, a field of transactions or an entire market, but for which the costs are not borne by all the participants of the transaction and are therefore not included in the pricing system (Akerlof, 1970, 2002; Spence, 2002; Stiglitz, 1975). In digital corporate communication that is replicated: a specific communicative transaction takes place online, but the costs are not borne by all the participants in the transaction.

As intimated earlier, a three-way interaction exists. First, an individual will transact with another entity to obtain a specific item whether that be a product, service or information. That entity not only supplies the item for which the transaction was initiated, but also stores and aggregates the data of all those who contact it online and, if they wish (and increasingly they do), analyse it for their own purposes, mostly using algorithms. The capability of organizations to collect data is enhanced as the technologies for interaction become more 'personal': for example, the use of chatbots encourages the divulgence of more and more personal information (Murtarelli et al., 2021). Data analytics are now advanced and organizations are able to provide personalized materials (goods, services, information) in return for the current transaction, and they can, with predictive analytics, forecast future needs and preferences in an instant. In addition, they can retain that data in perpetuity and use it for their gain in ways that are not yet known to the individual(s) supplying it.

Second, information about individuals' and organizations' business transactions and from other online activity, is available for third-party commercial organizations who specialize in data collection, to aggregate and trade. An example is when activity on LinkedIn is aggregated by a third party and sold to employers as a forecast of when and which employees are at risk of leaving for another job (Bennett, 2017). While the collection and aggregation of data therefore creates value for some, it does so by creating and perpetuating asymmetries to the detriment of data-contributing individuals (West, 2017; Zwitter, 2014). Consequently, the dominant critique of the economics of big data, rests on the (dynamically increasing) imbalance of benefits between the individual and data-aggregating firms. The leading critical economist Mazzucato (2017, 2018, 2019) speaks of 'digital feudalism' as the defining power structure of our times in which the few extract value from the many. Qiu (2015) describes how the many (data providing social media users) are estranged from their unpaid labour and from the value it creates for the few.

Individuals supplying data engage in transactions of their choosing, but simultaneously reduce their ability to exercise choice in subsequent and other transactions. The resulting lack of agency over their own data (and its subsequent use) is the real, but hidden cost of the transaction. Thus, the aggregation of data not only creates value for some, it also creates and perpetuates the hegemony of the data-aggregating parties over data-supplying individuals.

374 *Handbook on digital corporate communication*

The most obvious contributors to this effect are the owners of dominant algorithms like Google, Amazon and Facebook, who limit the choices (of books, pet toys, travel destinations, information, opinions, etc.) given to the consumer in the name of 'personalization'. The inhibition of choice becomes more obviously costly for individuals when the process is applied without nuance or judgement. An example of this is an insurance provider who uses zip codes to categorize people which leads to a poorer credit rating for some even though the individual may have perfectly good credit credentials (Cerquitelli et al., 2017; Lepri et al., 2017). Remedies in this market are typically extra-political and instead rely on market alternatives, e.g., peer-to-peer lending institutions, like *Lending Club* and *Prosper* whose credit scoring algorithms are transparent to both borrowers and lenders (unlike traditional banks), or the think-tank *ProPublica* (www.propublica.org) that proposes that individuals could negotiate their later-life health insurance premiums down in return for lifestyle-related data.

Classical economic theorists mostly exclude externalities from their analyses and assume that they will, over time, be included in the *price system* (like road charges for cars in Singapore to reduce the externality of congestion, or taxes on saturated fats in Denmark to counter the externality costs of ill-health). However, more critical theorists posit not only that the price system is incapable of properly reflecting externalities, but also that markets are constantly at risk of remaining unaware of them. In such cases externalities persist, i.e., the price of a good or service will remain too low, and it becomes more unlikely for a market to produce outcomes to all participants' benefit (Spence, 2012). Economic theory moreover warns that markets will eventually collapse when externalities are constantly reproduced because they become unacceptable to society: the adverse impacts are regarded as too great.

WHAT REMAINS THE SAME?

The argument that corporate communication ultimately contributes to the hegemony of corporate organizations over stakeholder groups remains as true as ever. At the core of a pre-digital research agenda is the identification of public relations (used here as a synonym for corporate communication) as a 'hegemonic practice' that – while purporting to engage in dialogue, symmetry- and consensus-building – chiefly seeks to "legitimize the perspectives and actions of corporate manager" and thus secures that the organization remains more powerful than its stakeholders and publics. (Holtzhausen, 2002, p. 251; L'Etang, 2005; Roper, 2005).

Indeed, some practitioner think tanks are advocating that public relations wholeheartedly adopt intelligence gathering and 'objective' data to help demonstrate business value. There is a relentlessness in the discourse about how these transactions enable the profession to prove business value (Weiner and Kochar, 2016), although some are aware of the power imbalances this creates (Valin and Gregory, 2020). Predominantly, however, in the current narrative, big data is not expected to empower stakeholders, as critiqued by Holtzhausen (2002), but instead to reproduce hegemony over them as described above.

Preserving the market for big data together with its recognized benefits to societies, such as the use of health big data to predict and limit the spread of disease via effective communication, means that its externalities need to be reined-in to avert the danger of the market becoming destructive to itself and society. As has been shown in other markets where current transactions incorporate the value of future behaviour (as shown in the ProPublica example given above), much more balanced transaction types can be achieved over time (Akerloff and Yellen, 1985a, 1985b; Stiglitz, 2000, 2002, 2006).

We contend that corporate communication's role in the market for big data, too, can be (re) organized such that

(a)   individuals are *aware* of any interaction involving their data in cases where that interaction contributes to the input for big-data business models (of reducing choice by algorithms in later transactions);
(b)   individuals are aware of the *value* of their data to firms and of the possible reduction of their later choices;
(c)   individuals have *second-tier choices* (beyond the original transaction) about whether, to what degree and until when they want their data to be stored, used, repurposed, or traded and are thus critically aware audiences to big data's algorithms (Kemper and Kolkman, 2019);
(d)   the aggregation of individuals (i.e., society) has a voice in the market as an input supplier and therefore a *third-tier* choice over what role the market plays in society.

Points (a) to (d) above have particular resonance for any digital corporate communication transition: (a) stakeholders first become aware of interactions that involve a digital communicative exchange and make judgements about whether they wish to proceed; (b) they come to a conclusion about the value of that communicative interaction to the other party involved; (c) they know that their interactions may be shared with others and choose to either allow that or to limit any perceived risk by, for example, demanding non-disclosure or confidentiality arrangements; (d) their participation in any digital communicative interaction may be aggregated into public opinion and those joint voices make choices about the permissions/accountabilities they make in the civic, economic and governance spheres.

CRITICAL EXAMINATION

Existing economic theory provides three major concepts for addressing negative externalities of a market-based activity which are now critically examined to investigate if they satisfy the four conditions stipulated above. The first is the correction of a market by government, specifically via taxation, as has first been proposed by Pigou (1920). It is traditionally deemed to be especially effective when private contractual arrangements (here: between data-commodifying organizations and data-supplying individuals) do not resolve the externalities. The idea is that by introducing a tax (equal to the marginal social cost of data aggregation) on each transaction between data-commodifying organizations and data-supplying individuals, prices for their data supply will go up, thus forcing firms to internalize the later costs to individuals of data aggregation. Such costs are therefore alleviated by government action through the taxes raised.

A Pigovian approach is successful in many other markets and is used in the examples of externalities provided earlier (e.g., for road usage in Singapore and for fat use in food production in Denmark), because they make the input more expensive and thus reduce externalities (like congestion of cities and hospital wards). However, road space and fat differ from big data in that the latter can hardly be quantified, nor a unit of analysis be identified and it is thus impossible to price and to tax. Popular appeals for Facebook, Google, Airbnb and its founders to pay appropriate amounts of taxes echo the Pigovian approach and might therefore be ideologically satisfying, but do not reduce the choice externalities of the market for big data. However, they are important because they signify there is a problem and therefore can be described as *symbolic* responses. Other Pigou-inspired responses are more than symbolic, but nevertheless – if taken in isolation – not sufficient. For example, the non-profit organization 'None of Your Business' (www.noyb.eu) calls for European Union fines on companies that gather individuals' data without making individuals sufficiently aware of the fact. While imposing specific fines has had some success (Kuchler, 2018), they aren't sufficient to permanently fulfil any of the four requirements mentioned above. We therefore classify them as a *proto*-remedies i.e., not full, but partial remedies. In sum, we contend that a Pigovian intervention alone would not be sufficient to alleviate the externalities of the market for big data, but they do have importance for pointing society's attention to externalities.

Economics offers the 'Coase theorem' as the second approach with which to respond to externalities. To its proponents (Anderson and Leal, 2001; Anderson and McChesney, 2003; Coase, 1960, 1988, 1995; Stigler, 1966), externalities are predominantly the result of ill-defined property rights. If only these rights were better assigned, input suppliers would be able to 'sell' their data at a price negotiated with the buyer (e.g., with data-commodifying organizations). Thus, if digital corporate communication required any information beyond that necessary for the transaction (such as date of birth, hobbies, etc.) and was going to keep and use that data for other purposes, it would have to pay the individual for the data supplied *and* for the loss of choice that they would have over the future use of that data. This theorem can help to overcome a key challenge of the market for big data, which is that the value of reducing an individual's later choices is currently not being understood as a transfer of some choice from one party to the other.

Nevertheless, while it is conceptually satisfying, the Coase theorem can't be applied in practice to the market for big data with ease, either. Responses based on the Coase theorem require that individuals organize themselves to coordinate their interests, agree on a negotiation process, bargain with data-commodifying organizations, and then formulate contracts for the sale of data and the reduction of future choice. To facilitate this, Posner and Weyl (2018) call for 'data labour unions' that could start 'data strikes'. However, scaling these responses up would be next to impossible given that even the simple informed consent given by individuals to businesses has been uncovered as 'the biggest lie on the internet' (Obar and Oeldorf-Hirsch, 2018). Furthermore, the practicalities of organizing and of constituting organizations that could undertake the required negotiations appear insurmountable. For these reasons, we also classify such calls as *symbolic* responses.

Other, more ambitious responses devised by governments, think-tanks or commercial organizations equally have the Coase theorem at their core. Nevertheless, they mostly fulfil two of our criteria, but not the last two as they do not go beyond making information about data transactions and aggregation available and therefore do not (re-)create choices for individuals. We therefore classify them as *proto*-remedies. Such Coasian proto-remedies include the standards by Alliance for Telecommunication Industry Solutions (ATIS) and European Telecommunications Standards Institute (ETSI) that guide the responses by telecommunications companies to requests for data from governments (Flyverbom et al., 2017). Other examples are the 'Honest Ads Act' introduced by a group of US senators in which advertisers on social media would be required to divulge to netizens which user classification made them see an advertisement. Likewise, they include movements to audit, have an 'FDA for algorithms' (Tutt, 2017) or at least identify the algorithms behind the collection of data, e.g., by the Data

Transparency Lab, the Web Transparency and Accountability Project at Princeton University, and the Message Machine at think-tank ProPublica.

A distinction needs to be drawn between – on the one hand – *symbolic responses* and *proto-remedies* and – on the other hand – what we call *corrective* and *deliberative* remedies. Corrective remedies are mostly inspired by the Coase theorem and can – at least conceptually – fulfil the first three criteria we advanced above by creating the choices for individuals that come with the ownership rights over their data. The European Union's GDPR[1] and the California Consumer Privacy Act[2] are such corrective remedies. They stipulate that any data collected must be approved by the individual and the repurposing and/or selling of the data for any other purposes is prohibited (O'Neil, 2016). In the case of the Californian law, consumers also have the right to "receive equal service and price whether or not they exercise their privacy rights" (Paul, 2019). Such correction is also the goal of the *Open Algorithms* project (OPAL) whose collaborators include Orange, the MIT Media Lab, the Data-Pop Alliance, Imperial College and the World Economic Forum. Nevertheless, corrective remedies are hard to execute. For example, Facebook simply moved 1.5 billion users in Asia-Pacific, Africa and Latin America from under Irish to US privacy laws just before GDPR took effect in its Irish headquarters (Ingram, 2018).

Corrective remedies need to be distinguished from *deliberative* remedies that are designed such that individuals can collaborate with data receivers to determine both the price of their data and of the reduction of their later choices, thereby taking part in the value creation made possible through their data-input. Such a remedy also permits them a third tier of choice about the role and rules of the market.

Where classical economic theory fails to embed market transactions within such third-tier societal choices, Ostrom's (1990, 1992, 2010) approach to common-pool resources serves to "explain phenomena that do not fit in a dichotomous world in which the market is separated from everything around it" (Ostrom, 2010, p. 641). This third concept fills a gap and points to an alternative response to the externalities described here. Ostrom's approach originally addressed the danger of the overuse of (natural) common resources to the detriment of – initially – other members of the community and, eventually, ending in the destruction of such good and/or market. Later, the concept was expanded to also apply to conflicts other than overharvesting, e.g., to conflicts about the methods in which value is created, maintained, distributed and appropriated (Schlager, 2002). In all such conflicts, design principles will and should determine the deliberation about the distribution of rights to produce, use and derive benefit from a certain market. These design principles cover the definition of boundaries; establish a balance between benefits and costs; and arrange for collective choice, monitoring, sanctions, conflict resolution, coordination and rights to organize (Ostrom, 1990, 2010).

Nevertheless, Ostrom's concept of common-pool resources is – like Pigovian and Coasian approaches – not entirely conceptually adequate. Algorithms and big data are not, strictly speaking, common pool resources, since they are practically an unlimited resource. However, we contend with others (Wilson et al., 2013, p. 522) that design principles can be applied to nearly any situation where people must coordinate to achieve common goals i.e., the collective of stakeholders which we call society. Singleton and Taylor (1992) describe that not just a rational need, but also a level of community increases the likelihood that user-groups will self-organize. Likewise, Ostrom (1990) discovers that existing institutional arrangements strengthen a community's ability to deliberate over design principles of a market. Deliberative responses inspired by Ostrom will therefore still need to be accompanied, or prepared by symbolic and proto-responses mentioned earlier that create a public awareness, agenda and propensity for collective action.

We suggest that the accelerating trend towards deliberative communities (Chwalisz, 2019; Thorold, 2020), called the 'deliberative wave' by the OECD (2020), is conceptually akin to the findings by Ostrom in that they are able to create second and third tiers of choice in and about the market for big data.

Deliberative decision-making is an approach "that allows participants to consider relevant information from multiple points of view" (Involve, 2020) and requires that representatives from all the relevant stakeholder groups involved and affected are given the time, space and resources to learn from a variety of expert sources which provide different perspectives on the issue under consideration. The experts and the discussion expose all the component parts of the different positions that can be taken on the issue, laying bare its complexities, competing claims and stances and potential ways forward with the consequences of decisions also being exposed. A key principle is that all participants have equal access to information and that it is shared. Those deliberating follow a process which ensures that no voices dominate, and where the respective parties learn and use the knowledge they acquire during the process to come to a communal views and rules. Examples of deliberative techniques include citizen assemblies which were used in Ireland in the debates leading up to the national referendum on abortion.

Deliberation is particularly helpful when addressing wicked, multi-layered problems such as climate change (Thorold, 2020). As yet, there are no examples to demonstrate how this might be enacted in the consideration of big data, but we would suggest this is the next logical step and would be usefully applied to issues such as the global governance of the market in big data and would serve to satisfy criteria three and four outlined above.

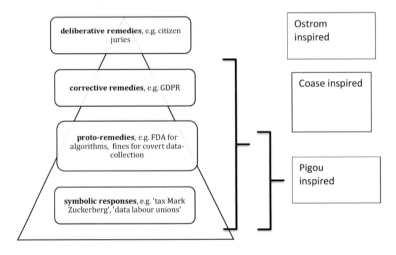

Figure 26.1   A taxonomy of responses to big data's externalities

A Conceptual Model for Addressing the Externalities of the Big Data Market

The discussion above points to a hierarchy of remedies which include Pigovian, Coasian and Ostromian approaches by considering issues of pricing, property rights and the requirement of the common pool, but it goes beyond them. Crucially it requires consideration of the four factors that we argue should be taken into account when seeking to preserve the big data market for digital corporate communication, i.e., that those who provide the input should be aware of any *transactions* involving their data, be made aware of its *value,* have *choices* and a form of choice over the role of that market in society.

In summary, Figure 26.1 describes a new taxonomy of society's responses available to address the externalities of the market for big data.

The taxonomy shows a hierarchy with deliberation at its apex. The taxonomy of responses and remedies to correct the current imbalances and imperfections of the big data market has drawn from economic theory, but its application to digital corporate communication is apparent. Increasingly, organizations are being held to account for their governance of big data (and AI) and corporate communications is being called on to explain and justify both organizational and its own uses of these technologies. The taxonomy above will assist them to consider their own responses. It could be argued that symbolic and proto-responses are just that and designed as deflections from the core issue of tackling the issue of choice and the restoration of agency to individuals and groups. They could be regarded as a price that is worth paying to re-enforce the hegemony of powerful organizations and institutions. Corrective remedies move the dial towards constraints on hegemony. Deliberative remedies require organizations and corporate communication to recognize that in the digital sphere at least, it is not acceptable for individual organizations and institutions to determine 'the rules'.

CONCLUSIONS AND FUTURE DIRECTIONS

This chapter has sought to expose the complexities, arguments and potential remedies around an issue that is increasingly permeating the public discourse: the power that the large data platforms and other commercial organizations have because they possess the resources and capabilities to collect and aggregate data and use analytics to predict and drive the behaviour of individuals. Digital corporate communication is a producer of big data and analytics because it collects, aggregates and analyses data from and about stakeholders. It is also a consumer of it because it obtains big data or uses it in analysed form to inform significant areas of its work such as identifying and categorizing stakeholders, creating content that will engage and/ or drive behaviour and evaluating responses. There is little literature yet on the wider societal implications of this, although much more on the use and benefits of such digital insights for organizational gain. The model provided here, drawn from economic theory, allows us to stand back and look at the implications of the externalities of the big data and analytics market and to provide remedies at the macroscopic level. These remedies all have major communication dimensions which range from the symbolic to the deliberative. They also require digital corporate communication to engage in responses that involve stakeholders at the individual, group, corporate and societal levels.

As yet, there are no examples of the big data and analytics market indulging in the critical self-reflection that would be required to provide such macroscopic insights. Therefore, this chapter calls for two specific future directions of work for the digital corporate communication community. First, to accelerate conversations within the community of practice itself on the implications of the practice being involved in big data market. This would require reflection and questioning on a range of issues raised, such as:

380 *Handbook on digital corporate communication*

- the purchasing power of the practice and if this can be used to influence any ameliorative or remedial actions in the market;
- careful consideration of the big data and analytics products and services available and the ethical implications of them.

There should be consideration of the nature of relationships with stakeholders and society that big data is opening up, for example, the ability to predict and change behaviour and the appropriate governance that should be put in place.

Second, to stimulate discussions in organizations and in society more widely on the issues around the impacts of the ubiquitous use of big data. This may include consideration of topics such as:

- how that big data shapes the nature of organizations, including the challenges it poses in decision-making and the dangers around the limitations of choice and data determinism;
- what society's relationship should be with the market in and organizations that hold the major repositories of data and whether regulation or other remedies should be put in place to ensure that society, not the market determines how the market develops and is governed.

A final observation is that the size of the big data and analytics market is large and growing, as is the digital transformation sector of which it is a part. If these conversations are not started now, society may well be in a similar position to where it was before the financial collapse of 2009–2011. The market will be regarded as too big and too powerful to be regulated effectively and society will ultimately pay the price.[3]

NOTES

1. Regulation (EU) 2016/679 of the European Parliament and of the Council of 27 April 2016 on the protection of natural persons with regard to the processing of personal data and on the free movement of such data, and repealing Directive 95/46/EC (General Data Protection Regulation). http://eur-lex.europa.eu/eli/reg/2016/679/oj 8; http://www.datatransparencylab.org/.
2. California Consumer Privacy Act of 2018 [1798.100 – 1798.199]. http://leginfo.legislature.ca.gov/faces/codes_displayText.xhtml?lawCode=CIV&division=3.&title=1.81.5.&part=4.&chapter=&article=.
3. Ethical approval: This chapter does not contain any studies with human participants or animals performed by any of the authors.

REFERENCES

Akerlof, G. A. (1970). The market for lemons: Quality uncertainty and the market mechanism. *Quarterly Journal of Economics, 84*(3), 488–500.

Akerlof, G. A. (2002). Behavioral macroeconomics and macroeconomic behavior. *American Economic Review, 92*(3), 411–433.

Akerlof, G. A. and Yellen, J. L. (1985a). A near rational model of the business cycle, with wage and price inertia. *Quarterly Journal of Economics, 100*, 823–838.

Akerlof, G. A. and Yellen, J. L. (1985b). Can small deviations from rationality make significant differences to economic equilibria? *American Economic Review, 75*(4), 708–720.

Anderson, T. L. and Leal, D. R. (2001). *Free market environmentalism.* Basingstoke: Palgrave Macmillan.

Anderson, T. L. and McChesney, F. S. (2003). *Property rights: Cooperation, conflict, and law.* Princeton: Princeton University Press.

Annenberg Center for Public Relations (2019). *2019 Global Communications Report. PR: Tech. The future of technology in communications.* USC Annenberg Centre for Public Relations, University of Southern California. https://annenberg.usc.edu/news/research-and-impact/usc-annenberg-study -predicts-technology-will-help-citizens-become-more.

Bambauer, D. (2014). Ghost in the network. *University of Pennsylvania Law Review, 162*(5), 1011–1091.

Bateman, C., Valentine, S., and Rittenburg, T. (2013). Ethical decision making in a peer-to-peer file sharing situation. The role of moral absolutes and social consensus. *Journal of Business Ethics, 115*(2), 229–240.

Bennett, D. (2017). The brutal fight to mine your data and sell it to your boss. *Bloomberg Businessweek,* 15 November. https://www.bloomberg.com/news/features/2017-11-15/the-brutal-fight-to-mine-your -data-and-sell-it-to-your-boss.

Bloomberg (2020). Big data and business analytics market size is projected to reach USD 512.04 billion by 2026. https://www.bloomberg.com/press-releases/2020-02-11/big-data-and-business-analytics -market-size-is-projected-to-reach-usd-512-04-billion-by-2026-valuates-reports.

Buhmann, A., Paßmann, J., and Fieseler, C. (2020). Managing algorithmic accountability: Balancing reputational concerns, engagement strategies, and the potential of rational discourse. *Journal of Business Ethics, 163*(2), 265–280.

Cerquitelli, T., Quercia, D., and Pasquale, F. (2017). *Transparent data mining for big and small data.* Cham: Springer.

Chwalisz, C. (2019). *A new wave of deliberative democracy.* Carnegie Europe, 26 November. https:// carnegieeurope.eu/2019/11/26/new-wave-of-deliberative-democracy-pub-80422

CIPR (Chartered Institute of Public Relations) (2021). *The AI and Big Data Readiness Report,* 23 November. https://cipr.co.uk/CIPR/Our_work/Policy/AI_in_PR.aspx.

Coase, R. H. (1960). The problem of social cost. *Journal of Law and Economics, 3,* 1–44.

Coase, R. H. (1988). *The firm, the market, and the law.* Chicago: University of Chicago Press.

Coase, R. H. (1995). *Essays on economics and economists.* Chicago: University of Chicago Press.

De George, R. (2003). *The ethics of information technology and business.* Oxford: Blackwell Publishing.

Flyverbom, M., Deibert, R., and Matten, D. (2017). The governance of digital technology, big data, and the new roles and responsibilities for business. *Business & Society, 58*(1), 3–19.

Galloway, C. and Swiatek, L. (2018). Public relations and artificial intelligence: It's not (just) about robots. *Public Relations Review, 44*(5), 734–740.

Gregory, A. and Halff, G. (2020). The damage done by big data-driven public relations. *Public Relations Review, 46*(2), article 101902. https://doi.org/10.1016/j.pubrev.2020.101902.

Holtzhausen, D. (2002). Towards a postmodern agenda for public relations. *Public Relations Review, 28,* 251–264.

Hong, W. and Thong, J. (2013). Internet privacy concerns: An integrated conceptualization and four empirical studies. *MIS Quarterly, 37*(1), 275–298.

Ingram, D. (2018). *Facebook to put 1.5 billion users out of reach of new EU privacy law.* https://www .reuters.com/article/us-facebook-privacy-eu-exclusive/exclusive-facebook-to-put-1-5-billion-users -out-of-reach-of-new-eu-privacy-law-idUSKBN1HQ00P.

Involve (2020). *Deliberative public engagement.* .http://www.involve.org.uk/resources/knowledge-base/ what/deliberative-public-engagement.

Kemper, J. and Kolkman, D. (2019). Transparent to whom? No algorithmic accountability without a critical audience. *Information, Communication & Society, 22*(14), 2081–2096.

Kuchler, H. (2018). The man who took on Facebook – and won. *Financial Times,* 5 April. https://www .ft.com/content/86d1ce50-3799-11e8-8eee-e06bde01c544.

Lepri, B., Oliver, N., Letouze, E., Pentland, A., and Vinck, P. (2017). Fair, transparent and accountable algorithmic decision-making processes. *Philosophy and Technology, 30*(4), 1–17.

L'Etang, J. (2005). Critical public relations: Some reflections. *Public Relations Review, 31,* 521–526.

Marketsandmarkets (2021). *Digital transformation market.* https://www.marketsandmarkets.com/ Market-Reports/digital-transformation-market-43010479.html?gclid=CjwKCAjw7IeUBhBbE iwADhiEMYc-uR8mR9Bjn0ygGGtlM1kQyODHjA_CZOkqjv4TQLBfNxx9nAk_IBoCml4QAvD _BwE.

382 *Handbook on digital corporate communication*

Mazzucato, M. (2017). *The value of everything*. London: Penguin.

Mazzucato, M. (2018). *The entrepreneurial state*. London: Penguin.

Mazzucato, M. (2019). Preventing digital feudalism. *Project Syndicate*, 2 October. https://www.project-syndicate.org/commentary/platform-economy-digital-feudalism-by-mariana-mazzucato-2019-10.

Murtarelli, G., Gregory, A., and Romenti, S. (2021). A conversation-based perspective for shaping ethical human-machine interactions: The particular challenge of chatbots. *Journal of Business Research*, *129*, 927–935.

Naughton, J. (2019). The goal is to automate us. *The Guardian*, 20 January. https://www.theguardian.com/technology/2019/jan/20/shoshana-zuboff-age-of-surveillance-capitalism-google-facebook.

Nunan, D. and Di Domenico, M. (2013). Market research and the ethics of big data. *International Journal of Market Research*, *55*(4), 505–520.

Nunan, D. and Di Domenico, M. (2017). Big data: A normal accident waiting to happen? *Journal of Business Ethics*, *145*(3), 481–491.

Obar, J. A. and Oeldorf-Hirsch, A. (2018). The biggest lie on the Internet: Ignoring the privacy policies and terms of service policies of social networking services. *Information, Communication & Society*, *23*(1), 128–147.

OECD (2020). *Innovative citizen participation and new democratic institutions: Catching the deliberative wave*. Paris: OECD Publishing.

O'Neil, C. (2016). *Weapons of math destruction*. New York: Penguin Books.

Ostrom, E. (1990). *Governing the commons: The evolution of institutions for collective action*. Cambridge: Cambridge University Press.

Ostrom, E. (1992). Institutions and common-pool resources. *Journal of Theoretical Politics*, *4*(3), 243–245.

Ostrom, E. (2010). Polycentric systems for coping with collective action and global environmental change. *Global Environmental Change*, *20*(4), 550–557.

Pasquale, F. (2015). *The black box society: The secret algorithms that control money and information*. Cambridge, MA: Harvard University Press.

Paul, K. (2019). California's groundbreaking privacy law takes effect in January. What does it do? *The Guardian*, 30 December. https://www.theguardian.com/us-news/2019/dec/30/california-consumer-privacy-act-what-does-it-do#:~:text=California's%20groundbreaking%20privacy%20law%20takes%20effect%20in%20January.,-What%20does%20it&text=Last%20year%2C%20California%20passed%20a,and%20how%20it%20is%20used.

Pigou, A. C. (1920). *The economics of welfare*. London: Macmillan.

Posner, E. A. and Weyl, E. G. (2018). *Radical markets: Uprooting capitalism and democracy for a just society*. Princeton: Princeton University Press.

Qiu, J. L. (2015). Reflections on big data: 'Just because it is accessible does not make it ethical'. *Media, Culture & Society*, *37*(7), 1089–1094.

Roper, J. (2005). Symmetrical communication: Excellent public relations or a strategy for hegemony? *Journal of Public Relations Research*, *17*(1), 69–86.

Schlager, E. (2002). Rationality, cooperation, and common pool resources. *American Behavioral Scientist*, *45*(5), 801–819.

Singleton, S. and Taylor, M. (1992). Common property, collective action and community. *Journal of Theoretical Politics*, *4*(3), 309–324.

Sivarajah, U., Kamal, M. M., Irani, Z., and Weerakoddy, V. (2017). Critical analysis of Big Data challenges and analytical methods. *Journal of Business Research*, *70*, 263–286.

Spence, A. M. (2002). Signaling in retrospect and the informational structure of markets. *American Economic Review*, *92*(3), 434–459.

Spence, A. M. (2012). Mind over market. *Project Syndicate*, 13 January. http://www.project-syndicate.org/commentary/mind-over-market.

Stigler, G. J. (1966). *The theory of price*. London: Collier-Macmillan.

Stiglitz, J. E. (1975). The theory of screening, education and the distribution of income. *American Economic Review*, *65*(3), 283–300.

Stiglitz, J. E. (2000). The contributions of the economics of information to twentieth century economics. *Quarterly Journal of Economics*, *115*(4), 1441–1478.

Stiglitz, J. E. (2002). *Globalization and its discontents*. New York: Penguin.

Stiglitz, J. E. (2006). *Making globalization work: The next steps to global justice.* New York: Penguin.

Thorold, R. (2020). Deliberative democracy. *RSA Journal, 1,* 48.

Tutt, A. (2017). An FDA for algorithms. *Administrative Law Review, 69,* 83–123.

Valin, J. and Gregory, A. (2020). *Ethics guide to artificial intelligence in PR.* CIPR. https://www.cipr.co.uk/CIPR/Our_work/Policy/AI_in_PR.aspx.

Weiner, M. and Kochar, S. (2016). *Irreversible: The public relations big data revolution.* Gainesville, FL: Institute for Public Relations.

West, S. M. (2017). Data capitalism: Redefining the logics of surveillance and privacy. *Business & Society, 58*(1), 20–41.

Wiesenberg, M., Zerfass, A., and Moreno, A. (2017). Big Data and automation in strategic communication. *International Journal of Strategic Communication, 11*(2), 95–114.

Wilson, D. S., Ostrom, E., and Cox, M. E. (2013). Generalizing the core design principles for the efficacy of groups. *Journal of Economic Behavior & Organization, 905,* 521–532.

Zuboff, S, (2019). *The age of surveillance capitalism.* London: Profile Books.

Zwitter, A. (2014). Big data ethics. *Big Data & Society, 1*(2), 1–6.

27. Digital corporate communication and public diplomacy
Jérôme Chariatte and Diana Ingenhoff

INTRODUCTION

Digitalization and globalization have made corporate communication international, either by companies increasingly operating transnationally or addressing stakeholders from various cultures through online technologies. While building international legitimacy and reputation, corporations are often confronted with the fact that international stakeholders evaluate them and their products based on their country of origin (Nes, 2018) and the activities of nation-states. Equally, however, various studies point out that companies can act as ambassadors for their home country and influence, intentionally or unintentionally, positively or negatively, the perception of nation-states and the diplomatic arena (Ingenhoff et al., 2018; Qu and Carpentier, 2021; White, 2015). Indeed, the activities of corporations and governments are aligned through globalization; increasingly governments are becoming corporatized and corporations are taking over functions formerly reserved for nation-states (Bolewski, 2022). For this reason, corporations need to understand how nation-states promote country images and build international relationships and how they themselves can shape the diplomatic discourse. Accordingly, companies are gaining diplomatic importance, especially through digitalization.

In 2020, the technology company Meta released a *Digital Diplomacy Facebook Guide*, which provides diplomats with best practices for conducting international relations on the social web (Meta, 2020). The notion of a company explaining to diplomats how to communicate and talk with international interaction partners may initially seem surprising. However, it illustrates the challenges and deficiencies encountered by diplomacy in today's digitized world. The days when diplomacy took place behind closed doors are long gone and diplomats and nation-states are confronted with a multitude of stakeholders raising their voices through digital platforms. According to Bjola and Zaiotti, "the global spread of new digital communication technologies has profoundly transformed the way individuals, states, and businesses operate and interact with the outside world" (2020, p. 1). Digital technologies affect the strategic communication of organizations and entire societies. However, diplomats and diplomatic organizations responsible for country image cultivation still struggle to address and engage with the players of today's digitalized society.

Therefore, digitalization raises several questions. How is public diplomacy changing through digital offerings? What role do non-state actors such as corporations play in the digital sphere, and how can they be considered and addressed? Moreover, what contributes to impactful digital diplomacy?

This chapter begins by introducing and defining *digital public diplomacy*. Next, changes in public diplomacy through digitalization are discussed, mainly relating to the rising power of sub-national stakeholders like corporations. This discussion critically examines diplomatic actors' ways of engaging and listening to these stakeholders. Further, a new evaluation proce-

Digital corporate communication and public diplomacy 385

dure and strategies for impactful digital diplomacy are proposed and illustrated in the example of Switzerland's public digital diplomacy activities.

DEFINITION OF DIGITAL PUBLIC DIPLOMACY AND PREVIOUS STUDIES

Public diplomacy is defined as strategic communication that involves the country's relationship building with publics in home and host countries to advance policies and actions and maintain a good country image (Ingenhoff and Chariatte, 2020; Melissen and Wang, 2019). The definition of public diplomacy has evolved over the years. Whereas traditional public diplomacy was mainly the one-way dissemination of information from diplomatic institutions, the new public diplomacy (Melissen, 2005) levels up towards a dialogue and relationship-building with relevant stakeholders. Cowan and Arsenault (2008) go further, adding a collaborative level to public diplomacy, which means that governmental diplomatic organizations and non-state actors such as corporations can work together to achieve communication goals. The second and especially the third level, which was more a theoretically elaborated ideal for a long time, becomes a reality through digital technologies.

Talking about digital public diplomacy suggests that it is merely a form of 'public diplomacy 2.0' involving the use of new digital platforms. This understanding is suggested by terms such as 'Facebook Diplomacy' or 'Twitplomacy' (Spry, 2019; Su and Xu, 2015). However, this limits online diplomatic activities to (1) specific channels that may no longer be relevant in years to come, as digital offerings are changing and developing drastically in a very short time (Cornut and Dale, 2019), making it difficult to establish a state of the art; and (2) a new soft power tool through which previous strategic diplomatic communication practices are maintained (Hedling and Bremberg, 2021). Indeed, the essence of diplomatic functions and communication also remains in the digital sphere to achieve strategic goals like representing a nation's interests (Cornut and Dale, 2019). At the same time, we can observe many changes in today's digitized society that need to be addressed and considered when undertaking digital public diplomacy.

Digital public diplomacy is the climax of a larger social, cultural and political change in recent years (Hayden, 2018). Thanks to globalization and new digital technologies, we can observe how various actors interact with each other, nurturing the idea of a network society (Castells, 2010). This new society is characterized by global interdependencies (e.g., in international trade), challenging the role of the powerful state and empowering stakeholder groups that raise their voices through digital technologies and shape the international discourse.

One example is transnational corporations that become global players. Having adopted digital technologies earlier than state actors, companies presumably show more competence in using new communication channels (e.g., social media) to address international stakeholders. Further, some international stakeholders may perceive international companies as closer and more trustworthy than states and companies are increasingly taking up diplomatic functions (Bolewski, 2022; White, 2020). This new corporate activity is called 'corporate diplomacy' and involves corporations' engagement in international environmental, societal and political issues (Ingenhoff and Marschlich, 2019). Their actions can serve a nation's public diplomacy, but they can also be driven by self-interest and the fulfilment of social expectations. We can observe a rising (digital) stakeholder activism coming to fruition in hashtags such as

386 *Handbook on digital corporate communication*

#FridaysForFuture used by the climate movement, calling for companies and society to take up international social and political responsibility.

Thus, digitalization fosters an important change in public diplomacy, namely that the nation-state is no longer the only player in the public diplomacy communication process (Dolea, 2018). Different sub-national actors (like corporations, activists and even cities and city mayors) emerge, raise their voices and co-create the country's image by using digital technologies such as social media, having low access costs and extensive reach (Bjola et al., 2020). Publics, which were long passive recipients, become real stakeholders who are not only affected but can affect the achievement of an organization's goals (Freeman, 1984). Therefore, digital public diplomacy means the adaptation and "strategy of managing change through digital tools and virtual collaboration" for diplomatic actors (Holmes, 2015, p. 15).

WHAT IS CHANGING?

To build relationships and collaboration, diplomatic state actors need to know the different stakeholder groups emerging, how they are interconnected and their potential and willingness to cooperate. In the following section, diverse stakeholder groups are presented and discussed in the digitalization context.

Regions and Cities

Digital platforms blur the boundaries between national and international actors, and bring international and domestic publics – which have been strongly neglected in previous research – into play (Bjola et al., 2019). A major group of domestic players is that of paradiplomatic actors, sub-national actors with a territorial character engaged in complementary, supportive or opposing actions parallel to the nation's diplomatic communication (Duran, 2016). These actors may include regions and cities (see also 'city diplomacy') entering the international political stage to represent themselves and their interests (Van der Pluijm and Melissen, 2007). This may include influencing their governments' national and international policies, strengthening separatist and nationalist motives, getting international attention and building international relationships to foster investments of companies and trade (Kuznetsov, 2014). Digital technologies allow cities to have a stronger international presence. Their place branding and digital public diplomacy activities can overlap online as cities position and market themselves (Dinnie and Sevin, 2020).

Cities use hashtag activism and co-creational aspects in their campaigns to make their city brand more authentic and foster tourism or investments, for example (Casais and Monteiro, 2019). The following examples show how economic interests and political engagement are interlinked: The region of Catalonia, the most prosperous region of Spain, has been in the international spotlight for a long time due to its aspirations for independence from Spain. It is attracting new attention through websites and social media by the Public Diplomacy Council of Catalonia and different Catalan institutions to promote the region and its unique culture, among other activities, and to attract international companies (Alexander and Royo i Marine, 2020; Johnson and Cester, 2015). During the Brexit process, sub-state actors like Scotland and the capital city of London showed their disapproval for leaving the European Union with online co-creation of campaigns such as #LondonIsOpen and #Leavealighton, mainly to ensure their economic prosperity and investments in their local corporations (Chariatte and Ingenhoff, 2021). These actions show that cities have some of the same interests as companies in entering the international discourse. Therefore, in the following discussion, we will shed light on the role of companies in public digital diplomacy.

International Corporations and Technology Companies

Companies play an increasingly important role at the international level; thus, diplomatic cooperation can be particularly interesting for corporations and states. On the one hand, governments may benefit from corporations' networks and, through their success, ensure economic welfare and stability. On the other hand, companies may gain additional resources and, in certain countries, address local stakeholders more easily with governmental support (Marschlich and Ingenhoff, 2022; Sevin and Dinnie, 2015). But the literature disagrees regarding the interaction of these two entities, especially in terms of who is the dominant actor in this relationship (Sondergaard, 2014; White, 2020). Further, to our knowledge until today no study has addressed corporate diplomacy and diplomatic collaborations in the digital sphere.

From a traditional public diplomacy perspective, corporations need to serve by promoting the country's image and values (Fitzpatrick et al., 2020). In contrast, political and international relations studies see government in the role of 'commercial diplomats' supporting corporations by negotiating and promoting business opportunities (Sevin and Dinnie, 2015). However, digitalization has facilitated the broad dissemination of business information and empowered companies to take over investment and trade negotiations (Ruël et al., 2015). Business and management literature highlight that corporations work independently and collaborate with foreign governments only for their own interests, such as profit-gaining and reaching new markets (White, 2020). This goes along with the findings of Fitzpatrick et al. (2020), who found that American companies are not particularly interested in working with their government unless the government helps them fulfil their role as corporate citizens by addressing global issues.

Corporate diplomacy is strongly interlinked with the concept of political corporate social responsibility (Ingenhoff and Marschlich, 2019). International corporations have long been pressured to respond to the expectations of their stakeholders, a response that involves social and political responsibility. Stakeholder pressures have been drastically augmented through the new information environment, as company misconduct can be digitally reported worldwide in minutes. Further, stakeholders of the millennial generation, being digital natives, especially value corporate political engagement and are increasingly pressuring companies online (Kesteleyn et al., 2014; Manfredi-Sánchez, 2022).

To reach and satisfy these stakeholders and get international attention quickly and cost-efficiently, corporations not only show socially responsible behaviour but also take a stand on political issues on social networking sites. This corporate activism is used to give issues more public attention, normalize them and thereby motivate policy changes (Eilert and Cherup, 2020). For instance, Deutsche Bank and PayPal advocated online against controversial LGBTQ policies in North Carolina (Hill, 2020). In the summer of 2021, Ben & Jerry's communicated on Twitter that it would stop selling ice cream in certain regions involved with the Israeli–Palestinian conflict, as it would be "inconsistent with its values" (Ben & Jerry's, 2021). Finally, HSBC UK's campaign "We are not an island", which, according to its statements, was not meant a priori to be a political statement, was discussed online as an anti-Brexit

388 *Handbook on digital corporate communication*

positioning (BBC, 2019). Therefore, digitalization fosters the activism and politicization of companies. However, this new activism is not without risks for corporations and may create some backlash (Eilert and Cherup, 2020).

As a result of digitalization, the corporate responsibility and business ethics literature has recently addressed so-called corporate digital responsibility. This describes the ethical responsibility of companies in digital matters, such as the handling of data, algorithms and artificial intelligence (Lobschat et al., 2021). This digital corporate responsibility has an impact on international relations and diplomacy as shown by the following examples of the technology industry.

Corporations like Google or Facebook are increasingly shaping diplomatic discourses and practices through their digital platforms. Diplomatic actors need to be aware that Facebook, Instagram, and others are not simply digital platforms or tools; behind them are people with interests that need to be negotiated (Hayden, 2018; Melissen and de Keulenaar, 2017). Countries like Denmark are aware of this and send so-called tech ambassadors to Silicon Valley to discuss political and regulatory issues (Klynge et al., 2020). Such action is necessary as tech companies define the diplomatic discourse by impacting the international news flow. People increasingly replace traditional media with online search engines and social media platforms as information sources. However, not all countries are equally present and framed online (Segev, 2018). To a certain degree, the presence of nation-states online is defined by the algorithms developed by tech companies. Algorithms may show users' information that mainly confirms their worldviews (e.g., filter bubbles), making it difficult for diplomatic organizations responsible for image management to convey new and varied representations of their country (Manor, 2016). Further, tech companies can be made responsible regarding their vast collections of personal data and how these can be used for political purposes, as shown by the Facebook Cambridge Analytica scandal around the US elections in 2016.

The format of the tech companies' platforms is also changing the way we communicate about countries. With its limit of 280 characters per message, Twitter shapes diplomatic communication, in which complex events must be communicated in a highly simplified manner. There is an online trend to communicate simplified worldviews and use visual and emotional content (e.g., Instagram and Snapchat), which impacts the online country's image (Duncombe, 2019; Thelander and Cassinger, 2017).

Overall, the role of corporations in diplomacy is not yet clearly defined and is changing through digitalization. Technology companies are taking an increasingly important role and need to take up ethical responsibility in shaping the international discourse. In general, corporations are increasingly pressured by their digital stakeholders to take up social responsibility (e.g., on social media), highlighting the influence of individuals on the diplomatic discourse.

CEOs, Citizens, Influencers and Activists

The fact that anyone can open their own profile on social media platforms means that individuals can also influence public (digital) diplomacy. In the digital context, considerable interest is given to so-called influencers, opinion leaders who communicate with others in multi-directional ways (Ingenhoff et al., 2021). These influencers can be political leaders (e.g., presidents, ministers, mayors) who impact the perception of nation-states and international relations (Balmas, 2018). The relevance of social media in this process has been demonstrated

Digital corporate communication and public diplomacy 389

by former US President Trump, who also polarized audiences through his Twitter communication and launched the social media platform 'Truth Social' in 2022.

Here too, private actors can play a role alongside political actors. Many CEOs of large companies establish a social media presence and use it to position themselves and their companies (e.g., through corporate social responsibility (CSR) communication), which may affect not only the corporation's but also the country's reputation (Kim and Ji, 2021). For instance, the former CEO of Goldman Sachs used Twitter for the first time to criticize Trump's decision to leave the Paris Climate Agreement (Gurdus, 2017).

A variety of other people have also achieved celebrity status, be it entertainers, athletes, lifestyle influencers on Instagram or scientists who may play a role in digital public diplomacy (Bergman Rosamond and Hedling, 2022). A comparative study of Switzerland, Austria and the Netherlands shows that ordinary citizens influence the public's perception of countries online (Ingenhoff et al., 2021). Countries like Sweden consider this and entrust citizens with their Twitter and Instagram channels to make their communication and place brands more personal and authentic (Christensen, 2013; Thelander and Cassinger, 2017). An example in which individuals challenge nation-states' activities is the case of WikiLeaks, which published online information challenging US diplomacy (Cull, 2011). Particularly through groupings, activism and social movements on the web, citizens can significantly influence international politics, as observed with the Arab Spring, starting in 2010.

To sum up, it can be stated that today's online diplomatic discourse is handled by an extensive variety of stakeholders, ranging from individuals to companies and regions that interact with diplomats, nation-states and among each other. State actors need to engage with these sub-state actors, consider both interests and build a coherent and integrated communication.

WHAT REMAINS (UNFORTUNATELY) THE SAME? A CALL FOR LISTENING

Public diplomacy is often practised similarly in the offline and online spheres. For example, most Ministries of Foreign Affairs (MFA) today have social media accounts, but they use them to show their presence, or their content is mainly shaped by institutional customs rather than stakeholder interests and dialogue (Spry, 2019). This implies that digital public diplomacy on social media is often still limited to the dissemination of information (Kampf et al., 2015; Manor, 2016). The core of digital tools, namely their potential for interaction, relationship building and knowing one's stakeholders, is not used (Bjola et al., 2019). Little is known about the expectations and motivations of non-state actors to engage in digital public diplomacy (Huang, 2020). Despite its importance, listening to key stakeholders is the least frequently used approach of MFAs in the digital sphere and the least studied aspect of public diplomacy (Dodd and Collins, 2017).

Listening to key stakeholders refers to the necessity to understand and consider publics' interests in the communication strategy by "systematically collecting and analysing the opinions of foreign publics" (Cull, 2010, p. 12). Despite a trend of data collection in times of datafication and big data, many measurements are recorded only for the purpose of 'measuring' without reflecting on them theoretically (Carballo et al., 2018). Practitioners lack tools and knowledge regarding what listening means or how to implement (digital) listening steps (Sommerfeldt and Buhmann, 2019). For instance, many people still understand listening as a monitoring and evaluation technique, which is done before and after a communication campaign to test its efficiency. According to Di Martino (2019), this kind of 'tactical listening' is not adapted, especially for the digital sphere. On social media, diplomatic actors need to show ongoing 'active listening', which implies engaging continuously with their stakeholders and showing them that there is a genuine interest in their opinions and that their ideas are considered, to build mutual trust. Further, with the speed of the internet, which allows negative electronic-word-of-mouth or fake news to spread rapidly (Bjola and Pamment, 2018), diplomatic actors need to be flexible, react rapidly and be open to changes: "Digitalization involves taking risks and engaging with the unknown, which in turn is at odds with the perception that diplomacy should display foresight and be risk-averse" (Hedling and Bremberg, 2021, p. 1596).

Thus, efficient listening and evaluation approaches need both summative and formative measurement steps, allowing for the continuous adaptation of communication strategies (Van Ruler, 2019). However, previous diplomatic activities and measurement models often fail to include formative measurement steps and do not focus on contextual factors. Therefore, the Listening and Evaluation Compass (LEC) (Ingenhoff and Chariatte, 2020) framework is proposed and discussed in the context of digitalization (Figure 27.1).

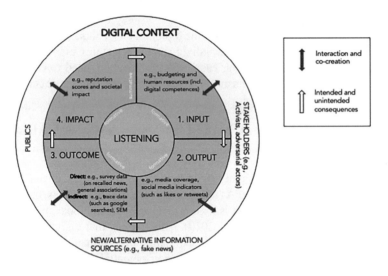

Source: Adapted from Ingenhoff and Chariatte (2020).

Figure 27.1 Listening and evaluation compass

The framework is based on the established input, output, outcome and impact levels. On all levels, listening steps are required as they are influenced by different stakeholders and a changing dynamic context – here, digitalization.

The input level comprises the resources and expenditures the public diplomacy entity (e.g., MFAs) invests in strategic communication and its related listening activities. Regarding personal resources, we can observe that digitalization requires specific knowledge, and today's job profiles in diplomatic institutions are changing. Information technology skills, such as programming websites and software, analysing big data and dealing with digital security issues, are required (Hayden, 2018; Melissen and de Keulenaar, 2017). Knowing how to use social media platforms for relationship-building – the core of public diplomacy – is also of primary importance. This includes knowing which channels are used today and in which regions (e.g., Vkontakte in Russia, Weibo in China). However, most of today's diplomatic actors are not 'digital natives' and show significant literacy issues regarding the digital sphere and online relationship-building.

The output level shows the direct reception and visibility communication activities have received in offline and online media. Especially in the context of online media, it is crucial to look for mis- or disinformation and filter relevant information out of big data sets thanks to automated and visual methods like data mining or semantic network analysis.

Regarding communication reach, social media gives diplomatic actors a range of new listening indicators such as likes, retweets, shares and replies. Thanks to social network analysis, diplomatic actors may determine who are the opinion leaders spreading the news. However, caution is needed when interpreting the relevance of such metrics. First, these indicators may be distorted (e.g., by bots), and second, they do not give insights into the effects of the communication messages (Bjola et al., 2020).

On the outcome level, surveys can assess stakeholders' topic awareness about the aim of the strategic communication (direct results), attitudes and behavioural intentions (indirect results). They can be analysed with the help of multivariate techniques such as partial least square structural equation modelling (see Ingenhoff and Chariatte, 2020). Further digital offerings provide new chances for the assessment of behaviours and public diplomacy activities. Trace data such as Google searches can reveal what people are looking at regarding travel, shopping or migration. Thanks to social network analysis, opinion leaders in the digital discourse can be identified.

Finally, the impact level is about measuring the impact of digital public diplomacy. This proves to be particularly difficult because, as mentioned, digital indicators of success do not allow conclusions to be drawn regarding real changes. Country image ratings and specific indices related to the communication objective can be helpful here.

The presented model is not rigid and does not need to be calculated through (Ingenhoff and Chariatte, 2020). There is no one-size-fits-all option, especially in the digital age, which is characterized by flexibility and the unexpected. Indeed, as shown in the next section, there are various challenges to digital public diplomacy listening and engagement activities.

CRITICAL EXAMINATION

The digitalization of public diplomacy activities is often accompanied by a certain optimism. Digital advances like social media are seen as opportunities for more democracy and direct exchange and co-creation between nation-states and relevant stakeholders. However, this idea of relationship-building and collaborative public diplomacy encounters some disruptions and is not entirely positive (Bjola et al., 2019). First, due to digital inequalities, the digital sphere is mainly characterized by elite actors (Pacher, 2018). For example, in several African countries, there is no (or only limited) access to the internet for large groups of the population. This is particularly unfortunate, as in Africa and Indo-Pacific regions, there is a younger population than in the Western world. This population easily grasps new technologies and shows higher

392   *Handbook on digital corporate communication*

involvement with foreign MFAs to get information and educational and development opportunities (Spry, 2019; Turianskyi and Wekesa, 2021). In general, little is known about the challenges and practices of digital public diplomacy in the Global South (Khan et al., 2021).

Second, it needs to be clear that some stakeholder groups do not necessarily want to collaborate and sometimes even counter the communication of diplomatic institutions because of diverging points of interest. Even worse, a nation's soft power can be harmed by digital phenomena like the spread of disinformation or fake news (Bjola and Pamment, 2018). Diplomatic actors need to be ready to communicate at any moment, to correct false information or react to negative electronic word-of mouth.

With positively minded actors, and possibly even more with critically minded ones, it is important to know, understand and engage with them properly to build efficient strategic communication. Despite the above-mentioned fact that an understanding of listening approaches is lacking, diplomatic actors often miss resources to evaluate all the communication steps, and it is not clear how to conceive impactful digital public diplomacy activities, as impact is difficult to make tangible.

Bjola (2016) points out that it is crucial to be aware of the measurement possibilities in the *listening* process, which is a fundamental principle for impactful digital public diplomacy. Indeed, there are five principles for impactful digital public diplomacy: listening, prioritization, hybridization, engagement and adaptation (Bjola, 2016). *Prioritization* implies formulating short- and long-term goals. *Hybridization* explains that digital public diplomacy cannot work independently and needs to be coordinated with traditional (public) diplomacy activities, whereas *engagement* includes reaching large audiences in real-time. *Adaptation* is the need to be flexible, to adapt to a dynamic environment and different actors. These five principles of success and the different actors engaging in the digital sphere will be visualized and addressed in the following case study.

CASE STUDY: SWITZERLAND'S DIGITAL PUBLIC DIPLOMACY ACTIVITIES

Switzerland's public diplomacy is managed by Presence Switzerland, a special unit within the Federal Department of Foreign Affairs of Switzerland (FDFA) established in 2001. As defined in the Federal Act of 24 March 2001, it is to support and maintain Switzerland's network of relationships and care for the country's image abroad. Regarding digitalization, the organization applies many of the five principles presented above.

Listening: Introducing the Image Monitor Switzerland

Before fixing the inputs of a new communication strategy, Presence Switzerland needs to analyse its stakeholders and how the country is internationally perceived. Related to the levels of the LEC model (Ingenhoff and Chariatte, 2020), Presence Switzerland analyses media on the *output* level, including digital media and social media platforms. For example, analysis of Instagram, Twitter and Facebook and related hashtags such as #Switzerland showed that aesthetic, entertaining and emotional news gained international attention online (FDFA, 2017, 2018, 2019, 2020a). For instance, the news item "Chocolate snow covers Swiss town", which referred to a malfunction of the ventilation system of the Lindt chocolate factory that distrib-

Digital corporate communication and public diplomacy 393

uted cocoa powder over the town of Olten, was frequently shared on online media (FDFA, 2020a). Another trending topic online was the disputes between environmental activists and Swiss bank Credit Suisse, and the role of its prominent ambassador, Roger Federer was also discussed (FDFA, 2020a).

These examples confirm our theoretical assumptions that the digital sphere is very emotional and that micro- (e.g., activists, celebrities) and meso-level (e.g., banks) actors can also contribute to a digital country image. Further, it becomes clear that people are interested in peculiar stories regarding Switzerland. Monitoring and listening to these phenomena can be used in public diplomacy communication, as was done by Presence Switzerland's partner Tourism Switzerland in 2019. By inviting a well-known South Korean K-pop band to Switzerland, Switzerland acknowledged the importance of celebrities in country promotion and became better known in the Asian region through the posts of these celebrities (FDFA, 2019).

On the *outcome level,* Presence Switzerland is conducting an international survey study on recalled news, associations, strengths and weaknesses of Switzerland in 19 countries on average on a biennial basis. The survey includes both closed and open-ended questions to capture the opinions and interests of the respondents about the country and refer to the five country image dimensions (Ingenhoff and Chariatte, 2020). Thanks to partial least squares analysis and importance-performance analysis, it is possible to find out the most important country image dimensions and the underlying value drivers. Further, in collaboration with the authors of this study, Presence Switzerland has analysed the survey data and complemented it with Google search analysis to learn more about the online search behaviour of relevant stakeholder groups and how digital platforms influence the information process about countries (see Ingenhoff et al., 2020). Together, these insights help build their communication strategy and address different states. Finally, Presence Switzerland considers the impact level by looking at various indicators such as the Nation Brands Index (Anholt, 2005).

These findings regarding the Swiss country perception can be useful for private corporations active in place-branding, such as Swiss Tourism and the MFAs, to compare themselves with other countries. However, it is important to note that MFAs not only look at their country image but also look if there are hints indicating that Swiss corporations are negatively perceived (e.g., regarding their ethical behaviour). This might be important regarding possible collaborations within their strategy, as discussed later on.

Prioritization: Formulating a Strategy

Prioritization involves planning and choosing short- and long-term goals regarding digitalization. The topic of digitalization is central to Switzerland and, for the first time, a focal point in its foreign policy strategy 2020–2023 (FDFA, 2020b). In its global communication strategy, Switzerland shows its awareness of different sub-national actors co-creating the diplomatic discourse by relying on a so-called multi-stakeholder approach, which can be seen in the different areas of practice. Regarding digital innovations, the government emphasizes the importance of collaboration with research institutions (e.g., Cern, universities) or big tech companies (e.g., Google or Meta) located in Switzerland, a major advantage Switzerland has over other countries. Further, Switzerland is trying to position the city of Geneva as a major hub for digital governance, relying on the city's long history of international governance. In 2018, Switzerland launched the Geneva Dialogue on Responsible Behaviour in Cyberspace to promote collaboration among companies regarding cybersecurity. As home to many

394   *Handbook on digital corporate communication*

blockchain companies, the Crypto Valley in the Swiss region of Zug is another example of establishing Switzerland as an important digital hub.

Specific to digital public diplomacy activities, there is also a strategy paper for Presence Switzerland, which is re-evaluated every four years (FDFA, 2021a), depending on changes in international opinion. In the Strategy for Communication Abroad 2021–2024, digital communication is described as relying on three aspects: developing its own communication channels, raising digital awareness about Switzerland and maintaining event platforms in times of digitalization (FDFA, 2021a), as described in the next section.

Engagement: Visibility and Interaction through Websites and Social Media

Digital communication channels are an important basis of digital strategy. In addition to a general information platform (www.eda.admin.ch/aboutswitzerland), Switzerland uses the 'House of Switzerland' storytelling platform to position itself (House of Switzerland, 2022). Storytelling strategies fit current digital trends of visual, emotional and personal communication (Hedling, 2020). The previous listening activities show that international publics mainly recall emotional and extraordinary Swiss narratives. The stories used are built around different events where Switzerland is participating (e.g., Olympic Games, World Exhibitions), but also around important actors shaping the Swiss country image, as stated by Presence Switzerland director: "Switzerland's image is closely related to the people and things that create it, such as Swiss brands, athletes and products. It is with such icons – and sometimes clichés – that we work" (House of Switzerland, 2022). The collaboration with these actors can also be seen on the website, which links to various tech and financial industry platforms. Further, FDFA sets guidelines on partnering with private sponsors (FDFA, 2021b). This shows that corporate diplomacy cooperation already exists and serves to promote business and include corporations in the strategic country image communication.

House of Switzerland further expands its digital presence through various social media channels managed by Presence Switzerland. These channels are used to share House of Switzerland's activities thanks to visuals (e.g., Instagram, Flickr, YouTube) and inform and engage with stakeholders (e.g., Facebook or Twitter), for example, by using quizzes. To foster social media interaction and promote Switzerland in a playful way, House of Switzerland has introduced 'Happy Lilly', a small wooden cow symbolizing Swiss values, on Facebook and Twitter. Social media users are invited to integrate the small wooden figure into their travel photos and share their views of Switzerland on their networks, thereby acting as Swiss ambassadors. The project stands out for its organic implementation, as Happy Lilly can be easily incorporated into users' everyday social media activities (Dinnie and Sevin, 2020).

The use of apps also proves to be an easy way for Ministries of Foreign Affairs to communicate with the public, and it addresses the trend of mobile technologies. Switzerland has developed the Travel Admin App, which Swiss citizens can use to quickly locate and contact Swiss representatives abroad in a crisis (FDFA, 2021c). Its functions could be further developed and, as some other countries have done, allow users to learn more about the activities of the Ministry of Foreign Affairs to foster engagement and understanding of each other (e.g., tracking visits and activities or reading the latest MFA press releases).

In the discussion of media, another focal point of the digital foreign strategy is to make Switzerland more visible and better known online. To foster the online presence of Swiss news and thus make Switzerland better known, the platform Swissinfo (www.swissinfo.ch)

is used. It was specifically designed to make Swiss news and information accessible internationally. The FDFA strategy paper on communication abroad also reveals that a great deal is being invested in search engine optimization, a necessary technique for dealing with the algorithms of online technologies. Finally, the country's appearance at international events and exhibitions such as the Olympic Games or the Expo 2020 in Dubai is essential to position the country. The role of digitization in this activity is explained in the next section.

Hybridization and Adaptation

The relevance of major events and exhibitions and the direct human contact associated with them cannot be entirely replaced by digital media. For this reason, Switzerland is focusing on hybrid offerings that are adapted to their stakeholders. A current example is the Pop-up Houses of Switzerland in various border regions and cities, aiming to present the Swiss economy and attract investors. The concept of pop-up houses, which can only be found in one location for a short time, is said to be particularly popular with digital natives. It is interesting to note that the pop-up houses are also digitally accessible, which enriches the experience of this offer and has allowed flexibility during the Covid-19 pandemic, which is characterized by restrictions regarding face-to-face events. These offerings are also made in collaborations with corporate actors, showing the diversity of actors involved in country promotion.

CONCLUSION AND FUTURE DIRECTIONS

Digitalization has empowered numerous new actors to shape diplomatic discourse, which poses various challenges. On the one hand, traditional diplomatic actors struggle to understand and interact with these new stakeholder groups, especially on new digital communication channels. On the other hand, rising diplomatic forces like corporations still need to sense the impact of digitalization or their potential to co-create the diplomatic discourse. Until today, no study has explicitly addressed digital corporate diplomacy.

This chapter gives corporate diplomatic actors insights into the functioning of public diplomacy in the digital age. It also provides insight for both traditional and new diplomatic actors on building impactful digital diplomacy. A particular interest is given to the notion of listening, which highlights the importance of knowing and understanding digital stakeholders and how they are networked. Diplomatic actors need to abandon the idea of total control and realize the necessity to be open, adaptive, engaging, and cooperative. The illustrative example of Switzerland's digital public diplomacy shows that collaboration with various actors (e.g., cities, corporations) has become essential to cope with the challenges of today's digitalization. Further, digital diplomatic actors need to realize the potential of digital communication platforms, encouraging visual, emotional, and personal discourse in times of where one can observe distrust towards political entities considered too distant from the population's concerns.

Adapting to these new communication trends is crucial, as diplomacy may become more hybrid as societal life is becoming increasingly digital. The Covid-19 pandemic, which started in December 2019, has strongly affected diplomatic relations and made clear how urgent and necessary it is to adapt to digitalization. Bilateral talks, conferences, and international meetings have depended on tech companies' services such as the virtual platforms Zoom

396 *Handbook on digital corporate communication*

and Skype. One can observe how nations (e.g., Sweden or USA) have been building virtual embassies serving as cultural hubs or places of engagement for several years (Manor, 2016). Nowadays, cities and nations like Seoul or Barbados are already planning to build embassies and representation offices in the Metaverse, a world of augmented reality, to offer administrative and consular services (Chandran, 2021). However, despite clear advantages (lower travel costs, secure negotiation locations), many diplomatic actors highlight how vital direct human contact is for diplomatic purposes. This is just one of the issues becoming crucial with the advent of augmented reality, artificial intelligence, the internet of things, and the Web.3.0 in diplomacy, which need to be addressed in future research.

REFERENCES

Alexander, C. and Royo i Marine, A. (2020). Prohibited sub-state public diplomacy: The attempt to dissolve Catalonia's *DIPLOCAT*. *Place Branding and Public Diplomacy*, *16*, 238–250.

Anholt, S. (2005). Anholt Nation Brands Index: How does the world see America? *Journal of Advertising Research*, *45*(3), 296–304.

Balmas, M. (2018). Tell me who is your leader, and I will tell you who you are: Foreign leaders' perceived personality and public attitudes toward their countries and citizenry. *American Journal of Political Science*, *62*(2), 499–514.

BBC (2019). *HSBC sparks controversy with ad campaign.* https://www.bbc.com/news/business-46782759.

Ben & Jerry's (2021). *Ben & Jerry's will end sales of our ice cream in the occupied Palestinian territory.* https://www.benjerry.com/about-us/media-center/opt-statement.

Bergman Rosamond, A. and Hedling, E. (2022). Celebrity diplomacy during the Covid-19 pandemic? The chief-state epidemiologists as the 'face of the Swedish experiment'. *Place Branding and Public Diplomacy*, *18*, 41–43.

Bjola, C. (2016). Getting digital diplomacy right: What quantum theory can teach us about measuring impact. *Global Affairs*, *2*(3), 345–353.

Bjola, C., Cassidy, J., and Manor, I. (2019). Public diplomacy in the digital age. In J. Melissen and J. Wang (eds.), *Debating public diplomacy* (pp. 83–101). Leiden: Brill Nijhoff.

Bjola, C., Cassidy, J. A., and Manor, I. (2020). Digital public diplomacy: Business as usual or a paradigm shift? In N. Snow and N. J. Cull (eds.), *Routledge handbook of public diplomacy* (2nd edition, pp. 405–412). London: Routledge.

Bjola, C. and Pamment, J. (eds.) (2018). *Countering online propaganda and extremism: The dark side of digital diplomacy*. London: Routledge.

Bjola, C. and Zaiotti, R. (2020). Going digital: Choices and challenges for international organizations. In C. Bjola and R. Zaiotti (eds.), *Digital diplomacy and international organizations: Autonomy, legitimacy and contestation* (pp. 1–18). London: Routledge.

Bolewski, W. (2022). Corporate diplomacy: Compass for public/private management in turbulent times. In S. P. Sebastião and S. Spínola (eds.), *Diplomacy, organisations and citizens* (pp. 139–154). Cham: Palgrave Macmillan.

Carballo, M., López-Escobar, E., and McCombs, M. (2018). Communication, public opinion, and democracy: New challenges. *Communication & Society*, *31*(4), 121–133.

Casais, B. and Monteiro, P. (2019). Residents' involvement in city brand co-creation and their perceptions of city brand identity: A case study in Porto. *Place Branding and Public Diplomacy*, *15*(4), 229–237.

Castells, M. (2010). *The rise of the network society: The information age: Economy, society and culture* (2nd edition). Hoboken, NJ: Wiley-Blackwell.

Chandran, R. (2021). *Analysis: Seoul, Barbados check into metaverse as governments eye virtual presence*. Reuters, 25 November. https://www.reuters.com/markets/currencies/seoul-barbados-check-into-metaverse-governments-eye-virtual-presence-2021-11-25/.

Chariatte, J. and Ingenhoff, D. (2021). Network of cleavages? British paradiplomacy in the (digital) international discourse around Brexit. In E. Segev (ed.), *Semantic network analysis in social sciences* (pp. 112–135). New York: Routledge.

Christensen, C. (2013). @ Sweden: Curating a nation on Twitter. *Popular Communication, 11*(1), 30–46.

Cornut, J. and Dale, N. (2019). Historical, practical, and theoretical perspectives on the digitalization of diplomacy: An exploratory analysis. *Diplomacy & Statecraft, 30*(4), 829–836.

Cowan, G. and Arsenault, A. (2008). Moving from monologue to dialogue to collaboration: The three layers of public diplomacy. *The Annals of the American Academy of Political and Social Science, 616*(1), 10–30.

Cull, N. J. (2010). Public diplomacy: Seven lessons for its future from its past. *Place Branding and Public Diplomacy*, 6, 11–17.

Cull, N. J. (2011). WikiLeaks, public diplomacy 2.0 and the state of digital public diplomacy. *Place Branding and Public Diplomacy, 7*(1), 1–8.

Di Martino, L. (2019). Conceptualising public diplomacy listening on social media. *Place Branding and Public Diplomacy*, 16, 1–12.

Dinnie, K. and Sevin, E. (2020). The changing nature of nation branding: Implications for public diplomacy. In N. Snow and N. J. Cull (eds.) *Routledge handbook of public diplomacy* (2nd edition, pp. 137–144). London: Routledge.

Dodd, M. D. and Collins, S. J. (2017). Public relations message strategies and public diplomacy 2.0: An empirical analysis using Central-Eastern European and Western embassy Twitter accounts. *Public Relations Review, 43*(2), 417–425.

Dolea, A. (2018). Public diplomacy as co-constructed discourses of engagement. In K. A. Johnston and M. Taylor (eds.), *The handbook of communication engagement* (pp. 331–345). New York: Wiley.

Duncombe, C. (2019). Digital diplomacy: Emotion and identity in the public realm. *The Hague Journal of Diplomacy, 14*(1–2), 102–116.

Duran, M. (2016). Paradiplomacy as a diplomatic broker: Between separating differences and engaging commonalities. *Brill Research Perspectives in Diplomacy and Foreign Policy, 1*(3), 1–56.

Eilert, M. and Cherup, A. N. (2020). The activist company: Examining a company's pursuit of societal change through corporate activism using an institutional theoretical lens. *Journal of Public Policy & Marketing, 39*(4), 461–476.

FDFA (2017). *Switzerland seen from abroad in 2017.* https://www.eda.admin.ch/dam/eda/en/documents/das-eda/landeskommunikation/PRS-Rapport-image-suisse-2017_EN.pdf.

FDFA (2018). *Switzerland seen from abroad in 2018. Switzerland's image on Twitter and in foreign media.* https://www.eda.admin.ch/dam/eda/en/documents/das-eda/landeskommunikation/PRS-Rapport-image-suisse-2018_EN.pdf.

FDFA (2019). *Switzerland seen from abroad in 2019.* https://www.eda.admin.ch/dam/eda/en/documents/das-eda/landeskommunikation/PRS_2019_analyse_EN.pdf.

FDFA (2020a). *Switzerland seen from abroad in 2020.* https://www.eda.admin.ch/dam/eda/en/documents/das-eda/landeskommunikation/prs-jahresanalyse-2020_EN.pdf.

FDFA (2020b). *Foreign policy strategy 2020–2023.* https://www.eda.admin.ch/dam/eda/en/documents/publications/SchweizerischeAussenpolitik/Aussenpolitische-Strategie-2020-23_EN.pdf.

FDFA (2021a). *Strategy for communication abroad 2021–2024.* https://www.eda.admin.ch/dam/eda/en/documents/publications/SchweizerischeAussenpolitik/strategie-landeskommunikation-2021-2024_EN.pdf.

FDFA (2021b). *FDFA Guidelines on partnering with sponsors.* Federal Department of Foreign Affairs. https://www.admin.ch/gov/en/start/documentation/media-releases.msg-id-81738.html.

FDFA (2021c). *Travel Admin App.* Federal Department of Foreign Affairs. https://www.eda.admin.ch/eda/en/fdfa/representations-and-travel-advice/travel-advice/travel-admin-app.html.

Fitzpatrick, K. R., White, C. L., and Bier, L. M. (2020). C-suite perspectives on corporate diplomacy as a component of public diplomacy. *Place Branding and Public Diplomacy*, 16, 25–35.

Freeman, E. R. (1984). *Strategic management: A stakeholder approach.* London: Pitman.

Gurdus, L. (2017). *Goldman Sachs CEO Lloyd Blankfein shares why he started speaking out on Twitter.* CNBC, 19 June. https://www.cnbc.com/2017/06/19/goldman-sachs-ceo-details-why-he-started-speaking-out-on-twitter.html.

398 *Handbook on digital corporate communication*

Hayden, C. (2018). Digital diplomacy. In G. Martel (ed.), *The encyclopedia of diplomacy* (pp. 1–13). New York: Wiley. https://doi.org/10.1002/9781118885154.dipl0068.

Hedling, E. (2020). Storytelling in EU public diplomacy: Reputation management and recognition of success. *Place Branding and Public Diplomacy, 16*, 143–152.

Hedling, E. and Bremberg, N. (2021). Practice approaches to the digital transformations of diplomacy: Toward a new research agenda. *International Studies Review, 23*(4), 1595–1618.

Hill, S. (2020). Politics and corporate content: Situating corporate strategic communication between marketing and activism. *International Journal of Strategic Communication, 14*(5), 317–329.

Holmes, M. (2015). Digital diplomacy and international change management. In C. Bjola and M. Holmes (eds.), *Digital diplomacy* (pp. 13–32). London: Routledge.

House of Switzerland (2022). *About us*. Federal Department of Foreign Affairs. https://www.houseofswitzerland.org/about-us.

Huang, E. Q. (2020). Facebook not statebook. Defining SNS diplomacy with four modes of online diplomatic participation. *International Journal of Communication, 14*, 3885–3902.

Ingenhoff, D., Buhmann, A., White, C., Zhang, T., and Kiousis, S. (2018). Reputation spillover: Corporate crises' effects on country reputation. *Journal of Communication Management, 22*(1), 96–112.

Ingenhoff, D., Calamai, G., and Sevin, E. (2021). Key influencers in public diplomacy 2.0: A country-based social network analysis. *Social Media + Society, 7*(1), 1–12.

Ingenhoff, D. and Chariatte, J. (2020). *Solving the public diplomacy puzzle: Developing a 360 degree listening and evaluation approach to assess country images*. Los Angeles: Figueora Press.

Ingenhoff, D. and Marschlich S. (2019). Corporate diplomacy and political CSR: Similarities, differences and theoretical implications. *Public Relations Review, 45*(2), 348–371.

Ingenhoff, D., Segev, E., and Chariatte, J. (2020). The construction of country images and stereotypes: From public views to Google searches. *International Journal of Communication, 14*, 92–113.

Johnson, M. A. and Cester, X. (2015). Communicating Catalan culture in a global society. *Public Relations Review, 41*(5), 809–815.

Kampf, R., Manor, I., and Segev, E. (2015). Digital diplomacy 2.0? A cross-national comparison of public engagement in Facebook and Twitter. *The Hague Journal of Diplomacy, 10*(4), 331–362.

Kesteleyn, J., Riordan, S., and Ruël, H. (2014). Introduction: Business diplomacy. *The Hague Journal of Diplomacy, 9*(4), 303–309.

Khan, M. L., Ittefaq, M., Pantoja, Y. I. M., Raziq, M. M., and Malik, A. (2021). Public engagement model to analyze digital diplomacy on Twitter: A social media analytics framework. *International Journal of Communication, 15*, 1741–1769.

Kim, S. and Ji, Y. (2021). Positive ripple effects of corporate leaders' CSR donations amid COVID-19 on corporate and country reputations. Multi-level reputational benefits of CSR focusing on Bill Gates and Jack Ma. *Public Relations Review, 47*(4). Online First. https://doi.org/10.1016/j.pubrev.2021.102073.

Klynge, C., Ekman, M., and Waedegaard, N. J. (2020). Diplomacy in the digital age: Lessons from Denmark's TechPlomacy initiative. *The Hague Journal of Diplomacy, 15*(1–2), 185–195.

Kuznetsov, A. (2014). *Theory and practice of paradiplomacy: Subnational governments in international affairs*. London: Routledge.

Lobschat, L., Mueller, B., Eggers, F., Brandimarte, L., Diefenbach, S., Kroschke, M., and Wirtz, J. (2021). Corporate digital responsibility. *Journal of Business Research, 122*, 875–888.

Manfredi-Sánchez, J. L. (2022). Corporate diplomacy in a post-COVID-19 world. In S. P. Sebastião and S. Spínola (eds.), *Diplomacy, organisations and citizens* (pp. 125–138). Cham: Palgrave Macmillan.

Manor, I. (2016). What is digital diplomacy, and how is it practiced around the world? A brief introduction. *The 2016 Annual Review of the Diplomatist Magazine*. http://www.diplomatist.com/dipoannual2016/index.html.

Marschlich, S. and Ingenhoff, D. (2022). Public-private partnerships: How institutional linkages help to build organizational legitimacy in an international environment. *Public Relations Review, 48*(1). Online First. https://doi.org/10.1016/j.pubrev.2021.102124.

Melissen, J. (2005). *The new public diplomacy*. Basingstoke: Palgrave Macmillan.

Melissen, J. and de Keulenaar, E. V. (2017). Critical digital diplomacy as a global challenge: The South Korean experience. *Global Policy, 8*(3), 294–302.

Melissen, J. and Wang, J. (2019). Introduction: Debating public diplomacy. *The Hague Journal of Diplomacy*, *14*(1–2), 1–5.

Meta (2020). *Introducing: Digital Diplomacy on Facebook Guide. A global best practices guide for ministries of foreign affairs, embassies, consulate offices and diplomats.* https://www.facebook.com/gpa/blog/digital-diplomacy.

Nes, E. B. (2018). The role of country images in international marketing. Country-of-origin effects. In D. Ingenhoff, C. White, A. Buhmann, and S. Kiousis (eds.), *Bridging interdisciplinary perspectives on the country image, reputation, brand and identity* (pp. 33–48). London: Routledge.

Pacher, A. (2018). Strategic publics in public diplomacy: A typology and a heuristic device for multiple publics. *The Hague Journal of Diplomacy*, *13*(3), 272–296.

Qu, Y. and Carpentier, F. R. D. (2021). Practicing public diplomacy by doing good: Examining the effects of corporate social responsibility on country reputation. *International Journal of Strategic Communication*, *15*(3), 193–213.

Ruël, H., Gesink, T., and Bondarouk, T. (2015). Electronic commercial diplomacy: A research model and an empirical analysis of embassy websites. *International Journal of Diplomacy and Economy*, *2*(4), 299–327.

Segev, E. (2018). Googling the world: Global and regional information flows in Google Trends. *International Journal of Communication*, *12*, 2232–2250.

Sevin, E. and Dinnie, K. (2015). Digital channels and technologies for commercial diplomacy: Conceptualization and future research propositions. *International Journal of Diplomacy and Economy*, *2*(4), 266–277.

Sommerfeldt, E. J. and Buhmann, A. (2019). The status quo of evaluation in public diplomacy: Insights from the US State Department. *Journal of Communication Management*, *23*(3), 198–212.

Sondergaard, M. (2014). Corporate business diplomacy: Reflections on the interdisciplinary nature of the field. *The Hague Journal of Diplomacy*, *9*(4), 356–371.

Spry, D. (2019). From Delhi to Dili: Facebook diplomacy by ministries of foreign affairs in the Asia-Pacific. *The Hague Journal of Diplomacy*, *15*(1–2), 93–125.

Su, S. and Xu, M. (2015). Twitplomacy: Social media as a new platform for development of public diplomacy. *International Journal of E-Politics*, *6*(1). https://doi.org/10.4018/IJEP.2015010102.

Thelander, Å. and Cassinger, C. (2017). Brand new images? Implications of Instagram photography for place branding. *Media and Communication*, *5*(4). https://doi.org/10.17645/mac.v5i4.1053.

Turianskyi, Y. and Wekesa, B. (2021). African digital diplomacy: Emergence, evolution, and the future. *South African Journal of International Affairs*, *28*(3), 341–359.

Van der Pluijm, R. and Melissen, J. (2007). *City diplomacy: The expanding role of cities in international politics.* The Hague: Netherlands Institute of International Relations.

Van Ruler, B. (2019). Agile communication evaluation and measurement. *Journal of Communication Management*, *23*(3), 265–280.

White, C. (2015). Exploring the role of private sector corporations in public diplomacy. *Public Relations Inquiry*, *4*(3), 305–321.

White, C. (2020). Corporate diplomacy. In N. Snow and N. Cull (eds.), *Routledge handbook of public diplomacy* (2nd ed, pp. 413-421). London: Routledge.

28. Digital corporate communication and public sector organizations

Hanna Reinikainen and Chiara Valentini

INTRODUCTION

As the number of citizens getting their information and news from digital platforms has increased, many interactions today between private citizens, businesses, non-governmental organizations (NGOs), and public sector organizations have moved online. This chapter specifically focuses on public sector organizations and their communications towards citizens in the evolving digital media ecosystem.

Public sector organizations are politically mandated and regulated organizations, such as ministries, political organizations, public administrations, federal agencies, and other governmental organizations, that provide services for citizens and realize political decisions (Fredriksson and Pallas, 2018). These organizations typically focus on specific areas – such as infrastructure, livelihood, transportation, education, and health care – and operate on national, regional, and/or municipal levels (Luoma-aho and Canel, 2020). Though each public sector organization has its own specific objectives and operates within certain environments and legal parameters, all such organizations share some common traits, such as their general austerity-oriented approach, their wide but fragmented public base, and their level of citizen activism, particularly in democratic societies where citizens' scrutiny of public sector management and services has steadily increased (Luoma-aho et al., 2019). Furthermore, their communications are often "goal-oriented" supporting "public sector functions, within their specific cultural/political settings", and helping these organizations in "building and maintaining the public good and trust between citizen and authorities" (Luoma-aho and Canel, 2020, p. 10). Public sector communication is not only communication by governmental organizations, but also by public foundations, agencies, authorities, and regulators and organizations involved in public–private joint operations, such as state monopolies (Luoma-aho and Canel, 2020).

To deliver these goal-oriented communications, public sector organizations often create departments or units dedicated to managing the organization's communications and external relations. In some countries, these 'public affairs offices' oversee all matters relevant to public information and relations with external publics, and they are not to be confused with the corporate public affairs function, which involves managing an organization's sociopolitical environment by influencing political decision-making (Harris and Fleisher, 2016). These units play key roles within public sector organizations, often acting as clearing houses for information on all organization activities by, for example, preparing and issuing news releases, coordinating interactions between organization officials and news media representatives, and otherwise accommodating journalists' information needs. Today, these public sector organizational units also administer their organization's digital presence, which involves managing websites, social media, multimedia, and livestreaming; creating and disseminating digital content; and coordinating the digital communications of other departments.

Digital corporate communication and public sector organizations   401

Many communication principles and stakeholder management approaches utilized by public sector organizations in Western countries are similar to those undertaken by corporate organizations. Hence, we argue that these organizations face parallel challenges in adapting to the transformations produced by digitalization that deserve a critical attention, particularly in respect to these organizations' emerging initiatives of digital corporate communication. As we posit in this chapter, digital public sector organization communication can be understood as *the management of digital technologies to improve communication with citizens and other internal and external stakeholders to maintain the organization's most valuable intangible assets, such as legitimacy and trust among citizens*. To support our assertions, we provide an overview of the main tenets of public sector communication in the new digital environment, and we discuss how public sector organizations use digital corporate communication to serve citizens and other stakeholders and how they have adapted to the new digital environment.

We first discuss the nature of the digital environment and then expand that discourse to address significant changes in communication modes and practices of public sector organizations. We also discuss relevant changes in digital public behaviour, considering the core communicative and engagement needs of public sector organizations. Next, we introduce the primary opportunities and drawbacks of undertaking digital corporate communication to achieve public-oriented communication goals by critically examining possible negative effects of the increased digitalization of public sector activities. Finally, we present an example of a public sector communication effort by the Finnish Tax Administration to illustrate the impact of digital transformation in such organizations. The chapter concludes with suggestions for future research on digital corporate communication in the context of public sector organizations.

DEFINITIONS OF THE TOPIC AND PREVIOUS STUDIES

Research on public sector organizations and their communication has historically centred around the concepts of legitimacy and public engagement. As public sector organizations are publicly funded and conduct work for the common good, they heavily depend on legitimacy (Wæraas, 2020), which refers to a public's perceived congruence between the goals, actions, and values of the organizations and those of the broader society (Suchman, 1995). Legitimacy for public sector organizations is thus "a license to operate" that is given by citizens, the main stakeholders of these organizations (Canel and Luoma-aho, 2019), through an evaluation of what they believe these organizations should do for society and what they actually do. Because citizens "award legitimacy to the extent that they judge the organization and its activities to be beneficial to them" (Wæraas, 2020, p. 48), public opinion is highly important for public sector organizations, even more so than for corporations. On the other hand, public engagement, understood as the capacity by citizens to participate in and influence the definition and discussion of public issues, has been found to affect public satisfaction with public sector activities and, hence, directly influencing public judgements about these organizations.

Given their civic nature, public sector organizations are subjected to strong judgements by diverse stakeholders. Their operative environment is normally more complex and politically driven than those of private, corporate, and not-for-profit organizations (Luoma-aho et al., 2019). Balancing different and, at times, conflicting interests and still be perceived to be beneficial to a wide public can be a challenge (Wæraas and Byrkjeflot, 2012). Yet, failing to meet stakeholder expectations can undermine these organizations' legitimacy and, as a result, it can increase citizens' scepticism towards the value of these organizations, and even open up public criticism. If citizens' evaluations of public sector organizations are negative over time, these organizations, at the worst, would not be able to survive and, at the best, they would have several difficulties in serving citizens' needs.

Gaining and maintaining legitimacy is thus an important organizational goal for public sector organizations. Communication has been recognized as a key element for building positive impressions of these organizations' activities towards citizens and thus protecting these organizations against legitimacy challenges (Ashforth and Gibbs, 1990). Indeed, particularly in the last decade, these organizations' communications have become more complex, fulfilling different purposes. While informing citizens about public activities, decisions, and services has remained an important communicative goal, other expressive and self-centred communications have increased to help these organizations promote positive images among stakeholders (Wæraas, 2020). Even digital corporate communication undertaken by these organizations has become more about influencing multiple stakeholder groups and advocating for organizational values and policies. Partly, this is because public sector organizations are facing more and more service offering competition from other non-public organizations, resulting in an increase of civic and business participation in democratic processes (Binderkrantz et al., 2014; Bunea, 2016). Hence, they need to advocate their offering and values more proactively to retain their legitimacy.

New public management (NPM) reforms (Lovari and Valentini, 2020) have increased the importance of communication as a tool for organizing and managing activities across departments and units, for negotiating and discussing policies, and for ensuring transparency and accountability regarding organizational intentions, behaviours, and actions. Public sector organizations in many Western societies have, in fact, responded to calls for transparency, openness, and citizen-oriented communication and have successfully launched services that are, for example, based on social media (Lovari and Materassi, 2021).

Notwithstanding the progress made, many public sector organizations are still organized bureaucratically (Deverell et al., 2015), bounded by internal protocols and regulations (Gunawong et al., 2019) that hinder the opportunities for building positive relationships with citizens (Canel and Luoma-aho, 2019). Other challenges brought by digitalization are related to these organizations' capacity to adopt innovative solutions, to use emergent digital tools (Zerfass et al., 2021), and to develop and apply strategies that support visual and informal communication (Mori et al., 2020). Limited digital competencies of public sector employees, poor national or regional digital infrastructures, inadequate political and economic agendas on digitalization, and/or the lack of an internal organizational and communication culture that supports digitalization are among the most common reasons for lagging behind (Lovari and Valentini, 2020).

On the bright side, previous studies on public sector organizations show encouraging signs of digitalization of public sector communication, examining how these organizations utilize social media, for example, for building engagement and trust towards public organizations (Lovari and Materassi, 2021; Lovari and Parisi, 2015), enhancing the function and performance of authority communication during crises and disasters like pandemics (Tampere et al., 2016; Tirkkonen and Luoma-aho, 2011), and for implementing new forms of influencer communication for public sector goals (Pöyry et al., 2022). Early research also offers insights on local governments' perceptions and uses of social media as a communication tool (Graham,

Digital corporate communication and public sector organizations   403

2014), the integration of social media into government communication (Figenschou, 2020), and the possibilities for using social media to de-bureaucratize government communication structures (Meijer and Torenvlied, 2016). Together, these studies show that many public sector organizations are actively adapting to the digital environment and experimenting with innovative and informal ways to connect with citizens and other stakeholders.

WHAT IS CHANGING?

In those countries with high Internet penetration and strong political support for a digital economy, digitalization has steadily changed practices and activities inside and outside public sector organizations (Kozolanka, 2015), especially the communication activities of their public affairs offices/communication departments. Through various digital technologies, these administrative units can now more systematically listen to and inform their key stakeholders. They have also become increasingly involved with communications in hybrid media systems where various actors, technologies, and practices are merged together in response to the declining gatekeeper role of traditional media (Chadwick, 2017).

Internally, digitalization has transformed the modes, means, and approaches of employee and leadership communications. Digital platforms such as enterprise social media have increased productivity among public sector employees by substituting for Intranets and other internal communication tools in coordinating human resources and communicating their efforts (Chun and Luna-Reyes, 2012). Additionally, these technologies have improved knowledge management by serving as a repository for workplace expertise that can be transformed and reused as needed (Agerdal-Hjermind and Valentini, 2015). Externally, digitalization has enabled public sector organizations to rely less on legacy media – a process called 'disintermediation' – to distribute their messages to citizens and more on direct communications to (and from) citizens. As communication to and with stakeholders becomes more direct, digital technologies provide public sector organizations with many opportunities to enhance transparency and accountability, offering stakeholders real-time accounts of what they are doing. However, the more public sector communications become disintermediated, the more challenges the organizations face regarding credibility, trust, and legitimacy.

Other important benefits of digital communication have been found in relation to strengthening the communicative effectiveness of crisis communication plans and to support branding, listening, and media relations efforts. The use of digital channels has also increased the opportunities for public participation in public and political matters which then produce higher levels of public satisfaction with these organizations' activities (Lovari and Valentini, 2020).

Simultaneously, the behaviours of the publics are also changing. Some digital publics have become "refracted", strategically circumventing official communication sources and consuming digital content "under the radar", such as through private groups, locked platforms, and instantaneous content (Abidin, 2021, p. 3). This poses an additional challenge to public sector organizations, particularly because these organizations may need to reach out to publics who refrain from processing official digital corporate communication for alternative, unofficial ones. On the opposite side, public sector organizations are also experiencing an increase in digital activism among those digital publics who are more vocal and more diversified in their interests, demands, and expectations (Thomas, 2013). Various interest groups and minorities have been provided with platforms for mobilizing and effectively influencing policies

404 *Handbook on digital corporate communication*

and decision-making (Soriano, 2015). The growing penetration of digital technologies has increased citizen empowerment, with more citizens speaking up, venting dissatisfaction, advocating causes, and demanding changes, publicly and anonymously. Such efforts may include, for example, ridiculing the legitimacy of public sector organizations through memes (Sihvonen et al., 2020) and expressing diverging critiques on digital platforms (Ojala et al., 2019). This has increased the visibility and amplification of citizens' and other stakeholders' sometimes-conflicting demands of public sector organizations. Such developments have forced these organizations to re-evaluate their communication efforts and consider innovative ways to engage with these active citizens, resulting in a major ongoing power shift in public sector communications: Public sector organizations are no longer viewed as *having power over citizens* but, instead, are seen as *sharing their power with* citizens (Thomas, 2013). For example, the public sector organizations' traditional one-way communication channel is transitioning into a constant, real-time dialogue with various citizen groups through varied platforms (Luoma-aho and Canel, 2020). This transformation has challenged public sector organizations' human resources capacity, as multiple real-time dialogues require enough trained communication professionals to interact with citizens.

Another challenge that has emerged is determining which voices and positions the senior management of these organizations should engage with when considering future directions for public services. The obedient, subservient citizen and diligent taxpayer is being replaced by customers and partners "who expect to be involved and to get value for their money" (Luoma-aho and Canel, 2020, p. 18), but a decision must be made as to who among these customers has legitimate claims to become involved partners when public sector organizations strive to serve everyone equally. While digital environments offer new possibilities for public organizations and their communication efforts, new ways of demanding accountability from public sector organizations are also rapidly coming to light.

A closer look at the type, frequency, and format of digital interactions between public sector organizations and their stakeholders reveals that messaging strategies have changed too. Digital users both share and seek more visual and metaphorical forms of expression (Kuronen and Huhtinen, 2017) and less formal communications; they expect more fluid and emotion-driven content (Papacharissi, 2015; Wahl-Jorgensen, 2018) and less constructed and bureaucratic content. For the most part, digital corporate communication in public sector organizations is still rather informative and fact-based, addressing the publics' cognitive needs rather than engaging them in participatory exchanges and addressing emotional elements. Because of this, public sector organizations are often organized in ways that promote slow and bureaucratic (Canel and Luoma-aho, 2019; Deverell et al., 2015) communication emphasizing textual, legal, and administrative jargon. To accommodate public sector communication to the publics' changing expectations, an alternative communication genre is needed. But changing public sector communication modes and approaches to communicating and interacting with stakeholders to follow the unpredictable, sometimes surprising, and constantly changing dynamics of the digital environment can be challenging.

To address this fluid environment, public sector organizations should first change their attitudes towards communication and stakeholder relations. They would need to 'go with the flow' and act quickly, seizing opportunities as they present themselves (Huhtinen and Rantapelkonen, 2014). In other words, public sector organizations would need to match the expectations of the platforms and, thus, communicate more personally and less bureaucratically (Lovari and Valentini, 2020).

WHAT REMAINS THE SAME?

The digitalization of public sector organizations dates back to the 1990s, when the process was primarily considered a technological adoption by civil servants to operate more effectively and efficiently (Lovari and Valentini, 2020). The real disruption in public sector management logic occurred in the late 2010s, when these organizations in democratic countries started to push for more open communication, participatory cultures, and collaboration across organizational boundaries (Chadwick, 2017). The process of technological adaption is continually ongoing, as new technologies are developed to improve security, data management, and work activities. While a lot is changing in and around public sector organizations, many things still remain the same: Public sector organizations still must serve citizens and other stakeholders equally, as they deliver the same services daily to demonstrate their accountability (Ojala et al., 2019), warrant their legitimacy (Wæraas, 2020), serve the public good, and carefully listen to the sentiments of citizens and other stakeholders (Canel and Luoma-aho, 2019). Their communications are still conceived under formal legal foundations; and have been characterized by a nonpartisan, objective, and calibrated account of information, independent from political circumstances; and shaped by overall transparency in its communicative intent (Pasquier and Villeneuve, 2012).

The main goals of public sector organizations have not changed either. The culture of public participation in policy formulation, service developments, and delivery (Mergel, 2012) has given public sector organizations new ways to use digital technology to communicate about, and market their activities. For some, public sector organization advocacy "offers a vehicle for more effectively meeting the needs of the populations served, many of which are underserved and relatively high risk" (Gray et al., 2020, p. 2), such as immigrants, refugees, disabled persons, and minorities. While often not adequately recognized, public sector advocacy has been important in reaching certain objectives, such as promoting general public health, workers' rights, and cultural competency (Brady et al., 2015; Carrizales et al., 2016; Rogers et al., 2020). These and similar public-oriented goals remain relevant, but they are now achieved through the strategic use of digital platforms. Digital advocacy essentially leverages the power of digital technology to inform, connect with people, and mobilize them to act regarding a cause or issue (Johansson and Scaramuzzino, 2019). Public sector organizations are slowly but steadily increasing their use of digital technologies to promote their services and goods because of the expanding marketization of public services and to attract more clients under the user choice-based transparency and exit options (Hansen and Lindholst, 2016).

CRITICAL EXAMINATION

As public sector organizations gain ground in applying innovative practices for using digital technologies in communication strategies, they must be cautious of potential problems. For example, public sector organizations' reliance on platforms and services provided by giant, multinational tech companies to support their communication efforts has been raised as an issue of concern. Moreover, the ethics of using data and algorithms on citizens for strategizing public sector communication and the possibly delusive openness and transparency that using social media may mean to public sector communication are other considerations of importance.

Transitioning into the digital age has meant a transition into a "platformed sociality" (van Dijck, 2013, p. 5), wherein digital platforms facilitate much of "our social, cultural, political, and economic interactions and exchanges" (Plantin and Punathambekar, 2019, p. 164). While the platforms allow new forms of socialization, they are also driven by corporate interests, and they subjugate users to algorithms that manipulate the kind of content they are exposed to, as well as to the usage of their personal data and, at times, to harmful content. This raises the question as to what responsibility is held by public sector organizations that take advantage of social media platforms in their communication efforts and, thus, contribute to validating practices that may negatively impact citizens. Public sector organizations have no control over many of the platforms they use, which means the consequences of using them may be unpredictable. For instance, in October 2021, a sudden outage took down Facebook, Instagram, WhatsApp, and Facebook Messenger for several hours, impacting multiple organizations that rely on these services in their operations (Lawler and Heath, 2021). This suggests that public sector organizations that are designed to provide services for citizens should consider the possible costs of interacting with citizens through forums that may suddenly become unavailable.

Digitalization has also established data as a central asset in society, with people's personal data being particularly valuable to many organizations and their operations (Roeber et al., 2015). Digital users generate data all the time through such acts as visiting websites, making online purchases, publishing social media posts, reacting to others' posts, using location services, and employing mobile applications (Twetman and Bergmanis-Korats, 2021). In digital corporate communication, personal data can be used, for example, to target citizens with specialized content and adapt to their content preferences (Wiesenberg et al., 2017). In best-case scenarios, the use of data in digital corporate communication means that public sector organizations can serve their citizens with relevant and timely information. In the worst-case scenarios, personal data are collected and used without consent, transparency, or control, or are used as a form of political manipulation, thus leading citizens to encounter unwanted and irrelevant content (Twetman and Bergmanis-Korats, 2021). This suggests that to maintain citizens' trust, public sector organizations should be extremely cautious about gathering, handling, and using personal data. Transparency, openness, and appropriate safety measures related to personal data are vital knowledge areas and competences for public sector communicators.

Public sector organizations that integrate digital engagement into their communication strategies must also ensure that information is accessible for all citizens, including those who need support with digital tools to overcome the digital divide (Lovari and Valentini, 2020). In practice, this involves considering such measures as using multiple languages within online services, accommodating the needs of visually- and hearing-impaired citizens, and above all, considering the extent to which various citizen groups are assumed to have access to and be literate in the digital technologies utilized (Sison, 2020).

In addition, public sector organizations must also ensure inclusiveness related to culture, ethnicity, gender, sexual orientation, age, and other diverse characteristics (Sison, 2020). While diversity management has traditionally referred to fostering an organization's internal diversity, within the context of communication, diversity management has been described as reconsidering diversity as "the range of individual opinions and societal discourses that get expressed and can find resonance in organizational settings" (Trittin and Schoeneborn, 2017, p. 306). Recognizing, cultivating, empowering, and showing sensitivity towards various voices is, therefore, decisive for public sector organizations. An important concern related to power relations among citizens and other stakeholders is that certain under-represented

Digital corporate communication and public sector organizations *italic heading in running header — omit*

individuals or groups may be less vocal than other citizens or stakeholders due to their backgrounds, which may lead to an overemphasis on input from the more vocal parties (Sison, 2020). This imbalance is often easy to detect in authentic situations, such as within discussions on online forums and platforms maintained by public sector organizations. Hate speech and toxic language is nowadays a concern for all organizations, but public sector organizations especially can be perceived as having greater responsibility in ensuring their digital platforms are safe for all participants and in encouraging opinions and participation among all citizens and stakeholders, including the traditionally less vocal groups.

Finally, digital corporate communication within the public sector also draws the attention of the fourth estate on the purpose of public sector communication. Journalists critique whether tax-funded organizations should engage in practices that resemble corporate public relations (Arolainen, 2014; Hiltunen, 2021), as these are often perceived to be overly promotional, less truthful, and at times, even deceitful. Such accounts can be interpreted as a longing for the more traditional one-way communication practices of public sector organizations, which no longer respond to the current communication environment. Another paradox is evident; while public sector communication on social media is often presented as advancing openness, transparency, and dialogue with citizens (Lovari and Valentini, 2020), journalists have noted that public sector representatives often appear reluctant to provide public information, as the organizations seek to protect their public image (Hiltunen, 2021). While public sector organizations' direct interaction with citizens is important, equally important is that journalists maintain access to public sector organizations' documents and the ability to critically assess their actions and practices. Balancing these factors reflects a strategic asset for legitimacy maintenance. Digital corporate communication by public sector organizations, therefore, should be authentic rather than creating a smokescreen of openness and transparency through carefully drafted messages sent directly to citizens while blocking journalists' access to information.

ILLUSTRATIVE EXAMPLE: THE FINNISH TAX ADMINISTRATION

In October 2020, the Finnish Association of Communications Professionals (ProCom) granted the Communication Act of the Year Award to the Finnish Tax Administration. The association reported that the Finnish Tax Administration had successfully changed its public perception by communicating messages about taxation – commonly considered an uninteresting topic – that were understandable, distinctive, and funny, thus challenging other public organizations to also communicate to citizens in more inviting ways (Tax Administration, 2020). Innovative communication by the Finnish Tax Administration included, for example, Instagram livestreams of a pack of newborn puppies; 'tax meditations' published on Spotify including a calm reading of tax laws, statutes, and clauses; live tweeting of an episode of the children's show *PAW Patrol* from the perspective of tax returns; autonomous sensory meridian response (ASMR) videos published on YouTube, with the rustling sound of a tax return form; and a gif character known as the 'epic tax guy', an alter ego of a classic tax collector. While these actions may sound like tomfoolery, the Finnish Tax Administration has emphasized that the overall strategy always steers all communications, and all actions are prompted by the goal to create content that resonates with and invites interaction from citizens (Halonen, 2020). Thus, the aim of this

408   *Handbook on digital corporate communication*

communication is to support the overall strategy of the Tax Administration, i.e., ensuring tax revenue, fair tax assessment, and a positive taxpayer experience (Tax Administration, 2022).

The Finnish Tax Administration has stated that much has changed in the way it relates to citizens (Hietamäki, 2020). While previously citizens were seen as subordinates and later as taxpayers, today's citizens are perceived as customers, and even (on social media) as friends. A cultural change has occurred in which the Finnish Tax Administration has shown an increase in its trust in its customers. For example, deductible receipts are no longer required to be included in tax returns; instead, customers are asked to save the receipts for a certain amount of time and then present them to the Tax Administration, if necessary (Hietamäki, 2020). The Finnish Tax Administration has also altered its approach to serving customers. For example, most tax returns in Finland are now processed digitally, with citizens declaring their taxes through an online system. Phone calls and in-person appointments at tax offices have been steadily declining, while website and social media activity has been increasing. The change in strategic approach has shown to pay off. In 2020, the Tax Administration's social media audience grew by more than 60,000 new followers, representing a growth of 150 per cent, and the number of visits to the Administration's website increased by more than seven million (Tax Administration, 2021).

These practices suggest the Finnish Tax Administration has exploited the advantages of the digital media environment and has embraced emergent changes in digital corporate communication, including new expectations of citizens and stakeholders; indeed, according to the Administration (Hietamäki, 2020), the organization has transformed its communication style from a one-directional, textual-based authoritative approach to a more modern, multi-channel strategy that emphasizes interaction, immediacy, and visuals, and which depends on interaction. However, the Finnish Tax Administration has emphasized that significant time is needed to develop digital strategies and plans for their implementation (Hietamäki, 2020). A bureaucratic public sector organization that has never engaged in meaningful, direct interactions with citizens cannot expect to abruptly begin using the organization's Instagram account in a more informal or friendly/funny way. Social media practices always need to align with and be drawn from the overall strategy of the organization.

While these digital activities assumed by the Tax Administration drive citizens to digital services, there will always be individuals who are not able to use digital technologies. Tax offices cannot be closed entirely. Yet, directing the mass of customers to use online services may release resources to serve those customers in person, who are somehow unable to use or prevented from using the digital services. Finally, while the more interactive approach seems to have gained a positive reception from the public, risks are always included; for example, if citizen approval of the Tax Administration using taxpayer money and resources for social media interactions declines. A bigger question is the general sentiment about the fairness of collecting taxes overall when citizens are freely left to decide what to submit and report. In this case, acceptance would start to widely erode, the value of digital corporate communication would also likely be questioned.

CONCLUSION AND FUTURE DIRECTIONS

The digital environment has permanently changed the communication playing field for public sector organizations. The current, fast-paced digital environment has little room for one-way,

Digital corporate communication and public sector organizations 409

bureaucratic communication, as citizens and other stakeholders expect real-time dialogue and instant reactions from public sector organizations (Luoma-aho and Canel, 2020). The legitimacy of and trust in public sector organizations is constantly tested by polarized behaviours: some citizens are "refracted" (Abidin, 2021, p. 3) and avoid the reach of digital corporate communication, while others vent their frustration publicly and loudly, voicing their needs and expectations critically (Ojala et al., 2019; Sihvonen et al., 2020). Balancing outreach efforts to address these varied stakeholders can be difficult and is probably not even desirable. Nevertheless, listening to different voices and finding new ways to engage various publics through digital communication are two top priorities of any public sector organization working for the public interest.

Importantly, the traditionally textual-based and informational communication culture of public sector organizations is being challenged through memes and fiery emotions. Some public sector organizations are successfully adapting to address these challenges by developing and implementing new communication practices, while others are still struggling with outdated strategies. Those public sector organizations that can address altered citizens' expectations are more likely to maintain their intangible assets and their license to operate among multiple stakeholders (Canel and Luoma-aho, 2019).

The case of the Finnish Tax Administration describes the interactive, visual, and intimate approach that one public sector organization has taken to communication, perceiving citizens as customers or even as friends (on social media), reflecting a successful response to today's digital environment and citizens' changed expectations. The Finnish Tax Administration's digital communication practices also introduced an interesting angle related to understanding the impact of trust in public sector organizations. Trust is commonly understood as a key intangible asset and a measure of organizational legitimacy (Canel and Luoma-aho, 2019), meaning public sector organizations that are highly trusted by citizens – the trustors in the relationship – are more likely to succeed in their endeavours. Thus, scholars studying public sector communication have traditionally shown great interest in the degree to which citizens and stakeholders trust public sector organizations and how those organizations can gain that trust in the digital environment (see e.g., Lovari and Materassi, 2021; Reinikainen et al., 2020).

However, the example of the Finnish Tax Administration reverses this situation. By placing a high level of trust in citizens, this Administration has become the trustor and the citizens the trustees in the organization–public relations dyad. For instance, this specific administration put its confidence in citizens' behaviours related to tax declarations. This suggests the need for research to study trust and public sector organizations in the digital environment, specifically examining the trust that public sector organizations have in their citizens. Also, relevant to consider is how citizens perceive this trust, for example, when they encounter public sector organizations on social media or when they use the organization's digital services. Other questions that future research can seek to answer include: Is trust evident or does it feel non-existent? What are the possible outcomes of such trust towards citizens? And how will such trust-related matters affect the public sector's accountability and legitimacy? Trust is rarely one-sided, often mutual; hence, the digital environment can be a place to foster trusting relationships between public sector organizations and citizens.

410 *Handbook on digital corporate communication*

REFERENCES

Abidin, C. (2021). From "networked publics" to "refracted publics": A companion framework for researching "below the radar" studies. *Social Media + Society*, *7*(1). https://doi.org/10.1177/2056305120984458.

Agerdal-Hjermind, A. and Valentini, C. (2015). Blogging as a communication strategy for government agencies: A Danish case study. *International Journal of Strategic Communication*, *9*(4), 293–315.

Arolainen, T. (2014). Valtio tiivistää strategista viestintää, media arvostelee [The state strengthens strategic communication, media criticizes]. In J. Rantapelkonen (ed.), *Strategisen viestinnän salat* [The secrets of strategic communication] (pp. 40–47). Helsinki: Maanpuolustuskorkeakoulu.

Ashforth, B. E. and Gibbs, B. W. (1990). The double-edge of organizational legitimation. *Organization Science*, 1, 177–194.

Binderkrantz, A. S., Christiansen, P. M., and Pedersen, H. H. (2014). A privileged position? The influence of business interests in government consultations. *Journal of Public Administration Research and Theory*, *24*(4), 879–896.

Brady, S. R., Young, J. A., and McLeod, D. A. (2015). Utilizing digital advocacy in community organizing: Lessons learned from organizing in virtual spaces to promote worker rights and economic justice. *Journal of Community Practice*, *23*, 255–273.

Bunea, A. (2016). Designing stakeholder consultations: Reinforcing or alleviating bias in the European Union system of governance? *European Journal of Political Research*, *56*(1), 46–69.

Canel, M. and Luoma-aho, V. (2019). *Public sector communication: Closing gaps between public sector organizations and citizens.* Hoboken, NJ: John Wiley & Sons.

Carrizales, T., Zahradnik, A., and Silverio, M. (2016). Organizational advocacy of cultural competency initiatives: Lessons for public administration. *Public Administration Quarterly*, *40*(1), 126–155.

Chadwick, A. (2017). *The hybrid media system: Politics and power.* Oxford: Oxford University Press.

Chun, S. A. and Luna-Reyes, L. (2012). Social media in government. *Government Information Quarterly*, *29*(4), 441–445.

Deverell, E., Olsson, E., Wagnsson, C., Hellman, M., and Johnsson, M. (2015). Understanding public agency communication: The case of the Swedish armed forces. *Journal of Public Affairs*, *15*(4), 387–396.

Figenschou, T. U. (2020). Social bureaucracy? The integration of social media into government communication. *Communications*, *45*(1), 513–534.

Fredriksson, M. and Pallas, J. (2018). Public sector communication. In R. L. Heath and W. Johansen (eds.), *The international encyclopedia of strategic communication.* Hoboken, NJ: John Wiley & Sons.

Graham, M. W. (2014). Government communication in the digital age: Social media's effect on local government public relations. *Public Relations Inquiry*, *3*(3), 361–376.

Gray, J. S., Kaslow, N. J., and Allbaugh, L. J. (2020). Introduction to the special issue: Advocacy in public service settings. *Psychological Services*, *17*(S1), 1–4.

Gunawong, P., Thongpapanl, N., and Ferreira, C. C. (2019). A comparative study of Twitter utilization in disaster management between public and private organizations. *Journal of Public Affairs*, *19*(4), e1932.

Halonen, K. (2020). Miten verottajasta tuli someilmiö? Selvitimme, kuka epic tax guy on oikeasti ja kuka verohallinnon Instagramissa vastaa seuraajien kysymyksiin [How did the Tax Administration become a social media phenomenon? We investigated who epic tax guy really is and who answers questions on the Tax Administration's Instagram]. *MeNaiset*, 30 August. https://www.is.fi/menaiset/ilmiot/art-2000006619856.html.

Hansen, M. B. and Lindholst, A. C. (2016). Marketization revisited. *International Journal of Public Sector Management*, *29*(5), 398–408.

Harris, P., and Fleisher, C. S. (2016). *The SAGE handbook of international corporate and public affairs.* London: Sage Publications.

Hietamäki, N. (2020). *10 oppia Verohallinnon viestinnästä* [10 learnings from the communication of the Finnish Tax Administration. A webinar presentation]. Meltwater Webinar. https://www.meltwater.com/fi/resources/10-oppia-verohallinnon-viestinnasta.

Hiltunen, H. (2021). External interference in a hybrid media environment. *Journalism Practice*, *16*(10), 2106–2124. https://doi.org/10.1080/17512786.2021.1905539.

Digital corporate communication and public sector organizations 411

Huhtinen, A. and Rantapelkonen, J. (2014). Rihmastoajattelu strategisena kommunikaationa [Rhizome-thinking as strategic communication]. In J. Rantapelkonen (ed.), *Strategisen viestinnän salat* [The secrets of strategic communication] (pp. 126–139). Helsinki: Maanpuolustuskorkeakoulu.

Johansson, H. and Scaramuzzino, G. (2019). The logics of digital advocacy: Between acts of political influence and presence. *New Media & Society*, *21*(7), 1528–1545.

Kozolanka, K. (2015). Communicating strategically in government. In D. R. Holtzhausen and A. Zerfass (eds.), *The Routledge handbook of strategic communication* (pp. 394–408). London: Routledge.

Kuronen, T. and Huhtinen, A. (2017). Organizing conflict: The rhizome of Jihad. *Journal of Management Inquiry*, *26*(1), 47–61.

Lawler, R., and Heath, A. (2021). Facebook is back online after a massive outage that also took down Instagram, WhatsApp, Messenger, and Oculus. *The Verge*, 5 October. https://www.theverge.com/2021/10/4/22708989/instagram-facebook-outage-messenger-whatsapp-error.

Lovari, A. and Materassi, L. (2021). Trust me, I am the social media manager! Public sector communication's trust work in municipality social media channels. *Corporate Communications: An International Journal*, *26*(1), 55–69.

Lovari, A. and Parisi, L. (2015). Listening to digital publics: Investigating citizens' voice and engagement within Italian municipalities' Facebook pages. *Public Relations Review*, *41*(2), 205–213.

Lovari, A. and Valentini, C. (2020). Public sector communication and social media: Opportunities and limits of current policies, activities, and practices. In V. Luoma-aho and M.-J. Canel (eds.), *The handbook of public sector communication* (pp. 315–328). Hoboken, NJ: John Wiley & Sons.

Luoma-aho, V. and Canel, M.-J. (2020). Introduction to public sector communication. In V. Luoma-aho and M.-J. Canel (eds.), *The handbook of public sector communication* (pp. 1–26). Hoboken, NJ: John Wiley & Sons.

Luoma-aho, V., Canel, M.-J., and Sanders, K. (2019). Global public sector and political communication. In K. Sriramesh and D. Vercic (eds.), *The global public relations handbook* (3rd edition, pp. 111–119). London: Routledge.

Meijer, A. J. and Torenvlied, R. (2016). Social media and the new organization of government communications: An empirical analysis of Twitter usage by the Dutch police. *American Review of Public Administration*, *46*(2), 143–161.

Mergel, I. (2012). *Social media in the public sector: A guide to participation, collaboration, and transparency in the networked world*. Hoboken, NJ: John Wiley & Sons.

Mori, E., Barabaschi, B., Cantoni, F., and Virtuani, R. (2020). Local governments' communication through Facebook: Evidences from COVID-19 pandemic in Italy. *Journal of Public Affairs*, *21*(4). https://doi.org/10.1002/pa.2551.

Ojala, M., Pantti, M., and Laaksonen, S.-M. (2019). Networked publics as agents of accountability: Online interactions between citizens, the media and immigration officials during the European refugee crisis. *New Media & Society*, *21*(2), 279–297.

Papacharissi, Z. (2015). *Affective publics: Sentiment, technology, and politics.* Oxford: Oxford University Press.

Pasquier, M. and Villeneuve, J.-P. (2012). *Marketing management and communications in the public sector*. London: Routledge.

Plantin, J.-C. and Punathambekar, A. (2019). Digital media infrastructures: Pipes, platforms, and politics. *Media, Culture & Society*, *41*(2), 163–174.

Pöyry, E., Reinikainen, H., and Luoma-aho, V. (2022). The role of social media influencers in public health communication: Case COVID-19 pandemic. *International Journal of Strategic Communication*, *16*(3), 469–484.

Reinikainen, H., Kari, J. T., and Luoma-aho, V. (2020). Generation Z and organizational listening on social media. *Media and Communication*, *8*(2), 185–196.

Roeber, B., Rehse, O., Knorrek, R., and Thomsen, B. (2015). Personal data: How context shapes consumers' data sharing with organizations from various sectors. *Electron Markets*, *25*, 95–108.

Rogers, M. R., Marraccini, M. E., O'Bryon, E. C., Dupont-Frechette, J. A., and Lubiner, A. G. (2020). Advocates in public service settings: Voices from the field. Psychological Services, 17(Suppl. 1), 44–55.

Sihvonen, T., Koskela, M., and Laaksonen, S.-M. (2020). Tunipaloja rajapinnoilla? Tampereen yliopiston legitimiteettikamppailut hybridissä mediatilassa [Tuni-fires on boundaries? Discursive struggles

412 *Handbook on digital corporate communication*

over the legitimacy of the Tampere University in the hybrid media system]. *Media & Viestintä*, *43*(4), 272–302.

Sison, M. D. (2020). Public sector communicators as global citizens: Toward diversity and inclusivity. In V. Luoma-aho and M.-J. Canel (eds.), *The handbook of public sector communication* (pp. 345–359). Hoboken, NJ: John Wiley & Sons.

Soriano, C. M. (2015). Strategic activism for democratization and social change. In D. R. Holtzhausen and A. Zerfass (eds.), *The Routledge handbook of strategic communication* (pp. 424–438). London: Routledge.

Suchman, M. C. (1995). Managing legitimacy: Strategic and institutional approaches. *Academy of Management Review*, *20*, 571–610.

Tampere, P., Tampere, K., and Luoma-aho, V. (2016). Facebook discussion of a crisis: Authority communication and its relationship to citizens. *Corporate Communications: An International Journal*, *21*(4), 414–434.

Tax Administration (2020). *Verohallinnon viestintä on valittu vuoden viestintäteoksi* [The communication of the Tax Administration awarded as the communication act of the year]. Verohallinto. https://www.vero.fi/tietoa-verohallinnosta/uutishuone/uutiset/uutiset/2020/verohallinnon-viestint%C3%A4 -on-valittu-vuoden-viestint%C3%A4teoksi/.

Tax Administration (2021). *Annual Report.* Verohallinto. https://www.vero.fi/en/About-us/finnish-tax -administration/year-2020/.

Tax Administration (2022). *Tax Administration Strategy.* Verohallinto. https://www.vero.fi/en/About -us/finnish-tax-administration/strategy/.

Thomas, J. C. (2013). Citizen, customer, partner: Rethinking the place of the public in public management. *Public Administration Review*, *73*(6), 786–796.

Tirkkonen, P. and Luoma-aho, V. (2011). Online authority communication during an epidemic: A Finnish example. *Public Relations Review*, *37*(2), 172–174.

Trittin, H. and Schoeneborn, D. (2017). Diversity as polyphony: Reconceptualizing diversity management from a communication-centered perspective. *Journal of Business Ethics*, *144*, 305–322.

Twetman, H. and Bergmanis-Korats, G. (2021). *Data brokers and security.* NATO Strategic Communications Centre of Excellence. https://stratcomcoe.org/publications/data-brokers-and -security/17.

van Dijck, J. (2013). *The culture of connectivity: A critical history of social media.* Oxford: Oxford University Press.

Wæraas, A. (2020). Public sector communication and organizational legitimacy. In V. Luoma-aho and M.-J. Canel (eds.), *The handbook of public sector communication* (pp. 45–58). Hoboken, NJ: John Wiley & Sons.

Wæraas, A. and Byrkjeflot, H. (2012). Public sector organizations and reputation management: Five problems. *International Public Management Journal*, *15*, 186–206.

Wahl-Jorgensen, K. (2018). The emotional architecture of social media. In Z. Papacharissi (ed.), *A networked self and platforms, stories, connections* (pp. 77–93). London: Routledge.

Wiesenberg, M., Zerfass, A., and Moreno, A. (2017). Big data and automation in strategic communication. *International Journal of Strategic Communication*, *11*(2), 95–114.

Zerfass, A., Buhmann, A., Tench, R., Verčič, D., and Moreno, A. (2021). *European Communication Monitor 2021. CommTech and digital infrastructure, video-conferencing, and future roles for communication professionals. Results of a survey in 46 countries.* EUPRERA/EACD. https://www. communicationmonitor.eu/2021/05/21/ecm-european-communication-monitor-2021/.

29. Digital corporate communication and co-productive citizen engagement
Louis Pierre Philippe Homont, María-José Canel and Vilma Luoma-aho

INTRODUCTION

Digital technologies are expanding the possibilities to disseminate information, and with it, new social demands for openness, interactivity, participation and information sharing in the public sector are emerging (Moon, 2018; Santos et al., 2019). Regarding citizen participation in the form of co-production, scholars argue that "the advent of the Internet's unique many-to-many interactivity and of ubiquitous communications promises to enable co-production on an unprecedented scale" (Linders, 2012, p. 446). This chapter attempts to explore this unprecedented scale by looking at how digital tools and technologies are enabling public sector and government organizations to enhance engagement with and among their stakeholders.

This chapter focuses on engagement in the form of co-production – a concept that, as is argued below, implies that citizens and authorities are equal participants in the production of public services (Tuurnas, 2020), and follows the assumption that co-production is valuable for it contributes to long-term relationships which in turn foster organizational intangible assets providing benefits for organizations, citizens and society at large (Canel and Luoma-aho, 2019). The scope of the chapter is confined to the public sector, which includes all those public authority organizations operating on several levels (national, regional and municipal), that provide public services and that have politically elected and appointed officials as well as public servants.

The goal of the chapter is to explore the relation between digital corporate communication and co-productive citizen engagement. The structure is as follows. First, the conceptual framework is presented. Second, the changes in ICTs that shape the way public sector organizations (PSOs) and citizens communicate for co-producing experiences are discussed. Benefits and risks of ICTs for co-production are then critically examined. Finally, an illustrative example of digital co-production is offered from which lessons are drawn about how to enhance co-productive citizen engagement.

DEFINITIONS OF THE TOPIC AND PREVIOUS STUDIES

The theory framework of this chapter links digital corporate communication and co-productive citizen engagement concepts. Starting from a broad concept, *corporate communication* has been defined as "a management function that offers a framework for the effective coordination of all internal and external communication with the overall purpose of establishing and maintaining favourable reputations with stakeholder groups upon which the organization is

414 *Handbook on digital corporate communication*

dependent" (Cornelissen, 2008, p. 5). One of the key issues in scholarly definitions is whether the purpose of this communication is confined to the benefit of the corporation or whether it includes the benefit of stakeholders.

Although it is beyond the scope of this chapter to elaborate on the normative debates that definitions trigger, this chapter aligns with Badham and Luoma-aho's definition of *digital corporate communication* (DCC) provided in Chapter 1 of this volume: "An organization's strategic management of digital technologies, digital infrastructures and digitalization processes to improve communication with internal and external stakeholders and more broadly within society for the maintenance of organizational tangible and intangible assets" (p. 9). We understand there is a normative implication in this definition to the extent that maintaining intangible assets also entails benefiting stakeholders, something which is more explicitly profiled in the following definition of *public sector communication*: "goal-oriented communication ... with the purpose of building and maintaining the public good and trust between citizens and authorities" (Canel and Luoma-aho, 2019, p. 33). Therefore, the key point that emerges from this theory framework is whether digital communication undertaken by public sector organizations builds some form of intangible value, and this allows refinement of the goal of this chapter in the following terms: to explore the extent to which digital corporate communication in the public sector may help build intangible value in the form of co-productive citizen engagement.

The concept of *citizen engagement* entails issues related to citizen–PSO dialogue, involvement and interaction (Piqueiras et al., 2020; Yang et al., 2021) that, again, fall beyond the scope of this chapter. It is the specific approach of this chapter (the possible intangible value generated with ICTs) that guides the conceptualization of this term as the "intangible asset that measures the capacity of an organization to get citizens involved in public administration processes" (Canel and Luoma-aho, 2019, p. 190). More specifically, here citizen involvement in public management is explored under the notion of '*co-production*' (Bovaird, 2007; Bovaird and Loeffler, 2012; Bovaird et al., 2015; Brandsen and Honingh, 2016; Tuurnas, 2020), and it builds on the following definition: "[the] relationship between a paid employee of an organization and (groups of) individual citizens that requires a direct and active contribution from these citizens to the work of the organization" (Brandsen and Honingh, 2016, p. 431). Co-production is a form of citizen engagement by which citizens engage with public sector organizations (Piqueiras et al., 2020).

The chapter explores how digital communication in the public sector may expand, increase and improve the relationship between public sector authorities and individual citizens to jointly work on public policies and services. There is still little systematic evidence about how digital technologies affect co-production in practice (Lember et al., 2019, p. 1680). For the purpose of this chapter, the following definitions are adopted: *Digital Citizen Engagement* (DCE) is "the use of new media/digital information and communication technologies to create or enhance the communication channels that facilitate the interaction between citizens and governments" (World Bank, 2016, cited in Malhotra et al., 2019, pp. 149–150); and *Digital Co-production* (DCP) is the "joint and collaborative web-based production of public services by the government and its citizens" (Moon, 2018, p. 295), including the utilization of digital platforms, social media and smartphone apps.

Digital corporate communication and co-productive citizen engagement 415

WHAT IS CHANGING IN THE DEVELOPMENT OF DIGITAL CO-PRODUCTION?

It has been argued that ICTs increase interactivity to an unprecedented scale (Linders, 2012, p. 446; Sorrentino et al., 2018). By enhancing the amount of information available for citizens and public sector organizations (Moon, 2018; Yang et al., 2021), ICTs provide a set of opportunities for governments to engage citizens (Cho and Melisa, 2021; Clifton et al., 2020; Meijer et al., 2018; Yuan, 2019). In this sense, Lember et al. (2019) argue that ICTs support a swifter, broader, more efficient and real-time flow of information between citizens and public sector organizations, thus affecting the scale and the way through which both sides interact. Given that co-production is associated with the establishment of dialogue (Loeffler and Bovaird, 2018), it seems reasonable to state that digital technologies could strengthen the positive outcome of this specific form of citizen engagement.

The definition of digital co-production is subject to debate about whether a new phenomenon can be identified. There are scholars who claim that the use of digital platforms would allow new forms of co-production (Cho and Melisa, 2021; Cordella and Palleti, 2017; Lember, 2018), while for others, it simply adds a new component to it. Alam considers that digital co-production enabled by social media platforms challenges traditional co-production in the sense that, since the latter is linked to face-to-face interactions and long-term relationships, considerable resources are required (Alam, 2021, p. 1089). Digital technologies bring higher possibilities for co-production to develop.

In analysing the possibilities that ICTs entail for digital co-production in the public sector, two areas of change may be examined according to who is initiating the communication, whether organizations or citizens.

Communicating with Citizens for Engagement

Public sector organizations may find in digital technologies better ways of reaching citizens. It has been extensively argued that ICTs represent key elements for public sector organizations to better understand citizens' preferences, needs and issues (Lember et al., 2019; Sideri et al., 2019; Yuan, 2019). A better understanding of stakeholders enables crafting better communication strategies to address them (Canel and Luoma-aho, 2019; Krishnan et al., 2018; Tuurnas, 2020). Among benefits, it is also mentioned that ICTs enable public sector organizations' communication with citizens by lowering the required costs and efforts (Cho and Melisa, 2021; Yang et al., 2021).

Elaborating on the new opportunities of technologies to engage citizens, Lember et al. identify the following (2019, pp. 1670–1672): sensing technologies may provide accurate real-time data and strengthen the ability of public administrations to attune with citizens' needs; social media facilitate gathering citizens' views; machine learning enables collecting and analysing citizens' inputs in a way that leads to a better understanding of social needs and preferences; and finally, actuation technologies such as robotics may help develop citizen engagement with less effort from citizens.

A specific area of analysis is that of public organizations' possibilities to manage citizens' motivation for engagement. If well-used, some digital tools can generate higher motivation levels (De Jong et al., 2019; Lember et al., 2019), for example, via the personalization of data and of services. Here, according to Krishnan et al. (2018) and Valdez-Mendia and

Flores-Cuautle (2022), personalization has to do with recognizing and treating users as individuals through messages that are crafted, taking into account their characteristics and contexts. In this sense, a gamification strategy, which consists of the collection of users' data through a game, may provide new incentives for citizens to participate in the crowdsourcing of public services (Mergel, 2016). By increasing citizen motivation, ICTs may ultimately positively affect citizens' participation in co-production (Clifton et al., 2020; Malhotra et al., 2019; Moon, 2018).

Citizen Communication with Governments to Engage in Public Management

The second area of analysis looks at changes from the citizen perspective. It has been stated that digital technologies change the way citizens can communicate with their governments (Jalonen et al., 2021; Moon, 2018). In fact, ICTs allow citizens to search and share information, and to create new forms of organization to collectively resolve problems (Jurgens and Helsloot, 2018). By providing features such as opinion maps, surveys, comments, solutions' simulation, voting and ranking ideas, digital tools facilitate the collaboration, discussion and sharing of ideas among citizens (Falco and Kleinhans, 2018, pp. 17–18). In addition, as they allow citizens to crowdsource data and report problems, digital tools enable citizens to engage in public services through co-production (Allen et al., 2020; Jalonen et al., 2021; Lember et al., 2019; Yuan, 2019).

WHAT REMAINS THE SAME?

The need to serve and engage citizens in democratic settings is almost as old as democracy itself. The ideals in public service remain much the same throughout different stages of development of technology or other trends in history. The aim of public value remains at the core of much public sector communication and collaboration with citizens (Canel and Luoma-aho, 2019).

As humans change slower than technologies develop, many times the affordances of technology do not manifest in reality as planned despite inclusion and transparency potential between the different stakeholders on new media platforms (Aten and Thomas, 2016). What remains the same in DCP is the fact that most citizens are still passive and uninterested in active collaboration with public sector organizations, no matter the technological advances enabling interaction (Delli Carpini, 2020). Technology merely enables participation, but does not motivate it, and sometimes it actually provides a false positive of being effective, as in the case of clicktivism, online activism and providing support via easy solutions such as likes on social media. Furthermore, as the adoption of digital technologies is often slow, one could argue that many public sector organizations globally still function with very little co-production in practice, relying on the traditional model of one-way informing of citizens about public management issues (Canel and Luoma-aho, 2019).

CRITICAL EXAMINATION: BENEFITS AND RISKS OF ICTs FOR CO-PRODUCTIVE CITIZEN ENGAGEMENT

In exploring the development of ICTs for supporting digital citizen engagement and co-production, several risks should be taken into account. Among those identified by the literature, there is the digital divide, understood as "the gap between people who have adequate access to information and communication technology and people who have poor or no access to [it]" (Lythreatis et al., 2022, p. 1). The digital divide can be evaluated in terms of Internet accessibility or of digital skills (Sorrentino et al., 2018, p. 283). Individuals' possibilities to participate in public and social issues are reduced, and with it, social and economic inequalities reinforced (Ragnedda, 2017, cited in Lythreatis et al., 2022, p. 1; Ribeiro et al., 2018). The digital divide could even lead to non-representative co-produced services, potentially enabling government illegitimacy (Linders, 2012). To face this risk, the use of smartphones and apps (Ye and Yang, 2020), and the equipment of citizens with basic ICT tools and digital skills (Sari et al., 2018) could be of help. If not properly equipped, governments could otherwise burnout the few participants in digital co-production (Linders, 2012), reduce motivation levels to co-produce and ultimately lower citizen engagement.

Digital co-production might also be associated with the emergence of a new kind of stakeholder, fakeholders, defined as "opinions, socio-bots and stakeholders artificially generated by either individuals or persona-creating software and algorithms to either oppose or support an issue" (Luoma-aho, 2015, p. 14). These fakeholders may damage co-production by practising one-sided interaction (Piqueiras et al., 2020), and hence influence decision-making to serve not joint interests but their own.

Scholars also point out the political issue of who has the control over production processes in digital co-production (Lember et al., 2019, p. 1675): ICTs allow for including external stakeholders in decision-making, and who the government finally includes in the process is subject to controversies. It could happen, for instance, that a specific party or socio-political activist group is in a better position to access co-production opportunities, thus creating power imbalances in the co-production of public services.

Finally, the 'echo chamber' phenomenon is also a risk for the development of digital co-production, and it occurs as "a mechanism [that] reinforces an existing opinion within a group, and, as a result, move the entire group toward more extreme positions" (Cinelli et al., 2021, p. 1). By fostering polarization, this phenomenon could nourish the clash of values among different co-producing stakeholders, which hinders the co-production process itself (Bovaird, 2007).

The implementation of digital tools for engaging citizens also engenders several challenges, among which there is the digital capacitation of officials (Clifton et al., 2020; Falco and Kleinhans, 2018; Khine et al., 2021; Kumar et al., 2017). Public sector organizations are having to undertake motivation strategies in order to battle potential resistance to change and involve employees in ways of doing which are different from those they are used to (Paletti, 2016; Wamsler et al., 2020). Finally, digital co-production challenges current regulations related to digital accessibility, privacy, data protection and security policies (Chen et al., 2020).

418 *Handbook on digital corporate communication*

ILLUSTRATIVE EXAMPLE: MADRID CITY COUNCIL'S MOBILE APP FOR CITY MANAGEMENT

It has already been mentioned that there is still little systematic evidence about how digital technologies affect co-production in practice, and this section presents an analysis of a government initiative, the Madrid Móvil app of the Madrid City Council. The focus of the analysis is whether the benefits and opportunities offered by ITCs in co-production may be associated with a higher intangible value, and the latter is looked at in terms of citizen participation. Data collection was carried out through the analysis of the information provided by Madrid City Council's website and apps, as well as via the use of this app by the authors.

Two areas are explored below. First, the extent to which the deployed digital corporate communication reflects the changes and possibilities for digital co-production that have already been discussed; and second, the extent to which the developed digital co-production may be associated with intangible value.

The Context

In 2014, Madrid City Council developed a smartphone app with the purpose of facilitating the local government's communication with citizens (VDA, 2014). Operationally, the app established connection with citizens by requesting their registration through email address, Facebook or a specific municipal account (an account through which the user can access services provided by the municipality). From there, several city council portals can be accessed to get involved in different activities such as the following. In the transparency portal users can access data and news feeds to follow up on the city council performance. Users can also arrange appointments for local services such as sports activities in public buildings. They can proactively get involved in public management using the "avisos" (notices) option with which they can create a geolocated post to report problems (i.e., ordure in public areas). An "aviso" has the following process: once the post is created, the user receives a ticket with information to follow up on the notice; this information includes the responsible municipal department and also the status (completed, in process, or rejected). It also has the possibility for other nearby users to support, report and comment on it. Finally, users are notified when the problem is actually solved (Madrid, n.d.a).

In terms of the policy cycle, this app allows citizens to get involved in co-production at the design as well as at the implementation phase of public policies. A single platform includes full information of local public services and the interaction of participants. A "social community of notices and petitions" is created that, as claimed by the organization, "enhances the possibility of sharing information among citizens and of engendering a shared view of the notices and petitions of the neighbourhood" (Madrid, n.d.a, para. 2).

New Opportunities for Local Government and Citizens to Communicate via ICTs

To what extent do ICTs support the Madrid City Council in the challenge of communicating with citizens to engage them in public management via the Madrid Móvil app? And, to what extent do ICTs enable Madrid's citizens to communicate with the Madrid City Council to engage in co-producing via the Madrid Móvil app? Table 29.1 shows information collected from the analysis. The rows indicate the different areas in which ICTs can operate (first

Digital corporate communication and co-productive citizen engagement 419

Table 29.1   *Madrid City Council's and citizens' new possibilities to engage in co-production via the Madrid Móvil app*

	Changes in communication due to ICTs (based on literature review)		Illustrative example
Areas of change	Opportunities presented by ICTs for public sector organizations	Opportunities presented by ICTs for citizens	What co-production via Madrid Móvil shows
Operational facilities	Less significant organizational resources. Lower costs of government actions for engaging citizens.	Easy access to public authorities. Less time is required to get involved in public management.	Involvement of citizens without requiring from them a face-to-face encounter or a visit to the official building. The resources that are implied in the Madrid Móvil app are the app development and maintenance, and development of artificial intelligence.
Real-time information	Real-time data collection.	Real-time reporting.	The app is available 24/7, allowing a real-time bi-directional communication between the organization and users.
Better data	Data crowdsourcing.	Problem reporting. Collective problem solving.	Data are created by users when they post "avisos", comment on, support and report other posts.
Better interaction	Multidirectional, interconnected and dynamic flow of information that reshapes the existing relationships.	Reliable information searching and sharing. New possibilities to access authorities and other citizens.	Real-time and bi-directional communication is enabled via the city council's portals and news feeds (from the municipality to users) and through "avisos" (from users to the municipality).
Mutual knowledge	New ways for the collection and analysis of citizens' views. Better understanding of citizens' needs.	Better information about how the organization performs.	Madrid Móvil allows exchange of information with which: the local government collects real-time information of citizens' needs; citizens can follow up on how the local government manages the city.
Co-produced public management	Engagement with citizens in public service design and delivery.	Collective problem discussion and solving via opinion maps, surveys, simulation of solutions, dissemination of ideas, voting.	The government and citizens are jointly involved in public service design and implementation through: - the exchange of information; - the co-arrangement of public services; - the sharing and commenting of information with other citizens; - transparent access to public information on public management.

Source: Authors' own elaboration.

column) presenting new opportunities both for the public sector organization (second column) and citizens (third column); these columns synthesize the review of literature presented in the first part of this chapter. The fourth column summarizes the analysis of these changes to this specific digital co-production initiative (Madrid Móvil).

The co-production that Madrid Móvil allows shows several of the opportunities that ICTs provide according to the literature review. The app represents a new way for both the local government and Madrilian citizens to exchange information in the following areas: more operational facilities (less time and human and technical capital are needed), real-time information

420   *Handbook on digital corporate communication*

and better data about each other, which ultimately enriches mutual interaction and knowledge. By allowing users to share their opinions and needs, to comment on other users' posts and to follow up on how the municipality is responding to their requests, Madrid Móvil (a) helps the local government to better understand and listen to citizens, and to collect information from them that enables efficiency and efficacy in public management; and (b) allows citizens to be better contextualized and aware of the organization's performance and other citizens' needs and reactions. What Madrid Móvil shows is that, ultimately, a better interaction, data and an increased mutual knowledge enable joint efforts for the co-production of public services.

Intangible Value Measured in Terms of Citizens' Participation

To what extent did this app build intangible value? Information for the analysis was provided by the open data webpage of the Madrid City Council (Madrid, n.d.b) regarding citizen participation, represented in the form of "avisos" received and solved. It has to be mentioned that the app is not the only channel available for posting notices. Citizens can also use traditional (or offline) channels such as the Madrid Council's phone number 010, the Citizen Attention Offices and the offices for specific public services such as the Canal Isabel II (the public company in charge of water cycle management).

Table 29.2 represents through-app notices versus non-app notices (meaning all the notices received via any channel other than the app). The table includes data for 2019 and 2020.

Table 29.2   Notices received and solved (Madrid Móvil versus non-Madrid Móvil)

"Avisos"	2019			2020		
	Received	Solved	% of solved over received	Received	Solved	% of solved over received
Via-Madrid Móvil notices	61,350	47,481	77.39	68,444	54,929	80.25
Non-Madrid Móvil notices	422,217	376,515	89.18	381,085	335,002	87.91

Source: Authors' own elaboration based on data from Madrid Open Data Platform (Madrid, n.d.b).

Data shows clearly that non-app channels are still much more used: in 2019, 422,217 notices were received through non-app channels, while only 61,350 notices came through the app. It seems Madrilian citizens are still not very familiar with the app. However, comparative data across time shows a slight increasing trend for use of the Madrid Móvil app: while through-app notices increased (from 61,350 to 68,444), the non-app notices decreased (from 422,217 to 381,085). This decrease can be explained by the lockdown caused by the Covid-19 pandemic in 2020, in which it was easier to resort to the app than other channels. Finally, it is interesting to note that the rate of solved notices increased for through-apps (from 77.39 per cent to 80.25 per cent) while it decreased for non-app notices (from 89.18 per cent to 87.91 per cent). There is not much data to account for this, but it could be reasonably stated that in circumstances such as a pandemic lockdown, Madrid Móvil ended up performing slightly better.

Table 29.3 specifies data for all the different channels, allowing for contrast of traditional channels with digital ones as well as for analysis of the app as compared with other digital channels.

Table 29.3   Notices received and solved (traditional channels versus digital channels)

	2019			2020		
	Received	Solved	% of solved over received	Received	Solved	% of solved over received
Traditional channels:	*343,644*	*310,008*	*90.21*	*270,669*	*246,878*	*91.21*
Telephone 010						
Canal Isabel II						
Citizen Attention Offices	334,008	302,539	90.58	260,894	239,545	91.82
Suggestions and	5	5	100	2	1	50
complaints	75	57	76	261	187	71.65
Urban woodland unit	9,220				6,947	
	336	7,231	78.43	9,039	198	76.86
		176	52.38	473		41.86
Digital channels:	*139,922*	*113,986*	*81.46*	*178,860*	*143,053*	*79.98*
Madrid Móvil app	61,349	47,481	77.39	68,444	54,930	80.26
Madrid City Website	52,295	44,012	84.16	105,223	83,512	79.37
Twitter	25,429	21,750	85.53	4,896	4,335	88.54
Email	53	48	90.57	80	73	91.25
Suggestions Council Portal	796	695	87.31	217	203	93.55
Total	483,566	423,994	87.68	449,529	389,931	86.74

Source: Authors' own elaboration based on data from Madrid Open Data Platform (Madrid, n.d.b).

Data shows, again, Madrid citizens' predominant resort to traditional channel use: notices received through traditional channels such as telephone and physical offices are, in 2019, more than double (343,644) those received through digital channels (139,922). The telephone is, by far, the most used channel (334,008 notices).

Looking at Madrid Móvil comparatively with other digital channels, it seems that, in 2019, this was the most used channel: almost half of the notices coming from the digital channels came through this app, doubling even social media networks such as Twitter. It seems that this tool was the first driver of citizens participation among digital channels.

The evolution from 2019 to 2020 shows a telling trend: there is an increase of digital channel use (from 139,922 to 178,860, equating to +27.83 per cent) and a decrease in the use of the traditional ones (from 343,644 to 270,669, equating to −21.24 per cent). Citizens' use of the Madrid City website almost doubled between 2019 and 2020 while use of the Madrid Móvil app increased less, from 61,349 to 68,444 received notices.

Overall, and despite the limitations of the presented data, it is reasonable to state that in circumstances such as a pandemic lockdown, Madrid Móvil ended up performing slightly better than other channels; that digital channels made up for the drawbacks that the pandemic could have caused for citizens to participate and get involved in co-production; and that an increase in citizens' use of digital communication may have helped them to get more familiar with digital tools, hence establishing a trend which in the future may be more solid in terms of citizen engagement.

Some comment can finally be made about how Madrid Móvil faces the risks associated to ICTs for digital citizen engagement and digital co-production. Regarding the digital divide, Madrid City Council still allows citizens to report problems and give suggestions through traditional channels and, as the data shows, the latter are available and more used by citizens.

422 *Handbook on digital corporate communication*

To address the problem of fakeholders, Madrid Móvil offers two solutions. First, users are required to register through an email address or by creating a municipal account; no one can post a notice without registering. Second, users can only post a notice if they are physically within the area (the app checks geo-localization).

Lessons Learned

The illustrative case shows that the use of digital technologies by public sector organizations for building citizen engagement is progressing within the context of other both online and offline channels. This case shows citizens' predominant use of the latter. Public sector organizations should combine online with offline communication in order to minimize the possible negative effects of the digital divide and of echo chambers. By keeping traditional ways of communicating with citizens, the engagement of non-digital-skilled citizens will be preserved, and thus digital co-production will not harm the representation of the social majority in the provision of public services.

In this illustrative example, ICTs appeared to make up for the difficulties caused by the pandemic to communicate with citizens and to get them involved in public management. Where there is cross-time comparative data, an increase in the use of digital channels is shown parallel to a decrease in offline ones. This may mean that citizens have become a bit more familiar with digital communication thanks to the pandemic, and that this higher familiarity will remain in the future in favour of the development of citizen participation and engagement. Overall, the use of digital communication may increase the participation of citizens in co-production of public services and policies.

CONCLUSION AND FUTURE DIRECTIONS

This chapter has explored how digital corporate communication employed by public sector organizations may build intangible value via co-productive citizen engagement. It analysed first the extent to which ICT allows organizations to reach out to citizens and get them to participate in public management; and second, the extent to which ICT enables citizens to interact better with public sector organizations and participate in public management. The exploration of an illustrative example of digital co-production has shown that the use of digital communication by public sector organizations for building citizen engagement is making its way within the context of other both online and offline channels; that ICTs made up for the difficulties caused by the pandemic to contact citizens and to get them to participate in public management, thus establishing a trend of increase in the participation of digital coproduction which may remain in the future; and that governments should keep working on strategies that avoid risks such as those of echo chambers, the digital divide and of fakeholders. Overall, the analysed example shows that citizen engagement became co-production via ICTs, enabling the local government and citizens improved interaction based on better and real-time data, mutual knowledge and joint efforts in public services; and that this digital co-production is associated with higher intangible value due to better possibilities of citizen participation. Further research should develop metrics and indicators to more specifically identify and assess the intangible value that digital corporate communication builds in the form of digital co-productive citizen engagement.

REFERENCES

Alam, L. (2021). Many hands make light work: Towards a framework of digital co-production to co-creation on social platforms. *Information Technology and People*, *34*, 1087–1118.

Allen, B., Tamindael, L. E., Bickerton, S. H., and Cho, W. (2020). Does citizen coproduction lead to better urban services in smart cities projects? An empirical study on e-participation in a mobile big data platform. *Government Information Quarterly*, *37*(1), 101412.

Aten, K. and Thomas, G. (2016). Crowdsourcing strategizing: Communication technology affordances and the communicative constitution of organizational strategy. *International Journal of Business Communication*, *53*(2), 148–180.

Bovaird, T. (2007). Beyond engagement and participation: User and community coproduction of public services. *Public Administration Review*, *67*(5), 846–860.

Bovaird, T. and Loeffler, E. (2012). From engagement to co-production: The contribution of users and communities to outcomes and public value. *Voluntas: International Journal of Voluntary and Nonprofit Organizations*, *23*(4), 1119–1138.

Bovaird, T., Van Ryzin, G., Loeffler, E., and Parrado, S. (2015). Activating citizens to participate in collective co-production of public services. *Journal of Social Policy*, *44*(1), 1–23.

Brandsen, T. and Honingh, M. (2016). Distinguishing different types of co-production: A conceptual analysis based on the classical definitions. *Public Administration Review*, *76*(3), 427–435.

Canel, M. and Luoma-aho, V. (2019). *Public sector communication: Closing gaps between public sector organizations and citizens*. Hoboken, NJ: John Wiley & Sons.

Chen, Q., Min, C., Zhang, W., Wang, G., Ma, X., and Evans, R. (2020). Unpacking the black box: How to promote citizen engagement through government social media during the COVID-19 crisis. *Computers in Human Behavior*, *110* (Virtual Issue). https://doi.org/10.1016/j.chb.2020.106380.

Cho, W. and Melisa, W. D. (2021). Citizen coproduction and social media communication: Delivering government's urban services through digital participation. *Administrative Sciences*, *11*(2), 1–15.

Cinelli, M., De Francisci-Morales, G., Galeazzi, A., Quattrociocchi, W., and Starnini, M. (2021). The echo chamber effect on social media. *PNAS*, *118*(9), e2023301118.

Clifton, J., Díaz-Fuentes, D., and Llamosas-García, G. (2020). ICT-enabled co-production of public services: Barriers and enablers – a systematic review. *Information Polity*, *25*(1), 25–48.

Cordella, A. and Paletti, A. (2017). Value creation, ICT, and co-production in public sector: Bureaucracy, opensourcing and crowdsourcing. In Association for Computing Machinery (ed.), *Proceedings of the 18th Annual International Conference on Digital Government Research* (pp. 185–194). https://doi.org/10.1145/3085228.3085305.

Cornelissen, J. (2008). *Corporate communication: A guide to theory and practice*. Thousand Oaks, CA: Sage Publications.

De Jong, M. D. T., Sharon, N., and Jansma, S. R. (2019). Citizens' intentions to participate in governmental co-creation initiatives: Comparing three co-creation configurations. *Government Information Quarterly*, *36*(3), 490–500.

Delli Carpini, M. X. (2020). Public sector communication and democracy. In V. Luoma-aho and M. J. Canel (eds.), *The handbook of public sector communication* (pp. 31–44). Hoboken, NJ: Wiley-Blackwell.

Falco, E. and Kleinhans, R. (2018). Beyond technology: Identifying local government challenges for using digital platforms for citizen engagement. *International Journal of Information Management*, *40*(C), 17–20.

Jalonen, H., Kokkola, J., Laihonen, H., Kirjavainen, H., Kaartemo, V., and Vähämaa, M. (2021). Reaching hard-to-reach people through digital means: Citizens as initiators of co-creation in public services. *International Journal of Public Sector Management*, *34*(7), 799–816.

Jurgens, M. and Helsloot, I. (2018). The effect of social media on the dynamics of (self) resilience during disasters: A literature review. *Journal of Contingencies and Crisis Management*, *26*(1), 79–88.

Khine, P. K., Mi, J., and Shahid, R. (2021). A comparative analysis of co-production in public services. *Sustainability*, *13*(12), 1–13.

Krishnan, B., Vijayakumar, A., Kumar, H., Balaji, R., Ghose, A., and Venkatachari, S. R. (2018). Digital citizen engagement framework: An approach to citizen centric smart cities of the future. *Intelligent Environments*, *23*, 28–37.

424 *Handbook on digital corporate communication*

Kumar, V. R., Kumar, S., and Ilavarasan, V. (2017). Government portals, social media platforms and citizen engagement in India: Some insights. *Procedia Computer Science*, *122*, 842–849.

Lember, V. (2018). The role of new technologies in co-production and co-creation. In T. Brandsen, T. Steen, and B. Verschuere (eds.), *Co-production and co-creation in public service delivery* (pp. 115–127). New York: Routledge.

Lember, V., Brandsen T., and Tõnurist, P. (2019). The potential impacts of digital technologies on co-production and co-creation. *Public Management Review*, *21*(11), 1665–1686.

Linders, D. (2012). From e-government to we-government: Defining a typology for citizen coproduction in the age of social media. *Government Information Quarterly*, *29*(4), 446–454.

Loeffler, E. and Bovaird, T. (2018). From participation to co-production: Widening and deepening the contributions of citizens to public services and outcomes. In E. Ongaro and S. Van Thiel (eds.), *The Palgrave handbook of public administration and management in Europe* (pp. 403–423). London: Palgrave Macmillan.

Luoma-aho, V. (2015). Understanding stakeholder engagement: Faith-holders, hateholders & fakehold-ers. *RJ-IPR: Research Journal of the Institute for Public Relations*, *2*(1). http://www.instituteforpr .org/understanding-stakeholder-engagement-fai.

Lythreatis, S., Kumar-Singh, S., and El-Kassar, A. N. (2022). The digital divide: A review and future research agenda. *Technological Forecasting and Social Change*, *175*, 121359.

Madrid (n.d.a). *Aplicación móvil – Madrid Móvil*. Madrid. https://bit.ly/3zXoXBb.

Madrid (n.d.b). *Avisos ciudadanos*. Datos abiertos. https://bit.ly/3AXqXdR.

Malhotra, C., Sharma, A., Agarwal, N., and Malhotra, I. (2019). Review of digital citizen engagement (DCE) platform: A case study of MyGov of Government of India. In ICEGOV2019 (ed.), *Proceedings of the 12th International Conference on Theory and Practice of Electronic Governance* (pp. 148–155). Melbourne: ICEGOV2019.

Meijer, A., Rodríguez-Bolívar, M. P., and Gil-Garcia, J. R. (2018). From e-government to digital era governance and beyond: Lessons from 15 years of research into information and communications technology in the public sector. *Journal of Public Administration Research and Theory* (Virtual Issue). https://static.primary.prod.gcms.the-infra.com/static/site/jpart/document/EGov-Introduction .pdf?node=691b14abd3cfe516876e&version=9612:e229f05e70f9d491413c.

Mergel, I. (2016). Social media in the public sector. In D. Bearfield and M. Dubnick (eds.), *Encyclopedia of Public Administration and Public Policy* (Vol. 3; pp. 3017–3021). New York: Routledge.

Moon, M. J. (2018). Evolution of co-production in the information age: Crowdsourcing as a model of web-based co-production in Korea. *Policy and Society*, *37*(3), 294–309.

Paletti, A. (2016). Co-production through ICT in the public sector: When citizens reframe the production of public services. In L. Caporarello, F. Cesaroni, R. Giesecke, and M. Missikoff (eds.), *Digitally supported innovation: A multi-disciplinary view on enterprise, public sector and user innovation* (pp. 141–152). Cham: Springer.

Piqueiras, P., Canel, M. J., and Luoma-aho, V. (2020). Citizen engagement and public sector commu-nication. In V. Luoma-aho and M. J. Canel (eds.), *The handbook of public sector communication* (pp. 277–288). Hoboken, NJ: Wiley-Blackwell.

Ragnedda, M. (2017). *The third digital divide: A Weberian approach to digital inequalities*. Abingdon: Routledge.

Ribeiro, M. M., Cunha, M. A., and Barbosa, A. F. (2018). E-participation, social media and digital gap: Challenges in the Brazilian context. In A. Zuiderwijk and C. C. Hinnant (eds.), *Proceedings of the 19th Annual International Conference on Digital Government Research: Governance in the Data Age*. New York: ACM.

Santos, T., Louca, J., and Coelho, H. (2019). The digital transformation of the public sphere. *Systems Research and Behavioral Science*, *36*(6), 778–788.

Sari, A. M., Hidayanto, A. N., Purwandari, B., Ayuning Budi, N. F., and Kosandi, M. (2018). Challenges and issues of e-participation implementation: A case study of e-complaint Indonesia. In Institute of Electrical and Electronics (ed.), *Third International Conference of Informatics and Computing (ICIC)*. Piscataway: Institute of Electrical and Electronics Engineers. https://doi.org/10.1109/IAC .2018.8780467.

Sideri, M., Kitsiou, A., Filippopoulou, A., Kalloniatis, C., and Gritzalis, S. (2019). E-government in educational settings: Greek educational organizations leadership's perspectives towards social media usage for participatory decision-making. *Internet Research*, *29*(4), 818–845.

Sorrentino, M., Sicilia, M., and Howlett, M. (2018). Understanding co-production as a new public governance tool. *Policy and Society*, *37*(3), 277–293.

Tuurnas, S. (2020). How does the idea of co-production challenge public sector communication? In V. Luoma-aho and M. J. Canel (eds.), *The handbook of public sector communication* (pp. 139–152). Hoboken, NJ: Wiley-Blackwell.

Valdez-Mendia, J. M. and Flores-Cuautle, J. J. A. (2022). Toward customer hyper-personalization experience: A data-driven approach. *Cogent Business & Management*, *9*(1), 2041384.

VDA (2014). Nueva aplicación móvil para avisar al ayuntamiento de incidencias urbanas. *Mirador de Madrid*, 29 August. https://elmiradordemadrid.es/nueva-aplicacion-movil-para-avisar-al-ayuntamiento-de-incidencias-urbanas/?amp=1.

Wamsler, C., Alkan-Olsson, J., Björn, H., Hanson, H., Oskarsson, T., Simonsson, E., and Zelmerlow, F. (2020). Beyond participation: When citizen engagement leads to undesirable outcomes for nature-based solutions and climate change adaptation. *Climatic Change*, *158*, 235–254.

World Bank (2016). *Evaluating digital citizen engagement*. Washington, DC: World Bank.

Yang, Y., Deng, W., Zhang, Y., and Mao, Z. (2021). Promoting public engagement during the COVID-19 crisis: How effective is the Wuhan local government's information release? *International Journal of Environmental Research and Public Health*, *18*(1), 118.

Ye, L. and Yang, H. (2020). From digital divide to social inclusion: A tale of mobile platform empowerment in rural areas. *Sustainability*, *12*(6), 2424.

Yuan, Q. (2019). Co-production of public service and information technology: A literature review. In *Proceedings of the 20th Annual International Conference on Digital Government Research (June 18, 2019. Dubai, United Arab Emirates)* (pp. 123–132). New York: ACM.

30. Digital corporate communication and disinformation

Mirko Olivieri, Rosa-Maria Mäkelä, Stefania Romenti and Vilma Luoma-aho

INTRODUCTION

Disinformation in the form of half-truths, false information and deliberative lies has always existed (Lewandowsky and van der Linden, 2021). Although there is nothing new in this phenomenon, the novelty is in the speed with which disinformation spreads in the information environment, as technological development, and, in particular, social media, has allowed a more rapid spread of news (Bovet and Makse, 2019). In other words, digitalization is a key aspect that has allowed and contributed to making disinformation a topical concern among policy makers, organizations, scholars and institutions. According to some authors, digitalization allows fake news to propagate more rapidly than it ever has before (Mills et al., 2019). Social media platforms, such as Facebook and Twitter, have been blamed because of fake news dissemination in virtual spaces (Jang and Kim, 2018; Spohr, 2017). This is due to their structure: on these platforms, content can be shared among users with no third-party filtering, fact-checking or editorial judgement (Allcott and Gentzkow, 2017), which facilitates the spread of fake news.

Nowadays, in the scenario characterized by, for example, the Covid-19 pandemic, the use of digital channels to retrieve information has grown exponentially and, consequently, disinformation has spread more easily, so much so that the World Health Organization has coined the term 'infodemic'. For instance, according to a recent Statista study (2020), 60 per cent of young people between the ages of 16 and 24 have recently used social media to acquire information on the coronavirus, and 59 per cent have found fake news related to that topic.

Indeed, the phenomenon of fake news affects not only society in general, but also organizations. In this context, digital corporate communication, understood as "an organization's strategic management of digital technologies, digital infrastructures and digitalization processes to improve communication with internal and external stakeholders and more broadly within society for the maintenance of organizational tangible and intangible assets" (Badham and Luoma-aho, Chapter 1 in this volume, p. 9), could be compromised by the spread of fake news (Fulgoni and Lipsman, 2017). More specifically, scholars demonstrate that fake news influences consumers' attitudes towards businesses (Di Domenico et al., 2021), conveys misleading beliefs (Lewandowsky et al., 2012), and creates confusion about past experiences with brands (Rapp and Salovich, 2018). Scholars have also found that corporate reputation could be strongly compromised by fake news (Berthon and Pitt, 2018), to the point of being subject to product boycotts for no reason (Obadă, 2019).

The aim of this chapter is to address the topic of disinformation and explore the role of digital corporate communication to counter the spread of this dangerous phenomenon. The first part of the chapter consists of a conceptual framework of the disinformation phenomenon:

Digital corporate communication and disinformation 427

definitions, theories and dimensions are analysed and compared. The chapter then focuses on what is changing as a result of digitalization (i.e., fake news spreading in the communicative overcrowding scenario) and yet what remains the same (i.e., the old threat of disinformation). The risks that disinformation causes for organizations is also discussed. An illustration of how the European Union tackled disinformation surrounding the Covid-19 pandemic is presented. The chapter concludes with implications for practitioners and future research directions regarding this topic.

DEFINITIONS OF DISINFORMATION AND PREVIOUS STUDIES

Disinformation has been extensively examined from different perspectives in academic literature, including communication studies. Disinformation includes "deceptive advertising (in business and in politics), government propaganda, doctored photographs, forged documents, fake maps, internet frauds, fake websites, and manipulated Wikipedia entries" (Fallis, 2015, p. 401). Scholars do not always refer to the phenomenon in the same way. In fact, the literature has identified various types of false information and authors have provided different definitions of the topic over the years.

Historically, the concept of disinformation has been associated with that of propaganda and, therefore, with communication strategies implemented in the political field. However, according to Lanoszka (2019), although the concepts of disinformation and propaganda partially overlap, they have different meanings and objectives. Indeed, while the purpose of propaganda is linked to persuading an individual with respect to a privileged point of view in order to reach political interests (Cull et al., 2003), the aim of disinformation is "to manipulate beliefs in order to take advantage of erroneous inferences" (Ettinger and Jeheil, 2010, p. 1).

Generally, a discussion of disinformation suffers from inaccurate definitions (Karlova and Lee, 2011). For example, the terms disinformation and misinformation are used interchangeably by various scholars (Losee, 1997), while at other times the two terms refer to variations of each other (Zhou and Zhang, 2007). Also, according to the recent study by La Cour (2020), the phenomenon of disinformation can manifest in different forms and can be used by different actors. La Cour (2020) identifies three most frequent prototypes of disinformation, which are (1) a "disinformation story", that is a singular false news in an information system; (2) a "disinformation campaign", that is a campaign which collects multiple false stories related to the same topic; and (3) a "disinformation operation", that is a "long-term effort to systematically deceive a foreign public" (La Cour, 2020, p. 708).

Table 30.1 shows various definitions of disinformation offered in academic literature.

Since the 2016 US presidential election (Guess et al., 2018), the disinformation phenomenon has been extensively studied and fake news, as invented information which imitates media contents in form but not in processes or organizational intentions (Lazer et al., 2018), has begun to enter the academic debate. For example, Tandoc et al. (2018) conducted a literature review of the fake news topic and found only 34 academic articles which used the term 'fake news' between 2003 and 2017. First, the authors raised the question of what is meant by the term 'news' and what is meant by 'fake'. *News* is defined as "information or reports about recent events", "recent information about people you know", "a printed or broadcast report of information about important events in the world, the country or the local area", according to the Cambridge Dictionary. Academics refer to this word as a new piece of information, an

428 *Handbook on digital corporate communication*

Table 30.1   *Definitions from academic studies about disinformation*

Category	Definition	Author(s)
Disinformation	"Disinformation is widely understood as content produced to generate profits, pursue political goals, or maliciously mislead, such as in the form of hoaxes"	Nielsen and Graves (2017)
	"Disinformation means that false information is strategically shared to cause harm"	Wardle and Derakhshan (2017)
	"It is widely understood as misleading content produced to generate profits, pursue political goals, or maliciously deceive"	Humprecht et al. (2020)
	"Any form of manifestly false information or content, which is originally uttered or written with the intent to do harm and subsequently disseminated"	La Cour (2020)
	"False, incomplete or misleading information that is passed, fed, or confirmed to a targeted individual, group, or country"	Shultz and Godson (1984)
	"Intentional falsehoods spread as new stories or simulated documentary formats to advance political goals"	Bennett and Livingston (2018)
	"Information that is intentionally created and uploaded on various websites, and thereafter disseminated via social media either for profit or for social influence"	Humprecht (2018)
Misinformation	"Unintentional publication of false or misleading information"	Wardle and Derakhshan (2017)
	"A category of claim for which there is at least substantial disagreement (or even consensus rejection) when judged as to truth value among the widest feasible range of observers"	Southwell et al. (2018)
	"Misinformation refers to claims that – unlike information – are not supported by the majority of societally accepted evidence adjudicators, and reflects content that may be inaccurate, uncertain, vague, or ambiguous"	Karlova and Fisher (2013)
Malinformation	"Malinformation occurs when genuine information is shared to cause harm, for example, by disclosing private information to the public"	Wardle and Derakhshan (2017)

Source: Authors' own elaboration.

account of a recent and interesting event, one that has a significant impact on people (Paschen, 2019; Tandoc et al., 2018). It is considered an output of journalism, so it is expected to be reliable, independent and accurate, given that it is the responsibility of journalism to report objective and true information in what it produces. According to the Cambridge Dictionary, *fake* is something "that is made to look real or valuable in order to deceive people" or that "is not what or who they claim to be"; "not real, but made to look or seem real", "something that is intended to look like and be mistaken for something else". Thus, fake characterizes something that is not genuine, an imitation, something false, counterfeit or fraudulent.

Tandoc et al. (2018) offered a categorization of fake news, as shown in Table 30.2.

From a review of the literature on disinformation and fake news, it emerges that there are different types of disinformation and fake news contents which, consequently, also have different objectives and contexts. For example, the intentions of the source change, which can be of two types (Allcott and Gentzkow, 2017): economic and/or ideological. On the one hand, economic reasons push organizations to spread fake news with the aim of increasing traffic on a specific website by generating clicks. Political organizations, on the other hand, spread fake news for propaganda purposes.

Generally, some elements of the definition of fake news are agreed among academics. For example, fake news is intentionally false but realistic information, fabricated with the intent to deceive and be taken as truth. Further, it needs the look and feel of real news (e.g., how web-

Digital corporate communication and disinformation 429

Table 30.2   Different types of fake news (Tandoc et al., 2018)

Fake news type	Description
Fabricated news	Information with no factual basis rendered in the style of news articles to create legitimacy
Satire and parody	Content that doesn't have the intention to harm but the possibility to fool. According to Wardle (2017), if effective and intelligent they could be considered forms of art
Materials manipulation	The contents (e.g., photographs, videos) are digitally altered or extracted from their original context (intentionally or unintentionally) to represent a different meaning
Advertorial	It seems to be a genuine news with content featuring statistics, sources, interviews, etc. but in fact it is an ad. Taking the format of news, it misleads in persuading it is authentic, hiding its one-sided claim
Propaganda	It is a news story which is created by a political entity with the intent to influence public opinion, especially on a political and ideological level, to benefit one side, and often discredit another. The aim is to persuade, rather than inform, with information, opinions, ideas of only one part

Source: Authors' own elaboration.

sites look, how articles are written and how photos include attribution). Hiding under a veneer of legitimacy, it takes on some form of credibility by trying to appear as real news.

Tandoc et al. (2018) suggest the expression 'fake news' can be considered an oxymoron, since news is supposed to be true and reliable, so in its definition it excludes the concept of falsity. Furthermore, they point out another problem in the definition of fake news: it is hard to affirm what is real and what is fake since news is socially constructed. Inadvertently, willing or not, journalists make a subjective judgement when they choose to include or exclude parts of the information and who they report it to. News is vulnerable not only to the preferences of journalists, but also to government and political institutions, advertisers and market forces. However, in all cases, it is expected to be accurate information based on truth. There are also opinion pieces in which authors explicitly say what they think, so they are not interpreted as fake news (Paschen, 2019).

Moreover, fake news can be categorized according to two dimensions: 'facticity' and 'intention to deceive' (Tandoc et al., 2018). *Facticity* means 'being a fact' and indicates the degree to which fake news relies on actual elements. If facticity is high, then the news is reliable and accurate. But if it is low, it means it is fictitious. *Intention to deceive* refers to the creator's or author's goal to cheat and misinform people, and that can be for many reasons, such as for profit or ideology.

WHAT IS CHANGING?

It is now widely accepted that the concept of fake news gained prominence in the public's consciousness during the 2016 US presidential election campaign (Guess et al., 2018). During this election, social media played a key role as a vehicle to spread news and build consensus, reaching as many users as possible for politic purposes. This phenomenon brought scholarly and wider public attention to the causes and effects of fake news. Frequently, in the case of a diffusion campaign of fake news, behind these fake contents is the contribution of organizations capable of creating damage to people, such as political opponents, institutions, or companies. As a result, the world of social media is radically changing the paradigms of information

430 *Handbook on digital corporate communication*

use. On the one hand, social media favours the spread of so-called "counter-information" (Colombo, 2014). On the other hand, social media increases the spread of false information (Howell, 2013).

With the rapid diffusion of social media, the phenomenon of disinformation has grown exponentially. According to a recent study by Statista (2020), among the sources of trustworthy news by medium, social media ranks last and is preceded by digital and printed newspapers, blogs, television and online news websites. Organizations are not immune to these type of developments. They need to be alert and ready to tackle untrue information being disseminated about them on social media.

Disinformation is facilitated by a plurality of touchpoints, both online and offline, available to users to seek information and therefore is characterized by communicative overcrowding. A large quantity of news born and spread quickly without being verified in advance risks generating social alarm, distorted visions of reality and orientations and behaviours which can have negative consequences on individuals and entire communities. These risks are even more evident in the case of scientific news, which is difficult to interpret and has repercussions on collective behaviours. Indeed, a study by Jennings et al. (2021) has shown that those who receive information from social media sources, such as YouTube, develop conspiratorial beliefs, and believe less in institutional sources.

In this uncertain scenario, social media plays a key role and often amplifies the spread of ambiguous content and fake news, which organizations need to be aware of (Berthon and Pitt, 2018). For example, research by Media Matters (2021) has shown that the TikTok algorithm frequently amplifies false news about Covid-19 and vaccines. The algorithm of TikTok, as well as that of many other social media such as Instagram, allows users to customize their feed so that they receive similar content based on the preferences and likes of users. Research by Media Matters has shown that, after liking some fake news content, a user's feed will be filled almost exclusively with similar content and therefore with fake news.

WHAT REMAINS THE SAME?

Internet users have moved away from traditional media and increasingly use social media channels not only to seek new information, but also opinions about organizations, brands and products. This popularity of social media communication among organizations depends on the viral dissemination of information via the Internet and the greater ability to reach audiences than traditional media. Organizations are now aware of the imminent need to focus on developing bilateral personal relationships with consumers and to foster interactions.

Thus, the advent of social media has democratized content and made information sharing quicker via digital channels, inevitably also favouring the diffusion of distorted content (Fulgoni and Lipsman, 2017). According to Burkhardt (2017), the first fake news dates back to the invention of the printing press: the spread of literacy made it possible to disseminate information rapidly and in this period the phenomenon has become more visible. In 1844, the American author Edgar Allan Poe wrote a hoax newspaper article saying that a balloonist crossed the Atlantic in just three days. Due to the details used by Poe in the storytelling, many readers believed the news, which later turned out to be false only when journalists failed to contact the balloonist. Therefore, fake news has existed for a long time but the motivations

Digital corporate communication and disinformation 431

that prompted the authors to write fake news are different. Some authors probably had good intentions, but others intended to harm something or someone (Burkhardt, 2017).

CRITICAL EXAMINATION

There are many risks of the fake news phenomenon for organizations. For example, as reputation is a resource on which organizations can capitalize, fake news represents a form of 'pollution', a toxin that risks compromising organizations' reputation-building strategies (Fulgoni and Lipsman, 2017). In this regard, Nyilasy (2019, p. 338) considers fake news a risk factor and an obstacle to building corporate reputation: "fake news is not merely media content – its intention is to influence people for the purposes of a particular persuasion goal" and "it is undeniable that this is sponsored messaging" that "spreads through mass media channels and has a persuasive intent". In fact, as also highlighted by Kwon et al. (2019), communication flows have always had a significant impact on the identity of organizations and their reputation.

In this vein, the impact of fake news on the reputation and other intangible assets of a company is accentuated by the wide accessibility of the Internet and the role social media have acquired in the management of communication flows. Indeed, due to the low barriers to entry on the web, producers of fake news are driven by economic reasons to create deceptive content: sensational headlines easily generate clicks and traffic that increase advertising volume and, by extension, revenue (Ormond et al., 2016). As a result, organizations can lose control of their communication messages, strategies and practices (Mills and Robson, 2019). According to a recent study by Jahng (2021), the increase in the circulation of fake news in the digital environment represents a challenge for crisis communication on social media. This challenge not only affects the reputation of organizations, but also undermines the relationship with the target audience. However, according to Jahng (2021), the awareness of users about the dangers of fake news and the knowledge of the characteristics of these contents could alleviate reputational damage to organizations. Currently, a study by Castellani and Berton (2017) reports that several companies have begun to implement strategies aimed at limiting the spread of fake news to avoid reputational damage, linked to credibility and trust or in terms of sales. According to this study, organizations affected by fake news have promoted communication campaigns with the aim of transmitting timely and transparent information through different channels, online and offline.

ILLUSTRATIVE EXAMPLE: THE COVID-19 'INFODEMIC'

Censis research reveals that the web remains a privileged environment in which disinformation and fake news are produced and developed (Censis, 2021). Almost 30 million Italians declared that during the health emergency situation related to Covid-19, they discovered news that turned out to be false or wrong on the Internet. Indeed, the circulation of fake news tends to intensify in periods dominated by great uncertainty. In the face of the health emergency caused by Covid-19, for example, the spread of disinformation increased exponentially, so much so that the World Health Organization coined the term 'infodemic'. As a result, health organizations and authorities around the world became increasingly aware of the damage disinformation can cause people. At the base of this phenomenon is the expectation of receiving reassuring news during tough times, and this increases the number of people willing to believe truthful news that apparently reassures and that appears plausible for the wide propagation of false news. According to Statista (2021), in May 2020 up to 6 per cent of all news and online posts related to Covid-19 was false or inaccurate. As can be seen in Figure 30.1, the peak in the dissemination of fake news was recorded in the initial phase of the pandemic (at the end of January 2020), with 7.3 per cent of the fake news information related to Covid-19.

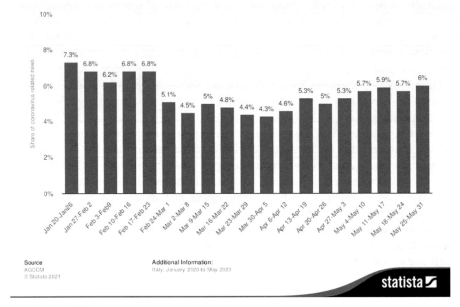

Source: Statista (2021).

Figure 30.1 Share of online fake news related to Covid-19 in the period January–May 2020

The European Union's Response to Disinformation

On 10 June 2020 the European Commission Vice President stated:

> The Coronavirus pandemic is also an infodemic. It is accompanied by a huge wave of disinformation and consumer hoaxes. It really showed that disinformation does not only harm the health of our democracies, it also harms the health of our citizens. It can negatively impact the economy and undermine the response of the public authorities and therefore weaken the health measures. (The European Commission Vice President Jourová, 10 June 2020)

Communicators in the European Union are becoming increasingly aware of a variety of disinformation tactics and processes (see e.g., EUvsDisinfo.eu; EUDisinfoLab, 2021). Disinformation is seen to fuel general anxiety, contribute to polarization, and to question science and experts. Furthermore, dis- and misinformation have, for example, been perceived

Digital corporate communication and disinformation   433

to feed into vaccine hesitancy (Eurofound, 2021). The EU has several means in place to tackle disinformation, and these actions and tools have been increasingly developed and strengthened during the past couple of years. As outlined in Table 30.3, there are several institutions, organizations and stakeholders tackling disinformation in the European Union, which poses both challenges and opportunities to the EU. On the one hand, the more there are players on the ground spotting and reviewing disinformation, the less disinformation goes unnoticed. On the other hand, due to the number of organizations and their communication professionals dealing with disinformation in the EU, creating effective and coordinated solutions to disinformation can be demanding.

Table 30.3   The EU's policy framework and instruments for tackling disinformation

Tool	Overseen by	Implication
EUvsDisinfo site Weekly disinformation reviews	– The EEAS (European External Action Service) Strategic Communication Division the East StratCom Task Forces Unit (ESCTF) – Holds a coordinating position within the EU when it comes to tackling disinformation by foreign actors, involves 140 EU delegations around the world	– Combines monitoring, analysis, public diplomacy, and strategic communications – Implements the Action Plan Against Disinformation and the Rapid Alert System – ESCTF monitors, identifies, and debunks pro-Kremlin disinformation e.g., on EUvsDisinfo site – ESCTF also aims to build resilience against disinformation in the Western Balkans and the Southern neighbourhood
The Rapid Alert System	– The EEAS coordinates the system in collaboration with the EU Member States – Coordinates with the G-7 Rapid Response Mechanism and NATO	– Facilitates information sharing – Exposes disinformation in real-time
The Code of Practice on Disinformation (CoPD)	– Coordinated by the European Commission	– An experiment for the technology industry to voluntary self-regulate – CoPD agreement made with major social media companies
The European Digital Media Observatory (EDMO)	– EDMO	– Coordinates the network of fact-checking organizations, researchers and media practitioners, teachers with technological platforms and public authorities – Aims to strengthen the media – Offers funding for research tackling disinformation
The European Democracy Action Plan (EDAP) and the Digital Services Act (DSA)	– European Council, European Commission, European Parliament	– Proposes legally binding tools especially regarding the accountability and transparency of digital platforms, and enhances the EU's democratic resilience – EDAP offers an opportunity to strengthen the Code of Practice – The DSA aims to develop rules for the online environment

Source: Table elaborated by the authors and adapted from Colomina et al. (2021).

The EU's Response to a Covid-19 Vaccine Disinformation Campaign

Both the European Medicine Agency (EMA) and the World Health Organization (WHO) became targets of Kremlin disinformation in March 2021. The disinformation story claimed that the EMA and WHO did not approve the Sputnik Covid-19 vaccine by deliberately ignoring its success. Sputnik V demanded a public apology from the chair of the EMA management

434 *Handbook on digital corporate communication*

board on Twitter after the EMA had discouraged the EU Member States from approving the vaccine (EUvsDisinfo, 2021a, 2021b).

In reality, the health regulators had not received enough information to review and prove the Sputnik V vaccine was safe for people to use. Neither EMA nor WHO had received the requested data from Russia, and some legal procedures to Russia were also still pending. EMA had earlier, in February 2021, announced that they would approve the vaccine if it met the applied standards (EMA, 2021). In October 2021, WHO did inform that data from Russian authorities was still pending. The vaccine disinformation campaign was proved by the European External Action Service (EEAS) Strategic Communication Division to be disinformation, and this was announced on the EUvsDisinfo website (EUvsDisinfo, 2021b). According to the EEAS Strategic Communication Division, the disinformation campaign was connected to a pro-Kremlin narrative that had been circulating since the launch of Sputnik V. It included a claim that the EU was not accepting Russia's primacy, and the EU did not approve of the Sputnik vaccine due to political reasons (EUvsDisinfo, 2021b).

It seems that only the EEAS EU Strategic Communication task force reacted to the disinformation publicly. The EUvsDisinfo published an article and a tweet on their website and Twitter account stating that "Pro-Kremlin disinformation seeks to portray Sputnik V and Russia as unfairly treated by the West and the EU" (EUvsDisinfo, 2021c). Interestingly, it appears that the EMA did not respond to the specific disinformation on their social media channels, even though they had published a press release clarifying their vaccine approval process earlier in February 2022. They stated that EMA would discuss next steps with the Sputnik V producing company as well as confirmed that they apply the same approach to every vaccine application (EMA, 2021).

The response to disinformation, in this case, appears to be institutionally coordinated: the EEAS East Strategic Communication task forces called out the false claims against the EMA's vaccine approval process. The benefit of this approach ensures that disinformation, for example, related to the Covid-19 vaccines stays aligned and accurate within the EU. A decentralized approach, however, would give more responsibility to the EU institution or organization to tackle disinformation based on the case at hand (Pamment, 2020). However, a faster response could potentially prevent false information from disseminating to larger audiences.

The challenge for the EU is that the producers of disinformation are not often bound by legal restrictions or the burden of bureaucracy the same way as the EU is, and their aim is to harass the climate of debate and undermine trust in institutions and organizations. Moreover, they touch upon local concerns that can be used to strengthen support for the harmful goals, and with the use of advanced technologies and means to raise attention. The adversaries may use sophisticated techniques, established networks, and narratives to reach their objectives (Pamment, 2020). It requires special attention for the EU to not compromise its fundamental values when finding solutions in addressing disinformation – intertwining public diplomacy and disinformation is not an option for the EU (Vériter et al., 2020). Hence, defining disinformation in the European Union law is a tricky task which has become evident in the recent discussions on the content of the Digital Services Act. There are doubts whether the regulation will address the definition of disinformation – in other words, content that can be harmful but not illegal per se (Shattock, 2021). This is because it could allegedly undermine freedom of expression (Shattock, 2021). Therefore, the discussion on expression of fundamental freedoms and legislating disinformation is likely to continue (Helm and Nasu, 2021; Osetti and

Digital corporate communication and disinformation 435

Bontcheva, 2020), and creating an ethical response to disinformation will continue to lie at the heart of the matter.

CONCLUSION AND FUTURE DIRECTIONS

In recent years, the phenomenon of disinformation, and, in particular, the propagation of fake news in the digital environment and on social media platforms, has assumed a key role in the academic debate of corporate communication (Di Domenico et al., 2021; Lazer et al., 2018). In addition, tackling it is likely to remain a priority of policy makers, organizations, and institutions. Indeed, although fake news is not a new phenomenon, social media platforms have facilitated its spread. On the one hand, this has become evident in compromising the right of users to be correctly informed, and on the other hand, by threatening and attacking the organizations based on fake content that undermines both their credibility and reputation.

It is not always easy to distinguish the true from the false on these digital platforms. In the era of the Covid-19 pandemic, during which the use of digital channels exploded around the world, fake content spread rapidly, decisively influencing behaviour and the choices of individuals. Many news items are inaccurate, deliberately distorted or completely unfounded. Oftentimes untrue information heavily affects users' perception of reality, alternating the tendency to underestimate the problem with feelings of panic.

For organizations, combating the spread of false news represents one of the arduous challenges to be faced in this complex scenario. The number of channels and spaces in which to interact with stakeholders has multiplied. Digital corporate communication, therefore, plays a central role in combating disinformation in the online environment. Many institutions and organizations, including European Union institutions analysed in this chapter, have understood the importance of digital communication to tackle this phenomenon. Through communications on social media and on dedicated websites, organizations daily try to face this challenge. According to the literature (e.g., Allcott and Gentzkow, 2017), among the intentions of the sources that disseminate fake news on social media there is not only the economic aspect, but also social and political issues that push fake news disseminators to carry out these polluting actions on the web.

Therefore, although social media are digital spaces in which fake news thrives, these channels represent a means for organizations to address the concerns of users and create and strengthen relationships of trust with stakeholders with effective digital corporate communication. This is evident, for example, in the EU; the European Union institutions have created policies, tools, and communication practices to tackle disinformation.

Hence, organizations nowadays seem to have gained awareness of the phenomenon of disinformation and that anyone can become a target of disinformation. This is demonstrated by the communication studies that have been developing around the topic of fake news in recent years (e.g., Berthon and Pitt, 2018; Di Domenico et al., 2021; Obadă, 2019).

Future reflections on this issue could concern the means of how organizations can effectively address disinformation targeted at them. In addition, discussion of ethical approaches to prevent the spread of disinformation from becoming uncontrolled by polluting the web would be of importance. In particular, the perception of users regarding the reliability of the source could be worthy of further analysis by scholars and professionals.

REFERENCES

Allcott, H. and Gentzkow, M. (2017). Social media and fake news in the 2016 election. *Journal of Economic Perspectives*, *31*(2), 211–236.

Bennett, W. L. and Livingston, S. (2018). The disinformation order: Disruptive communication and the decline of democratic institutions. *European Journal of Communication*, *33*(2), 122–139.

Berthon, P. R. and Pitt, L. F. (2018). Brands, truthiness and post-fact: Managing brands in a post-rational world. *Journal of Macromarketing*, *38*(2), 218–227.

Bovet, A. and Makse, H. A. (2019). Influence of fake news in Twitter during the 2016 US presidential election. *Nature Communications*, *10*(1), 1–14.

Burkhardt, J. M. (2017). History of fake news. *Library Technology Reports*, *53*(8). https://journals.ala .org/index.php/ltr/article/view/6497/8636.

Castellani, P. and Berton, M. (2017). Fake news and corporate reputation: What strategies do companies adopt against false information in the media? Toulon-Verona Conference "Excellence in Services".

Censis (2021). *Disinformazione e fake news durante la pandemia: il ruolo delle agenzie di comunicazione.* https://www.censis.it/sites/default/files/downloads/Rapporto%20Ital%20Communications -Censis_def.pdf.

Colombo, F. (2014). Web 2.0 e democrazia: un rapporto problematico. In P. Aroldi (ed.), *La piazza, la rete e il voto* (pp. 30–36). Rome: Fondazione Apostolicam Actuositatem.

Colomina, C., Sanchez Margalef, H., and Youngs, R. (2021). *The impact of disinformation on democratic processes and human rights in the world.* European Parliament Study requested by DROI Committee. https://www.europarl.europa.eu/RegData/etudes/STUD/2021/653635/EXPO_STU(2021)653635 _EN.pdf.

Cull, N. J., Culbert, D., and Welch, D. (2003). *Propaganda and mass persuasion: A historical encyclopedia, 1500 to the present.* Santa Barbara, CA: ABC-CLIO.

Di Domenico, G., Sit, J., Ishizaka, A., and Nunan, D. (2021). Fake news, social media and marketing: A systematic review. *Journal of Business Research*, *124*, 329–341.

EMA (2021). *Clarification on Sputnik V vaccine in the EU approval process.* https://www.ema.europa .eu/en/news/clarification-sputnik-v-vaccine-eu-approval-process.

Ettinger, D. and Jeheil, P. (2010). A theory of deception. *American Economic Journal: Microeconomics*, *2*(1), 1–20.

EUDisinfoLab (2021). Open letter to EU Policy-Makers: How the Digital Services Act (DSA) can tackle disinformation – EU DisinfoLab. 31 August. https://www.disinfo.eu/advocacy/open-letter-to-eu -policy-makers-how-the-digital-services-act-dsa-can-tackle-disinformation/.

Eurofound (2021). *COVID-19.* https://www.eurofound.europa.eu/topic/covid-19.

European Commission Vice President Jourová (2020). Speech by VP Jourová on disinformation, 10 June. https://ec.europa.eu/commission/presscorner/detail/en/SPEECH_20_1033.

EUvsDisinfo (2021a). *The culture of resentment revisited.* https://euvsdisinfo.eu/the-culture-of -resentment-revisited/.

EUvsDisinfo (2021b). *Disinfo: Sputnik V's success is ignored by the EMA and WHO.* https://euvsdisinfo .eu/report/sputnik-vs-success-is-ignored-by-the-ema-and-who.

EUvsDisinfo [@EUvsDisinfo] (2021c). *Pro-Kremlin disinformation seeks to portray Sputnik V and Russia as unfairly treated by the West and the EU.* https://euvsdisinfo.eu/the-culture-of...[Tweet]. Twitter. https://twitter.com/euvsdisinfo/status/1370639517770788864.

Fallis, D. (2015). What is disinformation? *Library Trends*, *63*(3), 401–426.

Fulgoni, G. M. and Lipsman, A. (2017). The downside of digital word of mouth and the pursuit of media quality: How social sharing is disrupting digital advertising models and metrics. *Journal of Advertising Research*, *57*(2), 127–131.

Guess, A., Nyhan, B., and Reifler, J. (2018). Selective exposure to misinformation: Evidence from the consumption of fake news during the 2016 US presidential campaign. *European Research Council*, *9*(3), 1–49.

Helm, R. and Nasu, H. (2021). Regulatory responses to "fake news" and freedom of expression: Normative and empirical evaluation. *Human Rights Law Review*, *21*(2), 302–328.

Howell, L. W. (2013). *Digital wildfires in a hyperconnected world.* Report Global Risks, 23.

Humprecht, E. (2018). Where 'fake news' flourishes: A comparison across four Western democracies. *Information, Communication & Society*, 21, 1–16.

Humprecht, E., Esser, F., and Van Aelst, P. (2020). Resilience to online disinformation: A framework for cross-national comparative research. *The International Journal of Press/Politics*, 25(3), 493–516.

Jahng, M. R. (2021). Is fake news the new social media crisis? Examining the public evaluation of crisis management for corporate organizations targeted in fake news. *International Journal of Strategic Communication*, 15(1), 18–36.

Jang, S. M. and Kim, J. K. (2018). Third person effects of fake news: Fake news regulation and media literacy interventions. *Computers in Human Behavior*, 80, 295–302.

Jennings, W., Stoker, G., Bunting, H., Valgarðsson, V. O., Gaskell, J., Devine, D., … Mills, M. C. (2021). Lack of trust, conspiracy beliefs, and social media use predict COVID-19 vaccine hesitancy. *Vaccines*, 9(6), 1–14.

Karlova, N. A. and Lee, J. H. (2011). Notes from the underground city of disinformation: A conceptual investigation. *Proceedings of the American Society for Information Science and Technology*, 48(1), 1–9.

Karlova, N. A., Natascha, A., and Fisher, K. E. (2013) A social diffusion model of misinformation and disinformation for understanding human information behaviour. *Information Research*, 18(1), https://informationr.net/ir/18-1/paper573.html.

Kwon, E. S., King, K. W., Nyilasy, G., and Reid, L. N. (2019). Impact of media context on advertising memory: A meta-analysis of advertising effectiveness. *Journal of Advertising Research*, 59(1), 99–128.

La Cour, C. (2020). Theorising digital disinformation in international relations. *International Politics*, 57(4), 704–723.

Lanoszka, A. (2019). Disinformation in international politics. *European Journal of International Security*, 4(2), 227–248.

Lazer, D. M. J., Baum, M. A., Benkler, Y., Berinsky, A. J., Greenhill, K. M., … Zittrain, J. L. (2018). The science of fake news. *Science*, 359, 1094–1096.

Lewandowsky, S., Ecker, U. K. H., Seifert, C. M., Schwarz, N., and Cook, J. (2012). Misinformation and its correction: Continued influence and successful debiasing. *Psychological Science in the Public Interest*, 13(3), 106–131.

Lewandowsky, S. and van der Linden, S. (2021). Countering misinformation and fake news through inoculation and prebunking. *European Review of Social Psychology*, 32(2), 348–384.

Losee, R. M. (1997). A discipline independent definition of information. *Journal of the American Society for Information Science*, 48(3), 254–269.

Media Matters (2021). TikTok's algorithm is amplifying COVID-19 and vaccine misinformation. https://www.mediamatters.org/tiktok/tiktoks-algorithm-amplifying-covid-19-and-vaccine-misinformation.

Mills, A. J., Pitt, C., and Ferguson, S. L. (2019). The relationship between fake news and advertising: Brand management in the era of programmatic advertising and prolific falsehood. *Journal of Advertising Research*, 59(1), 3–8.

Mills, A. J. and Robson, K. (2019). Brand management in the era of fake news: Narrative response as a strategy to insulate brand value. *Journal of Product & Brand Management*, 29(2), 159–167.

Nielsen, R. K. and Graves, L. (2017). "News you don't believe": Audience perspectives on fake news. https://reutersinstitute.politics.ox.ac.uk/sites/default/files/2017-10/Nielsen%26Graves_factsheet_1710v3_FINAL_download.pdf.

Nyilasy, G. (2019). Fake news: When the dark side of persuasion takes over. *International Journal of Advertising*, 38(2), 336–342.

Obadă, D. (2019). Sharing fake news about brands on social media: A new conceptual model based on flow theory. *Argumentum: Journal the Seminar of Discursive Logic, Argumentation Theory & Rhetoric*, 17(2), 144–166.

Ormond, D., Warketin, M., Johnston, A. C., and Thompson, S. C. (2016). Perceived deception: Evaluating source credibility and self-efficacy. *Journal of Information, Privacy and Security*, 12(4), 197–217.

Osetti, J. and Bontcheva, K. (2020). *Disinfodemic: Deciphering COVID-19 disinformation.* UNESCO Policy Brief #2. https://en.unesco.org/covid19/disinfodemic.

438 *Handbook on digital corporate communication*

Pamment, J. (2020). *The EU's Role in Fighting Disinformation: Developing Policy Interventions for the 2020s.* Carnegie Endowment for International Peace.

Paschen, J. (2019). Investigating the emotional appeal of fake news using artificial intelligence and human contributions. *Journal of Product & Brand Management, 29*(2), 223–233.

Rapp, D. N. and Salovich, N. A. (2018). Can't we just disregard fake news? The consequences of exposure to inaccurate information. *Policy Insights from the Behavioral and Brain Sciences, 5*(2), 232–239.

Shattock, E. (2021). Self-regulation 2:0? A critical reflection of the European fight against disinformation. *Harvard Kennedy School Misinformation Review.* https://doi.org/10.37016/mr-2020-73.

Shultz, R. H. and Godson, R. (1984). *Dezinformatsia: Active measures in Soviet strategy.* Sterling, VA: Brassey's Inc.

Southwell, B. G., Thorson, E. A., and Sheble, L. (2018). *Misinformation and mass audiences.* Austin: University of Texas Press.

Spohr, D. (2017). Fake news and ideological polarization: Filter bubbles and selective exposure on social media. *Business Information Review, 34*(3), 150–160.

Statista (2020). *Fake news in Italy.* https://www-statista-com.ezproxy.unicatt.it/study/44352/fake-news -in-italy/.

Statista (2021). *Share of online fake news related to coronavirus (COVID-19) in Italy between January and May 2020.* https://www-statista-com.ezproxy.unicatt.it/statistics/1109490/share-of-coronavirus -fake-news-italy/.

Tandoc Jr, E. C., Lim, Z. W., and Ling, R. (2018). Defining "fake news": A typology of scholarly definitions. *Digital Journalism, 6*(2), 137–153.

Vériter, S. L., Bjola, C., and Koops, J. A. (2020). Tackling Covid-19 disinformation: Internal and external challenges for the European Union. *The Hague Journal of Diplomacy, 15*(4), 569–582.

Wardle, C. (2017). "Fake news." It's complicated. https://medium.com/1st-draft/fake-news-its -complicated-d0f773766c79.

Wardle, C. and Derakhshan, H. (2017). *Information disorder: Toward an interdisciplinary framework for research and policy making.* Council of Europe Report. https://www.coe.in.

Zhou, L. and Zhang, D. (2007). An ontology-supported misinformation model: Toward a digital misinformation library. *IEEE Transactions on Systems, Man, and Cybernetics – Part A: Systems and Humans, 37*(5), 804–813.

PART V

FUTURE DIRECTIONS

31. Conclusion: future roles of digital corporate communication

Vilma Luoma-aho, Mark Badham and Alina Arti

INTRODUCTION

Digitalization is understood as a holistic process of societal change and development brought about by advances in technology and data processing, which occurs in society whether organizations are paying attention to it or not. As society becomes increasingly digitalized, for organizations, staying competitive and maintaining legitimacy requires changes ranging from minor incremental additions to technology to major business model transformations (Hensellek, 2020; Rachinger et al., 2019). In fact, we may be only at the beginning of development of technology for organizations and business. For example, the metaverse of Web 3.0 promises to democratize the Internet and de-centralize organizational power from just a few to the many (decentralized autonomous organizations) (Mattila et al., 2022). Further, robotic process automation is taking over routine tasks, thus freeing time for human creativity (Dhengre et al., 2020). The more technology enables, the more there is need for humanity: in fact, empathy and affect in communication are becoming new requirements for successful technologies (Skjuve et al., 2021), giving corporate communication the centre stage in organizational success.

CommTech is about digital technologies for managing and executing workflow and core organizational activities, and as the quantity of data and the complexity of organizational processes increase, corporate communication has new tasks ahead. At worst, failure to adopt and implement CommTech can lead to value no-creation or even value co-destruction, as digital stakeholders, employees and customers expect organizations to be accessible and communicative in the digital realm (Makkonen and Olkkonen, 2017). The biggest challenges to implementing CommTech are reported to be structural barriers, such as lack of IT support, budget or organizational culture supporting technology use (Zerfass et al., 2022). Further, organizational preparedness or lack of it is another reason, whereas digital competencies of communicators and imperfect technology appear to play a smaller role (Zerfass et al., 2022).

Utilization and acceptance of edge computing and other forms of 'just in time' data, combined with the behavioural economic 'nudging' of individuals towards the right decisions, become increasingly value based and ethical responsibilities of communication managers and leaders. Though complexity may increase, the choices made by organizations will become easier as AI and machine learning enable predictions that portray the potential organizational paths and their outcomes (Hirsch, 2018). When the voices of both human and non-human stakeholders abound in society, whose voice should the organization pay attention to? When pre-programmed functions cause harm to employees or society, who is responsible? How do organizations optimize partnerships when unexpected interests and issues emerge? When masses of data are available, how do organizations ensure its fair and ethical use? How can organizational messages stay relevant and above the spam of a digitally savvy environment?

Conclusion: future roles of digital corporate communication 441

This chapter concludes the *Handbook on Digital Corporate Communication* by reflecting on new functions that corporate communication will adopt in organizations when new technology emerges. This chapter summarizes five new roles for corporate communication emerging from the complex development of technology and calls for future studies to address the changes brought about by these. These future roles of corporate communication are examined next.

1. CORPORATE COMMUNICATION AS DIGITAL COMMUNITY BUILDER

The more complex technology becomes, the easier it is for society to polarize and individuals to remain in their own technological user bubbles (Barrett et al., 2021). With every iteration of the Internet, enabling technologies make creating a sense of community apparently easier (Al-Omoush et al., 2021). Despite this, achieving a sense of community online remains very difficult in practice, as expectations remain as diverse as the interests of the individuals working for and with an organization.

Inclusivity will become one of the greatest values for societies and organizations of the future, as the human need for a sense of community remains unchanged (Aral, 2020). Organizations will be held responsible for emerging engagement tasks, such as community building and fostering a sense of belonging (Jorio et al., 2021). Whereas polarization may occur unaided, a sense of community does not. Effort is needed from corporate communication to maintain a sense of belonging and community, especially when digital recruitment accelerates the potential for change and employees are looking for reasons to justify their loyalty.

Individuals group together in the digital realm in virtual metaverses and communities, which are seen as the form of communication proliferated by the 'Internet revolution' (Lim, 2014), as members in computer-mediated spaces engage in relational interactions or social ties and repeatedly share information and knowledge for mutual learning or problem solving. This grouping together, however, is no longer organization- or brand-centric (Luoma-aho and Vos, 2010); as even in the case of online brand communities, consumers, fans and faith-holders group together often without the knowledge of the focal brand (Bowden et al., 2017). This has meant little organizational control over what is discussed in those arenas, despite the power they hold for guiding individuals into purchases and opinions (Reinikainen et al., 2020).

Despite this lack of control, these online spaces are often open for brands and organizational representatives if they choose to take a supportive role (Zuboff and Maxim, 2002). Learning to support stakeholders and customers without driving the organizational agenda remains a challenge but those overcoming it will curate future faith-holders who can help the organization in challenging times and online firestorms that happen sooner or later in the digital realm.

2. CORPORATE COMMUNICATION AS ORGANIZATIONAL CONSCIENCE FOR AI

As advanced machine learning and artificial intelligence (AI) are getting closer to human levels of intelligence (Van der Maas et al., 2021), they are becoming the new assistants of corporate communication. This assistance takes different forms, ranging from real-time data analysis to

442 *Handbook on digital corporate communication*

predictive monitoring systems for management and employees (Akinosho et al., 2020; Aziz and Dowling, 2019; Lalmuanawma et al., 2020). However, it requires ethical consideration and guidance (Ayling and Chapman, 2022), and understanding of the role of empathy and emotions (Park et al., 2022). This is not new for corporate communication, as algorithms are already producing content for news media, and bots and AI are utilized for building and testing organizational crisis preparedness (Perez-Liebana et al., 2019; Wong, 2021).

Much of AI still remains in its infancy, as automated messages and tailored content appear as disturbing spam to those it attempts to 'help'. At best, AI and machine learning enable communication to become more targeted, real-time and accurate as there will be fewer human flaws and biases in the organizational processes (Hancock et al., 2020). Described at worst as the digital iron cage enabling the surveillance of employees (Faraj et al., 2018), AI in organizations can also be used by organizational management to guide, predict and reward employee communication and performance. AI can and will also be used for manipulation of content, as fakeholders utilizing deepfakes may strategically attack brands and organizations, thus realizing their worst fears (Albahar and Almalki, 2019). Monitoring stakeholder sentiment may prove the only way to prevent content hijackings for future corporate communication (Luoma-aho et al., 2018).

Data and information flows offer new ways to transform social realities as human activity increasingly becomes subject to programmed analytics and visualization techniques (Vuorisalo, 2018). This means multiple new sources and data points for managers providing information on stakeholder and customer choices and employee performance, and less guesswork for future needs of employees, supply chains and stakeholders (Merendino et al., 2018). Complexity of legislation around data increases along with the development of technology, and ethical breaches in accessing, testing and monitoring data for behavioural insight become more regular, especially in countries and regions with less democratic societies and data use restrictions.

Simultaneously, as different organizational devices connect online, the Internet of things (IoT) is forming stakeholders out of different organizational technologies and even non-human tangible structures (Luoma-aho and Paloviita, 2010). These non-human entities can support organizational aims such as ideal customer experience, but also make the organization vulnerable if control of these systems falls into unintended hands via hijacks, hacks or breaches (Lakshmanan, 2020). For organizations, the larger the role AI and machine learning take, the more important the ethics guiding it becomes (Buhmann et al., 2020). As unforeseen situations requiring contextual understanding and experience still remain challenging for algorithms (Alkhatib and Bernstein, 2019), much of corporate communication functions demanding creativity will be necessary for guiding algorithms in organizations. In fact, a new task is emerging for corporate communication: becoming the organizational conscience for AI (Buhmann et al., 2020).

Questions about nudging individuals to make the right choice based on data and making sense of information in organizations become issues that require increased transparency and long-term impact evaluations. New questions will need addressing, such as: What are the social costs of AI efficiency? How much privacy and intimacy loss makes an acceptable trade for useful targeting? What is the value of data once lost? What happens when an algorithm developed to serve an organization starts to serve itself or gets hijacked and used for harmful purposes?

Conclusion: future roles of digital corporate communication 443

For corporate communication, AI holds the power to support stakeholder voices otherwise left unheard and increase stakeholder capitalism (Jackson et al., 2021; O'Brien, 2020). This can only succeed if AI empowers and helps organizations to become more employee- and stakeholder-centred. Understanding and listening to emerging needs and expectations may prove to be one of the most valuable skills of future organizations, yet the limits of what kind of listening is acceptable are constantly renegotiated. Transparency has been suggested to be a solution in this development, but simultaneously there is a threat of becoming vulnerable by revealing too much (Buhmann and Fieseler, 2022).

3.   CORPORATE COMMUNICATION AS DIGITAL CO-CREATION ENABLER

The digital environment will empower not only organizations but also stakeholders, shareholders and customers to execute their creative ideas related to brands. For example, 3D printing can enable individuals to become producers and distributors of any corporate brand or product. Organizational faith-holding will take extreme forms, as fans and supporters will be able to not only live in brand-related virtual environments, but also immerse their lives into all things digital brand-related. Future sales will include not only the product, but its blueprints for reproduction, online community for exchanging such information and supporting its production, as well as the different brand-related digital non-fungible tokens (NFT) (Joy et al., 2022).

Strongly controlled brand management will become outdated, as organizations can no longer guard their immaterial rights and copyrights. Online communities and support groups will enable peers to build brand experiences and solve technical issues, while the focal brand and organizations behind it often take a backseat supporting role. For corporate communication, this change means giving up brand control. As fakes increase in both intangible and tangible formats (Giachanou et al., 2020), new corporate communication tasks will emerge, such as verification of product authenticity as well as enabling new sustainable ways to trade used and second-hand products via reliable platforms. Accordingly, corporate communication will need to step into the role of enabler of stakeholder and customer co-creation of products, services, activities and experiences.

Questions will need to be addressed related to where to draw the line in co-creation and copyrights, how to support faith-holding in its best forms, and what are the consequences of uncontrolled use of the brand and organizational intangible assets in the future?

4.   CORPORATE COMMUNICATION AS BOXTURNER

Whether a sign of moral panic or conscious consumerism, customers and stakeholders are looking for the values behind brands and organizations (Alldredge et al., 2021). Expectations are rising in society about transparency of organizational management, production and sales (Dethier et al., 2021). In practice, there are more demands from stakeholders, more shareholder activism and more boxturning in the digital realm. Similar to reading the small print behind advertising messages or 'turning the box' around to read the small print, *boxturning* refers to active stakeholders' and consumers' investigations of the facts behind organizational or brand claims. For corporate communication, boxturning means increasing challenges in advertising and marketing, as all organizational messages need to resonate with the stakeholders on a deeper level than before. Messages put out merely for marketing purposes will backfire: the new consumer boxturners look to test and verify every corporate claim in reality, and loudly report inconsistencies across the digital media. The emergence of boxturners highlights the urgency of understanding and measuring stakeholder expectations and experiences in real time.

Extreme forms of boxturning in the digital realm also are becoming more common and challenging organizations and brands (Koschate-Fischer et al., 2019). As cancel culture takes over in consumption, there are new and unexpected pressures for organizations and brands to change their behaviour, products or even withdraw from deals or collaborations in the name of satisfying stakeholders' demands (Edson and Charsky, 2021). Cancel culture and wokeism will keep organizations on their toes, as being found guilty in the eyes of stakeholders can lead to rapidly spreading bans and boycotts. These bans and boycotts also result from geopolitical polarization and ideological differences: brands and products originating from an unfavourable nation or location may find it challenging to explain their stance to loud, digital hateholders (Luoma-aho, 2015). Moreover, negative messages spread faster, and fake accusations may prove almost as powerful as real ones, as the speed of the digital realm keeps individuals from factchecking (Pfeffer et al., 2014).

Corporate communication will increasingly have to focus on digital issues management and framing, as organizational points of view compete for attention among stakeholder opinions. In practice, organizations claiming to be something they are not, or pretending to satisfy diverse needs inauthentically, will be accused of inauthenticity and woke-washing (Vredenburg et al., 2020). In addition, such accusations may plague entire industries, when individual brands or organizations get infected or suspected of some misconduct or undesired development.

5.   CORPORATE COMMUNICATION AS GLOBAL DIPLOMAT

The more isolated individuals appear inside their own societal groups, the easier it is to divide and conquer. Organizations will increasingly find themselves catering to an increasingly diverse group of customers across global markets (Sriramesh and Verčič, 2020), yet at the same time nationalistic endeavours may threaten existence in global markets. As the digital workforce becomes easier to recruit across cultures and sectors, new challenges emerge such as changing expectations and geopolitical tensions (Walter and Förster, 2019). These challenges can only be solved with the help of corporate communication.

Simultaneously, the country of origin for brands and organizations may prove to be either an enabler or a hindrance, as reputation in the digital realm is formed based on impressions associated with different nationalities (Chu et al., 2010; Hien et al., 2020). Stakeholders scattered across the globe tend to judge organizations based on their country of origin (Nes, 2018), including how these countries behave on the world stage. Major competition between different regions may cause organizations and brands to pick sides and markets, when belonging to one may exclude from another.

In the near future, as national governments fail to unite ideologically and socio-politically divergent populations, leading to increased distrust towards governments, organizations and brands will need to take on more of a society-building function (Bolewski, 2022). Organizations encouraging social aspects of responsibility such as diversity and inclusivity

Conclusion: future roles of digital corporate communication 445

will offer employees and other stakeholders a place to belong and contribute to, which will gain greater competitiveness and legitimacy for these organizations in an increasingly divided society (Stevens et al., 2008). For this to happen, corporate communicators need to step up and contribute their core competencies to help organizations fulfil this important function in society. With a heavy focus on dialogic communication, monitoring and relationship-building, corporate communicators are best positioned to transition into this global diplomat role.

CONCLUSION

Utilizing technology always carries risks and responsibilities as well. At its worst, communication technology left unattended or used unethically may contribute to digital division and exclusion, where major brands rule over masses without voice or access. If left alone, digital corporate communication (DCC) could become the strategic management of digital technologies to hijack and distort communication in organizations, in society, and with organizational stakeholders for the destroying of organizational intangible and tangible assets.

At its best, ethical and empowering DCC becomes a core revenue function enabling organizational success. For future studies, the challenge remains testing these suggested and other emerging roles of technology for corporate communication in terms of their impact in different cultural contexts and settings. As technology becomes ubiquitous, new trends may move communication in unpredictable directions, even back to analogue and thus away from technologies. Should that be the case, many of the lessons of digital corporate communication will endure: both in the digital and in the analogue, relationships, belonging, ethics, boxturning and diplomacy continue as enablers of organizational success.

REFERENCES

Akinosho, T. D., Oyedele, L. O., Bilal, M., Ajayi, A. O., Delgado, M. D., Akinade, O. O., and Ahmed, A. A. (2020). Deep learning in the construction industry: A review of present status and future innovations. *Journal of Building Engineering*, 32, 101827.

Albahar, M. and Almalki, J. (2019). Deepfakes: Threats and countermeasures systematic review. *Journal of Theoretical and Applied Information Technology*, 97(22), 3242–3250.

Alkhatib, A. and Bernstein, M. (2019). Street-level algorithms: A theory at the gaps between policy and decisions. *Conference on Human Factors in Computing Systems – Proceedings*, New York, 2 May 2019 (pp. 1–13). https://doi.org/10.1145/3290605.3300760.

Alldredge, K., Jacobs, J., and Teichner, W. (2021). Great expectations: Navigating challenging stakeholder expectations of brands. McKinsey & Co, 9 December. https://www.mckinsey.com/industries/consumer-packaged-goods/our-insights/great-expectations-navigating-challenging-stakeholder-expectations-of-brands.

Al-Omoush, K. S., Orero-Blat, M., and Ribeiro-Soriano, D. (2021). The role of sense of community in harnessing the wisdom of crowds and creating collaborative knowledge during the COVID-19 pandemic. *Journal of Business Research*, 132, 765–774.

Aral, S. (2020). *The hype machine*. New York: Penguin Random House.

Ayling, J. and Chapman, A. (2022). Putting AI ethics to work: Are the tools fit for purpose? *AI and Ethics*, 2, 405–429. https://doi.org/10.1007/s43681-021-00084-x.

Aziz, S. and Dowling, M. (2019). Machine learning and AI for risk management. In T. Lynn, G. Mooney, P. Rosati, and M. Cummins (eds.), *Disrupting finance: FinTech and strategy in the 21st century* (pp. 33–50). Cham: Palgrave Macmillan.

446 *Handbook on digital corporate communication*

Barrett, P. M, Hendrix, J., and Sims, J. G. (2021). *Fueling the fire: How social media intensifies U.S. polarization – and what can be done about it.* New York University, Stern Center for Business and Human Rights.

Bowden, J. L.-H., Conduit, J., Hollebeek, L. D., Luoma-aho, V., and Solem, B. A. (2017). Engagement valence duality and spillover effects in online brand communities. *Journal of Service Theory and Practice, 27*(4), 877–897.

Bolewski, W. (2022). Corporate diplomacy: Compass for public/private management in turbulent times. In S. P. Sebastião and S. Spínola (eds.), *Diplomacy, organisations and citizens* (pp. 139–154). Cham: Palgrave Macmillan.

Buhmann, A. and Fieseler, C. (2022). Deep learning meets deep democracy: Deliberative governance and responsible innovation in artificial intelligence. *Business Ethics Quarterly.* https://doi.org/10.1017/beq.2021.42.

Buhmann, A., Passman, J., & Fieseler, C. (2020). Managing algorithmic accountability: Balancing reputational concerns, engagement strategies, and the potential of rational discourse. *Journal of Business Ethics, 163*, 265–280.

Chu, P., Chang, C., Chen, C., and Wang, T. (2010). Countering negative country-of-origin effects. *European Journal of Marketing, 44*(7/8), 1055–1076.

Dethier, F., Delcourt, C., and Willems, J. (2021). Transparency of nonprofit organizations: An integrative framework and research agenda. *Journal of Philanthropy and Marketing*, e1725. https://doi.org/10.1002/nvsm.1725.

Dhengre, S., Mathur, J., Oghazian, F., Tan, X., and McComb, C. (2020). Towards enhanced creativity in interface design through automated usability evaluation. Eleventh International Conference on Computational Creativity_ICCC20, Coimbra, Portugal (pp. 366–369). https://www.academia.edu/66882190/Towards_Enhanced_Creativity_in_Interface_Design_through_Automated_Usability_Evaluation.

Edson, T. and Charsky, D. (2021). Developing authentic corporate activism initiatives. https://digitalcommons.ithaca.edu/cgi/viewcontent.cgi?.

Faraj, S., Pachidi, S., and Sayegh, K. (2018). Working and organizing in the age of the learning algorithm. *Information and Organization, 28*(1), 62–70.

Giachanou, A., Zhang, G., and Rosso, P. (2020). Multimodal multi-image fake news detection. In *2020 IEEE 7th International Conference on Data Science and Advanced Analytics (DSAA)* (pp. 647–654). IEEE.

Hancock, J. T., Naaman, M., and Levy, K. (2020). AI-mediated communication: Definition, research agenda, and ethical considerations. *Journal of Computer-Mediated Communication, 25*(1), 89–100.

Hensellek, S. (2020). Digital leadership. *Journal of Media Management and Entrepreneurship, 2*(1), 55–69.

Hien, N., Phuong, N., Tran, T., and Thang, L. (2020). The effect of country-of-origin image on purchase intention: The mediating role of brand image and brand evaluation. *Management Science Letters, 10*(6), 1205–1212.

Hirsch, B. (2018). Tie me to the mast: Artificial intelligence & reputation risk management. *Journal of Business Strategy, 39*(1), 61–64.

Jackson, B. R., Ye, Y., Crawford, J. M., Becich, M. J., Roy, S., Botkin, J. R., de Baca, M. E., and Pantanowitz, L. (2021). The ethics of artificial intelligence in pathology and laboratory medicine: Principles and practice. *Academic Pathology.* https://doi.org/10.1177/2374289521990784.

Jorio, H., Samira, K., and Machrafi, M. (2021). Corporate social responsibility, innovation and employees engagement: The case of Moroccan companies. *Journal of Economic and Social Development, 8*(1), 29–38.

Joy, A., Zhu, Y., Peña, C., and Brouard, M. (2022). Digital future of luxury brands: Metaverse, digital fashion, and non-fungible tokens. *Strategic Change, 31*(3), 337–343.

Koschate-Fischer, N., Hoyer, W. D., and Wolframm, C. (2019). What if something unexpected happens to my brand? Spillover effects from positive and negative events in a co-branding partnership. *Psychology & Marketing, 38*(8), 758–772.

Lakshmanan, A. (2020). *Literature review on the latest security & the vulnerability of the Internet of Things (IoT) & a Proposal to Overcome.* Technical Report. https://doi.org/10.13140/RG.2.2.13756.80006.

Lalmuanawma, S., Hussain J., and Chhakchhuak, L. (2020). Applications of machine learning and artificial intelligence for Covid-19 (SARS-CoV-2) pandemic: A review. *Chaos, Solitons & Fractals*, 139, 110059. https://doi.org/10.1016/j.chaos.2020.110059.

Lim, W. M. (2014). Sense of virtual community and perceived critical mass in online group buying. *Journal of Strategic Marketing*, *22*(3), 268–283.

Luoma-aho, V. (2015). Understanding stakeholder engagement: Faith-holders, hateholders and fakeholders. *Research Journal of the Institute for Public Relations*, *2*(1). https://instituteforpr.org/understanding-stakeholder-engagement-faith-holders-hateholders-fakeholders/.

Luoma-aho, V. and Paloviita, A. (2010). Actor-networking stakeholder theory for corporate communications. *Corporate Communications: An International Journal*, *15*(1), 47–69.

Luoma-aho, V., Virolainen, M., Lievonen, M., and Halff, G. (2018). Brand hijacked: Why campaigns and hashtags are taken over by audiences. In A. Laskin (ed.), *Social, mobile and emerging media around the world* (pp. 57–68). Lanham, MD: Lexington Books.

Luoma-aho, V. and Vos, M. (2010). Towards a more dynamic stakeholder model: Acknowledging multiple issue arenas. *Corporate Communications: An International Journal*, *15*(3), 315–331.

Makkonen, H. and Olkkonen, R. (2017). Interactive value formation in interorganizational relationships. *Marketing Theory*, *17*(4), 517–535.

Mattila, V., Dwivedi, P., Gauri, P., and Ahbab, M. (2022). Mapping out the DAO ecosystem and assessing DAO autonomy. *International Journal of Computer Science and Information Technology Research*, *10*(1), 30–34.

Merendino, A., Dibb, S., Meadows, M., Quinn, L., Wilson, D., Simkin, L., and Canhoto, A. (2018). Big data, big decisions: The impact of big data on board level decision-making. *Journal of Business Research*, *93*, 67–78.

Nes, E. B. (2018). The role of country images in international marketing. Country-of-origin effects. In D. Ingenhoff, C. White, A. Buhmann, and S. Kiousis (eds.), *Bridging interdisciplinary perspectives on the country image, reputation, brand and identity* (pp. 33–48). London: Routledge.

O'Brien, J. (2020). The moral foundations of stakeholder capitalism. *Law and Financial Markets Review*, *14*(1), 1–4.

Park, G., Yim, C., Chung, J., and S. Lee (2022). Effect of AI chatbot empathy and identity disclosure on willingness to donate: The mediation of humanness and social presence. *Behaviour & Information Technology*. https://doi.org/10.1080/0144929X.2022.2105746.

Perez-Liebana, D., Liu, J., Khalifa, A., Gaina, R. D., Togelius, J., and Lucas, S. M. (2019). General video game AI: A multitrack framework for evaluating agents, games, and content generation algorithms. *IEEE Transactions on Games*, *11*(3), 195–214.

Pfeffer, J., Zorbach, T., and Carley, K. M. (2014). Understanding online firestorms: Negative word-of-mouth dynamics in social media networks. *Journal of Marketing Communications*, *20*(1–2), 117–128.

Rachinger, M., Rauter, R., Müller, C., Vorraber, W., and Schirgi, E. (2019). Digitalization and its influence on business model innovation. *Journal of Manufacturing Technology Management*, *30*(8), 1143–1160.

Reinikainen, H., Munnukka, J., Maity, D., and Luoma-aho, V. (2020). 'You really are a great big sister': Parasocial relationships, credibility, and the moderating role of audience comments in influencer marketing. *Journal of Marketing Management*, *36*(3–4), 279–298.

Skjuve, M., Følstad, A., Fostervold, K. I., and Brandtzaeg, P. B. (2021). My chatbot companion: A study of human-chatbot relationships. *International Journal of Human-Computer Studies*, *149*, 102601.

Sriramesh, K. and Verčič, D. (eds.) (2020). *The global public relations handbook: Theory, research, and practice*. New York: Routledge.

Stevens, F. G., Plaut, V. C., and Sanchez-Burks, J. (2008). Unlocking the benefits of diversity: All-inclusive multiculturalism and positive organizational change. *The Journal of Applied Behavioral Science*, *44*(1), 116–133.

Van der Maas, H. L., Snoek, L., and Stevenson, C. E. (2021). How much intelligence is there in artificial intelligence? A 2020 update. *Intelligence*, *87*, 101548.

Vredenburg, J., Kapitan, S., Spry, A., and Kemper, J. (2020). Brands taking a stand: Authentic brand activism or woke washing? *Journal of Public Policy & Marketing*, *4*, 444–460.

448 *Handbook on digital corporate communication*

Vuorisalo, V. (2018). Algorithmic life and power flows in the digital world. In M. Lehto and P. Neittaanmäki (eds.), *Cyber security: Power and technology* (pp. 233–247). Berlin: Springer.

Walter, A. and Förster, S. (2019). The effects of globalization on human resources management in SMEs. *DSpace*. http://dspace.tsu.ge/xmlui/handle/123456789/502.

Wong, Y. K. (2021). Dealing crisis management using AI decision making. *International Journal of Computer Science, Engineering and Applications (IJCSEA)*, *11*(5), 15–22. https://doi.org/10.5121/ijcsea.2021.11502.

Zerfass, A., Moreno, A., Tench, R., Verčič, D., and Buhmann, A. (2022). *European Communication Monitor 2022. Exploring diversity and empathic leadership, CommTech and consulting in communications. Results of a survey in 43 countries.* Brussels: EUPRERA/EACD.

Zuboff, S. and Maxim, J. (2002). *The support economy: Why corporations are failing individuals and the next episode of capitalism.* New York: Allen Lane.

Index

2021 European Communication Monitor 6

Achmea 12, 364–5
ACID Test of corporate brand management 41
actionable audience 83, 85–6
activism 11
 Asian Pulp and Paper (APP) company 161–2
 civil society, engagement in 154
 corporations and activists 157–8
 definition 152
 future directions 162
 network theory 155–6
 stakeholder engagement 154–5
 supply chain network 153
 tools 159–60
 value chains, activist engagement in 157
activists 11, 67, 152–3, 155, 159–62, 167–8, 226, 388–9
 corporations and 157–8
 groups 39, 58, 135, 139, 160, 161, 162, 229, 417
 online 67, 72, 74
 see also activism
Adobe Experience Cloud 244
#adoptaunabotella 85
advanced information technology (AIT) 23
advertising value equivalence (AVE) 126
advertorials 56, 429
aggregation brandjack 224
aggregative frames 139–43
The AI and Big Data Readiness Report 284
'AIinPR' 283–4, 285
Airbnb 283, 375
algorithm-driven organization 315
algorithmic communication 316
algorithmic filtering 366
algorithmic leader 317, 318
algorithmic management and leadership 12, 311–12
 autonomy of workers 321
 communication principles 316
 corporate communication and 314–15
 definition 312–14
 Deliveroo case study 322
 e-leadership 23, 313, 314, 317
 employment relations 321
 future directions 323
 human resource management 321–2
 role of communication in 319–20

scientific management 317–18
substitutes-for-leadership theory 318
transformational leadership 317
algorithmic profiling 125
algorithms 12, 171, 213, 214, 255, 282, 290, 297, 313, 315, 318, 320, 374, 388, 430, 442
 AI and 65, 282, 288, 291, 297
 big data and 375, 377
 in corporate sustainability 316
 definition 170, 312
 in performance management 321–2
Alibaba 73, 343, 352
Allen, T. J. 25
Alliance for Telecommunication Industry Solutions (ATIS) 376
Alphabet 128, 299, 343
Amazon 157, 160, 282, 299, 346, 347, 348, 351, 374
 Alexa 12, 170, 343, 344, 346–9, 350
Amazon Associates Program 347
Amazon Influencer Program 347
AMEC 129
America's Army (2002) 271
antecedents, relationship outcomes and 105–6
Apple 55, 299, 343
 HomePod 343
application programming interfaces (APIs) 343
appraisal theory 194
Apsland, W. 299
Arenstein, S. 179
Argenti, P. 358
Aristotle 302
 Leviathan 357
 Politics 357
Arsenault, A. 385
Arthur W. Page Society for Global Communication Executives 6
artificial intelligence (AI) 11, 12, 46, 65, 71, 74, 97, 113, 118, 128, 166, 170, 175, 287, 297, 298, 299, 306, 363, 371, 440
 agents 71, 286
 automatized text analyses 124
 based voice assistants 343
 big data and 289, 291, 292, 299–300
 City of Sydney case study 305–7
 content personalization 301
 corporate communication and 170, 290, 291–2, 294, 303–4, 304
  as organizational conscience for 441–3

450 *Handbook on digital corporate communication*

deep learning 282
definition 281
in digital corporate communication 283–4
discursive engagement for 289–90
environmental scanning 171
epistemic concerns 288–90
ethical and reputational concerns 288
evidence concerns 288
extended intelligence and 298–9
framework 293, 294
future directions 294–5
governance, at Vodafone 292–4
for identifying risks 171
impact on corporate life 282–3
implications 290–92
intelligent user interfaces 284–7
limitations of 173–4
machine learning 170–71, 282
measurement and evaluation 128–9
misinformation campaigns 230
opacity 129, 288
outcome concerns 288
technologies 37, 300, 301, 307, 316, 344
see also extended intelligence; paracrises
Artificial Intelligence Act 294
Asian Pulp and Paper (APP) Company 11, 153, 161–2
Asia-Pacific Communications Report 302
Audiense 108
audio ads 347, 348
audio social networks 346, 347
augmented reality (AR) 12, 47–8, 277, 338, 396
automated content analysis (ACA) 170
automated leadership 313
automation 6, 39, 124, 127, 241, 283, 284, 290, 304, 312, 314, 343, 349, 440
autonomous sensory meridian response (ASMR) 407
avatars, in gamification 268, 270
Avolio, B. J. 23, 313

Back, L. 357
Badham, M. 56, 105, 152, 267, 298, 344, 371, 414
Bakhtin, M. 359
Bakir, V. 213
Balmer, J. M. T. 38
Barcelona Declaration of Measurement Principles 126
Barnard, C. I. 20, 26
Beger, R. 304
behavioural insights 363
Ben & Jerry's 387
Benoit, W. L. 225
Bentley, S. 366

Berocca (Bayer Consumer Health) 348
Berton, M. 431
big data 170, 287, 299–300, 372
algorithms and 375, 377
analytics and 371, 372–3, 379–80
artificial intelligence and 282, 291, 292
business analytics revenues 282–3
big data market 12, 371, 374
aggregation of data 373
Coase theorem 376, 377
corporate communication's role in 375
corrective and deliberative remedies 377, 379
deliberative decision-making 378
externalities of 372–4, 378–9
future directions 379–80
Ostrom's common-pool resources 377–8
Pigovian approach in markets 375–6
Bishop, B. 316
Bizzarri, M. 201, 202
Bjola, C. 384, 392
#BlackLivesMatter (racial equality) 160, 229
blogs 159
Bloomberg, J. 8
Boeing, character assassination at 11, 222, 226–8
Bogost, I. 268, 271
Bokányi, E. 322
Bollen, L. 93
#borderfreecoffee 70
Bowen, S. 366
Bowen, S. A. 24, 299–300, 300
boxturning 443, 444
boycott 152, 167, 193, 444
#boycottDolceGabbana 73–3
#boycottEltonJohn 72
#deleteuber boycott 11, 145–6, 147
NFL Boycott scandal 230–31
#boycottDolceGabbana 72–3
#boycottEltonJohn 72
brand communication 10, 34
British Monarchy 43–7
corporate brand 34–5
digital corporate 36
future directions 47–8
quaternary communication 39–40
total corporate brand communication mix 41–2
total corporate communication 35–6
developments in 37–9
brand endorsements 256
brandjacking 11, 228, 231
aggregation brandjack 224
CA campaigns 232
definition 222, 223
at McDonald's 223–5

reputational attacks and 229
brand journalism 56
Brandt, D. 366
BrandWatch 108
Braun, S. 23, 24
Brennan, J. S. 8
Brennen, J. S. 20
Brexit campaign 145
British Broadcasting Corporation's (BBC) 38, 39
'British' Commonwealth 44
British Government Communication Service's
    Evaluation Framework 2.0. 121
British Monarchy 10, 43–5
    corporate communication
        controlled based (secondary) 46
        corporate brand based (promissory) 45
        corporate identity based (primary) 45
        digital (quaternary) based 46–7
        feedback (responsory) based 47
        word-of-mouth based (tertiary) 46
British Post Office 43
Brockhaus, J. 6, 242, 243
Broom, G. M. 104
Brown and Williamson 225
Bruning, S. D. 104
Buber, M. 25, 359
Bughin, J. 8
Buhmann, A. 119, 121, 297
Burger King 347, 352
Burkhardt, J. M. 430
Burnside-Lawry, J. 360, 361
Bussie, J. 359
BuzzFeed 289
bystanders 193, 196, 199, 203
ByteDance 43

Caillois, R. 270
Calhoun, D. 227
California Consumer Privacy Act 377
Cambridge Analytica 70, 388
Camilleri, M. A. 299
cancel culture (CC) 145, 160, 229, 230, 231, 444
cancel tactics 160
capital markets 94–5
Caplan, R. 366
Cardon, P. W. 22, 24
CarParts corporation 98
"The Case for Extended Intelligence" 307
cashtags 97
Castellani, P. 431
Castells, M. 22
Catalonia 386
CCO theory 357
Centre for Strategic Communication Excellence
    297

CEOs 40–41, 146, 201, 202, 222, 226, 227, 229,
    230–31, 231, 347, 388–9
Chadwick, A. 51, 208, 212
challenge paracrisis cluster 170
Chamorro-Premuzik, T. 299
Change.org platform 152, 157, 159
Chan, N. K. 320
character assassination (CA) 11, 226, 229, 231
    at Boeing 226–7
    brandjacking and 232
    as challenge crisis 226, 228
    character-based reputation 225
    definition 222, 225
Chartered Institute of Public Relations (CIPR)
    283–4
chatbots 1, 12, 113, 282, 294, 304–5, 358, 363,
    373
Cheney, G. 316
Chen, F. 169
Chew, D. 187
Cho, M. 154–5
Christensen, L. T. 3
Cision Communications Cloud 244
Ciszek, E. L. 159, 160
cities, hashtag activism 386–7
citizen co-production 413, 414, 417
citizen engagement 12, 13, 414–16, 422
    see also co-productive citizen engagement
citizen participation 413, 418, 420, 422
City of Sydney case study 12, 305–7
Civil Learning Tool 136
civil society 154, 211, 212, 311
clicktivism 1, 152, 157, 416
climate change 58
Cloud Computing 299, 371
Coakley, G. 360
Coase theorem 376, 377
Cobb, S. 223
Cocolo Chanel 201
Colleoni, E. 139
CommTech (Communication Technology) 5–6,
    123, 240, 241, 242, 243, 246, 249, 440
communal relationship 104
communicated relational commitment 105
communicating entity 3
communication 4–5
    in algorithmic management and leadership
        319–20
    centrality of 357
    departments 6, 128, 129, 238, 240–42, 246–8
    digital effects shaping 9
    information vs. 359
    management of 3–4
    in organizational practices 319–20
    principles of 316

452 *Handbook on digital corporate communication*

as two-way dialogic process 359
communication functions and departments 238,
    246–7
  digitalizing 242
  digital transformation of 240–41, 243
communication management 11, 109, 154, 240,
    297, 304
communication networks 25, 257, 320
communication practitioners 6, 7, 11, 129, 184,
    242, 247, 249, 284, 289
communicatively constituted organizations
    (CCO) 311, 314, 316, 317, 319, 320
complaint management 11, 193
  collective goals 195
  complaining behaviour 196, 197, 203–4
  definitions of complaining 194–6
  in digital environments 198–201
  discrete emotions 194
  dissatisfaction 194
  future directions 202–4
  Gucci case study 201–2
  online firestorms 196–7, 200–201, 203
  personal goals 195
  public online complaints 196, 198
  redress seeking 195, 199
  venting 195, 200, 201
computer-human leadership (CHL) 313
computer-mediated communication (CMC) 21,
    22, 187
CONE Communications 78
Confederation of Swedish Enterprises' crisis 216
Connelly, C. E. 321
conspiracy logic 216
  and sustained futility of response 217–18
conspiracy theories 217, 222, 226
  hostile narratives and 209–10
contingency theory 166
conversational broadness 143, 146
conversational commerce 38
conversational human voice 82, 85, 105, 108, 109
conversational volume 143, 146
Coombs, W. T. 168, 179, 180, 181, 185, 189,
    225, 226
Cooper, L. 360
COP26 climate 58
co-production 13, 413, 414
  see also digital co-production
co-productive citizen engagement 13, 413
  benefits and risks of ICTs for 417
  digital co-production 414–16
  digital corporate communication and 414
  digital divide 417, 421–2
  future directions 422
  Madrid City Council, Madrid Móvil app of
    418–22

Coral bottle campaign 261–2
#coralliebtdeinekleidung 261
core functional digital infrastructure 243–4
Cornelissen, J. 3, 300, 358
corporate apologia 166
corporate brand 34–5
  based communication 41, 42, 45, 46
  emotional ownership 40
  employees importance 40–41
  legal ownership 40
  promissory corporate communication 41
  role of senior management and CEO 41
corporate communication 3, 7, 10, 34, 37, 52,
    103, 110, 119–20, 136, 238, 242–3, 266,
    267, 290, 300, 314, 328, 371, 372, 375
  academic research in 6–7
  adoption of digital technologies 11–12
  artificial intelligence and 290–92, 294, 303–4
  attributes of 2–5
  as boxturner 443–4
  definition 2, 5, 358, 413
  digital activism and 157
  as digital co-creation enabler 443
  as digital community builder 441
  digitalization in 1–2
  digitally-influenced effects in society 12–13
  digital transformation for 11, 240
  gamification in 272–5
  as global diplomat 444–5
  IUI technology 285–6
  as leadership enabler 315
  measurement and evaluation 119–20, 127–8
  as organizational conscience for AI 441–3
  organization-wide digital transformation and
    245–6
  public relations *vs.* 4
  visual contents for 326, 327
  see also digital transformation
corporate communicators 11, 47, 256–7, 289–90,
    292, 302, 303, 307, 445
corporate crisis communication 165, 166, 171,
    175
corporate digital communication 39, 41, 231
corporate diplomacy 385, 387, 394, 395
corporate failures 193, 194, 198
corporate identities 35, 36, 45
corporate influencers 11, 258
corporate leadership process 314
corporate life, artificial intelligence impact on
    282–3
corporate marketing 35, 37
corporate misconduct 193, 200, 202
corporate-owned voice assistants (OVA) 346
corporate public relations *see* corporate
    communication

corporate reputation 10, 64, 66, 69, 136
  artificial intelligence 71, 74
  changes in 67–9
  definition 65–6
  Dolce & Gabbana (D&G) 72–4
  future directions 74
  media landscape 68–9
  media reputation 67–8
  signals, fake news and 69–70
  in social media 64–5, 66
corporate social performance (CSP) 66
corporate social responsibility (CSR) 10, 78, 80,
    86, 231, 266
  definition 79
  initiatives 78–9, 82, 266
  motives 80
  programmes 231
  social assessments and 167–8
  social movements and 231
  see also CSR communication
corporate storytelling 266, 267, 271–2, 277
corporate visual identification see corporate
    identities
corporations 1, 57, 92, 96, 97, 100, 128, 162, 168,
    170, 228, 260
  activists and 152–5, 157–60
  corporate brands for 35
  in crisis 172–4
  gamification and 266, 269, 271–3, 275
  international 387–8
  stakeholders and 107–10, 167, 169
  support for LGBTQ+ communities 231
  transnational 385
Couldry, N. 357
Council on Extended Intelligence 306, 307
Covey, S. 359
Covid-19 153, 273, 283, 284, 371, 395, 426
  infodemic 431–2
    EU's response to disinformation 432–3
    vaccine disinformation campaign 13,
      433–5
  pandemic 18, 24, 59–60, 93, 100, 227, 243,
    276, 338
Cowan, G. 385
Craig, R. 357
Crandall, W. R. 185
Credit Suisse 393
crisis 165, 166, 168
  arenas 198
  command centre 172
  communication 11, 165, 166, 172, 208
    best practices in 182–3
    hostile hijacking and 211–12
  distinction between paracrisis and 169

management 22, 59, 136, 169, 172, 179, 180,
    185, 189
  response, delivery of 173
Crisis Arena Crossover (CAC) framework 56
crisis communication plan (CCP) 172
crisis communication team (CCT) 172
crisis life cycles 11, 179–80
  crisis communication 182–3
  crisis, phases 180, 181
  dialogic communication 186–7
  digital crisis life cycle framework 183–4,
    185, 187–9
  future directions 189
  new electronic payment service (e-pay)
    187–9
  operation of 180
  organizational listening 186
  social media 181
    organizational crises and 181–2
  strategic phase 180
crisis managers 172, 173, 174, 185
crowdfunding 98, 299
crowdinvesting 98
crowdsourcing 58, 98, 159, 228
The Crown 44
Crypto Valley 394
CSR communication 10, 79, 81
  actionable 78, 79
  challenges, solutions to 82–4
  credit-sharing framing approach in 80
  data misuse and privacy issues 82
  digital corporate communication 80
  future directions 85–6
  greenwashing 82
  Grupo Nutresa 84–5
  stakeholders scepticism and 81–2
CSR fit 82–3, 85
customer journey mapping 363
customer relationship management (CRM) tools
    94
cybersecurity 110, 113, 371, 393

Dapper Dan 201
Dark PR 144–5
data analytics 282, 299, 306, 367, 373
data-enabled platform 372
DataReportal 78
deepfakes 39, 230, 336, 337, 442
#deleteuber boycott 11, 145–6, 147
deliberative polling 363
Delisle, M.-P. 255
Deliveroo France 12, 317, 322
Deloitte 12
  Leadership Academy 275
  2018 Global Crisis Management Survey 179

Deterding, S. 270
Deutsche Bank 387
Dewey, J. 357
Diageo 348
dialogic communication 103, 105, 186–7, 189
dialogic theory 259
Di Domenico, M. 372
Diers-Lawson, A. 180, 181
digital 7
    activism 152, 153, 157, 160, 162, 229, 230,
       231
    activists 152, 155, 222, 229
    channels 167–8, 173, 175, 403
        direct *vs.* indirect 195
        disinformation and 426, 430, 435
    collectives 138, 144
        and communication ecosystems 139–40
        monitoring refraction of 141–3
    effects shaping communication 9
    intermediaries 55
    internal media 23, 24–5
digital citizen engagement (DCE) 414, 417, 421
digital communication 64–5, 92–3, 112, 137,
    140–41, 152, 157, 222, 323
digital co-production (DCP) 414, 418–22
    development of 415–16
    'echo chamber' phenomenon 417
digital corporate brand communication 34, 36, 39,
    42, 43, 48
digital corporate communication (DCC) 1–2, 38,
    103, 165, 209, 222, 230, 232, 238, 294,
    298, 300, 301, 313, 352, 353, 379, 445
    artificial intelligence in 283–4
    brand communication and 34, 35, 38, 40, 42,
       45, 47–8
    co-productive citizen engagement 413, 414,
       418, 422
    crisis life cycles and 182–3, 189
    CSR communication and 80
    definition 8–9, 36, 106, 118, 152, 193–4,
       267, 312, 371, 414
    digital voice communication and 343–4
    disinformation and 426, 435
    extended intelligence and 297, 298, 300–302,
       305, 307
    future roles of 440–45
    intelligent user interfaces impact on 286–7
    market for big data 371, 372, 375, 376, 379
    measurement and evaluation of 118, 119,
       120–22, 123–6, 128, 130
    organizational listening 358, 361, 366, 367
    practices 5–6
    public sector organizations 401, 402, 404,
       406–7, 408
    relationship management practice 113

research 2, 6–7
stakeholder relationship management 103,
    110–11, 112, 113
visual communication and 326, 327, 339
digital corporate communication management
    119, 123, 125–6
digital crisis life cycle framework 183, 184, 185,
    187–9
digital diplomacy 384–5, 387, 395
Digital Diplomacy Facebook Guide 384
digital environments 108, 139, 165, 198–201,
    227–8, 401, 404, 408
digital feudalism 373
digital hijacking 39
digital images 328, 329
digital infrastructure 7, 8, 10, 240, 242–4
digital internal communication 18, 20–22, 24,
    26, 29
digitalization 7, 10, 13, 18, 126, 238, 240, 314,
    328, 388, 426, 440
    changing measurement and evaluation
       118–19, 122, 127
    communication functions and departments
       242
    in corporate communication 1–2
    definition 8, 20–21, 239
    formal and informal communication
       networks 25
    internal communication and 22–3
    investor relations and 91, 94, 95, 96, 98–100
    issues management and 144–5
    leadership and 23
    media relations and 51, 54–6
    public diplomacy and 384, 386, 387, 391–2,
       395
    of public sector communication 402–3
    of public sector organizations 402, 405, 406
    stakeholder communications 241
    stakeholder journey 241
digital leadership 23
digitally-enabled service workers 320
digital marketing 7, 241
digital media 20, 23, 59, 157, 160–61, 328, 329,
    336, 400, 408
digital media-arenas (DMA) framework 345
digital optimizers 99
digital organizational listening 362–3
digital pioneers 99, 238
digital platforms 7, 22, 43, 276, 386, 388, 403
digital positioners 99
digital public diplomacy 12–13, 384, 385–6, 389,
    392–5
    see also public diplomacy
digital public relations 7, 241
digital publics 113, 329, 334–5, 403

digital public sector organization communication 401

Digital Services Act 434

digital space 110, 111, 152, 181

Digital Taylorism *see* scientific management 2.0

digital technologies 1, 2, 10, 37, 103, 107, 110, 121, 242–3, 246, 247, 351, 371, 384, 404
  access 107, 109
  communication processes and 5–6
  corporate communication and 11–13
  engagement 108, 109
  for functional support 244
  in management 312
  media relations and 51
  for stakeholder communications 241
  voices 107–8, 109

digital tools 11, 26, 93–5, 99, 100, 241, 244, 247, 248, 415–16, 417

digital transformation 7, 118, 297, 298, 299, 305, 314
  of communication functions and departments 240–41, 243
  of corporate communication 11
    agenda for research on 249
  definition 8, 239
  future directions 248–9
  obstacles of 247
  of organizations 244–6
  strategies 239
  see also corporate communication

digital transmitters 99

digital visual communication 326, 336, 337, 339

digital visual experience, realms of 330, 333–6

digital voice communication (DVC) 343, 344, 345–6, 350, 351, 353

digitization 7, 8, 20–21, 100, 395

Dilraba Dilmurat 73

Di Martino, L. 390

Dionisopoulos, G. N. 316

diplomatic actors 384, 386, 388, 390–92, 392, 395

disinformation 213, 218, 426, 431
  academic studies 427, 428
  campaign 13, 208, 211, 212, 214, 427, 433–5
  Covid-19 infodemic 431–5
  definition 210, 427
  fake news 426–9
  future directions 435
  hostile hijacking and 210–11
  operators 208, 209, 211, 214–15, 219
  prototypes of 427
  social media 429–30

disintermediation 283, 403

dissatisfaction 193, 194

distributed denial of service (DDOS) 152, 157, 160, 162

distributive justice 199, 200

diversity, equity, and inclusion (DEI) 98

Dobson, A. 360

Dolce, D. 72

Dolce & Gabbana (D&G) 72–4

Domino's Pizza 349

Dow Jones Sustainability Indices (DJSI) 84

Dowling, G. 66

Dozier, D. M. 159

Drupal 244

earned media 167–8

Easterbrook, S. 229

Edelman's 2021 Trust Barometer 78

Edelman's Earned Brand Study 230

Edwards, F. 152

Einwiller, S. A. 195, 199, 200, 365

e-leadership 23, 313, 314, 317

The Elites vs. the People (narrative) 209

Elizabeth II, Queen 44, 45

emails 21, 54, 58, 346

emotional ownership, corporate brand 40

engagement
  in civil society 154
  dimensions of 154–5
  organizational listening 363, 365
  stakeholder 154–5

enterprise risk management (ERM) 136

enterprise social media 319, 403

#entretodoscontribuimos 85

environmental activists 153, 161–2

Environmental Paper Network (EPN) 161

environmental, social and governance (ESG) 98

Esrock, S. L. 93

ETrade 97

Etter, M. 6, 64, 66, 67, 69

European Commission 432

European External Action Service (EEAS) 209, 434
  Strategic Communication Division 434

European Medicine Agency (EMA) 433–4

European Telecommunications Standards Institute (ETSI) 376

European Union 292, 294, 376, 386, 427, 434, 435
  Covid-19 vaccine disinformation campaign 13, 433–5
  disinformation tactics 432–3
  GDPR 12, 377

EUvsDisinfo 209, 210, 216, 218, 434

Ewing, M. 6

exchange relationship 104

experiential relationships 104

456 *Handbook on digital corporate communication*

extended intelligence (EI) 12, 297–8, 302, 304, 307
    artificial intelligence and 298–9
    big data and 299–300
    chatbots 304–5
    City of Sydney case study 305–7
    corporate communicators 302–3
    expanded capability 298–9
    face-to-face communication 303
    future directions 307
    see also artificial intelligence
extended reality (ER) 47, 48
externalities 373–9

Facebook 1, 12, 43, 57, 70, 78, 79, 80, 97, 107, 128, 137, 159, 161, 174, 178, 195, 199, 202, 213–14, 282, 327, 374, 375, 377, 388, 392, 394, 406, 418
Facebook Diplomacy 385
Facebook Insights 124
Facebook Messenger 406
Facebook Metaverse 273, 336
facticity 429
Factiva 129
Fahmy, S. 327
faith-holders 154, 441
fakeholders 70, 112, 209, 211, 212, 218, 417
fake news 64–5, 69–70, 70, 182, 426, 427, 428, 429, 431, 435
    see also disinformation
faux pas paracrisis 169–70, 174
The Favourite 44
Fearn-Banks, K. 179, 180
Federal Department of Foreign Affairs of Switzerland (FDFA) 392, 394, 395
Federer, R. 393
feedback based communication 41–2, 47
Feller, A. 156
Ferguson, M. A. 104
filter function 213–14
financial communication 10, 91–2, 95
Fink, S. 180
Finnish Association of Communications Professionals (ProCom) 407
Finnish Tax Administration 13, 401, 407–8, 409
first industrial revolution 37
First Marketing Revolution 38
Fitzpatrick, K. R. 387
Fiumara, G. 357
Flores-Cuautle, J. J. A. 415–16
Flynn, J. 360
Flyverbom, M. 316
Fombrun, C. 65
Forbes 223, 303
Fordism 318

formal communication networks 25
formative evaluation 120
Fortune 66
Fortune Global 500 companies 78, 93, 161
Four Realms of Digital Visual Experience (4ReDiVE) 326, 330, 333, 339
    aesthetic realm 334–5
    connection 333
    educational realm 335
    entertainment realm 333–4
    escapist realm 335–6
    participation 333
Fourth Industrial Revolution 23, 37–8, 287
Fourth Marketing Revolution 38
Frandsen, F. 185
Frankiewicz, B. 299
Freberg, K. 6
Frenzel, A. 8
#FridaysForFuture 386
Friedman, T. L. 223–4
Fujitsu Horizon computer system 43
The functions of the executive (Barnard) 26

Gabbana, S. 72, 73
Gadamer, H. 359
Galière, S. 322
Galloway, C. 344
game elements 270, 272, 273–4
GameStop 97–8
gamification 11, 12, 266, 273
    for brand–consumer relationships 275
    as buzzword 267
    in corporate communication 272–5
    as corporate storytelling 271–2
    definition 267
    'Deloitte Leadership Academy' 275
    effects of 268
    elements of 270–71
    future directions 276–7
    gamified
        communities 272
        external communication 269
        internal communication 269
    negative effects 273–4
    Nissan's 'Leaf' car 275
    procedural rhetoric and 271
    as a strategy 268
    as a tool 268
    users' perspective 270
gamified environments 270, 273, 274
Gartner 5, 73–4, 301
General Data Protection Regulation (GDPR) 289
Generation-Z 304
generic digital infrastructure 244
Geneva Dialogue on Responsible Behaviour 393

George, A. M. 180
George III, King 44
George, J. G. 152, 157
George VI, King 44
Gerdenitsch, C. 269
Gerlach, G. I. 27
German DPRG/ICV model 121
German Investor Relations Association 99
Gilmore, J. H. 333
GitHub 290
Glenn, E. 359
Global Council on Extended Intelligence 300
Global Strategic Communications Council
    (GSCC) 10, 58–9
GoFundMe 159
Goh, W. W. P. 303
Goldman Sachs 389
Golightly, N. 226–7
Gonzalez-Herrero, A. 180
Google 12, 43, 55, 128, 160, 214, 275–6, 282,
    347, 348, 350, 374, 375, 388, 391, 393
Google Analytics 124
Google Assistant 1, 352
Google Code Jam 275–576
GoogleDocs 58
Google Home 343, 349, 352
Google Scholar 79
Google Shopping 349
Greening, D. W. 66
Greenpeace 153, 161
greenwashing 82, 86
Grégoire, Y. 200
Greyser, S. A. 38
Grunig, J. E. 104
Grupo Nutresa 10, 84–5
GSMA 292, 293
The Guardian 71
Gucci 11, 193, 194, 200, 201–2
Gucci Changemakers 202
guilt by association, paracrisis cluster 169, 170

Habermas, J. 212
hacking 137, 157, 169, 170
Hahaganda (narrative) 210
Hall, R. 65
Han, G. 314
Hannák, A. 322
Hansen, H. K. 316
'Happy Lilly,' 394
Hargie, O. 365
Harms, P. D. 314
hashtags (#) 1, 97, 143, 162, 229, 386
    activism tactics 160
    hijacking 152, 159, 160, 162
Havas Worldwide Singapore 11, 187, 188

hearing, listening *vs.* 359–60
Heath, R. L. 158
Heineken® 12, 337–9
Heitmüller, E. 174
heuristic method 185
Hills, M. 299
Hinson, M. D. 6
Hirschman, A. O. 193
H&M 200
Hobbes, T. 357
Hoffmann, C. P. 99
Holladay, J. 181
Holladay, S. 225, 226
Holladay, S. J. 168
Holtzhausen, D. 374
Hond, F. den 316
'Honest Ads Act' 376
Hon, L. C. 104, 105
Hootsuite 107, 108, 124, 244
Horton, D. 256
hostile hijacking 208, 209
    connectivity 212–13
    conspiracy logic
        sustained futility of response and
            217–18
    crisis communication and 211–12
    disinformation operations 214–15
    filter function 213–14
    future directions 218–19
    hostile hijackers 211, 213
    hybridity and attention economy 212
    identity grievance campaigns 214
    link by association 216
    of organizational crises 11, 208, 209
    at Swedish organizations 215–18
    victimization and mask-slipping 217
    see also disinformation
hostile narratives 216
    and conspiracy theories 209–10
'House of Switzerland' storytelling platform 394
HSBC UK's campaign 387–8
Huang, Q. 108
Huang, Y. H. 104
Hübscher, R. 285, 286
humaning 112
human resource management (HRM) 321–2
Humphreys, L. 320
hybridity, attention economy and 212

identity grievance campaigns 214
IKEA 208
Illia, L. 145
image-based apps 11
image repair theory 166
images 326, 327, 336

458 *Handbook on digital corporate communication*

in corporate communication 328
visual social semiotics of 329–32
Imminent Collapse (narrative) 210
immunity to change phenomenon 27
The Independent 39
Indiegogo 159
influencer campaigns, strategy for 256–7
influencer content 159, 261
influencer marketing 253, 256
influencer relations 257–8
influencers *see* social media influencers
informal communication networks 25, 320
information and communication technologies
(ICT) 67, 118, 267, 272, 422
for co-productive citizen engagement 413,
415, 417
Madrid City Council 418–19, 421
information, communication *vs.* 359
information technology (IT) 22–3, 319, 390–91
in-skill purchasing (ISP) 349
Instagram 72, 73, 79, 84, 85, 107, 140, 143, 159,
174, 175, 184, 193, 201, 202, 255, 261,
328, 335, 336, 388, 389, 392, 406, 407,
408, 430
Instagram Insights 124
Institute for Public Relations 283
institutionalized actors 138–9
integrated evaluation framework (IEF) 121
integrated internal communication 19
'Intel Inside' jingle 346
intelligent user interfaces (IUIs) 284–7
intention to deceive 429
interactional justice 198–9
internal communication 10, 18
changes in 22–5
communication visibility/surveillance 27
critical perspective 26–7
definition 19–20
future research 29
leadership and 23–4
practices remaining same 25–6
pseudo involvement 26–7
reconceptualization of space and time 22–3
social bot in 22
strategic management of 19
Swedish Transport Administration 28–9
internal social media (ISM) 21
International Association for the Measurement
and Evaluation of Communication 121
international corporations 387–8
International Data Corporation (IDC) 111
International Journal of Listening 359
Internet 111, 157, 193, 430, 431, 441
internet of things (IoT) 23, 39, 282, 299, 371, 442
internet-related public relations 7

investment 91, 97, 98, 100
investor relations
adoption of digital communication 92–3
capital markets 94–5
definition 91
digital investor relations tools 93–4
digitalization and 91, 94, 95, 96, 98–100
disclosure of information 92, 96
financial communication and 10
future directions 100
non-financial disclosure 96–7
SAP SE 99–100
shareholders and 98
social media and 93, 97, 98
investor relations officer (IRO) 91, 92–3, 95, 96,
97, 99
investors 91, 95–6
see also investor relations
issues management (IM) 11, 135, 137, 231
audiences, issues of interest 141
crisis management and 136
definition 135
#deleteuber boycott 145–6, 147
digital collectives
and communication ecosystems 139–40
monitoring refraction of 141–3
in digital era 143–4
digitalization and 144–5
future directions 146–7
institutionalized actors 138–9
issue lifecycle 141, 142
issues prioritization 140–41
stakeholders' segmentation 137–8
issues prioritization 140–41
"It Gets Better" campaign 160
Ito, J. 302

Jabagi, N. 319
Jackson, P. R. 19
Jackson, S. L. 347
Jahng, M. R. 184, 431
James, E. H. 180
James, W. 357, 360
Jarrahi, M. H. 313, 315, 320
JD 73
Jennings, W. 430
Johansen, W. 185
John, E. 72
Johnen, M. 196
Johnson, R. G. 328
Johnston, K. A. 154, 155
Josserand, E. 320
journalism 10, 51, 57, 59, 71, 428
citizen 55, 213, 327
media relations and 56–7

journalist-centric media relations model 52–3
journalists 51–4, 52, 55, 56, 57–9, 126, 187,
212–14, 257–8, 407, 429
justice, notions of 198–9
Just, S. N. 247

Kahai, S. S. 23
Kaine, S. 320
Kalla, H. K. 19
Kamenchuk, O. 214
Kang, M. 159
Kaput, M. 301
Kegan, R. 27
Kelleher, T. 105
Kent, M. L. 159
KFC 347
Kickstarter 159
The King's Speech 44
Kiousis, S. 104
Kochar, S. 287
Koontz, H. 311
Kovacs, R. 161
Kowalski, R. M. 195
K-pop band 393
Kreiss, D. 8, 20
Kress, G. 330
Krishnan, B. 415
Kwon, E. S. 431

La Cour, C. 427
Lahey, L. L. 27
Laitinen, K. 22, 27
Lalić, D. 299
Lane Crawford 73
Langert, B. 228
Langley, Q. 224
Lanoszka, A. 427
Laskin, A. V. 98
Lauzen, M. M. 159
leaderboards 270, 272, 274
leadership 20, 23, 24, 311, 314, 315, 317, 318,
403
see also e-leadership
Leclercq, T. 272
Ledingham, J. A. 104
Leeman, M. 302
Lee, M. K. 313
Lee, Spike 201
legacy news media 52, 54
legal ownership, corporate brand 40
Legendary 7 campaign 338
legitimacy 3, 173, 226, 440, 445
digital 351
organizational 5, 228, 409

for public sector organizations 401–2, 404,
409
Legner, C. 8
Leichty, G. B. 93
Leidner, D. E. 152, 157
Lember, V. 415
Lending Club 374
Leonardi, P. M. 21, 24
Leonardo da Vinci 328
Lerbinger, O. 169, 299
Lewis, L. 247, 366
LexisNexis Newsdesk 129
LGBTQ+ communities 231
Lievonen, M. 223
Likely, F. 119, 121
Lin, H.-C. 256
link by association 216, 218
LinkedIn 124, 174, 255, 373
Lin, X. L. 183
listening 186, 357, 384, 389–91
architecture of 361, 362, 366, 367
digital corporate communication 358
hearing *vs.* 359–60
seven canons of 359–60, 361
Switzerland's digital public diplomacy
392–3
see also organizational listening
Listening and Evaluation Compass (LEC)
framework 390–91
Lock, I. 187
Lost Sovereignty/Lost National Identity
(narrative) 210
ludus ('gaming') 270
Luoma-aho, V. 70, 112, 152, 154, 223, 227, 267,
298, 344, 371, 414
Lutrell, R. 6
Lyft 312, 313, 317

machine learning 12, 124, 170, 171, 229, 282,
290, 364, 415
artificial intelligence and 118, 128, 440, 441
Macnamara, J. 121, 186, 302
The Madness of King George 44
Madrid City Council, Madrid Móvil app of 13,
418
"avisos" (notices) option 418
citizens' possibilities in co-production
418–20
lessons learned 422
notices received and solved 420–21
Madsen, V. T. 24, 25
Majesty Magazine 44
Malakyan, P. G. 23
managerialism 311
Marimekko 335

460 *Handbook on digital corporate communication*

Marin, A. 155
market for big data *see* big data market
marketing technology 123
Marr, B. 300
MarTech 123, 128, 241, 249
Mary, Queen 44
Mateescu, A. 316
Mattel 161
Mazzucato, M. 373
McCarthy, J. D. 152
McDonald's 11, 12, 222, 229
    "Bacon Hour" promotion 225
    brandjacking at 223–5
    Flagship Farmers campaign 228
    'I'm Lovin' it' audio 346
    McDonald's Nutrition Network (MNN) 224
    #MeetTheFarmers campaign 224, 225, 228
    Physicians' Committee for Responsible
        Medicine and 224–5, 228
    #SeriouslyMcDonalds 224, 225
McKinsey 8, 283
McStay, A. 213
meaningful stories 270
measurement and evaluation (M&E) 118, 122,
    123, 127, 130
    artificial intelligence for 128–9
    Barcelona Declaration of Measurement
        Principles 126
    corporate communication 119–20, 127–8
    of digital corporate communication 119,
        120–22, 123–5
        core elements 120
        data analysis 124
        data collection 123–4
        data usage 124–5
        evaluation types 120–21
        individual level (micro level) 128
        management 119, 123, 125–6
        organizational level (meso level) 128
        societal level (macro level) 128
    future directions 130
    key performance indicators 119, 122, 124–6,
        129
    SMART objectives 126–7
    stages of 121–2
    UNICEF 129–30
Mediacorp 187, 188
media environment 51, 54, 144, 212
media landscape 67–8, 108, 113, 146
Media Matters 430
media relations 10, 51, 54
    critical examination 57
    definition 52
    digitalization and 51, 54–6
    function of 53–4

future directions 59–60
Global Strategic Communications Council
    58–9
journalism 52, 56–7, 59
practitioners 52, 53
    and journalists 54
social media 54–5
specialists 56–7
media reputation 67–8
Meltwater 244
memes 13, 218, 230, 328, 333, 334, 337, 404, 409
Meniane, D. 98
Men, L. R. 20, 108, 109
Men, R. L. 300
Meta 43, 128, 343, 384, 393
#MeToo movement 160, 227, 229, 231
Meyers, G. C. 180
micro-blogging 160
Microsoft 128, 299, 343
microtargeting 125, 128
Miller, B. M. 105
Ministries of Foreign Affairs (MFA) 389, 390,
    392, 393
Minocher, X. 157
misinformation paracrisis cluster 169, 170
Mitchell, R. K. 154
MIT Media Lab 297, 298, 377
Mitroff, I. I. 180
mixed reality (MR) 47, 48
Möhlmann, M. 316
Mondelez 10, 112–13
Monsanto 231
Moore, S. 285, 286
Morel, B. 301
Moser, C. 316
Mrs Brown, Victoria and Abdul 44
MS Teams 244
Müller, M. G. 328–9
Murtarelli, G. 286
Musk, E. 347

Nadja Enke 159
Nair, P. 188
narrative strand 223
Nass, C. 343
National Health Service (NHS) Mandate 364
National Investor Relations Institute (NIRI) 91,
    92
Nation Brands Index 393
native advertising 56
natural language processing (NLP) 119, 281, 282,
    343, 363, 364
negative engagement 223
negative engagement online 196
Neill, M. S. 24, 366

Nelson, J. L. 303
Nespresso 349
Nestlé 162, 348
NETS 11, 187
    preparing phase 188
    programming phase 188
    responding phase 188
    reviewing phase 188–9
network theory 155–6
neutralizers 318
new public management (NPM) reforms 402
news media 51, 53, 54, 56, 67, 71, 143, 144, 169
newsrooms 51, 55
The New York Times 289–90
New Zealand Government Department of Internal
    Affairs 302
NFL Boycott scandal 230–31
Nguyen, A. 316
Nike 347, 352
Nisbet, E. 214
Nissan 12
    'Leaf' car 275
'None of Your Business' 376
non-fungible tokens (NFT) 37, 443
non-government organizations (NGOs) 59, 74,
    138, 139, 141, 154, 358
non-profit organizations (NPOs) 91, 358, 376
Norris, P. 229
Nunan, D. 372
Nyilasy, G. 431

obstructive marketing 223
#Occupy movement 139
OECD 378
Olaniran, B. 183
Oliver, S. 303
online complaint 193, 195, 199
    management 202–3, 204
online firestorms 196, 197, 200–201, 203, 441
online forums 320, 407
online hateholders 67
online petitions 159
Open Algorithms project 377
organizational change 244–5, 247, 366
organizational communication 2, 4, 19, 105, 182,
    184
organizational crises 10–11, 165, 181–2
    see also hostile hijacking
organizational intangible assets 3, 5, 413
organizational listening 12, 186, 357
    Achmea 364–5
    communication *vs.* information 359
    corporate communication 358
    definition 360–61
    delegation 360–61

    digital 362–3
    digital corporate communication 358, 361
    engagement methods 363
    future directions 367
    interpersonal communication 365
    issue of scale 360
    listening *vs.* hearing 359–60
    mediation 361
    social media and 366
    stakeholders and 360–61, 362
    systematic analysis of data 363
Organizational Listening Project 361, 364
organizational reputation 51, 67, 182
organization-public relationships (OPRs) 104,
    106, 108, 109, 155, 267
organizations 11, 179, 239, 366, 440, 444–5
    digitally-influenced issues affecting 10–11
    external communication 20
    functionalist research on 19
    human aspects in 25–6
    internal communication 19, 20
    news media and 55
    social media and 69, 182
    supporting digital transformation of 244–6
    use of dialogic communication 186–7
organization-stakeholder relationships (OSR) 5,
    12, 104, 339, 344, 346
organization-wide digital transformation 245–6,
    248
OrgTech 243
Orlikowski, W. J. 247
Ostermeier, M. 245, 246
Östling, L. 216, 217
Ostrom, E. 377–8
owned media 167–8, 328, 345, 353

Page Society 283
paida ('playing') 270
Palmieri, R. 95
Pamment, J. 211
Pang, A. 52, 180, 181–2, 184, 186, 187, 189
Papa John's brand 230–31
paracrises 11, 166, 175, 197
    challenge type of 169
    context 167–8
    definition 168–9
    distinction between crisis and 169
    frequency of occurrence 169–70
    online environment 168
    reputational risks 168–9
    social media and 181
    stakeholder challenge 168
    types 169–70
    VW case study 174–5
    see also artificial intelligence

462 *Handbook on digital corporate communication*

parasocial relationships (PSR) 256
Paris Climate Agreement 389
Park, Y. E. 159
Parmentier, M.-A. 255
parody social media 182
participatory action research (PAR) 363, 364
Pauchant, T. C. 180
PayPal 387
peer-to-peer (P2P) relationship 254
perceived automated social presence 344
performance graphs 270
person-brand capital 255, 258
PESO model 345
Peters, J. 357
Peterson, M. O. 328
Petrucci, A. 300, 302
P&G 348
Physicians' Committee for Responsible Medicine
    (PCRM), McDonald's and 224–5, 228
Pigou, A. C. 375
Pinsdorf, M. K. 179
Pinterest 328
podcasts 52, 159–60, 346, 347
Poe, E. A. 430
points, gamification 270
Politico 58
Ponzi, L. 69
pop-up houses 395
positivity/optimism of organization 105
Posner, E. A. 376
PostNord 216, 217–18
Pratt, C. B. 180
Presence Switzerland 12, 392–4
press releases 51, 53, 54, 84, 85, 93, 99, 215
primary corporate communication 36, 39, 45
procedural justice 198
procedural rhetoric 268, 271, 274, 276
process evaluation 120–21
professionalism 260
promissory corporate communication 41, 42, 45
ProPublica 374, 377
Prosper 374
public affairs offices 400, 403
public diplomacy 12–13
    activists 388–9
    CEOs 389
    citizens 389
    corporate diplomacy 385
    definition 385
    digitalization and 384, 386, 387, 391–2
    future directions 395–6
    influencers 388–9
    international corporations 387–8
    Listening and Evaluation Compass
        framework 390–91

regions and cities 386–7
social media and 389, 390, 391
Switzerland's digital public diplomacy
    392–5
technology companies 387–8
see also digital public diplomacy
public engagement 82, 108, 401
public online complaints (POCs) 196, 198,
    199–200, 202, 203, 204
public relations (PR) 2, 4, 7, 104, 105, 136, 253,
    291, 374
public sector communication 12, 400, 401, 404,
    405, 407, 414
    digitalization of 402–3
public sector organization (PSO) 13, 400, 409,
    413, 415–17, 422
    challenges to 403–4
    digitalization of 402, 405, 406
    diversity management 406–7
    Finnish Tax Administration 407–8
    future directions 408–9
    goal-oriented communications 400
    journalists' access to information 407
    legitimacy for 401–2, 409
    personal data 406
    platformed sociality 406
    stakeholders and 401–2, 404
    trust in 401, 402, 408, 409
Pump, Lil 201
Putnam, L. L. 19
PwC consulting group 299

Qiu, J. L. 373
quaternary corporate communication 39–40, 41,
    46–7
The Queen 44

Rasmussen, R. K. 247
Reddit 97, 98, 254
Reeves, B. 343
Reinikainen, H. 366
Reinke, K. 27
relationship outcomes 104–5
reputation 65, 167
    see also corporate reputation
reputational relationships 104
research instruments 119
responsiveness 105
responsory corporate communication 42, 47
rhetorical arena theory (RAT) 166
Rindova, V. P. 66
Roberts, J. 95
Roberts, P. 66
Robinhood 97
robots 71, 282, 286, 287, 294, 300, 313, 440

Romney, M. 328
Rosenblat, A. 317, 319
'Royal Channel' 46
Royal Family 43–4, 45
Royal Fashion YouTube channel 44
A Royal Night Out 44

Sahay, S. 366
Salmon, C. T. 304
Sanders, B. 333
Sanderson, J. 160
SAP 100, 242, 244
SAP SE 10, 99–100
SAS case 11, 215–18, 216, 217, 218
Sauter, M. 160
scansis 227
Schildt, H. 313
Schnatter, J. 230
Schön, D. 26
Schuett, J. 298
Schwab, K. 38, 287
scientific management 317
scientific management 2.0 313, 314, 318
searched media 345, 347, 352
secondary corporate communication 36, 39, 46
second industrial revolution 37, 317
Second Life 273, 276
Second Marketing Revolution 38
Securities and Exchange Committee 158
Seeger, M. W. 180, 183
Seiffert-Brockmann, J. 272
sensemaking 24–5, 246, 320
serious games 270, 274
service recovery 198, 199, 203
The Seven Habits of Highly Effective People (Covey) 359
Shanley, M. 65
shared or distributed leadership theory 315
shareholder 35, 92, 94, 95, 97–100, 98, 158, 161, 443
Shin, W. S. 186
Siah, J. 181, 184
Siemens Healthineers 11, 247–8
Silic, M. 269
Simmons, R. 201
Sina Weibo 160
Singleton, S. 377
situation crisis communication theory (SCCT) 166, 171
Sivarajah, U. 372
Sivunen, A. 27
Skype 396
Slack 22, 25
Slackbot 22
Smart City Strategic Framework 305

SMART objectives 126–7
Sng, K. 182
social badging 319
social bots, in internal communication 22, 29, 229
social corporate justice (SCJ) 231
social media 1, 6, 10, 54, 56, 67–9, 93, 170, 183, 227, 320, 366, 426, 435
    account hacking cluster 169, 170
    activism 157, 158
    in brandjacking 228
    campaigns 228, 231
    cancel culture and 229
    on corporate reputation 64–5, 66
    crisis 56, 73, 166, 168, 183
    CSR communication 78–9, 81, 86
    disinformation and 429–30
    internal 24–5
    misuse paracrisis cluster 169, 170
    organizational crises and 181–2
    public diplomacy and 389, 390, 391, 394
    relationship management 103, 107, 108, 111
social media crisis communication (SMCC) 166, 183
social media hype 181–2, 188
social media influencers (SMIs) 11–12, 182, 253, 257, 258
    advantages of collaborating with 259–60
    campaigns strategy 256–7
    challenges in collaborating with 260–61
    corporate communication 259
    corporate influencers 258
    definition 253
    future directions 262
    influencer–follower relationship 254, 255
    microcelebrity status 255
    parasocial relationships 256
    relations 257–8
    research 255–7
    specific roles of 254
    Unilever influencer campaign 261–2
social networks/social networking 25, 107, 108, 142, 155, 159, 319, 387, 391
The Society's CommTech guide 6
socio-technical systems theory 239
Sonderegger, A. 313
sonic branding and brand voice 346–7
Sony 349
Spence, A. M. 65
spoofs 336
Sports Network 328
Spotify 348, 407
Sputnik Covid-19 vaccine 433–4
Squid Game (television show) 338
Stackmann, J. 174

stakeholder relationship management 10, 103, 107, 109
  antecedents 105–6
  in digital era 106–7
  future directions 113
  indicators 104, 106, 110
  measures 105
  Mondelez 112–13
  outcomes 106
  risks and challenges in 110–11
  strategies 105, 106
  types 104, 106
  see also stakeholders
stakeholders 1, 4, 10, 41, 105, 106, 110, 124, 125, 128, 167, 212–13, 226, 291, 301, 389, 443–4
  activist 173, 226
  affecting corporate reputation 67
  big data market 374, 375
  communication
    CSR 81–2, 86
    digital technologies for 241
  consumers and 328
  corporate communication and 4
  corporate engagement with 158
  definition 154
  discourse, communicators and 289–90
  engagement 154–5
  experience with visual contents 333
  forms of 111–12
  gamification 272–3, 276
  international corporations and 387
  journey, digitalizing 241
  organizational listening and 360–61, 362
  post-digital classifications of 111–12
  in pre-digital communication era 137–8
  public sector organizations and 401–2, 404
  salience of 173
  see also stakeholder relationship management
Starbucks 70, 352
Stark, L. 317, 319
Statista study 426, 430, 432
stealing thunder 166
Steilen, S. 195, 199, 365
StockTwits 97
Stokols, D. 314
"The Story of Little Black Sambo" 201
strategic influencer communication 253, 255, 256, 258, 259, 261–2
Strategy for Communication Abroad 2021–2024 394
Strömbäck, J. 104
Sturges, D. L. 180
sub-national actors 386, 393

substitutes-for-leadership theory 318
summative evaluation 121
supply chain 11, 153, 155, 156, 161, 162, 293
supportive functional digital infrastructure 244
surveillance capitalism 128, 372
Sutherland, W. 313, 320
Swedish Democrats 217
Swedish National Board of Health and Welfare 208, 216, 218
Swedish Transport Administration 10, 28–9
Swiatek, L. 344
Swiss Federal Department of Foreign Affairs 13
Swissinfo 394–5
#Switzerland 392
Switzerland, digital public diplomacy 392
  engagement 394–5
  hybridization and adaptation 395
  listening 392–293
  prioritization 393–4
Sydney (Australia) case study *see* City of Sydney
Syvänen, S. 304

tactical listening 390
'Talisker Tasting Experience' app 348
Talkwalker 124, 129
Tandoc Jr, E. C. 427, 428, 429
Tan, K. Y. 184, 186
task sharing 105
Taylor, F. 317
Taylor, M. 154, 155, 186, 377
teammates, gamification 270, 272
Tencent 343
tertiary corporate communication 36, 39, 46
Tesla 343, 347
third industrial revolution 37
Third Marketing Revolution 38
Threatened Values (narrative) 209–10
T.I. (rapper) 201
TikTok 1, 43, 44, 86, 97, 137, 159, 174, 181, 184, 193, 254, 255, 282, 328, 336, 430
Tilson, D. 8
Tinkov, O. 230
tipping point 48, 143, 147
Todos por el planeta (All for the planet) campaign 84–5
total corporate brand communication (TCBC) 10, 34, 40, 41–2, 43–7, 47
total corporate communication (TCC) 34, 35, 36, 37–9, 41
Towers-Clark, C. 300
Toyoda, Y. 319
Tranovo, M. 73
transformational leadership 317
transnational corporations 385
Treem, J. W. 21

TrendKite 129
TripAdvisor 254
Troise, C. 299
Trump, D. 146, 389
Trump, M. 72
trust, in public sector organizations 401, 402, 408, 409
Tsai, W. S. 108, 109
TSheets 244
Tsyrenzhapova, D. 213
Tumblr 159, 328
Turban, D. B. 66
Turner, B. 180
TVEyes 129
tweetjacking 152, 160, 162
Twitch 254, 255
Twitter 7, 46, 54, 78, 79, 80, 84, 97, 99, 137, 160, 161, 174, 193, 195, 196, 199, 201, 202, 215, 217, 218, 224, 229, 327, 335, 337–8, 387–9, 392, 394, 426, 434
two-way communication 91, 93, 186, 209, 211, 316, 318, 343, 367

Uber 145–6, 283, 313, 314, 317, 319, 320
UNICEF 10, 129–30
Unilever influencer campaign 12, 261–2
United Nations 129
United Nations Global Compact 84
University of Beer 338
US Chamber of Commerce Foundation 78
user-generated content (UGC) 83, 155, 254, 257

Valdez-Mendia, J. M. 415–16
Valentini, C. 304
Valin, J. 284, 287
value chains 85, 155, 156, 157, 161
van Leeuwen, T. 330
Van Noort, G. 199
Veil, S. 159
Verčič, A. T. 18–19
Vernuccio, M. 186
Verstraete, M. 182
victimization and mask-slipping 217
Victoria, Queen 44
virtual reality (VR) 12, 48, 277, 302, 334, 338–9
visibility analysis 170
visual communication 12, 326, 329
    deepfake videos 336
    definition 326
    4ReDiVE framework 330, 333–6
    future directions 339
    Heineken® 337–9
    images 326, 327, 328
    visual content production 328–9
    visual semiotics 329–30

visual content 329, 333, 336, 338–9
    aesthetic realm 334–5
    for corporate communication 326, 327
    educational realm 335
    entertainment realm 333–4
    escapist realm 335
    Heineken® 337, 338
    production 326–7, 329–30, 335, 339
    shared online 337
visual semiotics 329–30
visual social semiotics 327, 331–5, 337
visual turn 326, 328, 339
vlogs 159
Vodafone, AI governance at 12, 292–4
voice affiliate programs 346, 347
voice apps 347–8
voice assistants (VAs) 11, 343–5, 345, 347, 349, 350, 351, 353
voice commerce 348–9
voice communication 12, 343
    convergence of corporate communication
        commerce and 352, 353
        marketing and 352, 353
    digital voice communication framework 344–6
    future directions 353
    organizations adopting VA 351
        limitations 351–2
    voice commerce 348–9
    voice corporate communication 346–7
    voice marketing 347–8
    see also voice assistants
voice corporate communication (VCC) 346–7
voice-enabled shopping 349, 350
voice marketing 347–8
voice of the consumer (VOC) 366
voice ordering automation 349, 350
voice publicity events 347
voice searches 348, 352
voice search optimization (VSO) 348
voice shopping events 349, 350
voice to text (VTT) 363
VW racist advertisement 11, 174–5

Waisbord, S. 182
Walmart 223, 346, 349
Wang Junkai, K. 73
Wang, P. 298
Wan, S. 182
Wardle, C. 210
webcare 199–200, 203
Weick, K. E. 19
Weiner, M. 287
Welch, M. 19
Wellman, B. 155

Wellman, M. L. 261
Werbach, K. 270
Werner, H. 175
Wesche, J. S. 313
Weyl, E. G. 376
WhatsApp 54, 406
Wigand, J. 225–6
WikiLeaks 389
Wikipedia 98, 159, 226, 254, 255, 352, 427
Wilcox, D. L. 184
Willemsen, L. M. 199
Williams, D. 183
Wilson, C. 6
The Windsors 44
Wohl, R. 256
Wolvin, A. 360
Woolley, S. 213
workers 146, 311, 312, 315–20, 321, 322
workplace communication 22
World Economic Forum 78, 287, 377

World Health Organization (WHO) 426, 431, 433, 434
World of Warcraft 276
Wright, D. K. 6

Xiong, Y. 159, 160

Yang, A. 155, 158
Yen, D. A. 38
Yoox-Net-a-Porter 73
The Young Victoria 44
YouTube 7, 43, 46, 51, 54, 159–60, 188, 193, 224, 254, 255, 328, 337, 394, 407, 430

Zaiotti, R. 384
Zald, M. N. 152
Zalmanson, L. 316
Zerfass, A. 242, 243, 304
Zoom 58, 100, 244, 303, 395